ERRATA: *American Society, Inc.*, Second Edition

page 31: following entry 31 in Table 4-1, read also—
"32. Security Pacific National Bank . . . . 5.0"

page 35, line 25: for "(p.00)" read "(p.44)"
line 40: for "(pp. 00-00)" read "(pp. 45-47)"

page 43, line 15: for "(p.00)" read "(p. 44)"
line 31: for "(pp. 00-00)" read "(pp. 45-47)"

pages 46 and 47: read page 47, then page 46.

page 75-77: in Table 6.1 read each section as if a rule were
beneath lines beginning with "Asset."

page 105, line 27: for "the initial coefficients factor" read
"the initial coefficients for factor"

page 107, line 17: for "and the standard post-, excluding" read
"and the standard post-fisc excluding"

page 112: beneath Table 10-1, read above "Notes" line—

| Mean | .4358 | .4427 | .420 | .4106 |
| Std. Dev. | (.0134) | (.0152) | (.0067) | (.0058) |

page 121, line 23: for "income" read "ratio"

page 122, line 37: for "far more" read "far less"

page 129: The title for Table 11-1 should read—
"The Poverty Picture—Excluding Government Benefits (Pretransfer Poor)"

page 133, line 11: for "transfers only" read "transfers lifted only"

page 146, Table 13-1: in title of table read "School Class of 1957[1]"
and in column headings, for "Officers[1]" read "Officers[2]"
In Notes, lines 1 and 2, substitute—
[1] Servicemen whose parental income was not ascertained are
excluded.
[2] This category includes two army warrant officers.

For Table 13-3 on page 150, substitute copy below.

Table 13-3. Percent "Poor," by Father's Occupation, Among Wisconsin Servicemen Killed in Vietnam through December 31, 1967, Classified by Rank, Compared to the Male Seniors in the Wisconsin High School Class of 1957[1]

	High School Cohort (N)	Privates (N)	ALL BRANCHES NCOs (N)	Officers (N)	All Ranks (N)
Workers					
Skilled	7.6% (675)	11.1% (18)	22.2% (27)	0 (5)	16.0% (50)
Semi-Skilled and Unskilled	17.5 (1341)	29.4 (51)	21.4 (70)	12.5 (8)	24.0 (129)
(Workers combined)	14.2%	24.6%	21.6%	7.7%	21.8%
Farm Owners	23.6 (839)	65.0 (20)	50.0 (20)	(1/2)	57.1 (42)
Middle Strata[2]	10.1 (1225)	20.0 (20)	30.6 (36)	10.5 (19)	22.4 (76)[3]
Total:	14.9% (4080)	31.2% (109)	27.5% (153)	11.8% (34)	26.9% (297)

1. Excluding those whose parental income and father's occupation were not ascertained.
2. Professionals, technicians, etc.; managers, officials, proprietors; clerical, sales, etc. The number of poor in each of these occupational groups is too small to calculate percentages for meaningful comparisons.
3. One manager is included whose rank was not ascertained.

For Table 13-4 on page 151, substitute copy below.

Table 13-4. Percentage Distribution of Occupations of Fathers of Wisconsin Servicemen killed in Vietnam through December 31, 1967, All Branches, Compared to the Occupations of Fathers of Male Seniors in the Wisconsin High School Class of 1957, Classified by Poverty Level[1]

	High School Cohort		Servicemen	
	Poor	Others	Poor	Others
Professional, Technical, etc.	2.6%	7.6%	6.3%	6.5%
Managers, Officials, Proprietors (non-farm)	10.7	14.2	3.8	13.8
Clerical, Sales, etc.	7.1	9.9	11.3	6.9
Skilled Workers	8.4	18.0	10.0	19.4
Semi-Skilled and Unskilled Workers	38.7	31.9	38.8	45.2
Farm Owners	32.6	18.5	30.0	8.3
	100%	100%	100%	100%
	(N=608)	(N=3472)	(N=80)	(N=217)

Subtotals (braces): Professional through Clerical — High School: Poor 20.4%, Others 31.7%; Servicemen: Poor 21.4%, Others 27.2%. Skilled and Semi-Skilled — High School: Poor 47.1%, Others 49.9%; Servicemen: Poor 48.8%, Others 64.6%.

1. Excluding those whose parental income and father's occupation were not ascertained.

page 154: in Table 13-6 for "Workers[3] " read "Workers."
                   for "Poor Semi- and Unskilled Workers" read
                      "Poor Semi- and Unskilled Workers[3] ."

page 201, line 32: for "movement of capital commodities" read "movement of capital and commodities"

page 229, line 20: read
"—for that is the meaning of the shift—is a turn to non-capitalist modes"

page 263: in Table 21-3, read line 1, "Type of Principal Employer" as if a rule were beneath it; also a rule is needed beneath line 8, "Other." In line 1 of footnote read "Sources: See Table 21-2."

page 341, line 15: for "oderly" read "orderly"

page 397, line 21: for "in solving" read "involving"

page 450, lines 3 and 4 of footnote: read "Books, 1966), pp. 12-28, by permission of the publisher. Copyright © 1966 by Basic Books, Inc. This is the first half of the original article."

page 470, line 4 of footnote: for "Robert" read "Richard"

pages 517-24: Read from page 517 to page 520 (omit pages 518, 519) and on through page 524 as part of the article on pages 487-517.

page 532: the heading of column two should read—
"Percent of Total Man-Days Idle
Through Work Stoppages"

AMERICAN SOCIETY, INC.

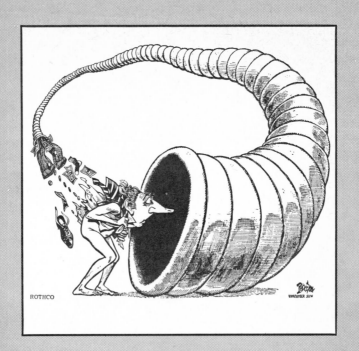

ROTHCO

SECOND
EDITION

AMERICAN SOCIETY, INC.

Studies of the Social Structure and Political Economy of the United States

Edited by

Maurice Zeitlin
University of California, Los Angeles

 Rand McNally College Publishing Company / Chicago

To the Memory of My Mother,
Rose Zeitlin

77 78 79 10 9 8 7 6 5 4 3 2 1

Contents

General
Introduction

In one way or another, the studies in this volume are related to the question: Whither America? They deal with the shape and movement of the social structure and political economy of the United States, and focus on the interaction between them. Implicitly, then, there is still another question—a rather more specific and inherently controversial one—that runs through this volume and ties the studies together. It was clearly posed at the turn of this century by Max Weber, the great German social scientist, who spent much of his intellectual and political life wrestling with it. "The question is: How are freedom and democracy in the long run at all possible under the domination of highly developed capitalism?"[1]

If this is not an academic question, it underlies—although rarely explicitly or in these words—much of the social science taught in American universities; and the answers given are typically impregnated by liberal ideology, often without the intention or awareness of the social scientists themselves. The point is that social theories are also, implicitly, forms of social advocacy: they are doctrines that contain hidden tenets about human nature and social reality. To the extent that they prevail among us, they have real social consequences and serve specific interests, because there are questions that cannot be raised within them or that their adherents dare not pose. Of course, social science practitioners—and I count myself among them—are bound by canons of "objectivity." They strive to provide answers to their questions and summary explanations (theories) that others can test and verify empirically. Yet by posing this theory (or specific proposition) rather than that, by wording it one way instead of another, by examining certain relationships and interconnections and not others, social research takes on irreducible *political* meaning: namely, the aspects of

1. From *Max Weber,* edited by H. Gerth and C. W. Mills (New York: Oxford University Press, 1946), p. 71.

the social order from which it deflects attention and the thoughts and practices it stifles or paralyzes. This can be revealed by critical analysis of the ideological content of research and theory; but such critique is inherently limited—both as polemic and valid knowledge—unless it is combined with reasoned empirical investigations of the world that start from different premises, ask different questions (or the same questions differently), seek relationships not sought in other theories, and counterpose explanations of substantive problems that make more sense than others, and that can be tested and modified by our own practical activity.

The present volume attempts, therefore, to *counterpose* alternative social theories and research whose questions and answers, whether explicitly or not, revolve around the same theme. In particular, this volume juxtaposes liberal and socialist formulations of the relationship between contemporary capitalism, social equality, and political democracy. However, this is no mere debate between political "viewpoints." Rather, the studies in this volume typically utilize social scientific reasoning and evidence to deal with the issues, whether or not they are written in a studied style of detachment or with passion and obvious political commitment. The point is that whatever the style in which theories are stated or the form in which the findings of empirical social research are presented, they play a role—when suitably interpreted—in confirming or disconfirming our view of the world, in determining what we believe is either possible or desirable and what has to be done to bring it about. Thus the questions that tie the selections in this volume together, while written mainly by university professors, are scarcely academic.

This volume is divided into six parts, each of which touches on the fundamental nature of American social reality from a different vantage point and focuses on a different, though closely related, set of issues. In the first and second parts, the objective is to set the record straight on some of the most basic dimensions of the "economy" and on the depth of the divisions in our social life. The sort of cultivated ignorance about such critical and fundamental features of our society as economic concentration and inequality in wealth and income (and how these features have changed over the past half century) is prevalent in America because, in part, few social scientists bother to study them, politicians rarely mention them, and the media usually ignore or distort them. Fortunately, there have been some excellent but usually recondite studies about these questions of how concentrated is production, who has the wealth, and who gets the money in America. The studies in Part One and Part Two provide some of the most reliable and valid answers available.

In Part Three, the specific question of "poverty" is raised—its extent, causes, and consequences. How "poverty" is measured, what is means to measure it one way or another, and how different methods affect our estimate of the number of Americans who continue to suffer it; what poverty means in their lives; and why they are poor, or why anyone has to be poor, in this country of ours—these are the questions at issue. The debate about the causes of poverty (alternative "theories of poverty") necessarily leads to the more basic issue that is the focus of Part Four: the nature of the class structure and the political economy of contemporary capitalism in the United States. What are the inner tendencies and decisive features of contemporary capitalism, and is it, in fact, even "capitalist" at all? Among the central issues debated here are the place of the large corporation in American society and what significance it has for that society's drift and thrust—indeed, for America's place in the world. Thus Part Four ends with a sharp exchange on the alleged "necessity" of American "imperialism."

Questions of "economics," as the debate in Part Four ought to make readily apparent, are also political questions. Thus, the issues in Part Five are: How, by whom, for what ends, and with what consequences is power in America exercised? What, in short, is the social meaning of political democracy in the context of the American economy? Does the national "power structure" (if there is one at all) consist of a protean complex of interacting organized and unorganized interests whose power, standing, and claims constantly shift and result in an essentially pluralistic governmental process? What role do "the masses" play in our "mass democracy"—and what role the so-called elite? Or are there people at the top who constitute a "ruling" or dominant capitalist class of the rich and the "well-born," and their active advocates? And how is the political process as a whole shaped and constrained by the most fundamental class relationships between labor and capital, both nationally and internationally?

How one answers these questions depends on what one thinks the struggle for power is all about and who the real antagonists are, whatever the appearances may be. In Part Six, therefore, that is the issue. The debate centers first on the source and meaning of the "disorders" in America's inner cities in the 1960s; and it moves, necessarily, to the overriding question: Are classes still decisive elements in our country's historical development? "What happened," as Galbraith asks, "to the class struggle?" Have American workers become integrated into the status quo, lacking in class consciousness and cynical about movements for social reform? Or are there worker revolts and daily struggles that go unnoticed and unreported elsewhere, and even deeper stirrings that portend profound changes in America's future?

Rarely do American social scientists—any more than their fellow Americans in other walks of life—try to answer such socially relevant and historically significant questions. In their concern with static models, in their rush to generalize, most social scientists ignore analysis of the historically specific social reality of contemporary America. That reality is usually accepted as given, while movement around and interaction within it, and the consequences for (or "correlates" of) individual values and behavior, are explored. Sociological studies of "social stratification" typically ignore the pattern of ownership of productive property and the skewed distribution of income, and thereby neutralize the question of class conflict and class domination. The prevailing econometric models of "microtheory," as well as the dictates of "macroeconomic" policy, are peculiarly myopic about the extent of economic concentration and monopoly power. Political science's prevalent focus on formal political processes and "decision-making, on the diffusion of appropriate civic values, or on the role of virtuous "elites" deflects this "science" from genuine analysis of the nature of political power in America.

Underlying academic social science as a whole is a conservative metaphysic (though usually in its peculiarly American "liberal" form). It is assumed that the social order in the United States (and capitalism in general), albeit imperfect, is essentially just, harmonious, and timeless, rather than inherently exploitative, contradictory, temporal, and as likely as any other historic social order to be transformed by emerging social forces and the activities of rational and creative human beings. There has been little difference in ideological content among the dominant products of each discipline in the social sciences; each has reinforced and fed the others. All around, they "discovered" that the major problems that had hitherto characterized advanced capitalist countries were solved in the United States. Socialism might have some symbolic value for the backward, but it is no more than a chimera in our own country.

This volume attempts, therefore, to reconstitute explicitly the debate in American social science that underlies it implicitly (though only asymmetrically and by indirection), and to bring socialist (or "radical") formulations to bear on the same issues dealt with by the prevailing liberal paradigms. These rarely confront one another directly. Therefore, by juxtaposing contrary and colliding interpretations and findings concerning the same "realities," the readings in this volume will, I hope, enlighten us more about the questions at issue than they would if read in isolation from each other. Their analytical gaps and inadequacies and their ideological content, as well as their insights and contributions to our ability to grapple with these questions, will be more readily seen in this context. Considering these studies together should also enable the reader to recognize the inseparable interrelationship between the questions and issues posed in the various studies.

If this volume is designed to contrast formulations from fundamentally different theoretical standpoints, it is also premised on the assumption that only a unified social science can adequately grapple with the issues posed. In fact, the academic division of labor along bureaucratically determined lines between "disciplines" that, on the one hand, separate the major aspects of social reality from one another and compel its students to see only within "departmental" boundaries, and, on the other, excludes certain questions from systematic consideration altogether, is both cause and consequence of the limitations of contemporary academic social science. This volume recognizes no such boundaries. Trained incapacity and professional psychosis are far more significant obstacles to relevant social research and theory than the government contracts, grants, and consultantships that fund so much current work in the social sciences. This is not to deny, of course, that such specific pressures and rewards (and not only the general structure of academia) undoubtedly also play a role in steering social research and theory away from *verboten* topics.

The fact is that the research projects of many prestigious professors and of centers, institutes, and "interdisciplinary programs" of leading universities have been funded, and their objectives have been coincident with, if not determined by, the CIA, the air force, or army research offices. Even the most incorruptible recipients of such "no strings attached" funds must have their scientific curiosity and breadth of vision and inquiry rather constrained by such sponsorship.[2] However, in addition to these sorts of contacts between U.S. intelligence agencies and the American academic community, which involved "many thousands of United States academics at hundreds of U.S. academic institutions"—contacts ranging, according to the Senate Intelligence Committee, from consultation in areas of expertise or "occasional debriefing to a continual operational relationship"—the CIA is now using "covert operational exploitation" of "several hundred American academics . . . located in over 100 American colleges, universities, and related institutes. At the majority of institutions, no one other than the individual concerned is aware of the CIA link."[3] The CIA's "long-developed clandestine rela-

---

2. The funding of such research through various covert "conduits" was widely publicized in 1967–1968. It led to President Lyndon Johnson's appointment of a special committee, headed by the then Under Secretary of State, Nicholas Katzenbach, to investigate and report on the CIA's covert funding of American educational and private voluntary associations and foundations. The Final Report of the Senate Intelligence Committee chaired by Senator Frank Church also contains brief revelations on the CIA's role in American academia. See U.S. Congress, Senate, 94th Cong., 2nd Sess., Select Committee to Study Governmental Operations with Respect to Intelligence Activities. *Foreign and Military Intelligence,* Book I (Washington, D.C.: U.S. Government Printing Office, 1976), chap. 10. Referring to "the CIA's intrusion into the foundation field in the 1960s," the Committee said, it "can only be described as massive. Excluding grants from the 'Big Three'—Ford, Rockefeller, and Carnegie—of the 700 grants over $10,000 given by 164 other foundations during the period 1963–1966 [alone], at least 108 involved partial or complete CIA funding. . . . In the same period, more than one-third of the grants awarded by the non-'Big Three' in the physical, life and social sciences also involved CIA funds" (p. 182).

3. *Foreign and Military Intelligence,* Book I, pp. 181; 189–91.

tionships with the American academic community" have specifically included "academic research and writing where CIA sponsorship is hidden." How this extensive interpenetration of American academia and intelligence agencies affected the climate of academic social thought is for the reader to judge. Nor can the effects on a whole generation of American intellectuals and academics of the epoch of Cold War scholarship, and the preceding wave of political trials under the Smith Act, the rash of congressional investigations, the blacklists in the media, the attacks on left-wing intellectuals in and out of the university, the loyalty oaths, and the justification of such purges by leading academic lights, be forgotten. After World War II, a special type of Cold War liberalism fastened itself upon the country; and neoscholastic, abstracted empiricist, and apologist social research prevailed and coprospered in American universities until sharply challenged by the theoretical and practical activity of a New Left born in the epoch of the civil rights and antiwar movements of the late 1960s. As a result, in recent years there has been genuine ferment and debate in the social sciences, and it is hoped that this second edition of *American Society, Inc.* will, like the first, make its own modest contribution to continuing and sharpening that debate.

In order to pinpoint the issues and clarify the arguments, I have written brief introductions to each part of this volume, introductions in which I have tried to accurately summarize the essentials of the selections presented. As editor, of course, I have tried to make the debate as pointed as possible by selecting works that exemplify the alternative theories. But I have not, in my various introductions, joined the debate myself, nor have I stated my own view of the specific issues. I should forewarn the reader (if it is not already clear) that I find the prevailing liberal formulations wanting and the socialist formulations persuasive —but if this has affected my presentation of opposing arguments in the various introductions, it was not intentional. In any event, the authors are there to speak for themselves, and readers are encouraged, in following the debate, to try to synthesize their own answers to the questions posed—or, if need be, to pose their own questions anew.

I should say, finally, that I have not designed this volume to be read only by undergraduate college students, although I certainly think it will serve them well. On the contrary, readers with advanced training and a high level of sophistication in the social sciences (including "professional" social scientists) can also learn a good deal from a close reading of this volume of studies of the social structure and political economy of the United States. What's more, since I am convinced that the questions at issue in this volume must sooner or later be confronted by all Americans, I have also tried to select studies written clearly, if not gracefully, so that readers untutored in the often mysterious dialect of the various social sciences can read and understand—and join—the debate.

Part 1

Economic Concentration
and
Corporate Ownership

No adequate theory of American reality can ignore the deeper divisions in our social life which frame our nation's productive activity. If production in America is eminently social, appropriation of the social product is peculiarly private: a few hundred large corporations, owned by a minute fraction of all Americans who get the bulk of the dividends and an extraordinarily uneven share of all the personal income, control most of the assets in this country and employ most of the workers in manufacturing.[1] The studies in Parts One and Two document this statement. What its implications are, however, are debated in later parts of this volume. In this part, the selections from U.S. Government publications report on the concentration of industry and banking among the nation's largest corporations, and on some important aspects of their ownership. In Part Two, we focus on the ownership of wealth and the distribution of income.

Economic Concentration and Corporate Ownership

By the 1920s the large corporation had become the decisive unit of production in the United States. In 1929, the 200 largest *nonfinancial* corporations (i.e., corporations other than banks, insurance companies, and other financial firms) already had *legal* control of nearly three-fifths (58 percent) of the net capital assets of all nonfinancial corporations, and the figure is probably somewhat higher today, according to detailed studies by Gardiner C. Means.[2] Actual control, through intercorporate holdings and various legal devices, is even greater.

In manufacturing, three main waves of mergers brought the most significant increases in concentration, but internal growth also was a major factor. On the basis of secret information available in the files of the Bureau of Internal Revenue to which he was given access, Means was able to estimate concentration in manufacturing alone, and also to take into account the majority ownership of smaller by large firms. His estimate is that the 100 largest *manufacturing* corporations controlled 44 percent of the net capital assets—the net land, buildings, and equipment—of *all* manufacturing corporations in 1929 and that their share increased to 58 percent in 1962. Even these estimates understate the actual level of overall concentration in manufacturing, because control can be exercised over other firms through minority holdings.

According to Willard F. Mueller, who was director of the Federal Trade Commission's Bureau of Economics when he did his analysis (Selection Number 1), some 180,000 corporations and 240,000 partnerships and proprietorships constitute the population of all manufacturing enterprises in the United States. In 1962, corporations held 98 percent of all manufacturing assets held by these companies. Without taking into account intercorporate holdings (which means the following are *under*-estimates), Mueller estimates that the 20 largest manufacturing corporations held an estimated 25 percent of *all* assets of manufacturing companies. The 50 largest held 36 percent, the 100 largest 46 percent, and the 200 largest 56 percent. The 419,000 smallest companies held only 25 percent of the total manu-

---

1. In 1970, the 500 largest industrial corporations employed roughly 15 million workers, or more than 75 percent of all employment in manufacturing, according to the *Statistical Abstract of the United States* (Washington, D.C.: U.S. Government Printing Office, 1971).

2. Gardiner C. Means, *Economic Concentration,* in *Hearings before the Subcommittee on Antitrust and Monopoly of the Committee on the Judiciary, United States Senate, 88th Cong., 2nd Sess., pursuant to S. Res. 262. Part 1: Overall and Conglomerate Aspects* (Washington, D.C.: U.S. Government Printing Office, July, 1964).

facturing assets. Thus the total assets of the 20 largest manufacturing corporations were about the same as those of the 419,000 smallest companies.

Concentration measured by net profits is even greater: The 20 largest manufacturing corporations held 31 percent of total *net capital assets* and received 38 percent of all profits after taxes. The net profits of the 5 largest corporations were nearly twice as large as those of the approximately 178,000 smallest corporations.

Regardless of the measure used, it is obvious that a relatively few immense corporations hold the great bulk of the financial resources of American manufacturing. Similar degrees of concentration exist in each of 28 selected industry groups. In fact, concentration in manufacturing has increased substantially since 1950. In just 12 years, the share of all manufacturing assets held by the 200 largest corporations increased by about 17 percent.

American industry is going through another great wave of mergers, with over 60 large mergers (among the 2,000 companies with at least $10 million in assets) each year since 1959. Since the end of 1950, one in five of the 1,000 largest manufacturing companies have disappeared because of mergers. Very few of them were losing money before being acquired. Many of the acquired companies were very profitable enterprises which, Mueller believes, could have offered effective competition to the large corporations if they had not acquired them.

The most recent relevant data on direct U.S. foreign investments (1957) analyzed by Howard Sherman (Selection Number 2) indicates that the average American firm investing abroad had a profit rate considerably higher than the average of all U.S. corporations. The value of direct foreign investment by the average American firm operating abroad was well over twenty times that of all U.S. firms. Therefore, foreign profits are probably a major source of the higher profit rates of the large corporations. Investment abroad is extremely concentrated. Less than 2 percent of the American companies investing abroad in 1957 held 57 percent of all U.S. investments abroad. The U.S. ownership of foreign investments is far more concentrated than even the very concentrated ownership of domestic assets. Less than 1 percent of the companies received over 60 percent of the earnings whereas 65 percent of the companies received less than 1 percent of the earnings. Thus it is evident that a few companies hold most U.S. investments abroad and receive most of the profits from these investments.

Banking Concentration

"The structure of the commercial banking system in the United States," as a report of the House Committee on the Judiciary points out, "is notable for two characteristics: (1) the absolute reduction of independent bank units since World War II as a result of a strong merger movement, and (2) a high degree of concentration of assets in the hands of a few large units."[3] The actual number of commercial banks declined from 14,539 in 1940 to 14,174 in 1950 and, with fluctuations in between, to 13,775 by the end of 1964. In fact, "the one-bank town is prevalent in the United States today," as the committee notes, and even "the typical metropolitan area is one in which assets are heavily concentrated in a few large banks,

---

3. U.S. Congress. *Interlocks in Corporate Management.* Staff Report to the Antitrust Subcommittee of the Committee on the Judiciary House of Representatives. 89th Congress, 1st Session. Washington, D.C.: Government Printing Office, 1965, p. 165.

with the small remaining share diffused among a substantial number of small units."[4]

Comprehensive surveys of ownership of large commercial banks and major corporations have been conducted in recent years by subcommittees of the House Committee on Banking and Currency and the Senate Committee on Government Operations. Selections 3, 4, and 5 are excerpted from these reports, and the principal findings in these selections may be summarized as follows:

At the end of 1964, the 100 largest commercial banks in the U.S. held 46 percent of all deposits in the 13,775 commercial banks in the country. The 14 largest, or one-tenth of 1 percent of all commercial banks, held a quarter of all commercial bank deposits. A similar pattern prevails in the 65 metropolitan areas studied: the three largest banks held more than half the deposits in 59 of the 65 areas surveyed.

In the trust business, concentration is even greater. Less than 2 percent of the banks held 61 percent of all trust assets in national banks. Analysis of data from the largest banks in ten major cities (49 banks in all) found that these 49 banks held well over half the total trust assets in all banks in the country. Just 30 of these banks held 52 percent of all trust assets. In seven of the ten cities, the banks studied held more than 90 percent of all bank trust assets in the area.

Bank Shareownership in Large Corporations

The trust departments of the 49 banks surveyed held 5 percent or more of the common stock in 147 (29 percent) of the 500 largest industrial corporations, as well as 17 of the 50 largest merchandising companies and 17 of the 50 largest transportation companies. These 49 banks were also represented on the boards of directors of 386 of the 500 largest industrial corporations. The pattern was the same among the 50 largest merchandising, as well as the 50 largest utilities, transportation, and insurance companies.

The Senate Committee on Government Operations reports (Selection Number 4) that bank trust departments manage assets substantially exceeding the assets of the largest one hundred corporations in the United States. Seventeen major commercial banks among the 32 institutional investors managed at least $5 billion investment portfolios in 1972. Trading in stock by institutional investors is mainly in the stock of the largest corporations, which, Senators Metcalf and Muskie state, tends to raise their prices, undervalue the stock of smaller firms, and force the latter to borrow at escalated rates from the largest banks, driving them deeper into debt. Not only did institutional investors account for an estimated 70 percent of the dollar value of New York Stock Exchange trading volume, but they held nearly 40 percent of the total stock outstanding listed on that exchange in 1970. These holdings are mainly in the largest corporations, where, as Senators Muskie and Metcalf note, the use of multiple nominees in ownership reports to federal regulators results in a "massive coverup of the extent to which holdings of stock have become concentrated in the hands of a very few institutional investors, especially banks." Analysis of useful data received from 89 or 324 of the nation's largest companies surveyed shows that their stock is concentrated among a handful of New York bank trust departments. Eight institutional investors held 2 percent or more of the stock in at least 10 of the 89 companies. Chase Manhattan, for

---

4. U.S. Congress, 1965, pp. 165–66.

example, held 2 percent more of the voting stock in 46 of the 89 companies, and Morgan Guarantee and First National City had 2 percent or more of the voting stock in 29 and 28 of them, respectively. Yet even ownership of 1 percent or 2 percent of the stock in large corporations whose stock holdings are dispersed can provide the basis for control of their basic policies. In turn, these corporations, "in which a few banks have substantial influence," as Senators Metcalf and Muskie put it, make decisions which affect "momentous public issues." Compared to them, "federal officials play a minor role." The Committee on Government Operations staff found that several New York banks combined held at least 10 percent of the total voting stock in 48 of the 89 major corporations which provided useful data. This was true of three of the four major oil companies reporting, twelve of the twenty-one other industrials, six of the ten airlines, eight of the seventeen railroads and other transportation companies, eight of the nineteen utilities, five of the eight retailers, five of the nine commercial banks, and the one major insurance company reporting. (See Table 4–5 in Selection Number 4.)

Who Owns the Banks?

The House Banking Committee's survey of the stockholding of the 210 largest banks holding over 60 percent of the total deposits in the country in 1966 shows that 94 percent of the surveyed banks held some of their own stock.[5] Nearly one-third of the banks exercised influence over the voting of 5 percent or more of their own shares. In the staff's view, as just noted, control of even 1 or 2 percent of the stock in a "publicly held" corporation gives tremendous influence over policies and operations. The diffusion of ownership is such that the holder of even a small percentage of the stock is one of the company's largest shareholders. Large shareholders are often able to exert control far beyond their ownership because they can also put representatives on the boards of directors of these companies. Management, in turn, pays a great deal more attention to a large shareholder who may own more than 100 times what the average shareholder owns. Two hundred ten of the largest commercial banks in the U.S., 258 insurance companies, and 189 mutual savings banks were listed as shareholders "of record" (that is, others may be the real owners) among the top 20 shareholders of record in the 300 largest commercial banks. These "major financial institutions" were stockholders of record in 275 of the 300 largest banks as of March 1966. In 72 percent of the 275 largest banks, at least 5 percent of the stock was owned by these major financial institutions. Five percent or more of the shares of nearly one-half of the 275 commercial banks could be voted exclusively by the major financial institutions reporting. In two-thirds of the 275 major banks, 5 percent or more of the shares were held by other major commercial banks. Almost one-half had 10 percent or more of their stock held by other major commercial banks. Almost one-third had 5 percent or more of their shares voted exclusively by other major commercial banks. In New York, for example, major banks hold and vote a significant percentage of shares in competing banks.

The survey of the Senate Committee on Government Operations revealed a similar pattern of ownership of the principal shareholdings in large commercial

---

5. Staff Report for the Domestic Finance Subcommittee of the House Committee on Banking and Currency, 90th Cong., 2nd Sess. *Commercial Banks and their Trust Activities: Emerging Influence on the American Economy* (Washington, D.C.: U.S. Government Printing Office, July, 1968).

banks (Selection Number 5). The committee requested a list of the 30 largest stockholders and the amount of stock each held, from the 50 largest commercial banks in 1970. Only nine provided the information requested; in eight of these the principle shareholder was the bank itself through various nominee accounts. In five, eight or fewer major New York banks combined held over 10 percent of the stock, and in two more, these New York banks held between 5 percent and 10 percent of the stock. Thus, supposedly competing financial institutions are tightly connected through common stock ownership, not to mention interlocking directorates. The question is, how do such significant common interests among the largest banks affect the competitive struggle for profits?

Unfortunately, there is a major problem with these very useful findings from congressional investigations. If there has been a "massive coverup," as Senators Metcalf and Muskie put it, of the extent to which the principal holdings in the nation's largest banks and corporations are concentrated in a few large bank trust departments and other financial institutions, the problem is that these "institutional holdings" themselves may merely hide the real principal owners of capital. There may be, in other words, an even more "massive coverup" of the extent to which the controlling blocks of stock in the largest banks and corporations in the United States are held by major capitalist families.

The prevailing view among American academics and intellectuals is that not major capitalists but so-called "managers" (or technicians) control the large corporations which are decisive in the American political economy. The question then becomes, where have all the capitalists gone? The answer given by leading academic social theorists such as Talcott Parsons is that a shift in corporate control to managers, "high progressive taxation," and other "changes in the structure of the economy, have 'lopped off' the previous top stratum" of principal capitalist families.[6] Yet the evidence on the concentration of wealth ownership presented in Part Two indicates that these families are still very much with us. Later, in Part Four, we shall extensively examine the arguments and evidence concerning this notion of a "silent" managerial revolution in our country.

---

6. "A Revised Analytical Approach to the Theory of Social Stratification," in *Class, Status and Power*, ed. Reinhard Bendix and S. M. Lipset. (Glencoe, Ill.: Free Press, 1953), p. 123.

Recent Changes in Industrial Concentration and the Current Merger Movement

1

Willard F. Mueller

I. THE MEASUREMENT OF INDUSTRIAL CONCENTRATION

There is no doubt that large U.S. manufacturing corporations have been growing at a rapid rate in recent years, both in terms of number and assets. In 1947, there were 113 corporations with assets of $100 million or more; by the end of 1962 their number had more than tripled to about 370. This substantial and rapid growth, by itself, is not to be equated with increases in industrial concentration. Increases in concentration occur only when growth is not distributed proportionately among companies.

This, then, is the distinction between increasing bigness and increasing concentration.

Concentration refers to:

> the ownership or control of a large proportion of some aggregate of economic resources or activity by a small proportion of the units which own or control the aggregate, or by a small absolute number of such units.[1]

Concentration may be measured in a variety of different economic sectors; the universe selected for measurement is largely a question of what is being analyzed. For example the *degree* of concentration may be measured for nonfinancial companies, all manufacturing companies, companies in identical "industries," or companies producing identical "products." The broader and more heterogeneous the universe, the more general the measure; the narrower and more homogeneous the universe, the more specific the measure. In one instance, the degree of

Reprinted from Willard F. Mueller, *Economic Concentration* in *Hearings before the Subcommittee on Antitrust and Monopoly of the Committee on the Judiciary, United States Senate, 88th Cong., 2nd Sess., pursuant to S. Res. 262. Part 1: Overall and Conglomerate Aspects* (Washington, D.C.: U.S. Government Printing Office, July 1964), pp. 11–29. Footnotes and tables have been renumbered.

1. J. S. Bain, *Industrial Organization* (1959).

concentration measures the control over the assets, income, or output of perhaps all manufacturing corporations; in another, only the control over the output of outboard motors. Thus, the terms "general" or "specific" refer to the universe being measured rather than the method of measurement employed or the variables selected for measurement.

Many methods have been developed to measure concentration. But all have essentially the same purpose: to measure the extent to which a small absolute or relative number of firms account for a large proportion of assets, income, or output.

Approximately a half-dozen variables have been employed to measure concentration. These include total assets, net capital assets, sales, value added by manufacture, value of shipments, income, and employment.

Total Assets and Net Capital Assets. Assets, both total and net capital assets (property, plant, and equipment less depreciation), have been widely used to measure economic concentration. Assets fairly accurately reflect the productive resources and financial strength of a corporation. The advantages and disadvantages of this measure have been discussed at considerable length.[2]

An advantage of using *total assets* is that they include financial as well as physical productive resources. On the other hand, *net capital assets* probably do a better job of taking into account the extent to which firms are vertically integrated. This may be one of the reasons the degree of concentration as measured by net capital assets and by net income differs by less than the degree of concentration as measured by total assets and net income. Another advantage of using net capital assets rather than total assets is that the former exclude intercorporate obligations and investment.[3]

Sales. Sales data are readily available for most companies. However, as most critics of this measure have pointed out, it disregards the extent to which firms are vertically integrated.[4] Although this is not a particular problem when measuring a firm's share of a given product, it makes this measure all but useless in measuring overall concentration of productive and financial resources in broad sectors of the economy; for example, all manufacturing.

Income Generated. Adelman suggests "income generated," which he considers to be "almost identical with that of the Census 'value added by manufacture,' " is the most appropriate single measure of economic

2. See, for example, *The Concentration of Productive Facilities* (Federal Trade Commission, 1949): 6, 7; M. A. Adelman, "The Measurement of Industrial Concentration." *The Review of Economics and Statistics* (November, 1951): 272–73; John M. Blair, "The Measurement of Industrial Concentration: A Reply," *The Review of Economics and Statistics* 52 (1952): 343–55.

3. *The Concentration of Productive Facilities* (Federal Trade Commission, 1949), p. 6.

4. Ibid., 5, and Adelman, op. cit., p. 222·

size.[5] Profits represent another form of income generated. Net profits constitute one of the most important indicators of the financial strength of a business enterprise. Therefore, in many respects it serves as a useful proxy of the concentration of economic power.

In the following section we shall use most of the above measures: (1) Total assets are used in measuring the extent of concentration in all manufacturing in 1962 (Table 1–1). (2) Total assets, net capital assets, and net income are used in measuring concentration among manufacturing corporations in 1962 (Table 1–2). (3) Total assets, net capital assets, net profits, and sales are used to measure concentration in 28 broad industry groups (Tables 1–3 and 1–4). (4) Total assets are used in measuring the share of assets held by the 200 largest manufacturing corporations in 1950 and 1962, and in measuring the share of assets held by the 113 largest manufacturing corporations in 1947, 1950, and 1962 (Tables 1–5 and 1–6).

II. CONCENTRATION IN AMERICAN MANUFACTURING

Introduction

The data on manufacturing corporations for the fourth quarter of the year 1962 are based on information submitted to the Securities and Exchange Commission and the Federal Trade Commission and used in the preparation by these agencies of the Quarterly Financial Report for Manufacturing Corporations.[6]

In a few instances, these special tabulations have been adjusted to include certain items which some companies omitted from their quarterly reports but which they included in their annual consolidated income and operating statements. No adjustments have been made in these preliminary figures which would consolidate companies under common ownership.

I would like to say that the following data on concentration have not adjusted in the same fashion as those of Gardiner Means; namely, of consolidating certain companies under common ownership. This is one of the reasons for the differences in our data on concentration and those presented by Dr. Means.

Also, the data which I shall summarize do not consolidate the assets of joint ventures. A brief examination of the largest manufacturing corporations indicates that, at a minimum, 15 joint ventures with combined assets of almost $900 million are included among the 1,000 largest U.S. manufacturing corporations. Thus, the following preliminary asset

---

5. Adelman, op. cit., p. 272.

6. A discussion of the history, sampling methods, and limitations of these data appears in each issue of these quarterly reports.

concentration figures underestimate the degree of concentration actually present in American manufacturing. Throughout this statement newspapers are not included among manufacturing companies.

Concentration of Assets in Total Manufacturing

In 1962, the population of American manufacturing enterprises consisted of about 180,000 corporations and 240,000 partnerships and proprietorships. These approximately 420,000 business units had combined assets of about $296 billion as of the fourth quarter of 1962. About 98.4 percent of these assets were held by corporations.

Table 1–1 and Figure 1–1 show the ownership distribution of manufacturing assets. The 20 largest manufacturing corporations (all of which had assets of more than $1.5 billion at year-end 1962) had $73.8 billion assets, or an estimated 25 percent of the total assets of *all* U.S. manufacturing companies. The 50 largest corporations accounted for 35.7 percent, the 100 largest for 46.1 percent, the 200 largest for 55.9 percent, and the 1,000 largest for almost three-fourths (74.8 percent) of the total assets of all manufacturing companies. These data demonstrate quite clearly the high degree of concentration in American manufacturing. In fact, whereas the 20 largest companies held 25 percent and the 1,000 largest held 74.8 percent of all manufacturing assets, the 419,000 smallest companies accounted for only 25.2 percent of total manufacturing assets. Thus, the total assets of the 20 largest manufacturing corporations were approximately the same as those of the 419,000 smallest.

Table 1–1. Concentration of Total Manufacturing Assets, 4th Quarter 1962

Corporate size group	Assets (millions)	All manu-facturing (percent)	Corpora-tions only (percent)
5 largest	$ 36,447	12.3	12.5
10 largest	54,353	18.4	18.7
20 largest	74,825	25.0	25.4
50 largest	105,421	35.7	36.2
100 largest	136,222	46.1	46.8
200 largest	165,328	55.9	56.8
500 largest	199,894	67.6	68.7
1,000 largest	221,279	74.8	76.0
Corporations with assets over $10,000,000[a]	237,410	80.3	81.6
All corporations[b]	291,022	98.4	100.0
Total manufacturing business[c]	295,690	100.0	—

Source: Bureau of Economics, Federal Trade Commission.
[a]There were 2,041 manufacturing corporations in operation the first quarter of 1963.
[b]This group includes about 180,000 manufacturing corporations.
[c]Includes asset estimates for approximately 240,000 manufacturing proprietorships and partnerships.

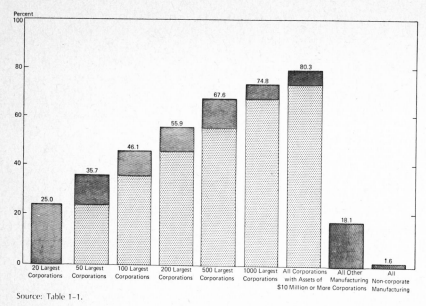

Source: Table 1-1.

Figure 1-1. Percent of Total Manufacturing Assets Accounted for by Various Groups of Firms: 1962

Asset and Profit Concentration Among Manufacturing Corporations, 1962

Three financial items were used to measure concentration among manufacturing corporations: total assets, net capital assets, and net income. The results of these comparisons are shown in Table 1-2 and Figure 1-2.

When concentration is measured in terms of net capital assets, it is greater than when total assets are used. Concentration measured in terms of net profits is greater than when either asset measure is used. For example, the 20 largest manufacturing corporations, with 25.4 percent of total corporate assets, accounted for 31.3 percent of total net capital assets and 38 percent of profits after taxes. The 100 largest manufacturing corporations in 1962 accounted for 57.6 percent of net profits, compared with 55.1 percent of net capital assets and 46.8 percent of total assets. The 1,000 largest corporations accounted for 86.4 percent of profits after taxes, 82.2 percent of net capital assets, and 76 percent of total assets.

The approximately 2,041 corporations with assets of $10 million or more earned 89.3 percent of all corporate profits, whereas the about 178,000 remaining corporations earned 10.7 percent. Also of significance, the net profits of the 5 largest corporations were nearly twice as large as those of the about 178,000 smallest corporations.

Table 1-2. Concentration of Assets and Income All Manufacturing Corporations, 4th Quarter 1962

Corporate size group	Total assets Millions	Total assets Percent	Net capital assets Millions	Net capital assets Percent	Profit after taxes Millions	Profit after taxes Percent
5 largest	$ 36,447	12.5	$ 17,502	15.3	$ 957	19.8
10 largest	54,353	18.7	27,783	24.3	1,434	29.6
20 largest	73,825	25.4	35,840	31.3	1,839	38.0
50 largest	105,421	36.2	51,057	44.6	2,315	47.9
100 largest	136,222	46.8	63,128	55.1	2,788	57.6
200 largest	165,328	56.8	73,447	64.1	3,265	67.5
500 largest	199,894	68.9	86,818	75.8	3,821	79.0
1,000 largest	221,279	76.0	94,178	82.2	4,178	86.4
All over $10,000,000[a]	237,409	81.6	99,443	86.8	4,321	89.3
All corporations[b]	291,022[c]	100.0	114,589	100.0	4,837	100.0

Source: Bureau of Economics, Federal Trade Commission.
[a]There were 2,041 corporations in this size class the 1st quarter of 1963. *Quarterly Financial Report,* 1963, p. 61.
[b]There were approximately 180,000 manufacturing corporations at the end of 1962.
[c]Adjusted. See text for explanation of adjustment.

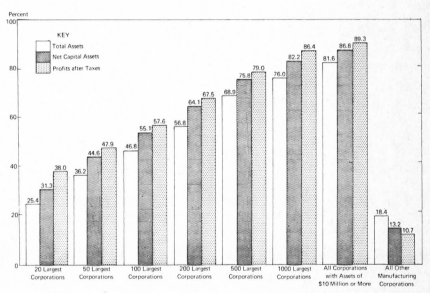

Source: Table 1-2.

Figure 1-2. Concentration of Manufacturing Corporations Assets and
Income: 1962

These data indicate unmistakably that, regardless of the measure
used, a relatively few immense corporations hold the great bulk of the
financial resources of American manufacturing.

Concentration in 28 Industry Groups, 1962

These are the 28 industries which appear in the Federal Trade Commission–Security and Exchange Commission's *Quarterly Financial Report on Manufacturing Corporations.*

The 20 largest manufacturing corporations, at year-end 1962, accounted for 25 percent of the total assets, 31 percent of the net capital assets and 38 percent of profits after taxes of all manufacturing businesses. While these data demonstrate that there is a high degree of concentration of economic resources, they tell us little of the degree of concentration in individual industries. To enlarge this area of the analysis, concentration measures have been computed for 28 individual industry groups. Table 1–3 contains estimates of the share of each industry group's sales, total assets, net capital assets, and income after taxes that are held by the 4 and 20 largest companies.

These data, while for broader industry groups than generally used to measure product concentration, do provide interesting insights into relative strength of the major producers in each industry group. Most major producers confront their competitors in a number of different related industries and produce a large number of common products. Also, while almost all of the companies covered by this analysis are diversified to some extent, the bulk of the diversification of these companies has been into related product areas.[7]

Table 1–3 provides a brief summary of . . . individual industry group data. . . . ([A table in the original showing concentration in 28 selected industry groups has been omitted here.—ED.]) Again, as in Table 1–2, the degree of concentration in each industry group may vary depending upon the financial variable employed. These data, like those in Table 1–2, reveal that profits and net capital assets are more concentrated than total assets. In every industry group, sales are the least concentrated. Regardless of the variable selected, however, in more than half the

---

7. A preliminary tabulation was made of the number of two, three, four, and five-digit classifications in which each of the 1,000 largest manufacturing corporations appeared, as reported in *Fortune*'s 1963 *Plant and Product Directory*. This tabulation indicates a high degree of diversification at the narrow five-digit product level, but a substantially smaller degree at the broader two-digit industry group level. (Examples of five-digit product classifications are margarine, roasted coffee, lace goods, and softwood plywood; examples of two-digit industry groups are food and kindred products, chemicals, and transportation equipment.)

These data indicate that while less than 5 percent of the 1,000 largest manufacturing companies are engaged in the production of goods confined to a single five-digit product class, over 25 percent manufacture products included entirely in a single two-digit industry group; and that only 21 percent of these companies were engaged in the production of as few as four five-digit products, but that 73 percent of the 1,000 largest companies accounted for their total output in four or less two-digit industry groups. Therefore, the above data, while not providing a precise picture of the structure of narrowly defined industries, have the virtue of showing concentration in a number of more or less closely related industries.

Table 1–3. Concentration of Sales, Total Assets, Net Capital Assets, and Profit After Taxes for 27 Selected Industry Groups, 4th Quarter 1962

	Number of industries							
	Sales		Total assets		Net Capital assets		Profits after taxes	
Percent of industry	4 largest	20[a] largest	4 largest	20[a] largest	4 largest	20[a] largest	4 largest	20[a] largest
90 to 100	—	4	—	4	—	4	—	5
80 to 89	1	1	—	3	1	5	1	6
70 to 79	1	2	2	4	—	3	2	2
60 to 69	—	4	—	4	1	4	1	7
50 to 59	1	5	2	2	3	5	6	—
40 to 49	6	2	8	6	7	3	4	5
30 to 39	5	5	5	2	9	1	5	—
20 to 29	6	2	4	1	1	2	4	2
10 to 19	5	2	4	1	4	—	2	—
Less than 10	2	—	2	—	1	—	2	—

Source: Bureau of Economics, Federal Trade Commission.

Note: Based on the data appearing in Table 1–4 except that textile products are not included.

[a]Includes 2 industry groups with less than 20 companies.

industry groups the 20 largest companies account for 50 percent or more of total sales, total assets, net capital assets, or profits after taxes.

In 23 of the 28 industry groups (about 82 percent), profits after taxes show either the highest concentration or concentration within 1 percentage point of the highest figure. In 20 of the industry groups, the 20 top companies earned over 60 percent of industry profits.

Considerable variations in the degree of concentration exist among industry groups. For example, the four largest producers of motor vehicles and parts accounted for 79.7 percent of that industry's total assets and 89.1 percent of its net profits; the four largest producers of tobacco products accounted for 72.7 percent of total assets and 72.5 percent of total net profits of that industry group. Both industries are highly concentrated and there is considerable disparity between the size of the four largest and all other producers of these products.

Rather high degrees of concentration also exist in rubber and miscellaneous plastic products, dairy products, primary iron and steel, alcoholic beverages, petroleum refining, industrial chemicals, other transportation equipment, and instruments and related products. In each one of these relatively broad industry groups, the four largest companies accounted for more than 40 percent of the total assets and more than 50 percent of the profits after taxes.

On the other hand, there are seven industry groups in which the four largest companies accounted for less than 20 percent of total assets. These include stone, clay, and glass products, fabricated metal products, textile products, metalworking machinery, other food products (except alcoholic beverages, dairy and bakery products), furniture and fixtures, and apparel. However, in all but two of the above industry groups the 20 largest companies in each group accounted for 40 percent or more of the profits after taxes.[8]

Concentration in Manufacturing, 1950 and 1962

In addition to the above estimates of concentration in 1962, we have prepared estimates of the share of total manufacturing assets held by the 200 largest manufacturing corporations in 1950 (Table 1–4). These data show that between 1950 and 1962 a substantial increase in total manufacturing assets occurred in this country.[9] During the period, the total assets of all manufacturing businesses increased by 106 percent and the total assets of all manufacturing corporations grew by 111 percent. However, the assets of the 200 largest manufacturing corporations increased by 141.3 percent during the same period.

The data presented in Table 1–4 reflect the relatively more rapid growth of the 200 largest American manufacturing corporations (all with assets of $200 million or more in 1962). In 1950, for example, the 20 largest companies accounted for 21.5 percent of total *corporate* assets. By 1962, the 20 largest companies' share had grown to 24.8 percent— an increase of 3.3 percentage points. The share of the 100 largest companies increased from 40.2 percent in 1950 to 45.7 percent in 1962—an increase of 5.5 percentage points, while that of the 200 largest compa-

Table 1–4. Concentration of Total Assets, 200 Largest Manufacturing Corporations, 1950 and 1962

Corporate size group	1950, total assets (millions)[a]	Percent of total All corpo-rations	Percent of total All manufac-turing	1962, total assets (millions)[a]	Percent of total All corpo-rations	Percent of total All manufac-turing
5 largest	$ 13,711	10.0	9.6	$ 35,299	12.3	11.9
10 largest	20,759	15.7	14.5	52,924	18.9	17.9
20 largest	29,682	21.5	20.7	72,179	24.8	24.4
50 largest	43,353	31.8	30.2	103,560	35.8	35.0
100 largest	55,388	40.2	38.6	133,000	45.7	45.0
200 largest	66,931	48.9	46.7	161,531	55.0	54.6
All corporations	137,719[b]	—	—	291,022[b]	—	—
All manufacturing	143,396[c]	—	—	295,690[c]	—	—

Source: Bureau of Economics. Federal Trade Commisssion.

[a]These asset figures differ from those appearing in Tables 1–1 and 1–2 because the asset data used here are those reported in *Moody's Industrial Manual* rather than those reported in the *FTC-SEC Quarterly Financial Report.*

[b]Estimate. (See text for explanation for basis of estimates.)

[c]Estimate of the total assets of all incorporated and unincorporated manufacturing corporations. (See text for explanation of basis of estimates.)

8. Sales concentration figures for each industry group . . . were not included in the above comparisons because of the limited usefulness for the analysis of broad industry groups.

9. The 1950 and 1952 data presented in this section were taken from corporation annual reports and *Moody's Industrial Manual.* Therefore, the 1962 figures contained in Table 1–4 are slightly lower than those contained in Tables 1–1 and 1–2.

nies increased from 48.9 percent in 1950 to 55 percent in 1962—an increase of 6.1 percentage points. These data show that concentration in manufacturing has increased substantially since 1959.

When noncorporate manufacturing companies are included in the comparison, the increase in concentration is even more pronounced. Whereas in 1950 the largest corporations held 38.6 percent of all manufacturing assets, by 1962 they held 45 percent of such assets—an increase of 6.4 percentage points. The share of the 200 largest companies increased from 46.7 to 54.6 percent, an increase of 7.9 percentage points. Hence, in just 12 years, their share of all manufacturing assets grew by about 17 percent.

Moreover, it must be recalled that this may well represent a minimum estimate of the actual increase in concentration of the period. As noted earlier, the assets of a number of joint ventures have not been credited to their parents.

Concentration in Manufacturing, 1947, 1950, and 1962

In 1950 the Federal Trade Commission published concentration estimates for the 113 largest manufacturing corporations of 1947 with assets of $100 million or more.[10] That study showed that in 1947 the 113 largest manufacturing corporations controlled 40 percent of the total assets and 46.1 percent of the net capital assets of all U.S. manufacturing businesses.

Table 1–5 presents estimates of the share of all manufacturing assets held by the 133 largest manufacturing corporations in each of the years 1947, 1950, and 1962. Considerable care should be taken in drawing any precise comparisons between these estimates. In 1951 substantial changes were made in the sample design of the *Quarterly Financial Report* program; therefore, we have adjusted the 1950 asset data on the basis of the 1951 change. However, we have no logical basis on which to make a similar adjustment in the 1947 data.

These data show that between 1947 and 1950 the share of all manufacturing assets held by the 113 largest companies increased from 40 to 43.5 percent (the 1950 unadjusted figure). It is further shown that between 1950 and 1962 the 113 largest increased their share from 40 (adjusted 1950 figure) to 46.6 percent. While the data for the three years are not directly comparable, they show quite clearly that between 1947 and 1962 the share of all manufacturing assets held by the 113 largest manufacturing corporations *probably* increased by about 10 percentage points, or by about 25 percent. . . .

The data contained in Tables 1–4 and 1–5 show that over the past 15 years the degree of concentration in the manufacturing segment of our economy increased at a rate comparable to increases in concentra-

---

10. *The Concentration of Productive Facilities* (Federal Trade Commission, 1947, 1950).

Table 1-5. Concentration of Total Assets, 113 Largest Manufacturing Corporations, 1947, 1950, and 1960

Year	Total manufacturing assets (millions)[a]	113 largest corporations	
		Total assets (millions)	Percent of total manufacturing
1947[b]	$105,369	$ 42,197	40.0
1950	132,032[c]	57,430[d]	43.5
1950	143,396[e]	57,430[d]	40.0
1962	295,690	137,786[d]	46.6

Source: Bureau of Economics, Federal Trade Commission.

Note: The data for the three years may not be compared directly because of the noncomparability of the total asset figures due to differences in sampling procedures. However, substantial comparability exists between the 1947 and the 1950 (unadjusted) figures, and between the 1950 (adjusted) and the 1962 figures.

[a]Includes estimates of unincorporated manufacturing firms.

[b]Federal Trade Commission, *Report on the Concentration of Productive Facilities, 1947*, 1949, p. 16.

[c]Unadjusted

[d]*Moody's Industrial Manual.*

[e]1950 data adjusted to allow for 1951 change in sample design.

tion which occurred in the 1920s.[11] At this time we have no data which indicates that this growth is subsiding. In fact, according to the latest copy of *Fortune* magazine which came to my attention yesterday, between 1962 and 1963 the assets of the 500 largest industrial corporations as measured by *Fortune* grew more rapidly than did all manufacturing assets during that period, suggesting that an additional increase in concentration occurred between 1962 and 1963. . . .

III. THE SCOPE OF THE CURRENT MERGER MOVEMENT

American industry is undergoing another important merger movement, and I am reasonably confident that this movement has played a major role in the post-World War II increases in overall concentration discussed earlier. I regret that we are unable, today, to provide you with very complete information of the scope and comparative significance of this movement. We are currently in the process of compiling and summarizing the merger information in our files. Although we have not completed this compilation, the information developed to date indicates some of the important dimensions of the current merger movement. . . .

Acquisitions of Large Manufacturing and Mining Concerns

As we pointed out earlier (Table 1-2), in 1962 the approximately 2,000 manufacturing corporations with assets of $10 million or more held about 81.6 percent of the total assets and 89.3 percent of the total profits of all manufacturing corporations.

11. N. R. Collins and Lee E. Preston, "The Size Structure of the Largest Industrial Firms, 1909–58," *The American Economic Review* (December, 1962): 987, Table 1.

This, then, is really the heart of American manufacturing—about 2,000 companies with assets of over $10 million. Consequently, substantial merger activity among firms in this size class could have a significant impact upon the structure of the American economy.

Table 1-6 summarizes the total number and value of assets for manufacturing and mining acquisitions occurring since 1948 in which the acquired concern had assets of $10 million or more in the year prior to acquisition. Although these "large" acquisitions represented only about 6 percent of all acquisitions recorded by the Federal Trade Commission since 1948, they very likely accounted for well over half of the value of assets of all recorded acquisitions.[12]

The first point to be noted from these statistics is the rising tide of merger activity among large concerns following 1948 to 1950. From a low of under 10 per year during 1948 to 1950, mergers moved upward, reaching a postwar peak of 66 in 1955; they then declined to 33 in the recession year of 1958. Beginning with 1959, there were over 60 large mergers each year.

Table 1-6. Acquisitions of Mining and Manufacturing Corporations with Assets of $10,000,000 and over, 1948–1963

Year	Number of acquisitions[a]	Total assets of acquired corporations (millions)[b]
1948	2	$ 39.6
1949	1	21.5
1950	3	135.7
1951	12	257.3
1952	12	313.8
1953	24	713.6
1954	30	1,165.4
1955	66	2,202.1
1956	53	2,052.9
1957	44	1,304.1
1958	33	943.1
1959	61	1,790.7
1960	61	1,861.0
1961	66	2,569.3
1962	61	1,651.6
1963	62	2,490.5
Total[c]	591	$19,512.2

Source: Bureau of Economics, Federal Trade Commission.
[a]See Appendix A for sources of merger data.
[b]Includes consideration paid, when asset data not available.
[c]Total does not include 10 nonmining and nonmanufacturing acquisitions with total assets of $265,700,000.

---

12. In 1963 the Federal Trade Commission recorded 1,018 manufacturing and mining acquisitions. The 62 of these with assets of $10 million or more had combined assets of $2.5 billion; 198 other acquisitions for which asset information could be obtained, or could be estimated, had combined assets of about $500 million.

During the entire 1948 to 1963 period at least 591 manufacturing and mining corporations with assets of $10 million or more merged or were acquired. These merged[13] corporations had total assets of $19.5 billion in the year prior to acquisition (Table 1–6).

One way to gauge the magnitude of these mergers is to compare them with the total number and assets of firms in this size class. Had these "large" firms not been acquired, and had they continued to operate in this size class in 1963, there would have been at least 26 percent more firms[14] in this size class in 1963 than there actually were (about 2,230).[15]

More significant, during each of the last five years, over 60 "large" firms were acquired each year. Whether or not this is a high merger rate is a question of judgment; but certainly, compared to the recorded wartime and immediate postwar merger rates, this is a high rate. During 1940 to 1947, 81 concerns with assets of $10 million or more were acquired,[16] and during 1948 to 1950 only six additional firms of this size class were acquired (Table 1–6). Clearly, the annual rate of the 1940 to 1950 period fell far short of current levels.[17]

The total value of assets acquired during 1948 to 1963 was equal to about 22 percent of total manufacturing and mining assets in 1948 and 8 percent of such assets in 1963.

Perhaps the most meaningful measure of the relative magnitude of these mergers is to compare them with the assets of all firms in the size class of firms with assets of between $10 and $250 million, since all but three of the acquired concerns fell in this size class.[18] Such a comparison

---

13. Throughout this discussion the terms "merger" and "acquisition" are used interchangeably to mean the disappearance of the whole or substantial part of a previously independent business entity, or a stock acquisition involving purchase by one company of over 50 percent of the stock of another company.

14. Of course, had they not been acquired, some of the firms may well have dropped from this size class because they failed or declined in size after 1948. On the other hand, an unknown—but perhaps larger—number of firms (not included in this count) with assets under $10 million when acquired, would have been in the $10 million class by 1963 had they not been acquired in the meantime.

15. There were in this size class 2,041 manufacturing corporations in the first quarter of 1963 (*Quarterly Financial Report,* FTC-SEC, op. cit., p. 61) and 189 mining corporations in fiscal year 1961 to 1962, the last year for which the Internal Revenue Service has such information.

16. *Report of the Federal Trade Commission on the Merger Movement* (1948), p. 27. Lintner and Butters place the number of such acquisitions at 58. Lintner and Butters, "Effect of Mergers on Industrial Concentrations, 1940–47," *Review of Economics and Statistics* (February, 1950):38.

17. During 1940 to 1947, 139 manufacturing and mining corporations with assets of $5 million or more were acquired. *Report of the Federal Trade Commission on the Merger Movement* (1948), p. 27. Since there were in 1947 about the same number of corporations with assets of $5 million or more as there were corporations with $10 million or more in 1963, the current merger rate among "large" firms clearly is higher than during the wartime merger movement.

18. Three acquired concerns had assets of over $250 million in the year prior to being acquired. The total assets of these three concerns were $839.5 million.

reveals that the assets of acquired concerns were 20 percent as great as the assets of all firms in the $10 to $250 million size class in 1963. And in recent years, the merger mortality rate (measured by assets) among firms in this size class exceeded 2 percent annually.

Acquisitions Involving the 1,000 Largest Manufacturing Corporations of 1950

Another indication of the relative volume of large mergers is the number of the 1,000 largest manufacturing corporations of 1950 which have disappeared because of mergers. Since December 31, 1950, at least 216, or over one in five, of the 1,000 largest manufacturing corporations of 1950 have merged or been acquired (Table 1–7).[19] These merger-caused disappearances were especially heavy among the companies ranking in the 501 to 1,000 largest class. A total of 139 corporations, or 27.8 percent, of those in this class were acquired. The comparable percentages for the 201 to 500 class were 20.7 percent, and for the top 200 class, 7.5 percent. These tabulations further reveal that over one-third of the disappearing companies were acquired by companies which ranked among the 200 largest corporations in 1950. The assets of the firms acquired by these 200 corporations represented about 66 percent of the total assets of all acquisitions involving the 1,000 largest corporations of 1950.

Finally I would like to discuss the pattern of acquisitions made by the 200 largest manufacturing corporations of 1962.

Table 1–7. Companies Ranked among the 1,000 Largest Manufacturing Companies in 1950 Disappearing through Mergers during 1951–1963

Nature of acquiring company	Total	Rank of acquired company, 1950		
		1 to 200	201 to 500	501 to 1,000
Company rank in 1950:				
1 to 200	82	8	35	39
201 to 500	52	4	12	36
501 to 1,000	29	1	6	22
Total by 1,000 largest of 1950	163	13	53	97
Other manufacturing companies	37	2	6	29
Companies not principally engaged in manufacturing	16	—	3	13
Total number of disappearances	216	15	62	139

Source: Bureau of Economics, Federal Trade Commission.

19. Kottke analyzed the number of acquisitions involving these concerns during the 1951 to 1959 period. Kottke, "Mergers of Large Manufacturing Companies, 1951–59," *The Review of Economics and Statistics* (November, 1959).

Acquisitions of the 200 Largest Corporations

Between January 1, 1951, and the end of 1963, the 200 largest manufacturing corporations made at least 1,956 acquisitions (Table 1–8). Asset estimates could be made for 1,080 (55 percent) of these; we believe that most of the 876 for which no asset estimates have been made were very small.

Of those acquisitions for which we have asset estimates, 308 (28 percent) had assets below $1 million and 611 (56 percent) had assets below $5 million; these 611 acquired units involved assets of about $875 million. On the other hand, the 339 acquired units with assets of $10 million or more involved total assets of over $13 billion, or about 88 percent of all assets acquired between 1951 and 1963 by the 200 largest manufacturing corporations.

Table 1–9 summarizes the asset values of acquisitions made by the 200 largest manufacturing corporations and compares the acquired assets with the 1950 and 1962 assets of the acquiring corporations, as well as with the growth in their assets between 1950 and 1962.

Firms in all size classes made a substantial volume of acquisitions (measured in assets) during the period (Table 1–9). The 10 largest corporations acquired the greatest volume of assets per firm, averaging about $143 million each; and as a group their acquired assets totaled $1,436 million.

The contribution of assets to the asset growth of the 200 largest firms varied, generally being relatively more important to firms in the smaller size classes. For example, acquired assets were equal to 2.8 percent of the asset growth of the five largest corporations and over 20 percent of

Table 1–8. Size of Acquisitions Made between 1951 and 1963 by the 200 Largest Manufacturing Corporations of 1962

Asset size of acquired units (millions)	Number of acquisitions	Total acquired assets (millions)[a]	Percent of total
Unknown	876	—	—
Under 1	308	$ 100.7	0.7
1 to 4.9	303	773.9	5.1
5 to 9.9	130	918.9	6.1
10 to 24.9	183	2,799.4	18.5
25 to 49	85	3,006.4	19.9
50 to 99.9	45	3,176.1	21.0
100 to 249.9	23	3,479.7	23.1
250 to 1,000	3	839.5	5.6
Total	1,956	$15,094.6	100.0

Source: Bureau of Economics, Federal Trade Commission.

[a]These figures include all acquisitions (including partial acquisitions) made by the acquiring companies during the period 1951 to 1963 and are not limited to acquisitions of mining and manufacturing companies. In instances where asset data were unavailable, consideration paid has been used. See Appendix A for sources of merger data.

the asset growth of the 51st to 200th largest corporations (last column, Table 1–9).

As shown earlier (Table 1–4), between 1950 and 1962 the 200 largest corporations' share of the total assets of manufacturing corporations increased by about 6.1 percentage points. Clearly, acquisitions played a central role in this increase in concentration. The $13,782,400,000 of assets acquired by these corporations were equal to 21.6 percent of their 1950 assets, 8.4 percent of their 1962 assets, and 15.7 percent of the growth in their assets between 1950 and 1962 (Table 1–9).

Only 16 of the 200 largest manufacturing corporations made no acquisitions during the period 1951 to 1962 (Table 1–10); another 15 companies made acquisitions, but asset information was available for none of these (Table 1–10); and for 69 other companies the value of assets acquired was less than 10 percent of their total asset growth between 1950 and 1962. However, for 35 companies acquired assets exceeded 40 percent of the total growth in their assets between 1950 and 1962, and in the case of 23 companies acquired assets exceeded 50 percent of their asset growth during the period (Table 1–10).

These facts indicate that although mergers played a significant role in the growth of most large corporations, their relative importance varied substantially among corporations.

Although we have not completed our analysis of the impact of mergers on the changing mobility of firms, I think it will show that in a good many cases . . . the reason for mobility among the largest corporations is that some firms are making very extensive use of mergers.

Table 1–9. Acquisitions Made between 1951 and 1962 by 200 Largest Manufacturing Corporations of 1962

Size of acquiring corporation[a]	Assets of group		Asset growth 1950–1962 (millions)	Number of acquisitions	Total assets acquired (millions)[b]	Acquired assets as percent of total		
	1950 (millions)	1962 (millions)				1950	1962	Asset growth
5 largest	$13,274.9	$ 36,447.3	$ 23,172.4	30	$ 651.1	4.9	1.8	2.8
6 to 10	7,403.3	17,905.8	10,502.5	35	782.5	10.6	4.4	7.5
11 to 20	8,237.0	19,471.6	11,234.1	47	278.3	3.4	1.4	2.5
21 to 50	12,389.0	31,597.0	19,208.0	232	2,905.8	23.5	9.2	15.1
51 to 100	11,910.7	30,625.9	18,715.0	709	4,888.9	41.0	16.0	26.1
101 to 150	6,833.3	17,654.8	10,821.4	434	2,223.0	32.5	12.6	20.5
151 to 200	4,305.4	11,625.1	7,319.6	382	2,052.8	47.7	17.7	28.0
Total 200	$64,353.6	$165,327.5	$100,973.1	1,869	$13,782.4	21.6	8.4	15.7

Source: Bureau of Economics, Federal Trade Commission.

[a]Companies ranked by total assets in 1962.

[b]These figures include all acquisitions (including partial acquisitions) made by the acquiring company during the period 1951–1963 and are not limited to acquisitions of mining and manufacturing companies. In instances where asset data were unavailable, consideration paid has been used. Asset information was available for 1,016 of these acquisitions.

Table 1-10. Acquired Assets as Percent of Asset Growth from 1950 to 1962 of the 200 Largest Manufacturing Corporations of 1962

Acquired assets as percent of total assets growth [a]	Number of acquiring corporations
0 [b]	31
Less than 10	69
10 to 19.9	26
20 to 29.9	22
30 to 39.9	17
40 to 49.9	12
50 to 59.9	8
60 to 69.9	4
70 to 79.9	3
80 to 89.9	5
90 to 99	1
100 and over	2

Source: Bureau of Economics, Federal Trade Commission.

[a] These figures include all acquisitions (including partial acquisitions) made by the acquiring companies during the period 1951 to 1963 and are not limited to acquisitions of mining and manufacturing companies. In instances where asset data were unavailable, consideration paid has been used.

[b] Includes 15 companies which made acquisitions but for which asset data were not available and 16 companies which made no acquisitions.

Acquisitions by 25 Corporations

A relatively few corporations accounted for a large share of the assets acquired by the 200 largest corporations; 10 companies accounted for 25.5 percent and 25 companies acquired 47.8 percent of all the assets acquired by the 200 largest corporations (Table 1–11). These leading 25 acquirers made at least 477 acquisitions. The 159 of their acquisitions for which asset data are available totaled $6,584 million. The 50 leading acquirers made 773 acquisitions; they acquired about 70 percent of the total assets of all companies acquired by the top 200 corporations.

Financial Status of Large Acquired Concerns

One final aspect of recent mergers which may be of interest is the financial status of the large firms which were acquired.

We have found that very few large acquired corporations were failing concerns, or even losing money in the year prior to being acquired. In fact, a substantial percentage were very profitable enterprises. As shown in Table 1–12, only 17 of the 165 acquired corporations for which we have financial information were losing money in the year prior to being acquired.[20] These concerns represented only 10.3 percent of all corporations for which we obtained such financial information.

On the other hand, 58 of the acquired corporations enjoyed earnings on net worth of over 10 percent and 90 of over 7.5 percent in the year

---

20. The data in Table 1–12 are for the acquired corporations summarized in Table 1-7 for which we have developed financial information.

Table 1-11. Twenty-five Leading Acquiring Manufacturing Corporations, 1951-1962

Rank by volume of acquisitions[a]	Number of acquisitions	Number for which assets available	Total assets acquired (millions)[b]	Percent of total assets acquired by 200 largest corporations
5 leaders	181	49	$ 2,216.4	16.1
6 to 10	103	33	1,293.9	9.4
11 to 15	84	37	1,215.0	8.8
16 to 20	48	15	994.5	7.2
21 to 25	61	25	864.3	6.3
Total 25 companies	477	159	6,584.1	47.8
Total 50 companies	773	289	9,621.6	69.8
Total 200 companies	1,869	1,016	$13,782.4	100.0

Source: Bureau of Economics, Federal Trade Commission.

[a]Acquiring corporations ranked by volume of assets acquired during 1951 to 1962.

[b]These figures include all acquisitions (including partial acquisitions) made by the acquiring companies during the period 1951 to 1962 and are not limited to acquisitions of mining and manufacturing companies. In instances where asset data were unavailable, consideration paid has been used. See Appendix A for source of merger data.

Table 1-12. Net Income after Taxes as Percent of Net Worth for 165 Acquired Corporations

Rate of return[a] (percent)	Number of companies
Negative	17
0.0 to 2.4	16
2.5 to 4.9	12
5.0 to 7.4	30
7.5 to 9.9	32
10.0 to 14.9	37
15.0 to 19.9	14
20.0 and over	7
Total	165

Source: Bureau of Economics, Federal Trade Commission.

Note: [The figures] show rates of return for 165 of the 216 acquired corporations reported in Table 1-7.

[a]Computed from data contained in Moody's Industrial Manual.

preceding acquisition. This suggests that many of the acquired concerns were very profitable enterprises, and had they not been acquired they most likely would have continued as healthy economic enterprises capable of offering effective competition.

APPENDIX A: SOURCES OF ACQUISITION DATA

The merger data summarized in the accompanying tables were reported in company annual reports and prospectuses: *Moody's Industrial Manual, Standard Corporation Records,* and various newspapers, especially the *Wall Street Journal.* Table 1-6 includes only those acquired companies for which it was possible to obtain information on assets, consideration paid, or which were among the 1,000 largest manufacturing companies in 1950, as reported in *Report of the Federal Trade Commission on Industrial Concentration and Product Diversification in the 1,000 Largest Manufacturing Companies: 1950,* January 1957, pp. 650–56. (All companies in the latter group had assets of at least $11.5 million in 1950.) Frank J. Kottke, "Mergers of Large Manufacturing Companies, 1951–59," *The Review of Economics and Statistics,* November 1959, p. 430. Acquired companies which were among the 1,000 largest in 1950, but whose assets when acquired were unknown, were assumed to have assets equal to the assets of the smallest firm in their size class in 1950, i.e., $11.5 million for those companies ranking among the 501 to 1,000 largest and $40 million for those ranking among the 201 to 500 largest. Where only the consideration paid was known, this figure was used as an estimate of the assets of the acquired concern. Where only the sales of the acquired company were known, assets were estimated by applying an asset to sales ratio common to the industry in which the acquired concern operated.

Although the time series derived from the above sources do not include all "large" acquisitions, it is most accurate for the period 1959 to 1963. *News Front* (management's news magazine, New York City) directories of various years were consulted to obtain asset information beginning in 1959.

Concentration of Foreign Investment

2

Howard J. Sherman

The latest complete and official study of profits on foreign investment by size of firm is a 1960 study for 1957 data. Therefore, these profit rates of firms abroad will be compared with rates for all firms in the 1957 data. In 1957, the profit rate (total profit before tax, divided by total equity) of all American corporations was 13 percent.[1] The average equity (total equity divided by total number of firms) of all American corporations was $391,705.[2] American firms investing abroad had a considerably higher profit rate (profit before tax from direct investment abroad divided by value of direct investment abroad), namely 15.4 percent.[3] Moreover, the average American firm operating abroad had very high average equity (value of direct investment abroad divided by number of companies investing abroad), namely $8,983,642.[4] It would appear, therefore, that higher rates of foreign earnings are one source of the higher observed profit rates of the larger American firms.

As averages may be deceptive, it is useful to cite some of the more detailed data recently available on the characteristics and performance of American firms abroad. There is pictured in the 1957 data mentioned above revealing extreme concentration in the holding by U.S. companies of investments abroad.[5] Thus, the largest-sized class of companies is classified as those holding direct foreign investments of over $100 million dollars. This class of companies included only 1.6 percent of all companies, but owned 57.2 percent of all U.S. investments abroad. At

Reprinted from Howard J. Sherman, *Profits in the United States: An Introduction to a Study of Economic Concentration and Business Cycles* (Ithaca, N.Y.: Cornell University Press, 1968), pp. 136–38. Used by permission of the author and Cornell University Press. Copyright © 1968 by Cornell University. Footnotes have been renumbered.

1. Calculated from U.S. Treasury Department, Internal Revenue Service, *Statistics of Income, Corporation Income Tax Returns for 1957* (Washington, D.C.: U.S.G.P.O., 1960).
2. Ibid.
3. U.S. Department of Commerce, Office of Business Economics, *United States Investments in Foreign Countries* (Washington, D.C.: U.S.G.P.O., 1960), pp. 144–45.
4. Ibid., p. 144.
5. Ibid., p. 145.

the other end of the spectrum, 24.7 percent of the companies with foreign investments each invested less than $100 thousand dollars, and all together held only 0.1 percent of the U.S. foreign investment. Even the next 26.1 percent of companies, each investing $100 to $500 thousand abroad, held only 0.7 percent of all U.S. foreign investment. In fact, in 1957 only 2,812 U.S. companies had any investment abroad. Clearly, the U.S. ownership of foreign investments is far more concentrated than even the very concentrated ownership of domestic assets.

The same picture of extreme concentration may be seen in Table 2–1, which shows earnings from United States investments abroad. It shows that less than 1 percent of the companies received 61.4 percent of the earnings, whereas 64.9 percent of the companies received less than 1 percent of the earnings. Thus the data indicate that a few companies hold most of the United States investment abroad, and that a few companies (presumably the same large companies for the most part) receive most of the earnings from United States investment abroad.

None of this, however, is sufficient proof that earnings abroad are a significant explanatory factor of the higher profit rates of large firms. It may be accepted that profit rates earned abroad are higher than domestic profit rates. It may also be accepted that earnings abroad are quite concentrated. Two questions, nevertheless, remain unanswered. Is the investment and profit concentration of United States corporations any higher abroad than domestically? If so, does the greater profit rate earned abroad produce enough in quantitative terms to have a significant effect on average profit rates by asset size? Comparisons with earlier data indicate that answers to these questions may help explain the facts, but a much more detailed study would be required to prove their importance.

Table 2-1. Earnings on Foreign Investments by Size of Earning in 1957

Net earnings of direct investments by size of earnings (lower limit)	Number of companies (all industries)	Amount of earnings	Companies (percent)	Earnings
$25,000,000	25	$2,464,000,000	0.9	61.4%
10,000,000	30	443,000,000	1.1	11.0
5,000,000	58	411,000,000	2.1	10.2
2,500,000	72	242,000,000	2.6	6.0
1,000,000	139	209,000,000	4.9	5.2
500,000	138	91,000,000	4.9	2.3
100,000	524	123,000,000	18.6	3.1
1	944	28,000,000	33.6	0.7
0	335		11.9	0.0
Deficit firms	547	−133,000,000	19.4	losses
Total	2,812	$3,881,000,000	100.0	100.0[a]

Source: U.S. Department of Commerce, Office of Business Economics, *United States Investments in Foreign Countries* (Washington, D.C.: U.S.G.P.O., 1960), adapted from Table 56, p. 145.

[a]Here 100.0 percent equals $4,014,000,000 which is $3,881,000,000 plus $133,000,000 deficit.

Concentration of Banking

3

House Committee on Banking and Currency

The latest figures on the concentration of banking in general ... show that as of the end of 1964, the 100 largest commercial banks in the United States held 46.3 percent of all the deposits in the 13,775 commercial banks in the United States. Of these 100 giant banking institutions, the 14 largest, representing one-tenth of 1 percent of all commercial banks in the country, held 24 percent of all commercial bank deposits. Looking at particular metropolitan areas ... FDIC figures indicate that in every one of 65 major metropolitan areas recently surveyed the three largest banks held more than 30 percent of all commercial bank deposits in the area; in 59 of these 65 areas the three largest banks held over 50 percent of all commercial bank deposits, and in 46 of these areas, almost three out of four, the three largest banks held over 70 percent of all commercial bank deposits in the area.

In the trust business, ... indications are that concentration is even greater than in banking in general. Taking trust assets of banks under Federal charter (i.e., national banks) as of the end of 1965, only 26, or 1.7 percent, accounted for $54.7 billion, or 61.2 percent, of all trust assets in national banks. Only 114 national banks held more than $75 billion in trust assets or over 83 percent of the trust assets in all national banks. No comparable statistics are available for state-chartered banks.

In addition, it should be noted that a recent study by the Securities and Exchange Commission indicates that 20 large banks manage almost half of all noninsured private pension fund assets.[1]

Reprinted from the Staff Report for the Domestic Finance Subcommittee of the House Committee on Banking and Currency, 90th Cong., 2nd. sess. *Commercial Banks and Their Trust Activities: Emerging Influence on the American Economy* (Washington, D.C.: U.S. Government Printing Office, July 1968, (Subcommittee Reprint of Staff Report on "Bank Stock Ownership and Control," December 29, 1966), pp. 804–8; and pp. 83; 88–92. Footnotes have been renumbered.

1. United States Congress, House of Representatives Committee on Interstate and Foreign Commerce, 89th Cong., 2nd sess., "Report of the Securities and Exchange Commission on the Public Policy Implications of Investment Company Growth" (Washington, D.C.: December 2, 1966).

... [N]ationwide, commercial banks are today the most important single institutional investor group and are likely to maintain this position indefinitely.... It is also clear ... that concentration in the bank trust business is extremely high and far greater than in commercial banking in general.... Data were obtained from the 49 banks in the 10 cities chosen for detailed study.[2] These 49 banks were asked to submit information on various aspects of their trust department and other operations....

The Subcommittee obtained replies from all 49 banks surveyed. Two of the banks reported that they had no trust assets at all. The amount of total trust assets held by the remaining 49 banks range from $16.8 billion held by the Morgan Guaranty Trust Co. of New York City down to $10,175,000 in trust assets held by the Peoples Union Bank and Trust Co. of Pittsburgh, Pa.

In comparing the coverage in this detailed survey with the overall trust department survey of 2,890 banks, ... we find that these 49 banks hold $135.2 billion in trust assets, or 54.03 percent of all the trust assets in the nationwide survey. Just 30 of the largest banks in the Subcommittee's 49-bank survey hold 51.73 percent of all trust assets in the nationwide survey. Therefore, the coverage obtained by studying in detail the submissions of 49 banks in 10 cities would seem adequate to develop a picture of bank trust department financial activities in general....

In terms of percentage of total trust assets in each of the 10 Standard Metropolitan Areas studied, the banks surveyed hold in the aggregate between 79.2 percent and 99.9 percent of the total bank trust assets in each respective metropolitan area. In 7 of the 10 cities, the banks studied hold over 90 percent of all bank trust assets in the area....

---

2. The 10 cities are Baltimore, Boston, Cincinnati, Chicago, Cleveland, Detroit, Hartford, New York City, Philadelphia, and Pittsburgh. In seven cities the five largest banks by deposit size were chosen, while in New York the six largest banks were used. In Cincinnati and Detroit four banks were surveyed.

Principal Shareholdings in Major Corporations by Banks and Other "Institutional Investors"

4

Senate Committee on Government Operations

BACKGROUND

Congressional committees, federal agencies, and scholars are considering substantive issues created by the dominant role of institutional investors—bank trust departments, insurance companies, investment companies, pension funds, and others, such as foundations and universities—in major corporations. At least 32 institutions are known to manage investment portfolios in excess of $5 billion each. (They are listed in the table below.)

Their decisions can alter the stability of the market and individual companies. To minimize impact on medium and small companies, large institutional investors tend to concentrate their investments in large companies. This has led to the two-tier market, in which stocks of the largest companies trade at a considerably higher multiple of earnings than those of many medium and smaller companies, which encounter difficulty in raising equity capital.

Institutional Investors' Role

The role of institutional investors is of course not limited to the acquisition and sale of stock and the right, in many cases, to vote it. Some institutional investors make loans to companies in which they invest, or provide insurance coverage. Their representatives often sit on the companies' boards of directors. Sometimes institutional investors help facilitate or block mergers.

Reprinted from U.S. Congress. Senate. Subcommittees on Intergovernmental Relations (chaired by Senator Muskie) and on Budgeting, Management, and Expenditures (chaired by Senator Metcalf) of the Senate Committee on Government Operations (chaired by Senator Sam J. Ervin, Jr.), *Disclosure of Corporate Ownership.* 93d Cong., 2nd sess. (Washington, D.C.: Government Printing Office, 1974), pp. 1–3; 5–7; 9–11; 15–16; 21–22; 24–28. Footnotes and tables have been renumbered, and certain subheads edited. Pages 1 through 3 are an "Introduction" by Senators Lee Metcalf and Edmund S. Muskie.

The institutional investors' effect on medium-sized and smaller companies, and those companies' inability to pierce through nominee accounts to communicate with their own stockholders, was described to a Senate subcommittee this summer by the chairman of the Committee of Publicly Owned Companies, C. V. Wood, Jr., who is also president of McCulloch Oil Corporation. Speaking for the leadership of 469 companies with $43 billion in assets, 1.8 million stockholders, and 1.1 million employees, he testified that the institutional investors have run up the price of the stock of the big companies with which they have personnel and business relationships. Trading in stocks of smaller and medium-sized companies languishes; their stock prices sink to new lows despite good earnings. Because the market undervalues the stock, the

Table 4-1. Thirty-two Institutional Investors With Assets Under Management Of $5 Billion And Over, End Of 1972

Investor	Assets (Billions)
1. Morgan Guaranty Trust Company	$27.4
2. Bankers Trust Company, New York	19.9
3. Prudential Insurance Company of America	18.3
4. First National City Bank, New York	17.2
5. U.S. Trust Company of New York	17.0
6. Metropolitan Life Insurance Company	16.5
7. Equitable Life Assurance Society	16.4
8. Chase Manhattan Bank	16.2
9. Travelers Corporation	13.1
10. New York Life Insurance Company	11.5
11. Manufacturers Hanover Trust Company	10.9
12. Mellon National Bank and Trust Company	10.5
13. Investors Diversified Services	9.7
14. First National Bank of Chicago	8.4
15. Continental Illinois National Bank and Trust Company	8.2
16. Aetna Life and Casualty Group	8.2
17. Scudder, Stevens and Clark	7.2
18. Bank of America	7.1
19. Harris Trust and Savings Bank	7.0
20. Wilmington Trust Company	7.0
21. First National Bank of Boston	6.8
22. Northern Trust Company, Chicago	6.7
23. Chemical Bank, New York	6.5
24. National Bank of Detroit	6.5
25. Loomis, Sayles and Company	6.3
26. Northwestern Mutual Life Insurance Company	6.1
27. Lionel D. Edie and Company	6.1
28. Wells Fargo Bank	6.0
29. Equitable Trust Company of Baltimore	5.5
30. Girard Bank, Philadelphia	5.2
31. Crocker Citizens National Bank	5.0

Sources: *Business Week*, June 2, 1973. *Fortune*, July 1973. *1973 Money Market Directory*.

smaller companies cannot raise money in the market for replacement or expansion of facilities. So they have to borrow the capital they need, increasing their debt-equity ratio to dangerous highs. They borrow at escalated interest rates from the banks which are driving them deeper into debt. They cannot break through the maze of nominee accounts held by institutional investors to communicate directly with their beneficial shareholders. As a consequence, Chairman Wood testified, the smaller and medium U.S. corporations have become prime targets of the foreign companies which have recently taken over U.S. companies from bases in Italy, France, Switzerland, Germany, the United Kingdom, and Saudi Arabia.[1]

The multiple levers of corporate management available to institutional investors present fundamental questions regarding public policy. These matters cut across the concerns of a number of different agencies and congressional committees. Together they present questions about the nature of our industrial society—how it will be directed and controlled.

There is as yet no consensus regarding what additional government controls, if any, should be placed on institutional investors. Indeed, there is respectable opinion that institutional controls produce beneficial effects, such as more rational and expert market analysis, and more effective oversight of corporate management. . . .

Despite agencies' requests for identification of those security holders with highest voting powers, the companies frequently report "nominees" or "street names" which represent the stock held by institutions which frequently are not named in the reports.

A single institutional investor may use a dozen or more different "street" names. Although some agencies tell companies to list security holders "in order of voting power," holdings of the same institutional investor frequently are not consolidated in reports to the federal regulatory commissions. The commissions nevertheless accept the unconsolidated, unresponsive, and misleading data, and place it in their public files.

The Nominee List

Only through use of the *Nominee List,* published by the American Society of Corporate Secretaries[2] can one translate the nominees to

---

1. Some years ago the FPC's request to obtain voting right information on more than 10 security holders was denied by the Budget Bureau, on the advice of one of its business advisory committees on Federal reports.

2. A government regulatory agency official, a newspaper editor, and an attorney reported in 1971 that the American Society of Corporate Secretaries refused to sell them a copy of the *Nominee List.* The 1971 edition was printed in the *Congressional Record* on June 24, 1971, (Vol. 117, No. 98—Part II). Subsequently the Society decided to sell the *Nominee List,* which is updated and issued early each year, for $20. The Society's address is 1 Rockefeller Plaza, New York, N.Y. 10020.

institutions. An excerpt from the Comptroller General's April 10, 1973, letter . . . describes the findings of the General Accounting Office on this point:

> We examined a limited number of reports and applications requiring ownership information. It appeared that for large regulated companies the names of nominees are often shown in lieu of the names of stock owners. The presence of nominees in the ownership data was confirmed by officials of each of the agencies, who told us that the companies were not in a position to know who the stock owners were. The officials stated that the companies could only report the names of the stockholders of record, which includes nominees.
>
> Using the *Nominee List,* published by the American Society of Corporate Secretaries, we were able to identify the person or organization the nominees represented. For example, the 1972 annual report submitted to the Interstate Commerce Commission by one of the country's largest railroads included 24 nominees among the list of the 30 largest stockholders. The 24 nominees represented two insurance companies and 12 banks.[3]

Use of Multiple Nominees

 . . . . The holdings of institutional investors, especially banks, are often hidden from view of regulators and the public through use of multiple nominees—"Hemfar & Co.," "Lerche & Co.," "Kane & Co.," "Bark & Co.," "Pace & Co.," and many more. In response to the federal regulators' request for the addresses of these "security holders" the companies report simply "New York, N.Y.," "Boston, Mass.," or "Pittsburgh, Pa.," occasionally adding a post office box number. These nominee names are not in the city directory. They are not in the telephone book. Letters to some nominees whose post office box is listed have not been answered.

---

3. The ownership reports filed with the ICC by railroads which have become subsidiaries of conglomerate holding companies are even less informative than the example used here. Each subsidiary railroad simply lists the name of its parent company.

Conglomerates have practically taken over the railroad industry in the short span of 11 years. In 1962 two major railroads were acquired by parent holding companies. By June 15, 1973, 16 major railroads, which account for approximately two-thirds of the total industry revenues and ton-miles, were controlled by conglomerate holding companies.

On August 9, 1973, the Interstate Commerce Commission advised Congress of questionable and improper practices of the railroad conglomerates. The ICC requested legislation which, among other things, would require reports to the ICC by any persons having legal or beneficial ownership, as trustee or otherwise, of more than 1 percent of the stock of major railroads.

The ICC's report and recommended legislation (S. 2460) appears in the Sept. 20, 1973, Congressional Record pp. 17102–07.

The consequence of this continuing use of nominees in ownership reports to federal regulators is a massive coverup of the extent to which holdings of stock have become concentrated in the hands of very few institutional investors, especially banks.

THIRTY TOP STOCKHOLDERS OF EIGHTY-NINE COMPANIES

This report is an analysis of the responses received from 324 of the nation's largest companies in response to a request last year for identification of their 30 top stockholders, the amount of common stock each held, and the total number of voting shares of common stock. The letters to the chief executive officer of each company stated that if the company records did not conveniently identify the actual owner of the stock the street name (nominee) would suffice.

Eighty-nine of the 324 companies responded fully to the query. Partial information was supplied by 74. Subsidiary companies responded in 20 instances. Eighty-three replied without submitting relevant data and 58 did not reply. . . .

The comprehensive industry-by-industry analysis of these replies was prepared by Julius W. Allen, senior specialist in business economics at the Congressional Research Service, Library of Congress, with the assistance of Miss Eugénie Dieringer.

Eighty-nine Companies Deserve Commendation

The 89 companies which fully responded to the query deserve commendation. Their willingness to cooperate contrasts sharply with the unresponsiveness of most of the other companies. The most unresponsive companies were generally those subject to minimal public disclosure requirements—banks, retail companies, industrial and insurance companies, and miscellaneous transportation companies. Policy considerations alone do not appear to justify this inattention. For instance, banks not only manage huge blocks of stock as trustees. They also provide large amounts of capital in the form of loans to the same companies (which make conflicts of interest a definite possibility). They have their own officers sitting on the portfolio companies' boards of directors (which makes it difficult to avoid self-dealing on the basis of inside information). Thus policy considerations would seem to cut the opposite way. It is fair to infer that nondisclosure is more the consequence of governmental apathy than corporate necessity.

It is important to note that not all of the stockholdings analyzed [here] necessarily carry voting rights. Banks may have sole, partial or no voting rights in stock they hold.[4] . . .

---

4. The 1968 Patman Committee study of 13,598 employee benefit accounts managed by 43 banks showed that the banks had sole voting rights in all stock investments in 81.5 percent (11,087) of the accounts. (House Banking and Currency Subcommittee on Domestic Finance, *Commercial Banks and Their Trust Activities: Emerging Influence on the American Economy*, Vol. 1, p. 510.)

Using the *Nominee List,* Mr. Allen and associates on our staffs translated nominees into the actual institutional investors. They found that frequently the "30 top stockholders" were but 20 or so, because holdings of the same institutional investor were listed separately in two, three, or more accounts. Nominees used by the various investors are included in the tabulations within Mr. Allen's report.

Cede & Co. The stock reported in the nominee name "Cede & Co." has not been translated because it is in a different category. A few words of explanation and caution about Cede & Co. are in order.

Cede (pronounced "seedy") & Co. is technically a nominee for a nominee. It was created in 1966 and became fully operational in 1969 as the nominee for the Stock Clearing Corporation, a wholly owned subsidiary of the New York Stock Exchange, which furnished stock clearing service to member brokerage firms. Listings under Cede & Co. formerly represented deposits in the Exchange's Central Certificate Service. In May, 1973, the business of CCS was transferred to a new Exchange subsidiary, the Depository Trust Company, for which Cede & Co. is now the nominee.

Cede & Co., as record holder of securities of New York issuers, is entitled to vote stock, but does so only on instructions of the Depository Trust member to whose account such securities are credited. . . .

Concentration in New York Bank Trust Departments. The concentration of stockholdings in a whole range of companies—energy, manufacturing, transportation, communications, and retail trade—among a handful of New York bank trust departments is portrayed in Table 4–3 (p. 00). It lists the holders of 2 percent or more of the voting stock in three or more of the 89 cooperating companies. Following Cede & Co., which was the holder of record of 2 percent or more of the stock in 55 of the 89 companies, were the trust departments of four New York banks.

Chase Manhattan held 2 percent or more of the stock in more than half (46) of the companies.

Morgan Guaranty and First National City Bank held 2 percent or more of the stock in almost one-third (29 and 28) of the companies.

Bankers Trust held 2 percent or more of the stock in almost one-fourth (21) of the companies.

Ranking slightly below Bankers Trust were the New York brokerage house, Merrill Lynch, Pierce, Fenner & Smith, with 2 percent or more of the stock in 19 reporting companies, the Bank of New York in 17 companies, and State Street Bank of Boston in 16 companies.

Table 4–4 (pp. 00–00) shows the holdings of the above eight institutions in the 89 cooperating companies. These are the institutions which held 2 percent or more of the stock in 10 or more of the 89 reporting companies, arranged by industry groups. Thus, for example, Chase Manhattan's trust department held between 9 and 6.9 percent of the stock in each of four airlines, between 8.3 and 5.3 percent of the stock in each of six railroads, and more than 5 percent of the stock in each of five industrials, in addition to lesser amounts of stock in other companies in each of the categories. Table 4–4 also shows that the above eight institutions together held 20 percent or more of the stock in a number of companies.

The Top of the Pyramid. Were this report presented in geometric terms and were full data on bank ownership available, the top of the pyramid might well be the final page of Table 4–4 which shows the holdings of the eight above institutions in banks. As noted previously, the response from banks to the query regarding 30 top stockholders was poor; only nine of the 50 queried responded fully. The nine cooperating banks include two which are also among the eight major institutional investors mentioned above. First National City Bank reported that Chase Manhattan's trust department held 2.7 percent and Morgan Guaranty's trust department held 2 percent of First National City Bank's stock. Bankers Trust reported that Chase Manhattan held 2.4 percent, and State Street of Boston 2.1 percent of Bankers Trust's stock.

Bank Nominees Dominate Holdings

Data from banks which submitted partial responses show that bank nominees dominate the holdings of the 30 top security holders in banks. More than one-fourth of the stock in Wells Fargo was reported held by 21 unidentified bank nominees. The 30 top security holders in J. P. Morgan, holding more than one-fourth of the stock in that bank, included 22 unidentified bank nominees. Fifteen percent of the stock in Chase Manhattan was reported held by 22 unidentified bank nominees. The reported bank holdings, in most instances, were several times greater than the combined holdings of other institutional and individual investors among the top security holders. . . .

THE MULTIPLE LEVERS OF CONTROL

Inadequate Disclosure a Recurring Theme. Control of a small block of stock in a widely held company by a single or few like-minded financial institutions provides them with disproportionately large powers within the company. The House Banking and Currency Subcommittee on Domestic Finance, in its 1968 study *Commercial Banks and Their Trust Activities: Emerging Influence on the American Economy,* considered a 5 percent or larger holding of one class of stock significant in judging the potential influence of a bank trust department's stockholding in a particular corporation. The subcommittee emphasized that "even 1 or 2 percent of stock in a publicly held corporation can gain tremendous influence over a company's policies and operations."

Control Presumed

Congress has established various ownership percentages, usually 10 percent, as the benchmark at which control by an institution or individual holding can be presumed. It is noteworthy that in 1970 sections 13(d) and 14(d) of the Securities and Exchange Act of 1934 were amended to reduce from 10 percent to 5 percent the levels of ownership at which a person seeking shares of a company would be required to report his holdings. This appears to reflect the feeling that at these levels such a person could acquire substantial leverage in the company. S 2460, recently recommended by the ICC, ... would require reporting of 1 percent or more holdings of any class of stock in a railroad having operating revenues exceeding $5 million annually. S 2506, the Oil and Gas Regulatory Reform Act of 1973 now being considered by the Senate Commerce Committee, would require oil pipeline applicants to report "the name and address of each shareholder with voting rights to one per centum or more of the shares, together with the number and percentage of any class of voting shares of the entity which such shareholder is authorized to vote."

The levers of control available to principal stockholders derive from several sources. One of these sources, regarding which detailed information is presented here, is the purchase, sale, holding, and voting of stock. [See Table 4–5 for a summary of stockholder data on 89 firms.] As prelude to our discussion of the other levers of control we note that, as in the case of stockholdings, a recurring theme is inadequate disclosure by institutional investors, especially banks, to the Government, to stockholders, and even to portfolio companies.

Information Not Included in "IIS" Report. The SEC's *Institutional Investor Study* report concluded that some institutions, particularly banks, have personnel and business relationships with portfolio companies which may tend to reinforce any power conferred as a result of stock holdings, create potential conflicts of interest and lead to misuse of inside information. The *IIS* report found a strong statistical correlation between bank stockholdings and personnel and business relationships. However, the SEC did not collect and publish information regarding the personnel and business relationships of identified institutional investors. Nor did it publish details regarding the personnel and business relationships of unidentified, individual institutional investors.

Inadequate Information on Corporate Interlocks. Comprehensive and current information regarding such relationships between individual bank trust departments and their portfolio companies is difficult to assemble either from agency files or standard references. Some major banks were not responsive to a recent request by the Congressional Research Service of the Library of Congress for a report on their corporate interlocks with other corporations, funds, and universities.

Chase Manhattan did not respond to repeated requests, written and oral, from the Congressional Research Service. Morgan Guaranty Trust supplied information regarding interlocks with publicly owned domestic corporations and domestic foundations and universities. However,

Morgan did not report interlocks with closely held companies, foreign corporations or subsidiaries and other affiliates of domestic corporations. Furthermore, Morgan supplied CRS only with interlocking positions, without providing the names of the directors or officers who held them.

Interlocks extend well beyond the election of an institutional representative to the portfolio company's board of directors, or a portfolio company's official on the board of the financial institution. Interlocks provide major banks with levers throughout the industries in which they hold major blocks of stock. These interlocks also extend into the federal agencies which regulate portfolio companies, as was documented in the hearings by the Subcommittee on Intergovernmental Relations which preceded enactment of PL 92–463, the Federal Advisory Committee Act. . . .

CONCLUSIONS AND RECOMMENDATIONS

Neither companies nor ordinary stockholders have information which they need, to protect their own interests, regarding stock ownership and the personnel and business relationships between portfolio companies and institutional investors, principally banks. The federal government does not have sufficient information in these areas upon which to base reasoned public policy. Much of the information collected by federal agencies regarding stock ownership, displayed in public files and shared with state agencies and the public, is meaningless or misleading despite the clear policy stated in the Federal Reports Act of 1942 that information collected by federal agencies should be tabulated so as to "maximize the usefulness of the information to other federal agencies and the public."

The information needed regarding the several levers of corporate control is held by a few institutional investors, principally six superbanks headquartered in New York. These institutional investors have the capacity to report their holdings quickly and fully.[5] Similar reports on personnel and business relationships with portfolio companies would be even easier to make.

Effect of Concentration

Congress and some Federal commissions have on occasion established limits on institutional levers of corporate control, principally regarding stockholders. But neither the Congress, nor the commissions,

---

5. "We will know sometime today what our position was in various companies yesterday . . ."—Edward T. Ryan, vice president, Chase Manhattan, FCC Administrative Conference with the American Bankers Association, Sept. 1, 1970, Docket 18751.

"Sure, we'll disclose as often as you like—every week, if necessary."—Roger Kennedy, vice president, Ford Foundation, *Business Week*, June 2, 1973.

nor the executive branch can fully evaluate the total effect of concentration—the impact of the several levers of corporate control exercised by banks and other major investors throughout industry groups and the economy as a whole.

Meanwhile, the portfolio companies in which a few banks have substantial influence make many decisions affecting public policy. Oil companies deal with foreign nations regarding oil supply and cost. Pipeline companies deal with the Soviet Union for natural gas. Utilities exercise the right of eminent domain. Milling companies and the Soviet Union arrange grain sales which sharply affect domestic price, supply, transportation, and storage. These are momentous public issues in which Federal officials play a minor role, much of it after basic decisions have been agreed upon by American companies and foreign governments. . . .

DISCLOSURE IS THE PREREQUISITE

Whatever solutions the federal government chooses to the mounting problems resulting from economic concentration, the prerequisite is the regular collection and disclosure of information from institutional investors on stock holdings and the personnel and business relationships between institutional investors and portfolio companies.

Equally important, the information must be centrally available to the federal government and the public, at one location, most appropriately the Library of Congress. Such information, insofar as it is now reported, is scattered among three federal banking agencies, 50 State insurance commissions, the SEC (for investment companies), various other federal and state regulatory commissions, and the files of hundreds of universities, foundations, and funds.

Proprietary Owners Should Be Identified

Proprietary owners of 1 percent or more of the stock in publicly held companies should be identified. Reports on their voting rights and their corporate personnel and financial relationships should be filed, on a quarterly basis, with the Library of Congress. This information should be published, for regulatory review and stockholder information.

Straightforward and regular reporting of these matters will vastly simplify the job of regulatory commissions, and provide Congress with basic information which it always needs and never has. It will also afford ample time and minimum inconvenience to those stockholders who wish to discuss issues and candidates for corporate elections—prior to proxy solicitation—with representatives of the large institutional investors who usually cast the deciding votes.

Stockholders Face Obstacles. Stockholders at present face formidable obstacles. Considerable expense and effort is required, months prior to annual meetings, for stockholders to comply with SEC rules, to receive consideration of modest, additional agenda items or even one candidate for the board of directors, then to locate and present their case to the few institutional investors who by proxy and often casually will decide the outcome of the election. Because of these cumbersome procedures the typical corporate election today features a "Russian ballot"—bearing a single slate of nominees for the board of directors. Some company ballots do not even provide for casting a no vote.

If Congress, like Salome, decides to lift the seven veils, which in this instance shroud the ownership of stock, care must be taken that the lists of principal proprietary owners do not get lost in "Cede & Co," the nominee for the new subsidiary of the New York Stock Exchange, Depository Trust Company, which has replaced the Central Certificate Service division of Stock Clearing Corporation. The urgent need to reduce the paperwork burden of the securities industry must not be permitted to render meaningless the effort to provide timely access to the voter lists which are fundamental to affecting change within corporate and political systems.

OVERSIGHT NEEDED

Much can be done toward reaching the objectives suggested above without new legislation. The regulatory commissions suffer from lack of oversight by Congress, the Office of Management and Budget and the General Accounting Office. . . .

FINDINGS ON LEADING STOCKHOLDERS

The Institutional Investor Study Report of the Securities and Exchange Commission, issued in 1971, points out that institutions as a group (excluding endowments, foundations, investment counseling accounts, and various minor types of institutionally managed portfolios for which data are not available prior to 1952) increased their share of total stock outstanding from less than 7 percent in 1900 to about 19 percent in 1952. A more comprehensive definition of financial institutions places estimates of institutional holdings at about 24 percent of outstanding corporate stock in 1952, a figure that increased to 26 percent by 1958 where, with some fluctuations, it remained through the following decade.[6] However it should be noted that these investments have been concentrated heavily in the shares of the larger, publicly traded corporations. Thus, as the same study notes, three successive Census of Share-ownership surveys conducted by the New York Stock Exchange

---

6. U.S. Securities and Exchange Commission. Institutional Investor Study Report. Summary Volume (92nd Congress, 1st Session, House Doc. No. 92-64, Part 8), p. ix.

of the ownership of securities listed on that Exchange show that from 1962 to 1965 and 1970, institutional holdings increased from 31.1 percent to 35.5 percent to 39.4 percent, respectively.[7] In fact, John C. Whitehead, chairman of the Securities Industry Association, is reported to have said this year: "In 1963, institutional investors accounted for 35 percent of the dollar value of New York Stock Exchange trading volume. That percentage today is over 70 percent. In some stocks, 90 percent of volume is institutional."[8]

Equity Holdings of Financial Institutions

Paul Kolton, president of the American Stock Exchange, estimated this year that total equity holdings of financial institutions amounted to $310 billion divided as [shown in Table 4–2].[9]

Some of the potential danger that such concentration portends was well outlined in the recent *Business Week* article from which the statistics just cited are taken: "Are the Institutions Wrecking Wall Street?" (*Business Week*, June 2, 1973, pp. 58–66.) This article reaches the following conclusion:

> It is a fact that institutions [mutual funds, insurance companies, pension funds, and bank trust departments] trade stocks in such huge quantities that they accentuate price swings in the market—all the more so because institutions increasingly limit their investing to a relative handful of stocks. What has emerged is a highly volatile market in a few issues, a lackluster market in most issues—and a closed door to many of the companies that want to take their shares public. Beyond all that—and one prime reason the small investor has deserted the market—are allegations that institutions, because of their huge holdings, are privy to inside information of which the small investor is left ignorant.

Two-tier Market

Similarly the lead article in the July 1973 issue of *Fortune*, "How the Terrible Two-Tier Market Came to Wall Street," by Carol J. Loomis, starts out with the summary statement: "The big banks have used their

Table 4-2. Estimated Total Equity Holdings of Financial Institutions, 1974

Institution	Holdings (billions)
Banks	$170
Mutual funds	45
Insurance companies	42
Foundations, investment counselors, and smaller institutions	53

7. Ibid., p. ix.
8. *Business Week,* June 2, 1973, p. 58.
9. Ibid., p. 58.

trust and pension-fund dollars to create a situation unique in history. For a good many corporations it spells trouble in raising equity capital." The two-tier market refers to one market of a select few securities, usually with very high price-earnings ratios, so-called glamour stocks, which institutional investors favor to the virtual exclusion of the other market which consists of less favored stocks which nonetheless have substantial investment merit. As the article states (p. 83):

> The two-tier market owes its existence to the actions, and the nonactions, of both institutional and individual investors. But market conditions at the moment suggest that control of the situation lies in the hands of the institutions, and that the two-tier market will disappear only if they—and in particular those giants, the bank trust departments—decide to swerve from the investment policies on which they have leaned very heavily in the last few years. The power of the institutions to shape events seems right now more awesome than ever before—and also more subject to attack.

Bank Trust Departments

Finally, another aspect of the same problem is confronted by Martin E. Lybecker, writing in the April 1973 issue of the *Yale Law Journal,* when he states:

> Among the most powerful (and most anonymous) of our nation's financial institutions are bank trust departments. They manage assets substantially exceeding the assets of the largest one hundred corporations in the United States. In fact, bank trust departments have larger securities portfolios than all other institutional investors combined. As a result, certain commercial banks have the power to control major corporations.
>
> Yet the regulation of bank trust departments seems cursory in many respects compared to that applied to other institutional investors. Only superficial data are gathered by bank examiners, whose responsibilities relate primarily to the bank's other departments. Even less information is made available to the public.[10] . . .

SUMMARY TABLES

Precautionary Note

A precautionary note needs to be stressed . . . which applies to . . . the tables in this report. The data showing holdings by trust departments of banks and other financial institutions indicate aggregate holdings without any indication as to the voting power inherent in such holdings. These holdings will include some with full voting authority,

---

10. Lybecker, Martin E. Regulation of bank trust department investment activities. *Yale Law Journal,* 82 (April, 1973):997.

some with contingent or partial voting power, and some with no voting rights.[11]

This precaution is especially important in interpretation of data on Cede and Company, the nominee of the New York Stock Exchange through its subsidiary corporation, the Depository Trust Company. Under the rules of the stock exchange, Cede and Company only votes stock on the instruction of member firms belonging to the Depository Trust Company in whose name the stock is registered, even though there is no legal restriction to Cede's right to vote stock it holds. Thus the fact that Cede and Company is the largest, or a sizeable, holder of stock in a given company should not be interpreted as giving it actual voting strength in the stock of such a company. . . .

. . . Tables 4–3 and 4–4 provide an overview of the extent to which major institutions hold 2 or more percent of the stock of the 89 reporting companies. Table 4–3 (p. 00) includes all those institutional investors which held 2 or more percent of the *voting stock* of three or more of the 89 reporting companies. The totals are broken down into the industry categories which are utilized in this report.

Thus it can be seen that, based on returns from 89 corporations, Cede and Company held 2 or more percent of 55 out of these companies, followed by Chase Manhattan with 2 percent or more of 46 companies, Morgan Guaranty with 2 percent or more of 29 companies, and First National City Bank with 2 percent or more of 28 companies. Twenty-four institutional investors held 2 percent or more of at least three companies among the 89 reporting companies. These include (besides Cede and Company, the nominee of the New York Stock Exchange) eight New York banks, three Boston banks, two Chicago banks, two Minneapolis banks, six other banks, and two New York brokerage houses.

Top Institutional Holders

More detail is shown in Table 4–4 (p. 00–00) which takes the top eight institutional holders of this table, those with 2 percent or more of more than 10 out of the 89 reporting companies, and shows the actual percentages of total voting stock held by these eight holders in specific companies, arranged in the same sequence followed throughout the main body of the report, that is by industry group and within the group by size of company. Thus it can be seen, for example, that Cede and Company, among the 55 companies in which it held 2 percent or more of the voting stock, held 32.6 percent of the stock of the Chicago

---

11. Part II of [the original] document deals with stock in which institutional investors have sole voting rights. Part III deals with stock in which institutional investors have sole or partial voting rights.

Table 4-3. Holders of 2 Percent or More of Voting Stock in Three or More of 89 Fully Reporting Companies in 1972, by Industry Group

	Total number of companies	Industrials Petroleum	Other	Transportation Airlines	Railroads	Other	Utilities Communication	Electricity and gas	Retail trade	Banks	Life insurance
(Total reporting)	(89)	(4)	(21)	(9)	(15)	(2)	(4)	(16)	(8)	(9)	(1)
Cede & Co.	55	4	13	8	6	2	3	11	7	1	0
Chase Manhattan Bank	46	2	15	5	8	1	2	6	4	2	1
Morgan Guaranty	29	3	6	5	3	0	0	3	6	2	1
First National City Bank	28	1	6	3	4	0	2	5	1	5	1
Bankers Trust	21	2	6	5	2	0	1	1	2	2	0
Merrill Lynch, Pierce, Fenner & Smith Inc.	19	0	4	3	7	0	0	3	2	0	0
Bank of New York	17	0	3	4	4	1	1	1	3	0	0
State Street of Boston	16	0	3	4	2	0	1	0	4	1	1
Manufacturers Hanover	9	0	3	0	3	0	0	2	0	1	0
First National of Chicago	8	0	3	1	1	0	0	1	1	1	0
National Shawmut of Boston	6	0	1	4	0	0	0	0	1	0	0
Continental Illinois, Chicago	6	1	1	2	1	0	0	0	1	0	0
Commerce Bank of Kansas City	6	0	1	0	2	0	0	1	1	1	0
First National of Boston	5	0	4	1	0	0	0	0	0	0	0
National Bank of Detroit	5	0	4	1	0	0	0	0	0	0	0
Chemical Bank of New York	5	0	0	0	2	0	1	0	1	1	0
Northwestern National, Minneapolis	5	0	0	2	0	0	0	0	3	0	0
First Jersey, Jersey City	5	0	0	2	0	0	0	1	2	0	0
Brown Brothers, Harriman	4	0	1	0	0	0	0	1	2	0	0
U.S. Trust	3	0	2	0	0	0	1	0	0	0	0
Bank of Delaware	3	0	0	0	1	0	0	0	0	2	0
Mellon National Bank, Pittsburgh	3	0	0	0	0	0	0	0	1	2	0
Girard Trust, Philadelphia	3	0	0	0	0	0	0	1	1	1	0
First National Bank of Minneapolis	3	0	0	0	0	0	1	0	1	1	0

Table 4–4. Eight Institutional Holders of 2 Percent or More of Voting Stock in 10 or More of the 89 Reporting Companies with the Percentage of Voting Stock Held in these Companies in 1972

	Cede & Co.	Chase Manhattan Bank	Morgan Guaranty	First National City Bank	Bankers Trust	Merrill Lynch, Pierce, Fenner & Smith	Bank of New York	State Street of Boston
Industrials								
A. Oil Companies								
Mobil Oil	2.3	5.2	2.9	—	6.1	—	—	—
Atlantic Richfield	2.3	4.5	—	2.7	—	—	—	—
Continental Oil	4.4	—	2.2	—	5.8	—	—	—
Ashland Oil	7.0	—	2.1	—	—	—	—	—
B. Other Industrial Companies								
Ford Motor	—	3.5	—	2.9	—	—	—	2.2
General Electric	—	3.6	2.7	—	—	—	—	—
Chrysler	12.1	4.0	—	—	—	2.2	—	2.0
Westinghouse	—	2.1	5.0	—	—	—	—	—
RCA	—	4.2	—	—	—	3.2	—	—
Union Carbide	3.2	5.2	—	—	2.4	2.0	—	—
Kraftco	2.1	—	—	2.4	—	—	—	—
Greyhound	8.1	—	—	—	—	—	—	—
Litton Industries	8.4	9.0	—	—	—	—	—	—
Caterpillar Tractor	—	—	2.1	5.0	—	—	—	—
Monsanto	3.1	7.4	2.4	—	—	—	—	—
Dow Chemical	—	2.0	—	—	2.1	—	—	—
United Aircraft	4.6	4.0	7.0	—	3.1	—	4.0	—
Xerox	4.3	2.5	3.9	6.1	2.5	—	—	—
R. J. Reynolds	—	2.8	—	—	—	—	—	—
Bendix	4.9	—	—	10.9	4.9	—	—	—
United Brands	20.5	8.0	—	—	—	2.5	—	—
Textron	4.7	—	—	4.1	—	—	2.2	—
CPC International	—	—	—	—	—	—	—	—
Warner-Lambert	2.4	4.7	—	—	2.8	—	—	—
Raytheon	5.5	2.0	—	—	—	—	4.2	3.7
Transportation *A. Airlines*								
United Airlines	3.7	8.3	2.5	3.1	6.3	—	—	2.4
American Airlines	2.9	9.0	4.3	3.3	8.1	—	4.7	—
Pan American World Airways	15.0	2.7	2.0	—	3.7	2.3	3.7	3.6
Northwest Airlines	4.8	6.9	2.1	—	4.9	—	6.5	—
Braniff Airways	15.3	—	—	3.7	5.8	3.5	4.4	4.1
Western Air Lines	—	7.3	5.1	—	—	5.7	—	—
Pacific Southwest Airlines	21.3	—	—	—	—	—	—	6.5
North Central Airlines	10.6	—	—	—	—	—	—	—
Frontier Airlines	10.7	—	—	—	—	—	—	—

Table 4–4. (cont.)

	Cede & Co.	Chase Man- hattan Bank	Morgan Guaranty	First National City Bank	Bankers Trust	Merrill Lynch, Pierce, Fenner & Smith	Bank of New York	State Street of Boston
Northeast Utilities	3.0	—	—	—	—	—	—	—
Pennzoil	—	2.8	—	7.5	—	3.0	—	—
Baltimore Gas & Electric	4.2	2.1	—	—	—	—	—	—
Allegheny Power	5.9	1.8	—	3.6	—	—	—	—
Transcontinental Gas Pipeline	4.3	—	—	—	2.0	—	—	—
Pennsylvania Power & Light	3.8	—	—	—	—	—	—	—
Long Island Lighting	4.6	5.1	3.9	3.0	—	—	—	—
Potomac Electric	6.1	—	—	—	—	—	—	—
Pacific Power & Light	—	—	—	—	—	2.5	—	—
Cleveland Electric Illuminating	3.3	—	—	—	—	—	—	—
Retail								
Safeway Stores	5.3	10.5	3.0	—	—	2.5	—	—
Gamble–Skogmo	5.4	—	—	—	—	—	—	3.1
Grand Union	13.6	2.5	3.3	—	—	—	—	—
R.H. Macy	2.4	3.4	6.2	—	—	—	3.3	2.6
Interstate Stores	18.7	3.7	4.1	4.0	2.7	—	5.1	—
Cook United	6.0	—	—	—	4.2	—	2.2	2.9
Melville Shoe Corp.	2.2	—	6.7	—	—	—	—	—
Pueblo International	—	—	2.7	—	—	9.7	—	3.4
Banks								
First National City	—	2.7	2.0	4.3	—	—	—	—
Chemical New York Corp.	2.2	—	—	—	—	—	—	—
Bankers Trust	—	2.4	—	—	5.7	—	—	2.1
First Bank System (Minneapolis)	—	—	—	3.9	—	—	—	—
Republic National Bank of Dallas	—	—	—	—	—	—	—	—
Girard Trust	—	—	—	3.2	—	—	—	—
First National Bank in Dallas	—	—	—	10.2	—	—	—	—
Citizens & Southern	—	—	3.6	6.7	2.3	—	—	—
Shawmut Associaton	—	—	—	—	—	—	—	—
Insurance								
Travelers Insurance	—	3.0	6.0	2.0	—	—	—	3.8

	Cede & Co.	Chase Manhattan Bank	Morgan Guaranty	First National City Bank	Bankers Trust	Merrill Lynch, Pierce, Fenner & Smith	Bank of New York	State Street of Boston
B. Railroads								
Penn Central	18.9	—	—	—	—	2.7	—	—
Burlington Northern	—	6.7	—	—	4.5	2.5	6.1	4.2
Norfolk & Western	—	4.2	2.1	—	—	—	—	—
Chesapeak & Ohio	—	—	—	—	—	4.4	—	—
Seaboard Coast Line Industries, Inc.	4.4	6.2	3.2	2.8	—	—	—	—
Southern Railway	—	8.3	3.5	2.0	—	—	2.0	7.1
Missouri Pacific	—	—	—	—	—	—	—	—
Chicago Rock Island & Pacific	—	—	—	—	—	—	—	—
Chicago Milwaukee Corp.	32.6	2.8	—	—	—	4.4	—	—
St. Louis- San Francisco	—	6.5	—	—	3.9	2.5	2.6	—
Rio Grande Industries	7.7	5.7	—	4.0	—	—	5.4	—
Kansas City Southern Industries	13.9	5.3	—	2.1	—	—	—	—
Soo Line	8.4	—	—	—	—	—	—	—
Reading	—	—	—	—	—	3.6	—	—
Gulf, Mobile & Ohio	—	—	—	—	—	5.8	—	—
C. Other Transportation								
Seatrain Lines	4.2	3.1	—	—	—	—	4.4	—
Spector Industries	15.1	—	—	—	—	—	—	—
Utilities								
A. Communications								
AT & T	—	—	—	—	—	—	—	—
General Telephone & Electronics	3.8		—	2.3	—	—	—	—
Continental Telephone	2.4	4.9	—	5.1	—	—	2.8	—
Western Union	6.9	4.3	—	—	6.2	—	—	4.1
B. Other Utilities								
American Electric Power	5.5	2.8	—	—	—	—	—	—
Virginia Electric and Power	—	—	3.1	5.6	—	3.7	—	—
Texas Eastern Transmission Co.	—	—	—	—	—	—	2.6	—
Texas Utilities	—	2.9	2.1	2.4	—	—	—	—
American Natural Gas	5.4	—	—	—	—	—	—	—
Niagara Mohawk Power	6.9	—	—	—	—	—	—	—

Milwaukee Corporation; 21.3 percent of the stock of Pacific Southwestern Airlines; 20.5 percent of the stock of United Brands; and 15 or more percent of the stock of five other companies. Similarly it can be seen that Chase Manhattan Bank, among the 46 companies in which it held 2 or more percent of the stock, includes five airlines, in four of which its holdings ranked between 9.0 and 6.9 percent; eight railroads, in six of which its holdings ranked between 8.3 and 5.3 percent; and 17 industrial companies, in five of which its holdings exceeded 5 percent of the company's outstanding stock.

Summary Information

Table 4–5 (pp. 49–52) is a more general summary table of the information supplied by the 89 [firms] that provided information on their top 30 stockholders of record. The information is arranged by industry division and subdivision (e.g., industrial corporations are divided into oil companies and all other industrial companies) and within each division companies are arranged by size. Five columns of data are provided as follows: (1) the percentage of total *voting stock* held by 30 top stockholders; (2) the percentage of total *voting stock* held by New York banks that are among the 30 top stockholders; (3) the percentage of total *voting stock* held by the single largest stockholder; this is divided into three groups: (*a*) where the largest stockholder is a New York bank; in this case the particular bank is indicated by a letter symbol; (*b*) where the largest stockholder is Cede and Company, the nominee of the New York Stock Exchange; and (*c*) where the largest stockholder is neither a New York bank nor Cede and Company. All of the data in this table are taken from the individual tabulations and text [of the original report]. . . .

Table 4-5. Summary of Stockholder Data Supplied by 89 Respondents Supplying Data on 30 Largest Stockholders in 1972

	Percent of stock held by 30 largest stockholders	Percent of stock held by New York banks within the 30 largest stockholders	Percent held by largest single stockholder except where largest stockholder is a New York bank or Cede & Co.	Largest percent of stock held by a New York bank[1]	Percent held by Cede & Co.
I. Industrials					
A. Oil Companies					
Mobil Oil	29.0	17.4	—	6.1 BT	2.3
Atlantic Richfield	26.3	11.7	—	4.5 CM	2.3
Continental Oil	30.8	13.3	—	5.8 BT	4.4
Ashland Oil	22.6	3.0	—	2.1 MG	7.0
B. Other Industrials					
Ford Motor	35.7	11.2	12.2[2]	3.5 CM	1.6
General Electric	21.1	14.0	—	3.6 CM	1.6
Chrysler	41.2	8.2	—	4.0 CM	12.1
Westinghouse	23.1	11.7	—	5.0 MG	1.7
RCA	24.0	7.2	—	4.2 CM	—
Union Carbide	26.7	12.9	—	5.2 CM	3.2
Kraftco	26.7	7.3	—	2.4 FN	2.1
Greyhound	20.0	2.7	—	.9 MG	8.1
Litton Industries	45.5	11.9	—	9.0 CM	8.4
Caterpillar Tractor	30.0	13.2	5.2[3]	5.0 FN	1.3
Monsanto	31.9	12.4	—	7.4 CM	3.1
Dow Chemical	26.1	7.1	2.2[4]	2.1 BT	1.1
R.J. Reynolds	27.6	7.1	3.0[5]	2.8 CM	—
United Aircraft	44.7	20.6	—	7.0 MG	4.6
Xerox	31.9	19.8	—	6.1 FN	4.3
Bendix	37.4	17.9	—	10.9 FN	4.9
Textron	39.1	6.3	11.3[6]	4.1 FN	4.7
United Brands	69.5	10.7	—	8.0 CM	20.5
CPC International	23.2	6.6	—	1.5 MG	—
Warner-Lambert	28.3	14.3	—	4.7 CM	2.4
Raytheon	42.6	7.8	—	4.2 BNY	5.5
II. Transportation					
A. Airlines					
United Airlines	47.1	21.9	—	8.3 CM	3.7
American Airlines	44.6	30.8	—	9.0 CM	2.9
Pan American World Airways	49.2	13.6	—	3.7 BT	15.0
Northwest Airlines	53.0	22.5	—	6.9 CM	4.8
Braniff Airways	56.1	17.1	—	5.8 BT	15.3

Table 4-5. (cont.)

	Percent of stock held by 30 largest stockholders	Percent of stock held by New York banks within the 30 largest stockholders	Percent held by largest single stockholder except where largest stockholder is a New York bank or Cede & Co.	Largest percent of stock held by a New York bank[1]	Percent held by Cede & Co.
Western Air Lines	64.0	13.8	27.4[7]	7.3 CM	—
Pacific Southwest Airlines	56.8	3.7	—	1.9 MH	21.3
North Central Airlines	26.1	—	—	—	10.6
Frontier Airlines	66.2	.2	46.7[8]	.2 BNY	10.7
B. Railroads					
Penn Central	42.4	1.7	—	.8 IT	18.9
Norfolk & Western	37.0	9.1	15.3[9]	4.2 CM	—
Burlington & Northern	36.0	30.0	—	6.7 CM	—
Chesapeake & Ohio	19.7	4.3	4.4[10]	1.5 MH	—
Southern	40.2	18.5	—	8.3 CM	—
Missouri Pacific	72.2	1.6	60.7[11]	1.2 FR	—
Chicago-Rock Island & Pacific	92.0	78.1	—	77.4 CB[12]	—
Chicago, Milwaukee, St. Paul & Pacific	68.5	5.2	—	2.8 CM	32.6
St. Louis-San Francisco	48.2	19.8	15.0[13]	6.5 CM	—
Reading	70.6	1.5	38.3[14]	1.1 FT	—
Kansas City Southern	49.3	10.0	—	5.3 CM	13.9
Rio Grande Industries	54.2	19.2	—	5.7 CM	7.7
Soo Line	73.7	1.0	55.7[15]	1.0 CB	8.4
Gulf, Mobile & Ohio	52.0	3.2	18.8[16]	1.5 MH	—
Seaboard Coast Line	40.1	15.8	—	6.2 CM	4.4
C. Other					
Seatrain Lines[17]	88.3	11.0	26.5[18]	4.4 BNY	4.2
Spector Industries	72.0	.3	—	.3 CN	15.1
III. Utilities					
AT&T	7.5	3.0	—	1.1 CM	.7
American Electric Power	25.5	13.3	—	3.5 MH	5.5

	Percent of stock held by 30 largest stockholders	Percent of stock held by New York banks within the 30 largest stockholders	Percent held by largest single stockholder except where largest stockholder is a New York bank or Cede & Co.	Largest percent of stock held by a New York bank[1]	Percent held by Cede & Co.
General Telephone & Electric	18.1	4.7	—	2.3 FN	3.8
Texas Eastern Transmission	26.9	9.8	—	2.6 BNY	—
Virginia Electric & Power	29.9	16.1	—	5.6 FN	—
Pennzoil United	40.9	18.6	—	7.5 FN	—
Texas Utilities	25.8	11.0	—	2.9 CM	1.3
American Natural Gas	29.3	10.1	—	2.3 SB	5.4
Niagara Mohawk Power	16.9	7.5	—	2.7 MM	6.9
Northeast Utilities	14.1	2.8	—	1.0 BT	3.0
Transcontinental Gas Pipeline	27.1	2.5	4.3[19]	2.0 BT	4.3
Continental Telephone	29.4	15.2	—	5.1 FN	2.4
Allegheny Power System	27.9	9.3	—	3.6 FN	5.9
Baltimore Gas & Electric	24.6	4.8	—	2.1 CH	4.2
Pennsylvania Power & Light	18.6	2.1	—	.9 MG	3.8
Potomac Electric Power	14.8	1.2	—	.8 CH	6.1
Long Island Lighting	26.4	14.3	—	5.1 CM	4.6
Pacific Power & Light	10.0	.4	2.5[20]	.3 MG	—
Western Union	43.0	17.8	—	6.2 BT	6.9
Cleveland Electric Illuminating	24.1	3.2	—	1.4 MG	3.3
IV. Retailing Companies					
Safeway Stores	33.5	18.4	—	10.5 CM	5.3
Gamble-Skogmo	55.1	7.2	7.9[21]	2.5 IT	5.4
Grand Union	45.2	12.6	—	3.3 MG	13.6
R.H. Macy	44.5	15.5	—	6.2 MG	2.4
Interstate Stores	63.6	24.4	—	5.1 BNY	18.7
Cook United	57.4	8.5	11.7[22]	4.2 BT	6.0

Table 4-5. (cont.)

	Percent of stock held by 30 largest stockholders	Percent of stock held by New York banks within the 30 largest stockholders	Percent held by largest single stockholder except where largest stockholder is a New York bank or Cede & Co.	Largest percent of stock held by a New York bank[1]	Percent held by Cede & Co.
Pueblo International	76.9	2.7	23.2[23]	2.7 MG	—
Melville Shoe	42.9	10.2	8.3[24]	6.7 MG	2.2
V. Commercial Banks					
First National City[17]	22.4	14.0	—	4.3 FN	1.5
Chemical New York[17]	23.8	11.1	—	5.4 CB	2.2
Bankers Trust-New York	28.4	15.6	—	5.7 BT	1.2
First Bank System	40.6	8.5	8.4[25]	3.9 FN	1.8
Republic National of Dallas	35.8	6.6	6.4[26]	3.2 MH	—
Girard Co.	29.1	5.9	5.7[27]	3.2 FN	—
First National Bank in Dallas	34.4	13.4	—	10.2 FN	—
Citizens & Southern National	42.5	14.1	10.8[28]	6.7 FN	—
Shawmut Association	15.0	1.6	1.3[29]	.6 MG	—
VI. Life Insurance Companies					
Travelers	34.0	14.4	—	6.0 MG	1.8

Note: Respondent companies are arranged by size within each industry group.

1. Banks are designated by the following symbols: BNY—Bank of New York; BT—Bankers Trust; CB—Chemical Bank; CM—Chase Manhattan; FN—First National City; FR—Franklin National; FT—Fiduciary Trust; IT—Irving Trust; MG—Morgan Guaranty; MH—Manufacturers Hanover; MM—Marine Midland; SB—Savings Bank Trust.

2. Ford Motor Co. employees stock plan.

3. First National of Chicago.

4. First National of Boston.

5. Mercantile Safe (Baltimore).

6. Textron employee stock savings program.

7. Kirk Kerkorian (director Western Air Lines).

8. RKO General, Inc.

9. Pennsylvania Company.

10. Merrill Lynch, Pierce, Fenner & Smith Inc.

11. Mississippi River Corp.

12. Chemical Bank is the exchange agent under Union Pacific RR Co.'s exchange offer of September 1964.

13. Scherck, Stein & Franc.

14. Baltimore & Ohio RR.

15. Canadian Pacific Limited RR.

16. Chicago Title & Trust Co.

17. Figures reflect top 29 stockholders only.

18. Howard M. Park.

19. First National City Houston as trustee of Transcontinental Gas Pipelines employee stock plan.

20. Merrill Lynch, Pierce, Fenner & Smith Inc.

21. Continental Illinois Bank.

22. Cleveland Trust.

23. Harold Toppel.

24. Ward Melville and beneficial shares in trust.

25. First Trust Co. of St. Paul.

26. Republic National Bank of Dallas.

27. Girard Trust.

28. Citizens & Southern.

29. National Shawmut.

"Ownership of Large Commercial Banks"

5

Senate Committee on Government Operations

Requests for the names of top stockholders and amounts of holdings went from Senator Lee Metcalf to the 50 largest banks in 1970 based on assets. Twenty-four of the 50 declined to provide any of the information requested, mostly due to reasons of confidentiality. Frequently cited as authority for not supplying the information were the National Banking Act (12 U.S.C. 484), and regulations of the Comptroller of the Currency (Ruling 7.6025), which limit the disclosure of bank records by banks to anyone other than the Comptroller of the Currency except as authorized by law.

Nevertheless, nine banks did provide the information requested, including three of the 10 largest banks in the United States which also happen to be three of the six largest banks in New York City. Thus it would appear that there was, to say the least, considerable divergence of interpretation as to what barriers, real or imaginary, exist in providing the information requested. It may also be of interest to note that two of the nine fully reporting banks are in Dallas, Texas, where the county requires banks to file a certified list of shareholders which then becomes a matter of public record.

Partial Responses

Eleven of the banks provided very limited information, information they believed might be helpful without at the same time being specific as to particular holdings. Thus the Bank of America, the largest bank in the United States, indicated that no shareholder held more than 6

Reprinted from U.S. Congress. Senate. Subcommittees on Intergovernmental Relations and on Budgeting, Management, and Expenditures of the Senate Committee on Government Operations, *Disclosure of Corporate Ownership.* 93d Cong. 2nd sess. (Washington, D.C.: Government Printing Office, 1974), pp. 115–16; 124–25. Report prepared by Julius W. Allen, assisted by Eugénie Dieringer, Congressional Research Service, The Library of Congress.

percent of the 69,003,590 outstanding shares, with the largest block of shares, 3,855,576, or 5.6 percent of the outstanding shares, held by a trustee in trust for the employees of the bank.

Chase Manhattan, the third largest bank, did not name the 30 top holders of its stock, but did indicate the amount held by type of holder, e.g., bank nominees, insurance companies, brokers. From the data it supplied the following information can be gleaned: of the total of 31,881,747 common shares outstanding, 6,508,219, or 20.0 percent, were held by the top 30 holders as shown in Table 5-1:

Table 5-1.   Chase Manhattan Stockholders

	Number of shares	Percent of total stock outstanding
22 bank nominees	4,839,047	15.1
3 insurance companies	463,790	1.3
2 investment bankers and brokers	428,251	1.3
1 individual (David Rockefeller)	337,500	1.0
1 nominee (unspecified)	245,703	.7
1 corporation	193,928	.6

J. P. Morgan & Co., reporting somewhat along the lines of Chase Manhattan, but not in as much detail on an individual account basis, disclosed that 4,871,000 or 27 percent of the 18,267,207 shares of the company, were held by the top 30 stockholders. These 30 stockholders consisted of 17 nominees of 10 commercial banks, the nominees of three insurance companies, a nominee of the Stock Clearing Corporation (Cede & Company), two insurance companies, a stock exchange member firm, and five nominees of Morgan Guaranty Trust Company of New York, a wholly owned subsidiary of J. P. Morgan & Co., Inc.

Charter New York Corporation indicated that the two largest holders of its shares were a nominee for a national securities exchange (almost certainly Cede and Co.), with 300,433, or 4.1 percent of the total of 7,210,028 shares outstanding, and a bank nominee with 250,000 shares, about 3.4 percent. No other entity owned as much as 100,000 shares or 1.4 percent of the total.

Wells Fargo of San Francisco reported along the same pattern as Chase Manhattan. It indicated that the top 30 stockholders held 3,049,946, or 32.6 percent of the total of 9,287,040 outstanding shares, as broken down as shown in Table 5-2.

Franklin New York Corporation reported two major holders of voting securities, Loews Corporation with 20.2 percent of the outstanding voting securities, and Sol Kittay, a director of the corporation, with 1.7 percent of the outstanding voting securities. In July, 1972, Loews sold most of its holdings to Fasco International Holdings, S.A., controlled by the Italian financier, Michele Sindora. As of Dec. 31, 1972, Fasco Inter-

Table 5-2. Wells Fargo Stockholders

	Number of shares	Percent of total stock outstanding
21 bank nominees	2,399,861	25.8
4 insurance companies	282,625	3.0
New York Stock Exchange (Cede and Co.)	168,400	1.8
2 individuals	123,951	1.3
1 corporation	39,200	.4
1 stockbroker	35,509	.3

national owned about 18.3 percent of Franklin New York Corporation's voting stock. No other person is believed to control or hold power to vote 5 percent or more of the outstanding voting securities of the corporation.

First Pennsylvania reported the same kind of information as Chase Manhattan and Wells Fargo. The 30 largest stockholders accounted for 3,859,298 or 31.5 percent of the 12,241,922 shares of voting common stock outstanding. This is broken down into the categories shown in Table 5-3.

Wachovia Corporation of Winston-Salem reported only that the bank's employees' profit-sharing plan is the largest stockholder with 3 percent of the voting stock, and that no individual shareholder approached this percentage.

Manufacturers National Bank of Detroit disclosed solely that the 30 largest stockholders consisted of 15 nominees, 10 individual holders, three institutional holders and two brokers. No identities were disclosed.

The NCNB Corporation (North Carolina National Bank) of Charlotte disclosed one stockholder with more than 10 percent of the total.

Table 5-3. First Pennsylvania Stockholders

	Number of shares	Percent total stock outstanding
11 nominees for bank fiduciary accounts	1,713,731	14.0
6 individuals	783,628	6.4
3 brokers	339,760	2.8
2 nominees for mutual funds	241,958	2.0
2 insurance companies	228,226	1.9
1 nominee for Central Certificate Service (Cede and Company)	148,593	1.2
2 nominees for pension trusts	116,852	1.0
1 nominee for a corporation	112,398	.9
1 State teachers pension fund	97,700	.8
1 custodian for foreign accounts	76,452	.6

Jefferson-Pilot Corporation held 11.25 percent of the outstanding common stock of the NCNB Corporation.

The National Bank of North America, of New York, N.Y., is 98 percent owned by the C.I.T. Financial Corporation.

Failure to Respond

Six banks did not reply to Senator Metcalf's letter. They were:

Marine Midland
First National Boston Corporation
Lincoln First Banks of Rochester, New York
Bank of California, San Francisco
Valley National Bank of Arizona
National Bank of Commerce of Seattle

We turn now to the tabulations and summaries of the responses from the nine banks which provided all, or virtually all, of the information requested by Senator Metcalf, arranged in order of assets of the banks in 1971. Two banks, First National City Corporation and Chemical New York Corporation, both included their treasury holdings among the top 30. Since such stock is not voting stock it was excluded from the tabulations; thus for these two companies 29 rather than 30 top holders are disclosed. [The original report lists the names of the 30 largest shareholders and their nominees in Table 15, pp. 116–24.—] . . .

First National City Corporation. This, the second largest commercial bank in the nation was the largest bank reporting its 30 largest stockholders as requested. Subtracting the treasury stock, as noted above, the remaining 29 stockholders accounted for 22.4 percent of all voting common stock of the corporation. Only three stockholders (all were banks listed under their nominees) held 2 or more percent of the stock of First National City. These were:

	Percent
First National City itself	4.3
(in 4 nominee accounts)	
Chase Manhattan	2.7
(in 3 nominee accounts)	
Morgan Guaranty	2.0
(in 3 nominee accounts)	

Eight New York banks held 14.0 percent of the voting stock of First National City through their nominee accounts.

Chemical New York Corporation. The 29 largest holders of voting stock of Chemical New York Corporation, the seventh largest bank in the United States, held 23.8 percent of such stock. Only two stockholders held 2 or more percent of the voting shares of common stock:

	Percent
Chemical New York Bank	5.4
(through four nominees of its subsidiary, Chemical Bank (New York))	
Cede and Co.	2.2
(the nominee of the New York Stock Exchange)	

Eight New York banks combined held 11.1 percent; as already noted nearly half of that was held by nominees of Chemical New York Corporation itself.

Bankers Trust Company (New York). The picture here is quite similar to that of Chemical New York. The 30 largest holders of Bankers Trust common stock account for 28.4 percent of such stock. Four stockholders held 2 or more percent of such stock, led again by the bank itself through three nominees and one trust account, with 5.7 percent; followed by:

	Percent
Commerce Bank of Kansas	2.6
(through three nominee accounts)	
Chase Manhattan	2.4
State Street Bank of Boston	2.1
(through two nominees)	

Eight New York banks combined held a total of 15.6 percent of the common stock of Bankers Trust.

First Bank System (Minneapolis). The First Bank System (Minneapolis) identified by name the 19 of the largest stockholders that were bank nominees and beyond that designated the kind of holder and amount of shares (e.g., insurance company, mutual fund, charitable foundation, individual, family estate) of the other 11 holders without disclosing the names of such holders.

The 30 largest shareholders accounted for 40.6 percent of First Bank System's capital stock. By far the largest holder was the First Bank System itself, through the various nominees of the member banks of the System. These include: (1) two nominees of the First Trust Company of St. Paul, Brack and Company with 7.1 percent of the stock,[1] and Sod and Company with 1.2 percent of the stock; (2) two nominees of First National Bank of Minneapolis, with 5.1 percent of the stock between them; and (3) one nominee of the Northern City National Bank of Duluth with 1.1 percent of the stock. Thus, the nominees of three member banks of the First Bank System held among them 14.6 percent of the stock of the system.

---

1. The largest single account in Brack and Company was the Employee's Deferred Payment Profitsharing Trust Plan, with 2 percent of the total stock of the First Bank System.

The only other holders of more than 2 percent of the stock were two New York banks, First National City with 3.9 percent in three nominee accounts, and Morgan Guaranty with 2.8 percent in two nominee accounts. Five New York banks held a total of 8.5 percent of the shares of the First Bank System.

Republic National Bank of Dallas. The 30 largest stockholders accounted for 35.8 percent of the outstanding common capital stock of the bank. Five shareholders held 2 or more percent of the stock, headed, as in the case of the other banks mentioned above, by the bank itself which, through two nominees, held 6.4 percent of the stock, followed by:

	Percent
Hoblitzelle Foundation of Dallas	4.9
Manufacturers Hanover of New York (through 2 nominee accounts)	3.2
Bank of Delaware, Wilmington	3.2
Southland Life Insurance Co.	2.9

Four New York banks combined held 6.6 percent of the stock of Republic National Bank of Dallas.

Girard Bank. The 30 top stockholders accounted for 29.1 percent of the common stock of the Girard Bank. Six held 2 or more percent of the stock, led again by the bank itself with 5.7 percent through two nominee accounts of its subsidiary, Girard Trust Bank. Other leading holders are:

	Percent
First National City of New York (through 2 nominees)	3.2
Providence National of Philadelphia (through 2 nominees)	3.0
First Pennsylvania Bank, Philadelphia	2.8
Fidelity Bank, Philadelphia	2.0
Insurance Co. of North America, Philadelphia	2.0

Four New York banks accounted for 4.5 percent of the stock of the Girard Bank, and six Philadelphia banks, including Girard itself through nominees, 14.5 percent.

First National Bank in Dallas. The top 30 stockholders accounted for 34.4 percent of the common stock of the First National Bank in Dallas. Four of these 30 held 2 or more percent of the stock of the bank:

	Percent
First National City of New York (through four nominees)	10.2
First National Bank in Dallas (in five nominee accounts)	5.1
Bank of Delaware, Wilmington	3.1
N. P. Powell of Tyler, Texas	2.5

Four New York banks combined held 13.3 percent of the common stock of First National Bank in Dallas.

Citizens and Southern National Bank. The response from Citizens and Southern National Bank of Atlanta, Georgia, is not strictly comparable to the other eight banks (or any of the other reporting companies) whose tabulations are summarized here. In some ways it is the most informative response received. Instead of treating a single nominee account as one of the largest stockholders, Citizens and Southern chose to consider all of the nominees of a single bank or other financial institution as one account. Thus, information is supplied on the holdings of at least 54 nominee accounts including 17 in Morgan Guaranty of New York, and 11 of Citizens and Southern, itself. The inclusion of all nominees would tend to increase the concentration of holdings among the top 30 companies, and of those banks with many nominees in particular, as compared with other reporting banks.

With this caveat, it can be seen that Citizens and Southern National Bank reported that 42.5 percent of its stock was held by the 30 largest stockholders. Five firms, all banks through their nominees, held over 2 percent of the total stock of Citizens and Southern National Bank. They were, in order of size of holdings:

	Percent
Citizens and Southern	10.8
(itself, through 11 nominees, as noted above, and as trustee in one instance)	
First National City	6.7
(in three nominee accounts)	
Mellon National Bank, Pittsburgh	4.5
(in three nominee accounts)	
Morgan Guaranty	3.6
(in 17 nominee accounts)	
Bankers Trust	2.3
(in four nominee accounts)	

Six New York banks combined held 14.1 percent of the common stock of Citizens and First National, with the three New York banks just mentioned accounting for 12.6 percent.

Shawmut Association. In reporting its largest stockholders, Shawmut actually listed 31 holders (the 29th, 30th, and 31st all holding equally 5,000 shares). Omitted was the holding of one unnamed individual with 5,460 shares, or 0.2 percent of the total outstanding.

On the basis of this tabulation, Shawmut Association has far less concentration of its common stock holdings than the other reporting banks, with the top 31 holders accounting for only 15.0 percent of the stock. No single holder had as much as 2 percent of the shares. Three New York banks combined held 1.6 percent and five Boston banks held 3.4 percent of the shares. Olsen & Company, a nominee of National

Shawmut Bank of Boston, Trust Department, subsidiary of Shawmut Association, was the largest holder with 24,206 shares or 1.3 percent of the total; this represents primarily shares held for exployees of affiliated banks in the holding company under profit sharing and stock purchase plans.

A few at least tentative conclusions can be reached from the information in this section of the report. Perhaps most striking is the small number of banks supplying the information requested, and the fact that those that did report fully were spread fairly evenly by size among the 50 banks circulated (i.e. three in the first quintile; one in the second quintile; two in the third quintile; one in the fourth quintile; and two in the fifth quintile). Second is the fact that the principal holder in eight of the nine reporting banks was the bank itself through various nominee accounts. The extent of bank discretion in voting or influencing the voting of such shares would be worthy of further exploration.

A concomitant question also worthy of consideration is why so rarely any holders outside of banks appear in the list of holders of more than 2 percent of bank stock.

Part 2

Wealth and
Income Inequality

How concentrated are wealth and income, and how has this changed in the past half-century in the United States? The studies presented here on wealth and income inequality attempt to answer these questions. Measuring the concentration of wealth and income is extraordinarily difficult, and "findings" are highly affected by the sources and types of data employed as well as the assumptions, concepts, and (frequently) educated guesses involved in assembling and analyzing the relevant information. While specialists differ little in their estimates of wealth concentration, there *is* debate concerning the trends in income concentration.

The Concentration of Wealth

The rich, as *Business Week* notes, "are much harder to count or interview than other Americans, and even government economists with access to Internal Revenue Service data have a tough time figuring out the share of the nation's wealth held by the rich."[1] Wealth is liable to be both consciously hidden and unintentionally concealed through holdings in business and other organizations and financial intermediaries. James D. Smith and Stephen D. Franklin, following the precedent set by Robert J. Lampman,[2] limit their analysis to the personal sector and make no adjustments for hidden wealth holding. Using the "estate multiplier technique," which treats those who died in a given year as a stratified sample of the living population, Smith and Franklin estimate the relative share of wealth held by the richest 0.5 percent of all individuals in selected years between 1922 and 1969, and for the richest 0.5 percent and 1.0 percent of the population between 1953 and 1969. Their estimates of wealth distribution *understate* the degree of concentration in any given year, since they had to conceptually align their present estimates with earlier estimates, which meant sacrificing certain improved methods of measurement currently available. They conclude that wealth concentration has become somewhat less concentrated in the last half century; most of the decrease occurred, however, as the result of the Great Depression in which many fortunes near the pinnacle of the wealth pyramid plummeted. Since 1945, the distribution of wealth in the United States has remained essentially unchanged. The wealthiest 1 percent of the population held 27.5 percent of the net worth of all persons in 1953, 27.4 percent in 1962, and 24.9 percent in 1969. The shares held by the richest 0.5 percent in those years, respectively, were 22.0 percent, 21.6 percent and 19.9 percent.[3] The only striking change during this period was an apparent increase in dispersion of corporation stockholdings. There was a nearly 500 percent increase in the number of shareholders between 1952 and 1970, spurred by

---

1. "Who Has the Wealth in America," *Business Week,* August 5, 1972, pp. 54–56.

2. *The Share of Top Wealth-holders in National Wealth, 1922–1956.* (Princeton: Princeton University Press, 1962).

3. Careful estimates have been made on the basis of manuscript census reports of the size distribution of wealth in the United States during the nineteenth century, and the share of the wealth held by the richest 1 percent of Americans. Remarkably, the estimates indicate that the share held by them in 1860, on the eve of the American civil war, was 24 percent or almost precisely the same share they (24.9 percent) held a century later, in 1969. The estimates of the share held by the richest 1 percent for selected years were as follows: 1810, 21 percent; 1860, 24 percent; and 1900, 26 to 31 percent. See Robert E. Gallman, "Trends in the Size Distribution of Wealth in the Nineteenth Century: Some Speculations," in *Six Papers on the Size Distribution of Income,* ed. Lee Soltow. (New York: National Bureau of Economic Research; Columbia University Press, 1969). See also the comment by Soltow and the reply by Gallman.

the boom in mutual funds during the 1960s. Smith and Franklin provide the first available estimates of the concentration of trust assets, which are clearly the most concentrated of all substantial types of wealth: In 1969, 85 percent of the value of trusts were held by the richest 0.5 percent, and 92 percent by the richest 1 percent. (Recall also, as noted in the introduction to Part One that most trust assets are held by a few large banks: less than 2 percent of the banks hold 61 percent of all trust assets in national banks.) In 1969, the richest 1 percent also held 14 percent of the market value of all real estate, 51 percent of the corporate stock, 36 percent of the bonds, and 14 percent of the cash held by all persons in the United States. These estimates, remember, were made to assure accurate measurement of temporal changes in concentration. Smith and Franklin emphasize that the individual figures given have a downward bias of 10 percent to 15 percent from their best estimates of concentration—that is, concentration of wealth is even greater than these figures show. In another paper, Smith estimates the share of the national wealth held in 1969 by the richest 4 percent of the adult population as follows: "They owned over a quarter of the nation's real estate [27.4 percent], three-fifths of all privately held corporate stock [63.3 percent], four-fifths of the state and local bonds [78.4 percent], two-fifths of the business assets (excluding business real estate) [39.5 percent], a third of the cash [32.6 percent], and virtually all of the notes, mortgages, and foreign and corporate bonds."[4] All told, the richest 4 percent of Americans owned 37 percent of the net worth of all Americans. Indeed, after subtracting their debts, Smith points out, they were "worth over a trillion dollars, enough to have purchased the entire national output of the United States plus the combined output of Switzerland, Denmark, Norway, and Sweden in 1969."

The University of Michigan's Survey Research Center, using data collected through interviews rather than data on estate tax returns, estimates that in 1970 the richest 5 percent of family units had upwards of 40 percent of all the personal wealth—an estimate quite close to Smith's—and that the bottom *half* of wealthholders accounted for only 3 percent of the net worth of all Americans. The top 20 percent of family units had three times the net worth of the bottom 80 percent. To get another view of the holdings of the rich, Dorothy Projector and Gertrude Weiss analyzed data from interviews conducted by the Census Bureau under the auspices of the Federal Reserve System.[5] They found that, in 1962, less than 1 percent of all consumer units (families and unrelated individuals) had wealth of $500,000 or more, and less than 0.5 percent had wealth of $1,000,000 and over. On the other end, 10 percent of all consumer units had a total wealth of less than one dollar, and another 16 percent more than one dollar but less than $1,000. Twenty-six percent of all consumer units in America, in other words, had less than $1,000 of "wealth," including liquid assets, checking and savings accounts, and "investments," including real estate, stocks, and bonds. No comparable survey of such scope has been completed since the Projector-Weiss study.

---

4. "The Concentration of Personal Wealth in America, 1969," *Review of Income and Wealth,* Series 20, No. 2 (June, 1974):143–80.

5. Dorothy Projector and Gertrude Weiss, *Survey of Financial Characteristics of Consumers* (Washington, D.C.: Federal Reserve System, August, 1966).

Income Distribution

The concentration of wealth, of course, is closely related to the concentration of income. Property ownership is the principal source of income for the wealthy, while the typical American family gets most of its income from wages and salaries. According to Projector, Weiss, and Thoresen, the 20 percent of consumer units with the highest incomes received 64 percent of the total of business and property income in 1962 (the most recent year for which comprehensive official data have been analyzed), whereas the lowest 20 percent got 2 percent.[6] Of all income in wages and salaries, in contrast, the top 20 percent income bracket got 45 percent compared to the lowest 20 percent, which got 1 percent. The Gini coefficient summary measure neatly summarizes these differences between the concentration of income from wages and salaries compared to business and property.[7] For all income, from any source, the coefficient is .43; for wages and salaries, it is .52; but for business and property income, it is .93. This measure reflects the fact that more than one-third of the total population has no business or property income, and that most of this income is concentrated in the upper brackets. The higher the income bracket, the larger the precentage of consumer units (families and un-related individuals) in it that get income from property ownership. Receipt of income from (1) dividends on publicly traded stock, (2) rents and royalties, and (3) trusts and estates is particularly concentrated in the top income brackets, while receipt of interest income is less concentrated. In the $100,000 or more income bracket, 97 percent had income from the first, 69 percent from the second, and 56 percent from the third type of property, compared to the following percentages among all consumer units with income from these respective types of property: 12 percent, 12 percent, and 1 percent. In the $100,000 bracket, 96 percent had interest income, but 53 percent of all Americans also had some income from interest. Most significant, however, is the actual *share* of the *total* income from these different sources which the consumer units in the various income brackets received. Of the total dollars of property income received by all the consumer units, the top 5 percent took in 47 percent, broken down as follows: 64 percent of the dividends from publicly traded stock; 37 percent of the rents and royalties; 64 percent of all income from trusts and estates; and 30 percent of all interest income (Table 1).

---

6. Dorothy S. Projector, Gertrude S. Weiss, and E. T. Thoresen, "Composition of Income as Shown by the Survey of Financial Characteristics of Consumers," in *Six Papers on the Size Distribution of Wealth and Income,* ed. Lee Soltow.

7. The Gini coefficient is based on the "Lorenz curve," which graphically represents the distribution of wealth and income by plotting percentages of income recipients or wealth-holders on the horizontal axis and percentages of total income and wealth on the vertical axis, both expressed cumulatively. The "line of equality" corresponds with the 45 degree line or diagonal, and the deeper the banana-shaped segment enclosed by that line and the Lorenz curve, the greater the inequality. The Gini coefficient is the ratio of *(a)* the banana-shaped area between the Lorenz curve and the line of equality to *(b)* the entire area lying under the line of equality. The Gini coefficient varies from one, or perfect *in*equality," to zero, or "perfect equality," of income or wealth distribution. Put simply, the closer the coefficient is to one, the greater is the inequality of the distribution (see figure below).

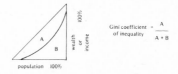

Table 1. Distribution of Property Income for 1962 (percentage of total dollars of specified types of property income received by income groups)

Group characteristic	Total property income	Stock dividends[a]	Interest income	Total	Other dividends[b]	Rents and royalties	Trusts and estates
						Other property income	
All units	100	100	100	100	100	100	100
1962 income:							
Negative	0	0	0	−1	0	−1	0
$0-2,999	8	3	14	8	1	10	4
$3,000-4,999	9	5	12	10	0	14	0
$5,000-7,499	10	10	11	10	0	12	3
$7,500-9,999	12	8	18	11	1	13	9
$10,000-14,999	14	11	16	16	12	15	19
$15,000-24,999	11	12	10	10	7	8	15
$25,000-49,999	14	21	7	14	24	12	17
$50,000-99,999	11	11	9	11	54	13	1
$100,000 and over	11	19	3	11	1	4	31

Group characteristic	Total property income	Stock dividends[a]	Interest income	Total	Other dividends[b]	Rents and royalties	Trusts and estates
						Other property income	
Units ranked by size of income:							
Lowest tenth	1	1	3	1	0	2	0
Second	3	1	6	4	0	4	2
Third	4	2	6	4	0	5	2
Fourth	4	2	6	5	0	7	0
Fifth	4	2	5	4	0	5	0
Sixth	6	7	6	6	0	7	1
Seventh	4	3	6	4	0	4	2
Eighth	7	1	12	8	0	9	5
Ninth	12	14	12	12	1	13	9
Highest tenth	53	68	39	53	98	42	78
90-95th percentile	7	4	8	7	5	5	14
Above 95th percentile	47	64	30	46	93	37	64

Source: D. S. Projector, G. S. Weiss, and E. T. Thoresen, "Composition of Income as Shown by the Survey of Financial Characteristics of Consumers," in *Six Papers on the Size Distribution of Wealth and Income*, ed. Lee Soltow (New York: National Bureau of Economic Research; Columbia University Press, 1969), p. 139. Reprinted and adapted with the permission of the National Bureau of Economic Research.

Note: Details may not add to totals because of rounding. Zero is used to indicate no cases reported or a percentage of less than one-half of 1 percent or a mean of less than one-half of one dollar.

[a]Publicly traded stock.

[b]Dividends from closely held corporations, not managed by unit.

If both wealth and income are highly concentrated, the question is to what extent the distribution has changed over time. As we have seen, the concentration of wealth at the top has remained steady at least since the end of the Second World War, and perhaps since the Civil War. Apparently income distribution has also stayed more or less the same since World War II, though some authorities conclude it has become more unequal, as we discuss below briefly. A study for the Joint Economic Committee of Congress by economists Lester C. Thurow and Robert E. B. Lucas, based on Census Bureau data, shows that though real income has climbed since 1947, the income shares going to the richest and poorest fifths in 1970 are close to the 1947 pattern. The poorest fifth of American families received about 5 percent of the country's total family income while the top fifth received 42 percent in almost every year since 1947. That is a ratio of eight to one. But there is a growing absolute discrepancy between the average real incomes of the top and bottom income fifths; between 1949 and 1969, according to Thurow and Lucas, the gap widened from less than $11,000 to more than $19,000 in constant 1969 dollars. Based on Commerce Department projections of schooling and age distribution, and making the rather tenuous assumption of full employment, it is estimated that income shares in 1985 will be about the same as in 1965, a year of relatively low unemployment.[8]

In Selma F. Goldsmith's study "Changes in the Size Distribution of Income" (Selection Number 7), she reviews and reanalyzes findings from many different studies of income distribution in the United States from the Great Depression (1929) to 1955. During that quarter century, there was a rise in real mean family income of about 1.5 percent before taxes and 1 percent after taxes. The question, though, is how the *distribution* of income changed. Goldsmith compares her findings from census data on changes in relative family income shares to the analysis by Simon Kuznets of the relative income shares of the top 5 percent of individual income recipients, based on income tax returns. Kuznets concluded that there was a drastic reduction of about 40 percent in the share of income received by the top 5 percent of individuals between 1929 and 1948.[9] Goldsmith's family data indicate a similar though somewhat dampened decline. This decline is imputed to an increase in the relative *importance* of wages and salaries as income sources and to changes in the relative *distribution* of various types of income. The greatest narrowing of income apparently came during the Great Depression and during the Second World War, though even this conclusion is disputed, as we shall see. Even after the loss of fortunes and the mass organization of industrial workers during the thirties, and the subsequent wage and price controls, full employment economy, and high labor demand of the Second World War, "income distribution has remained remarkably resistant to redistributive efforts," as *Business Week* sums it up.[10]

The fact is that there are several critical limitations to using personal income data: variations from year to year; inadequate differential cost-of-living indexes for rich and poor over time; inability to identify and compare shifts of specific individuals or families; and inadequate data on the number and composition of the lower

---

8. "More Money, but the Shares Stay the Same," *Business Week,*, April 1, 1972, pp. 56–57.

9. Shares of Upper Income Groups in Income and Savings. New York: National Bureau of Economic Research, 1953.

10. "More Money," April 1, 1972.

income strata. A more important limitation results from the failure to take into account income, such as "expense accounts" and fringe benefits of many kinds, which the higher income strata receive from corporations. In addition, specific tax allowances, such as depletion allowances, also increase the actual income received but not noted by the wealthy. Kuznets relied on income tax data but did not take underreporting into account. Excluding capital gains from the income measure also underestimates the income of the higher brackets. However, Goldsmith concludes that although measurements of these types of incomes are not available, and although these measurements doubtlessly would show the decline in income shares to be smaller, their impact would not be sufficient to change the general pattern.

Most important, however, is the failure to distinguish between the relative distribution of income *emerging from production* compared to the distribution of *personal* income. National income *includes* and personal income *excludes* elements of production not paid out to persons. Some of these elements are undistributed corporate profits, corporate inventory valuations, taxes on corporate profits, and contributions for social insurance. Undistributed corporate earnings, which go predominantly to the top income strata, account for a larger relative share of the national income in the post–World War II period than in the prewar period. When such factors are taken into account, the alleged increase in income equality is seen very differently. Converting to national income measurements reduces the percentage decline in the income of the top 5 percent from 1929 to 1950–1955 by about one-third (from 30 percent to 20 percent). From 1939 to 1950–1955, the corresponding reduction is about three-fourths (from 20 percent to only 5 percent). And this 5 percent decline is probably a statistical rather than a real one. Therefore, Goldsmith concludes that if income is measured in terms of *national* income rather than personal income flows, there probably was no reduction between 1939 and 1950–1955 in the relative share of income received by the top 5 percent.

In his early (1954) critique of Kuznets's studies, Victor Perlo (Selection Number 8) came to conclusions similar to those of Goldsmith. His major point is that studies such as that of Kuznets focus on the distribution of income among individuals or families rather than among classes. By using this approach, says Perlo, Kuznets ignores the vast increase in corporate profits since 1929. Trends in the distribution of income from production have been the opposite of what Kuznets claimed for personal income, with the greatest increase occurring in the share going to corporate capitalists.

Perlo argues that mere shifting of income among individuals and families within the same capitalist class, as income is split among descendants, would show up as decreased income concentration by Kuznets's method. Perlo also criticizes studies which use income tax statements without taking into account underreporting by those in the higher brackets—underreporting done to the greatest extent on income from dividends, interest, and rent and to the least extent on income from wages and salaries. Moreover, Kuznets estimates the income of those in the lower brackets by subtracting the income-tax-reported incomes of the top 5 percent from Commerce Department total income figures, thus exaggerating the incomes of the lower income brackets by the same amount that incomes of the wealthy are underestimated. The alleged declining trend results, according to Perlo, largely from the increasingly important systematic tax evasion and avoidance which began as a "big business" in the 1930s with the introduction of ostensibly progressive income taxes. Perlo also discusses the role of undistributed profits, coming to conclusions similar to Goldsmith's. A third weakness is Kuznets's failure to adjust for the tendency of the wealthy to split incomes.

Perlo claims his studies reveal that, taken together, these three main errors in Kuznets's approach wholly eliminate the evidence Kuznets adduces for an increase in income equality. If fact, Perlo's calculations are that the upper 5 percent had one-third of the national income in both 1929 and 1948 (the period of Kuznets's study), and the upper 1 percent had about one-sixth of the national income in each of these years. Perlo's estimates of concentration are considerably higher than those in more recent studies—to which, however, Perlo would probably offer many of the same objec.ions as he did to the estimates by Kuznets. Calculations based on figures from the U.S. government's Office of Business Economics and from the Internal Revenue Service put the average annual share of family personal income received by the top 1 percent income bracket at 8 percent in the period from 1946 to 1967.[11]

In a comprehensive analysis of the "post-fisc" distribution of income in 1950, 1961, and 1970 (covering roughly the period since Goldsmith's and Kuznets's studies), Morgan Reynolds and Eugene Smolensky (Selection Number 9) attempt to detect changes in the final income distributions during these two decades. "Post-fisc" distribution means that all government taxes and expenditures are allocated to households in each of these periods, in addition to income from wages, salaries, and investments. The dispersion of income in each of these years is measured by the Gini coefficient. The problem is how to allocate government taxes and expenditures to income classes. For instance, state and local taxes rose from a ratio of 42 percent of federal taxes in 1950 to 51 percent in 1961 and 58 percent in 1970. Since state and local taxes are probably more regressive than federal taxes, this means the total tax bill has probably become more regressive also. Furthermore, the corporate income tax declined from 27 percent of federal tax receipts in 1950 to 16 percent in 1970, while Social Security and payroll taxes grew much more rapidly than all federal taxes—from less than 9 percent in 1950 to 26 percent in 1970. These changes imply that in the past two decades the federal tax burden itself has actually become more regressive, that is, it falls more heavily on the lower income brackets than on the higher ones. Reynolds and Smolensky conducted a number of "experiments" which make different, more or less progressive or regressive, assumptions about how taxes and government expenditures are actually distributed. They find that conventional assignments of government expenditures and taxes by income bracket yield distributions of income that are very similar in 1950, 1961, and 1970. There were no major changes in final income distributions even with the rapid growth of government expenditures (from 20 percent of Net National Product in 1950 to 35 percent in 1970) and sizable changes in the composition of taxes and expenditures. Reynolds and Smolensky conclude that despite a sizeable increase in government benefits accruing to the lower income levels, aggregate income inequality in the United States was virtually unaltered between 1950 and 1970.

This conclusion is not accepted by everyone who has studied the trend in income inequality since the Second World War. Several studies have found that

11. Edward C. Budd, "Postwar Changes in the Size Distribution of Income in the U.S.," *American Economic Review* 60:2 (May, 1972), Table 4, p. 253.

income inequality has not remained stable, but in fact *increased* during the post-war period. Danziger and Smolensky (Selection Number 10), therefore, present four time series on income inequality between 1947 and 1973 based on different sources of data and on different methods of measurement, income concept, and unit of observation. The results are conflicting trends, depending on the years included and the income unit analyzed, which they cannot yet explain satisfactorily. (For instance, there is a trend toward *increased* income *in*equality among male, full-year, wage and salary workers, 1958 to 1969, and among all earners included in the Social Security population, 1951 to 1969.) There are also conflicting findings on the "cyclical pattern of income inequality"; for instance, whether (as has been commonly assumed) inequality decreases when unemployment falls or wages rise. The only conclusion that is clearly sustained by Danziger and Smolensky's analysis is that even small differences in how a standard measure of income inequality is calculated can alter the direction of the trends. This underlines once again how important it is to examine quantitative "findings" with special attention to the concepts and methods of measurement used in their "discovery" —particularly when the findings concerning equality carry, as Danziger and Smolensky note, "an enormous emotional and ideological charge."

Concentration of Personal Wealth, 1922-1969

6

By *James D. Smith and Stephen D. Franklin*

This paper presents estimates of the concentration of personal wealth in the United States from 1922 to 1969. These estimates lead us to conclude that the distribution of wealth (1) became significantly more equal in the 1930s and early 1940s, two periods of massive government intervention in the marketplace, and (2) has remained essentially unchanged since 1945.[1]

In what follows, we compare the wealth held by the richest 1.0 and 0.5 percent of the population to that of all persons. The wealth of the richest 1.0 and 0.5 percent was estimated by the estate multiplier technique.[2] The wealth of all persons was derived from national balance sheets.[3]

The estimates presented here for the period before 1953 were developed by Robert J. Lampman using highly aggregated Internal Revenue Service (IRS) data. For 1953 and 1958 we use detailed estimates (from special IRS tabulations) by Lampman and Smith, modified slightly to

Reprinted from James D. Smith and Stephen D. Franklin, "The Concentration of Personal Wealth," *American Economic Review* 86 (May, 1974):162–67, by permission of the publisher and authors. James D. Smith and Stephen D. Franklin are from the Urban Institute and the Pennsylvania State University respectively. The work reported here is part of the Urban Institute's research program on income and wealth distribution. The support of the National Science Foundation is gratefully acknowledged.

1. We wish to make clear that our concern is with temporal change and that we have sacrificed best estimates for individual years to achieve consistency over the time series. Individual figures have a downward bias of 10 to 15 percent from our best estimates of concentration. (Best estimates for 1969 may be found in Smith; similar estimates for other years will appear later.)

2. Detailed descriptions of the methodology and attendant problems can be found in Smith and Staunton Calvert, Robert J. Lampman, and Smith.

3. National Balance sheets were constructed for a person's sector using data supplied by the Board of Governors of the Federal Reserve System. Helen Stone Tice did the basic work on these special sector balance sheets. Smith provides a detailed description of the balance sheet.

take account of current knowledge. Estimates for 1962, 1965, and 1969 are new detailed estimates developed by the authors using microdata files of estate tax returns prepared by the IRS for its routine publications. Here we focus on the years since 1953.

Information available from estate tax returns varies from year to year, so a number of adjustments were made to bring the estimates for individual years into conceptual alignment with one another. The alignment problem was exacerbated because the IRS has destroyed tapes of returns filed before 1963, leaving only Lampman's and Smith's printed tabulations for 1953 and 1958.[4] It was impractical to reestimate the distributions for 1953 and 1958 by better methods based on current knowledge. Consequently, the estimates for 1962, 1965, and 1969 were made consistent with those for 1953 and 1958 after they were slightly adjusted.[5] The result is a time series of wealth distributions which understates the degree of concentration in any given year but is consistent and permits comparisons over time.

As applied here, the estate multiplier technique treats decedents in a given year as a stratified sample of the living population whose estates would have been required to file tax returns had they died during the year. As with any sample, estimates of population parameters can be made by weighting observations by the reciprocals of their sampling rates. For samples "drawn" by death, the sampling rates are mortality rates. The mortality strata used here are age, sex, and social class.

We first look at the overall concentration of wealth from 1922 to 1969 and at the detailed estimates for 1953 to 1969, and then discuss briefly the estimation of trust assets.

I. CHANGES IN THE GENERAL CONCENTRATION OF WEALTH, 1922–1969

Wealth in the United States has become less concentrated in the last half century. The diminution has not been great, however, and it all occurred during periods when the market system was functioning under duress or was in administrative abeyance, specifically, the Great Depression and World War II.

---

4. A further problem resulted from the fact that the IRS erased the age field from the 1965 tape. This was most unfortunate because of all years for which the IRS has coded estate tax returns, 1965 had the most detailed classification of information. The erased data was restored by a stochastic process which took into account the relationship between age and other characteristics observable in the files for 1962 and 1969.

5. We adjusted Lampman's basic estimates for 1953 to include an amount represented by decedents whose age was unspecified on estate tax returns. Smith's estimate for 1958 was distorted by a sampling fluke—the inclusion of an outlier, i.e., a totally atypical individual (with a very large estate held entirely in annuities). We therefore adjusted his figure by distributing this outlier's assets. (Had the outlier's assets been left unadjusted, the estimate of the total value of annuities would have been raised by over $16 billion.)

Lampman, in his classic study of the distribution of wealth, found the highest measurable concentration on the eve of the Great Depression. According to his figures, the richest 0.5 percent of Americans in 1929 owned 32.4 percent of the net wealth of all individuals, no doubt a reflection of the phenomenal rise in the price of stock—long the dominant asset in the portfolios of the rich—at that time.

But the collapse of the market in October of 1929 and its plummet downward to 1932 carried with it the fortunes of many near the pinnacle of America's wealth pyramid. Whether 1932 was the nadir of America's affluent we do not know, but by 1933 the top 0.5 percent had lost 22 percent of the share of wealth it held four years before. Lampman found that the share of the richest 0.5 percent then rose somewhat— from 25.2 percent in 1933 to 28.0 percent in 1939—but later fell sharply to only 20.9 percent in 1945. And 1949 saw the most egalitarian distribution of American wealth measured to date. In that year the top 0.5 percent of wealth-holders held only 19.3 percent of all personally held net wealth.

By 1953, Lampman found, the share of the top 0.5 percent had risen sharply to 22.7 percent (22.0 percent after our subsequent adjustments). His rough estimate for 1954, based on published data, showed about the same share, 22.5 percent. His estimate for 1956, also based on published data, showed a substantial increase to 25.0 percent.

Following Lampman, Smith estimated that the top 0.5 percent held 21.7 percent of the nation's personal wealth in 1958, a figure not significantly different from Lampman's for 1953. And IRS estimates imply that the top 0.5 percent held 23.4 percent of the wealth of all persons in 1962.[6]

It might seem, then, that the trend toward equality in the two decades following the market's crash in 1929 reversed itself after World War II. But our examination of the old evidence and our new estimates for 1958, 1962, 1965, and 1969 do not support this conclusion. In our view, observable point-to-point differences in the estimated concentration of wealth since 1945 are due to inconsistencies and inadequacies in IRS data, sampling errors, short-run stock market variations, and a valuation bias in the basic data which understates the wealth of the rich in declining market periods by permitting estates to select between the most beneficial of two valuation dates.

---

6. We believe, on the basis of information provided us by the Metropolitan Life Insurance Company, that the mortality rates used for the 1962 estimates resulted in a significant overstatement of the wealth of persons with over $60,000 gross assets.

We also believe that preliminary IRS estimates for 1969 (see Vito Natrella) are too high. They imply that persons with gross assets over $60,000 owned 47.4 percent of total wealth in 1969; adjusted to reflect underestimation biases, the implied share of such persons will exceed 50 percent.

In Figure 6–1 we have plotted estimates of the share of the nation's personal net worth held by the richest 0.5 percent of all individuals since 1922, along with Standard and Poor's stock price index. One can perceive a generally downward trend in concentration up to the mid-1940s. After that it appears that the trend line is flat. It also appears that, after 1945, periods when the actual wealth share was above (below) the trend were generally preceded by periods of market increases (declines).

II. THE DETAILED CONCENTRATION OF WEALTH, 1953–1969

Table 6–1 gives estimates of the shares of specific assets held by the richest 0.5 percent and richest 1.0 percent of the population in 1953, 1958, 1962, 1965, and 1969.

The only striking change over this period was a decline in the concentration of corporate stockholdings. The richest 0.5 percent of the population held 86 percent of the value of personally owned stock in 1953, but only 44 percent in 1969.[7]

It is worth noting that 1965 is the first year for which an estimate of the concentration of trust assets by size of individuals' wealth is available. Although the estimates for other years are derived estimates based on the 1965 measurement and a procedure described below, the 1965 estimate is a direct one. It is clear that trusts are the most concentrated of all substantial types of wealth: 85 percent of the value of trusts were in the hands of the top 0.5 percent of wealth-holders and 93 percent were held by the richest 1.0 percent in 1965.

Before discussing the estimation of trust assets, we once again wish to emphasize that the values shown here understate shares of wealth owned by the top 0.5 percent of wealth-holders because maintaining consistency with the published data for 1953 and 1958 prevented the application of refinements usable on the 1962, 1965, and 1969 microdata.

III. ESTIMATION OF TRUST ASSETS

In 1962 and 1969 the IRS recorded trust assets by type of property (real estate, stock, etc.), but not a separate total for trusts. In 1965 it did exactly the reverse. The data for 1953 and 1958 included trust interests in "other property." Since the value of trust assets held by the wealthy is substantial, we attempted to make the estimates consistent across years by estimating the total value of trust interests of the top 0.5 percent and 1.0 percent of the population in those years where trusts

---

7. This is consistent with New York Stock Exchange figures showing an increase of nearly 500 percent in the number of shareholders between 1952 and 1970.

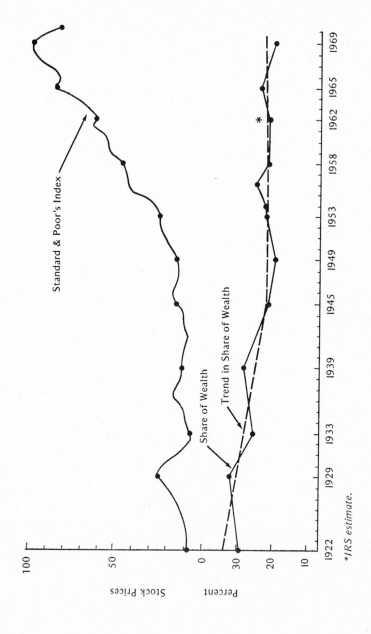

Figure 6–1. Share of Wealth Held by Richest 0.5 Percent of Population, and Stock Prices, 1922–1969

*IRS estimate.

74

Table 6–1. Shares of Richest 0.5 Percent and 1.0 Percent of Persons in National Wealth, 1953, 1958, 1962, 1965, and 1969

	1953				
	Value (billions) Held by Richest			Share (percent) Held by Richest	
Asset	100.0%	0.5%	1.0%	0.5%	1.0%
Real estate[a]	$ 439.0	$ 45.0	$ 68.0	10.3	15.5
Corporate stock[b]	151.5	116.6	130.8	77.0	86.3
Bonds	72.8	33.0	8.3	45.3	52.6
Cash[c]	160.1	20.9	28.8	13.1	18.0
Debt instruments[d]	34.0	8.2	10.9	24.1	32.1
Life insurance (CSV)[e]	64.5	6.6	9.1	10.2	14.1
Miscellaneous and trusts[f]	243.3	30.0	38.6	12.3	15.9
Trusts	20.5	17.5	18.8	85.4	91.7
Miscellaneous	222.8	12.5	19.8	5.6	8.9
Total assets	$1144.7	$242.8	$305.7	21.2	26.7
Liabilities	$ 140.0	$ 21.3	$ 29.0	15.2	20.7
Net worth	$1004.7	$221.5	$276.7	22.0	27.5
Number of persons (millions)		0.80	1.60		

	1958				
	Value (billions) Held by Richest			Share (percent) Held by Richest	
Asset	100.0%	0.5%	1.0%	0.5%	1.0%
Real estate[a]	$ 621.5	$ 62.5	$ 93.9	10.1	15.1
Corporate stock[b]	264.1	175.9	199.2	66.6	75.4
Bonds	87.0	31.3	36.0	36.0	41.4
Cash[c]	216.0	22.5	32.8	10.4	15.2
Debt instruments[d]	43.7	12.5	16.3	28.6	37.3
Life insurance (CSV)[e]	79.9	7.5	11.3	9.4	14.1
Miscellaneous and trusts[f]	343.2	45.6	52.8	13.3	15.4
Trusts	30.3	25.8	27.9	85.1	92.1
Miscellaneous	312.9	19.8	24.9	6.3	7.9
Total assets	$1625.1	$332.0	$414.4	20.4	25.5
Liabilities	$ 227.4	$ 29.2	$ 38.3	12.9	16.8
Net worth	$1396.7	$302.8	$376.1	21.7	26.9
Number of persons (millions)		0.87	1.74		

Table 6-1. (cont.)

	1962				
	Value (billions) Held by Richest			Share (percent) Held by Richest	
Asset	100.0%	0.5%	1.0%	0.5%	1.0%
Real estate[a]	$ 770.0	$ 79.6	$117.8	10.3	15.3
Corporate stock[b]	426.4	227.3	264.4	53.3	62.0
Bonds	94.5	33.2	38.4	35.1	40.6
Cash[c]	278.3	28.9	42.5	10.4	15.3
Debt instruments[d]	51.5	16.5	21.8	32.0	42.3
Life insurance (CSV)[e]	93.8	7.1	10.7	7.6	11.4
Miscellaneous and trusts[f]	425.5	NA	NA	—	—
Trusts	46.1	NA	NA	—	—
Miscellaneous	379.4	39.8	52.7	10.5	13.9
Total assets	$2093.9	$432.4	$548.3	20.7	26.2
Liabilities	$ 314.0	$ 47.8	$ 61.0	15.2	19.4
Net worth	$1779.9	$384.6	$487.3	21.6	27.4
Number of persons (millions)		.93	1.87		

	1965				
	Value (billions) Held by Richest			Share (percent) Held by Richest	
Asset	100.0%	0.5%	1.0%	0.5%	1.0%
Real estate[a]	$ 917.7	$ 94.4	$135.8	10.3	14.8
Corporate stock[b]	596.6	317.2	364.9	53.2	61.2
Bonds	103.6	57.5	63.2	55.5	61.0
Cash[c]	366.0	43.7	62.7	11.9	17.1
Debt instruments[d]	53.3	19.8	25.4	37.1	47.7
Life insurance (CSV)[e]	107.2	6.5	10.9	6.1	10.2
Miscellaneous and trusts[f]	514.1	85.3	101.8	16.6	19.8
Trusts	57.5	49.0	52.7	85.2	91.7
Miscellaneous	456.6	36.3	49.1	8.0	10.8
Total assets	$2601.0	$575.4	$712.7	22.1	27.4
Liabilities	$ 413.3	$ 57.0	$ 73.1	13.8	17.7
Net worth	$2187.7	$518.4	$639.6	23.7	29.2
Number of persons (millions)		.97	1.94		

	1969				
	Value (billions) Held by Richest			Share (percent) Held by Richest	
Asset	100.0%	0.5%	1.0%	0.5%	1.0%
Real estate[a]	$1188.8	$117.0	$170.7	9.8	14.4
Corporate stock[b]	832.5	366.3	423.3	44.0	50.8
Bonds	198.9	63.7	71.5	32.0	35.9
Cash[c]	495.0	48.1	71.2	9.7	14.4
Debt instruments[d]	85.3	21.9	29.6	25.7	34.7
Life insurance (CSV)[e]	127.2	8.4	13.8	6.6	10.8
Miscellaneous and trusts[f]	705.8	107.0	133.2	15.2	18.9
Trusts	70.4	60.0	64.5	85.2	91.6
Miscellaneous	633.7	47.0	68.7	7.4	10.8
Total assets	$3561.4	$672.4	$848.8	18.9	23.8
Liabilities	$ 557.5	$ 75.8	$100.5	13.6	18.0
Net worth	$3003.0	$596.7	$748.1	19.9	24.9
Number of persons (millions)		1.01	2.03		

Note: "Richness" is measured in terms of gross assets. Net worth is preferred to gross assets as a classifier, but the microdata for 1953 and 1958 which would have permitted such an arrangement have been destroyed by the Internal Revenue Service. The microdata for 1962, 1965, and 1969 were therefore ordered by gross assets to produce estimates consistent with Lampman's and Smith's for 1953 and 1958 respectively.

[a]Real estate is shown at its market value without deduction of mortgages, liens, or other incumbrances. In 1953 and 1958 only real estate located in the United States is included. In 1962 the value of real estate located outside the United States was brought into the estimate by a change in the law which made foreign real estate subject to estate taxes. The amount of such real estate is, however, seriously underrepresented because the law took effect late in 1962. Only estates for decedents who died after October 16, 1962, and who had acquired foreign real estate (except by gift or inheritance) after February, 1962, were required to report it on estate tax returns. In 1965 and 1969 foreign real estate was included along with other real estate.

Included in real estate are land and structures for personal and business use. All other business assets are included in the "miscellaneous" category. Real estate held in trust is included here to the extent of the trust interest. A relatively small proportion of trust assets is in real estate, but the absolute value of all trust assets is understated here for reasons explained in the text.

[b]Corporate stock includes the value of all common and preferred issues, shares in domestic or foreign firms whether traded or closely held, certificates and shares of building and loan and savings and loan associations, Federal Land Bank stock, and other instruments representing an equity interest in an enterprise. Accrued dividends are also included. Stock held in trust is included, but the absolute value is understated.

[c]Cash includes balances in checking and savings accounts, currency on hand or in safety deposit boxes, cash balances with stock brokers, and postal savings accounts. Cash in trust is included, but understated.

[d]Debt includes all legal obligations except loans on life insurance policies.

[e]Life insurance (cash surrender value—CSV) is the amount individuals could expect to receive were they to surrender their policies to the carriers. It takes account of policy loans, accrued dividends, and unearned premiums.

[f]"Miscellaneous and trusts" includes all assets owned in trust *except real estate* and all assets other than real estate, corporate stock, bonds, cash, debt instruments, and life insurance (CSV) not held in trusts. Included are such items as consumer durables, personal effects, business assets (excluding real estate), mineral rights, tax sale certificates, judgments, lifetime transfers, and growing crops if not included in the value of real estate. This classification is shown here as an information item to explicate certain adjustments described in the text. It should not be summed with other assets to arrive at a total asset figure because trust assets are included within the individual asset types.

Miscellaneous assets are those described under miscellaneous and trusts less trust assets. The miscellaneous asset category is added to other assets to arrive at total assets.

Trusts represent the actuarial value of reversionary and remainder interests in trusts. This actuarial value is substantially less than the total market value of assets held in trusts. On the basis of analysis reported in the text the national balance sheet totals (100 percent) have been adjusted to the reporting concept used for estate tax purposes.

The separate value of trusts could be estimated directly only for 1965. For other years indirect estimates were made by a method described in the text. The value for trusts is shown as an information item. The assets held in trust have been distributed to specific asset categories.

are included in the "other property" category and then allocating this total among specific asset types (stocks, bonds, etc.) based on the composition of trust assets in national balance sheets.

The value of trust assets reportable on estate tax returns is an actuarial value. It is, in general, the present value of future payments which may be contingent upon such events as the death of another person. Although the valuation of trust assets in this manner may be appropriate for estate tax purposes, it understates the immediate market value of trust assets in which persons have a financial interest. Consequently, the value of trust assets estimated by the estate multiplier technique cannot be compared directly to national balance sheet totals, which represent the market value of trust assets, without regard to restrictions imposed by trust instruments. To determine the extent to which the value of trust assets is understated, we estimated the number of trusts valued at over $60,000 by the estate multiplier method using the 1965 file (the one file on which they are identified). The estimated number of trusts over $60,000 was 118,925. Next, the number of such trusts was counted off, starting with the largest, in the array of fiduciary income tax returns filed for trusts in 1965.[8] The reported income of the counted-off trusts was then capitalized at the rate which the reported income of all trusts bore to the value of trust assets in the 1965 national balance sheets, or about 5.7 percent. The capitalized income of these 118,925 largest trusts amounted to $94.9 billion. The trust assets estimated by the estate multiplier method for the same number of largest trusts in 1965 was $51.5 billion. On this basis, we concluded that conceptually we were limited to estimating only 54.3 percent of balance sheet trust assets. Consequently, we reduced the value in the national balance sheet to 54.3 percent *for purposes of making estimates of the share of trust assets held by the richest 1.0 and 0.5 percent of the population.*

Interests in trusts for the years 1953 and 1958 were estimated for the top 0.5 percent and 1.0 percent of the population using the information provided from 1965 returns. It was assumed that the share of trusts held by the wealthy was the same in each year as in 1965. After an estimate was made for trusts, the value was allocated to stocks, bonds, notes and mortgages, and cash in the same proportion which each asset represents of the total trust assets held by all persons. For the 1969 data, contrary to the IRS reports that trust assets were distributed by asset type, there is strong evidence that, in fact, the total value of trusts was included in "other property." The original estimates for 1969 showed that the share of stocks and bonds (the largest components of trust assets) had dropped to 39 percent and 25 percent respectively and that their share of miscellaneous property had risen to about 17 percent. The estimates

---

8. See U.S. Department of Treasury, p. 22.

for 1969 shown in Table 6–1 are based on the assumption that trust assets had not been allocated and were shown in "other property."

REFERENCES

R. J. Lampman, *The Share of Top Wealth-Holders in National Wealth,* Princeton 1962.

V. Natrella, "Discussion," in J. D. Smith, ed., *Personal Distributions of Income and Wealth,* forthcoming.

J. D. Smith, "The Concentration of Wealth in America," *Review of Income and Wealth,* forthcoming.

J. D. Smith and S. Calvert, "Estimating the Wealth of Top Wealth-Holders from Estate-Tax Returns," *Proc. of the Bus. and Econ. Sec., Amer. Statist. Assn.,* 1965.

New York Stock Exchange, *Census of Shareholders,* New York 1972.

U.S. Dept. of Treasury, *Statistics of Income 1965, Fiduciary, Gift and Estate Tax Returns,* Washington 1966.

Changes in the Size Distribution of Income

7

Selma F. Goldsmith

This paper attempts to summarize some recent findings concerning changes that have taken place in income distribution in the United States during the past 25 years. The discussion is directed primarily at the question of whether or not there has been a reduction over this period in relative income differences among families and individuals. If so, how large has it been, and to what extent are the available figures influenced by particular concepts and definitions?

To those who are working in this field it will be apparent that the materials presented here are not essentially new but merely summarize some of the statistical findings and analyses that have recently appeared or will shortly appear in a number of journal articles, government publications, and other sources. However, these materials are sufficiently scattered and the subject important enough that a summary should prove useful. It must be obvious that the limitations of this paper make it impossible to cover many important aspects of this broad subject.

Although there is some argument as to its exact magnitude, partly as a result of problems of appropriate deflation procedures, there is general agreement that there has been a very substantial increase in total and average real income over the past quarter century. In terms of the personal income series of the Office of Business Economics, total real income flowing to families and unattached individuals increased between 1929 and 1955 at an average annual rate of approximately 3 or 2.5 percent a year, depending on whether income is measured before or after federal individual income taxes. The number of families and unattached individuals sharing in the income total has increased at an average rate of about 1.4 percent per year. Thus, real mean family income has risen at an average yearly rate of about 1.5 percent on a before-tax

Reprinted from Selma F. Goldsmith, "Changes in the Size Distribution of Income," *American Economic Review* 47:2 (May, 1957):504–18, by permission of the publisher. Footnotes have been renumbered.

basis or slightly over 1 percent on an after-tax basis, from 1929 to 1955.

The increase in average real income has been reflected in a very substantial upward shift in the income-size distribution of consumer units (families and unattached individuals). For example, with family incomes expressed in terms of 1950 prices—and ignoring for the moment certain important problems of comparability of data—we find that the proportion of consumer units with before-tax incomes over $3,000 increased from one-third in 1929 to two-thirds in 1954. The proportion above $4,000 rose from one-fifth to one-half and the proportion above $5,000 from about 13 to 35 percent.[1]

The income-size distributions available for selected intermediate years within the 1929 to 1954 period indicate that a very large part of the upward shift in real incomes occurred between 1941 and 1944. For example, about one-half of the 1929 to 1954 increase of 33 percentage points in the proportion of consumer units with real (1950 dollar) incomes over $3,000 took place between 1941 and 1944. However, the available price indexes do not reflect certain hidden price increases that occurred during the war so that the deflated figures overstate somewhat the wartime rise in real incomes and understate the increase in the early postwar years.

Of equal significance with the absolute income figures are estimates of the changes in relative income distribution over the past 25 years. I propose first to summarize what the available figures show and then to appraise as best we can the validity of these findings.

The two statistical series on income-size distribution to which we can turn, present essentially the same pattern for the post-1929 period; namely, a marked decline in the percentage share of total income accruing to the top income group.

The first of these series, developed by Professor Kuznets, presents annual data on relative income shares received by successive top percentiles of the population; e.g., by the 5 percent of men, women, and children covered on those individual income tax returns reporting the largest per capita incomes in each year.[2] The second series, developed by my colleagues and myself, is on a family rather than a population basis and covers the full range of family incomes for selected years.[3] The top 5 percent in this series refers to families and unattached individuals having the largest family personal incomes in each year.

---

1. Selma F. Goldsmith, "Relation of Census Income Distribution Statistics to Other Income Data," to be published in volume 23 of *Studies in Income and Wealth* (National Bureau of Economic Research).

2. Simon Kuznets, *Shares of Upper Income Groups in Income and Savings* (National Bureau of Economic Research, 1953).

3. Office of Business Economics, "Income Distribution in the United States by Size, 1944–50," a Supplement to the *Survey of Current Business* (U.S. Department of Commerce, 1953); "Income Distribution in the United States, 1950–53," and "1952–55," *Survey of Current Business* (March, 1955), (June, 1956); Selma Goldsmith, George Jaszi, Hyman Kaitz, and Maurice Liebenberg, "Size Distribution of Income since the Mid-thirties," *Review of Economics and Statistics* (February, 1954).

Starting with Kuznets's series, in 1929 the incomes received by the top 5 percent of the population amounted to about 32 percent of the total income receipts of all individuals (measured before income taxes and excluding net capital gains). In 1939, this relative share had dropped to 28 percent, reflecting mainly a loss in relative share by the topmost percentile of the population. After 1939 declines were registered by all bands within the top 5 percent. By 1946, the relative share of this top group had fallen to 20 percent and in 1948 it is estimated at somewhat over 19 percent (Table 7–1). For the 1929 to 1948 period as a whole, this represented a decline of 40 percent in the relative share of before-tax

Table 7–1. Percentage Shares of Income Received by Top 5 Percent, Selected Years

| Year | Top 5 percent of population (Kuznets) | | | Top 5 percent of Consumer units | |
	Economic income variant (1)	Disposable income variant (2)	Economic income variant plus realized net capital gains (3)	Family personal income (4)	Income after federal individual income tax liability (5)
1929	32.2	33.8	34.8	30.0	29.5
1935–36	28.8	27.9		26.5	
1939	27.8	26.8	27.8	25.8	24.8
1941	25.7	23.0		24.0	21.5
1944	18.7	15.8		20.7	
1946	20.0	17.7	21.4	21.3	
1947	19.4			20.9	
1948	19.4				
1952				20.5	18.2
Percent decrease:					
1929 to 1946	38	48	38	29	
1939 to 1946	28	34	23	17	
1929 to 1948	40				
1929 to 1952				32	38
1939 to 1952				21	27

Sources: Columns 1 and 2, which represent, respectively, before-tax income exclusive of capital gains, and income after federal individual income taxes but inclusive of realized net capital gains, from Simon Kuznets, *Shares of Upper Income Groups In Income and Savings* (National Bureau of Economic Research, 1953), pages 453, 635, 637 (with 1948 extrapolated by Kuznets' "basic variant" series, page 599). For column 1, an estimate of 17.4 is obtained for the year 1953 by applying to data from *Statistics of Income, Part 1, 1953* (U.S. Treasury Department) and from July, 1956, issue of *Survey of Current Business* (U.S. Department of Commerce) the various adjustments used by Kuznets to derive his economic income variant series. (Shares, pages 280, 302, 360–361, 366–367, 387, 412–413, 423–424, 571, 577, and 579.) Comparability between 1953 and the earlier years in column 1 is impaired, however, by the introduction of the split-income provision in 1948. Column 3 derived by adding to column 1 Kuznets' adjustment to include net capital gains (page 599, column 5 minus column 1) and subtracting his adjustment for unwarranted inclusions (page 622, column 4 minus column 1). Column 4, which represents personal income before income taxes flowing to families and unattached individuals and excludes capital gains and losses, for 1952 from "Income Distribution in the United States, by Size, 1952–55," *Survey of Current Business* (June, 1956), 1946 and 1947 from "Income Distribution in the United States, by Size, 1944–50," a supplement to the *Survey of Current Business* (1953); 1941, 1935–36 and 1929 from Selma Goldsmith, George Jaszi, Hyman Kaitz, and Maurice Liebenberg, "Size Distribution of Income since the Mid-thirties," *Review of Economics and Statistics* (February, 1954); 1939 derived by interpolation between 1935–36 and 1941 using column 1 as a basis. Column 5, which represents column 4 minus federal individual income tax liabilities other than those on net capital gains, for 1952 and 1941 derived from sources listed for column 4 for those years; 1929 and 1939 obtained by subtracting from amounts underlying column 4 federal individual income tax liabilities excluding liabilities on net capital gains, estimated from data in *Statistics of Income, Part 1, 1929 and 1939* (U.S. Treasury Department).

income received by the top 5 percent of the population. Kuznets has recently conjectured that this narrowing of relative income differences is part of a long-time secular swing that followed a period of widening income inequality during the second half of the last century.[4]

The family income distributions show a similar though somewhat dampened post-1929 decline for the top income group. The relative share of the top 5 percent of consumer units is estimated at 30 percent in 1929 and at under 21 percent in 1944 and in the postwar period.

Both the Kuznets and family income series represent before tax incomes and, in deriving both of them, data from federal individual income tax returns represented the primary source material. The difference between them reflects a number of factors, such as differences in the basic unit of measurement (the family versus the person), in the concept of income, and in the adjustments that were made in the basic tax-return statistics by Kuznets, on the one hand, and by the various sets of persons who initially developed the family distributions for selected prewar and postwar years, on the other.

The family income distributions also tell us how the decrease in relative income share of the top 5 percent of the consumer units was spread among other income groups. Between 1929 and 1947, for example, the 9 percentage points of decline in the share of the top 5 percent were offset by the following gains: 3½ percentage points by the lowest 40 percent of families and unattached individuals, 2¼ points by the middle quintile, 2¾ points by the fourth quintile, and ¾ points by the 15 percent of consumer units directly below the top 5.[5]

A salient point is that for the lowest 40 percent of consumer units, the period of greatest relative gains was between 1941 and 1944. Since 1944, there has been little change in the relative distribution of family income according to the available figures.

Kuznets has also developed a series in terms of disposable income (i.e., income after federal individual income taxes and inclusive of capital gains). For the top 5 percent of the population, the relative share in total disposable income dropped from almost 34 percent in 1929 to well under 18 percent in 1946, the last year for which this series is available. This represented a decrease of 48 percent, 10 points more than the 38 percent drop in the before-tax income share from 1929 to 1946 (Table 7–1).

These decreases in relative income shares are reflected strikingly in the average income figures for the top income sector. Kuznets's per capita disposable income of the top 5 percent is about one-eighth lower in 1946 than in 1929, even in current dollars; i.e., before allowance for

4. Simon Kuznets, "Economic Growth and Income Inequality," *American Economic Review* (March, 1955).
5. Goldsmith, op. cit.

the higher prices prevailing in the latter year (Table 7–2). On a before-tax basis the current-dollar per capita income of the top 5 percent just about kept up with the rise in the consumer price index for the period 1929 to 1946 but fell behind by 1948.[6] However, attention must be called to the limited applicability of the consumer price index in this context. Not until we are able to develop differential cost-of-living indexes appropriate for the various income groups and can solve the problem of how to deflate the portions of income used for income taxes and saving, will we be in a position to measure with precision changes in the distribution of real income.

Several related statistical series lend support to the finding that there has been a reduction in relative income differences in the post-1929 and particularly in the post-1939 period. The before-tax income measures include:

1. *Changes in the Relative Importance of the Various Types of Income in the Personal Income Total.* Since 1929 there has been a striking increase in the percentage that wages and salaries and transfer payments constitute of the personal income total flowing to families and unattached individuals. These payments together accounted for 61 percent of total personal income in 1929, 67 percent in 1939, and 73 percent in 1950 to 1955 (Table 7–3). In contrast, there was a marked reduction in the shares of dividends and interest—types of income that are heavily concentrated in the upper end of the family income scale.[7]

2. *Changes in the Relative Distribution of the Various Types of Income.* By examining the shares of the top 5 per cent in separate types of income, Kuznets found that the relative shares of this top group, based on data from tax returns, declined from 1929 to 1948 for wages and salaries, dividends, interest, and—to a lesser extent—for rental income. More recently, Herman Miller compared the wage and salary data reported in the last two Decennial Censuses of Population for detailed occupation and industry groups and found three factors making for a narrowing of income differentials within the wage and salary sector between 1939 and 1949: (a) decreases in relative income dispersion for men within practically all of the 118 occupations and 117 industries he studied; (b) relatively greater gains in median wage and salary income for low-paid than for high-paid occupations and industries; and (c) an increase in the

---

6. Geoffrey Moore showed that this fall took place within the top 1 percent of the population. See "Secular Changes in the Distribution of Income," AEA *Papers and Proceedings* (May, 1952).

7. For a discussion of the relative importance of wages and salaries and other income shares in national income, see Edward F. Denison, "Income Types and the Size Distribution," AEA *Papers and Proceedings* (May, 1954), and "Distribution of National Income; Pattern of Income Shares since 1929," *Survey of Current Business* (June, 1952). Also, Jesse Burkhead, "Changes in the Functional Distribution of Income," *Journal of the American Statistical Association* (June, 1953), and George J. Schuller, "The Secular Trend in Income Distribution by Type," *Review of Economics and Statistics* (November, 1953).

Table 7-2. Average Income of Entire Population and of Top 5 Percent, Selected Years

Year	Average income per capita (Kuznets)				Consumer price index 1947–49 = 100
	Economic income variant		Disposable income variant		
	Total population	Top 5 percent	Total population	Top 5 percent	
1929	$ 674	$4,339	$ 690	$4,666	73.3
1939	537	2,982	528	2,831	59.4
1941	700	3,594	664	3,052	62.9
1946	1,234	4,926	1,166	4,118	83.4
1948	1,400	5,421			102.8
Percent increase:					
1929 to 1946	83	14	69	-12	14
1939 to 1946	130	65	121	45	40
1929 to 1948	108	25			40

Sources: Averages (see Table 7-1 for definitions) derived from Simon Kuznets, *Shares*, pp. 635, 637, 641, 644 (with 1948 extrapolated from 1947 by Kuznets' "basic variant" series). Consumer price index from Bureau of Labor Statistics.

Table 7-3. Percent Distribution of Family Personal Income by Major Types of Income and Relative Importance of Compensation of Employees in National Income, Selected Years

	1929	1939	1949	1950–55 average
Family personal income:				
Wages and salaries and other labor income	59.6	63.3	64.8	67.5
Transfer payments	1.7	4.0	5.9	5.4
Subtotal	61.3	67.3	70.7	72.9
Business and professional income:				
Farm	7.1	6.1	6.4	5.2
Nonfarm	10.5	10.2	10.7	9.8
Dividends and interest	14.7	12.6	8.2	8.3
Rental income	6.4	3.8	4.0	3.8
Total	100.0	100.0	100.0	100.0
Compensation of employees as a percent of national income originating in:				
Economy as a whole	58.2	66.1	65.2	67.3
Ordinary business sector (corporations, partnerships, and proprietorships)	61.2	65.8	64.0	66.4
All other sectors	46.9	67.2	69.8	70.7
All nonfarm corporations	74.5	80.9	75.8	76.6
Manufacturing corporations	75	81	74	75

Sources: Upper bank derived by adjusting U.S. Department of Commerce personal income series from *Survey of Current Business* (July, 1956), as described on pages 17–18 and 67 of "Income Distribution in the United States, by Size 1944–1950," U.S. Department of Commerce, 1953. Lower bank, except last line, derived from Table 12 (and underlying data) of 1954 *National Income* supplement and July, 1956, issue of *Survey of Current Business*. Last line derived from *Survey of Current Business* (November, 1956):20.

proportion of workers classified in occupations with comparatively little income dispersion.[8] Unfortunately similar data are not available from the Census for 1929.

Of particular interest to those in the teaching profession is Miller's finding that when the industries are ranked by size of median wage or salary and grouped into deciles, the educational services industry dropped from the third highest decile in 1939 to the fourth from the bottom in 1949.

3. A Narrowing of Relative Income Differences, as Measured by Mean Incomes, between the Farm and Nonfarm Population. Because average incomes are lower for farm than for nonfarm consumer units—even with allowance for income received in kind—a narrowing in this differential, barring other changes, will work in the direction of reducing relative income differences in the overall income distribution. Per capita income of persons on farms was three times as large in 1949 as in 1939—reflecting in part the relatively low level of farm income in the earlier year—whereas the corresponding ratio was two and one-half for persons not living on farms.[9] Despite the fall in farm incomes in the past few years, the ratio of per capita income in 1952 to 1955 to that in 1939 is still substantially higher for farm residents than for nonfarm.

Another recent study that has bearing on the subject under discussion is the analysis of changes since 1929 in income distribution by states that has been made by members of the staff of the Office of Business Economics.[10] As part of this study, per capita incomes in the various states for selected years are expressed as percentages of the national average, and these percentages are compared over time. Two major conclusions emerge.

First, "there has been a significant narrowing over the past quarter of a century in the relative differences in average-income levels among states and regions. . . . As shown by the coefficient of variation, relative dispersion in the state per capita income array was reduced by nearly 40 percent from 1927–1929 to 1953–1955."

Second, the period of greatest narrowing of state per capita incomes was that of the war years, 1942 to 1944. Only a small part of the reduction in dispersion occurred in the prewar period, and "the regional differentials obtaining in 1944 were carried over with only moderate alteration into the postwar period and since then have tended to remain relatively stable in most regions."

---

8. Herman P. Miller, *Income of the American People* (New York, 1955), and "Changes in the Industrial Distribution of Wages in the United States: 1939–49," to be published in vol. 23 of *Studies in Income and Wealth* (National Bureau of Economic Research).

9. *Farm Income Situation* (No. 159, Agricultural Marketing Service, U.S. Department of Agriculture), July 17, 1956.

10. *Personal Income by States Since 1929,* a supplement to the *Survey of Current Business* (1957).

These findings are remarkably consistent with those for the relative distribution of family income by size. As was noted earlier, the period of greatest gain in relative income share for the two lowest quintiles in the family income size distributions was between 1941 and 1944, and after 1944 the available data show little change in the relative distribution of family personal income by size. Of course, the narrowing of state differentials in average income does not of itself prove that there was a reduction in the relative dispersion of income by size, but it does lend credence to the finding that such a reduction took place.

We turn now to certain limitations in the income statistics. To save time I shall simply list four of the general ones: *(a)* Income for a single year is not a satisfactory measure of income inequality. *(b)* We do not have differential cost-of-living indexes appropriate for various income groups; so that we cannot measure with precision changes in the distribution of real income. *(c)* The available statistics on the number and composition of families at the lower end of the income scale are particularly unsatisfactory. *(d)* When we compare income shares of a given quintile or the top 5 percent in two periods, we are not comparing what has happened to an identical group of families, because the families comprising the quintile may be quite different in the two periods. For certain purposes, as, for example, in interpreting the change in the income share of the top quintile or top 5 percent of families over, say, a five- to ten-year time span, it would be extremely helpful to know the extent to which the families comprising the top sector differed in the terminal periods. Unfortunately, such family income data do not exist.

Next are several more specific limitations in the concept or coverage of the income measure that is used in determining relative income shares. Included in what follows are several points raised by George Garvy at the meeting of the American Economics Association three years ago and by Joseph Pechman at the latest Conference on Research in Income and Wealth of the Association.[11]

It is argued, in the first place, that various types of deferred compensation and a sizable amount of income in kind charged to business expense escape measurement in all of the income-size distribution series. Since these types of income presumably have grown in relative as well as absolute importance in the postwar period and since they accrue to a greater extent to upper than to middle or lower income groups, their

11. George Garvy, "Functional and Size Distributions of Income and Their Meaning," AEA *Papers and Proceedings* (May, 1954), and Joseph A. Pechman, "Comments on Mrs. Goldsmith's Paper," to be published in vol. 23 of *Studies in Income and Wealth.* Also see, J. Keith Butters, Lawrence Thompson, and Lynn Bollinger, *Effects of Taxation: Investments by Individuals* (1953), pp. 104–9; reviews of Kuznets's *Shares* etc., by Dudley Seers, *Economic Journal* (June, 1955), and Victor Perlo, *Science and Society* (Spring, 1954); Robert J. Lampman, "Recent Changes in Income Inequality Reconsidered," *American Economic Review* (June, 1954); and George Garvy, "A Report on Research on Income Size Distribution in the United States" (National Bureau of Economic Research, 1955, mimeographed).

exclusion from the basic statistics has the effect of exaggerating the decline in the relative share of total income received by the top income sector. Liberal expense accounts, free vacations, deferred compensation contracts, stock options given to corporate executives, and employer contributions to private pension, health, and welfare funds (these contributions are excluded from the family income-size distribution statistics though not from the monthly and annual personal income series) are the main items that have been listed.

Second, special tax allowances introduced in recent years, such as liberalized depreciation and depletion allowances, operate in the direction of understating the real income shares of top income groups in the postwar period. The splitting of dividend income among the children in the family for the purpose of reducing income tax liabilities would work in the same direction to the extent that the practice has grown in recent years, and full allowance for this factor cannot be made on the basis of the available statistics.

Aside from their effect on upper income shares, the items listed thus far, with one exception, have an important element in common: in the present state of our knowledge, reliable statistical magnitudes cannot be assigned to them. The exception relates to employer contributions to private pension funds for which reasonably good annual totals can be derived. However, this item is probably much more widely distributed than the others on the list and its inclusion would presumably have only a minor effect on the relative income share of the top 5 percent. (It may be noted that contributions to private pension funds are excluded from the family income measure in order to treat these funds in the same manner as public funds; i.e., benefits from them rather than contributions to them are included in family income.)

Third, another limitation of the statistics which, in this case, has been addressed only to the Kuznets series relates to understatement of reportable amounts of income by top-sector taxpayers. Kuznets measured top-sector incomes as the amounts reported by taxpayers on unaudited income tax returns (except for adjustments to add tax-exempt interest and imputed rent). It is argued that the percentage of understatement in reportable amounts of income for upper bracket taxpayers may be larger in recent than in prewar years and that the introduction of an allowance for this factor into the Kuznets series would dampen the post-1929 or post-1939 decline in the relative income share of the top percentiles of the population.

Unlike Kuznets's series, the family income distributions have been adjusted to allow for income understatement on tax returns in all years and, with the possible exception of 1929, this adjustment included at least some of the income brackets in which the top 5 percent of consumer units resided. However, mainly because a sufficiently detailed description of methodology is not available in the case of the family distribution for 1929, it is not possible to determine the magnitude of the adjustment for understatement of income that was applied in the top sector of tax returns in that year and compare it with the corresponding adjustment for the postwar period. As was noted earlier, the post-1929 decline in the relative income share of the top 5 percent is smaller in the family distributions than in the Kuznets series where no adjustment for this factor is made. This suggests that the statistical adjustment for income understatement in the family distributions has been relatively larger in postwar years than in 1929, but until a complete reworking of the 1929 distribution is attempted this cannot be definitely asserted. (It may be noted that the 1929 distribution included in the family income series represents the Brookings Institution's set of estimates for that year [*America's Capacity to Consume* (1934)] adjusted to remove capital gains and losses, which are excluded from the income definition used in family distributions for later years, and to reduce the Brookings' allowance for understatement of business income on tax returns for closer comparability with the figures for later years. Thus the resulting 1929 distribution incorporates a smaller allowance for income understatement in the upper income sector than the original Brookings Institution estimates, but the magnitude of the allowance that remains could not be determined.)

Fourth, an important point that has been raised frequently by all of those concerned with the statistics on relative income distribution is the effect of the exclusion of capital gains from the income measure. The tax incentive to convert property and even other types of income into capital gains is of course well known, and it is argued that the practice has become increasingly widespread in recent years, particularly within the upper income sector.

By limiting capital gains and losses to the realized amounts reported on individual income tax returns (i.e., before statutory percentage reductions and limitations on losses) and by attributing these amounts to the year in which they were realized—both of these are, of course, debatable procedures—Kuznets measured the effect on upper income shares of adding net capital gains to ordinary income. On the basis of his figures, the percentage decline in the relative before-tax income share of the top 5 percent is the same for the period 1929 to 1946 whether or not capital gains are included (38 percent; see Table 7–1). For 1939 to 1946, the percentage decline is reduced by the inclusion of realized capital gains by about one-sixth (from 28 to 23 percent), and it appears likely that the reduction for the post-1939 period would be more significant if the series were brought up through 1955.

We cannot assign reliable measures to the other factors that have been listed but there is little doubt that taken together they would serve to reduce the post-1929 decline in upper income shares. How large must they be if they were to eliminate the decline entirely? Using Kuznets's series, rough estimates of these amounts can be derived.

In 1946 the aggregate income of the top 5 percent of the population was 35 billion dollars exclusive of capital gains and 39 billion with realized net capital gains included—20.0 and 21.4 percent of the respective income totals for that year (Table 7–1). In order for the relative share of the top 5 percent to have been as large as in 1929—32.2 percent exclusive of capital gains or 34.8 percent with net capital gains included —a minimum of some 30 to 35 billion dollars would have to be added to the 1946 amounts. It is difficult to imagine that the factors listed above can account for magnitudes of anything like this size.

To reach 1939 rather than 1929 levels, the amount which would have to be added to the income of the top 5 percent in 1946 is in the neighborhood of 18 billion dollars if income is measured exclusive of capital gains, or 15 billion if realized capital gains are included. Again, it seems highly unlikely that the adjustments could be this large.

When we consider the postwar period by itself, the relative magnitudes involved are smaller but nevertheless substantial. The personal income flow to families and unattached individuals in 1955 was at an annual rate of somewhat under 300 billion dollars. Thus if the factors listed above accounted for 3 to 4 billion and accrued entirely to the top 5 percent of consumer units, the relative income share of this top group would be increased by 1 percentage point; i.e., from the presently estimated 21 percent to 22 percent; if they totaled 6 to 8 billion, the increase would be 2 percentage points, etc. In the present state of our statistical knowledge we cannot say which figure would be closest to the actual situation.

Intriguing in this connection is the decrease that has taken place between 1950 and 1953 in the number of federal individual income tax returns reporting high incomes. The number of tax returns decreased in practically all income brackets (before income taxes) above $200,000 between 1950 and 1951, in all brackets above $50,000 between 1951 and 1952, and in all brackets above $30,000 between 1952 and 1953, the last year for which these statistics are available.[12] These decreases are in marked contrast to the general upward shift that took place lower on the income scale. For example, the number of returns reporting incomes between $10,000 and $30,000 was 50 percent larger in 1953 than in 1950, whereas the number above $200,000 was one-third smaller.

The decreases may well be connected with the stability in dividend payments to individuals in the years 1950 to 1953 and the decline in statutory amounts of net capital gains reported on tax returns in 1952 and 1953. Both of these represent important components of total income

---

12. *Statistics of Income, Part 1, 1950, 1951* and *1952,* and *Preliminary Report for 1953* (Internal Revenue Service, U.S. Treasury Department).

for top income tax returns. Total dividends to persons remained close to nine billion dollars in each of these years and the excess of statutory capital gains over losses reported on individual income tax returns declined from about three billion in 1950 to 1951 to two and one-half billion in 1952 and to slightly over two billion in 1953.

Nevertheless, in view of the general increase in incomes and in particular the almost certain increase in upper bracket salaries in this period, the decrease is puzzling and merits close investigation, particularly if it should not be reversed in 1954 and 1955—years in which dividends increased sharply and realized capital gains almost certainly did. Such an investigation would require a more detailed tabulation of high-income returns than has been customary—in particular an exhaustive tabulation of all deductions and of all items relevant to the tax shelters that have been noted.

Fifth, the points noted thus far lie within the framework of personal income as the basic measure of the income flow to consumers. Of concern to many of us has been the fact that the relative distribution of income as it emerged from production may have changed over time in a different way from the distribution of personal income.[13]

The major differences between the production measure of the income flow—national income—and the personal income measure are that national income includes and personal income excludes elements of production not paid out to persons—undistributed corporate profits, the corporate inventory valuation adjustment, taxes on corporate profits, and contributions for social insurance—whereas the reverse is the case for elements of income received by persons but not accruing in production—transfer payments and government interest.

In particular, the fact that the undistributed earnings of corporations have accounted for a larger relative share of national income in the postwar period than before the war, coupled with the fact that they accrue to a relatively large extent to top-income groups, suggests that the post-1929 or post-1939 decline in the income share of the top sector would be smaller when such earnings are taken into account than when they are excluded from the income base.

Using Kuznets's data, Allan Cartter recently demonstrated that by including undistributed corporate profits and corporate income taxes in the income measure—allocating them between the top 5 percent and all other income groups combined on the basis of Kuznets's distribution of dividends—the decline in the relative income share of the top 5 percent of the population from 1937 to 1948 was reduced from the one-fourth shown by Kuznets to only 5 percent (if corporate income taxes are not

---

13. The effects on relative income distribution of other modifications in income definition such as adding to family personal income the value of free government services and subtracting excise, sales, property, and other taxes in addition to individual income taxes cannot be covered within the confines of this paper.

shifted; to 13 percent if part of these taxes are assumed to be shifted).[14] This appears at first glance to be in striking contrast to Kuznets's own calculations which showed that for the period 1939 to 1946 the inclusion of undistributed corporate profits had only a moderate effect on the decline in the relative income share of the top 5 percent. (The decline shown by Kuznets was 34 percent for disposable income and 27 percent for disposable income plus these profits. Kuznets assumed no shifting.)

The difference in these results reflects in part differences in the time period studied. Cartter's takeoff point, 1937, was a year with very much smaller undistributed corporate profits than 1939; and in 1948 these retained earnings represented a larger share of the national income total than in 1946. Thus Cartter's choice of the time period 1937 to 1948 would be expected to produce more striking results than 1939 to 1946.

But the main difference is due to the definition of undistributed corporate profits. Kuznets included only undistributed profits per se, whereas Cartter distributed corporate income taxes as well. Since factor incomes measured before rather than after income taxes are more useful for many types of economic analysis, it is preferable to impute these taxes along with undistributed profits to obtain a measure of the share of the upper income group in total national product measured at factor costs.

On the basis of rough allocations between the top 5 percent and the other 95 percent of consumer units of undistributed corporate profits, the corporate inventory valuation adjustment, corporate income taxes, and the other items of definitional difference between personal and national income, the following conclusions are reached: From 1929 to the average of 1950 to 1955, converting from a personal income to a national income basis reduces the percentage decline in the relative income share of the top 5 percent of the population by about one-third (i.e., the decline is reduced from about 30 to about 20 percent). The exclusion of transfer payments accounts for only a small part of the reduction; the major part is due to adding corporate income taxes along with retained corporate earnings (Table 7–4).

From 1939 to 1950–1955 the corresponding reduction is about three-fourths. In place of a 20 percent decline in the relative share of the top 5 percent in personal income, there is a decline of only about 5 percent on a national income basis (i.e., the relative share of the top 5 percent in national income is estimated at about 27 percent in 1939 and about 26 percent in 1950 to 1955). Again, the major reason for the dampening of the decline is the inclusion of retained corporate earnings and particularly corporate income taxes. The 5 percent decline is too small to be regarded as statistically significant, and in fact may be due entirely to

---

14. Allan M. Cartter, "Income Shares of Upper Income Groups in Great Britain and the United States," *American Economic Review* (December, 1954).

Table 7–4. Percentage Shares of Top 5 Percent of Consumer Units in Family Personal Income and Rough Estimates of Corresponding Shares Using Various Other Definitions of Income, Selected Years

	1929	1939	1950–55 average	Percent decrease[a] 1929 to 1950–55	1939 to 1950–55
1. Family personal income (before income taxes)	30.0	25.8	20.7	31	20
2. Family personal income after federal individual income tax liability	29.5	24.8	18.5	37	25
Family personal income plus:					
3. Undistributed corporate profits	31	27	22	29	16
4. Undistributed corporate profits and corporate income taxes	32	28	26	20	7
5. Undistributed corporate profits, corporate income taxes, and inventory valuation adjustment	33	27	25	22	6
6. Family personal income minus transfer payments	31	27	22	28	19
7. National income (= line 5 minus transfer payments and government interest, plus contributions for social insurance)	33	27	26	21	5
8. National income minus corporate and individual income taxes	31	25	20	36	20

Sources: Lines 1 and 2 from sources cited in Table 7-1, columns 4 and 5. Lines 3-5 estimated by distributing each of the 3 corporate profits items [*Survey of Current Business* (July, 1956), Table 1] between the top 5 and the other 95 percent of consumer units in proportion to Kuznets's estimates of the distribution of dividend receipts (*Shares*, p. 649). For lines 6 and 7, rough estimates of the corresponding distribution of the other income items listed were derived as explained in *Review of Economics and Statistics* (February, 1954), page 20. Line 8 obtained by subtracting corporate income taxes (see line 4) and federal individual income tax liabilities (see line 2) from amounts underlying line 7.
[a]Based on unrounded figures.

limitations of the statistics such as those listed under the first three points above. In other words, if income is measured in terms of the value of national production at factor costs rather than in terms of personal income flows, there appears to have been no reduction in the relative share of the top 5 percent of consumer units for the period 1939 to 1950–1955. On the other hand, if income is measured after income taxes, the decline since 1939 is sizable (Table 7–4) but as is true also for the post-1929 period as a whole, the reduction is overstated to an unknown extent by limitations in our income-share measures.

A Review of "Shares of Upper Income Groups in Income and Savings"

8

Victor Perlo

Dr. Simon Kuznets [in his book, *Shares of Upper Income Groups in Income and Savings*] concludes that the shares of the upper income groups in total income have declined sharply since 1929, and especially since 1939. The share of the top 1 percent of the population in his "basic variant" of income falls from 14.65 percent in 1929 to 8.38 percent in 1948. The share of the top 5 percent falls from 26.36 percent to 17.63 percent over the same period. After-tax income shares drop still more rapidly.

These conclusions have received an unusual amount of publicity, probably more than any other piece of economic research in the United States in a long time. They have become part of official folklore, with references in government publications and presidential speeches. Arthur F. Burns, chief economic adviser to the President, speaks of a "social revolution" involved in Kuznets's results, and newspaper commentators have shown still less restraint in their panegyrics.

Most of the publicity preceded publication of the volume. It was based on a preliminary pamphlet which gave the main results, but only a sketch of the methods used, and on newspaper interviews and speeches. Since the appearance of the lengthy volume itself in the spring of 1953, there has not been serious discussion or criticism in formal economic circles. However, scattered comment has criticized particular aspects of the work.

The Kuznets work reflects years of painstaking labor by a skilled staff. Different statistical series were reconciled with care and accuracy. Technical pitfalls were avoided, in such matters as the handling of tax-exempt interest and fiduciary income. To an extent unusual for a work of this type, the raw material is given which enables the student

Reprinted from *Science and Society* 18:2 (Spring, 1954): 168–73 by permission of the publisher. The selection originally appeared as a book review.

to retrace the steps taken. Many of the tables can prove invaluable to research workers.

But technical virtuosity is not the main requirement. Most vital are the assumptions and definitions which underlie the calculations. Here Kuznets adopts a series of major premises which are wholly invalid. Even more fundamentally, he concentrates attention on a secondary problem. The main question in the field is the distribution of income among different classes in society, rather than among individuals. Commerce Department figures show that between 1929 and 1948 corporate profits increased 244 percent, farm income 212 percent, income of unincorporated nonfarm enterprises 177 percent, and private wages and salaries 156 percent (all before taxes). Thus trends in the distribution of income from production have been the opposite of Kuznets's conclusions, with the share of the most powerful economic group, the large corporate interests, increasing the most.

In terms of social policy, it makes little difference—within certain limits—how many capitalists share in the distribution of corporate profits. Suppose, for example, the Rockefeller and du Pont fortunes are divided among an increasing number of family members, so that the shares of the leading Rockefeller and du Pont are less than formerly; while the total Rockefeller and du Pont incomes are rising relative to the national income. Then, according to Kuznets's approach, there is less concentration of income. But in reality, in terms of class groupings, there is more concentration. It is difficult to believe that a sufficient broadening of the top capitalist groups occurred to result in markedly different trends as between the class distribution of income and the distribution of individual incomes. Therefore, the undeniable trend towards greater class concentration of private income provides a test and a check which should be applied to evaluate any study of the shares of top-bracket individuals.

It is within this narrower framework that Kuznets adopts biased premises. He assumes—except for minor technical adjustments—that wealthy individuals report on income tax returns all of their incomes, not only as required by law, but as required to show their true income status. He assumes that wealthy stockholders have no stake in undistributed corporate profits. He assumes that wealthy people make no efforts to pad their numbers of dependents or split incomes for tax purposes. These assumptions are stated in Kuznets's text only in qualified form. But his calculations are premised on their absolute validity.

1. TAX-RETURN INCOME VERSUS ACTUAL INCOME

Kuznets measures upper-bracket incomes as equal to those reported on tax returns, save for technical adjustments. Upper-income individuals have a powerful incentive to report as little net taxable income as possible, either by plain hiding of income, or by "interpretations" which reduce income and increase deductions. It is common knowledge that the "art" of keeping income low for tax purposes has become a big business today. It has become the main occupation of accountants, and is a service widely advertised by business advisory concerns.

The general amount and character of income unreported for tax purposes has been studied. Selma F. Goldsmith, also of the National Bureau of Economic Research, estimated that in the period 1944 to 1946, 14 percent of all personal income was not reported. While only 5 percent of wages and salaries were unreported, 29 percent of entrepreneurial income, 24 percent of dividends, 63 percent of interest, and 55 percent of rent income went unreported. In short, nonreporting reaches huge dimensions exactly in the types of property income characteristic of the higher income groups. The wage earners, whose main earnings are taxed at the source, have little or no opportunity to get out of their tax payments.

However, even if the poor could and did evade taxes as much as the rich, this would not be reflected in Kuznets's method. He uses tax returns only for the top income groups. He does not use the tax returns of the poor. He uses the Commerce Department estimates of total income receipts. These are compiled mainly from reports of outpayments by government and business. There is generally no motive for biased reporting, and reasonable accuracy in the total results. Kuznets's estimates of lower-bracket incomes are the residuals obtained by subtracting the income-tax returns of the wealthy from the Commerce Department totals. Thus the incomes of the poor are exaggerated by the same amount that those of the wealthy are underreported.

This shows that Kuznets attributes too low a share in total income to the top brackets. It doesn't yet touch the declining trend in that share. Here, the answer is equally simple. It is common knowledge, as explained by the New Deal tax expert Randolph Paul in his *Taxation for Prosperity,* that systematic tax evasion and avoidance began during the 1930s, and were raised to the level of a big business during World War II. This business has been continually "perfected" since.

Thus the bias in Dr. Kuznets's figures is least in 1929, greater by 1939, and really huge in post-World War II years. The "declining shares" of the upper income groups are largely statistical measures of the declining extent to which they report their income for tax purposes.

One would think that Kuznets would give serious consideration to nonreporting of income. Indeed, a chapter is devoted largely to the reliability of tax return data. It includes impressive facts, such as a summary of the Internal Revenue Bureau audits of 1948 upper-income tax returns. Two-thirds of the audited returns had errors, and 88 percent of the main errors consisted of underreporting of income. The Bureau assessed net additional taxes of 7.2 percent on all audited returns, and over 10 percent on those with errors. Such audits are necessarily superficial. Legal loopholes take care of much unreported income. Tax agents are concerned only with the residual, and on this, the normal practice is for tax agents and tax accountants to "compromise."

In a series of tables, Kuznets shows the reduction *ad absurdum* of his own method. For recent years, when most people filed income tax returns, he shows the incomes of the lowest 20 percent of the population as a residual, by subtracting tax-return income from total income. For 1948 the per capita income of this lowest 20 percent comes out to 108 percent of the average for all people; their dividend and interest receipts to 128 percent of the average, and their rent receipts to 270 percent of the average. This lowest group is shown as receiving more property income, of all kinds, per capita, than the group comprising the second layer from the top in income (the 6 to 10 percent bracket).

How does Kuznets get around such impressive pieces of evidence? He claims they provide ground for "assuming" that underreporting is largely in the lower income brackets, and for the "inference" that in the upper income brackets underreporting is trivial. At the crucial point, really by ignoring his own evidence and a mountain of additional evidence not considered, Kuznets saves his calculations by assumption and inference. Here is the "scientific" method of apologetics—129 long tables of statistics, checked well for precision and internal consistency, combined with refusal to apply data, and substitution of absurb general assumptions when faced with the vital question—are the correct figures put into the calculating machines?

2. UNDISTRIBUTED CORPORATE PROFITS

Kuznets omits undistributed corporate profits from his estimate of upper-bracket income (and total income as well). Incomes derived from corporate enterprise are the main forms of income of the highest brackets. Traditionally, and in 1929, most corporate profits were paid out in dividends. The wealthy individual spent part on consumption, reinvested the remainder to increase his profit base and power position. Today, in large part because of higher tax rates, most corporate profits are not paid out in dividends, but reinvested directly. To the wealthy individual, it doesn't make too much difference, except for the tax saving. Lawrence Seltzer, in his *The Nature and Tax Treatment of Capital Gains and Losses*, another recent National Bureau publication, shows that, by and large, the reinvested profits are reflected in the market prices of the stocks. The individual investor can take out his profit, if he wishes, by selling part of his stock, and paying the lower rate of tax on capital gains. Securities companies stress the value of so-called "growth stocks" to investors for this reason (e.g. the *United Investment Report* of the United Business Service, January 11, 1954).

Undistributed corporate profits (also incompletely reported) jumped from $2.5 billion in 1929 to $13.5 billion in 1948, and four-fifths of this amount accrued to the credit of the top 5 percent of income receivers. By omitting undistributed profits, Kuznets converts a formal shift in the method of recording profits, a shift to the advantage of the wealthy, into a purely fictitious reduction in their income shares.

3. INCOME SPLITTING AND DEPENDENTS

A third source of error is in Kuznets's identification of the top 1 percent and 5 percent of income receivers. He makes no adjustments for the tendency of wealthy persons to split incomes, to increase their exemption claims as tax rates rise, and in particular, no adjustments for changes in the law in 1944 and 1948, which permitted additional exemptions. The effects of these law changes are identifiable and roughly measurable from income tax statistics. Thus, Kuznets's top 1 percent in 1948 represents a smaller proportion of the population than his top 1 percent in 1929. To a certain extent, therefore, the "decline" shown in the share of the upper income groups simply reflects a narrowing of Kuznets's count of these groups.

The above discussion points out three errors in Kuznets's premises, all working in the same direction. Each time, the assumption is biased to show a declining trend in top-bracket shares.

Do these errors account for all or only part of the decline in the share of the upper income groups shown by Kuznets? Butters, Thompson, and Bollinger, in their excellent book *Effects of Taxation, Investment by Individuals* (Cambridge, Mass., 1953), note that Kuznets overstates the decline in upper income shares by failing to take account of unreported income. They consider it unlikely that this factor is sufficient to account of all of the decline shown. Geoffrey H. Moore, of the National Bureau of Economic Research, made alternative calculations including the allocation of a prorata share of undistributed corporate profits to wealthy individuals. This substantially reduced, but did not eliminate, the downward trend in the share of the top brackets.

It is true that no one bias, by itself, accounts for all of Kuznets's results. The present writer, in conjunction with the Labor Research Association, has assayed corrections for all three of the main errors in Kuznets's work. In our opinion, these are minimal corrections. But in their combined effect, they wholly eliminate the downtrend. These calculations, roughly, show the upper 5 percent with one-third of the national income in both 1929 and 1948, and the upper 1 percent with about one-sixth of the national income in each of these years.

The Kuznets work, regardless of intentions, provides valuable propaganda backing for current attempts to reduce taxes on the wealthy, and to increase them on the poor as well as for reactionary steps in other economic fields. Refutation of Dr. Kuznets's conclusions is important for those who consider that economic concessions to ordinary people, and not to wealthy, are needed to help people cope with the difficult times ahead.

Public Budgets and the U.S. Distribution of Income: 1950, 1961, and 1970

9

Morgan Reynolds and Eugene Smolensky

This paper compares size distributions of income in 1950, 1961, and 1970 after allocating all government taxes and expenditures to households (final income). The motive, of course, is to detect changes in final income distributions over two decades. This study contributes to revived interest in distributional matters by exploring the response of measured income dispersion to a more comprehensive definition of household income, one that includes the benefits and burdens of government at all levels in one country over a considerable time interval. There have been many forerunners in this kind of enterprise, and there are several contemporary studies, but they have not been directed toward producing a systematic, intertemporal comparison of final income distributions for the United States.[1] In this study, data bases constructed

This article by Reynolds and Smolensky was written especially for this edition of *American Society, Inc.*

Morgan Reynolds and Eugene Smolensky are Assistant Professor, Texas A & M University and Professor, University of Wisconsin—Madison, respectively.

We wish to thank the Ford Foundation and the RANN division of the National Science Foundation for financing this research. The research reported here was supported in part by funds granted to the Institute for Research on Poverty at the University of Wisconsin by the Office of Economic Opportunity pursuant to the provisions of the Economic Opportunity Act of 1964. The conclusions are the sole responsibility of the authors.

Earlier drafts of this paper were presented at the meetings of the Public Choice Society, April 1975, Chicago, and at meetings of the Western Economic Association, June 1975, in San Diego. A version with a complete description of data and sources is available from the authors.

1. For some prominent examples, see Alfred H. Conrad, "Redistribution through Government Budgets in the United States, 1950," in *Income Redistribution and Social Policy*, ed. A. T. Peacock (London: Jonathan Cape, 1954); W. Irwin Gillespie, "Effects of Public Expenditures on the Distribution of Income," in *Essays in Fiscal Federalism*, ed. R. A. Musgrave (Washington, D.C.: Brookings Institution, 1965); G. A. Bishop, *Tax Burdens and Benefits of Government Expenditures by Income Class, 1961 and 1965* (New York: Tax Foundation, Inc., 1967); M. Reynolds and E. Smolensky, "The Post-Fisc Distribution; 1961 and 1970 Compared," *National Tax Journal* 27 (December, 1974):515–30; J. Pechman and R. Okner, "Who Bears the Tax Burden?" (Washington, D.C.: Brookings Institution, 1974); R. Musgrave, K. Case, and H. Leonard, "The Distribution of Fiscal Burdens and Benefits," *Public Finance Quarterly* 2 (July, 1974): 259–300.

for three earlier studies are combined with equivalent incidence assumptions to produce comparable measures of dispersion in final incomes for 1950, 1961, and 1970.[2]

ESTABLISHING A SET OF EXPECTATIONS

The National Income Accounts reveal some relevant trends for 1950 to 1970. Net National Product (NNP) in current dollars has grown from $265 billion in 1950 to $886 billion in 1970, the increase in each decade being about 80 percent. During these years government has grown much faster, raising the ratio of government expenditures at all levels from 20 percent of NNP in 1950 to 31 percent in 1961 to more than 35 percent in 1970. From a purely accounting point of view, the relative growth of the government is a factor that reduces inequality in the after-tax, after-expenditure pattern of distribution because public output is more equally distributed than private output.[3]

Post-fisc distributions are affected not only by the relative size of government but also by the composition of receipts and expenditures. First, consider the composition of taxes. Total state and local taxes have risen from 42 percent of total federal taxes in 1950 to 51 percent in 1961 and to 58 percent in 1970. This implies a gradual decline in the degree of progressivity of the overall tax structure, since state and local tax structures are generally believed to be less progressive than the federal tax structure.[4] Among state and local taxes, two groups of taxes have grown most rapidly—the personal income tax, and sales taxes, excises, and fees—with each type of tax raising its relative share in tax receipts by five percentage points. Property taxes fell from 43 percent of all state and local receipts in 1950 to 33 percent in 1970. This would commonly be interpreted as indicating a decline in the degree of regressivity in the average state-local tax structure because property taxes are often viewed as the most regressive tax with respect to current income. Obviously, however, this interpretation is sensitive to assumptions concerning who ultimately bears the burden of the tax (i.e., the "incidence" of the tax).

The structure of federal taxes has changed more dramatically than have the tax totals for all state and local governments combined. The corporate income tax declined from 27 percent of federal tax receipts in 1950 to 16 percent in 1970, while excise and customs taxes have declined

---

2. Data is drawn from Conrad, "Redistribution through Government Budgets," in Tax Foundation, *Tax Burdens and Benefits;* and Reynolds-Smolensky, "Post-Fisc Distribution."

3. If income originating in the government sector also were more equally distributed than income originating in the private sector, even greater equality in the pretax, pretransfer distributions would result.

4. For present purposes, progressivity is defined with respect to current money income rather than alternatives like permanent income, or proxy measures for it like house values or consumption expenditures.

from 20 percent in 1950 to 10 percent in 1970. Social Security payroll taxes have grown much more rapidly than all federal taxes, increasing their share from less than 9 percent to 26 percent. Receipts from the personal income tax have grown slightly faster than all federal taxes, increasing their share by four percentage points to 46 percent. Although a judgment about the net change in the degree of progressivity in the federal tax structure depends upon incidence assumptions, these changes appear to decrease progressivity. The large changes are declining corporate income taxes but growing payroll taxes, which is generally regarded as a regressive change except by those who believe that the corporate tax is borne in the end almost exclusively by consumers. The relative decline of federal excise receipts and the relative increase in personal income taxes can be viewed as largely offsetting each other. Accordingly, it appears that the federal tax structure has become less progressive while state and local government receipts, on average, have become less regressive.

It is somewhat more difficult to generate expectations about the distributive effects of expenditures because of the relatively recent development of relevant incidence assumptions. First, consider the relative size of state-local expenditures compared to federal expenditures. State-local expenditures have increased much more rapidly than have federal expenditures, rising from 38 percent of federal expenditures in 1950 to 56 percent in 1961 to 74 percent in 1970.[5] This change cannot be evaluated a priori because there is no consensus about whether the benefits of federal expenditures are more or less progressive than state and local expenditures.[6]

Among federal expenditures, there have been sizable declines between 1950 and 1970 in the share spent for veterans' benefits, interest, and agriculture. Budget shares increased in three primary areas: national defense, other "indivisible" government expenditures, and, most dramatically, Social Security payments—the last grew from less than 6 percent of the federal budget in 1950 to 23 percent in 1970. If allocated across income classes in a conventional manner, these shifts in the structure of federal outlays are increasingly pro-poor. The only major budget changes in aggregate state and local outlays are a sharp growth

5. Put in different terms, the ratios of state-local expenditures to NNP have risen from 5.6 in 1950 to 15.0 percent in 1970 while federal expenditures have risen more slowly from 14.6 percent in 1950 to 20.4 percent in 1970. Note that $24 billion of state-local expenditures financed by federal grants-in-aid for 1970 appear in state and local expenditures, not in federal expenditures.

6. Gillespie finds state-local government more pro-poor in expenditure incidence than the federal government "Effects of Public Expenditures," pp. 164–65, and the Tax Foundation does not explicitly make an expenditure comparison between levels of government, although taxes are compared. Since grants-in-aid and many other factors undoubtedly alter state expenditure and tax schedules, it may not be meaningful to arithmetically separate the effects of levels of government.

in the share of educational expenditures, from 24 to 41 percent, and a reduction in the share for streets and highways from more than 21 percent in 1950 to less than 12 percent in 1970. Public assistance and similar transfer programs are not a higher share of state-local budgets in 1970 than in 1950 and 1961. Other compositional changes at the state and local level are difficult to assess, but it appears likely that expenditure patterns are more pro-poor in later years.

On balance, the combined distributive impact of all levels of government upon the distribution of final income cannot be confidently predicted from these factors. Most of the changes in the size and composition of governments, however, appear to be increasingly pro-poor. Only the expansion of state-local governments relative to the federal government and the apparently lower progressivity of the federal tax structure are factors reducing the pro-poor direction of the fisc, at least as they are conventionally evaluated.

Methods for Comparing Post-Fisc Distributions

There is no consensus about *the* best way to describe a size distribution of income, much less about a way to compare size distributions over time.[7] Some methods of measuring dispersion—or inequality—are more popular than others, and we have chosen what seems to be the most popular and hence most familiar index of income inequality—the Gini coefficient or concentration ratio. The Gini coefficient is simply the average income difference between all pairs of households.[8] The Gini coefficient has no simple normative interpretation.[9]

Distributive comparison depends upon consistent data bases. As might be expected, the data are not identical in the previous studies for 1950, 1961, and 1970. However, it proved feasible to transform the published data to equivalent income, budget, and incidence concepts which permit robust inferences about the probable trend of post-fisc

---

7. For informative discussions about measuring dispersion, see Harold Lydall, *The Structure of Earnings* (London, Oxford University Press, 1968), pp. 137–41; Thomas Stark, *The Distribution of Personal Income in the United Kingdom, 1949–1963* (London: Cambridge University Press, 1972), pp. 137–53; D. G. Champernowne, "A Comparison of Measures of Inequality of Income Distribution," *Economic Journal* 84 (December, 1974):787–816; Peter Wiles, *Distribution of Income: East and West* (Amsterdam: North Holland, 1974), pp. ix–xii.

8. For an example, see Reynolds-Smolensky, "The Post-Fisc Distribution," p. 520. If distributions of income vary greatly in their shape, a single intersect of dispersion can be misleading. For example, Lorenz curves can intersect but have identical Gini coefficients. Since this occurs in some comparisons, careful interpretation is warranted, especially when differences between Gini coefficients are small. Comparisons of the relevant Lorenz curves support the assertions that are made subsequently.

9. See A. B. Atkinson, "On the Measurement of Inequality," *Journal of Economic Theory* 2 (September, 1970):244–63; E. Sheshinski, "Relation Between a Social Welfare Function and the Gini Index of Income Inequality," *Journal of Economic Theory* 4 (February, 1972): 98–100; P. Dasgupta, A. Sen, and D. Starret, "Notes on the Measurement of Inequality," *Journal of Economic Theory* 6 (April, 1973):180–87.

inequality over time. We are confident that remaining noncomparabilities and errors are small enough to permit valid inferences when numerical results show large differences among distributions.[10]

One more measurement issue deserves attention before the statistical results are described—the definition of the initial income base. A number of aggregate income bases can and have been used, possibly because each is appropriate for answering a particular question but also because little attention is generally given to this issue. In an intertemporal comparison, uniformity of definition is perhaps more important than finding the most appropriate aggregate income base; nonetheless, an income base must be selected. Our income base adds up to net national product rather than say, personal income. This seems appropriate because ultimately all claims to net output accrue to people; since we are dealing with all government taxes and expenditures, we should compare tax burdens and imputed expenditure gains with total output and hence total income by income group, from which taxes come and expenditures go.[11] Of course, other aggregate income concepts roughly of the same magnitude as NNP would yield similar distributive comparisons.

NNP is initially distributed across income classes by a distribution of factor earnings (factor NNP).[12] The Gini coefficient (x 1000) for factor NNP in 1970 is 446; for money NNP it is 400.

Post-Fisc Distributions

Table 9–1 shows the results of selected measures of initial and final income inequality. Row 1 shows the Gini coefficients for initial factor

---

10. A complete statistical appendix is available upon request from the authors.

11. Bishop has defended the use of net national product as the income base. See G. A. Bishop, "Income Redistribution in the Framework of the National Income Accounts," *National Tax Journal* 19 (December, 1966):378–90. Also see Jacob P. Meerman, "The Definition of Income in Studies of Budget Incidence and Income Distribution," *The Review of Income and Wealth* 20 (December, 1974):515–22. For a contrary view see Charles E. McLure, Jr., "On the Theory and Methodology of Estimating Benefit and Expenditure Incidence" Mimeographed manuscript (Houston: Rice University, 1974).

12. In our previous article, money income rather than factor income was the base. Money income includes cash transfers. Another major change from our previous article is to substitute the *Michigan Survey of Consumer Finances* (1962) for the Bureau of Labor Statistics *Consumer Expenditures and Income: Survey Guidelines,* Bulletin 1684, 1971, distribution of households and income for 1961. The BLS distribution was more compact than other reported distributions of household income in 1961 for two reasons: the BLS survey has more detailed questions about income sources, which raises income generally, and more importantly, the deduction of personal taxes reduces high incomes disproportionately. To make pre- and post-fisc distributions comparable over time, the Michigan SCF initial distribution was used because it was the basis for the 1950 study and the Michigan data was a representative pretax distribution compared to others for 1961. All BLS distributors for taxes and expenditures were also rescaled upward to conform to the Michigan SCF distribution of initial income. The basic assumption in the adjustment procedure is that only the households near the brackets are affected by the shift from post-to pretax income intervals.

Table 9-1.   Gini Coefficients for Selected Experiments, 1950, 1961, 1970 Factor NNP

Distributive Experiment	(Gini X 1,000)		
	1950	1961	1970
1. Initial Factor NNP	436	436	446
2. Normal	363	342	339
3. Normal Except General Expenditures by Income	384	378	375
4. Regressive	394	388	384
5. Progressive	328	289	284
Column Mean	381	367	366

NNP, or the pretax and preexpenditure distribution. By the Gini index, dispersion is slightly higher in 1970 (446) than in 1950 and 1961 (436).

Row 2 shows the first measure of post-fisc inequality of income. We have labeled it "normal" because it depends upon incidence assumptions for taxes and expenditures that can be termed the conventional, intermediate assumption of previous studies, especially those for 1961 and 1970.[13] Incidence is intermediate in the sense that more regressive or progressive assumptions are plausible. Key assumptions are that personal income taxes are borne by the income earners, estate and gift taxes are paid by the highest income class, the corporate income tax is borne equally by dividend recipients and consumers, excise and sales taxes are ultimately paid entirely by consumers. Social Security payroll taxes are borne entirely by employees, and the property tax is paid by consumers of housing in the residential sector and consumers of general output for commercial property taxes. The incidence of expenditures is assumed to fall entirely on recipients rather directly identified as beneficiaries—for example, automobile owners for highway expenditures or children under 18 for elementary and secondary expenditures. The general expenditures of government for which direct beneficiaries cannot be readily identified are arbitrarily distributed half by the distribution of households and half by share of initial income. The rationale is that households benefit on some egalitarian basis as well as in proportion to income. These expenditures are about one-half of federal and one-third of state and local outlays.

The Gini coefficients produced by this normal post-fisc experiment are much smaller in each year than are the initial coefficients factor income. By this measure there were sizable redistributions of net output toward the lower end of the income distribution due to government activity. Post-fisc dispersion is smallest for 1970 (339), followed by 1961

---

13. For a detailed description of these incidence assumptions, see Tax Foundation, *Tax Burdens and Benefits,* pp. 7–12; and Reynolds-Smolensky, "The Post-Fisc Distribution," pp. 522–24.

(342) and 1950 (363). Note, however, that the post-fisc Gini for 1950 is only 7 percent larger than the Gini ratio for 1970.

Now consider some alterations to the post-fisc distribution. Row 3 results when all normal incidence assumptions are preserved except that the general expenditures of government are distributed according to factor income alone. This allocation reflects the view that the indivisible expenditures of government are neutral with respect to the distribution of income rather than favoring lower income households. The difference in post-fisc concentration ratios between 1950 and 1961 is substantially reduced and the trivial difference between the post-fisc Gini ratios of 1961 and 1970 is unchanged. In other words, the relatively high Gini coefficient for 1950 is not preserved once general expenditures are no longer presumed to be redistributive. General expenditures at the federal level increased threefold between 1950 and 1961, and at the state-local level they grew even more rapidly, exceeding a fivefold increase.

In the next experiment taxes and expenditures are distributed more regressively. This variant distributes expenditures in the normal way except that general government expenditures are distributed via factor income. The incidence assumptions for two taxes, however, are changed from the standard—corporate income taxes are entirely shifted forward to consumption expenditures, 60 percent of property taxes are distributed by housing expenditures, and 40 percent of property taxes by consumption expenditures, a slightly more regressive distribution. These more regressive tax assumptions raise Gini coefficients by only ten points in 1950 and 1961 and 9 points in 1970 (row 4), compared to the normal with neutral general expenditures (row 3). These are very small increases in income inequality as measured by Gini coefficients. The equal rise in the Gini in each year leaves the trend in the post-fisc distribution unaffected.

Next, relatively progressive incidence assumptions were adopted. The changes from the normal assumptions are (1) the corporate income tax and sales-excise taxes are distributed one-third by dividends, one-third by wages and salaries, and one-third by consumption expenditures; (2) the Social Security tax is distributed 50 percent by covered payrolls, 25 percent by dividends, and 25 percent by consumption expenditure; and property taxes are distributed 40% by housing expenditures, 30 percent by dividends, and 30 percent by consumption expenditures.[14] All expenditures are distributed normally except for general expenditures, which are assigned according to the distribution of households. These incidence assumptions lower the Gini coefficients by a large amount compared with normal assumptions (row 2 minus row 5): 35 points for 1950, 53 points for 1961, and 55 points in 1970.

---

14. The progressive distribution of property taxes reflects recent arguments that some part of these taxes are borne by all owners of capital in the economy; see H. Aaron, R. A. Musgrave, et al., "The Property Tax: Progressive or Regressive?" *American Economy Association: Papers and Proceedings* 64 (May, 1974):212–35.

Distributing the large increase in general expenditures between 1950 and 1961 according to the distributions of households is the major factor producing this trend.

To summarize these experiments, as well as others not reported here, post-fisc distributions are more equal in all years than are distributions of factor income. They are generally smaller by significant amounts. Post-fisc inequality is lowest in 1970 but the difference between years is trivial in most comparisons, especially when compared to the differences between the pre-and post-fisc distributions in any year.[15] Finally, the variation in Gini coefficients as incidence assumptions are altered is smallest in 1950 and largest in 1970 when government is relatively larger.

Before turning to a statistical analysis of the sources of change in the Gini coefficient, it is interesting to consider what has happened to those at various places in the distribution since 1950. Table 9–2 shows the shares of income at various percentiles in the pre-, the standard post-, and the standard post-, excluding any direct distributional consequences of general expenditures. These results coincide with the rankings discussed earlier. The most striking feature of Table 9–2 is the virtual constancy of post-fisc shares by quintile. The factor income shares reveal modest declines for the lowest quintile as well as the middle 60 percent and a corresponding rise in the top quintile, as well as the top 5 percent. Post-fisc distributions reveal no trend, which is the same result which we have encountered time and time again.

Sources of Declines in Gini Coefficients

If all taxes and expenditures were distributed by the initial distribution of income, Gini coefficients would be identical for the initial and post-fisc distributions. If all taxes and expenditures but one were dis-

Table 9–2. Predicted Share of Income, Quintiles, 1950, 1961, and 1970

	Factor Income			Normal Post-Fisc			Normal Post-Fisc w/o GE		
	1950	1960	1970	1950	1960	1970	1950	1960	1970
				(percentage of income)					
Lowest 20 percent	3.6	3.3	2.9	6.4	6.4	6.7	5.6	5.2	5.4
Middle 60 percent	48.5	47.7	46.5	53.7	53.8	54.2	52.6	31.9	52.2
Highest 20 percent	48.0	49.0	50.6	39.9	39.8	39.1	41.8	42.9	42.4
Highest 5 percent	14.7	15.1	15.8	11.6	11.5	11.2	12.3	12.7	12.5

15. Kakwani and Podder have suggested both a functional form and a procedure for determining when two Gini coefficients are statistically significantly different. Making use of the Kakwani-Podder functional form and the standard Chow test we cannot reject the hypothesis that observed differences in the post-fisc distributions are simply due to chance. On the other hand normal post-fisc coefficients are significantly more equal than those for initial distributions in each year. See: N. C. Kakwani and N. Podder, "On the Estimation of Lorenz Curves From Grouped Observations," *International Economic Review* 14 (June, 1973):278–92, and G. C. Chow, "Tests of Equality Between Sets of Coefficients in Two Linear Regressions," *Econometrica* 28 (July, 1960):591–605; also see J. Johnston, *Econometric Methods* (New York: McGraw-Hill, 1963):136–38.

tributed by the initial distribution of income, any difference between the initial and post-fisc distributions could be attributed to the effects of that single tax or expenditure. Of course, this would be true only in an arithmetic sense, as is true of our other calculations, because the direct and indirect economic effects of the tax or expenditure are not included. Nonetheless, this technique provides a way to disaggregate the sources of lower post-fisc Gini coefficients in an additive manner. The size of any changes in Gini coefficients depends upon the size of the tax or expenditure and the nature of the incidence assumptions.

Table 9-3 shows the results of disaggregating the difference between initial and respective post-fisc coefficients under normal incidence assumptions. Each line was calculated by distributing all taxes and transfers by the initial distribution of factor income except for the item in question. Thus the decline due to Social Security taxes was calculated by distributing "other transfers," "specific federal expenditures," "the personal income tax," and so forth by initial income, but the Social Security tax was distributed by its standard distributor. Some striking features emerge. First, every expenditure category lowers the Gini coefficient, but not all taxes have that effect. For example, the effect of the declining progressivity of the tax structure (normal incidence) is traced out in line 2. By 1970 the tax structure actually increases the Gini ratio. The direction of change was common to each tax (except for the small change in personal state and local income taxes). The federal personal income tax became less progressive while the other taxes became more regressive. One surprise is that the growing regressivity of "other taxes" appears as important as the declining progressivity of the federal personal income tax. The same secular decline in the redistributive impact of the tax structure occurs if alternative but consistent incidence assumptions are used.

The decrease in Gini coefficients due to transfer payments grows dramatically between 1950 and 1970, almost entirely due to the growth in Social Security payments. The decreases in inequality due to other specifically allocable expenditures show only a slight upward trend, with state-local impact growing and the federal effect declining slightly. Finally, there does not seem to be a large trend in the total decrease in concentration ratios due to the fisc if general expenditures are treated as neutral. If general expenditures are believed to be redistributive toward lower incomes, however, there is a trend toward larger differences between initial and post-fisc Gini coefficients.

CONCLUSION

This paper demonstrates that conventional assignments of government expenditures and taxes by income class yield distrutions of final income that are very similar for the years 1950, 1961, and 1970. Some may find these results surprising, or even disappointing. We could find no major changes in final income distributions despite rapid growth of government, sizable changes in the composition of taxes and expenditures, and increasing concern about distributive effects among intellectuals and bureaucrats. Critics might contend that this failure to find a change confirms the hopeless inadequacy of crude research methods. We do not wish to deny deficiencies of this and related studies, but we suspect that the explanation for our results lies elsewhere. As Tullock suggests, numerous variables weaken the relationship between current income and government redistribution.[16] Most government benefits are distributed independently of income and depend upon characteristics like being a farmer or aged or a veteran, or driving an automobile, or going to a public college. Thus, much redistribution is back and forth within the middle-income groups, and only a portion of the large and growing share of income controlled by government is directed toward modifying the size distribution of final income. However, this paper is only an attempt to assess the "facts" about postwar distributions of final income rather than an attempt at causal analysis.[17]

Table 9-3. Sources of Declines in Gini Coefficients Normal Incidence, 1950, 1961, 1970

	Factor NNP		
	Gini X 1,000		
	1950	1961	1970
1. General Government	20	36	36
2. Taxes	10	5	-8[a]
a. Personal Income	15	15	8
1. Federal	15	14	7
2. State-Local	0	1	1
b. Social Security	-4[a]	-2[a]	-6[a]
c. Other	-2[a]	-8[a]	-10[a]
3. Transfer Payments	25	36	53
a. Social Security	8	20	34
b. Other	16	17	20
4. Other Specific Expenditures	16	18	26
a. Federal	13	7	9
b. State-Local	2	10	17
5. Total	73	95	106

[a]Negative sign indicates that the item raises rather than lowers the post-fisc Gini coefficient relative to initial inequality.

16. G. Tullock, "The Charity of the Uncharitable," *Western Economic Journal* 9 (December, 1971):379–92.

17. For an interesting survey of ideas attempting to explain some of the data, see James D. Rodgers, "Explaining Income Redistributions," pp. 165–205 in Harold M. Hochman and George E. Peterson, eds., *Redistribution Through Public Choice* (New York: Columbia University Press, 1974).

Income Inequality: Problems of Measurement and Interpretation

10

Sheldon Danziger and Eugene Smolensky

The recent literature has confused rather than clarified our perception of the behavior of income inequality during the post-World War II period. Several studies have concluded that inequality has been increasing over the long term (Brittain 1972, Gastwirth 1972, Henle 1972, Schultz 1972) while others have indicated that it has not changed (Budd 1970, Reynolds and Smolensky 1975, Thurow 1970). There has also been disagreement as to the course of income inequality during the business cycle. The conventional wisdom, that inequality increases during recessions and declines during revival, has been both confirmed (Metcalf 1972, Mirer 1973b, Schultz 1969, Thurow 1970) and challenged (Mirer 1973a, Tuckman and Brosch 1975). The confusion stems from inconsistencies in data, computational procedures, time period, and conjectural interpretations about the empirical results. We present and analyze the long-term trend in Section I and fluctuations around that trend associated with the general business cycle in Section II.

I. MEASUREMENT PROBLEMS ASSOCIATED WITH LONG-TERM TREND

Measures of inequality are sensitive to the choice of computational procedure, time period, income concept, and recipient unit. These attributes are varied in Table 10-1, which presents four time series on inequality. The Gini coefficient is the summary measure.[1] Columns 1

This article by Danziger and Smolensky was written especially for this edition of *American Society Ink.* This paper was supported by funds granted to the Institute for Research on Poverty at the University of Wisconsin–Madison by the Department of Health, Education, and Welfare pursuant to the Economic Opportunity Act of 1964. The opinions expressed are those of the authors.

1. The Gini coefficient, or concentration ratio, is the average income difference between all pairs of income receiving units. It ranges from total equality, .000, to total inequality, 1.000.

and 2, based on Internal Revenue Service (IRS) data (U.S. Department of the Treasury 1975), measure inequality in "adjusted gross incomes" for all tax returns filed. Columns 3 and 4, based on Current Population Survey (CPS) data (U.S. Bureau of the Census 1975), measure inequality in "Census money income" for families and unrelated individuals. Adjusted gross income excludes nontaxable transfer income, but includes realized capital gains and losses; Census money income includes cash transfers but excludes capital gains.[2] In addition, there is not a one-to-one correspondence between income tax filing units and the Census Bureau's definition of families and unrelated individuals. Finally, because of the manner in which the data are published, IRS Gini coefficients are computed using actual class means for all income intervals while CPS Gini coefficients use class midpoints and an estimate of the mean for the uppermost income class. (See Gastwirth for a complete discussion of the measurement problem posed by this reporting difference.)

Column 1 reproduces the data presented by Gastwirth (1972, p. 312) to support his view that the trend in inequality was increasing. Column 2 uses the same data base for the entire postwar period. These two series are highly correlated for the years in which they overlap (correlation coefficient is .996). Column 3 reproduces the data presented by Budd (1970, p. 255) to support his view that the trend was stationary, while column 4 extends the time period using the same underlying data. For the 21 years where the two CPS series overlap, the simple correlation coefficient is only .797, emphasizing the sensitivity of inequality measures to estimation procedures. Budd did not compute Gini coefficients using the standard procedure and "since they have been computed from smooth curves rather than linear segments, they exceed somewhat values computed by others" (Budd 1970, p. 252).

Table 10–2 displays several simple regressions revealing the conflicting secular trends that can be calculated for the period when different end points or different income concepts are used. Each regression takes the form: $\text{Gini} = \alpha_1 + \alpha_2 \text{Time}$.

Lines 1 and 2 show that for the IRS data in the 1955 to 1969 period, income inequality was increasing year by year, and that this trend is not likely to be due to chance factors. For nearly the same period (1955–1968), the CPS data (Table 10–1, column 3) show that income inequality was declining, but this finding may simply be due to chance. Line 3 shows that the trend for the IRS data for the longer period (Table 10–1, column 2) was toward greater inequality, but the trend is not so pronounced as for the shorter period. However, the trend in the CPS data

---

2. Transfer income does not result from services rendered during the period. Private transfers include receipts from charity; public transfers include social security, welfare, and other payments from government programs. The value of in-kind transfers, such as food stamps, are not included in these data.

Table 10-1. Inequality in the Post-World War II Period

	(1) IRS Gini Coefficient (Gastwirth)	(2) IRS Gini Coefficient	(3) CPS Gini Coefficient (Budd)	(4) CPS Gini Coefficient
1947		.4177	.430	.4150
1948		.4283	.424	.4072
1949		.4260	.428	.4145
1950		.4321	.431	.4145
1951		.4284	.416	.4017
1952		.4261	.416	.4153
1953		.4248	n.a.	.4089
1954		.4309	.429	.4193
1955	.4372	.4335	.420	.4145
1956	.4361	.4325	.415	.4067
1957	.4366	.4327	.418	.4031
1958	.4418	.4383	.416	.4051
1959	.4486	.4457	.422	.4091
1960	.4450	.4416	.423	.4152
1961	.4515	.4462	.432	.4241
1962	.4503	.4469	.421	.4129
1963	.4534	.4496	.418	.4103
1964	.4574	.4530	.419	.4106
1965	.4630	.4583	.417	.4082
1966	.4670	.4626	.413	.4073
1967	.4705	.4652	.416	.4044
1968	.4748	.4733	.406	.3988
1969	.4732	.4669		.4046
1970		.4525		.4094
1971		.4542		.4127
1972				.4173
1973				.4163

Notes: [Figures are derived as follows:]

Columns 1 and 2: Internal Revenue Service Data (IRS).

Adjusted Gross Income (excludes transfers, includes capital gains); all filing tax returns; actual class means for all intervals. Column 1 is data presented by Gastwirth (1972, p. 312). Column 2 is computed by the authors.

Columns 3 and 4: Current Population Survey Data (CPS).

Census Money Income (includes transfers, excludes capital gains); Families and unrelated individuals; class midpoints and a Pareto estimate for the openended interval. Column 3 is data presented by Budd (1970, p. 255). Column 4 is computed by the authors.

(Table 10-1, column 4) for the longer period was stationary. In the CPS data the Gini coefficient reached a maximum in 1961 and a minimum in 1968. Analysis of the 1947 to 1960 or the 1947 to 1973 period (Table 10-1, column 4) reveals no trend, while the 1947 to 1961 period shows an increase and the 1947 to 1968 period shows a decrease in inequality.

The differences in income concept and recipient unit that distinguish the IRS and CPS series suggest several explanatory hypotheses for their opposite trends. It has been suggested, for example, that the distribution of market earnings has shown a trend toward increased inequality because of a younger and increasingly female labor force (Kuznets 1972, 1974; Blinder 1975). Lines 5 and 6 of Table 10-2 show that two of the

Table 10-2. The Trend of Inequality in the Post-World War II Period

Dependent Variable: Gini Coefficient of	Constant	Time Trend (t-statistic)	R^2
1. IRS Data, 1955–1969 (Gastwirth)	.4302	.00294 (18.6)	.964
2. CPS Data, 1955–1968 (Budd)	.4224	–.00055 (1.50)	.158
3. IRS Data, 1947–1971 (Computed by the authors)	.4179	.00191 (11.6)	.853
4. CPS Data, 1947–1973 (Computed by the authors)	.4115	–.00006 (0.44)	.008
5. Male, full-year wage and salary workers, 1958–1969 (Henle)	.2550	.00192 (4.65)	.684
6. Earnings of the Social Security population, 1951–1969 (Brittain)	.4630	.00121 (4.40)	.533

available series on earnings inequality among individuals (Henle, Brittain) do show a trend toward greater inequality. Government transfers however may have run counter to the trend in earnings. The IRS data is a pretax, *pretransfer* distribution, while the CPS is a pretax, *posttransfer* distribution.

The role of transfers, however, may be more complicated, and their impact on inequality as measured less certain since

> The preponderance of federal transfers has gone to retired persons and a small part to women heading families; . . . the recipients, especially old people, are better off, both absolutely and relatively than they used to be; but . . . the equalizing effect of all this on the income distribution is offset by a combination of two other factors. One is early retirement. . . . The other is the increased tendency of adults at all ages to head their own households (Rivlin 1975, p. 5).

Rivlin is suggesting that the direct effect of transfers is to equalize incomes, but the indirect effect is to increase inequality by altering the number and the composition of recipient units. In particular, there will be more units headed by the young, the old, and females. Since these units have lower than average incomes, transfers indirectly increase inequality.

Danziger and Plotnick (1975) used CPS microeconomic data (available since 1965) to account for the distributional impact of changes both in demographic composition and in cash transfers. The changing composition of recipient units has affected measured inequality. About half of the increase in inequality can be accounted for by demographic change (1965–1972). Both the IRS and CPS data capture the change in the recipient unit, but the direct effect of transfers is excluded from the IRS data because they are not in adjusted gross income.

Danziger and Plotnick also found that between 1965 and 1972 both those distributions which count transfers in household income and those which do not became more unequal for the entire population and for most demographic groups. Government transfers dramatically reduce inequality for certain groups, especially the aged, but have only a modest effect on the aggregate degree of inequality. However, there is little difference between the impact of the transfer system in 1965 and in 1972, despite the rapid rise in transfers. This coincides with the findings of Reynolds and Smolensky (1974, 1975).

To summarize the sources of difference between the IRS and CPS data: We have found that the choice of beginning and ending points affects the trend in each series, but does not explain the differences between them. The presence of transfers in the CPS but not the IRS data affects their levels, but also fails to explain the differences in trend.

Based on a survey of all the available literature, a best guess at what happened to the trend in inequality since World War II is as follows: Earnings inequality increased throughout the period. The shifting composition of household types also increased income inequality over the long term. Cash transfers reduce inequality every year, but they do not impart any trend in the period for which we have data (1965–1972). In 1947, however, cash transfers were very small. Hence, over the longer interval they have probably damped the trend directly while inducing greater inequality indirectly. A more thorough analysis awaits a well-specified modeling of the behavioral interactions among the labor market, the transfer system, and demographic trends.

II. INTERPRETATION PROBLEMS ASSOCIATED WITH CYCLICAL FLUCTUATIONS

The conventional wisdom asserts that for business cycles whose amplitudes are relatively small, as during the past World War II period, inequality increases during recession and decreases during prosperity. Metcalf, however, has found the relationship between the cycle and inequality to be quite complex. In particular his analysis implies that the growing significance of transfers could upset the conventional relationship.

We can expect the following distributional response to a movement from recession to tight employment. The mean of the income distribution moves with an increase in output. As the unemployment rate falls and real wages rise, the lower tail of the distribution improves relative to the median. The upper tail of the distribution improves relative to the median when the nonwage share of personal income increases. This is more likely to occur in recessions rather than in the early stages of a boom, however, for the increased profit share found during boom periods is slow in finding its way into the personal income stream. Overall, the upper tail of the distribution tends to be fairly stable, in absolute terms, over the cycle. Equivalently, it improves relative to the median during recessions and declines during periods of tight employment.

Given this general pattern, families and individuals in the lower tail of the distribution who are not "related" to the labor force tend to be harmed during inflationary periods, relative to the median. The extent of this harm, and the harm suffered by labor force oriented groups in a recession, depends upon the level of transfer payments. Not surprisingly, at a given level of wages and employment, the lower tail of the income distribution is improved relative to the median by increased levels of transfer payments (Metcalf 1972, pp. 66–67).

Gramlich (1974) suggests that during the recession of 1970, workers in lower-paying occupations suffered relatively smaller losses in expected income because a greater proportion of their loss was recouped by transfers. Conceivably, therefore, inequality may actually decrease during a recession. In addition Mirer (1973a) found that for the recession of 1970 better-paying occupations (professional and technical, and managerial workers) suffered a greater loss of potential income than did lower-paying occupations (service workers, general laborers). Mirer cautions, however, that these results may be peculiar to the end of the Vietnam War and the resulting heavy unemployment in the high-technology industries.

Simple regressions on the cyclical pattern of income inequality for the two periods 1955 to 1969 and 1947 to 1973 yield one striking result: the results for the 1955 to 1969 time period diverge widely from those for the 1947 to 1973 period. The results for the shorter period show that increases in the female labor force participation rate, the civilian unemployment rate, and the rate of growth of Gross National Product all increase inequality, while increases in transfers per household and the rate of change of wholesale prices reduce inequality.[3] The results for the 1947 to 1973 period are generally inconclusive; only the coefficient on the unemployment rate is significant. These results are too crude to serve as the basis for a comprehensive analysis of the cyclical pattern. They are reported to emphasize the sensitivity of the results to the time period under study and the uncertainty surrounding the impact of the business cycle on inequality.

III. SUMMARY

The differences among the findings with regard to both trend and cycle stem from the fact that the income distribution has been quite stable, so that whether the researchers find inequality increasing or decreasing over the long-term or over the business cycle is affected by what may seem to be small differences in definitions and measurement

---

3. The regressions estimated are similar to those presented by Schultz (1969) and Thurow (1970). The dependent variable is the CPS Gini coefficient. Besides those listed in the text, other independent variables include the rate of growth of real GNP, wages as a percent of personal income, and a time trend.

procedures. It can be argued that too much emphasis is being placed on the results if they are subject to instability from minor factors. Whether inequality is increasing or decreasing, by no matter how small an amount, seems to carry an enormous emotional and ideological charge. For that reason there needs to be available a consistent and accurate record of the past, with all the qualifications quantified. Such a record does not exist.

BIBLIOGRAPHY

Benus, J. and Morgan, J. 1975. "Time Period, Unit of Analysis, and Income Concept in the Analysis of Income Distribution." In *The Personal Distribution of Income and Wealth,* edited by J. D. Smith, Chapter 7. New York: Columbia University Press.

Blinder, A. S. 1975. "Distribution Effects and the Aggregate Consumption Function." *Journal of Political Economy* 83 (June).

Brittain, J. A. 1972. *The Payroll Tax for Social Security.* Washington: Brookings Institution.

Budd, E. C. 1970. "Postwar Changes in the Size Distribution of Income in the U.S." *American Economic Review* 60 (May).

Danziger, S. and Plotnick, R. 1975. "Demographic Change, Government Transfers, and the Distribution of Income." Institute for Research on Poverty Discussion Paper #274-75. University of Wisconsin–Madison.

Gastwirth, J. L. 1972. "The Estimation of the Lorenz Curve and Gini Index." *Review of Economics and Statistics* 54 (August).

Gramlich, E. M. 1974. "The Distributional Effects of Higher Unemployment." *Brookings Papers on Economic Activity,* 1974:2.

Henle, P. 1972. "Exploring the Distribution of Earned Income." *Monthly Labor Review,* 95 (December).

Institute for Social Research. 1973. *A Panel Study of Income Dynamics.* University of Michigan, Ann Arbor.

Kuznets, S. 1972. "Demographic Aspects of the Distribution of Income Among Families: Recent Trends in the United States." Yale University Economic Growth Center Discussion Paper #165.

———. 1974. "Income-Related Differences in Natural Increase: Bearing on Growth and Distribution Income." In *Nations and Households in Economic Growth,* edited by P. A. David and M. W. Reder. New York: Academic Press.

Lindert, P. 1974. "Fertility and the Macroeconomics of Inequality." Institute for Research on Poverty Discussion Paper #219-74. University of Wisconsin–Madison.

Metcalf, C. 1972. *An Econometric Model of Income Distribution.* Chicago: Markham.

Mirer, T. 1973a. "The Distributional Impact of the 1970 Recession." *Review of Economics and Statistics* 55 (May).

————. 1973b. "The Effects of Macroeconomic Fluctuations on the Distribution of Income." *Review of Income and Wealth.* No. 19, Series 4.

Pechman, J. and Okner, B. 1974. *Who Bears the Tax Burden?* Washington: Brookings Institution.

Plotnick, Robert D. 1975. "Transfers, Labor Supply, and the Income Distributions: Towards a General Equilibrium Analysis." Institute for Research on Poverty, unpublished.

Radner, D. and Hinrichs, J. 1974. "Size Distribution of Income in 1964, 1970, and 1971." *Survey of Current Business* 54 (October).

Reynolds, M. and Smolensky, E. 1974. "The Post-Fisc Distribution: 1961 and 1970 Compared." *National Tax Journal* 27 (December).

————. 1975. "Post-Fisc Distribution of Income: 1950, 1961, and 1970." Institute for Research on Poverty Discussion Paper #270–75. University of Wisconsin–Madison.

Rivlin, A. M. 1975. "Income Distribution—Can Economists Help?" *American Economic Review* 65 (May).

Schultz, T. P. 1969. "Secular Trends and Cyclical Behavior of Income Distribution in the United States, 1944–1965." In *Six Papers on the Size Distribution of Wealth and Income,* edited by L. Saltow. New York: Columbia University Press.

————. 1972. "Long-Term Change in Personal Income Distribution: Theoretical Approaches, Evidence, and Explanations." Santa Monica: Rand Corporation.

Thurow, L. C. 1970. "Analyzing the American Income Distribution." *American Economic Review* 60 (May).

————. 1975. *The Generation of Inequality.* New York: Basic Books.

Tuckman, H. P. and Brosch, G. 1975. "Changes in Personal Income and Their Effect on Income Shares." *Southern Economics Journal* 41 (July).

U.S. Bureau of the Census. 1975. *Money Income in 1973 of Families and Persons in the United States.* Current Population Reports, Series P-60, No. 97. Washington: U.S. Government Printing Office.

U.S. Department of the Treasury. Internal Revenue Service. 1975. *Statistics of Income, Individual Income Tax Returns, 1972.* Washington: U.S. Government Printing Office.

Part 3

Poverty: Extent, Causes, and Consequences

The rise of the civil rights movement and the later rebellions of the black populations of one after another major city put the question of mass poverty on the
political agenda in this country. Since then, how has the so-called War on Poverty
affected the number of poor? The answer depends, in the first place, on how we
define "poverty." Usually poverty is measured using budgets which supposedly
cover the costs of goods and services needed to satisfy what investigators define
as basic requirements. This means, which "few Americans realize," (as a leading
authority on income distribution observes) "that we have a poverty definition
which artificially deflates the number of poor and makes the problem seem less
serious than it is."[1] It is now over a decade since the official definition of absolute
poverty was adopted, and it was based on a food plan (the Economy Budget)
designed by the Department of Agriculture for *emergency* use. The official poverty
line adopted by the Social Security Administration was calculated by determining
what it would cost—using this emergency food plan—to feed a nonfarm family of
four in 1963. Adjustments for smaller and larger families, with one or two adults,
male or female, in the household, were then made. Studies of the spending habits
of American families at the time showed that about a third of their *posttax* income
went for food over a wide range of income brackets. The SSA multiplied the cost
of the Agriculture Department's economy diet for emergency use by three to
determine the amount of income below which a family would be considered
officially poor. Remarkably, the SSA also measured this income on a *prettax* basis,
so that the actual disposable income available to such officially poor families after
payment of taxes might be even less. The poverty line was adjusted backward to
1959 on the basis of changes in the cost of living index and it has been adjusted
upward each year since 1963 in the same way. In 1972, the official poverty line
for a nonfarm family of four headed by a man was set at $4,277. This means that
the amount they had to spend on food—one-third of this sum—was $1,426 a year,
or 98 cents per person per day! The poverty thresholds that year varied from
$2,823 for couples under 65 years old with a male earner to $7,000 for families
of seven or more persons. For 1975, the poverty line would be about 28 percent
higher after adjusting for inflation. The amount calculated for food costs, it should
be emphasized, makes the tenuous assumption that the poor can buy food at the
prices assigned by the Agriculture Department. The calculation of how food costs
differ for families of varying size and composition is based on different arithmetical
factors—for instance, a factor of three for a nonfarm family of four, but 3.70 for
a couple and 5.92 for unrelated individuals. As Robert D. Plotnick and Felicity
Skidmore point out, however, such figures, "while wrapped in the apparent objectivity of budget studies, contain a generous dose of subjective judgment. The
official thresholds simply reflect one rather stringent view of how much income
is needed by different families to reach a minimum 'level of decency' relative to
average American standards. Their wide acceptance testifies only to their *political
acceptability* and not the intrinsic validity of the definition."[2]

---

1. Herman P. Miller, "A New Look at Inequality, Poverty, and Underemployment in the United States
—Without Rose-Colored Glasses," *Review of Black Political Economy* 3:2 (Winter, 1973): 28.

2. *Progress Against Poverty: A Review of the 1964–1974 Decade.* Institute for Research on Poverty,
Poverty Policy Analysis Series No. 1. (New York: Academic Press, 1976), p. 37.

The number of people who are counted as poor according to official poverty statistics, moreover, includes only those whose incomes are still below the official poverty line when government "cash benefits" have been counted in their income. The most basic question, though, is how effective the ordinary functioning of American capitalism is at producing a minimum decent standard of living for everyone. Next, it can be asked, say Plotnick and Skidmore (Selection Number 11), how effectively the government fills "the holes left by the market mechanism." To answer these questions, they devised an original measure, using OEO and CPS data and based on the official poverty line, of the extent of "pretransfer poverty." This allows them to estimate how many Americans are poor before receiving cash benefits from various government social programs, and how this has changed since the launching of the "War on Poverty."

"Relative Poverty"

Plotnick and Skidmore distinguish between "absolute" and "relative" poverty in their analysis of changes in the incidence of poverty and in the composition of the poor between 1965 and 1972. "Absolute" poverty refers to the official poverty threshold of a fixed amount of real cash income below which a family or individual is considered poor. "Relative" poverty is also related to the official poverty lines. Each family's current cash income is divided by the SSA poverty line. This yields a fraction (or "welfare ratio") by which the family exceeds or falls below the SSA minimum decency level. Families with ratios below .44 of the median ratio were defined as the "relative poor." This fraction was used, rather than the more common relative measure, which is one-half the median income, because in this way the same households that were defined as poor by the absolute measure in 1965 (the base year for Plotnick and Skidmore's analysis of changes in poverty) are also classified as being relatively poor. (In 1965, the median "welfare ratio" was 2.25, so any family below the official poverty line necessarily had a welfare ratio less than 1/2.25 of the median, or .44) Thus, changes by either the absolute or relative definition are measured against exactly the same (1965) base, but the measures can move in different directions. The relative definition is one indicator of the degree of inequality of the distribution of income. Over time, a *smaller* proportion of the population could fall below the absolute poverty line while a *larger* proportion fell a specified distance below the typical standard of living.

The Extent of Poverty

So how many poor are there in America by these various measures and definitions? In 1965, there were over 40 million "pretransfer" poor people in the United States, and the number had scarcely changed by 1972. Similarly, there was little shift in the proportion of all households that were living in poverty: 25.7 percent of all households were classified as pretransfer poor in 1965, and 24.8 percent in 1972.

An increase in average family income benefited households headed by able-bodied men more than other poor households, but an increase in overall unemployment also fell more heavily on them. As Plotnick and Skidmore point out, a low unemployment rate and relative economic growth are not enough to ensure minimally decent standards of living for people who are too old to work, disabled, discriminated against, or who have to stay home to care for their children. To help them requires specific government action through various social programs.

How effective has government antipoverty policy been? When government expenditures are added to private income sources, how has the number of poor changed? This is called "posttransfer poverty." In 1965, Plotnick and Skidmore found that 10.5 million households, or 17 percent of the total, were in "posttransfer poverty," and this decreased to 10 million households, or 14 percent of all of them, by 1972. Government cash programs plus in-kind transfers lifted almost 50 percent of households over the official poverty line in 1965, and 72 percent in 1972. In other words, a half of the poor in 1965 and nearly three-quarters of the poor in 1972 would have stayed poor if their private earnings were their only income and they had not received assistance from the government.

Even including these government transfers, though, "relative poverty" did not decline between 1965 and 1972. In fact, the number of relatively poor rose from 17.3 percent to 18.1 percent of all households in that period. These "sharp contrasts," as Plotnick and Skidmore emphasize, between the findings based on the absolute and relative definitions of poverty show how crucial such definitions are in our thinking about changes in poverty. By the official absolute definition, there has been gradual progress in eliminating poverty, at least until the mid-1970s economic crisis; but by the relative definition, Plotnick and Skidmore conclude, the "distribution of income, not including government benefits, has worsened. The poor are further away from being able to support themselves at typical American living standards than they were in 1965." Government spending compensated somewhat, but it did not reverse the trend.

This means that millions of American children are still deprived of the kinds of food they need to grow to healthy adulthood; that they are compelled to live "in overcrowded quarters, with no decent place to play"; that they have to go "without preventive health care"; that they have "little chance for more than a high school education"; and that their mothers are likely to have to work outside the home when they are young. These, in Lenore E. Bixby's words (Selection Number 12), are among some of the measurable consequences of poverty and low income in general. In her article, she documents the effects of inadequate income on children and their families.

Children from low-income families suffer from poor nutrition and overcrowded housing in rundown neighborhoods. Even crude data dividing them into low and high income groups show that the low income children get dental and medical examinations far more often, though these differences do not reflect the need for such care.[3] When they come of age, they are less likely to go to college, and if they do go, to make it through to graduation.

The smaller the husband's earnings, the more likely the wife is to work outside the home and the worse the arrangements to care for the children of such working mothers. Many are simply left on their own. Even those cared for are often left with an older child under eighteen. Working at a second job—"moonlighting"—is probably much more frequent among the fathers in low-income families than others, and the result is that they also have less contact with their children than

---

3. According to the Joint Commission of Mental Health of Children and Youth, poverty and conditions that go with it are likely to cause higher rates of poor physical and mental health, and the latter also run a higher risk of becoming poor. See *The Child Mental Health Crisis* (New York: Harper and Row, 1970).

more well-off fathers. In consequence, combined divorce and separation rates are higher in low-income families.[4]

Not only do the poor suffer more during their lifetimes compared to well-off Americans, but they also have less of a chance of staying alive. Their mortality rates are substantially higher than other Americans in ordinary times and, as research on death in Korea and Vietnam among American troops shows, men from poor families were also overrepresented among those killed there. Kenneth Lutterman, James W. Russell, and I investigated the extent to which the civilian class situation of the American fighting man determined his life chances in the armed forces and the likelihood of his death on the battlefields of Vietnam (Selection Number 13). We found that the alleged universalistic standards of the armed forces were affected by the class origins of the enlisted men and officers. Based on individual data on all 380 servicemen from Wisconsin who died in Vietnam through 1967, we found that 27.2 percent came from families classified as "poor" by official standards, in contrast to the comparable cohort figure of 14.9 percent in the population. That is, nearly twice as many sons of poor families died in Vietnam as would have if their share of the dead had been "equitable" or proportional. The disproportionate representation of the poor was even greater among nonofficers.

Most striking is the finding that within each class, among workers, farmers, and the middle strata, the poor were also overrepresented among the dead. In each class, the men from poor families were at least twice as likely as others to be killed in Vietnam. On the other hand, even if we consider poverty level, we still find differential class mortality. Among the poor, the differences in casualty rates between the sons of workers, farmers, and the middle strata scarcely differed. However, among those who were not poor, the sons of farmowners and those from middle-strata families, were quite *under* represented among the servicemen killed, while the percentage of workers' sons among the dead was nearly one and one-third times that in their high-school cohort.

The sons of the poor were probably overrepresented among the troops killed in Vietnam because, in the first place, they were least likely to qualify for—or know of—specific types of draft deferments, especially college deferments; the same may apply to the sons of the "nonpoor" manual workers compared to their counterparts from middle-class and farming families. Yet this explanation is insufficient, because we also find that poor servicemen were more likely to die in "hostile action" or actual combat.

Deaths in Vietnam occurred not only in actual combat, but also from accidents and personal illness. Separating deaths due to hostile action from deaths by other causes, we found a general tendency for servicemen from poor families—in all ranks combined and in all branches of the service—to be somewhat more likely to die in hostile action than their counterparts from families that were not poor. What's more, in each class, among workers', farmers', and middle-class sons—again, with all branches and ranks combined—the servicemen from poor families were more likely than the nonpoor to be killed in hostile action. On the other hand,

---

4. Catherine S. Chilman observes that "Many people erroneously conclude [because family breakdown is more prevalent among poor people] that family breakdown (including illegitimacy) *causes* poverty. It is far more likely that the reverse is true: poverty is a leading cause of family instability." She cites comparative studies by Philps Cutright which show that "when the effects of education, occupation, and income are considered together in their impact on divorce and separation, he finds the critical factor is income." "Families in Poverty in the Early 1970s," *Journal of Marriage and the Family* 37:1 (February, 1975):57.

when poverty level is taken into account, the differences between these classes were not systematic. However, of all strata, poor workers had the highest proportion of deaths from hostile action. We suggest that these differences in death from hostile action occurred because jobs in the armed forces carry different amounts of risk with them, and job allocation probably fell along the lines set by the social origins and relative class situation of enlisted men. The poor (and poor workers in particular) were probably least likely to be assigned to administrative, supply, or other less risky positions, and therefore were most likely to be exposed to hostile action and the risk of death.

Theories of Poverty

Poverty persists for millions of Americans, and their lives are painful and brief compared to their more fortunate countrymen. What determines the poor fortune of some and the good fortune of others? Is the problem some quality peculiar to the poor themselves that prevents them from making it out of poverty? Or does the problem of poverty inhere in the political economy of capitalism, which constantly creates and recreates poverty in its everyday workings because it is a system of production for private profit rather than the satisfaction of social needs?

The prevailing theories of poverty can be broadly classified as "cultural" or "structural," as David Elesh terms them (Selection Number 14) in his critical review of their substantive validity and policy relevance. Cultural theories explain poverty by the traits of the poor themselves; their values, attitudes, and behavior patterns supposedly prevent them from being "socially mobile." In contrast, "structural" theories, says Elesh explain poverty by the conditions under which the poor live: unemployment, underemployment, poor health, and poor education. The poor have distinctive traits, but these are seen as adaptations to inimical structural conditions. Thus, as Elesh observes, both theories characterize the poor similarly, but place different interpretations on the meaning of these traits.

Elesh claims that there are "ten traits which form a kind of poverty syndrome" in the writings of structural and cultural theorists. Successive generations of the same family are assumed to remain poor and to exhibit this syndrome. If cultural theory claims that "cultural transmission" from one generation to another perpetuates the cycle of poverty, structural theory argues that specific conditions, by "guaranteeing failure," turn out "independently produced lookalikes."

Based on his review of the internal evidence presented in the case studies of these theorists themselves and on the "methodologically rigorous research of others," Elesh finds that either the ostensible facts or imputed effects of the poverty syndrome are contradicted for seven of the ten traits. In his view, the internal and/or external evidence does *not* show a clear or systematic relationship between poverty and any of the following alleged traits of the poor: a matrifocal family, a lack of social organization beyond the extended family, an inability to delay gratification, fatalism, historical ignorance, political alienation, and a lack of class consciousness. If the poverty syndrome characterizes some of the poor, the numbers involved are unknown; on balance, the evidence for the poverty syndrome is weak. Thus the cultural theory, which claims these traits are the *causes* of poverty, "is particularly suspect," Elesh believes. However, structural theory is also found wanting since it sees these traits as *effects* of poverty, yet the syndrome apparently does not really exist. Neither theory is able to explain the actual variation in the presumed characteristics of the poor. Thus, Elesh concludes, these theories are of "dubious validity and policy relevance." While he has no theory to replace them, he suggests further research into subgroup variations among the poor along a number of dimensions, such as differences in ethnic and racial subcultures; residential, occupational, and industrial segregation; geographical location; and discrimination, which he hopes might allow more fruitful thoery construction and policy guidance.

The prevailing theories (and even such empirical critiques as Elesh's) take the existence of poverty as given and ask what sorts of individuals are likely to suffer from it. In contrast, Harry Caudill's analysis (Selection Number 15) focuses on the specific historical combination of political economic forces which created poverty itself througout a vast area of the United States, transforming it from a booming into a "depressed" area. For six decades, Caudill contends, absentee corporations held Appalachia's mineral wealth in their control, with the result that the region's booms and busts depended on the profit rates of the corporations. The courts upheld and enlarged corporate control and privileges gained in the nineteenth century, so that with the advent of new technology, the region was despoiled. Thousands of acres of timber were cut by the companies without compensating the owners; waters were diverted and polluted; livestock died of hunger and thirst; roads were run through fertile gardens; poisonous waters were sluiced onto crop land; and coal grit was hurled onto fields of corn—all with the aid and approval of the courts.

The companies were granted rights they had never paid for, says Caudill, and gained control over the present estate and future heritage of the land. New methods of surface or strip mining replaced or supplemented tunneling. Huge sheets of coal half a mile long, eight feet thick and fifty wide were bared in a few days. Because it was cheaper to the companies, the region's men were put out of work and its streams and land ruined. Auger mining accentuated and perhaps finalized the region's desolation. Yet the companies prevented even minimal attempts by the state to reclaim and stabilize the land, Caudill contends, and state governors failed to enforce even moderate legislation to restrain the mine owners.

The essential element in all this, according to Caudill, is that the region has constituted a colonial appendage of corporations centered in the industrial East and Middle West. Timber, coal, crops, and workers were exploited for the profits of the corporations; the corporations corrupted or intimidated public officials. The result was that little money remained to maintain decent schools, libraries, hospitals, and other institutions necessary for a decent life.

The only organized resistance came from the United Mineworkers Union, which, after violent struggles, was able to improve the working and living conditions of the miners and to build health facilities for the miners. However, says Caudill, the union accepted the domination of the big companies and tried to protect the miners in the big mines at the expense of those in the small ones. As a result, low wages and dangerous working conditions came to predominate once more. In an attempt to change these conditions, the UMW called a major strike in 1959. The strike failed, however, at the cost of several months of violence during which miners were killed and the National Guard was called in.

The Federal Government, meanwhile, continued to act as if in collusion with the mineowners, Caudill concludes, failing to make even token enforcement of minimum wage requirements of the Fair Labor Standards Act. Fewer and fewer have remained at work. The coal industry, faced with competition from petroleum and natural gas, itself went into rapid decline, taking with it what remained of the region and its people.

Is the poverty of Appalachia an aberration, or is it merely one historically specific and dramatically clear expression of processes inherent in capitalism, a system whose basic social relationships and objectives of production generate and regenerate poverty? For Barry Bluestone (Selection Number 16), the answer is evident—these dynamics of capitalism can be summed up in terms of "the law of uneven development" in Marxian theory. As Bluestone puts it, the maximization of private profits seldom coincides with the "maximization of total social return." Investment flows where profits are expected and declines where they are not. What is not profitable, whether specific products or infant industries, will not receive further investment and, consequently, will tend to deteriorate. Particularly when an industry becomes relatively concentrated, Bluestone argues, the static equilibrium models, in which diminishing returns to any single investment are supposed to prevent a long-run dichotomization between industrial sectors or classes, are inapplicable. Reinvestment in the relatively more capital intensive, concentrated, and more profitable industries, combined with disinvestment in the less profitable, tends to separate out two unevenly developed economic sectors. In time, wages decline comparatively in the industries that have "undergone drastic secular deterioration in relative capital intensity, concentration, profits, and wage levels," and the result is a "massive working poor" segment of the working class, who make up over half the poor in the nation. Since the situation of the aged and disabled among the poor who are no longer in the labor force is largely a consequence of their previous labor force status, the secular deterioration between industries affects them as well as currently employed poor workers.

The same pattern of "uneven development," Bluestone argues, occurs in investments in so-called "human capital," by which academic economists term the particular skills and training possessed by an individual. The unequal distribution of wealth and income and of consequent differential investment in learning in the home, decent schools, and higher education combines with the separation of cities from suburbs, blacks from whites, and working class neighborhoods from more well-off neighborhoods to "assure a secular deterioration in human capital terms" between the rich and the poor.

The modern state tends both to reinforce and stabilize the overall pattern of uneven development among industries and classes, Bluestone argues. Through subsidies, tax policies, and expenditures, the already concentrated, capital-intensive, profitable industries receive disproportionate state assistance to the detriment of others. This, in turn, leads to "revolutionary implications" if not corrected by other state policies, such as the progressive income tax, welfare, and manpower training programs. The latter, as analyses of the stability of "post-fisc" distribution indicate, have so far successfully offset the inherent tendency to even greater inequality. This means that the stability of American capitalism increasingly rests on "massive state intervention." Here lies the ultimate source of the "recurrent fiscal crises of the state." In Bluestone's view, "the state is forced constantly to expand the public transfer economy in order to ameliorate the dynamic *effects* of the functioning of the private sector." Under capitalism, it is the "only significant alternative to explosive political discontent." The question, Bluestone concludes, is whether this will mean the gradual "downfall of capitalism" through increased public intervention, or its more rapid abolition through political organization by the left.

Clearly, then, a central issue in the attempt to grapple with the deeper divisions in our social life revolves around the nature of contemporary American capitalism and, in turn, what this has to do with the struggle for power. These questions are taken up in the following parts of this book.

Progress Against Poverty: 1964-1974

11

Robert D. Plotnick and Felicity Skidmore

In 1964 the War on Poverty was declared. A regular report on the state of that war would seem reasonable. This article analyzes the whole of the period since the Office of Economic Opportunity was established and the war declared.

WHO ARE THE POOR WHO NEED GOVERNMENT HELP?

Official poverty statistics include as poor only those whose incomes remain below the poverty line even after government cash benefits—social insurance programs, like Social Security, and public assistance programs, like AFDC—have been counted in their income.

In any given year, the economy generates a set of earnings, property income, and private payments from one individual to another (for example, alimony) that together determine how much money different people have before specific government intervention. For the poor, the overwhelming proportion of this income comes from earnings. To be able to assess how effective our economy is at producing minimum decent standards for all—and then to judge how effective government is at filling the holes left by the market mechanism—we need to identify those who are unable to make it over the poverty line by their own effort.

We have calculated such a measure—which we term pretransfer poverty—for the first time, and charted its progress using data from the OEO Survey of Economic Opportunity and the Current Population Survey. (See Table 11-1).

This text is taken from an article by Felicity Skidmore in *Focus,* Spring-Summer, 1976, the newsletter of the Institute for Research on Poverty, University of Wisconsin-Madison, and from certain sections of Robert D. Plotnick and Felicity Skidmore, *Progress Against Poverty: A Review of the 1964–1974 Decade.* Institute for Research on Poverty, Poverty Policy Analysis Series No. 1. New York: Academic Press, 1975. By permission of the authors and the Institute for Research on Poverty.

Table 11-1. The Poverty Picture—Excluding Government Benefits

	1965		1968		1972	
	number (millions)	percentage of total	number (millions)	percentage of total	number (millions)	percentage of total
1. Poor persons	40.8	21.3	35.8	18.2	39.4	19.2
2. Poor families	9.4	19.5	8.4	16.6	9.6	17.7
3. Poor unrelated individuals	6.2	50.7	6.5	47.3	8.0	47.9
4. Poor households (#2 + #3)	15.6	25.7	14.9	23.2	17.6	24.8

Between 1965 and 1972, the absolute number of households whose earnings could not carry them over the poverty level rose from 15.6 million to 17.6 million. Because the total number of U.S. households increased over the period, this represented a small percentage decrease—from 25.7 percent to 24.8 percent. In 1968, after three years of strong economic growth and falling unemployment, the incidence of household poverty had dropped to almost 23 percent, but over the whole period 1965 to 1972 the drop was less then one percentage point.

Two major factors influencing earned income are the rate of economic growth and the rate of unemployment. We found that families headed by working-age women, the elderly, and unrelated individuals were much less responsive to changes in general economic conditions, and families headed by able-bodied men were much more responsive than the overall average.

1. A 1 percent increase in average family pretransfer income was associated with a *decline* in poverty of:
    a. 1.0 percent for all families
    b. 2.1 percent for families headed by a white man under 65
    c. 3.0 percent for families headed by a black man under 65
    contrasted with:
    a. 0.3 percent for families headed by a white or black woman under 65

2. A 10 percent increase in the national unemployment rate was associated with a poverty *increase* of:
    a. 2.7 percent for all families
    b. 5.8 percent for families headed by white men under 65
    c. 3.4 percent for families headed by black men under 65
    as contrasted with:
    a. 2.3 percent for families headed by white women under 65
    b. 0.1 percent for families headed by black women under 65

Overall economic activity, obviously, most affects those who can work. For those who do not work by reason of age, child care responsibilities, disability, or discrimination, a low unemployment rate and healthy economic growth are not enough to ensure minimally decent living standards. For this reason, we must also be concerned with the progress of specific government action to alleviate poverty.

GOVERNMENT SPENDING ON SOCIAL PROGRAMS

Government, at all levels, spends a substantial part of the taxes it collects on social programs specifically directed toward improving the economic and social well-being of its citizens as individuals. (All government expenditures, of course, affect the well-being of the population in some way, if only through the tax system that has to finance them. We limited the analysis to social programs with identifiable recipients.) These include expenditures on cash benefits—such as Social Security and public assistance—as well as programs that provide food, housing, manpower training, health, and education.

Clearly, not all these expenditures are explicitly designed for low-income groups. Many are designed to promote the well-being of the population in general. It is not to be expected, therefore, that the proportion going to the poor should ever approach 100 percent.

Much of it does go to the poor, however—much more, in fact, than they receive from programs directly aimed at fighting poverty. It is interesting to find out *how* much, to see how (or whether) the proportion has changed, and to trace which programs are the most important in money terms. (Table 11–2 shows the statistical picture of what we call social welfare expenditures (SWE), for those interested in the detailed figures.)

Table 11–2. Total Social Welfare Expenditures (SWE) and Percentage Going to the (Pretransfer) Poor

	1965		1968		1972	
	dollars (billions)	percentage to poor	dollars (billions)	percentage to poor	dollars (billions)	percentage to poor
Total	74.5	42	109.2	40	184.9	43
Cash Transfers	36.6	57	45.6	54	80.1	53
Social Security	16.5	62	22.7	58	38.3	58
Public Assistance	4.8	89	5.5	81	10.8	87
Nutrition	0.9	37	1.0	39	3.7	70
Food Stamps	10.04	95	0.9	92	1.9	85
Housing	0.3	51	0.4	70	1.8	55
Health	5.7	55	14.1	55	24.6	56
Medicaid			3.3	77	7.5	75
Medicare			4.4	47	7.0	48
Social (and OEO) Services	1.4	64	2.6	73	5.3	72
Employment and Manpower	0.7	63	2.0	79	3.9	72
Education	27.1	18	40.6	18	62.2	19

In 1965, $75 billion—or 39 percent of all public spending—was spent by all levels of government on social welfare. By 1972 this had climbed in absolute terms to $185 billion, and as a proportion of all public spending, to 46 percent.

Programs specifically designated as programs for low-income groups accounted for only 12 percent of the 1965 expenditures on social welfare, of which the OEO-initiated programs accounted for less than one-twentieth. By 1972 programs designated as low-income had risen to 18 percent of the total social welfare budget, of which OEO-initiated programs were still a small part—accounting for slightly over one-sixth.

Throughout the period, cash assistance was the largest major category, although as a percentage of total SWE it declined from 49 percent to 43 percent. The next largest throughout was education; its share also declined, but only from 36 percent to 33 percent. The big gainers in proportional terms were goods-and-services (in-kind) benefit programs, mainly because of Medicaid and Medicare and to a lesser degree because of a growth of OEO-related and employment and manpower programs.

How much of all this went to the poor? In absolute terms, the amount going to the poor increased from $31 billion in 1965 to $79 billion in 1972. And of the amount that went to the poor, a rising fraction has come from programs based on some low-income criterion for eligibility—24 percent in 1965, 35 percent in 1972—also largely attributable to the growth of Medicaid and Medicare, plus public assistance and Food Stamps.

As a fraction of the total SWE, however, the amount going to the poor stayed virtually stable (roughly 42 percent) in both years. This is primarily because education remains such a large component, and (as Table 11–2 shows) only 18 to 19 percent of educational expenditures go to the poor.

HOW EFFECTIVE HAS ANTIPOVERTY POLICY BEEN?

Official Poverty Statistics

How effective has antipoverty policy been? In answer to this question, we first assess progress by the government's official definition. Official statistics and government cash-benefit programs (Social Security, Unemployment Insurance, supplemental benefits, and AFDC, for example) were added to private income sources to arrive at the income definition used to assess poverty status.

By this measure (call it *posttransfer* poverty) there were significant though modest decreases in poverty over the period (as can be seen from Table 11–3). Before cash transfers were counted, the proportion of (pretransfer) poor households declined only very slightly (from 25.7 percent in 1965 to 24.8 percent in 1972). Addition of government cash benefits decreased the 1965 figure by 9 percentage points and the 1972 figure by 11 percentage points. Thus, in 1965, 10–1/2 million American households were (posttransfer) poor, constituting 17 percent of the total; by 1972 this had dropped to 10 million, or 14 percent of the total.

Contrasting this with the previous poverty measure, we can see how much progress against poverty government was able to make through its cash benefit (cash transfer) programs.

As this overall progress took place, the composition of those in poverty changed. Compared to 1965, the 1972 posttransfer poor more often lived in female-headed households and in households with young heads. Heads of posttransfer poor households in 1972 were also more likely than their 1965 counterparts to have a high school or college education and less likely to have held any job during the year.

Table 11–3. The Poverty Picture—Including Government Benefits (post-transfer poverty)

	1965		1968		1972	
Absolute Poverty	number (millions)	percentage of total	number (millions)	percentage of total	number (millions)	percentage of total
1. Poor persons	29.9	15.6	25.1	12.8	24.5	11.9
2. Poor families	6.0	12.4	5.1	10.0	5.1	9.3
3. Poor unrelated individuals	4.5	36.7	5.0	32.8	4.9	29.2
4. Poor households (#2 + #3)	10.5	17.3	10.1	15.7	10.0	14.0
Relative Poverty						
1. Poor persons	29.9	15.6	28.7	14.6	32.3	15.7
2. Poor families	6.0	12.4	5.8	11.6	6.8	12.5
3. Poor unrelated individuals	4.5	36.7	5.1	36.7	6.1	36.3
4. Poor households (#2 + #3)	10.5	17.3	10.9	17.0	12.9	18.1

Looking at the effect of the cash system on the poverty status of various groups, we can see how this change came about. In 1965, 33 percent of all pretransfer poor households were taken out of poverty by cash transfers. By 1972, this figure had risen by 44 percent. *But* the relative generosity of the cash benefit system varied widely across various population groups.

The elderly were heavily favored throughout the period; female-headed families, although starting out relatively well, made minimal progress (see Table 11–4).

Other Poverty Definitions

To put these figures into a wider perspective, we show two other measures of poverty progress:

1. A *relative* measure, designed to show how the fortunes of the low-income population are moving in comparison to the "typical U.S. standard of living." This gives a more pessimistic measure of progress than the official statistics.

2. A *cash plus in-kind* measure, designed to take into account, in addition to cash income, income received in goods and service benefits from government (Food Stamps, public housing, Medicare, and Medicaid). This gives a more optimistic picture of progress than the official definition.

In 1965, government cash programs took 33 percent of households out of poverty as officially measured. In 1972, these programs took 44 percent over the official poverty line. Cash plus in-kind transfers, in contrast, lifted about 50 percent of households over the official poverty line in 1965 and 72 percent in 1972.

These cash transfers only 34 percent over the relative poverty line in 1972.

Table 11–4. Percentage Taken Out of Poverty by Government Cash Benefits

Households headed by:	1965	1972
Aged	51	63
Non-aged men with children	11	23
Non-aged persons, no children	19	26
Non-aged women with children	22	23

RELATIVE POVERTY

Estimates of changes in relative poverty* are shown in the lower half of Table 11–3 (p. 132). . . . Relative poverty did *not* decline between 1965 and 1972, but remained fairly constant. Figure 11–1 displays this lack of change. The incidence of poverty among persons was 15.6 percent in 1965 and dipped slightly over the next three years to 14.6 percent (a change . . . that can be traced to the tight labor market of 1966 to 1968). Relative poverty then increased. By 1972, about the same fraction of the population was poor as in 1965. The fractions of families and unrelated individuals in poverty showed similar patterns. Since the total population grew, the number of relative poor persons, families, and individuals actually rose.

The sharp contrasts between the findings based on absolute and relative approaches indicate the crucial role played by the choice of definition in assessing changes in poverty. The official (absolute) measure of poverty shows gradual progress in reducing poverty (at least until 1974) through a combination of economic growth and increasingly generous government transfer programs. The relative perspective indicates little or no progress in eliminating poverty.

---

*"Relative poverty" is defined in the introduction to Part Three.—Ed.

MAJOR CHANGES IN THE POVERTY PICTURE SINCE 1964

1. A larger percentage of persons than ten years ago live in families where earnings and other private income are unable to lift them out of poverty.
2. Government social welfare expenditures—including expenditure on cash, goods, and service benefit programs—have grown enormously in the last decade. Because of it the proportion of the population living in poverty, even with government aid, has been reduced.
3. Programs providing cash constitute a steadily declining proportion of the benefits going to the poor.
4. Benefit programs providing goods and services to the poor (mainly food and medical care) have grown substantially, both in absolute terms and as a proportion of the total benefit package.
5. This renders the government's own poverty definition, which counts only cash income, an increasingly inappropriate tool to measure progress against poverty.

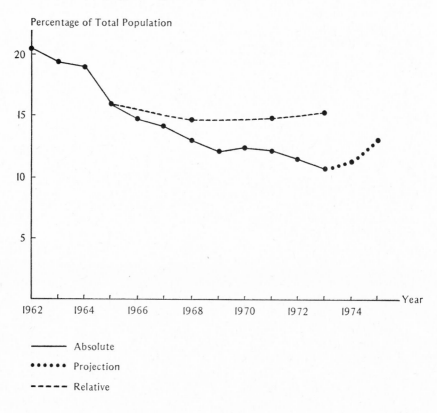

Figure 11-1. The Poverty Picture—Including Government Benefits (post transfer poverty)

6. Families headed by an able-bodied man have done proportionally least well out of the growth in government cash benefit programs. The proportion lifted out of poverty by cash benefits, unlike the aged or female-headed households, did not grow at all between 1965 and 1972, and has probably not increased much since.

7. Finally, the distribution of income not including government benefits has worsened. The poor are further away from being able to support themselves at typical American living standards than they were in 1965. The growth of government benefits over the period served to compensate for this, but did not reverse the trend.

Some Effects of Low Income on Children and Their Families

12

Lenore E. Bixby

To be a child in a family with inadequate income often means to be a child deprived of the kinds of food he needs to grow to healthy adulthood. It often means living in overcrowded quarters, with no decent place to play; going without preventive health care; and having little chance for more than a high school education. For about one in four it means that there is no father in the home; the mother is likely to work while the child is still very young. . . .

EFFECTS ON LIVING CONDITIONS

Low income characteristically means poor nutrition, poor housing, little or no preventive medical care. The facts hardly need documentation, but the extent of deprivation suffered by low-income families has been made clear in various studies.

Nutrition

A clear relationship between family income and the quantities of nutrients provided by the diet of nonfarm families was found by the Department of Agriculture in its 1955 Household Food Consumption Survey.[1] For the 8 million or more children on farms, where income typically is lower than it is in cities, adequacy of diet is less closely related to income. In seasons of the year when homegrown and home-preserved fruits and vegetables have generally been used up, however, farm diets provide less vitamin A and vitamin C—important nutrients for children—than do city diets.

Reprinted from the *Social Security Bulletin* 24 (1961):12–17, by permission of the publisher. Footnotes and tables have been renumbered.

1. Report No. 6, March 1957.

Housing

There are many examples of the inverse relationship between income and overcrowding and of the direct correlation between income and the physical qualities of housing, the extent of conveniences, the quality of the neighborhood, and so on. Moreover, broken families whose incomes tend to be low are likely to share the home of relatives. In 1959, almost a fourth of the one-parent families but only 2 percent of the married couples with children lived in a relative's home.[2]

The fact that overcrowded housing in rundown neighborhoods—with lack of privacy at home and lack of proper play space—may have unfortunate effects on children needs no underlining.

Medical Care

The National Health Survey,[3] like previous surveys, found that the amount of medical care received by a family was related to the family income. The frequency of visits to the dentist provides not only a measure of the amount of dental care received but an index of ability to obtain preventive health care in general. It is therefore significant that there are substantial variations with family income in the number of dental visits by children. Among children aged 5 to 14, for example, those in families with incomes of $4,000 or more visited a dentist three times as often as did the children in families with incomes of less than $4,000. The variations would be more apparent if data were available for finer income intervals.

Children in families with incomes of $4,000 or more also visited physicians more frequently than those in lower-income families. The differences are most striking at the younger ages—0 to 4 and 5 to 14—where children in the higher-income families saw a doctor one-and-one-half times as often as children in lower-income families.

It is clear from the Survey that the difference does not reflect variations in need for medical care. The amount of family income—using the same broad income classification—was not related to the number of days missed from school because of illness or the number of days of restricted activity or days spent in bed because of disability.

EFFECTS ON EDUCATION

Children in homes with inadequate income are less likely to go to college than those whose families are better off. When they do go, they are less likely to stay to graduate.

---

2. Derived from Bureau of the Census, *Current Population Reports,* Series P-20, *Population Characteristics,* No. 100.

3. Public Health Service, *Health Statistics from the U.S. National Health Survey:* C–1, *Children and Youth: Selected Health Characteristics, United States July 1957–June 1958* (October, 1959).

An Office of Education study, published in 1958, reported lack of financial resources as a major cause of transfer or of dropping out of college completely. For students who stayed to graduate, the median income of the families was $1,000 higher than for students who dropped out by the end of the first term, and it was almost $500 higher than for all nongraduates. Students' ability, however, as measured by placement tests, bore almost no relationship to family income.[4] . . .

A sample survey just completed for the Office of Education by the Michigan Survey Research Center shows a sharp correlation between family income and actual or expected college attendance. Of the children aged 20 to 29 in 1960, for example, the proportion that had attended or were attending college was about five times as large when family income exceeded $7,500 as when it was less than $3,000, as shown in Table 12–1.

It is interesting that for younger children there is a similar relationship between parents' income and plans for the child to attend college. The younger the child, however, the more likely his family is to be planning for his college education.

A recent report by the Bureau of Labor Statistics compares the experience of high school graduates in seven communities with that of students who dropped out of high school or who graduated but did not go on to college.[5] It shows that economic need was not a major reason for dropping out of high school, if the phrase is interpreted to mean that the family could not supply the child with the necessities for school attendance. A study of two Louisiana parishes (counties) where information was obtained on the occupation of the father suggests, however, that dropouts are much less common among the upper socioeconomic groups.[6] The parents' interest in education seemed to be related to their socioeconomic status.

Table 12–1. Proportion of Children Attending College, by Income

1959 income of family	Percent
Less than $3,000	12
3,000–4,999	25
5,000–7,499	28
7,500–9,999	55
10,000 and over	65

Source: John B. Lansing, Thomas Lorimer, and Chikashi Moriguchi, *How People Pay for College,* September 1960, p. 108, Table 41.

4. Robert E. Iffert, *Retention and Withdrawal of College Students,* Bulletin 1958, No. 1.
5. *School and Early Employment Experience of Youth: A Report on Seven Communities, 1952–57,* BLS Bulletin No. 1277, August 1960.
6. Alvin L. Bertrand and Marion B. Smith, *Environmental Factors & School Attendance: A Study in Rural Louisiana.* Louisiana Agricultural Experiment Station, Bulletin No. 533, May 1960.

The study by the Bureau of Labor Statistics provides telling evidence of lower earning power and higher unemployment rates among dropouts. Undoubtedly, further evidence exists that young people who drop out of school early have only a limited choice of jobs and lower earnings potential and that, as a result, the unfavorable economic situation in which they grow up tends to be perpetuated for them and for their children.

EFFECTS ON EMPLOYMENT OF FAMILY MEMBERS

Working Mothers

Despite the large number of married women who now work—many from choice—it is still true that the smaller the husband's earnings the more likely the mother is to work. Among mothers with preschool children (under age 6) the proportion in the labor force in 1959 was more than three times as large when the husband earned less than $3,000 than when his earnings exceeded $10,000.[7]

Mothers are also much more likely to work when there is no father in the home to share family responsibilities than when he is present. In March, 1959, the proportion of mothers in the labor force varied with the age of the children and the presence of the father, as shown in Table 12–2.

The Children's Bureau has just released a report summarizing what is known and what is not known about the effects of a mother's employment on the development and adjustment of the individual child and also on family structure and functioning.[8] The evidence, though incomplete and inconclusive, suggests "that the quality of the family

Table 12–2. Proportion of Mothers in Labor Force (percent)

Age of children in years	Married, husband present	Widowed, divorced, or separated
6–17, none younger	40	66
Under 6	19	45
None under 3	25	53
Some under 3	16	40
Total under 18	28	57

Source: Jacob Schiffman, "Family Characteristics of Workers, 1959," Reprint No. 2348, from the *Monthly Labor Review* (August 1960), Table 5.

7. Jacob Schiffman, "Family Characteristics of Workers, 1959," Reprint No. 2348, from the *Monthly Labor Review* (August, 1960) Table 5.

8. Elizabeth Herzog, *Children of Working Mothers,* Children's Bureau Publication No. 382, 1960.

life influences the effects of a mother's outside employment more than her employment influences the quality of the family life."

Woefully little is known about the quality of substitute care, which can be crucial for a child's development and adjustment if the mother does work. There is no doubt, however, that total lack of care is hazardous. A national survey undertaken in 1958 by the Bureau of the Census for the Children's Bureau showed that 1 in 13 of the children under age 12 whose mothers worked full time were left to take care of themselves.[9] A study made by the Bureau of Public Assistance of families receiving aid to dependent children in late 1958 shows that 1 in 9 of the children under age 12 whose mothers worked full time were left on their own.[10] The difference suggests that lower incomes are associated with less adequate arrangements for care. Moreover, about one-third of the relatives taking care of the child, when arrangements for care were reported, were under age 18. Because of their age, it seems likely that they were older siblings who might be out of school for the purpose.

Teenagers Helping Out

There is some evidence that teenagers are brought into the labor force when the father loses his job. A special survey of unemployment in Utica, New York, shows that when men aged 45 to 54 became unemployed the number of family members (other than the wife) in the labor force increases from 4 out of every 10 to 7 out of 10.[11]

"Moonlighting" Fathers

Low earnings may cause a man with heavy family responsibilities to "moonlight"—to take on a second job—a course that surely has an effect on family life and the children's relationship to the father. A recent report by the Bureau of Labor Statistics shows that in December, 1959, for example, 6.5 percent of the married men held two or more jobs simultaneously.[12] This was about twice as high a proportion of multiple jobholders as for other men and three times as high as for women.

Information is lacking on the extent to which need or opportunity leads a worker to take a second job. It is noteworthy, however, that 40 percent of the men with more than one job reported the occupation in their primary jobs as farmer, laborer, service worker, or factory opera-

9. See Henry C. Lajewski, "Working Mothers and Their Arrangements for Care of Their Children," *Social Security Bulletin,* (August, 1959).

10. Bureau of Public Assistance, *Characteristics and Financial Circumstances of Families Receiving Aid to Dependent Children,* Bureau Report No. 42, 1960, Table 28.

11. A. J. Jaffe and J. R. Milavsky, *Unemployment, Retirement, and Pensions,* paper presented at the Fifth Congress of the International Association of Gerontology, San Francisco, August 1960.

12. Gertrude Bancroft, "Multiple Jobholders in December, 1959," *Monthly Labor Review* (October, 1960).

tive—typically low paid. On the other hand, professional and technical men led all others in the rate of dual jobholding, presumably because their experience and skill open opportunities for extra work, and some, such as teachers, strive for a level of living higher than their salaries provide.

Migratory Workers

It is impossible even to outline in this summary report the hazards for child life when a family follows the migratory stream. The evidence is clear that it is a very low earning potential that creates our migratory labor force, and that the children of migrant workers have the least opportunities for proper development. In many cases they themselves work at a very young age, and many of them do not have the advantage of even an elementary school education or minimal health protection.

EFFECTS ON FAMILY STABILITY

As already suggested, poor and overcrowded housing and pressure for earnings to supplement or substitute for those of the father may affect family life unfavorably.

There is relatively little direct evidence on the relationship between income level and divorce and separation rates. Paul Glick's analysis of Census data for 1950, however, shows the rates of separation for women (standardized for age) varying inversely with years of school completed[13] which is one of the best indicators of socioeconomic status. Divorce rates were found lowest for women with four or more years of college and highest for those with one to three years of high school (the problem dropout group), but the rate for those who had no secondary schooling was also relatively low. When divorce and separation rates for

Table 12-3. Divorce and Separation Rates per 1,000 Women (standardized for age)

Years of school completed	Combined	Divorce	Separation
Elementary:			
0-8	10.7	3.8	6.9
High school:			
1-3	9.9	4.9	5.0
4	7.0	4.0	3.0
College:			
1-3	7.1	4.7	2.4
4 or more	5.4	3.4	2.0
Total	8.7	4.1	4.6

---

13. Paul G. Glick, *American Families,* a volume in the Census Monograph Series, New York, 1957, Chap. 8, especially Table 102.

women aged 15 to 54 are combined, it seems clear that family disruption is associated with low economic status, as shown in Table 12–3.

A special study of 1950 data for Philadelphia shows that divorce as well as desertion tends to be inversely correlated with occupational levels.[14] These findings raise a question on the validity of the cliché that desertion is the poor man's divorce—one that is supported, however, by Dr. Glick's finding that divorced men had higher incomes than men separated from their families. In any case, much more research is needed on the relationship between family stability and economic status.

The impact that family breakdown has on children may be inferred more directly from the way the proportion of families with children under age 18 that include only one parent—usually the mother—varies according to the education of the family head.

In March, 1959, the 2.2 million one-parent families (including those with a widowed parent) represented 9 percent of the nation's 25 million families with children. The percentage of families that contained only one parent varied according to the education of the family head, as shown in Table 12–4.

These data suggest that when the family head has a college degree, the child has four times as good a chance of living in a home with two parents as when the head never went beyond elementary school. Some but certainly not all of the difference reflects the fact that widows are older and therefore tend to have less education.

No evidence is available on the relationship of illegitimate first conceptions and economic status. Certainly it is clear that the well-to-do have a better chance than the poor of avoiding and of concealing an illegitimate birth. Moreover, it probably would not be disputed—though factual evidence is sparse—that multiple illegitimate births generally occur to women in the lowest socioeconomic groups.

Table 12-4. Percentage of Families with One Parent, by Educational Attainment

Years of school completed	Percent
Elementary:	
0-8	11.7
High school:	
1-3	9.5
4	8.2
College:	
1-3	6.3
4 or more	2.9

Source: Bureau of the Census, Current Population Reports, Series P–20, Population Characteristics, No. 100, Table 6. Comparable data on the education of the head are not available for subfamilies.

14. William M. Kephart, "Occupational Level and Marital Disruption," American Sociological Review (August, 1955).

Death in Vietnam: Class, Poverty, and the Risks of War

13

Maurice Zeitlin, Kenneth G. Lutterman, and James W. Russell

Has every young American man had an equal chance of getting killed in the war in Vietnam, whatever his social origins? This is the central empirical question of this article. Socially relevant and politically significant, this question is also important from a sociological standpoint. There is ample evidence that the "life chances" of the poor and of workers in general suffer by comparison to those of more privileged strata in the United States. This is true not only of such diverse "opportunities" or "rewards" as formal education, access to health and medical care, decent housing, and humane working conditions, but of mortality rates themselves. In a recent analysis of more than thirty studies—many of them in the United States—of "Social Class, Life Expectancy, and Overall Mortality," Aaron Antonovsky concluded that "despite the variegated populations surveyed, the inescapable conclusion is that class influences one's chances of staying alive. Almost without exception, the evidence shows that classes differ in mortality rates. . . . What seems to be beyond question is that, whatever the index used and whatever the number of classes considered, almost always a lowest class appears with substantially higher mortality rates. Moreover, the differential between it and other classes evidently has not diminished over recent decades."[1] Most relevant here is Antonovsky's conclusion that "when men are quite helpless before the threat of death, life chances will tend to be equitably distributed." The risks of death in war would seem to fit that category all too well, placing all fighting men on a par in their relative helplessness before the threat of death in combat.

13

Reprinted with permission from Maurice Zeitlin, Kenneth G. Lutterman and James W. Russell, "Death in Vietnam: Class, Poverty, and The Risks of War." Politics and Society 3, No. 3 (Spring 1973): 313–28.

1. Antonovsky's article appeared in the *Milbank Memorial Fund Quarterly* 65:2 (April, 1967), and is reprinted in *Structured Social Inequality,* ed. Celia S. Heller (New York: Macmillan, 1969).

Thus, our leading empirical question also has a special—and poignant—theoretical relevance: Does war equalize the threat of death? To what extent does the civilian class situation of the American fighting man determine his life chances in the armed forces, and the likelihood of his death on remote battlefields? Despite its importance, the question is apparently all but unresearched. A study by Mayer and Hoult of casualties in the Korean war, did find that, in Detroit, "the lower the relative economic standing of a man's home area, or the greater the number of nonwhites in his area, the more likely it was that he would be a war casualty."[2] However, aside from their important study, based on ecological analysis, we have found no others focusing on this question. So far as we know, moreover, ours is the only study to use income and occupational data on the individual servicemen themselves, and to differentiate them by their branch of service and rank.

METHODS AND DATA

This study is based on data gathered systematically on every serviceman from the state of Wisconsin killed in the war in Vietnam through December 31, 1967. The names, rank, branch of service, date and cause of death, and nearest of kin of all but one of the 380 Vietnam dead from Wisconsin were obtained from the State of Wisconsin Department of Veterans Affairs. Data on the occupations and income of the parents of the servicemen were obtained through the cooperation of the Wisconsin Department of Taxation. We were not able to ascertain the parental income of seventy-one servicemen, or the father's occupation of seventy-eight servicemen, and they were excluded from the analysis, as is indicated in the specific tables in this article. We adjusted gross family income, with some slight modification, in accordance with the Office of Economic Opportunity's scale of poverty thresholds by size of family for 1959.[3] Thus, it should be clear that the "poor" in this study represent a minimum estimate, by official standards.

The occupational and income distributions of the casualties' parents were compared to the distributions of these attributes in a one-third random sample of the parents of male seniors in all of the public, private, and parochial schools in 1957 in Wisconsin. We believe that this matching cohort is much more adequate for the purposes of our analysis than any available from Census data. The 1957 sample provides a reasonably accurate estimate of the social characteristics of the parents of sons close to the age of draft liability, which the Census cannot provide.

---

2. Albert J. Mayer and Thomas F. Hoult, "Social Stratification and Combat Survival," *Social Forces* 34 (December, 1955):155–59.

3. U.S. Office of Economic Opportunity, *Dimensions of Poverty*, Supplement I (Washington, D.C.: U.S. Government Printing Office, June 5, 1966).

However, the high school cohort presents one important problem: 11 percent of the school population has dropped out before reaching the senior year of high school. This cohort, therefore, probably understates the proportion of poor and manual workers among all age-peers of the 1957 seniors in the high school cohort. However, since school dropouts are quite likely to be very underrepresented in the pool of inductees also, this may not be a major drawback for our proposes. Eighty percent of the "young men rejected for military service between 1958 and 1960 . . . because they could not pass the Army's examination in basic scholastic skills . . . were school dropouts."[4]

FINDINGS

What, then, do we find concerning the relative representation of young men from different social origins among the servicemen who died in Vietnam? Our evidence clearly shows that the poor are highly *over* represented: whereas only 14.9 percent of the high school cohort came from poor families, nearly twice that proportion, or 27.2 percent, were poor among the casualties of war.[5] The disproportion is especially striking among army privates, those most likely to have been draftees: there, 35.2 percent were from poor families. It should also be noted that, in contrast to the situation among privates and noncoms, the poor are *under* represented among the officers killed in Vietnam (Table 13–1).[6]

---

4. Abraham J. Tannenbaum, *Dropout or Diploma* (New York: Teacher's College Press, Columbia University, 1966), p. 32. The 1957 cohort sample was gathered under the supervision of K.G. Lutterman and William H. Sewell, for a study of the "effects of family background and ability on earnings"; we are grateful to them for making it available for this study. The parents of the high school cohort are likely to be slightly older on the average than the parents of those who died in Vietnam from 1962 through 1967. However, since the parents of both groups are in their prime from an earnings standpoint, we presume this difference to be irrelevant to our analysis. It should be noted also that because we required a precise cohort for comparison, it was preferable not to extend the study beyond the casualties through 1967.

5. This overrepresentation of the poor is not the result of any disproportionate numbers of black servicemen among the poor. We attempted to identify the "race" of servicemen from photos accompanying their obituaries. To the extent to which this provided us with reliable evidence, we found only nine blacks (2.4 percent) among the 380 dead servicemen. We have no information on the racial composition of the high school cohort. Using the less adequate Census figures, there were in Wisconsin in 1960, 1.8 percent blacks among males between the ages of five and nineteen. We obtained no information on the parental income or fathers' occupations of these black servicemen, so they are excluded in the tables in the text.

6. Given the structure of the conscription army until now, it seems plausible that sons from poor families would be less likely to acquire the education, skills, and motivations required to rise into the officers' ranks. What is known of the social composition of armed forces officers supports this supposition: Unskilled and service workers' sons were found, in the one study which has come to our attention, to constitute 5.3 percent of the officers in the army. Among Regular Army enlisted men, that is, excluding draftees, the proportion rises to 14.1 percent. From an unpublished study by Rufus Browning cited by Charles H. Coates and Roland J. Pellegrin, *Military Sociology* (University Park, Maryland: The Social Science Press, 1965), pp. 267–73.

Table 13-1. Percent "Poor" Among the Parents of Wisconsin Servicemen Killed in Vietnam through December 31, 1967, Classified by Branch of Service and Rank, Compared to the Parents of Male Seniors in the Wisconsin High School Class of 1957

| | High School Cohort | Army | | | |
		Privates	NCOs	Officers[1]	All Ranks
Poor	14.9%	35.2%	28.0%	9.5%	28.7%
Others	85.1	64.8	72.0	90.5	71.3
	100%	100%	100%	100%	100%
	(N = 4080)	(N = 71)	(N = 82)	(N = 21)	(N = 174)

| | High School Cohort | Marines, Navy, Air Force | | | | |
		Privates	NCOs	Officers	N.A.	All Ranks
Poor	14.9%	26.8%	26.6%	14.3%	—	25.2%
Others	85.1	73.2	73.4	85.7	(1)	74.8
	100%	100%	100%	100%		100%
	(N = 4080)	(N = 41)	(N = 79)	(N = 14)	(N = 1)	(N = 135)

| | High School Cohort | All Branches | | | | |
		Privates	NCOs	Officers	N.A.	All Ranks
Poor	14.9%	32.1%	27.3%	11.4%		27.2%
Others	85.1	67.9	72.7	88.6	(1)	72.8
	100%	100%	100%	100%		100%
	(N = 4080)	(N = 112)	(N = 161)	(N = 35)	(N = 1)	(N = 309)

Note: Servicemen whose parental income was not ascertained are excluded. This category includes two army warrant officers.

In his Master's thesis, James W. Russell also examined the relationships of career-status—that is, whether servicemen were professional soldiers or draftees—with servicemen's deaths in Vietnam. This is clearly a distinction relevant to battle survival. He found the same essential relationships between class, poverty, and mortality rates among non-career and career men, although these relationships, as we might expect, were strongest among non-career men. Increased experience, training, and commitment would diminish the effects of one's civilian background on one's life's chances in combat ("Who Dies in Vietnam?" University of Wisconsin, 1968).

What about workers' sons? Have they, too, borne a disproportionate share of the casualties in Vietnam? We find that they have, although by no means as great as that borne by the undifferentiated poor: in the high school cohort, 51.9 percent are workers' sons compared to 60.3 percent of the war dead. That is, workers' sons are overrepresented by roughly a sixth (1.162 times their proportionate share); and the overrepresentation is not particularly different for the sons of the skilled as contrasted to the semiskilled and unskilled. The sons of fathers in no other occupational group are overrepresented among the casualties as a whole. Once again, however, it is striking that whereas skilled workers' sons are more or less proportionately represented among dead officers, and the sons of the less skilled are *under*represented among dead officers, the sons of professionals and technicians are highly *over*represented among the officers, as are the sons of managers, officials and proprietors, although to a lesser extent (Table 13–2).

Given that poverty cuts across the occupational strata, although greatest among semi- and unskilled workers and small farm proprietors in Wisconsin,[7] the question is how poverty affects the life chances of individuals *within* the different occupational groups; were the poor more likely to be killed in Vietnam, whatever their class? The answer is clear: the poor in every occupational group are overrepresented among the war dead (Table 13–3). Looking at the casualties in all ranks combined, we observe that the poor are overrepresented by at least twice their share in all occupational groups, excepting the semi- and unskilled, perhaps because the latter form a more homogeneous stratum than the other occupational groups. The sons of poor farmers were particularly hard hit, constituting nearly two-and-one-half times their proportionate share of the casualties. It is also interesting to note that whereas the sons of poor semi- and unskilled workers, and of poor farmers, are most overrepresented among privates, the sons of skilled workers and of the middle strata are most overrepresented among noncoms—an unfortunate and unforseen consequence, perhaps, of their "social mobility" in the armed forces.

An equally important question concerning the relationship between class and poverty is whether the sons of workers, farmers, or middle strata families are proportionately represented among the casualties, *once we take poverty level into account.* For example, did even the sons of well-off (nonpoor) workers die disproportionately in the war compared to servicemen from other social origins, or does taking poverty level into account eliminate the class differences in casualty rates? The answer is that among the poor, the differences between the occupational groups diminish considerably. In fact, taken as a whole, the differences in casualty rates between the classes virtually disappear, among the poor. Their relative proportions in the cohort and among the casualties are roughly identical: workers, for example, constitute 47.1 percent of the cohort poor and 48.8 percent of the servicemen who were from poor families. However, among those who were *not* poor, the sons of farm owners, and [sons] from middle strata families, are quite *under*represented among the well-off servicemen killed in Vietnam, while even well-off workers' sons are *over*represented. This is true of both skill-groups among the workers, as well as of the workers as a whole: 49.9 percent of the cohort nonpoor were from workers' families contrasted to 64.6 percent among the casualties who were not poor, or roughly one and one-third times their proportionate share (Table 13–4). That even

---

7. The following is the distribution of poverty in the 1957 male cohort among the specific occupational groups constituting the "middle strata": 5.7 percent of the professionals and technicians; 11.7 percent of the managers, proprietors, and officials; and 11.1 percent of the clerical and sales group fell below the poverty line.

Table 13-2. Percentage Distribution of Occupations of Fathers of Wisconsin Servicemen Killed in Vietnam through December 31, 1967, Classified by Rank and Branch of Service, Compared to the Occupations of Fathers of Male Seniors in the Wisconsin High School Class of 1957[1]

| Occupational Groups | High School Cohort[2] | Army | | | |
		Privates	NCOs	Officers	All Ranks
Professional, Technical, and Kindred	7.5%	1.4%	2.5%	23.8%	4.6%
Managers, Officials, and Proprietors (non-farm)	11.9	9.7	12.5	23.8	12.7
Clerical, Sales, and Kindred	10.8	6.9	6.3	14.3	7.5
Skilled Workers	14.6	15.3	22.5	14.3	18.5
Semi-Skilled and Unskilled Workers	37.3	47.2	40.0	19.0	40.5
Farm Owners	17.8	19.4	16.3	4.8	16.2
	100% (N = 4846)	100% (N = 72)	100% (N = 80)	100% (N = 21)	100% (N = 173)

| Occupational Groups | High School Cohort[2] | Marines, Navy, Air Force | | | | |
		Privates	NCOs	Officers	N.A.	All Ranks
Professional, Technical, and Kindred	7.5%	10.0%	5.3%	23.1%		8.5%
Managers, Officials, and Proprietors (non-farm)	11.9	10.0	˙6.7	15.4	(1)	9.3
Clerical, Sales, and Kindred	10.8	—	13.3	7.7		8.5
Skilled Workers	14.6	20.0	12.0	15.4		14.7
Semi-Skilled and Unskilled Workers	37.3	42.5	53.3	30.8		47.3
Farm Owners	17.8	17.5	9.3	7.7		11.6
	100% (N = 4846)	100% (N = 40)	100% (N = 75)	100% (N = 13)	— (N = 1)	100% (N = 129)

1. Excluding those whose father's occupation was not ascertained.
2. Technically, the distribution in the cohort is of the occupations of heads of households, though the overwhelming majority were fathers.

Table 13-2 (Continued)

Occupational Groups	High School Cohort	All Branches				
		Privates	NCOs	Officers	N.A.	All Ranks
Professional, Technical, etc.	7.5%	4.5%	3.9%	23.5%		6.3%
Managers, Officials, and Proprietors (non-farm)	11.9	9.8	9.7	20.6	(1)	11.3
Clerical, Sales, etc.	10.8	4.5	9.7	11.8		7.9
Skilled Workers	14.6	17.0	17.4	14.7		16.9
Semi-Skilled and Unskilled Workers	37.3	45.5	46.5	23.5		43.4
Farm Owners	17.8	18.8	12.9	5.9		14.2
	100% (N = 4846)	100% (N = 112)	100% (N = 155)	100% (N = 34)	(N = 1)	100% (N = 302)

1. Excluding those whose father's occupation was not ascertained.
2. Technically, the distribution in the cohort is of the occupations of heads of households, though the overwhelming majority were fathers.

workers who were *not* poor constitute a disproportionate share of the casualties in Vietnam underscores the pervasive and profound effect of the class structure on the individual's life chances; it is further evidence that the workers' location in the class structure of the United States, be their income sufficient to keep them above the poverty level or not, imposes disproportionate and cumulative disadvantages on them which severely restrict their life chances, indeed, their very survival, compared to individuals in other and more privileged classes.

INTERPRETATION

The question is, what processes lead to the disproportionate burden of the war's casualties being borne by the poor and by workers, even when they are not poor? The most plausible explanation is that they are overrepresented among the dead because they are overrepresented in the pool of draftees in the first place. That this country's system of military recruitment is, indeed, a "selective service" has been widely accepted; Senator Edward Kennedy, for example, has charged that the draft, because it virtually exempted college students, bore "down most heavily on the lower income brackets." Wisconsin's Republican Congressman Alvin O'Konski concluded, long before this study was completed in his state: "They say the poor are always with you . . . If the draft goes on as it has, they may not be with us much longer."[8] Stewart

8. Quoted in Jacquin Sanders, *The Draft and the Vietnam War* (New York: Walker and Co., 1966), p. 13, which was originally a *Newsweek* cover story on the draft; and in Bruce K. Chapman, *The Wrong Man in Uniform* (New York: Trident Press, 1967), p. 86.

Table 13-3. Percent "Poor," by Father's Occupation, Among Wisconsin Servicemen Killed in Vietnam through December 31, 1967, Classified by Rank, Compared to the Male Seniors in the Wisconsin High School Class of 1957[1]

	High School Cohort (N)	All Branches: Privates (N)	All Branches: NCOs (N)	All Branches: Officers (N)	All Branches: All Ranks (N)
Workers	14.2%	24.6%	21.6%	7.7%	21.8%
Skilled	7.6% (675)	11.1% (18)	22.2% (27)	0 (5)	16.0% (50)
Semi-Skilled and Unskilled	17.5 (1341)	29.4 (51)	21.4 (70)	12.5 (8)	24.0 (129)
Farm Owners	23.6 (839)	65.0 (20)	50.0 (20)	(1/2)	57.1 (42)
Middle Strata[2]	10.1 (1225)	20.0 (20)	30.6 (36)	10.5 (19)	22.4 (76)[3]
Total	14.9% (4080)	31.2% (109)	27.5% (153)	11.8% (34)	26.9% (297)

[1]Excluding those whose parental income and father's occupation were not ascertained.

[2]Professionals, technicians, etc.; managers, officials, proprietors; clerical, sales, etc. The number of poor in each of these occupational groups is too small to calculate percentages for meaningful comparisons.

Alsop, not usually given to radical pronouncements, has stated bluntly that the Selective Service System "is quite clearly based on class discrimination."[9] Others have argued, however, that because the mental, "moral," and physical disqualification rates tend to disproportionately exempt poor Americans from military service, they are probably *not* overrepresented in the armed forces. In short, "the 'disadvantaged' do have an advantage in escaping the draft."[10]

A systematic ecological analysis of differential induction rates in Wisconsin, by Davis and Dolbeare, found that "the income related bias in present deferment policies is sufficiently great to overcome the countervailing effects of higher proportions of unfitness in the lower income areas and to establish an income-based pattern of military service. . . .

9. "The American Class System," *Newsweek* (29 June 1970): 88. Alsop reports also that "Yale, Harvard, and Princeton, to cite three obvious examples, together have graduated precisely two-repeat, two—young men, in the whole course of the war, who were drafted and killed in action in Vietnam." He adds, however, that they had, respectively, 34, 13, and 13 young men who volunteered and were killed in Vietnam.

10. Chapman, *Wrong Man in Uniform,* pp. 81–86.

Table 13-4. Percentage Distribution of Occupations of Fathers of Wisconsin Servicemen Killed in Vietnam through December 31, 1967, All Branches, Compared to the Occupations of Fathers of Male Seniors in the Wisconsin High School Class of 1957, Classified by Poverty Level[1]

	High School Cohort				Servicemen			
		Poor	Others			Poor	Others	
Professional, Technical, etc.		2.6%	7.6%			6.3%	6.5%	
Managers, Officals, Proprietors (non-farm)	20.4%	10.7	14.2	31.7%	21.4%	3.8	13.8	27.2%
Clerical, Sales, etc.		7.1	9.9			11.3	6.9	
All Middle Shata	20.4		31.7					
Skilled Workers		8.4	18.0			10.0	19.4	
	47.1%			49.9%	48.8%			64.6%
Semi-Skilled and Unskilled Workers		38.7	31.9			38.8	45.2	
Farm Owners		32.6	18.5			30.0	8.3	
		100%	100%			100%	100%	
		(N=608)	(N=3472)			(N=80)	(N=217)	

The induction rate is higher in the low income areas and lower in the high income areas. This suggests," Davis and Dolbeare also point out, "that the higher service experience of registrants in low income areas is not due to enlistments, but quite the opposite, to inductions."[11] Thus, since the sons of the poor and of manual workers are generally far less likely to go to college, or to graduate, "college deferments" essentially defer the government from drafting those from the more privileged strata of American society.

In addition, more subtle processes may be involved than the mere enforcement of existing regulations. Draft board members are empowered to some extent to decide on deferments, to decide "who serves when not all serve." Most of them are from the middle strata (and white). Among local board members in the metropolitan areas of the United States, only 6.6 percent were from manual occupations during the period encompassed by this study; outside of metropolitan areas, the figure was 7.3 percent. In the state of Wisconsin, the figure was 8.3 percent.[12] We have little direct evidence regarding how the social com-

---

11. James W. Davis and Kenneth M. Dolbeare, *Little Groups of Neighbors: The Selective Service System* (Chicago: Markham Publishing Co., 1968), pp. 145–46.

12. National Advisory Commission on Selective Service, *In Pursuit of Equity: Who Serves When Not All Serve?* (Washington, D.C.: Government Printing Office, 1967), pp. 75 and 79.

position of the draft boards affects the individual's chances of being drafted. One study of local boards in an urban area by a participant observer found that board members tended to rely on their evaluations of the registrant's personal appearance or even his choice of words in a letter when deciding on hardship or occupational deferments—the types of deferments most likely to be required, and the only available, for the sons of workers and the poor. Board members' judgments reportedly were based on such values as "thrift, education, morality, nativism, etc."[13]

In a very fundamental way, then, the operation of the Selective Service System, whatever its peculiarities, is exemplary of certain general processes involved in the relationship between the "state" and the class structure. The Selective Service System was established to operate in such a way, *whatever the conscious motivations involved,* as to protect the privileged strata from the ravages of wars fought in their interests. By giving legal and institutional support to the general social processes which redound to the cumulative disadvantage of the workers and poor in our political economy, the state (in this case the Selective Service System), as well as the personnel who compose its administrative apparatus, adversely affects the interests of the poor and of the workers while protecting and advancing the interests of the privileged and dominant classes.

The very same social processes may be recapitulated in the "universalistic" armed forces themselves. Even when they end up in uniform, those from professional, technical, or other middle strata homes may be less likely to see combat than workers' or poor families' sons. Subtly or explicitly, "well-qualified and intelligent young men" may be encouraged to take administrative or noncombat posts—which would not, in the first place, seem to require much encouragement. In general, the MOS or job assignment received by individual servicemen may be influenced by their social origins and, perhaps, particularly by the formal education and skills brought with them (verbal and mechanical) from civilian life. Radar operatives or artillerymen, for instance, are probably less likely to have direct contact with the "enemy" or enemy action that subjects them to concentrated small arms fire than riflemen or infantrymen. Similarly, men in supply service battalions or administrative MOS classifications are probably less subject to risk from enemy action.

To some extent, the nature of a war against a popularly based guerrilla movement, as in Vietnam, may diminish such differential risks. In wars with relatively clear rear and forward positions, where the front is identifiable, and where the terrain is relatively open, the distinction

---

13. A study for an unpublished dissertation by Gary Wamsley, cited in *Little Groups of Neighbors,* pp. 81–82.

between "safe" and "hazardous" assignments is likely to be greater than in an expeditionary war against a national liberation movement. Here, the "enemy" is everywhere; fixed positions are few; women and children may be "enemy troops"; and "fighters by night and workers by day" and hidden snipers abound in the fight "against U.S. and allied forces in Vietnam."[14] When the NLF is capable of penetrating even the American Embassy in Saigon, a "safe" MOS will do little to protect its possessor.

The question then is whether or not, aside from the differential effects of the draft, there may be class effects on the rates of death in combat. Once in the armed forces, do fighting men from certain classes still continue to have greater life chances than others? Or here at last do all men, whatever their social origins, find themselves more or less equally "helpless before the threat of death," thus evening out their relative life chances? The Defense Department distinguishes in its casualty lists between "deaths resulting from hostile action" and "deaths resulting from other causes," such as the same sort of accidents or diseases that might kill in civilian life. If one's social origins affect one's chances of death in combat, we should find noticeable differences between the proportions of poor and nonpoor, and of workers and nonworkers, killed in "hostile action" in Vietnam. For this type of internal analysis, no external cohort is necessary or relevant.

What we find is that there is a very slight but noticeably systematic pattern of differences between the combat-death rates of the poor and the nonpoor (Table 13–5). In all ranks combined, in the army and other services, servicemen from poor families were somewhat more likely to be killed in hostile action than those who were not poor. This is true of privates *and* noncoms in the army, although this does not hold true of privates in the other services. The difference in combat death rates between the poor and the nonpoor is greatest among the noncoms in both the army and in the other services. Indeed, among the privates of all branches combined, the difference is negligible. We cannot test the following plausible explanation, but it is worth suggesting that this may result from the greater homogeneity of MOS assignments among privates than among noncoms, as well as the greater equality of the privates' helplessness before the threat of death.

When we look at the relationship between classes, poverty, and the rate of death in hostile action, one relatively clear pattern emerges (despite the paucity of cases in some categories): Among the sons of workers, farmers, and the middle strata, combining all ranks and branches of the armed forces, more sons of the poor died in hostile

14. Paraphrasis and quotes from Col. Robert B. Riggs, "Made in USA," *Army,* (January, 1968):24–31, reprinted in Maurice Zeitlin, ed., *American Society, Inc.* (Chicago: Markham Publishing Co., 1970).

Table 13-5. Percent Killed in "Hostile Action" Among "Poor" and Other Wisconsin Servicemen Killed in Vietnam Through December 31, 1967, Classified by Rank and Branch of Service[1]

| | Army | | | |
	Privates (N)	NCOs (N)	Officers (N)	All Ranks (N)
Poor	92% (25)	87% (23)	(1/2)	88% (50)
Others	89 (46)	78 (59)	74 (19)	81 (124)

| | Marines, Navy, Air Force | | | |
	Privates (N)	NCOs (N)	Officers (N)	All Ranks (N)
Poor	75% (11)	91% (21)	(2/2)	86% (34)
Others	80 (30)	79 (58)	75 (12)	78 (101)[2]

| | All Branches | | | |
	Privates (N)	NCOs (N)	Officers (N)	All Ranks (N)
Poor	87% (36)	89% (44)	(3/4)	87% (84)
Others	85 (76)	79 (117)	74 (31)	80 (225)[2]

[1] Excluding those whose parental income was not ascertained.
[2] Including one serviceman killed in hostile action, whose rank was not ascertained.

Table 13-6. Percent Killed in "Hostile Action" Among Poor and Other Wisconsin Servicemen Killed in Vietnam through December 31, 1967, Classified by Rank, and by Class[1]

| | All Branches | | | |
	Privates (N)	N.C.O.s (N)	Officers (N)	All Ranks (N)
Workers[3]				
Poor	88% (17)	95% (21)	(1/1)	92% (39)
Others	85 (52)	79 (76)	75 (12)	81 (140)
Farm Owners				
Poor	92 (13)	80 (10)	(0/1)	83 (24)
Others	(6/7)	70 (10)	(1/1)	78 (18)
Middle Strata				
Poor	(4/4)	82 (11)	(2/2)	88 (17)
Others	87 (16)	84 (25)	59 (17)	78 (59)[2]
	Privates (N)	N.C.O.s (N)	Officers (N)	All Ranks (N)
Poor Semi- and Un- skilled	93% (15)	93% (15)	(1/1)	93% (31)
Other Semi- and Un- skilled	83 (36)	82 (55)	(5/7)	82 (98)

[1] Excluding those whose parental income and father's occupation were not ascertained.
[2] One manager is included whose rank was not ascertained.
[3] We have sufficient numbers of sons of semi- and unskilled workers to view the relationship in this group alone.

action than their more privileged fellow fighting men. The differences between the classes, on the same poverty level, are not systematic, although, again, one fact stands out: Of all groups, the highest proportion of combat deaths is among poor workers' sons (Table 13–6).

We believe, therefore, that the cumulative evidence presented here clearly supports this conclusion: The sons of the poor and of the workers have borne by far the greatest burden of the war in Vietnam, in the measured but immeasurable precision of death.[15]

---

15. We should point out here that this distinction between deaths in hostile action and from other causes does not affect the findings presented in Tables 13–1 to 13–4. When the same relationships are examined among only those who were killed in hostile action, the relationships do not differ in any essential way.

Poverty Theories and Income Maintenance: Validity and Policy Relevance

14

David Elesh

This paper challenges the substantive validity and policy relevance of theories of poverty, particularly as they apply to proposals for income maintenance programs. Two basic types of theories are defined and evidence for them assessed. As the theories are almost entirely based upon case studies, the assessment chiefly utilizes methodologically more rigorous research. The policy relevance of the theories is examined in terms of poverty policy in general and income maintenance programs in particular, and an alternative perspective to the poverty theories built upon the findings presented earlier is explored.

THE THEORIES OF POVERTY

Theories of poverty can be broadly classified into two types: cultural and structural. Cultural theories find the explanation for poverty in the traits of the poor themselves. These theories assert it is the valuational, attitudinal, and behavioral patterns of the poor which prevent them from being socially mobile. In contrast, structural theories explain poverty in terms of the conditions under which the poor live: unemployment, underemployment, poor education, and poor health. The distinctive traits of the poor central to the explanation of the cultural theorists are, for the structural theorists, responses or adaptations to the hostility of the structural conditions the poor face. Structural theorists accept the cultural theorists' characterization of the poor; they merely place another interpretation on it.[1]

Reprinted from *Social Science Quarterly*, 54:2 (Sept. 1973): "Poverty Theories and Income Maintenance: Validity and Policy Relevance," by David Elesh, pp. 359–71. The research reported here was supported by funds granted to the Institute for Research on Poverty at the University of Wisconsin by the Office of Economic Opportunity pursuant to the provisions of the Economic Opportunity Act of 1964. The author is grateful to James D. Wright for editorial assistance. The conclusions, however, are the sole responsibility of the author.
1. This classification of poverty theories is quite similar to Valentine's characterization of poverty theories as describing the poor as either in a "self-perpetuating subsociety with a defective, unhealthy subculture" or an "externally oppressed subsociety with an imposed, exploited subculture." However, the present distinction between the cultural and structural models differs from that between Valentine's models in three principal ways: (1) the poverty syndrome (defined below) is here taken to grow out of persistent structural conditions while Valentine is vague about its origins; (2) the structural theory, as pre-

Table 14-1 shows the extent of agreement between the two theories in terms of the following ten traits, which form a kind of poverty syndrome frequently mentioned in the literature.[2] Although this list of traits was developed from the extensive discussion of Lewis, the evidence overlap in Table 14-1 clearly reveals the generality of his list.[3]

1. A community with little social organization beyond the extended family
2. A mother-centered family organization
3. Little class consciousness
4. General feelings of helplessness, fatalism, dependency, and inferiority
5. A strong present-time orientation, including a desire for excitement
6. Little historical knowledge
7. An alienation from political institutions
8. An early initiation into sexual activities
9. An emphasis on masculinity
10. Middle-class aspirations and values which are not translated into behavior

Both types of theorists also believe that successive generations of the same family remain poor. For the cultural theorists, the poverty syndrome explains the poverty cycles. Thus, the matrifocal family isolated from the larger society, imbued with feelings of inferiority, dependence, alienation, present-time orientation, etc., is thought by cultural theorists to socialize its young to the same poverty syndrome. The problem therefore lies within the poor family. Alternatively, the structural theorists explain the poverty cycle in terms of the persistence of inimical structural conditions. Liebow stated the argument well:

> No doubt, each generation does provide role models for each succeeding one. Of much greater importance for the possibilities of change, however, is the fact that many similarities between the lower class Negro father and son (or mother and daughter) do not result from "cultural transmission" but from

---

sented here, frequently interprets the various facets of the poverty syndrome as being at least rational responses to the hostility of structural conditions while Valentine's comparable model (second) interprets these facets as uniformly pathological; (3) the practical policy implications of the theories described below are shown to be less different than in Valentine's characterization. Valentine also offers a third model, a combination of the previous two, as a basis for future research. While an improvement, this model assumes that the poor have distinctive values by virtue of their poverty, an assumption for which, as Valentine himself notes, there is no real evidence. For this reason and because there is no literature testing the third model, it is irrelevant to the present discussion. See Charles A. Valentine's important book, *Culture and Poverty* (Chicago: University of Chicago Press, 1968), esp. Chapter 6.

2. The term, "poverty syndrome," is used here because of its lack of association with either the cultural or structural perspectives. While cultural theorists view these traits as definitional of the culture of poverty, others have expressed doubt as to whether the traits comprise a substantively meaningful culture.

3. Oscar Lewis, "The Culture of Poverty," *Scientific American* 215 (October, 1966): 19–25; *La Vida* (New York: Random House, 1966).

Table 14-1. The Poverty Syndrome and Poverty Researchers

Attributes	Cultural Theorists			Structural Theorists		
	Lewis	Miller	Reissman et al.	Rainwater	Clark	Liebow
1. Little social organization	X		X	X	X	X
2. Mother-centered family	X		X	X	X	X
3. Little class consciousness	X					
4. Feelings of fatalism, etc.	X	X	X	X	X	X
5. Present-time orientation	X	X	X	X	X	X
6. Little historical knowledge	X					
7. Alienation from politics	X		X		X	X
8. Early sex	X	X	X	X	X	X
9. Masculinity	X	X	X	X	X	X
10. Middle-class aspirations	X		X	X	X	X

Sources: Oscar Lewis, La Vida (New York: Random House, 1966); Walter Miller, "Lower Class Culture as a Generating Milieu of Gang Delinquency," Journal of Social Issues 14(March, 1958); Frank Reissman, et al., "Low Income Behavior and Cognitive Style," in Frank Reissman, et al., eds. Mental Health of the Poor (New York: Free Press, 1964); Lee Rainwater, "Crucible of Identity: The Negro Lower-Class Family," in Talcott Parsons and Kenneth B. Clark, eds., The Negro American (Boston: Beacon Press, 1966); Kenneth Clark, Dark Ghetto (New York: Harper & Row, 1965); Elliot Liebow, Tally's Corner (Boston: Little, Brown, 1967).

the fact that the son goes out and independently experiences the same failures, in the same areas, and for much the same reasons, as his father. What appears as a dynamic, self-sustaining cultural process is, in part at least, a relatively simple piece of social machinery which turns out, in rather mechanical fashion, independently produced look-alikes. *The problem is how to change the conditions which, by guaranteeing failure, cause the son to be made in the image of the father.* [4]

The frame of reference for both theories extends across national, cultural, ethnic, racial, and other boundaries, but both types of theorists appear to agree that the poverty syndrome is an outgrowth of capitalist societies such as the United States and would not appear in socialist countries.[5] Thus there appears to be a means for determining whether a society would display the poverty syndrome.

Within a society, however, the situation is not so clear. Neither cultural nor structural theories contains any mechanisms capable of explaining those poor who do not fit the poverty syndrome, although some theorists recognize that not all poor display it. Lewis, for example, has estimated that only 20 percent of the American poor exhibit the poverty syndrome. His explanation for this low percentage is that it is simply "because of the advanced technology, the high level of literacy, the development of mass media, and the relatively high aspiration level of all sectors of the population. . . ."[6]

---

4. Elliot Liebow, Tally's Corner (Boston: Little, Brown, 1967), p. 233, emphasis added.
5. Oscar Lewis, "The Culture of Poverty," in Daniel P. Moynihan, ed., On Understanding Poverty (New York: Basic Books, 1969), pp. 187–200; and Liebow, Tally's Corner, pp. 224–31.
6. Lewis, "The Culture of Poverty" (1969), p. 196.

Such an explanation is inadequate on two counts. First, the factors listed are not further elucidated. Second, with one exception, they nowhere appear as part of his theory. And the one exception, the high level of aspiration, is stated to be unimportant in the theory: "People with a culture of poverty are aware of middle-class values; they talk about them and even claim some of them as their own, but on the whole they do not live by them."[7] The implication of this statement is clear: it is not aspirations but the discrepancy between aspirations and behavior which is important. Consequently, Lewis's explanation is at best ad hoc; the reader cannot relate the ostensible reasons for the low prevalence of the poverty syndrome to its purported causes. The structural theorists fare no better. Although they assert that inimical structural conditions cause the poverty syndrome, they are silent as to why these conditions should not affect everyone in poverty equally.

THE VALIDITY OF THE POVERTY THEORIES

Since the evidence for the poverty syndrome largely rests upon case studies, it is appropriate to ask the extent to which it is supported by more methodologically rigorous research. Unfortunately, there are few studies designed to confirm the syndrome; therefore it is necessary to draw data from a variety of sources. Correlatively, there is the question of whether the researchers' conclusions are consistent with their own reported findings.

More rigorous evidence contradicting either the ostensible facts of the poverty syndrome or its imputed effects can be found for five of the ten basic elements: the matrifocal family, the lack of social organization beyond the extended family, the feelings of dependency, fatalism, etc., the lack of class consciousness, and the inability to delay gratification. The most widely discussed element is the matrifocal family structure, which, contrary to the impression given by many poverty theorists, is not the prevalent family form among the poor—at least in the United States: 66 percent of poor families are male-headed.[8] According to the cultural theorists, female-headed families cannot provide the masculine role image necessary for successful socialization; thus male children from these families will have lower intelligence scores, less education, higher unemployment rates, higher crime rates, and a variety of other poverty-maintaining liabilities. Some support for this view is found in the Duncans' analysis of a special Current Population Survey conducted by the U.S. Census, which revealed that family instability reduced the son's status attainment by five points on the Duncan SES Index when

---

7. Ibid., p. 190.

8. U.S. Bureau of the Census, *Current Population Reports,* Series P-60, No. 68; *Poverty in the United States: 1959 to 1968* (Washington, D.C.: U.S. Government Printing Office, 1969). Although matrifocality is a broader concept than female-headed families, the terms are usually used interchangeably in the poverty literature and thus are here.

race and education were controlled.[9] However, the effect of being black was almost four times that of family instability, suggesting a far less substantial role for family instability than indicated by the theories. Moreover, if a female head was regularly employed, the absence of a male head had no effect on her children's occupational success. And contrary to the poverty cycle concept, male children from female-headed families were *more* likely to be in an intact marriage than those raised in male-headed households. While these findings require further research, it is clear that the matrifocal family does not have large or irreparable effects upon occupational success. Indeed, if the female head works regularly, it may have no effect.

More generally, there is little evidence for a generational transmission of poverty. Blau and Duncan found that the correlation between father's and son's occupational status scores is .4 in the United States.[10] Similarly, only 10.5 percent of the sons of "service workers," 7.1 percent of the sons of "manufacturing laborers," and 9.9 percent of the sons of "other nonfarm laborers" are in the same occupations as their fathers.[11] More generally, only 21.4 percent of the sons of "service workers," 22.3 percent of the sons of "manufacturing laborers," and 16.5 percent of "other nonfarm laborers" were in *any* of the three categories. Father's occupation is also weakly related to son's income: the correlation is less than .2.

Since the poverty syndrome is ostensibly universally characteristic of the poor, subgroup variations directly challenge its validity. The claim that the poor have little social organization is one example. In an analysis of survey data from Detroit, Chicago, and a Washington, D.C. suburb, Orum found that 63 percent of the low-status group reported at least one group affiliation in response to the question, "How many organizations such as church and school groups, labor unions, or social, civic, and fraternal clubs do you belong to?"[12] Given such a high participation rate, it is difficult to argue that there is little social organization among the poor. Moreover, Negroes, who because of the cumulative nature of their status disadvantages might be expected to have fewer affiliations than whites, had more.[13] More recently, Olsen found that in a survey of Indianapolis, low SES blacks were more active than low SES whites on 15 different dimensions of political and social activity. In other words, in precisely the group in which one would expect to find

9. Beverly Duncan and O. D. Duncan, "Family Stability and Occupational Success," *Social Problems,* 16 (Winter, 1969): pp. 273–85.

10. Peter M. Blau and O. D. Duncan, *The American Occupational Structure* (New York: John Wiley and Sons, 1967).

11. Ibid., p. 28.

12. Anthony M. Orum, "A Reappraisal of the Social and Political Participation of Negroes," *American Journal of Sociology* 72 (July, 1966), 32–46.

13. Among those with an eighth-grade education or less, 45 percent of the blacks had an affiliation as against 30 percent of the whites.

the least amount of social organization given their cumulative disadvantages, one finds, comparatively speaking, the most.[14]

The same point can be made about the feelings of fatalism, dependency, and inferiority, which ostensibly describe all poor people. Using data from a survey designed to discover the characteristics of male heads of poor families which received and did not receive AFDC-UP funds in California, Irelan, Moles, and O'Shea sought to determine whether subgroups of the poor differed in the above feelings and found substantial variation by ethnicity.[15] In general, Spanish-speakers tended to be the most dependent and fatalistic, followed by blacks and whites. The authors related their results directly to Lewis's concept of the culture of poverty, concluding, "these findings suggest that a systematic consideration of ethnic groups other than the Spanish-speaking might have led Lewis to different conclusions about the existence, scope, and intensity of the culture of poverty."[16]

Similarly, subgroup variations challenge the supposed absence of class consciousness among the poor. Leggett surveyed class consciousness in Detroit in a sample whose incomes were classified as being less than or greater than $5,000 and found the low income group to have more consciousness.[17] Moreover, the group with the greatest proportion of families under $5,000, blacks, had the most consciousness, suggesting that consciousness increases as income decreases. Once again, the poverty theorists have no explanation for the subgroup variations.

Another feature of the poverty syndrome—the strong present-time orientation—is also unsupported. After reviewing the existing experimental and survey data, Miller, et al., found: (1) that the incidence of the present-time orientation among the poor is unknown; and (2) that a number of studies show no status differences in time orientation. They conclude that "the verdict on the DGP [present-time orientation] is 'not proved.' "[18]

Where the poverty syndrome is not challenged by external evidence, it is often contradicted by internal. For example, Lewis's assertions that the poor are politically alienated and lack historical knowledge neglect his own reports of their taking political leadership,[19] lobbying local

---

14. Marvin E. Olsen, "Social and Political Participation of Blacks," *American Sociological Review* 35 (Aug., 1970): 682–97.

15. Lola M. Irelan, Oliver C. Moles, and Robert M. O'Shea, "Ethnicity, Poverty, and Selected Attitudes: A Test of the 'Culture of Poverty' Hypothesis," *Social Forces* 47 (June, 1969): 405–13.

16. Irelan, et al., "Ethnicity, Poverty, and Selected Attitudes," p. 413. On the measure of fatalism, no significant difference between ethnic groups was found for the families on AFDC-UP.

17. John C. Leggett, *Class, Race, and Labor* (New York: Oxford University Press, 1968), pp. 97–118.

18. S. M. Miller et al., "Poverty and Self-Indulgence: A Critique of the Non-Deferred Gratification Pattern," in L. A. Ferman et al., eds., *Poverty In America* (Ann Arbor: University of Michigan Press, 1968), p. 432.

19. Oscar Lewis, *Five Families* (New York: Basic Books, 1959).

politicians, and being aware of the subtleties of politics in several Latin American countries.[20] Similarly, Gans reports on the West Enders' political passivity, and then later acknowledges that local politicians in the West End, as elsewhere, must provide political favors and vote correctly on issues of local concern.[21] From such contradictory evidence it is difficult to ascertain a syndrome of poverty—much less an explanation.

Omitted in these "explanations" of poverty is any account of the poor who do not display the poverty syndrome. To some extent this is because the case-study researcher, constrained to show that his data are generalizable, usually creates a stereotype from which explanation proceeds. Initial caveats as to the limitations of the data are quickly forgotten; discussion becomes centered on the stereotype, with the data playing only a subsidiary role. We hear not of *some* young lower-class Negroes but of "*the* young lower-class Negro."[22] Usually there is little evidence that we are speaking of probabilistic social processes; in their place we have the determinism of stereotypical descriptions.

On balance, the evidence for the poverty syndrome is weak. It may characterize certain subgroups of the poor, but the numbers involved are unknown. The cultural theory is particularly suspect, since these symptoms supposedly are *causes* of poverty. The structural theory also is challenged, though not so directly. While the poverty syndrome is not the cause of poverty, it is believed to be its effect. Consequently a failure to find it indicates a fundamental defect in the cause-effect linkage.

However, this is not to say that *elements* of the poverty syndrome may not for particular groups and particular times operate as the two types of poverty theorists suggest. It is the attempt to generalize from such particulars that is suspect. No one would deny that both culture and structure play some role in poverty, but it can be questioned as to whether the roles currently assigned to them are accurate. Most importantly, the theories do not appear able to explain the large variations in the presumed characteristics among the poor.

THE POVERTY THEORIES AND INCOME MAINTENANCE POLICY

Unfortunately, despite their deficiencies, these theories continue to serve as the rationale for policy efforts.[23] It is therefore worthwhile to examine their policy implications. In particular, their relation to programs of income maintenance will be examined. Two points are made:

20. Lewis, *La Vida,* pp. 82–85.

21. Herbert Gans, *The Urban Villagers* (New York: Free Press, 1962), pp. 173–76.

22. Lee Rainwater, "Crucible of Identity: The Negro Lower-Class Family," in Talcott Parsons and Kenneth B. Clark, eds., *The Negro American* (Boston: Beacon Press, 1966), p. 239.

23. Peter Marris and Martin Rein, *Dilemmas of Social Reform* (New York: Atherton Press, 1967); and Daniel P. Moynihan, *Maximum Feasible Misunderstanding* (New York: Free Press, 1969).

First, in practice, the policy implications of the two theories only marginally differ. Second, despite their generality and seeming universal applicability to poverty policy, the theories have little to say about income maintenance programs.

At first glance, the two theories would appear to offer dramatically different solutions for poverty. The cultural theorists suggest a direct attack on the values and behaviors that support the poverty cycle. Unless such a direct attack is undertaken, the syndrome will presumably continue. Thus, a broad range of social services designed to resocialize the poor to valuational and behavioral patterns useful in social mobility must be provided. Alternatively, the structural theorists assume that structural change of the employment, education, health, and housing markets is required. Because the poverty syndrome consists of reactions to structural conditions, its elimination necessitates the elimination of its causes.

In practice, however, the distinction usually makes little difference. Both theories minimize the possible effectiveness of remedial efforts for the adult poor because both believe that prior socialization insulates them from all such programs. While it is parental socialization in one case and environmental socialization in the other, they are nonetheless believed to be equally effective. Liebow noted the response of men structurally socialized to the existence of real opportunity:

> Each man comes to the job with a long job history characterized by his not being able to support himself and his family. Each man carries this knowledge, born of his experience, with him. He comes to the job flat and stale, wearied by the sameness of it all, convinced of his own incompetence, terrified of responsibility—of being tested still again and found wanting. . . . Convinced of their own inadequacies, not only do they not seek out those few better-paying jobs which test their resources, but they actively avoid them, gravitating in a mass to the menial, routine jobs which offer no challenge—and therefore pose no threat—to the already diminished images they have of themselves.[24]

Lewis has made the same point in cautioning that the elimination of the poverty syndrome will take more than a single generation.[25] It follows that for both types of theorists those most likely to benefit from poverty programs are the very young and succeeding generations. It follows also that if poverty programs designed to change the poor's labor, education, health and housing markets are to have any effect on adults, resocialization must be attempted. Conversely, for resocialization programs to be meaningful, structural changes must be undertaken. Thus, we find Lewis calling structural changes "absolutely essential and of the highest priority"[26] and Liebow, alternatively, praising the Office

24. Liebow, *Tally's Corner,* pp. 53–54.
25. Lewis, "The Culture of Poverty" (1969), p. 199.
26. Ibid., p. 199.

of Economic Opportunity's more modest efforts to change values.[27] The policy differences, then, between the two theories is more one of emphasis, or possibly of priorities, than of concrete action programs.

What does this mean in terms of income maintenance programs? Income maintenance programs are clearly not indicated by cultural theory since they do not involve direct attempts to change the poverty syndrome. They merely alter the economic condition of the poor through income supplements. Consequently, since the cultural theorists argue that the poverty syndrome must be directly assaulted if there is to be any hope of change for the currently adult (and perhaps even younger) generations, they would predict no short-term gains. It follows that to the extent to which the poverty syndrome can be identified and is affected by income maintenance in the short run, the cultural theory is undermined.

The meaning of income maintenance for the structural theory is not so clear. For some types of programs income maintenance involves structural change; for others it does not. It depends upon the particular market with which one is concerned and whether the income supplement is cash or in kind (e.g., job guarantees). To illustrate, it is useful to consider the effects of both cash and in-kind transfers on the employment, education, and health-service markets.

Employment

1. Cash Transfers. Most commentators have considered unemployment and underemployment as a fundamental cause of the poverty syndrome. Thus, to have impact on the syndrome, a cash-transfer program must improve the labor market for the poor. But, as payments are made to individuals, the supply side of the market, such payments are likely to have little effect on the demand for the poor workers. This means the transfers will help the poor insofar as they permit them to improve their position in terms of the existing demand for labor, for instance, by facilitating migration, better training, etc.

However, structural theorists consider only change on the demand side of the labor market as "true structural change."[28] Attention is focused on the necessity for a full-employment economy and direct federal intervention in the labor market either to stimulate full employment or to guarantee it through some form of job insurance program. Consequently, change on the supply side of the market is likely to be seen as only an incomplete solution, or palliative, and ambiguously related to the implications of the structural theory. So, although cash

---

27. Liebow, *Tally's Corner*, p. 226.

28. That is, it appears that "true structural change" is restricted to changes on the corporate, institutional, and governmental levels; Kenneth B. Clark, *Dark Ghetto* (New York: Harper and Row, 1965); Liebow, *Tally's Corner;* Rainwater, "Crucible of Identity."

transfers may attenuate the poverty syndrome, they may not be taken as a genuine confirmation of the structural theory.

2. In-Kind Transfers. Income maintenance programs involving in-kind transfers imply that the federal government directly or indirectly will supply jobs. Such proposals of direct supply involve structural reform consistent with the imagery of the structural theorists insofar as they assure jobs at some minimum wage. They also may provide skills transferable to private industry.

However, there are disadvantages to such programs. First, it would be difficult for the government to provide the better-paying semiskilled or skilled labor jobs without competing with private enterprise and arousing considerable political opposition. (Note that cash-transfer programs are not obviously competitive to established political interests.) Second, as a consequence, the jobs the government could offer would in all probability be menial. Third, since the government could not put itself in competition with private industry it could not develop an organizational structure permitting advancement.[29] Fourth, given the kind of jobs the government is likely to provide, the transfer value of learned skills is likely to be minimal. In sum, the major, and perhaps sole, benefit of a direct supply program the poor would appear to be job security.

Indirect supply programs are more difficult to assess. It seems likely that they would be less costly than direct supply programs in that the overhead and startup costs would be at least partially borne by private enterprise. Moreover, there is the possibility of occupational mobility. Alternatively, such programs can be "played" for the subsidies, possibly producing as much or more turnover as the poor currently experience. For example, employers might hire blacks for traditionally Negro occupations which have been placed under federal subsidy. Since, for blacks nothing has changed except that the occupational discrimination has federal support, turnover may be as high as if there had been no program.

Given these deficiencies of in-kind employment programs, it is not clear that they would alter the status quo. Insofar as they do not, the structural theory would imply that they would have little effect on the poverty syndrome.

Education

1. Cash Transfers. Transfers to parents may be either unrestricted cash grants or vouchers redeemable for educational expenses. The unrestricted grants render the educational effects contingent on parental decisions concerning more fundamental questions of employment and

---

29. While poverty agencies can serve this function, they cannot employ more than a small fraction of the poor.

housing. If employment or housing is improved, then the children may attend better schools, have better study conditions at home, etc. Alternatively, vouchers would have direct effects because they could not be used for any other purpose.[30] Children's school performance could be expected to improve to the extent it is related to educational expenditures (not very, if one believes the Coleman report),[31] and to the extent the educational system does not adjust its prices to maintain the status quo.

Programs which pay children directly for academic achievement change the educational market by advancing the cash payoffs for educational attainment. They also shorten the lag in the labor force's response time to changes in the occupational structure due to technology: fewer people will be available for the lower-skilled occupations for which demand is declining.

In terms of structural theory and the poverty syndrome, the implication of these programs is as follows: unrestricted grants are unlikely to influence the educational market and consequently have no significant bearing on the poverty syndrome; vouchers may attenuate the syndrome if the supplements enable the educational system to make expenditures for improved quality and pupil performance is sensitive to the improvement; direct payments to children should markedly diminish the syndrome over the intermediate (and perhaps, the short) term since the children no longer face the old attenuated and unstable reward system.

2. In-Kind Transfers. Transfers in kind in education involve income-conditioned provision of education. Existing educational efforts in the poverty program (e.g., Head Start) constitute such transfers and by definition are structural changes. Should they reduce the poverty syndrome, they would help to confirm the structural theory.

Health Services

1. Cash Transfers. There are two basic types of cash transfers which may affect the health of the poor: restricted and unrestricted cash grants. Restricted grants may be in the form of health insurance or a voucher system. Both differ from the unrestricted cash transfer in that they commit the individual to definite expenditures for health. Whether the health of the poor would be improved by greater use of health services than, say, by greater expenditures for food (which might result in a more adequate diet) is open to question.

But regardless of the kind of cash transfer, because of the extreme shortage of physicians and other health services, it is dubious that any

---

30. Of course, they might be sold at a discount for cash as sometimes occurs with food stamps.

31. James Coleman et al., *Equality of Educational Opportunity* (Washington, D.C.: U.S. Government Printing Office, 1966), esp. Chapter 3.

cash transfer program could bring about structural change. Indeed, it seems quite possible that the net effect of cash transfers would only be to raise prices beyond the reach of the transfer recipients.

2. *In-Kind Transfers.* The provision of in-kind transfers implies the supply of medical services and would require a reorganization of current medical practices, possibly some form of socialized medicine. It would require more physicians and increased use of paraprofessionals to relieve the physician of those activities which do not need his training. It might well require changes in the settings in which physicians work, their relationship to hospitals, their corporate organization, and the manner in which they are paid. Such changes would clearly be structural and might reduce the poverty syndrome by increasing the ability to work. However, the radical nature of the changes suggests that there would be few short-term effects.

To summarize, this discussion of the application of the poverty theories to income maintenance programs indicates that they provide limited guidance for the creation or selection of one, rather than another, program. Rather than theory guiding programs, it would seem that programs provide opportunities to "test" theory. At the same time, it is not entirely clear what would constitute a disconfirmation of the theories. Would all elements of the poverty syndrome have to be affected by a program or would change of only some be sufficient? Certainly, some elements are more susceptible to change by an income maintenance program (or any poverty program) than others. For example, we are more likely to affect a person's sense of political alienation than his family structure. Poverty theorists give us little guidance on this point. Moreover, some programs are not equally relevant to both theories. While all income maintenance programs constitute "tests" of the cultural theory, the same is not true of some cash transfer programs in relation to the structural theory, due to some uncertainty about what is "structural change."

AN ANALYTICAL ALTERNATIVE TO THE THEORIES OF POVERTY

Although this analysis has found poverty theories to be of dubious validity and policy relevance, it also has pointed to a number of lines along which theory construction and policy guidance might be more fruitfully developed. Among these are differences in ethnic and racial subcultures, residential segregation, and discrimination. Related to these are differences in terms of occupational and industrial segregation, geographic location, and "immigrant generation." These variables are not intended to be a theoretical substitute for the poverty theories but rather an analytic framework within which theories of specific processes producing and sustaining poverty may be constructed. This section will outline some of the implications of these variables and relate them to the same three areas of income maintenance discussed earlier to indicate their utility for policy guidance.

If, as Lewis asserts, poor Jews' values mediate their economic condition, it should not be surprising if the same is true for other groups. For example, Gans's West End Italians frowned upon attempts to be upwardly mobile which required leaving the community. As in the southern Italian agrarian society from which they came, the West Enders' lives revolved about their peer relationships and not their livelihoods. The quality of personal relationships was held to be more important than occupational success, and it was expected that, if a decision had to be made, the latter would be sacrificed for the former. Simultaneously, if a man was unemployed, he was likely to turn to his peer group for assistance in finding work. Similarly, if a man wanted to find better housing, he would likely ask his peer group for help. So long as he remained within the norms, the peer group was a network of assistance and information. It follows that income maintenance programs that do not permit groups such as the West Enders to maintain their peer relationships are likely to be ineffective among them.

Program effects may thus vary with the strength of group ties, and ethnic subcultures will exert control to the extent they are not forced to compete with other value systems. Competition is minimized chiefly as a byproduct of residential concentration. The more residentially concentrated a group is, the more likely it is that the social contacts of its members will be restricted to the group. Competition is also minimized through industrial concentration. If a particular group is numerically dominant in an industry, social contacts with nongroup members will again be limited. Moreover, since in these instances the common group membership is often used for job acquisition, maintenance, and advancement, the group member is likely to feel more constrained to observe group norms. The control of the transportation industry in New York by the Irish and the Jewish domination of the garment industries are but two examples of industrial concentration.[32] Occupational segregation also narrows social contacts in much the same fashion (e.g., Irish policemen and Italian bakery workers).

To be sure, the theoretic and policy significance of subcultural variations does not simply depend on the value groups may place upon peer relationships as opposed to occupational advancement. There are a number of other subcultural variables of relevance, some of which have been noted by the poverty theorists: the breadth of friendship and kin networks and the value placed upon mutual assistance within them, family structure, sex role definitions, and parental role definitions. A

32. Daniel P. Moynihan and Nathan Glazer, *Beyond the Melting Pot* (Cambridge: MIT Press, 1966).

variable of particular importance is "immigrant generation," that is, whether the poor group in question is first-generation Italian, Puerto Rican, urban black, etc. It is, of course, in the first generation that the cultural differences between an immigrant group and the larger society will be greatest. These differences are likely to produce both voluntary and involuntary social, residential, occupational, and industrial segregation. During succeeding generations, many of the linguistic and other cultural differences are removed by the educational and occupational systems and many of the discriminatory barriers thus also fall. The implication for income maintenance programs is that responses would increase with succeeding generations.

Among the remaining variables, discrimination is the most important. For many of the poor, notably blacks, discrimination is a fundamental barrier to upward mobility. The degree of this discrimination varies across groups and consequently varies in its effects. Generally speaking, to the extent discrimination creates residential, occupational, and industrial segregation, it impedes upward mobility by denying access to avenues of advancement.

Certainly, the effects of any income maintenance program must be viewed as contingent on discrimination. And since the majority of the poor are subject to it, ways must be found to either bypass or alter the markets in which it operates if these programs are to be effective.

There are, then, a number of variables useful for the creation of poverty theory and programs. Indeed, the foregoing discussion suggests that some relatively concrete predictions can be made about the effects of income maintenance programs in specific areas.

Employment

Aside from direct application to places of employment, jobs are most frequently obtained through friends and relatives.[33] Assuming constant motivation, it follows that the more extensive a person's friendship and kinship network, the more easily he will find a job or change jobs. Moreover, the greater the value placed upon mutual assistance within the network the easier the job hunt. Although there is not enough systematic knowledge to rank more than a few of the subgroups of the poor in these terms, it is enough to suggest that blacks would rank below, for example, Puerto Ricans and Italians. For this reason transfer programs are likely to have smaller employment effects among blacks than among the latter two groups. On the other hand, the response of Italians may be the strongest.

Blacks also should respond more poorly compared to most other

33. Melvin Lurie and Elton Rayack, "Racial Differences in Migration and Job Search," in L. A. Ferman, et al., eds., *Negroes and Jobs* (Ann Arbor: University of Michigan Press, 1968); and H. L. Sheppard and A. H. Balitsky, *The Job Hunt* (Baltimore: Johns Hopkins Press, 1966).

groups because they have poorer training, face greater discrimination, and live in more disadvantageous locations.[34] Moreover, in large part because of the difficulty of obtaining housing, blacks are less likely to move to the suburbs where the potential jobs are concentrated. And since discrimination in the labor market carries over into preparation for it, blacks will have less job training than whites of equal income.

Alternatively, blacks may be less affected by subcultural values which emphasize peer-group relationships over occupational values than those groups with more developed relational networks. However, predictions here require further research.

Education

The two types of cash transfer programs, transfers to parents and transfers to children, have rather different effects. As indicated earlier, the educational effects of transfers to parents depend on more basic job and housing decisions. Therefore, educational responses should follow the same ranking as work responses, with blacks at or near the bottom of the array and groups with less residential and occupational segregation, larger relational networks, and less social discrimination ranking higher.

On the other hand, transfers to children may be able to counteract a group's disadvantages. One feature of transfers to children is that they may be most effective among those who have rejected the established reward structure, for example, older, black, and relationally isolated children. Those children who accept the existing system are likely to be working closer to their capabilities and, consequently, to show a lower level of response. If this argument is correct, the ranking of group responses predicted on the basis of transfers to parents would be largely inverted by transfers to children.

In-kind educational transfers are like cash transfers to parents in that they do not affect the established reward structure. This means that the payoffs to whatever educational programs are undertaken depend upon all those factors which currently limit the translation of education into economic and social status. The response ranking should therefore be the same as that suggested for the employment effects of cash transfers.

Health Services

The current shortage of physicians and health services limits the potential response to cash transfers for health care for all groups. Although the distribution of health services does respond modestly to

---

34. Robert M. Guion, "Employment Tests and Discriminatory Hiring," in Ferman et al., *Negroes and Jobs;* Ray Marshall, *The Negro and Organized Labor* (New York: John Wiley and Sons, 1965); D. R. Fusfield, "Training for Minority Groups," in Ferman et al., *Negroes and Jobs.*

aggregate income, recent evidence suggests that the proposition is untrue if the potential client is black.[35] The best prediction that can be made of group demands for health services is that they will reflect current differences in the availability of such services. In all likelihood, this would mean that blacks will give the lowest response.

Group responses to in-kind health service transfers depend upon the structure of the transfer program and the groups to whom the transfers are directed. As this is a political problem, predictions are hazardous. It can be expected that those who have traditionally been excluded from political process will continue to be so. If so, the blacks will rank near the bottom once again.

CONCLUSION

In this paper the major competing theories of poverty have been described and evaluated in terms of the existing empirical evidence and their relevance to income maintenance policy. Both theories were found to be of dubious validity. The major criticism was that neither theory could account for subgroup variation in the central characteristics claimed to be highly associated with poverty. This problem, together with their highly general nature, also meant that theories could offer little guidance for poverty policy. However, the discussion of poverty theories did suggest a number of dimensions along which poverty could be more usefully analyzed for the purposes of both theory construction and policy formation. The dimensions suggested are in no sense exhaustive nor are their interrelationships fully known. But exploration of their completeness and their interrelationships is far more likely to be of value for further research on the cultural and structural theories of poverty.

---

35. David Elesh and Paul M. Schollaert, "Race and Urban Medicine: Factors Affecting the Distribution of Physicians in Chicago," *Journal of Health and Social Behavior* 13 (Sept., 1972): 236–50.

The Rape of the Appalachians

15

Harry Caudill

Strip mining, a branch of the industry which had previously been practiced in such flat coalfields as western Kentucky and southern Illinois,
invaded the Cumberlands on a vast scale [in the 1950s].

For nearly sixty years the greater part of the region's mineral wealth
had lain in the iron clutch of absentee corporations. They had prospered
and bankrupted and prospered again. But through their triumphs and
tragedies, their successes and failures, the corporations had clung to all
the old rights, privileges, immunities, powers and interests vested in
them by their nineteenth-century land and mineral deeds. These relics
from a laissez-faire century were construed to authorize the physical
destruction of the land and the abject impoverishment of its inhabitants. With strip mining and its companion, the auger-mining process,
the shades of darkness moved close indeed to the Cumberlands.

The courts have written strings of decisions which not only uphold
the convenants and privileges enumerated in the ancient deeds and
contracts but which in the opinion of many lawyers, greatly enlarge
them as well. We have seen that when the mountaineer's ancestor (for
the seller is, in most instances, long since dead) sold his land he lived
in an isolated backwater. Coal mining was a primitive industry whose
methods had changed little in a hundred years and which still depended
entirely on picks and shovels. To the mountaineer "mining" meant
tunneling into a hillside and digging the coal for removal through the
opening thus made. That the right to mine could authorize shaving off
and destroying the surface of the land in order to arrive at the underlying minerals was undreamed of by buyers and sellers alike.

But technology advanced. The steam shovel grew into a mighty mechanism and was replaced by gasoline and diesel-powered successors. "Dozers" and other efficient excavators were perfected. Ever cheaper and safer explosives came from the laboratories. These marvelous new tools enabled men to change the earth, abolishing its natural features and reshaping them as whim or necessity might require. And as these developments made possible a radically new application of the privileges granted in the yellowed mineral deeds, the courts kept pace. Year by year they subjected the mountaineer to each innovation in tools and techniques the technologists were able to dream up. First, it was decided that the purchase of coal automatically granted the "usual and ordinary" mining rights; and then that the usual mining rights included authority to cut down enough of the trees on the surface to supply props for the underground workings. This subjected thousands of acres to cutting for which the owners were uncompensated. It gave the companies an immensely valuable property right for which they had neither bargained nor paid.

Next came rulings which gave the companies the power to "divert and pollute" all water "in or on" the lands. With impunity they could kill the fish in the streams, render the water in the farmer's well unpotable and, by corrupting the stream from which his livestock drank, compel him to get rid of his milk cows and other beasts. They were authorized to pile mining refuse wherever they desired, even if the chosen sites destroyed the homes of farmers and bestowed no substantial advantage on the corporations. The companies which held "long-form" mineral deeds were empowered to withdraw subjacent supports, thereby causing the surface to subside and fracture. They could build roads wherever they desired, even through lawns and fertile vegetable gardens. They could sluice poisonous water from the pits onto crop lands. With impunity they could hurl out from their washeries clouds of coal grit which settled on fields of corn, alfalfa, and clover and rendered them worthless as fodder. Fumes from burning slate dumps peeled paint from houses, but the companies were absolved from damages.

The state's highest court held in substance that a majority of the people had "dedicated" the region to the mining industry, and that the inhabitants were estopped to complain of the depredations of the coal corporations, so long as they were not motivated by malice. Since malice seldom existed and could never be proved, this afforded no safeguard at all. The companies, which had bought their coal rights at prices ranging from fifty cents to a few dollars per acre, were, in effect, left free to do as they saw fit, restrained only by the shallow consciences of their officials. When the bulldozer and power shovel made contour strip-mining feasible and profitable in mountainous terrain, the court promptly enforced the companies' right to remove the coal by this unusual and wholly unforeseen method.

The court spurned as unimportant the fact that competent engineers swore only 20 percent of the coal in a virgin boundary could be recovered even when both strip and auger mining were employed in unison. It brushed aside proof that strip mining destroys the land and eradicates the economic base on which continued residence within the region is predicated. It substantially adjudicated away the rights of thousands of mountaineers to house and home. It bestowed upon the owner of a seam of coal the right to destroy totally the surface insofar as any known system of reclamation is concerned. It delivered into the hands of the coal corporations the present estate and future heritage in the land—in effect an option to preserve or ruin present and future generations. These fateful decisions of the state's highest court, decisions medieval in outlook and philosophy, are now buttressed by the hoary doctrine of *stare decisis* and can be dislodged only by social and political dynamite. And while there is strong reason to suppose that the court as presently constituted views these decisions with uneasiness and dismay, its relatively enlightened judges feel duty-bound to apply them in new appeals. This long line of judicial opinions opened the way for what may prove to be the final obliteration of the plateau's future as a vital part of the nation and its history.

It is probable that this process of judicially straitjacketing the mountaineers for the benefit of the coal companies reached its apogee in a decision handed down by the Court of Appeals on November 15, 1949. The appeal came up from the Circuit Court of Pike County. It involved one of the earliest stripping operations to be undertaken in eastern Kentucky. The Russell Fork Coal Company had cut the top off a mountain on Weddington Fork of Ferrells Creek, leaving ten acres of loose earth, mixed to a great depth with stones and fragments of trees. This vast mass of unstable rubble lay on the upper reaches of a narrow valley, on the floor of which several families made their homes. It was created in an area which had been battered by flash floods throughout its history, so that even the feeblest of minds could have anticipated their recurrence at almost any time. On the night of August 2, 1945, the calamity came in the form of a cloudburst and, foreseeably, thousands of tons of dirt, rocks, and shattered tree trunks from the devastated mountain were flung down the hillside into the raging creek. Like a titanic scythe the rolling rubble swept downstream, working havoc among the houses, stores, and farms. When the dazed inhabitants recovered sufficiently, they sued the coal company for damages on the reasonable assumption that its digging had triggered a misfortune which nature, left undisturbed, would not have visited upon them. The appellate bench reversed the verdict of the jury and the judgment of the trial court. It ruled, in effect, that the rain was an Act of God which the coal operator could not have foreseen and that, had the rain not fallen, the rubble would have remained safely in place. Besides, the stripping had been done in the "same manner as was customary at all strip mines." Usurping the factfinding prerogative of the jury, the judges, sitting as a self-appointed superjury, found the stripper innocent of wrongdoing and negligence.

In another case several years later, a mountaineer claimed that a company had plowed up his mountainsides, covered his bottomland with rubble, caused his well to go dry and, in his words, had "plumb broke" him. After he had heard all the evidence and arguments of counsel the trial judge dismissed the case. In doing so he told the mountaineer, "I deeply sympathize with you and sincerely wish I could rule for you. My hands are tied by the rulings of the Court of Appeals and under the law I must follow its decisions. The truth is that about the only rights you have on your land is to breathe on it and pay the taxes. For all practical purposes the company that owns the minerals in your land owns all the other rights pertaining to it."

By 1950 there were hundreds of "worked-out" ridges along whose edges ran slender banks of outcrop coal. It was of high quality but only extended into the hill a hundred feet or so. Tunnel and pillar mining had long since withdrawn most of the coal, leaving only a few supporting pillars and barrier walls. In order to remove the mineral by conventional methods, a thick barrier pillar must be left intact on the outer fringes of the seam. It comprises the principal support for the overlying mountain, affording stability and tending to prevent "squeezes"—those uncontrollable shiftings of the mountain which occur when too much coal is taken out. Then, too, as a practical matter all the mineral cannot be removed from the inside. As the miners approach the outside the roof of stone becomes increasingly "rotten" so that on the outer edges it is extremely difficult to shore up, no matter how thickly timbers and roof bolts are applied. Hence the bands of outcrop coal were a loss in so far as the owners were concerned and were written off as such.

Nor had all the coal in the interior of the mountains been removed. In the earlier years of the industry some 50 to 60 percent was recovered and the rest was required for supports. As techniques and tools improved, the percentage of recovery steadily rose. Finally in the most thoroughly mechanized mines—those employing roof bolts, conveyors, shuttle cars, and coal moles—recovery soared to 85 or 90 percent and some operators boasted that they "brought it clean," removing all except the outcrop. This permitted colossal "general falls" to bring the roof crashing down behind them as the machines rapidly chewed their way through the pillars in the pullback to the entries. But in all the mines the outcrop remained. In some places where the Big Bosses had first driven their headings nearly forty years before, the seams had been of extraordinarily high quality and very thick. For example, Consolidation Coal Company began its operations in 1912 in seams more than eight feet thick but by 1948 it had developed especially designed machines to work in veins only thirty-six inches thick. Engineers were tantalized by the old workings where thick bands of mineral lay temptingly near the outside of the mountains. Truck roads could be "dozed" to them at little cost and the rural highway program had already brought roads near countless such hollowed ridges.

But the engineers could devise no means of recovering the coal from the inside. The problem of roof supports was insoluble. Heartened by the powerful new earthmoving machines they resorted to "surface mining." If the coal could not be tunneled out from the interior it could be gouged out from the exterior. Dynamite and bulldozer could remove the "overburden." The coal could be "pop shot" with light charges of explosives, and loaded by giant shovels directly into trucks.

The recovery of coal by the "open-cut" method had previously never been feasible in the mountains, though it had occasionally been practiced in the low hills on the fringes of the plateau. But by 1950, strip mining was not only feasible but was increasingly profitable.

Typically a strip-mine operator needed only a tiny crew of men. He required two bulldozers, one of which could be substantially smaller than the other. He required an air compressor and drill for the boring of holes into the rock overlying the coal. He also required a power shovel for use in loading the coal from the seam into the trucks. These four machines could be operated by as many men. To their wages were added those of a night watchman and two or three laborers, and the crew was complete. With these men and machines the operator first built a road from the nearest highway up the hillside to the coal seam. The bulldozers pursued the seam around the hillside, uprooting the timber and removing all the soil until the coal was reached. Then the dirt was scraped from the sloping mountainside above to expose the crumbling rock. This cut proceeded along the contours of the ridge for half a mile. Then rows of holes were drilled in the rock strata and were tamped with explosives. When the explosives were set off, most of the dirt and rock was blown violently down the mountainside. The remainder lay, soft and crumbly, on top of the coal. The "dozers" then bestrode the shattered "overburden," and with their steel snouts shoved it down the steep slopes. This process left the outer edge of the outcrop exposed. A sheet of coal eight feet thick, fifty feet wide, and half a mile long could thus be bared within a few days.

Next, holes were drilled in the glittering black seam of coal. Small charges of dynamite loosened thousands of tons of the mineral, leaving it easily available to the shovel's big dipper. A number of truckers were hired to haul it away, at a cost of perhaps seventy-five cents a ton. It was carried to the nearest ramp or tipple where it was cleaned, sized, and loaded into gondolas.

It is instantly apparent that this method of recovery is vastly cheaper than shaft or drift mining. Six or eight men can thus dig more coal from the outcrop than five or six times their number can mine underground. The bulldozers, shovels, and drills are expensive, but not more so than their subterranean counterparts. They can produce a ton of coal for little more than half the cost imposed on a competitor in a deep pit. Where the strip mine lies close to the loading ramp so that the haul bill can be minimized, the price differential is even more striking.

In the flat country of western Kentucky, where thousands of acres had already been devastated by strip mining, the coal seams lie only thirty to sixty feet beneath the surface. The overburden is scraped off and the coal is scooped out. Inevitably such topsoil as the land affords is buried under the towering heaps of subsoil. When the strippers move on, once-level meadows and cornfields have been converted to jumbled heaps of hardpan, barren clay from deep in the earth. This hellish landscape is slow to support vegetation and years elapse before the yellow waste turns green again. In the meantime, immense quantities of dirt have crept into the sluggish streams, have choked them, and brackish ponds have formed to breed millions of mosquitoes.

The evil effects of open-cut mining are fantastically magnified when practiced in the mountains. Masses of shattered stone, shale, slate, and dirt are cast pellmell down the hillside. The first to go are the thin remaining layer of fertile topsoil and such trees as still find sustenance in it. The uprooted trees are flung down the slopes by the first cut. Then follows the sterile subsoil, shattered stone, and slate. As the cut extends deeper into the hillside the process is repeated again and again. Sometimes the "highwall," the perpendicular bank resulting from the cut, rises ninety feet; but a height of forty to sixty feet is more often found. In a single mile, hundreds of thousands of tons are displaced.

Each mountain is laced with coal seams. Sometimes a single ridge contains three to five veins varying in thickness from two-and-a-half to fourteen feet. Since each seam can be stripped, a sloping surface can be converted to a steplike one.

After the coal has been carried away, vast quantities of the shattered mineral are left uncovered. Many seams contain substantial quantities of sulphur, which when wet produces toxic sulphuric acid. This poison bleeds into the creeks, killing minute vegetation and destroying fish, frogs, and other stream dwellers.

Strip mining occurs largely in dry weather. In late spring, in summer, and in early fall the bulldozers and shovels tear tirelessly at the vitals of the mountains while trucks rumble away with their glittering cargoes. Above the operations and their haul roads lie mantles of tawny dust. In the hot sunshine the churned earth turns powder dry and the jumbled spoil banks lie soft almost to fluffiness.

The seam seldom lies less than a hundred feet above the base of the mountain. Sometimes it is near the top. Again it may lie midway between base and crest. But wherever the seam is situated the spoil bank extends downward like a monstrous apron. Stones as large as army tanks are sent bounding and crashing through trees and undergrowth. Lesser stones find lodgment against trees and other obstacles, and behind them countless tons of soil accumulate.

During the hot season the nearby creek takes on a sallow hue after even the slightest shower. People living along its bank watch apprehensively as the rising highwall deepens the loose earth on the dead and blasted slopes. They remember the horror of other years when flash floods pounded hillsides scratched by hoes and bull-tongue plows. They guess what will ensue if a similar downpour falls upon the ravaged slopes which overlook their farms and homes.

Then come the rains of autumn and the freezes and thaws of winter. The descending water flays the loose rubble, carrying thousands of tons of it into the streams and onto the bottoms. The watery scalpel shaves inches from the surface in almost instantaneous sheet erosion. At the same time it carves gullies which deepen until the streams reach the undisturbed soil far beneath. The rain has a kindlier effect, however, and eventually lessens its ravages by compacting the surface. Gradually the beating drops create a hard shell which affords considerable protection to the underlying dirt. Then in late November the saturated spoil banks freeze. In the icy grip of winter they lie hard as ice and perfectly stable. The freezing water pushes the dirt outward, leaving deep fissures extending far underground. When warmer weather melts the ice the earth crumbles and subsides downhill in tremendous landslides. Snows and rains then saturate the loosened masses again and the process is repeated until the displaced soil reaches the stream beds.

Within a few years after the "strip operator" has slashed his way into the hillside the unresting elements have carried away most of his discarded overburden. The dirt has vanished, leaving immense expanses of sere brown sandstone and slabs of sickening gray slate. A few straggly clusters of broom sage and an occasional spindly sycamore take root and struggle to survive.

Initially the strippers worked only in the outcrop of exhausted mines, but as their machines and techniques improved, they pushed into virgin seams. The great cuts appeared on the sides of ridges from which no coal had yet been withdrawn. They scalped away only a thin filament on the outer edges of the hill, leaving the body of the coal bed undisturbed. The coal auger made its appearance as a device for removing that portion of the outcrop which could not be reached by stripping. As a rule of thumb ten feet of overburden can profitably be removed for each foot of coal in the seam. When the highwall rose straight up so far it could not be advantageously increased, much of the outcrop remained. The auger allowed the recovery of a large part of the remaining mineral. It is a gigantic drill which bores straight back into the coal seam, spewing out huge quantities of the mineral with each revolution of the screw. The drills range from seventeen inches to six feet in diameter. When the point has penetrated the entire length of the bit a new section is attached and the drilling continues. Eventually it extends some seventy yards under the hill, piercing the entire barrier pillar.

The bore holes must be somewhat smaller in diameter than the seam is thick, and a few inches are left between the insertions. Consequently, the auger can bring out little more than half the coal. Initially its use was justified on the ground that it prevented the loss of the otherwise unrecoverable barrier pillars, but after the already disemboweled hills were stripped and augered the big bits moved into virgin ridges and began to rend seams which had never felt a pick. Usually stripping preceded the augers, but after a time some auger men dispensed with strip mining altogether. They simply made cuts sufficient to face up the seams, then the monstrous screws were set to work while the lines of trucks labored to carry away their product.

Where augering is done in a previously unmined ridge the crumbly "bloom" and a few yards of weathered roofstone is shoved over the hillside. Then the bore holes follow each other in interminable procession around the meandering ridge. They proceed along the edges of sharp spurs, around the "turn of the point," and back to the main ridge again. When the end of the ridge is passed, the cutting and boring continues on its reverse side. Thus the bore holes from one side of the mountain extend toward the ends of those drilled from the other side. Under these circumstances coal production is fantastically cheap. A well-financed operation augering in a four- to six-foot seam can realize a net profit of close to a dollar on the ton even in the depressed coal market prevailing as this is written in 1962. A six-foot auger turning uninterruptedly can load fifteen tons in less than one minute. If the fleet of trucks can keep pace with the bulldozers and augers, the profit can be fabulous, amounting to millions of dollars in a few years. Quite naturally the possibility of such quick and easy enrichment has excited many coal companies and the politicians through whom they dominate the state and county governments.

Strip and auger mining have one very real advantage over conventional methods: they eliminate the need for men to go under the hill. In augering, only the revolving steel bits pierce the mountainside, and their human attendants need never follow them. The peril of fire and slate-fall which dogs the underground miners in even the safest pits does not pursue the surface workman. But when this is said, nothing more in defense of the process can be forthcoming.

Augering in virgin ridges is fantastically wasteful. Rarely do the bits extend into the mountain more than a quarter of its width. Hence, even if the boring proceeds from both sides, a solid block is often left in the center of the ridge which contains at least 50 percent of the seam's original tonnage. When allowance is made for the huge quantities left between the holes and over and under them, another 25 percent of the seam's content is unretrieved. Competent mining engineers have testified that such an augering project is highly successful if 20 percent of the total coal is removed. Nor can the remainder be mined at a future time without totally destroying the terrain.

It will at first appear that shafts could be driven into the hill for mining the remaining coal by conventional methods, but unfortunately when the ridge has been augered on both sides this is no longer possible. The bore holes are so close together they leave no pillars of sufficient thickness to support the roof. Within a few years after air is admitted into the seam a chemical reaction causes the remaining coal to crumble. The weight of the overlying rock and soil crushes down through the thin walls remaining between the holes. The coal marooned in the center of the mountain is thus sealed against the outside world. Moreover, tunnel and pillar mining requires ventilation as well as roof supports, and if a reliable air supply is to be maintained at the working faces this exterior wall cannot be reduced under forty feet in thickness without running the risk that the mountain's weight will crack and shatter it, allowing the precious oxygen to leak out. Thus, even if an entry is managed it must operate within the confining limits of a forty-foot barrier pillar following the furthermost penetrations of the auger bits. Generally, when this indispensable safeguard is deducted, too little coal is left to justify the expense of mining it. Thus the auger skims off a thin layer of cream and leaves the balance of a rich and vitally important coal bed in such a state that mining engineers can presently offer no hope for its ultimate recovery. Prudence cannot permit the continued gross wastage of so vital a resource.

Open-cut strip mining does not always follow the meandering borders of the ridge. A different procedure is used when the vein lies near the top of the hill. Then the strippers blast and carve away the stone and soil overlying the coal, shoving it over the brink of the mountain until at last the entire seam lies black and glistening in the sunlight. Such an operation can transform a razorback spur into a flat mesa. Sometimes the hill's altitude is decreased by 20 per cent while its thickness is much increased. When the strippers have departed and the rains and freezes have flayed such a decapitated mountain for a season or two, it takes on an appearance not unlike the desolate, shattered tablelands of Colorado. But these manmade mesas lie in a rainy area and the layers of loose soil cloaking the slopes will not stay in situ. Wraithlike, the rubble melts away, only to reappear at countless places downstream.

Stripping and augering spread at an accelerating rate through the 1950s. For a long time they were viewed as a tentative and minor industry, one that could deface splotches of land but was unlikely to ever afford serious competition for conventional mines or to constitute a real threat to the region's soil, water, and natural beauty. But this casual viewpoint has been dispelled. In 1954 Kentucky's Governor Lawrence Wetherby advocated a mild bill designed to restrain the operators from the worst of their abuses. Immediately the holding companies and the industry reacted as if they had been stung by a huge bee. Lobbyists dragged out all the timeworn arguments again and the lawmakers were solemnly assured that strip and auger mining are good for the region's economy, creating jobs and bringing prosperity to Main Street. A diluted version of an initially weak bill was passed but successive governors have failed to enforce even its mild strictures. For all practical purposes the operators are permitted to conduct their affairs in complete absence of supervision or control. Little effort is made to reclaim or stabilize the land, and indeed, reclamation is rarely possible once the surface has been so violently disturbed. . . .

THE SCENE TODAY

The present crisis is compounded of many elements, human and material. They have produced what is probably the most seriously depressed region in the nation—and the adjective applies in much more than an economic sense. They have brought economic depression, to be sure, and it lies like a gray pall over the whole land. But a deeper tragedy lies in the depression of the spirit which has fallen upon so many of the people, making them for the moment at least listless, hopeless, and without ambition.

The essential element of the plateau's economic malaise lies in the fact that for a hundred and thirty years it has exported its resources, all of which—timber, coal, and even crops—have had to be wrested violently from the earth. The nation has siphoned off hundreds of millions of dollars' worth of its resources while returning little of lasting value. For all practical purposes the plateau has long constituted a colonial appendage of the industrial East and Middle West, rather than an integral part of the nation generally. The decades of exploitation have in large measure drained the region. Its timber wealth is exhausted and if its hillsides ever again produce arrow-straight white oaks, tulip poplars, and hemlocks, new crops of trees will first have to be planted and allowed to mature. Hundreds of ridges which once bulged with thick seams of high-quality coal have been emptied of all that lay in their vitals and their surfaces have been fragmented for the pitiful remnants in the outcrop. While billions of tons still remain undisturbed they lie in inferior seams and are of poorer quality. The magnificent veins through which Percheron horses once hauled strings of bank cars have been worked out.

Even more ruinous than the loss of its physical resources is the disappearance of the plateau's best human material. Most of the thousands who left were people who recognized the towering importance of education in the lives of their children, and craved better schools for them than Kentucky afforded. Too many of those who remained behind were without interest in real education as distinguished from its trappings. If their children attended the neighborhood schools the parents had done their duty. Too often they were far less ambitious and such ambition as they possessed was to evaporate in the arms of Welfarism and in the face of repeated failures.

From the beginning, the coal and timber companies insisted on keeping all, or nearly all, the wealth they produced. They were unwilling to plow more than a tiny part of the money they earned back into schools, libraries, health facilities, and other institutions essential to a balanced, pleasant, productive, and civilized society. The knowledge and guile of their managers enabled them to corrupt and cozen all too many of the region's elected public officials and to thwart the legitimate aspirations of the people. The greed and cunning of the coal magnates left behind an agglomeration of misery for a people who can boast of few of the facilities deemed indispensable to life in more sophisticated areas, and even these few are inadequate and of inferior quality.

Only one facet of the industry ever sought to return to the region any substantial part of the wealth it produced. The United Mine Workers' program of health, welfare, and retirement benefits funneled back to the coal counties millions of dollars otherwise destined for the pockets of distant shareholders. To compound the tragedy of the plateau, even this program is today showing unmistakable signs of breakdown and failure. The union and the trustees of its fund were headed for inevitable trouble after the end of the second boom in 1948. Its seeds germinated in the same soil that sprouted the difficulties of the late 1920s: the industry was grossly overexpanded and was prepared to produce twice as much coal as its markets could consume. In 1948 the tremendous new truck-mining industry was overgrown and, hard though they struggled to mechanize their mines with the castoff relics of their big competitors, the little operators were never really able to compete. A widespread double standard blanketed the coalfields. The big rail mines were sternly forced to comply with the wage and hour contracts negotiated year after year with the United Mine Workers, but John L. Lewis and his associates looked the other way where the truck mines were concerned. Fearing that if these small pits were shut down the resulting labor surplus might break the contracts in the big mines, they tolerated clandestine wage cuts. It became customary for the truck-mine operator to sign the contract and then ignore it. He paid his workmen five or ten dollars per day less than the scale wage and sent only a token contribution to the Health and Welfare Fund. Thus the truck mines existed for a decade, by sufferance of the union.

Then in the spring of 1959 the United Mine Workers undertook to change all this. Wages in many of the truck mines had sunk to ridiculous levels and in others the miners were "gang working" as partners and dividing the meager profits equally. But however they managed and toiled, many were earning no more than eight dollars a day and some as little as four dollars. Despite the pious provisions of the Federal Wage and Hour Law most operators paid as little as the miners could be persuaded to accept. But for a man with a wife and "a gang of young'-uns," with no money, no property and nowhere to go, any income is better than none. Thus when the union suddenly attempted to force the small pits to comply fully and faithfully with the contract their efforts ended in ignominious defeat. The miners in the little "dog-holes" had lost faith in the "organization." It had let them work at ever-lessening wages for ten years, preaching automation and higher pay to men who grew increasingly desperate with each passing year. In their cynical eyes John L. Lewis, once their hero and idol, had become a traitor to their interests.

When the 1959 strike was called, the response was far from uniform. Some of the workmen quit and picketed those who attempted to work. The strike dragged on for months amid recurrences of violence reminiscent of the 1930s. Men were slain, ramps and tipples were blasted and burned, and eventually the state's National Guard was sent into the troubled counties to preserve order. But the strike failed. In the long run practically all the truck miners deserted the union and went back to work. Today they mine many trainloads of coal daily but pay nothing into the Welfare Fund. Their miners no longer pay union dues. Their locals have folded up and disappeared. In retaliation against them the U.M.W. Fund trustees canceled their hospital cards and Welfare benefits and thousands of truck-mine laborers are now stranded at the mercy of their employers and the customers who buy their coal. It is a harsh world for everyone, but in all America there is no worker—not even the imported Mexican "wetback"—who occupies a position more exposed and helpless than the men who dig coal in these little pits.

The federal government makes only a token effort to enforce the minimum wage requirements of the Fair Labor Standards Act. Almost always when complaints are called to the attention of the United States Attorneys, they are too busy to deal with them and the miner in question receives a form letter advising him to bring suit for back wages in "a court of competent jurisdiction." But lawsuits cost money and the miner has none, so the suit is not brought, the delinquency is not collected and the low wages continue. His union has ostracized him as a yellow dog and a scab. Some of the magnificent union hospitals stand half-empty while their skilled physicians resign in disgust because there are so few patients to attend.[1] The truck-mine operator is earning little on the coal he sells and competition from the increasing numbers of strip and auger companies constantly deflates the price of his product. While other Americans are enjoying prosperity, planning expensive vacations in new automobiles, and buying corporate stocks in unprecedented numbers, the truck miner who is fortunate enough to have a job works for minuscule wages and wonders from payday to payday whether his employer will be able to pay even the pittances for which he has contracted.

Even worse, the federal government treats him as a second-class citizen when it comes to safety. Of all the things John L. Lewis can boast of having accomplished for all his followers, the Federal Mine Safety Code is the most important. But Congress gave Lewis only half a loaf, specifically restricting the act's application to mines employing fifteen or more men. Small pits were left to the tender mercies of their bosses and of state inspectors; the carnage continued in them unabated. Most of the plateau's coal counties now go two or three years at a time without a fatal accident in a railroad mine, but the dreary reports of dead and mangled bodies continue to filter with chilling frequency from the little operations. Truck mines produce approximately 12 percent of the plateau's coal output and 33⅓ percent of its killed and injured miners. Strangely enough, the state's senior senator, himself an eastern Kentuckian, is an outspoken defender of this industrial mayhem, and for several years has almost singlehandedly staved off federal safety enforcement in the small coal mines.

So the miners, the employed workmen who by hundreds make a skimpy living in the truck mines of the plateau, live on a downward spiral which for several years has appeared to be nearing rock bottom. With low wages, lack of union membership and protection, and in most instances without even Workmen's Compensation coverage, such a miner is fortunate to keep corn bread and beans on the dinner table in the poor shack he so often calls home.

So trifling were his wages that in many instances the "dog-hole miner" could not survive without the free food doled out to him monthly from the great stores of the United States Department of Agriculture. Though his situation was unusually severe, a miner recently remarked to me that for eleven eight-hour shifts of work he collected twenty-nine dollars in wages. It is apparent that he, his wife, and three children would starve to death if his labor afforded their only support. It is true that some truck mines are so efficiently organized and have grown so large that they are able to pay decent wages, though few

1. In October of 1962, the trustees of the Fund announced that four of its hospitals in the plateau would be permanently closed on June 30, 1963.

attempt the union scale. The largest ones, however, mine as much as a thousand tons a day and their owners pay twenty dollars for an eight-hour shift. Their miners live reasonably well but it should not be inferred that they set the standards for the industry. In most areas truck mining has degenerated into a ghastly economic mire which holds miner and operator alike enchained. Often the employer is fortunate if he can earn twenty dollars a day for himself, and his employees are lucky if they take home eight or ten dollars. In those pits in which the miners work as partners they are practically unsupervised by safety bosses. Each coworker thinks of himself as his own boss and of equal voice in the management of the mine and, in consequence, none can enforce safety discipline. Yet they continue to dig coal from the thinning seams, producing it for incredibly low prices and adding to a coal glut which can only depress prices, earnings, and wages still further.

Here and there a few rail mines still operate. During the last fifteen years there has been a relentless consolidation as the bigger companies steadily bought up the smaller ones. With roaring machines and shrunken crews, these corporate giants continue to pour coal from the black veins into the clattering tipples. But where nearly eight thousand men once toiled for United States Coal and Coke Company in the Big Black Mountain, fewer than seventeen hundred are now at work. Where five thousand miners once went under the hill for Consolidation Coal Company at Jenkins and McRoberts, nine hundred survivors are still on the payroll. But at neither place has coal production lessened. To the contrary, with advancing mechanization it has steadily swollen.

These fortunate hundreds earn a basic union wage in excess of twenty-four dollars a day and enjoy all the benefits the union contract bestows. They present a sharp contrast to the pauperized dog-hole miners. The two, and frequently they are blood brothers, are prince and pauper. The workman for Inland Steel, Bethlehem Mines, International Harvester, and United States Steel owns his home in a camp or in one of the rural areas. He has improved the house and installed a furnace and plumbing. His home is neat and well-painted. He drives and owns a late-model automobile and his children attend school regularly. He hopes to send at least some of them to college, perhaps to the University of Kentucky. He has a thousand dollars or so on deposit in a local bank. The magnificent facilities at the Miner's Memorial Hospitals exist primarily for his care. When he or any member of his family is ill or injured, doctors, surgeons, and hospitalization cost him nothing. The trustees have lowered the retirement age, and when he reaches his sixtieth birthday he can leave the mines and draw from the Fund a monthly retirement check of seventy-five dollars. The mine in which he works is well-ventilated and under the orders of Federal Safety Inspectors has been made as safe as human ingenuity can vouchsafe. If, despite the precautions, he is injured, compensation benefits up to a total of

$15,300 await him. His union shelters him from coercion by company officials and has long since forced the closing of the scrip office. In most camps the company store is little more than a memory.

But there are portents of trouble for these union miners and their organization. The United Mine Workers has shrunk its membership and raised the living standards of those who remain. In so doing it has kept abreast of progress because progress is bigness, efficiency, technological advancement, and organization. At the same time, it has created a favored class, a sort of blue-collar royalty amid a populace of industrial serfs. The combination of giant companies and giant union is driving the truck mines from the scene. Each spring the beginning of the lake trade finds fewer truck mines in operation. Within a few more seasons, the rail-mine operators can confidently expect the last of their small competitors to have been relegated to the scrap heap of history. But they are confronted with competition from other quarters—savage rivalry they cannot dispose of in so cavalier a fashion.

The rising crescendo of strip and auger mining is pouring growing quantities of extremely low-priced coal onto the market. So long as unspoiled ridges invite the bulldozers and big screws, the Big Bosses will face a gruesome dilemma. At great cost to their stockholders they have made ready to market clean and high quality coal. Ironically, this product is now becoming old-fashioned. The trend is toward lower prices and quality, and therefore the huge complex washeries may be little more than outmoded symbols of a departed time. In consequence, the union and its members are losing their economic and political importance. When coal was dug by simple tools and machines the many men who operated them could give fiscal chilblains to industrialists and government officials across the land. The nation was dependent upon coal, and hence on the miner's skills, but this dependence is seeping fast away. In coal production the cornerstone is still the dust-blackened, blue-collar miner, but he is surrendering his primacy to the white-collar expert whose skill and cunning has worked a far-reaching revolution in so short a time. The growing petroleum glut and the network of natural gas pipelines lessen coal's importance with each passing season. Within a few years tireless atomic reactors will provide much of the electric power now made from coal. Though the nation will surely grow steadily, coal is unlikely ever again to be a prime industry. Its path is downward, and the men and communities who are dependent upon it are tied to a descending star. Since coal is, for all practical purposes, the plateau's only industry, the region and its people are tied to an industrial albatross.

Capitalism and Poverty in America: A Discussion

16

By Barry Bluestone

In this brief paper I wish to highlight the nature or *functioning* of a capitalist economy rather than explore poverty's manifest functions. Hopefully this may lead to a better understanding of why poverty does not disappear in a system defined by private property and an incessant search for private profit.

The key to the dynamics of capitalism lies in the law of uneven development. Those who are in the position to make new investments (capitalists) will tend to reinvest in those particular product lines, machinery, and workers promising the highest return. Conversely, investment will tend to decline where potential expected profit is relatively low. In the static equilibrium economics of the neoclassical paradigm, diminishing returns to any single investment supposedly militate against a long-run dichotomy between sectors of the economy or between classes in society. Yet the simple dynamics of profit maximization, especially in a period of monopoly capital, produce a tendency toward a "secular deterioration of terms of trade" between nations, between industries, and between social classes.

This occurs for two reasons. First, investment in a dynamic economy tends not only to increase the capital intensity of the product or factor in question, but also changes the quality of the factor so as to make further investments technologically profitable. Capital investment in a given product, for instance, often increases the market value of the product, thereby strengthening the profitability of renewed investment. Higher past profits can also be used for research and development, which further expand the market for these goods. Profits also allow expanded advertising, which reinforces this tendency. On the other hand, new capital, products or people that originally fail to meet the test of the market, like many infant industries, seldom receive additional investment and consequently are doomed to deterioration.

The second reason for a dichotomization within society derives from the potential redistributive effect of any given investment. While it may be true that continued investment runs into diminishing marginal returns, capitalists will tend to link efficiency and distribution criteria in reinvestment decisions. Private investors will tend to reinvest their capital in areas which promise the highest relative return *only if such investment does not tend to alter the long-run income distribution in such a way as to reduce their own relative standing.* The capitalist has both a psychological and political stake in an unequal distribution of income, and consequently often measures his success not by the absolute amount of his accumulation, but by the relative surplus he accumulates compared with others. Individual capitalists will thus tend to invest in their "own" rather than contribute to the economic viability of competing individuals or groups. Seldom will the maximization of private returns constrained by this distributional objective coincide with the maximization of total social return. The outcome, of course, is uneven development where the rich become richer and the poor more impoverished. It is important to realize that this is not an aberration of capitalism, but precisely its traditional and necessary nature.

The most discussed case of "secular deterioration," or uneven development, is found in the realm of international trade between developed and Third-World countries. Left-liberal economists have for a number of years argued that capitalist trade has led to the enrichment of the developed capitalist world and the impoverishment of the nations of Latin America, Africa, and noncommunist Asia. "Circular causation with cumulative effect" is the surrogate terminology for the law of uneven development.[1]

What plagues trade between nations, however, is precisely evident *within* developed capitalist economics themselves. The tendency toward uneven development can be seen clearly in the development of industries in the United States. In tracing wage histories since the Second World War, one finds that the wage differential between "high-wage" and "low-wage" industries has increased secularly. In 1947 the set of industries with lowest wages paid straight-time hourly rates which averaged 75 percent of the average wages prevailing in the highest-wage industries in the nation. Apart from slight cyclical variation in wage increases during the ensuing period, the wage ratio between these two sets of industries fell to 60 percent by 1966. The low-wage industries granted smaller wage increases (in percentage as well as absolute terms) in all but four years during the two-decade period.[2]

---

1. Gunnar Myrdal is responsible for coining this phrase.

2. These results are presented in an unpublished paper by the author, entitled "The Secular Deterioration of Wage Terms Among Industries in the United States (1947–1966)," Fall, 1968.

Econometric evidence indicates that, regardless of the level of unemployment or the general state of the economy, the secular deterioration of wage terms cannot be reversed. It is natural to the system, if not functional. Reinvestment in the more capital-intensive, more concentrated, and more profitable industries follows precisely from the profit-maximization rule. Conversely, relatively less investment is undertaken in the less profitable industries. Over time, then, the capital intensity of the two sets of industries as well as productivity levels diverge, and finally wage terms deteriorate.

The result is the creation of a massive working-poor proletariat. In 1968 over 10 million workers—one in five private nonsupervisory employees—earned less than $1.60 an hour in the United States.[3] The working poor make up well over half the poor in the nation, and naturally they are concentrated in those industries which have undergone the drastic secular deterioration in relative capital intensity, concentration, profits, and wage levels. Since the economic status of persons no longer in the labor force—the aged and the disabled, for instance—depends to such an extent on previous labor force status, the secular deterioration between industries affects the nonworking poor as well as the currently low-paid. In this way, capitalism creates and recreates poverty as a part of the normal functioning of the system.

But uneven development is not restricted to industrial dichotomization alone. The same pattern of secular deterioration is clearly evident in investment decisions regarding "human capital." Reinvestment is made precisely in those children in whom already significant investments have been made. Socialization in the home is obviously biased in favor of the wealthy, who can afford educational playthings, home libraries, and summer vacations for their children. The unequal distribution of educational resources in the home is then mirrored in the school system. Studies of schooling ranging from preschool programs to higher education have shown that the distribution of educational resources is severely class- and race-biased.[4] Numerous studies have proven the degree to which educational investment is dichotomized between city and suburb, between white schools and black, and between vocational and college preparatory programs. Beyond high school the dichotomization continues, as public and private college and university resources are distributed overwhelmingly on the basis of class and race. In this way the socialization process is structured so as to maintain and intensify social class divisions from one period to the next.[5] From preschool to college, the children of the wealthy continue to receive

3. *Manpower Report of the President,* April, 1968, table 5, p. 27.
4. See the now famous Coleman Report, *Equality of Educational Opportunity* (Washington: U.S. Government Printing Office, 1966), on primary and secondary schooling. For an analysis of higher education, see W. Lee Hansen and Burton Weisbrod, *Benefits, Costs, and Finance of Public Higher Education* (Chicago: Markham, 1969).
5. See Sam Bowles, "Unequal Education and the Reproduction of the Social Division of Labor," *Review of Radical Political Economics* (Fall-Winter 1971).

additional investment, while the children of the poor are pushed out of the education stream at an early point in their lives. At birth the rich and poor begin with nearly equal abilities, but with time the educational investment process assures a secular deterioration in human capital terms between the two.

Capitalism thus tends to produce a *dual economy* both in the structure of industries and in the class structure of the labor force. The dual economy performs several critical functions necessary to the continued viability of a hierarchically stratified production system. But the dual economy is not some artificial construct of conspiring capitalists. Rather it is the normal and natural outcome of a system based on private investment decisions.

In a number of ways, the modern state reinforces the tendency toward uneven development in the private sector. The distribution of effective corporate income taxes, structured through depreciation and depletion allowances, investment tax credits, and specific-industry loopholes, benefits the more concentrated and powerful industries to the detriment of others. Government purchases, now amounting to nearly one-third of total expenditures in the United States, are also sharply skewed toward the highly concentrated defense industries and their suppliers. As with unequal tax treatment, unequal expenditure between industries reinforces secular deterioration through a dichotomization of capital intensity, concentration, profits, and finally wages. In addition to tax and expenditure policy, the state is using an increasing amount of subsidization in such a way as to further contribute to the natural trend of capitalism. The $250-million guaranteed loan to Lockheed Aircraft is the latest and most glaring example of this policy. In addition, through the public education system and the "grants economy," the state directly contributes to the uneven development of "human capital" and the dichotomization of social classes. Thus the state is partially responsible for the rate at which the dual economy has developed.

A trend toward greater disparity between industries and individuals would necessarily materialize in the course of capitalist development if it were not for the fact that such a trend is considered politically untenable. The revolutionary implications of ever greater income disparity are well known and generally appreciated. The state therefore must make an attempt to offset the powerful forces tending toward dichotomization of the economy. The object of state policy therefore becomes to stabilize the historically developed unequal distribution of income.

Historically the state has relied on three devices to accomplish this difficult task. One is the mildly progressive federal income tax. While the tax system is generally proportional, taking a roughly equal percentage of income from all families, a slight measure of progressivity exists between the very poor and the very rich. This tends somewhat to offset the effects of uneven development. A second device has been welfare. For those who have suffered the worst ravages of the secular deterioration process, the state provides subsidies. These too tend to reduce the economic effect of uneven development and thus to offset the tendency toward political instability. Manpower programs, aimed at countering secular deterioration of "human capital" investment, round out the current bag of government policies intended to offset the tendency toward dichotomization of income distribution. Through subsidization of institutional and on-the-job training as well as remedial education, the state attempts to increase the marketability of "disadvantaged" sectors of the work force.

In general, the state has been successful so far in offsetting the inherent tendency toward uneven development. This can be seen in statistics of aggregate income distribution, which clearly indicate that the distribution of after-tax and transfer income has remained approximately constant, at least since the Second World War and possibly since the turn of the century. The poorest one-fifth of all families perennially receive approximately 5 percent of total income after account is taken of taxes and welfare. The richest fifth are left with a little more than 40 percent year after year, while the wealthiest 5 percent normally receive between 14 and 17 percent of total after-tax and transfer income.[6] The degree of stability in the income distribution is reflected in the wealth distribution which, while extremely unequal by any definition, has remained equally unequal since the American Civil War. (The Gini coefficient of inequality of wealth in 1860 has been estimated at about .82 compared to .76 in 1962.)[7] It taxes the imagination to believe that this amazing stability in income and wealth has been the result of purely random counterbalancing forces. It makes more sense to assume that this apparent stability is the result of explicit state policy.

What is more crucial to realize, however, is that this high degree of stability has only been achieved through increasingly massive state intervention. The forces leading to uneven development are extremely powerful and in constant operation. To keep the income distribution fixed over time requires the state to run ever faster to remain in the same place. This is clearly indicated by statistics on both manpower programs and welfare. Between 1961 and 1970, the total outlay on manpower and human-resource development programs at the federal level grew from $184 million to over $2.6 billion a year.[8] Total federal aid to the poor through income-security programs, commodity and service programs

---

6. U.S. Census Bureau, *Current Population Reports,* Series P-60, No. 75, p. 22; and Edward C. Budd, *Inequality and Poverty* (New York: Norton, 1967), pp. xiii, xvi.

7. Lee Soltow, ed., *Six Papers on the Size Distribution of Wealth and Income* (New York: National Bureau of Economic Research, 1969), p. xii. The Gini coefficient is a widely used statistical measure of inequality.

8. *U.S. Budget,* Fiscal 1970, Special Analyses K and M.

(including housing, health, food, and compensatory basic education), manpower policy, and economic and community development grew nearly threefold in this period from $9.7 billion to $27.8 billion. The welfare picture is even more illuminating. In the ten-year period ending in 1967, the AFDC caseload doubled from 2.5 million to 5 million families. In the following four years, the caseload doubled once again, and the total AFDC cash outlay tripled. In the one year ending in April, 1971, the caseload had increased again by nearly 25 percent, and the costs had skyrocketed by more than 36 percent.[9] At this rate the caseload will once again double in less than three years while the costs will double in approximately two.

Yet these increasingly massive inputs of training and subsidy have only barely served to offset the increasing tendency toward secular deterioration between rich and poor. The income distribution has not become more equal, even in the face of these equalizing transfers. In response to an apparent acceleration in the pace of uneven development, the state now proposes large public-employment programs and even larger transfer schemes. The Nixon Family Assistance Plan is the most recent legislative approach to stemming the dynamic income distribution effect inherent in the capitalist economy. In one form or another this multi-billion-dollar bill will doubtless be signed into law and will temporarily offset the effect of uneven development. The state is thus forced constantly to expand the public transfer economy in order to ameliorate the dynamic *effects* of the functioning of the private sector.

Ultimately this ever-expanding process causes recurrent fiscal crises of the state. The manpower crisis was followed by the poverty crisis, which has now in turn given way to a welfare crisis. Each new stopgap measure has required a manifold increase in public expenditures in order to keep pace with developments in the private sector and to stifle potential political instability.

Within the context of a capitalist economy, expanding public welfare programs are the only significant alternative to explosive political discontent. And they will remain the only alternative, for to remove the *cause* of uneven development would require the replacement of the fundamental principle of capitalism—private investment decision. Within a capitalist economy, then, poverty is the natural outcome. Whether it is "functional" or not is an incidental question. The ultimate contradiction of capitalism is that it tends inevitably to lead to a secular deterioration between classes in society. In the long run this secular deterioration or uneven development leads to political instability. The only recourse to this process imposes an ever greater economic cost on the bourgeois state. Whether the downfall of capitalism as we know it

---

9. *Public Assistance Statistics,* National Center for Social Statistics, U.S. Department of Health, Education, and Welfare, Report A-2, November, 1970.

will come slowly, as the perceived need for political stability in the face of uneven development forces ever greater public intervention, or whether it comes more quickly through political organization will depend on the strength of the left. The slower method is by far the more costly in terms of human suffering.

Part 4

Contemporary Capitalism

That the large corporation has become the decisive unit of production in the United States is clear; what remains at issue is the significance of its ascendance for the class structure and political economy of contemporary capitalism. If, in fact, our political economy is still "capitalist"—have we entered a "postindustrial society"? The debate revolves mainly around whether or not there has been a shift in the control of large corporations from capital to bureaucracy, or indeed to the "technostructure," resulting in the abolition of the imperatives of profit maximization that once governed the political economy. Rarely explicit in this debate, but always implicit, is the question: Are classes and class conflict still decisive elements in the historical development of the United States? Galbraith's answer, in one of his favorite phrases, is that the class struggle in America is "a dwindling phenomenon" (see his article in Part Six). This, he says in *The New Industrial State,* is because a historical shift matching the earlier one from land to capital is underway in America, from capital to the technostructure. Power has passed, we are told by Galbraith (Selection Number 17), to the association of men with the diverse technical knowledge and experience required by modern technology and corporate planning. The requirements of technology and size have increased the corporation's need for specialized talent and the organization of this talent. Organized intelligence is, in fact, a new factor of production, and thus the technostructure is the new locus of power in the business enterprise and American society. Borrowing extensively from the arguments put forth earlier by Adolph Berle, Jr.[1] Galbraith argues that this transfer of power is the result of processes such as the separation of ownership and control in large corporations, increasing size, the ability of the corporations to finance from internal savings, and their dominant economic position.

Control of capital and control of markets are indispensable to planning. Control of supply and demand, economies of scale, and monopoly will serve the corporations' planning function. Decisions within the technostructure are now rooted in the organization, where technology and planning are uninfluenced by outsiders. The security of profits which the large corporations have—contrary to popular myth, Galbraith says the large corporations simply do not lose money—removes them from the influence of the market. They control—rather than are controlled by—the market. Thus, with the technostructure as controlling intelligence, says Galbraith, the giant corporations are now the basic planning units of our society; and he concludes that though their economic dominance cannot be doubted, neither can their widespread benefits.

That the corporations plan for their survival and expansion is scarcely debatable, but the question is: in whose interest is such "planning" and with what social consequences? Taking issue with Galbraith from the standpoint of neoclassical economics and arguing in defense of "the cold wind of competition" is Walter Adams (Selection Number 18). In Adams's view, the dominance of large corporations is not the result of any so-called technological imperatives. Rather, this is a rationalization for monopoly and for government policies which further it. Technological size and administrative size differ substantially. *Technical* efficiency may

---

1. Adolph Berle, Jr. and Gardiner C. Means, *The Modern Corporation and Private Property* (New York: Macmillan, 1932); Berle, *The 20th Century Capitalist Revolution* (New York: Harcourt, Brace, 1954).

require *smaller* rather than larger plants. In fact, of the 60 most important inventions in recent years, most came from research *not* done by large corporations. Most research is now done by the federal government, paid for by the people, and used for the private benefit of the corporations. It is "the socialization of risk and the privatization of profit and power," says Adams.

Innovations are taken over and used by the larger corporations once they have been proved successful by smaller domestic companies and/or foreign competitors. The large corporations themselves are not the innovators. The competitive market, "not industrial planning, carried on by private monopolists under public supverision," is the best instrument to serve society, Adams believes. TVA's competition with the electric power industry, the airline oligopoly's competition from non scheduled airlines, and the effects of foreign competition on the steel giants led to improved products at lower prices, indicating that "monopoloid" planning is done in the interests of monopoly power, not society at large. Competition, says Adams, along with the government policies designed to promote competition rather than monopoly, are necessary for progress, innovation, and the general welfare.

Daniel Bell (Selection Number 19) is not so sanguine as Galbraith about the uses of corporate power, which he acknowledges is "the predominant power in society." Nor does he think that "competition" is the answer. The problem is how to effectively limit corporate power, for competition alone cannot prevent private costs and social costs from diverging. The questions for the political economy of the future, according to Bell, are: who should bear these costs—the so-called "externalities" of competition—and in what amounts? The "economizing mode" —based on the false proposition that individual satisfaction is the unit in which costs and benefits are to be reckoned and that the sum of individual decisions is equivalent to a social decision—has to be replaced by the "sociologizing mode", in which an effort is necessary to judge society's needs more consciously on the basis of an explicit conception of the "public interest." This, says Bell, involves two basic decisions, namely: what is the "right" distribution of income? and, what should be the relative size of the private and public sectors? "The heart of the matter," Bell believes, "is the question of the nature of the corporation." Has it, or should it, become a servant of society in a system of pluralist power? The corporation may be a private enterprise, but it is not really private property, argues Bell; ownership is largely a legal fiction, and "owners" merely have a legitimate claim to a share of the profits. The corporation's management must operate "as trustees for members of the enterprise as a whole—not just stockholders, but workers and consumers too—and with due regard to the interests of society as a whole." We are, Bell argues, moving toward a "postindustrial society" in which "the most important economic decisions will be made at the political level, in terms of consciously defined 'goals' and 'priorities.' " This movement away from "governance by political economy to governance by political philosophy" is, Bell concludes, "the long-run historical tendency in Western society."

Bell's view is also implicitly shared by Nobel Prize economist Paul A. Samuelson, who reflects the common academic assumption that the American economy can now be subjected to rational control: government policies ("governance by political philosophy"?) can now be designed and implemented to spur economic activity and prevent depression. In Samuelson's view (Selection Number 20), the "Keynesian revolution" in economics now enables governments to sustain full employment by rationally determined spending, taxes, and monetary policies. Clearly, he says, capitalism no longer needs war to prime the pump, and if it ever did, and to assert such a view is foolish. The problem of war in the late twentieth century is as much attributable to strictly political conflicts between the so-called communist countries themselves (China and Russia) or between them and capitalist countries as it is to any alleged propensities to war inherent in capitalism. Certainly, Samuelson argues, the mid-1970s cost-push inflation has nothing "to do with insufficiency of domestic markets, and cold- or hot-war escapades can do nothing to make it better." The fact is, he says, "not a single mixed economy has had any problem these last thirty years with chronic insufficiency of purchasing power."

If Samuelson does not say so explicitly, his reasoning implies that classes and their interrelationships are not central to the American political economy. This is the prevailing view among academic social scientists. In their view, a class theory of the division of the social product, state policy, social conflict, and historic change has become inapplicable to the United States, largely because of the alleged separation of ownership and control in the large corporation. Of course, if this shift in control from the capitalist to the industrial bureaucrat in America's economic heartland has not occurred, then the various versions of this managerial theory held in the United States have no genuine empirical foundations, whatever their aesthetic or political allure.

Based on a systematic review of the discrepant findings of numerous studies and of critical problems of method and measurement, I find (Selection Number 21) that the alleged separation of ownership and control in the large corporation may well be merely a socially plausible but deceptive "pseudofact." Even the fount of the conventional wisdom, Berle and Mean's widely cited but seldom read *The Modern Corporation and Private Property,* had information which permitted them to classify as definitely under management control only 22 percent of the 200 largest corporations—and of the 106 industrials, only 3.8 percent!

I argue that in order to locate the actual centers of corporate control, we have to discover the effective kinship unit among the principal owners of capital. Without research into the web of kinship relations binding apparently unrelated individuals into a cohesive owning unit for purposes of control, analysis of the locus of control in the large corporation is hobbled at the outset. Appropriate social research will reveal, I argue, that the large corporations and banks in America are units in a class-controlled apparatus of private appropriation, and that the whole gamut of principal functionaries and owners of capital participate in varying degrees, and as members of the same dominant social class, in its direction. I also suggest that increased economic concentraion, the fusion of formerly separate large capitals, and the establishment of an effective organizational apparatus of interlocking directorates among large corporations, accompanied by the social and economic interweaving of once opposed financial and industrial interests within the dominant class, has heightened its cohesiveness and capacity for common action and unified policies.

Yet if the concentration and centralization of capital has heightened this class' self-organization, it has also posed critical economic problems which require state "intervention." There is a tendency toward stagnation in a capitalist economy dominated by a small number of large corporations, because the profits they reap tend to exceed the available profitable investment outlets. Therefore, argues Paul

M. Sweezy (Selection Number 22), government spending has become essential for spurring profitable investment and preventing the underemployment of men and productive capacity—and a new major depression. The bulk of government spending has been for the military, not for eliminating poverty or reconstructing our decaying cities; thus, says Sweezy, war and the preparation for war, not the rational economic policy claimed by liberals, have been decisive in keeping the economy afloat. Conducting an "experiment," Sweezy found that when (a) the real level of unemployment and (b) employment resulting directly or indirectly from military spending are measured and combined, roughly 25 percent of the American labor force (adjusted to include hidden unemployed) was really out of work; that is, could not be employed profitably by private capital apart from military spending. This, says Sweezy, is not much of a change from an estimated 30 percent of the adjusted labor force really unemployed in 1938, a period of economic upturn following the Great Depression.

So why has there been relative prosperity in other Western capitalist countries, particularly Germany and Japan, which have the *highest* levels of employment and the *least* military spending in the capitalist world? The answer, Sweezy argues, is that "capitalism is a global system and not a collection of separate national economies," and prosperity in these countries has largely depended on the situation in the world economy's most decisive unit, the economy of the United States. For instance, the Korean war was a major stimulus to profitable exports for Germany and Japan that made their "economic miracles" possible, in addition to such critical economic stimuli as postwar reconstruction and "automobilization" in these countries. Thus, the critical role of military spending is the only adequate explanation for world capitalism's relatively stable performance in the past three decades, Sweezy concludes.

This relative stability was shaken in the mid-1970s when American workers were unemployed in numbers not seen since the Great Depression and prices rose precipitously to record levels. In explaining this (or any) crisis, mainstream economist typically focus on short-term events, on "accidents" like the Arab oil embargo or the Russian wheat deal; but they ignore capitalism's inherent vulnerabilities to such "accidents" and to disruptions in the cycle of production and realization of profit. Production under capitalism is "guided" by calculations of profitability: capital flows where the profits are, or *appear* to be; yet investment decisions taken elsewhere can quickly decrease the profitability of any given investment. If so, investment lags, production slows down, and employment falls, setting off further disruptions of production throughout the economy. David M. Gordon (Selection Number 23) argues that it is in this "anarchy of production," as Marx termed it, that the real roots of the crisis lie. For example, he suggests, bad harvests around the world had an explosive effect on prices because there was a steady decline in world grain reserves over the decade. The reserves declined because the large grain companies were cornering and partially limiting supplies; also, considerable productive land was not planted in our country because of government acreage-retirement and price-subsidy programs—both of primary benefit to the largest producers. Similarly, an "accident" like the oil embargo fit the long-term strategy of the large oil companies, who used it in an attempt to extend their control of production and refining in the United States at the expense of the "independents" and expand their exploration against environmentalist opposition. The point is, actions taken by such large companies in pursuit of their own profits have drastic effects on interdependent industries which, in turn, reverberate throughout the economy. Further, Gordon argues, the anarchy of production extends to the world economy, compounding the problems posed for effective government stabilization policies. Business cycles in the advanced capitalist countries increasingly converge as European, Japanese, and American multinationals, the latter facing stepped-up competition at home and abroad by the former, move capital rapidly around the globe. On the one hand, this makes government "fine tuning" all the more difficult and, on the other, reduces the large corporations' ability to grant marginal wage increases at home as international competition heightens.

Combined with this historically, Gordon argues, has been the constriction of American expansion by antiimperialist movements abroad and the black rebellions at home. Most basically, government fiscal and monetary policies cannot adequately cope with capitalism's inherent class contradiction between capital and labor. Policies designed to achieve higher levels of employment also increase workers' bargaining power and militancy; profits are eroded, investment slows down, and production is disrupted. The government is then compelled to implement policies to raise *un*employment so as to curb workers' demands and rekindle investment. Here, Gordon concludes, lies the ultimate irrationality and basic contradiction of capitalism—the class struggle—which talk of "accidents" as the source of economic problems, or talk of the curative powers of government policy, merely serve to obscure.

American Imperialism?

Many of the issues already posed sharply in the debate about the nature of the American political economy are also critical in understanding the meaning of American imperialism and foreign intervention, both military and political. At bottom, S. M. Miller, Roy Bennett, and Cyril Alapatt reject the notion that "economic imperialism is a necessity" for the United States and other advanced capitalist countries because they believe that "truly fundamental changes" similar to those noted by Galbraith have occurred in these economies (Selection Number 24). In particular, they also accept the view that capitalism is now controllable by rational state policy, and that "different varieties of capitalist planning" now mitigate what were once considered insoluble internal market problems. On theoretical grounds, Miller et al argue, the view that imperialism is economically imperative for the United States and that military outlays are essential to high growth levels is untenable. The empirical question about the necessity of imperialism, they say, can be put as follows: Of what domestic significance are U.S. economic interests in "low-income" or "Third World" countries, and does protecting them compel U.S. military-interventionist action?

The answer, Miller et al say, is that these investments are *not* "necessary" for the U.S. economy, and political-military rather than economic reasons are usually decisive in foreign intervention by the U.S. government. Their basic argument can be summarized as follows: Foreign exports are negligible as a share of GNP in the United States, and most exports are to other *developed* countries. Compared to such countries as Japan, England, and Germany, foreign trade is relatively less important in the United States economy. United States direct foreign investment is only a small percentage of all its investment; most of it is in developed rather than low-income countries; and none of the low-income countries has U.S. direct investment large enough to "warrant great economic concern" by the United

States—though the investment may be of concern to specific firms. Income from direct investments in low-income countries is a negligible 3 to 4 percent of the total income of all U.S. companies, and the share is declining. It is not at all clear, according to Miller et al, that the United States is particularly dependent on raw material imports, or that it could not easily develop artificial substitutes or domestic sources to replace them. The economic benefits gained from "exploitation of weaker nations" are far outweighed by the huge military costs of intervention. They believe, then, that such foreign military intervention clearly springs from political and military rather than economic roots. The counterrevolutionary and interventionist policy of the United States could be reversed by "progressive political groups" organized to "offset the demands made by narrow, economically motivated interest groups." The economy would not collapse, Miller, Bennett and Alapatt conclude, "if particular economic interest groups were unable to control overseas U.S. political military activities in certain areas."

Asking whether or not "economic imperialism is a necessity," Harry Magdoff responds (Selection Number 25), is as relevant and off the mark as the question: "Is Manhattan necessary for the United States?" After all, manufacturing on that island is an insignificant percentage of total U.S. output, and the corporate and financial headquarters now there could be relocated elsewhere on the mainland. The point is, Magdoff says, that scientific inquiry has to discover the right questions to ask before it can give the right answers, and an abstractly speculative question like the one posed by Miller et al ignores the essential historic and structural question of how economic, political, and strategic interests have formed an essential unity and interacted in the course of the historical development of American capitalism—and other major capitalist countries—since the turn of the century or earlier. This means, then, that an analysis of imperialism is inherently inadequate if it is limited to asking about direct investment and foreign trade in the underdeveloped world. Magdoff argues that modern imperialism, as distinct from the territorial expansion and rapaciousness of the past, refers to an historically distinctive structure, characterized as follows: (1) The entire globe has been fitted into world capitalism as a system, and the most advanced countries are decisive in the movement of capital commodities around it. (2) Various countries at different stages of development are intricately interdependent in this global system, and the underdeveloped countries are "industrial and financial dependencies" of the advanced metropolitan areas. (3) Large oligopolistic corporations primarily determine economic change and government economic policy. They seek to control their supplies of raw materials and protect their markets, wherever they are, from other corporate contenders; and governments must assist them if the economy, in which they are decisive, is to function efficiently. (4) There is an "intensive competitive struggle among advanced capitalist nations" for dominance over each other, and not merely over their dependencies.

The crux of imperialism today is not trade and investment with the so-called Third World countries, Magdoff argues, but "the rivalries associated with the investment operations of advanced capitalist nations" in an interdependent world capitalist system. The United States, through its military might and financial and industrial strength, is preeminent in that system, says Magdoff, and has had the primary responsibility for maintaining it as a whole.

The Technostructure and the Corportion in the New Industrial State

17

John Kenneth Galbraith

The tendency to an excess of savings, and the need for an offsetting strategy by the state, is an established and well-recognized feature of the Keynesian economy. And savings . . . , are supplied by the industrial enterprise to itself as part of its planning. There is high certainty as to their availability, for this is the purpose of the planning.

At the same time the requirements of technology and planning have greatly increased the need of the industrial enterprise for specialized talent and for its organization. The industrial system must rely, in the main, on external sources for this talent. Unlike capital it is not something that the firm can supply to itself. To be effective this talent must also be brought into effective association with itself. It must be in an organization. Given a competent business organization, capital is now ordinarily available. But the mere possession of capital is now no guarantee that the requisite talent can be obtained and organized. One should expect, from past experience, to find a new shift of power in the industrial enterprise, this one from capital to organized intelligence. And one would expect that this shift would be reflected in the development of power in the society at large.

This has, indeed, occurred. It is a shift of power as between the factors of production which matches that which occurred from land to capital in the advanced countries beginning two centuries ago. It is an occurrence of the last fifty years and is still going on. A dozen matters of commonplace observation—the loss of power by stockholders in the modern corporation, the impregnable position of the successful corporate management, the dwindling social magnetism of the banker, the air of quaintness that attaches to the suggestion that the United States is run from Wall Street, the increasingly energetic search for industrial talent, the new prestige of education and educators—all attest the point.

This shift of power has been disguised because, as was once true of land, the position of capital is imagined to be immutable. That power should be elsewhere seems unnatural and those who so argue seem to be in search of frivolous novelty. And it has been disguised because power has not gone to another of the established factors as they are celebrated in conventional economic pedagogy. It has not passed to labor. Labor has won limited authority over its pay and working conditions but none over the enterprise. And it still tends to abundance. If overly abundant savings are not used, the first effect is unemployment; if savings are used one consequence is a substitution of machine processes for unskilled labor and standard skills. Thus unskilled labor and workers with conventional skills suffer, along with the capitalist, from an abundance of capital.

Nor has power passed to the classical entrepreneur—the individual who once used his access to capital to bring it into combination with the other factors of production. He is a diminishing figure in the industrial system. Apart from access to capital, his principal qualifications were imagination, capacity for decision, and courage in risking money including, not infrequently, his own. None of these qualifications are especially important for organizing intelligence or effective in competing with it.

Power has, in fact, passed to what anyone in search of novelty might be justified in calling a new factor of production. This is the association of men of diverse technical knowledge, experience, or other talent which modern industrial technology and planning require. It extends from the leadership of the modern industrial enterprise down to just short of the labor force and embraces a large number of people and a large variety of talent. It is on the effectiveness of this organization, as most business doctrine now implicitly agrees, that the success of the modern business enterprise now depends. Were this organization dismembered or otherwise lost, there is no certainty that it could be put together again. To enlarge it to undertake new tasks is an expensive and sometimes uncertain undertaking. Here one now finds the problem of an uncertainly high supply price at the margin. And here one finds the accompanying power. Our next task is to examine in some depth this new locus of power in the business enterprise and in the society. . . .

In the past, leadership in business organization was identified with the entrepreneur—the individual who united ownership [and] control of capital with capacity for organizing the other factors of production and, in most contexts, with a further capacity for innovation.[1] With the rise of the modern corporation, the emergence of the organization re-

---

1. To act with confidence beyond the range of familiar beacons and to overcome that resistance requires aptitudes that are present in only a small fraction of the population and [they] define the entrepreneurial type as well as the entrepreneurial function." Joseph A. Schumpeter, *Capitalism, Socialism, and Democracy,* Second Edition (New York: Harper, 1947), p. 132.

quired by modern technology and planning and the divorce of the owner of the capital from control of the enterprise, the entrepreneur no longer exists as an individual person in the mature industrial enterprise.[2] Everyday discourse, except in the economics textbooks, recognizes this change. It replaces the entrepreneur, as the directing force of the enterprise, with management. This is a collective and imperfectly defined entity; in the large corporation it embraces chairman, president, those vice-presidents with important staff or departmental responsibility, occupants of other major staff positions, and, perhaps, division or department heads not included above. It includes, however, only a small proportion of those who, as participants, contribute information to group decisions. This latter group is very large; it extends from the most senior officials of the corporation to where it meets, at the outer perimeter, the white- and blue-collar workers whose function is to conform more or less mechanically to instruction or routine. It embraces all who bring specialized knowledge, talent or experience to group decisionmaking. This, not the management, is the guiding intelligence—the brain—of the enterprise. There is no name for all who participate in group decisionmaking or the organization which they form. I propose to call this organization the Technostructure.

THE CORPORATION

Few subjects of earnest inquiry have been more unproductive than study of the modern large corporation. The reasons are clear. A vivid image of what *should* exist acts as a surrogate for reality. Pursuit of the image then prevents pursuit of the reality.

For purposes of scholarly inquiry, the corporation has a sharp legal image. Its purpose is to do business as an individual would but with the added ability to assemble and use the capital of several or numerous persons. In consequence, it can undertake tasks beyond the reach of any single person. And it protects those who supply capital by limiting their liability to the amount of their original investment, insuring them a vote on the significant affairs of the enterprise, defining the powers and the responsibilities of directors and officers, and giving them access to the courts to redress grievance. Apart from its ability to mobilize capital and its lessened association with the active life of any individual, the corporation is not deemed to differ functionally from the individual proprietorship or partnership. Its purpose, like theirs, is to conduct business on equitable terms with other businesses and make money for the owners.

Such corporations do exist and in large numbers. But one wonders if the natural interest of the student of economics is the local paving firm

2. He is still, of course, to be found in smaller firms and in larger ones that have yet to reach full maturity of organization. I deal with this evolution in the next [section].

or body repair shop. Or is it General Motors and Standard Oil of New Jersey and General Electric?

But these firms depart sharply from the legal image. In none of these firms is the capital pooled by original investors appreciable; in each it could be paid off by a few hours' or a few days' earnings. In none does the individual stockholder pretend to power. In all three cases, the corporation is far more influential in the markets in which it buys materials, components, and labor and in which it sells its finished products than is commonly imagined to be the case with the individual proprietorship.

In consequence, nearly all study of the corporation has been concerned with its deviation from its legal or formal image. This image—that of "an association of persons into an autonomous legal unit with a distinct legal personality that enable it to carry on business, own property, and contract debts"[3] —is highly normative. It is what a corporation should be. When the modern corporation disenfranchises its stockholders, grows to gargantuan size, expands into wholly unrelated activities, is a monopoly where it buys and a monopoly where it sells, something is wrong.

That the largest and most famous corporations, those whose names are household words and whose heads are accorded the most distinguished honors by their fellow businessmen, should be considered abnormal must seem a little dubious.

Additionally, it must be evident that General Motors does not have much in common with the Massachusetts Institute of Technology professors who pool their personal funds and what they can borrow from the banks and their friends to supply some erudite item to the Department of Defense and thus, in their modest way, help to defend the country and participate in capital gains. Their enterprise, created, owned, and directed by themselves and exploiting the advantages of the corporate form, approaches the established image. General Motors as clearly does not.

The answer is that there is no such thing as *a* corporation. Rather there are several kinds of corporations all deriving from a common but very loose framework. Some are subject to the market; others reflect varying degrees of adaptation to the requirements of planning and the needs of the technostructure. The person who sets out to study buildings on Manhattan on the assumption that all are alike will have difficulty in passing from the surviving brownstones to the skyscrapers. And he will handicap himself even more if he imagines that all buildings should be like brownstones and have load-carrying walls and that others are abnormal. So with corporations.

---

3. Harry G. Guthmann and Herbert E. Dougall, *Corporation Financial Policy,* Second Edition (New York: Prentice-Hall, Inc., 1948), p. 9.

2

The most obvious requirement of effective planning is large size. This, we have seen, allows the firm to accept market uncertainty where it cannot be eliminated; to eliminate markets on which otherwise it would be excessively dependent; to control other markets in which it buys and sells; and it is very nearly indispensable for participation in that part of the economy, characterized by exacting technology and comprehensive planning, where the only buyer is the federal government.

That corporations accommodate well to this need for size has scarcely to be stressed. They can, and have, become very large. But because of the odor of abnormality, this adaptation is not stressed. The head of the largest corporation is automatically accorded precedence in all business conventions, meetings, and other business rites and festivals. He is complimented for his intelligence, vision, courage, progressiveness, and for the remarkable rate of growth of his firm under his direction. But the great size of his firm—the value of its assets or the number of its employees—is not praised although this is its most striking feature.

Nothing so characterizes the industrial system as the scale of the modern corporate enterprise. In 1962 the five largest industrial corporations in the United States, with combined assets in excess of $36 billion, possessed over 12 percent of all assets used in manufacturing. The 50 largest corporations had over a third of all manufacturing assets. The 500 largest had well over two-thirds. Corporations with assets in excess of $10,000,000, some 2000 in all, accounted for about 80 percent of all the resources used in manufacturing in the United States.[4] In the mid-1950s, 28 corporations provided approximately 10 percent of all employment in manufacturing, mining, and retail and wholesale trade. Twenty-three corporations provided 15 percent of all the employment in manufacturing. In the first half of the decade (June, 1950–June, 1956) a hundred firms received two-thirds by value of all defense contracts; ten firms received one-third.[5] In 1960 four corporations accounted for

---

4. Hearings before the Subcommittee on Antitrust and Monopoly of the Committee of the Judiciary, United States Senate, Eighty-eighth Congress, Second Session, Pursuant to S. Res. 262. Part I. *Economic Concentration. Overall and Conglomerate Aspects* (1964), p. 113. Data on the concentration of industrial activity in the hands of large firms, and especially any that seem to show an increase in concentration, sustain a controversy in the United States that, at times, reaches mildly pathological proportions. The reason is that much of the argument between those who see the market as a viable institution and those who feel that it is succumbing to monopolistic influences has long turned on these figures. These figures are thus defended or attacked according to predilection. However, the general orders of magnitude given here are not subject to serious question.

5. Carl Kaysen, "The Corporation: How Much Power? What Scope?" in *The Corporation in Modern Society*, ed. Edward S. Mason, (Cambridge: Harvard University Press, 1959), pp. 86–87.

an estimated 22 percent of all industrial research and development expenditure. Three hundred and eighty-four corporations employing 7,000 or more workers accounted for 87 percent of these expenditures; 260,000 firms employing fewer than 1,000 accounted for only 7 percent.[6]

Planning is a function that is associated in most minds with the state. If the corporation is the basic planning unit, it is appropriate that the scale of operations of the largest should approximate those of government. This they do. In 1965, three industrial corporations, General Motors, Standard Oil of New Jersey, and Ford Motor Company, had more gross income than all of the farms in the country. The income of General Motors, of $20.7 billion, about equaled that of the three million smallest farms in the country—around 90 percent of all farms. The gross revenues of each of the three corporations just mentioned far exceed those of any single state. The revenues of General Motors in 1963 were fifty times those of Nevada, eight times those of New York and slightly less than one-fifth those of the Federal Government.[7]

Economists have anciently quarreled over the reasons for the great size of the modern corporation. Is it because size is essential in order to reap the economies of modern large scale production?[8] Is it, more insidiously, because the big firm wishes to exercise monopoly power in its markets? The present analysis allows both parties to the dispute to be partly right. The firm must be large enough to carry the large capital commitments of modern technology. It must also be large enough to control its markets. But the present view also explains what the older explanations don't explain. That is, why General Motors is not only large enough to afford the best size of automobile plant but is large enough to afford a dozen or more of the best size; and why it is large enough to produce things as diverse as aircraft engines and refrigerators, which cannot be explained by the economies of scale; and why, though it is large enough to have the market power associated with monopoly, consumers do not seriously complain of exploitation. The size of General Motors is in the service not of monopoly or the economies of scale but of planning. And for this planning—control of supply, control of demand, provision of capital, minimization of risk—there is no clear upper limit to the desirable size. It could be that the bigger the better. The corporate form accommodates to this need. Quite clearly it allows the firm to be very, very large.

---

6. M. A. Adelman, Hearings before the Subcommittee on Antitrust and Monopoly of the Committee on the Judiciary, United States Senate, Eighty-Ninth Congress, First Session, Pursuant to S. Res. 70, Part III. *Economic Concentration. Concentration, Invention and Innovation* (1965), pp. 1139–40.

7. Data from *Fortune*, U.S. Department of Agriculture, and *Statistical Abstract of the United States.*

8. Cf. Joe S. Bain, "Economics of Scale, Concentration, and the Condition of Entry in Twenty Manufacturing Industries," *The American Economic Review* 64:1 (March, 1954).

3

The corporation also accommodates itself admirably to the needs of the technostructure. This, we have seen, is an apparatus for group decision—for pooling and testing the information provided by numerous individuals to reach decisions that are beyond the knowledge of any one. It requires . . . a high measure of autonomy. It is vulnerable to any intervention by external authority for, given the nature of the group decisionmaking and the problems being solved, such external authority will always be incompletely informed and hence arbitrary. If problems were susceptible to decision by individuals, no group would be involved.

One possible source of such intervention is the state. The corporate charter, however, accords the corporation a large area of independent action in the conduct of its affairs. And this freedom is defended as a sacred right. Nothing in American business attitudes is so iniquitous as government interference in the *internal* affairs of the corporation. The safeguards here, both in law and custom, are great. There is equally vehement resistance to any invasion by trade unions of the prerogatives of management.

There is also, however, the danger of intervention by the owners—by the stockholders. Their exclusion is not secured by law or sanctified by custom. On the contrary, either directly or through the agency of the Board of Directors, their power is guaranteed. But being legal does not make it benign. Exercise of such power on substantive questions requiring group decision would be as damaging as any other. So the stockholder too must be excluded.

In part this has been accomplished by the simple attrition of the stockholder's power as death and the distribution of estates, the diversifying instincts of trusts and foundations, the distributional effects of property settlements and alimony, and the artistic, philanthropic, and social enjoyments of nonfunctional heirs all distribute the stock of any corporation to more and more hands. This process works rapidly, and the distribution need by no means be complete to separate the stockholder from all effective power. In the mid-1920s, in the first case to draw wide public attention to this tendency, it became known that Colonel Robert W. Stewart, the Chairman of the Board of Directors of the Standard Oil Company of Indiana, had, in concert with some of the men who later won immortality as the architects of the Teapot Dome and Elk Hills transactions, organized a highly specialized enterprise in Canada called the Continental Trading Company. This company had the sole function of buying crude oil from Colonel E. A. Humphreys, owner of the rich Mexica field in east central Texas, and reselling it to companies controlled by the same individuals, including Standard Oil of Indiana, at a markup of twenty-five cents a barrel. It was an excellent business. No costs were involved, other than a small percentage to the Canadian lawyer who served as a figurehead and went hunting in Africa whenever wanted for questioning, and for mailing back the proceeds after they had been converted into Liberty Bonds. (If some of these had not been used, carelessly, to bribe Secretary of the Interior Albert B. Fall and others to pay the deficit of the Republican National Committee, Continental might have forever remained unknown, as was unquestionably intended.) It was Colonel Stewart's later contention that he had always intended to turn over the profit to Standard Oil of Indiana. But, absentmindedly, he had allowed the bonds to remain in his own possession for many years and had cashed some of the coupons. In 1929 Standard of Indiana was only 18 years distant from the decree which had broken up the Standard Oil empire of John D. Rockefeller of which it had been an important part. The Rockefellers still owned 14.9 percent of the voting stock of the Indiana Company and were deemed to have the controlling interest. They reacted sternly to the outrage; the elder Rockefeller had, on notable occasions, imposed a somewhat similar levy on his competitors, but never on his own company. With the aid of the publicity generated by the Teapot Dome scandal, his own high standing in the financial community, his brother-in-law Winthrop W. Aldrich (who solicited proxies), and a very large expenditure of money, John D. Rockefeller, Jr., was able to oust the Colonel, although not by a wide margin.[9] (The latter had the full support of his Board of Directors.) In the absence of the scandal and his ample resources, Rockefeller, it was realized with some shock, would have had little hope.

In most other large corporations, the chance for exerting such power would have been less and it has become increasingly less with the passage of time. Professor Gordon's prewar study of the 176 largest corporations showed that at least half of their stock was held in blocks of less than 1 percent of the total outstanding. In less than a third of the companies was there a stockholder interest large enough to allow of potential control, i.e., the election of a Board of Directors, and "the number of companies in which any large degree of *active* leadership is associated with considerable ownership is certainly even smaller."[10] That was a quarter of a century ago; the dispersion of stock ownership, which was then much greater for the older railroad corporations than

9. Cf. Adolf A. Berle, Jr., and Gardiner C. Means, *The Modern Corporation and Private Property* (New York: Macmillan, 1934), pp. 82–83. Of the 8,465,299 shares represented, Rockefeller got the votes of 5,510,313. Stewart retired on a pension of $75,000 a year. M. R. Werner and John Starr, *Teapot Dome* (New York: The Viking Press, Inc., 1959), pp. 274–75.

10. R. A. Gordon, *Business Leadership in the Large Corporation* (Washington: Brookings, 1945), Chap. II. The median holdings of management were 2.1 percent of the stock. In 56 percent of the companies, management owned less than one percent; in only 16 of the companies did it own as much as 20 percent of the stock outstanding. A more recent study by Mabel Newcomer, *The Big Business Executive* (New York: Columbia University Press, 1955), showed that by 1952 there had been a further reduction in management holdings.

for newer industrial corporations, has almost certainly continued.[11] It means that to change control more stockholders must be persuaded, against the advice of management, to vote their stock for someone whom, in the nature of the case, they do not know and will not be disposed to trust. The effort must also contend with the tendency of the indifferent to give proxies to management. It is also in face of the requirement that the loser of a proxy battle, if he is an outsider, must pay the cost. And it must contend finally with the alternative, always available to the dissatisfied stockholder, of simply selling his stock. Corporate size, the passage of time, and the dispersion of stock ownership do not disenfranchise the stockholder. Rather, he can vote but his vote is valueless.

4

To be secure in its autonomy, the technostructure also needs to have a source of new capital to which it can turn without having, as a quid pro quo, to surrender any authority over its own decisions. Here capital abundance enters as a factor. A bank, insurance company, or investment banker cannot make control of decision, actual or potential, a condition of a loan or security underwriting if funds are readily available from another and more permissive source and if there is vigorous competition for the business.

The complexity of modern technological and planning decisions also protects the technostructure from outside interference. The country banker, out of his experience and knowledge of the business, can readily interpose his judgment, as against that of a farmer, on the prospects for feeder cattle—and does. Not even the most self-confident financier would wish to question the judgment of General Electric engineers, product planners, stylists, market researchers, and sales executives on the culturally advanced toaster taken up in the last chapter. By taking decisions away from individuals and locating them deeply within the technostructure, technology and planning thus remove them from the influence of outsiders.

But the corporation accords a much more specific protection to the technostructure. That is by providing it with a source of capital, derived from its own earnings, that is wholly under its own control. No banker can attach conditions as to how retained earnings are to be used. Nor can any other outsider. No one, the normally innocuous stockholder apart, has the right to ask about an investment from retained earnings that turns out badly. It is hard to overestimate the importance of the shift in power that is associated with availability of such a source of

---

11. This is explicitly confirmed by a study by R. J. Larner, "The 200 Largest Nonfinancial Corporations," *The American Economic Review* 56:4 Part 1 (September 1966): 777–87, which appeared just as [*The New Industrial State*] was going to press.

capital. Few other developments can have more fundamentally altered the character of capitalism. It is hardly surprising that retained earnings of corporations have become such an overwhelmingly important source of capital.

5

There remains one final source of danger to the autonomy of the technostructure. That arises with a failure of earnings. Then there are no retained earnings. If new plant is needed or working capital must be replenished, there will have to be appeal to bankers or other outsiders. This will be under circumstances, i.e., the fact that the firm is showing losses, when the right of such outsiders to inquire and to intervene will have to be conceded. They cannot be told to mind their own business. Thus does a shortage of capital, though limited in time and place, promptly revive the power of the capitalist. And it is in times of such failure of earnings, and then only, that the stockholder of the large corporation can be aroused. In large corporations, battles for control have been rare in recent times. And in all notable cases involving large corporations—the New York Central, Loew's, TWA, the New England railroads, Wheeling Steel, Curtis Publishing—the firm in contention was doing badly at the time. If revenues are above some minimum—they need not be at their maximum for no one will know what that is—creditors cannot intervene and stockholders cannot be aroused.

Here too the corporation, and the industrial system generally, have adapted effectively to the needs of the technostructure, though surprisingly the nature of the adaptation has been little noticed. The adaptation is simply that big corporations do not lose money. In 1957, a year of mild recession in the United States, not one of the 100 largest industrial corporations failed to return a profit. Only one of the largest 200 finished the year in the red. Seven years later in 1964, a prosperous year by general agreement, all of the first 100 again made money; only 2 among the first 200 had losses and only 7 among the first 500. None of the 50 largest merchandising firms—Sears, Roebuck, A & P, Safeway, et al.—failed to return a profit. Nor, predictably, did any of the 50 largest utilities. And among the 50 largest transportation companies, only 3 railroads and the momentarily unfortunate Eastern Airlines failed to make money.[12]

The American business liturgy has long intoned that this is a profit and loss economy. "The American competitive enterprise system is an acknowledged profit and loss system, the hope of profits being the

---

12. *The Fortune Directory,* August 1958, August 1965.

incentive and the fear of loss being the spur,"[13] This may be so. But it is not true of that organized part of the economy in which a developed technostructure is able to protect its profits by planning. Nor is it true of the United States Steel Corporation, author of the sentence just cited, which has not had losses for a quarter of a century.

6

As always, no strong case is improved by overstatement. Among the 200 largest corporations in the United States—those that form the heart of the industrial system—there are few in which owners exercise any important influence on decisions. And this influence decreases year by year. But there are exceptions. Some owners—the du Pont, and in lesser measure the Firestone and Ford, families are examples—participate, or have participated, actively in management. Thus they earn influence by being part of the technostructure and their influence is unquestionably increased by their ownership. Others, through position on the Board of Directors, have power in the selection of management—in decision on those who make decisions. And yet others may inform themselves and intervene substantively on individual decisions—a merger, a plant acquisition, or the launching of a new line.

In the last case, however, there must always be question as to how much the individual is deciding and how much has been decided for him by the group which has provided the relevant information; the danger of confusing ratification with decision must again be emphasized. And in all circumstances it is important to realize that corporate ceremony more or less deliberately disguises the reality. This deserves a final word.

Corporate liturgy strongly emphasizes the power of the Board of Directors and ultimately thus of the stockholders they are assumed to represent. The rites which attest this point are conducted with much solemnity; no one allows himself to be cynical as to their substance. Heavy dockets, replete with data, are submitted to the Board. Time is allowed for study. Recommendations are appended. Given the extent and group character of the preparation, rejection would be unthinkable. The Board, nonetheless, is left with the impression that it has made a decision.

Corporate procedure also allows the Board to act on financial transactions—changes in capital structure, declaration of dividends, authorization of lines of credit. These, given the control by the technostructure of its sources of savings and capital supply, are frequently the most routine and derivative of decisions. But as elsewhere noted, any association with large sums of money conveys an impression of power. It brings it to mind for the same traditional reasons as does a detachment of soldiers.

---

13. United States Steel Corporation. *Annual Report, 1958.*

With even greater unction although with less plausibility, corporate ceremony seeks also to give the stockholders an impression of power. When stockholders are (or were) in control of a company, stockholders' meetings are an occasion of scant ceremony. The majority is voted in and the minority is voted out, with such concessions as may seem strategic, and all understand the process involved. As stockholders cease to have influence, however, efforts are made to disguise this nullity. Their convenience is considered in selecting the place of meeting. They are presented with handsomely printed reports, the preparation of which is now a specialized business. Products and even plants are inspected. During the proceedings, as in the report, there are repetitive references to *your* company. Officers listen, with every evidence of attention, to highly irrelevant suggestions of wholly uninformed participants and assure them that these will be considered with the greatest care. Votes of thanks from women stockholders in print dresses owning ten shares "for the excellent skill with which you run *our* company" are received by the management with well-simulated gratitude. All present show stern disapproval of critics. No important stockholders are present. No decisions are taken. The annual meeting of the large American corporation is perhaps our most elaborate exercise in popular illusion.

Competition, Monopoly, and Planning

18

Walter Adams

In *The New Industrial State,* Galbraith once again examines the reality of corporate giantism and corporate power, and outlines the implications for public policy. He finds that the giant corporation has achieved such dominance of American industry that it can control its environment and immunize itself from the discipline of all exogenous control mechanisms —especially the competitive market. Through separation of ownership from management, it has emancipated itself from the control of stock-holders. By reinvestment of profits (internal financing), it has eliminated the influence of the financier and the capital market. By brainwashing its clientele, it has insulated itself from consumer sovereignty. By possession of market power, it has come to dominate both suppliers and customers. By judicious identification with and manipulation of the state, it has achieved autonomy from government control. Whatever it cannot do for itself to assure survival and growth, a compliant government does on its behalf—assuring the maintenance of full employment; eliminating the risk of, and subsidizing the investment in, research and development; and assuring the supply of scientific and technical skills required by the modern technostructure.

In return for this privileged autonomy, the industrial giant performs society's planning function. And this, according to Galbraith, is not only inevitable (because technological imperatives dictate it); it is also good. The market is dead, we are told; and there is no need to regret its passing. The only remaining task, it seems, is to recognize the trend, to accept it as inexorable necessity, and presumably not to stand in its way. . . .

Reprinted from Walter Adams, *Planning, Regulation, and Competition* in *Hearing before Subcommittees of the Select Committee on Small Business,* United States Senate, 90th Cong., 1st sess. (Washington, D.C.: U.S. Government Printing Office, June 29, 1967), pp. 11–16, 34.

Here is a blueprint for technocracy, private socialism, and the corporate state. The keystone of the new power structure is the giant corporation, freed from all traditional checks and balances, and subject only to the countervailing power of the intellectual in politics—those Platonic philosopher-kings who stand guard over the interests of the Republic. Happily, this blueprint need not cause undue alarm: first, because Galbraith's analysis rests on an empirically unsubstantiated premise; and second, because even if this analysis were correct, there would be more attractive public policy alternatives than Galbraith suggests.

Galbraith's contention that corporate giantism dominates American industry requires no adumbration. On that there is consensus. But Galbraith fails to prove that this dominance is the inevitable response to technological imperatives, and hence beyond our control. Specifically, he offers little evidence to demonstrate that Brobdingnagian size is the prerequisite for, and the guarantor of:

(1) operational efficiency;

(2) invention, innovation, and technological progress; and

(3) effective planning in the public interest.

Let me comment briefly on each of these points, and in so doing indicate that the competitive market need not be condemned to the euthanasia which Galbraith thinks is inexorable, and perhaps even desirable.

EFFICIENCY

In the mass-production industries, firms must undoubtedly be large, but do they need to assume the dinosaur proportions of some present-day giants? The unit of technological efficiency is the plant, not the firm. This means that there are undisputed advantages to large-scale integrated operations at a single steel plant, for example, but there is little technological justification for combining these functionally separate plants into a single administrative unit. United States Steel is nothing more than several Inland Steels strewn about the country, and no one has yet suggested that Inland is not big enough to be efficient. A firm producing such divergent lines as rubber boots, chain saws, motorboats, and chicken feed may be seeking conglomerate size and power; it is certainly not responding to technological necessity. In short, one can favor technological bigness and oppose administrative bigness without inconsistency.

Two major empirical studies document this generalization. The first, by Dr. John M. Blair, indicates a significant divergence between plant and company concentration in major industries dominated by oligopoly. It indicates, moreover, that between 1947 and 1958, there was a general tendency for plant concentration to decline, which means that in many industries technology may actually militate toward optimal efficiency in plants of "smaller" size.[1]

The second study, by Prof. Joe Bain, presents engineering estimates of scale economies and capital requirements in 20 industries of above-average concentration. Bain finds that "Concentration by firms is, in every case but one, greater than required by single-plant economies, and in more than half of the cases very substantially greater."

In less precise language, many multiplant industrial giants have gone beyond the optimal size required for efficiency. Galbraith acknowledges the validity of Bain's findings, but dismisses them by saying, "The size of General Motors is in the service not of monopoly or the economies of scale, but of planning. And for this planning ... there is no clear upper limit to the desirable size. It could be that the bigger the better."[2]

If size is to be justified, then, this must be done on grounds other than efficiency. I shall return to this point.

TECHNOLOGICAL PROGRESS

As in the case of efficiency, there is no strict correlation between giantism and progressiveness. In a study of the 60 most important inventions of recent years, it was found that more than half came from independent inventors, less than half from corporate research, and even less from the research done by large concerns.[3] Moreover, while some highly concentrated industries spend a large share of their income on research, others do not; within the same industry, some smaller firms spend as high a *percentage* as their larger rivals. As Wilcox points out, "The big concern has the ability to finance innovation; it does not necessarily do so. There is no clear relationship between size and investment in research."[4]

Finally, roughly two-thirds of the research done in the United States is financed by the federal government, and in many cases the research contractor gets the patent rights on inventions paid for with public funds. The inventive genius which ostensibly goes with size would seem to involve socialization of risk and privatization of profit and power.

The U.S. steel industry, which ranks among the largest, most basic, and most concentrated of American industries—certainly part of the industrial state that Professor Galbraith speaks of—affords a dramatic

1. U.S. Senate Antitrust and Monopoly Subcommittee, *Economic Concentration*, pp. 1541–51..

2. Ibid., p. 76.

3. Jewkes, Sawers, and Stillerman, *The Sources of Invention*, Chap. 4.

4. *Public Policies Toward Business*, 3rd ed., p. 258.

case in point. It spends only 0.7 percent of its revenues on research and, in technological progressiveness, the giants which dominate this industry lag behind their smaller domestic rivals as well as their smaller foreign competitors. Thus, the basic oxygen furnace—considered the "only major breakthrough at the ingot level since before the turn of the century"—was invented in 1950 by a miniscule Austrian *firm* which was less than one-third the size of a single *plant* of the United States Steel Corp. The innovation was introduced in the United States in 1954 by McLouth Steel which at the time had about 1 percent of domestic steel capacity—to be followed some 10 years later by the steel giants: United States Steel in December, 1963, Bethlehem in 1964, and Republic in 1965. Despite the fact that this revolutionary invention involved an average operating cost saving of $5 per ton and an investment cost saving of $20 per ton of installed capacity, the steel giants during the 1950s, according to *Business Week*, "bought 40 million tons of the wrong capacity—the open-hearth furnace" which was obsolete almost the moment it was put in place.[5]

Only after they were subjected to actual and threatened competition from domestic and foreign steelmakers in the 1960s did the steel giants decide to accommodate themselves to the oxygen revolution. Thus, it was the cold wind of competition, and not the catatonia induced by industrial concentration, which proved conducive to innovation and technological progress.[6]

PLANNING IN THE PUBLIC INTEREST

Modern technology, says Galbraith, makes planning essential, and the giant corporation is its chosen instrument. This planning in turn requires the corporation to eliminate risk and uncertainty, to create for itself an environment of stability and security, and to free itself from all outside interference with its planning function. Thus it must have enough size and power not only to produce a "mauve and cerise, air-conditioned, power-steered, and power-braked automobile"[7]—unsafe at any speed—but also enough power to brainwash customers to buy it. In the interest of planning, producers must be able to sell what they make—be it automobiles or missiles—and at prices which the techno-structure deems remunerative.

Aside from the unproved premise—technological necessity—on which this argument rests, it raises crucial questions of responsibility and accountability. By what standards do the industrial giants plan, and

---

5. *Business Week* (Nov. 16, 1963):144–46.
6. Adams and Dirlam, "Big Steel, Invention, and Innovation," *Quarterly Journal of Economics* (May, 1966).
7. *The Affluent Society*, p. 253.

is there an automatic convergence between private and public advantage? Must we, as a matter of inexorable inevitability, accept the proposition that what is good for General Motors is good for the country? What are the safeguards—other than the intellectual in politics—against arbitrary abuse of power, capricious or faulty decisionmaking? Must society legitimatize a self-sustaining, self-serving, self-justifying, and self-perpetuating industrial oligarchy as the price for industrial efficiency and progress?

This high price need not and should not be paid. The competitive market is a far more efficacious instrument for serving society—and far more viable—than Galbraith would have us believe. Let me illustrate:

(1) In the electric power industry a network of local monopolies, under government regulation and protection, was long addicted to the belief that the demand for electric power was inelastic—that rates had little to do with the quantity of electricity used. It was not industrial planning, carried on by private monopolists under public supervision, but the yardstick competition of TVA which demonstrated the financial feasibility of aggressive rate reductions. It was this competitive experiment which proved that lower electric rates were not only possible but also profitable—both to the private monopolists and to the customers they served.

(2) In the airline oligopoly, also operating under the umbrella of government protectionism, the dominant firms long suffered from the same addiction. They refused to institute coach service on the grounds that it would eliminate first-class service and—through a reduction in the rate structure—bring financial ruin to the industry. Again it was the force and discipline of competition—from the small nonscheduled carriers, operating at the margin of the industry—which proved that the giants and their overprotective public regulators were wrong. As this committee observed, it was the pioneering and competition of the nonskeds which "shattered the concept of the fixed, limited market for civil aviation. As a result, the question is no longer what portion of a fixed pie any company will get, but rather how much the entire pie can grow."[8]

Again, a bureaucracy-ridden, conservative, overcautious, overprotected industry was shown to have engaged in defective planning—to its own detriment as well as the public's.

(3) In the steel industry after World War II, oligopoly planning resulted in truly shabby performance. There was an almost unbroken climb in steel prices, in good times and bad, in the face of rising or falling demand, increasing or declining unit costs. Prices rose even when only 50 percent of the industry's capacity was utilized. Technological change

---

8. *Senate Report No. 540*, 82d Cong., first sess., 1951.

was resisted and obsolete capacity installed. Domestic markets were eroded by substitute materials and burgeoning imports. Steel's export-import balance deteriorated both in absolute and relative terms; whereas the industry once exported about five times as much as it imported, the ratio today is almost exactly reversed, and steel exports are confined almost exclusively to AID-financed sales guaranteed by "Buy American" provisos. We may be confident that if this deplorable performance is to be improved, it will come about through the disciplining force of domestic and foreign competition, and not through additional planning or an escalation of giant size. It will come about through an accommodation to the exigencies of the world market, and not by insensitive monopolistic pricing, practiced under the protectionist shelter of the tariffs which the industry now seeks.

Without multiplying such examples, it is safe to say that monopoloid planning is done in the interest of monopoly power. Seldom, if ever, is society the beneficiary.

In conclusion, I would note that industrial giantism in America is not the product of spontaneous generation, natural selection, or technological inevitability. In this era of "Big Government," it is often the end result of unwise, manmade, discriminatory, privilege-creating governmental action. Defense contracts, R. & D. support, patent policy, tax privileges, stockpiling arrangements, tariffs, subsidies, etc., have far from a neutral effect on our industrial structure. Especially in the regulated industries—in air and surface transportation, in broadcasting and communications—the writ of the state is decisive. In controlling these variables the policymaker has greater freedom and flexibility than is commonly supposed; the potential for promoting competition and dispersing industrial power is both real and practicable.[9]

It seems to me that Professor Galbraith keeps coming back to the charade of antitrust, but a competitive society is the product not simply of negative enforcement of the antitrust laws; it is the product of a total integrated approach on all levels of government—legislative, administrative, and regulatory. An integrated national policy of promoting competition—and this means more than mere enforcement of the antitrust laws—is not only feasible but desirable. No economy can function without builtin checks and balances which tend to break down the bureaucratic preference for letting well enough alone—forces which erode, subvert, or render obsolete the conservative bias inherent in any organization devoid of competition. Be it the dictates of the competitive market, the pressure from imports or substitutes, or the discipline of yardstick competition, it is these forces which the policymaker must try to reinforce where they exist and to *build into* the economic system

---

9. Adams and Gray, *Monopoly in America* (Macmillan, 1955).

where they are lacking or moribund. The policy objective throughout must be to promote market *structures* which will *compel* the conduct and performance which is in the public interest.

The disciplining force of competition is superior to industrial planning—by the private or public monopolist, the benevolent or authoritarian bureaucrat. It alone provides the incentives and compulsions to pioneer untried trails, to explore paths which may lead to dead ends, to take risks which may not pay off, and to try to make tomorrow better than the best. . . .

If indeed as Professor Galbraith tells us . . . the new industrial state is not the product of operational efficiency, if indeed it is not the virtuosity of technological progressiveness that explains giantism in American industry, then what is the justification for this giantism? Why do we have to tolerate it?

Professor Galbraith claims that the great virtue of the giant corporation is that it has the ability to plan. And he said giantism gives these corporations, and I am quoting his statement now, "gives *them* advantages in planning *their* own future and assuring *their* own survival."

Well, that is just the point. The planning that is done by these giants is motivated by private advantage, not public benefit. Is this a happy social instrument to be used? Are we going to tolerate it or are we going to do something about it?

"The Subordination of the Corporation in the Coming Post - Industrial Society"

19

Daniel Bell

In the post-industrial society, . . . there will be an enormous growth in the "third sector": the nonprofit area outside of business and government, which includes schools, hospitals, research institutes, voluntary and civic associations, and the like. Yet with all that, the business corporation remains, for the while, the heart of the society. About 55 percent of the Gross National Product originates in the corporate sector; about 9.5 percent of Gross National Product is invested annually by nonfinancial corporate firms for new plants and equipment.[1]

When we speak of the corporation in any familiar sense, we usually think of the industrial giants and of the "magic number" 500 that *Fortune* magazine has popularized. And there are clear reasons for this focus. Actually there are, in round numbers, about 1,500,000 corporations in the United States. But if we break down the total, they are distributed in this fashion:

Retail and wholesale trade—450,000
Finance, real estate and insurance—400,000
Services—200,000
Manufacturing—195,000
Construction—115,000
Agriculture and mining—45,000

If we take the manufacturing sector as the prototype of industrial America, we find that these 195,000 corporations have about $500 billion in assets. But about 192,000 corporations (or 98 percent of the total)

Reprinted with permission from Daniel Bell, "The Subordination of the Corporation in the Coming Post-Industrial Society," *The Coming of Post-Industrial Society: A Venture in Social Forecasting.* Copyright 1973 by Daniel Bell, Basic Books, Inc. Publishers, New York.
1. All the data are from the *Statistical Abstract of the United States* (1971).

are under $10 million in asset size, and this group of 98 percent of all corporations owns only 14 percent of all industrial corporate assets. Slightly more than 500 firms, with more than $25 million in assets, account for 83 percent of all corporate assets; 200 firms, each with more than $250 million in assets, account for 66 percent of all industrial assets, while 87 firms, each holding more than a billion dollars in assets, account for 46 percent of the total $500 billion assets.

These 500 industrial corporations, which in 1970 employed 14,-600,000 workers, or more than 75 percent of all employment in manufacturing, symbolize a degree of power which has been a source of recurrent concern for public policy. This concern is evident, once again, today; but for reasons far different than those, say, of thirty years ago, when a firm such as General Motors would spend millions of dollars for thugs, tear gas, and guns to fight the violence of labor organizing. Corporate power clearly is the predominant power in the society, and the problem is how to limit it. The concern for public policy, summed up in the phrase "social responsibility," derives from the growing conception of a communal society and the controls which a polity may have to impose on economic ventures that generate unforeseen consequences far beyond the intentions, or powers of control, of the initiating parties.

For almost half a century, this idea of divergence between private cost and social cost was almost completely neglected. Now with the rising concern with environmental spoilation, the second-order consequences of technological change and the increase in "externalities," the problem has moved into the center of social policy. In the next decade one of the major social questions will be the determination of who is to pay the costs of such externalities and how the amounts will be assessed. Which costs ought to be borne by the parties that generate the costs and which, legitimately, should be borne by the society as a whole will be one of the most difficult questions in the political economy of the future. What we have now is only the beginning awareness of the problem. What we lack is a genuine total cost matrix which, for particular instances, would be able to assess the costs and benefits of particular actions and policies.

THE SOCIOLOGIZING MODE

Important as all these issues are, they do not go to the heart of the matter, which is that the economizing mode is based on the proposition that *individual* satisfaction is the unit in which costs and benefits are to be reckoned. This is an atomistic view of society and reflects the utilitarian fallacy that the sum total of individual decisions is equivalent to a social decision. Yet the aggregate of individual decisions has collective effects far beyond the power of any individual to manage, and which often vitiate the individual's desires. Thus every individual may value the freedom and mobility which a personal automobile provides, yet the aggregate effect of so many autos on the roads at once can lead to clogged transportation. We might all accept in the abstract the principle that the automobile has become a vehicle of uglification; yet lacking a social decision about which alternative modes of transportation might best serve an area, I might have, willy-nilly, to go out and buy a car. Each of us individually may see the consequences of an individual action, but lacking a social mechanism to assess it we become helpless, drift, and thereby accelerate it.

In effect, in contrast to the economizing mode of thought, one can specify—I apologize for the heavy-handed clumsiness—a sociologizing mode, or the effort to judge a society's needs in more conscious fashion,[2] and (to use an old-fashioned terminology) to do so on the basis of some explicit conception of the "public interest."

Two fundamental questions are involved.

First, the conscious establishment of social justice by the inclusion of all persons *into* the society. If the value system of a society is made more explicit as a means of guiding the allocative system (pricing) of a society, this value system must also establish, however roughly, the "right" distribution of income in the society, the minimum income available to all citizens, etc.

The second is the relative size of the public and the private sector. Economic goods, to put it in textbook fashion, are of two types, individual and social. Individual goods are "divisible"; each person buys the goods or services he wants—clothes, appliances, automobiles—on the basis of free consumer choice. Social goods are not "divisible" into individual items of possession, but are a communal service—national defense, police and fire protection, public parks, water resources, highways, and the like. These goods and services are not sold to individual consumers and are not adjusted to individual tastes. The nature and amounts of these goods must be set by a single decision, applicable jointly to all persons. Social goods are subject, therefore, to communal or political, rather than individual, demand.

A man cannot ask for and individually buy in the marketplace his share of unpolluted air, even if he were willing to pay extra for it. These are actions that have to be taken in coordinated fashion through public channels. We can assign the costs of air pollution to its source, whether industrial, municipal, or individual, in order to force culprits to reduce

---

2. One can say, theoretically, that the price system could manage the problem, e.g., when the costs of individual congestion became high it would then become profitable for alternative modes of transportation to compete with the private car. But the price system, in this instance, relies on *trial and error* to assess the result. The difficulty is that such assessments, *after the fact,* are likely to be futile—an enormous amount of resources would have been misallocated, and a preemptive "system" of transportation will have been established. Under such a system, clogged highways will eventually result in the building of more highways.

the pollution, or we can use the money for remedial measures. In the same way, the laying out of roads, the planning of cities, the control of congestion, the organization of health care, the cleaning up of environmental pollution, the support of education—all these, necessarily, become matters of public policy, of public concern, and often (though not necessarily) of public funding.

To say, in effect, that the public sector of the society has to be expanded is not to assume naively that the failures of the market will now be remedied. Each arena has its own problems, and the beginning of political wisdom is to recognize the ineluctable difficulties in each. Public decisionmaking can easily be as irrational and counterproductive as private decisionmaking. The major sociological problem ahead will be the test of our ability to *foresee* the effects of social and technological change and to *construct alternative courses* in accordance with different valuations of ends, at different costs. . . .

THE TURNING POINT FOR THE CORPORATION

The question of "social responsibility" is, I believe, the crux of a debate that will become crucial in the next few years. One position has been put forth by Milton Friedman:

> What does it mean to say that the corporate executive has a "social responsibility" in his capacity as businessman? If this statement is not pure rhetoric, it must mean that he is to act in some way that is not in the interest of his employers. For example, that he is to refrain from increasing the price of the product in order to contribute to the social objective of preventing inflation, even though a price increase would be in the best interests of his corporation. Or that he is to make expenditures on reducing pollution beyond the amount that is in the best interests of the corporation or that is required by law in order to contribute to the social objective of improving the environment. Or that, at the expense of corporate profits, he is to hire "hard-core" unemployed instead of better qualified available workmen to contribute to the social objective of reducing poverty. . . .

> In a free-enterprise, private property system, a corporate executive is an employee of the owners of the business. He has direct responsibility to his employers. That responsibility is to conduct the business in accordance with their desires, which generally will be to make as much money as possible while conforming to the basic rules of the society, both those embodied in law and those embodied in ethical custom.[3]

There are two different kinds of answers to Friedman. Both were given recently by Alden Clausen, the new president and chief executive officer of the Bank of America, the biggest bank in the world.

---

3. From "The Social Responsibility of Business Is to Increase Its Profits," in *The Sunday Times Magazine* (September 13, 1970). The argument is elaborated in Friedman's book, *Capitalism and Freedom.*

For Clausen, one crucial question is: In what social context does the corporation operate today? As an article in *Fortune* by John Davenport reported: "To keep this giant money machine profitably growing is the first business of Alden Winship (Tom) Clausen. . . . It is of some significance that . . . his thoughts turn often to: how to alleviate if not cure the blight now spreading at Hunter's Point and south of Market Street [in San Francisco]; how to crack the city's hard-core unemployment; how to cope with student unrest at Berkeley or down the peninsula at Stanford."

In defending these objectives, Clausen confronted directly the views of Friedman. As the article in *Fortune* reported:

> At the moment Clausen and his associates are less interested in modifying their bank's capital structure than in charting a course through a period when capitalism itself is under intense attack. . . .
>
> . . . Business, he argued, has to concern itself with nonbusiness problems today if it wants to be around tomorrow. The Friedman view is okay in the short pull. "But in the long pull, nobody can expect to make profits—or have any meaningful use for profits—if the whole fabric of society is being ripped to shreds."
>
> There is, equally, a different question, apart from social expediency: Below the surface of this clash of views, there lies an important but seldomly explicated or confronted question about the nature of the corporation. Friedman sees the corporation as fundamentally an "artificial person" and the corporation manager as simply an agent of individual shareholders. Clausen sees the corporation as having a kind of life of its own, and hence having a certain freedom of choice in balancing its contribution to the long-range needs of the community against the immediate demands of owners.

And as the writer John Davenport, himself a distinguished conservative, comments: "There may be dangers lurking in Clausen's view of corporate autonomy, but there is surely something unrealistic in the view that society is just an atomized collection of individuals."[4]

The heart of the matter is the question of the nature of the corporation. Is the corporation primarily an instrument of "owners"—legally the stockholders—or is it an autonomous enterprise which, despite its particular history, has become—or should become—an instrument for service to society in a system of pluralist powers?

A classic debate on that question was initiated forty years ago in the pages of the *Harvard Law Review* by A. A. Berle and Merrick Dodd. Berle held to the view at the time (he later revised his views) that all corporate powers are powers in trust for the benefit of the stockholders. Dodd argued that legally such was the case, but the use of private property was deeply affected with a public interest and that the directors should be viewed as trustees for the enterprise as a whole—for the corporation

---

4. John Davenport, "Bank of America Is Not for Burning," *Fortune* (January, 1971).

viewed as an institution—and not merely as "attorneys for the stock-holders." Berle responded that, since one could not offer "a clear and reasonably enforceable scheme of responsibilities to someone else," Dodd's proposal would place the control of the organization entirely in the hands of management. The problem, as he saw it, was: If there is not a prior legal statement of responsibility to the stockholders, how does one prevent management from exercising arbitrary social and political powers, or from becoming overreaching and self-seeking?

This legal—and sociological—issue remains. Is the manager primarily a trustee for absentee investors? Or is the role of the manager, as Frank Abrams put it when he was chairman of the board of Standard Oil of New Jersey, to conduct his affairs "in such a way as to maintain an equitable and working balance among the claims of the various directly interested—stockholders, employees, customers, and the public at large."

PRIVATE PROPERTY OR PRIVATE ENTERPRISE?

The modern business corporation has lost many of the historic features of traditional capitalism, yet it has, for lack of a new rationale, retained the old ideology—and finds itself trapped by it.

Unhappy is a society that has run out of words to describe what is going on. So Thurman Arnold observed in connection with the language of private property—the myths and folklore of capitalism—which even thirty years ago was hopelessly out of date. *The point is that today ownership is simply a legal fiction.*

A stockholder is an owner because, in theory, he has put up equity capital and taken a risk. But only a minor proportion of corporate capital today is raised through the sale of equity capital. A more significant portion of capital comes through self-financing—by the success of the enterprise itself. In the last decade, more than 60 percent of the capital investment of the nation's 1,000 largest manufacturing firms was financed internally. Retained capital is the basis of the rise in net assets of large corporations. And the growth of retained capital is the product of managerial skill. (Equally, a large portion of new capital is raised by debentures, which becomes a fixed charge against earnings, rather than through floating equity or risk stock. Debentures hinge on the stability of the company and the prospect of repayment—again a managerial problem.)

If one were to follow the logic of Friedman's argument, as he does —it is his strength and weakness that he always follows the logic of his argument, to the very end—one would have to outlaw or at least discourage self-financing. Under the "pure" theory of market capitalism, a firm risks a stockholder's capital and then pays back any profits—in the form of dividends—to its legal owners, the stockholders. If it seeks to risk that money again, it should ask those stockholders to reinvest that money, rather than withhold it from them and reinvest it by managerial decision. Friedman argues that it is only the "double taxation" (through corporate and personal income tax) of dividends that prevents such a desirable state of affairs from emerging. But I should say that such a state of affairs is neither desirable nor possible. Given the pattern of stock ownership today—particularly with the growth of mutual funds, pension funds, and trust funds—the stockholder is often an "in-and-out" person with little continuing interest in the enterprise. Such an in-and-out procedure may be a useful discipline for management and a measure of economic performance—but then it becomes a form of countervailing power, not ownership. True owners are involved directly and psychologically in the fate of an enterprise, and this description better fits the employees of the corporation, not its stockholders. For these employees, the corporation is a social institution which they inhabit. It is politically and morally unthinkable that their lives should be at the mercy of a financial speculator.

In other words, the corporation may be a *private enterprise* institution, but it is not really a *private property* institution. (If the assets of the enterprise are primarily the skill of its managerial employees, not machinery or things—and this is preeminently true in the science-based industries, in communications, and in the so-called "knowledge industries"—then property is anyway of lesser importance.) And if ownership is largely a legal fiction, then one ought to adopt a more realistic attitude to it. One can treat stockholders not as "owners" but as legitimate claimants to some fixed share of the profits of a corporation—and to nothing more.[5]

THE MEANING OF "A CORPORATION"

What then is a corporation? If one goes back to the original meaning of the term (as a social invention of the late Middle Ages to meet some novel problems), a corporation was an instrument for self-governance

---

5. There are about 31 million shareholders in the United States, most of whom have only a small holding in the enterprise. The New York Stock Exchange survey of shareownership (1970) showed that of 30,520,000 shareholders surveyed (out of a total of 30,850,000) about 12,500,000 had portfolios worth less than $5,000, and 6,400,000 had between $5,000 and $10,000. Thus a total of 18,900,000 shareholders, or 62 percent, had portfolios of less than $10,000.

Institutional investors generally now hold an increasing proportion of the outstanding equity securities of major American corporations. As of the end of 1970, the New York Stock Exchange estimated that $161.9 billion, or 25.4 percent of all equity securities of companies listed on the Exchange, were held by institutional holders. If one excludes unregistered mutual funds, investment partnerships, nonbank trusts, and foreign institutions, the Exchange estimated that the total of all institutional holdings would exceed 40 percent. (I am indebted to Professor Philip Blumberg of the Boston University Law School for the data.)

for groups carrying on a common activity (artisan guilds, local boroughs, ecclesiastical bodies); it often had common economic assets, and its existence would persist beyond the lives of its individual members. Those who were "members" of the corporation were those directly responsible for its activities, those who were the legatees of the past members, and those chosen to carry on the work.

A business corporation today—like a university today—can be viewed in this original sociological conception of the term. Indeed, if one begins to look on the business corporation more and more on the model of the university, then the fallacy of ownership becomes more apparent. Who "owns" Harvard or the University of Chicago? Legally the "corporation," as composed by the overseers or the trustees. But in any sociological sense this is meaningless. The university is a self-selective ongoing enterprise of its members (administration, faculty, students, and alumni, with differential responsibilities and obligations) who seek to carry out its purposes with due regard to the interests of the particular community which constitutes the university—and also to the larger community that makes the university possible.

As a business institution, the "corporation" is the management and the board of directors, operating as trustees for members of the enterprise as a whole—not just stockholders, but workers and consumers too —and with due regard to the interests of society as a whole. But if this view is accepted, there is a significant logical corollary—that the constituencies which make up the corporation themselves have to be represented within the board of corporate power. Without that, there is no effective countervailing power to that of executive management. More important, without such representation, there would be a serious question about the "legitimacy" of managerial power.

The private enterprise system has been the primary institution of Western society not because of its coercive power but because its values —economizing and increasing output of material goods—were congruent with the major consumer values of the society. With all its obvious imperfections the system "worked." Today, however, those values are themselves being questioned, not in the way socialists and radicals questioned them a generation ago—that they were achieved at the cost of exploiting the worker—but at the very core, the creation of more private goods at the expense of other social values. I return to a point made earlier that unlike the polity no one, meeting collectively, "voted in" our market economy. But now votes are being taken.

It seems clear to me that today we in America are moving away from a society based on a private-enterprise market system toward one in which the most important economic decisions will be made at the political level, in terms of consciously defined "goals" and "priorities." The dangers inherent in such a shift are familiar enough to anyone acquainted with the liberal tradition. In the past, there was an "unspoken consensus," and the public philosophy did not need to be articulated. And this was a strength, for articulation often invites trials by force when implicit differences are made manifest. Today, however, there is a visible change from market to nonmarket political decisionmaking. The market disperses responsibility: the political center is visible, the question of who gains and who loses is clear, and government becomes a cockpit.

But to be hypnotized by such dangers is little less than frivolous. No social or economic order has a writ of immortality, and the consumer-oriented free-enterprise society no longer satisfies the citizenry, as once it did. So it will have to change, in order that something we still recognize as a liberal society might survive.

Whether such a change will represent "progress" is a nice metaphysical question that I for one do not know how to answer. This is a society that has rested on the premises of individualism and market rationality, in which the varied ends desired by individuals would be maximized by free exchange. We now move to a communal ethic without that community being as yet wholly defined. In a sense, the movement away from governance by political economy to governance by political philosophy —for that is the meaning of the shift—is a turn to r :capitalist modes of social thought. And this is the long-run historical tendency in Western society.[6]

---

6. This essay has dealt with the business corporation in the American context, but in the Soviet Union many of the same problems occur in the relation of the bureaucratic state enterprise to the society as a whole. Under the Soviet planning system, each enterprise is responsible for meeting the production and profit goals of the central plan. Where the enterprise "overfulfills" the plan it is allowed to retain a portion of the profits for its social investment fund, which is used to build housing for its workers, expand clubhouse facilities, and the like. Thus there is an incentive to "economizing," since the enterprise does not want to absorb the social costs that it generates. The large Soviet paper plants at the edge of Lake Baikal, for example, dangerously polluted the lake but strenuously resisted the idea of "internalizing" those additional costs. Insofar as the Soviet Union is committed so singlemindedly to the idea of "economic growth" and the "economizing" mode in the way I have used it, one can say that the Soviet system is actually state capitalism in which the maximization of production of each enterprise is the primary goal of the society. Yet inevitably in a complex society no enterprise can run its show in a single-purpose fashion, and protests do arise; and the state must also confront the problem of how to allocate the social costs. For a discussion of this problem in the Soviet Union, see Marshall Goldman, *The Spoils of Progress: Environmental Pollution in the Soviet Union* (Cambridge, Mass., 1972).

Taking Stock of War

20

Paul A. Samuelson

Three questions deserve hard-headed and unflinching investigation.

1. Are great, or little, wars inevitable because of the capitalist class's pursuit of profits? If not inevitable, are wars nevertheless more likely than under noncapitalist regimes (socialism, feudalism, the modern mixed economy)?

2. Are there particular groups of capitalists who profit from war—merchants of death in the form of munitions makers and, more generally, an entrenched and powerful military-industrial complex? Are there imperialistic investors abroad, whose pecuniary interests are furthered or preserved by war? Is it the lobbying and political power of such interests that contribute importantly to the occurrence and duration of great and little wars?

3. Leaving aside the parochial interests of the plutocratic or property-owning classes, is it the case that all the citizens of a market economy have a recognized or covert interest in war—for the reasons, first, that capitalism must break down in depression if it does not find imperialistic ventures that spend money and destroy surplus goods, and, second, that high living standards of the few advanced nations can be maintained only by exploitation of the teeming billions who live in the impoverished, underdeveloped nations?

To answer these questions, begin with the writings of ideologues: defenders of nineteenth-century capitalism (Adam Smith's followers, Hayek, Milton Friedman, Barry Goldwater, your great-uncle), [and] revolutionary critics of Victorian capitalism (Karl Marx and Friedrich Engels, Rosa Luxemburg and V. I. Lenin, Paul Sweezy and Paul Baran, Jack Gurley and Sam Bowles, your freshman brother at Yale).

You find your work has just begun. One sweeping, monistic explanation cancels out another. Alas, there is no substitute for tedious analysis of historical experience, unsparing analysis of what makes the macroeconomics of the mixed economy tick, and sophisticated insight into the checks and balances of realistic power politics.

Let's begin by answering a couple of the easy questions. Of course, particular groups benefit from war. Generals, for one (and they both antedate the market system and postdate it). Sergeants, for another. Assembly line workers on bombers, their spouses, their unions, their congressmen. And let's not forget the corporations whose activities are specialized to the defense industry.

But little or nothing follows from this. Somebody stands to benefit from every dollar of the gross national product. The plowshare industry stands to gain from peace, just as the sword industry gains from war. ITT has so well hedged a portfolio that only God knows—certainly Harold Geneen doesn't—where its pocketbook interests lie.

"Wait a minute," you will say. "Aren't you forgetting that war expenditures may be an add-on to gross national product—the something extra that permits underconsuming capitalism to get rid of its unemployment and its declining rate of profit?"

No. I am simply remembering that this is 1973, not 1903 or 1933. We are almost forty years into the Age of Keynes. I believe that Luxemburg and Lenin (and Hobson and Alvin Hansen) were right to worry about the sustainability of full employment in William McKinley's balanced-budget laissez-faire. However, not a single mixed economy has had any problem these last thirty years with chronic insufficiency of purchasing power. (Go down the list: the United States, Britain, France, Japan, Germany, little Belgium.)

Nor in the century to come—1973 to 2073—will the ancient scourge of intermitten-shortage-of-purchasing-power reoccur in the old form.

("What about recession and stagflation, professor? Don't deny they still happen!" Of course they do. And in 1983 or 2013 they may still occur to plague the mixed economy. But Sweezy and Bowles know what Lenin and Luxemburg couldn't know—that the disease of cost-push inflation which is involved in stagflation has nought to do with insufficiency of domestic markets, and cold- or hot-war escapades can do nothing to make it better.)

After the few easy answers of somebody-gains-somebody-loses-from-war and wars-no-longer-needed-to-prime-the-pump we are left with hard questions.

1. A World War III between Russia and China, two noncapitalistic countries, is as likely as between any two market economies and as likely as a war between the United States and either Russia or China or both of them.

2. The fact that the mixed economies of North America, Western Europe, and elsewhere will not willingly go through a communist revolution or the socialist societies of Eastern Europe and Asia will not

willingly go through a counterrevolution or take over, would produce acute or chronic warfare in the future. In this sense, "capitalism plus communism" might be deemed potential causes of war.

3. Revolution and insurrection cannot always be distinguished from war. The fact that wealth and power are unequally distributed, within nations and between nations, must be regarded as a potential cause of conflict and war.

4. Adam Smith's "invisible hand of self-interest" leads you to pick the best growth stock, the best hi-fi, and to vote for Richard Nixon. That same hand will lead other people to take over in the future foreign copper mines and oil concessions. And who is to say that the invisible hand which leads people to the ballot box will not someday lead them also to the barricades and the front line trenches?

Corporate Ownership and Control: The Large Corporation and the Capitalist Class

21

Maurice Zeitlin

The originating question of this article is, how has the ascendance of the large corporation as the decisive unit of production affected the class structures and political economies of the United States, Great Britain, and other "highly concentrated capitalist" countries?[1] In particular, our concern is with the alleged "separation of ownership and control" of the large corporation and the presumed impact of this separation on the internal structures, if not actual social existence, of the "dominant" or "upper" classes in these countries. This article does not provide any answers to this difficult issue; rather it questions the evidence for the accepted ones, which underlie what Ralf Dahrendorf (1959), a leading proponent of the prevailing view, has called the "astonishing degree of consensus among sociologists on the implications of joint-stock companies ... for the wider structure of society" (p. 42). This consensus extends, it should be emphasized, to other social science disciplines. E. S. Mason, though himself dissatisfied with economic theories derived from the prevalent view, wrote recently (1967): "Almost everyone now agrees that in the large corporation, the owner is, in general, a passive recipient; that, typically, control is in the hands of management; and that management normally selects its own replacements" (p. 4). Peter

Reprinted from Maurice Zeitlin, "Corporate Ownership and Control: The Large Corporation and the Capitalist Class," American Journal of Sociology 79 (No. 5):1073–1119. All rights reserved by the author.

I have benefited from critical comments on an earlier draft of this article by many colleagues of diverse and often opposing theoretical persuasions, all of whom are absolved of any responsibilities for what follows. Thanks are due Michael Aiken, Robert Alford, Daniel Bell, G. W. Domhoff, Lynda Ewen, Robert Larner, Ferdinand Lundberg, Harry Magdoff, Robert K. Merton, Barrington Moore, Jr., Harvey Molotch, Willard F. Mueller, James O'Connor, Victor Perlo, and Paul M. Sweezy. The comments of the anonymous referees for the *AJS* were also useful. I am particularly grateful to the editors of the *Journal,* especially to Florence Levinsohn, for their careful reading and cogent criticisms.

1. Bain (1966, p. 102) refers here to the United States, England, Japan, Sweden, France, Italy, and Canada, which were included in his study.

Drucker (1971), himself an early managerial theorist, writes that ideas concerning the separation of ownership and control represent "the most conventional and most widely accepted theses regarding American economic structure" as expressed in "the prevailing and generally accepted doctrine of 'managerialism' " (pp. 50–51). For Robert A. Dahl (1970), the facts are "resounding"; indeed, it is "incontrovertible" that ownership and control have been "split apart." In his view, "the question that was not asked during the great debate over socialism versus capitalism has now been answered: ownership has been split off de facto from internal control" (p. 125).

The question is whether this "astonishing consensus" derives from the findings of appropriate social research or from an unwitting acceptance of what Robert K. Merton has termed "the socially plausible, in which appearances persuade though they may deceive."

Thus, this article poses a type of question which, however simple, "is often undervalued in sociology"—a question which "calls," in Merton's words (1959), "for discovering a particular body of social fact. It might at first seem needless to say that before social facts can be 'explained,' it is advisable to ensure that they actually are facts. Yet, in science as in everyday life, explanations are sometimes provided for things that never were. . . . In sociology as in other disciplines, pseudofacts have a way of inducing pseudoproblems, which cannot be solved because matters are not as they purport to be" (pp. xiii–xv). Such pseudofacts may, of course, also serve to deflect attention from critical aspects of social structure, determinant social relations, and basic social processes. They may inspire not merely "explanations," but "inferences" and "theories" as well, which further confuse and obscure social reality. The methodological premise of this article, then, as well as its irreducibly minimal rationale, is the "obvious and compelling truth that 'if the facts used as a basis for reasoning are ill-established or erroneous, everything will crumble or be falsified; and it is thus that errors in scientific theories most often originate in errors of fact.' "[2]

THE "THEORY"

The prevailing view is that the diffusion of ownership in the large corporation among numerous stock owners has resulted in the separation of ownership and control, and, by severing the connection between the family and private property in the means of production, has torn up the roots of the old class structure and political economy of capitalism. A new class of functionaries of capital, or a congeries of economic "elites" in control of the new forms of productive property, appear: nonowning corporate managers displace their capitalist predecessors.

---

2. (Merton 1959, p. xiii.) The internal quote is from Claude Bernard.

"The capitalist class," as Pitirim Sorokin (1953) put it, is "transformed into the managerial class" (p. 90). In Talcott Parson's view (1953), "The *basic phenomenon* seems to have been the shift in control of enterprise from the property interests of founding families to managerial and technical personnel who as such have not had a comparable vested interest in ownership" (pp. 122–23; italics added).

In the view of these writers, a class theory of contemporary industrial society, based on the relationship between the owners of capital and formally free wage workers, "loses its analytical value as soon as legal ownership and factual control are separated" (Dahrendorf 1959, p. 136). This class theory is, therefore, inapplicable to the United States, England, and other countries in which ownership and control have been severed: it cannot explain nor serve as a fruitful source of hypotheses concerning the division of the social product, class conflict, social domination, political processes, or historic change in these countries. Thus, Parsons and Smelser (1957) refer to the separation of ownership and control as "one particular change in the American economic structure which has been virtually completed within the last half-century"—a "structural change in business organization [that] has been associated with changes in the stratification of the society." The families that once "controlled through ownership most of the big businesses . . . by and large failed to consolidate their positions as *the dominant class* in the society" (p. 254; italics added).

This "shift in *control* of enterprise from the property interests of founding families to managerial and technical personnel," according to Parsons (1953), is the "critical fact" underlying his interpretation that "the 'family elite' elements of the class structure (the Warnerian 'upper-uppers') hold a secondary rather than a primary position in the overall stratification system" (p. 123). The shift in control, "high progressive taxation," and other "changes in the structure of the economy, have 'lopped off' the previous top stratum," leaving instead "a broad and diffuse one with several loosely integrated components. *Undoubtedly* its main focus is now on occupational status and occupational earnings. Seen in historical as well as comparative perspective this is a notable *fact*, for the entrepreneurial fortunes of the period of economic development of the nineteenth century, especially after the Civil War, notably failed to produce *a set of ruling families on a national scale* who as family entities on a Japanese or even a French pattern have tended to keep control of the basic corporate entities in the economy" (p. 123; italics added). Thus, in Parson's view, a " 'ruling class' does not have a paramount position in American society" (p. 119).

Similarly, Daniel Bell (1958) has argued that a "silent revolution" has subverted the former "relations between power and class position in modern society." In his view, "The *singular fact* is that in the last seventy-five years the established relations between the systems of property and family . . . have broken down," resulting in "the breakup of 'family capitalism,' which has been the social cement of the bourgeois class system" (italics added). If, in general, "property, sanctioned by law and reinforced by the coercive power of the State" means power, and if a class system is maintained by the "fusion" of the institutions of the family and private property, economic development in the United States has "effected a radical separation of property and family." Therefore, in his view, if "family capitalism meant social and political, as well as economic, dominance," that is no longer the situation in the United States. "The chief consequence, politically, is the breakup of the 'ruling class' "—"a power-holding group which has both an established *community* of interest and a *continuity* of interest" no longer exists in the United States (pp. 246–49).

The profound implications of the acceptance of the separation of ownership and control as a social fact are, according to Parsons, that the former relations between classes have been replaced by an occupational system based on individual achievement, in which "status groups" are ordered hierarchically in accordance with their functional importance. Further, as Dahrendorf has put it (1959), the basic social conflict is no longer between capital and labor because "in postcapitalist society the ruling and the subjected classes of industry and of the political society are no longer identical; . . . there are, in other words, in principle [*sic*], two independent conflict fronts. . . . This holds increasingly as within industry the separation of ownership and control increases and as the more universal capitalists are replaced by managers" (pp. 275–76). The political economy of capitalism and the class interests which it once served have been replaced by a sort of capitalism without capitalists (Berle 1954)–if not postcapitalist society–shorn of the contradictions and class conflicts that once rent the social fabric of "classical capitalism." The basis of social domination in such societies, as these theorists would have it, is no longer class ownership of the means of production, and such a class clearly does not "rule" in any sense, economically, socially, or politically. "The decisive power in modern industrial society," in Galbraith's (1971) representative formulation, "is exercised not by capital but by organization, not by the capitalist but by the industrial bureaucrat" (p. xix).

Assuredly, the answer to this "theory"–particularly the propositions concerning the separation of ownership and control–rests on empirical grounds (Bell 1958, p. 246). However, logic, concepts, and methodology are certainly intertwined and inseparable aspects of the same intellectual process of discovering the "facts."

One common source of conceptual and analytic confusion in the writings on the issue of ownership and control derives from a teleology of bureaucratic imperatives. Bureaucratization is implicitly assumed to be an inexorable historic process, so that even the propertied classes and their power have fallen before its advance. Parsons and Smelser (1957) have written, for example, that the "kinship-property combination typical of classical capitalism was *destined,* unless social differentiation stopped altogether, to proceed toward 'bureaucratization,' towards differentiation between economy and polity, and between ownership and control" (p. 289; italics added).

The tendency toward the bureaucratization of enterprise, and of management in particular, is taken as an index of the appropriation of the powers of the propertied class by the managers. This confuses the (*a*) existence of an extensive administrative apparatus in the large corporation, in which the proportion of management positions held by members of the proprietary family may be negligible; and (*b*) the locus of control over this apparatus. Dahrendorf (1959) for instance, noting that the managers of large enterprises generally have neither inherited nor founded them, concludes from this that these new managers, "utterly different than their capitalist predecessors," have taken control for themselves. In place of the "classical" or "full capitalist," there stands the bureaucratic manager and "organization man" (pp. 42, 46). From the observation that in the large corporation, functions that (allegedly) were fulfilled in the past by a single owner-manager are now institutionalized and split up among differing roles in the bureaucratic administrative organizations, it is concluded that bureaucratic management (if such it is) means bureaucratic control. However, there is nothing in bureaucratic management itself that indicates the bureaucracy's relationship to extrabureaucratic centers of control at the apex or outside of the bureaucracy proper, such as large shareowners or bankers, to whom it may be responsible.

Max Weber (1965) clearly conceptualized this relationship, referring to the "appropriation of control over the persons exercising managerial authority by the interests of ownership." If "the immediate appropriation of managerial functions" is no longer in the hands of the owners, this does not mean the separation of *control* from ownership, but rather "the separation of the managerial *function*" from ownership. "By virtue of their ownership," Weber saw, "control over managerial positions may rest in the hands of property interests *outside the organization as such*" (pp. 248–49; italics added).

It is precisely this relationship between propertied interests and the bureaucracy, and between "capitalists" and "managers," which has received at best inadequate and usually no attention among those who report that they have seen a "corporate revolution" silently abolish private ownership in the means of production. Thus, Daniel Bell (1961) can write that "private productive property, especially in the United States, is largely a fiction" (p. 44), and Dahrendorf (1959) can claim: "Capital—and thereby *capitalism*—has *dissolved* and given way in the economic sphere to a plurality of partly agreed, partly competing, and partly simply different groups" (p. 47; italics added).

Two issues, then, have to be separated: (1) whether the large corporations continue to be controlled by ownership interests, despite their management by functionaries who may themselves be propertyless; (2) whether the undisputed rise of managerial functions means the rise of the functionaries themselves. Do they constitute a separate and cohesive stratum, with identifiable interests, ideas, and policies, which are opposed to those of the extant owning families? Are the consequences of their actions, whatever their intentions, to bring into being social relationships which undermine capitalism? How, with their "rise," is "the incidence of economic power" changed? (Bendix 1952, p. 119).

These are not merely analytically distinguishable issues. A number of social scientists, "plain marxists" preeminent among them,[3] concede the reality of the split between ownership and control in most large corporations. However, they reject the implication that this renders inapplicable to the United States and other developed capitalist countries a theory which roots classes in the concrete economic order and historically given system of property relations, and which focuses in particular on the relationship between the direct producers and the owners of the means of production. In their view, whatever the situation within the corporation as the predominant legal unit of ownership of large-scale productive property, the "owners" and "managers" of the large corporations, taken as a whole, constitute different strata or segments—when they are not merely agents—of the same more or less unified social class. They reject the notion, as Reinhard Bendix has observed (1952), "that people in the productive system constitute a separate social group because they serve similar functions and that they are powerful because they are indispensable" (p. 119). Rather, the corporations are units in a class-controlled apparatus of appropriation; and the whole gamut of functionaries and owners of capital participate in varying degrees, and as members of the same social class, in its direction (cf. Baran and Sweezy 1966, chap. 2; Miliband 1969, chap. 2; W. A. T. Nichols 1969, pp. 140–41; Playford 1972, pp. 116–18). This classic theory, as we discuss below in detail, demands research concerning the ensemble of social relations, concrete interests, and overriding commitments of the officers, directors, and principal shareowners of the large corporations in general. Rather than limiting analysis to the relationship between the "management" and principal shareowners of a given corporation, the analysis must focus on the multiplicity of their interconnections with other "managements" and principal shareowners in other large corporations, as well as the owners of other forms of large-scale

---

3. "Plain marxists" (uncapitalized) was C. Wright Mills's (1962) phrase to characterize thinkers to whom Marx's "general model and . . . ways of thinking are central to their own intellectual history and remain relevant to their attempts to grasp present-day social worlds" (p. 98). He listed such varied thinkers as Joan Robinson, Jean Paul Sartre, and Paul M. Sweezy, as well as himself, as plain marxists.

income-bearing property.[4] Were research to show that the putative separation of ownership and control within the large corporation is a "pseudofact" and that identifiable families and other cohesive owner-ship interests continue to control them, this might surprise certain "plain marxists," but it would, of course, be quite consistent with their general class theory.[5] Most important, were "managers" and "owners" to be found to occupy a common "class situation" (Weber 1968, p. 927),

---

4. Domhoff (1967, pp. 47–62) and Kolko (1962, pp. 60–69), who may also be considered "plain marxists," reject as incorrect both the separation of ownership and control within the large corporation and argue that "managers" belong to the same social class as the "owners." Their books contain brief empirical studies of the ownership of stock (Kolko) and "upper-class membership" (Domhoff) of large corporate directors. This is also the view of Ferdinand Lundberg (1946, 1968), who in particular lays stress on the need to study the kinship relationships among the owners and executives—a point we discuss in some detail below.

5. Though it might not accord with their "economic" theory. As we discuss briefly below, Baran and Sweezy (1966, chap. 2) discard the concept of "interest groups" or "communities of interest" binding together a number of corporations into a common system. They argue "that an appropriate model of the economy no longer needs to take account of them" (p. 18). Further, they also assert (without evidence) that they "abstract from whatever elements of outside control may still exist in the world of giant corporations because they are in *no sense essential* to the way it works" (p. 20; italics added). Unfortunately the issue is one which would require a new article, if not full-length monograph, to grapple with, and extended discussion here is impossible. However, I have not yet seen an explanation of why Baran and Sweezy have concluded that the question of "outside" or familial control is irrelevant to understanding the American political economy, nor why they should be so insistent on this point. They have not explained how the continuation of communities of interest and familial control groups would alter the ability of the system to face the problem of what they term "the tendency of surplus to rise," which is the central issue of their essay and cornerstone of their neomarxian theory of "monopoly capitalism." If, as they argue, (*a*) the large corporations tend, in their interaction, to produce a "surplus" of investment funds in excess of private investment outlets; and (*b*) this disparity between a rising surplus and available investment outlets is a chronic threat of crisis in our political economy, how would this tendency be affected by the existence of controlling ownership interests in the "giant corporations"? How would this tendency be affected by "interest groups" able to coordinate the prices, production, sales, and investment policies of ostensibly independent corporations? Would not such groups, rather than the individual corporation, constitute the "basic unit of capital"? An original thinker like Paul M. Sweezy might be expected to grapple with this question, rather than merely asserting its irrelevance. When he authored the NRC report on interest groups in 1939, he wrote: "This study should be regarded as doing no more than posing the problem of the larger significance of the facts which it seeks to portray" (Sweezy 1953, p. 184). He ended his essay by a couple of questions concerning their significance to which, to my knowledge, he has yet to speak: "What is the significance of the existence of more or less closely integrated interest groups for the pricing process? What are its implications for the relation between economic and political activity?" These questions seem to me to be quite as relevant today as when Sweezy first asked them. Indeed, when he republished this study in 1953, nearly two decades after its original appearance, he wrote: "No . . . study [of interest groups] . . . has been made in recent years, though there is an *obvious need* for one. I hope that the republication of this earlier attempt to deal with what was and *remains one of the crucial aspects of our whole social system* will stimulate the interest of younger social scientists and provide them with both a starting point and some useful methodological pointers" (pp. 158–59; italics added). Perhaps I may immodestly hope that this article by a "younger social scientist" will stimulate the interest of Paul M. Sweezy to explicitly deal with the issues he has so far avoided, but which he once thought of paramount importance!

the theory that ownership and control of the large corporations reside in the same social class would be confirmed. In contrast, either set of findings would tend to invalidate the essential assumptions, propositions, and inferences of managerial theory. In any event, each alleged implication requires careful analysis and empirical testing on its own.

MANAGERS AND CAPITALISTS: THE HISTORIC CONTROVERSY

The theory of managerial capitalism has hoary antecedents. Not only did Marx himself make rather confusing Hegelian comments about the emergence of the corporation, but the theory of a society in which the capitalist class is gradually replaced by an administrative stratum no longer devoted to the interests of property was being enunciated even while the epoch of "finance capital" and the large corporation was dawning in late nineteenth- and twentieth-century Germany. Eduard Bernstein and Konrad Schmidt, Social Democratic theoreticians of what came to be known as "revisionism," argued that the property form of the corporation presaged and was part of a gradual alteration in the essence of capitalism. The splitting up of property into shares brought with it "armies of shareholders" representing a new "power over the economic life of society. The shareholder," wrote Bernstein (1961), "takes the graded place in the social scale which the captains of industry used to occupy before the concentration of businesses" (p. 54). The capitalist class, said Schmidt, was undergoing a process of "expropriation by stages." The "decomposition of capital" was leading to the gradual extension of the rights of "sovereignty" over property to society as a whole. The capitalist was being transformed "from a proprietor to a simple administrator."[6]

This was substantially the thesis of a work which appeared three decades later in 1932, in the United States and which has been the most enduring source of the theory of managerial capitalism: *The Modern Corporation and Private Property,* by Adolph Berle, Jr., and Gardiner C. Means. "The dissolution of the atom of property," they wrote (1967), "destroys the very foundation on which the economic order of the past three centuries has rested" (p. 8). They reported that 65 percent of the 200 largest corporations appear to be "controlled either by the management or by a legal device involving a small proportion of ownership" (p. 110). The latter category, "control through a legal device," such as pyramiding, is clearly a form of ownership control, as Larner (1970) points out, "since it is based on stock ownership and not on a strategic

---

6. For a contemporary polemic against these views, written in 1899, see Luxemburg (1970), pp. 16–20. Several colleagues, including Professors Merton and Bell, who read this article in an earlier draft, urged me to discuss "Marx's confusing Hegelian comments." Those who are interested in this discussion will find it in the Appendix.

Table 21-1. Type of Control of the 200 Largest Corporations, 1929, According to Berle and Means

Type of Control	RR		PU		Ind.		Totals	
	N	Percent	N	Percent	N	Percent	N	Percent
Private ownership	2	4.8	2	3.8	8	7.5	12	6.0
Majority ownership	1	2.4	3	5.8	6	5.7	10	5.0
Minority control:								
"Presumed"	0	0	5	9.6	24	22.6	29	14.5
Others	4.5	10.7	2.5	4.8	10.5	9.9	17.5	8.7
Legal device	7.5	17.8	19	36.5	14.5	13.7	41	20.5
Management control:								
"Presumed"	0	0	5	9.6	39	36.8	44	22.0
Others	26	61.9	14.5	27.9	4	3.8	44.5	22.3
In receivership	1	2.4	1	1.9	0	0	2	1.0
Total	42	100	52	100	106	100	200	100

Note: RR = railroads; PU = public utilities; Ind. = industrials; "minority control" was assumed to be present when a single individual or cohesive group was found to own at least 20 percent of the corporation's stock; "presumed" refers to Berle and Means's classification of firms believed to be widely distributed and presumably under specified type of control.

position in management. The legal device simply reduces the share of stock ownership required for control" (p. 132). Berle and Means classified 44 percent of the top 200 corporations as actually under management control. However, they claimed to have "reasonably definite and reliable information" on at most two-thirds of the companies (Berle and Means 1967, p. 84). Indeed, they cited, in a detailed and extended table covering 20 pages of their book (pp. 86–105), the source of their information on each corporation and, most important, noted those corporations about whose locus of control they were merely surmising. Thus, they listed 73 corporations under the heading "majority of stock *believed to be widely distributed* and working control held either by a large minority interest or by the management" (italics added). Of these, 29 were considered *"presumably"* under the control of a minority interest, while 44 were *"presumably"* under management control. Indeed, of a total of 88½ corporations which they classified under management control,[7] they provided *no* information on 44, which they could only consider "presumably" management controlled. Among industrials, they classified fully 39 of the 43 management-controlled corporations as only "presumably" under management control. Thus, they had information which permitted them to classify as definitely under management control only 22 percent of the 200 largest corporations, and of the 106

---

7. If one corporation was controlled by another through ownership, but the latter itself was found to be under management control, it was classified by Berle and Means as "ultimately management controlled." If it was ultimately under the "joint control" of a minority interest and management, or other combinations, they counted the corporation as one-half in each of the categories. Thus, the figure 88½ corporations under management control.

industrials, only 3.8 percent! Yet numerous scholars over the years have cited the work by Berle and Means (when giving citations at all) as the main or only source of their own assertions that ownership and control were split apart in the large corporations. In part, this may be explained by the fact that Berle and Means presented their summary table and conclusions (pp. 109–10) without any mention of their earlier qualifications concerning the adequacy and validity of their information. If we take the information contained in parts J and K of their Table 12 on pages 103–5, a correct summary of their findings, with the necessary qualifications made explicit, would be as shown in Table 21–1.

In 1945 R. A. Gordon published a study, based in part on a secondary analysis of the Temporary National Economic Committee (TNEC) data, which came to conclusions much like those of Berle and Means. He wrote that "the real revolution [in property rights] has already largely taken place; the great majority of stockholders have been deprived of control of their property through the diffusion of ownership and the growth in the power of management" (1966, p. 350).

Quite recently Robert J. Larner duplicated the Berle-Means methods in his own study of the 500 largest nonfinancial corporations in the United States and concluded that the "managerial revolution" in process in 1929 was now "close to complete." Corporations in which the largest individual stockholder or members of a single family or a group of business associates were found *not* to own 10 percent or more of the voting stock were classified by Larner as under "management control." By this criterion, he classified 84 percent of the top 200 and 70 percent of the next 300 largest nonfinancial corporations in 1963 in the United States as "management controlled."[8] John Kenneth Galbraith (1968), who had relied on Berle and Means's and Gordon's studies to advance his own interpretation of the loss of stockholder control in the "new industrial state" not merely to management, but to the new "techno-structure," found that Larner's findings, some of which appeared as Galbraith's book was going to press, "explicitly confirmed" his view of the process (p. 90).

In contrast to these studies and others following similar methods of analysis and classification are several studies by analysts taking a quite different approach. These researchers have argued that without an investigation of the specific situation in a given corporation and of the interconnections between the principal shareholders, officers, and directors and other corporations, the actual control group is unlikely to be identified.

---

8. (Larner 1970, p. 21) Berle and Means had used 20 percent as the minimum necessary for minority ownership interests to maintain control. In a note to a new edition of their work, Berle and Means (1967), refer to Larner's original article in the September, 1966 *American Economic Review* as "a study [which] has duplicated the 1929 analysis for 1963, making only one significant change in concept" (p. 358), the reduced amount (10 percent) necessary for ownership control.

Thus studies which appeared at virtually the same time as that of Berle and Means, by Anna Rochester (1936) and Ferdinand Lundberg (1937), respectively, concluded (as Lundberg put it) that "a very small group of families," through their ownership interests and control of the major banks, were still in control of the "industrial system" (1946, pp. 506–8). Analyzing the same corporations that Berle and Means claimed were under management control, Lundberg found that "in most cases [the largest stockholding] families had themselves installed the management control or were among the directors," while several others were "authoritatively regarded in Wall Street as actually under the rule of J. P. Morgan and Company." "Exclusion of stockholders from control, within the context as revealed by Berle-Means," Lundberg concluded (pp. 506–8), "does not mean that large stockholders are excluded from a decisive voice in the management. It means only that small stockholders have been [excluded]." The National Resources Committee (NRC) also conducted a study of the control of the largest U.S. corporations during the same period. Unlike either Berle and Means or Gordon, the NRC study included not only the 200 largest nonfinancial corporations but also the 50 largest banks, which permitted its author (Paul M. Sweezy) to discover centers of "outside" control or abiding influence which were missed by the former studies. The NRC study also took account of corporation histories and information on the careers of key officers and directors as well as of information on primary interlocks between corporations. Almost half of the top 200 corporations and 16 of the banks were found to belong to eight different "interest groups" binding their constituent corporations together under a significant element of common control by wealthy families and/or financial associates and investment bankers (NRC 1939, pp. 100–103; 306–17; Sweezy 1953).

Of 43 industrial corporations which Berle and Means categorized under "management control," 36 appeared on the lists of top corporations studied by the TNEC (Goldsmith and Parmelee 1940) and NRC in the late thirties. Victor Perlo compared their findings concerning these particular corporations and found that of these 36, the TNEC located "definite centers of control" for 15 and the NRC for 11; in addition, Perlo's own research (1957) revealed that another seven were under the control of identifiable ownership interests, leaving only three industrial corporations on the original Berle and Means list for which other investigators did not locate definite control centers (p. 49).

Differences in the findings of recent studies also indicate the wisdom of considering the empirical question as open: Don Villarejo studied the locus of control in 250 of the largest industrial corporations (though not other types of nonfinancial corporations) on the 1960 *Fortune* list. He concluded (1961/62) that of the 232 corporations on which he obtained usable data "at least 126 corporations," or 54 percent, and perhaps as many as 141, or 61 percent were controlled by ownership interests; that is, he found "the existence of concentrated ownership to the extent of securing potential working control of the corporation in question" (p. 68). His findings were criticized by Larner (1970) "as open to challenge because he aggregated the stockholdings of directors, investment companies, and insurance companies in each corporation without providing specific evidence, such as family or business relationships, to suggest a community of interests or to indicate the likelihood of either intragroup or intergroup cooperation" (p. 22). This criticism of Villarejo's work may or may not be correct, but it is remarkable that Larner should make it, since it is at least as applicable—if not more so—not only to Berle and Means's original study, which Larner chose to emulate procedurally, but also to Larner's own findings. Larner certainly does not present systematic evidence of the kind he requires of Villarejo, yet he concluded that most large corporations were under "management control." It is relevant, therefore, that *Fortune,* using essentially the same definitions and procedures as Larner, and taking 10 percent as the minimum necessary for proprietary control, found in 1967 that 147 corporations of the top 500 were controlled through ownership interests, or over half again as many as Larner's 95 (Sheehan 1967).

PROBLEMS OF METHOD AND MEASUREMENT

Further brief review of recent contradictory findings concerning the control of the largest corporations in the United States highlights the most significant problem faced by investigators of this subject: the data needed for adequate measurement are, in the first place, often inaccessible. As Joseph Kahl (1957) points out, power, "because it is potential. . . . is usually impossible to see. Furthermore, where it exists it tends to be deliberately hidden; those who sit among the mighty do not invite sociologists to watch them make their decisions about how to control the behavior of others" (p. 10). Two separate problems of "inaccessibility of the data," the relative importance of which cannot be settled a priori, require investigation so that we can assess the limitations to our understanding: first, there is no official list of the largest corporations, ranked by assets, sales, or profits. Investigators must have access to the sources of information that will allow them to compile such a list or even make reasonable guesses. Studies in recent years have relied largely on *Fortune*'s 500 as their primary source of a list of which corporations to investigate. Thus, even the Patman Committee on Banking and Currency of the House of Representatives used that list in its analysis of interlocking relationships between large commercial banks and the largest corporations (Patman Report 1968, p. 91). In 1966 *Fortune* plainly disclosed that over the years since it had been publishing its list it had been omitting "privately owned or closely held companies that do not publish certified statements of their financial results." On the basis of *Fortune*'s knowledge, it now named 26 companies which it believed "had sufficient sales in 1965 to qualify for the 500 list" (Sheehan 1966). (Because of a high ratio of sales to assets, some of these firms might not rank among the top 500 if we knew their assets.) Obviously any adequate generalization about the ability of families to maintain control through ownership, indeed private ownership, of very large firms would have to take account of such previously ignored privately owned firms. Were these added to the "list," there would be not merely five privately owned firms as found by Larner, but 31, over six times as many as previously counted among the 500 largest. Whether other such large privately owned firms have still escaped notice is an important question to which there is no presently reliable answer.

Perhaps of greater importance as a source of inaccessibility of the relevant information is the fact that new methods of control, some of which rely on secrecy, have been devised by the principal shareowning families. The extent (though not the fact) of this secrecy is, once again, unknown. The problem, put most simply, is to discover who are the actual "beneficial owners" of the shareholdings held by the "shareholders of record." Shareholdings may appear in the name of voting trusts, foundations, holding companies, and other related operating corporations in which the given family has a dominant interest. "Use of nominees [brokers, dealers, bank trust departments], also known in the securities trade as 'street names' or 'straws' [usually nonfinancial firms listed as record shareholders but whose control is not publicly known] to hide beneficial ownership of stock is a common corporate practice today," as Senator Lee Metcalf recently noted (1971). Corporations *"habitually list nominees rather than beneficial owners,"* whatever the supposed formal reporting requirements (Metcalf and Reinemer 1971). In this way, the presence of principal proprietary families may be hidden or rendered scarcely noticeable among the reports of stock ownership filed with the Securities and Exchange Commission, which are required by law to list the stockholdings of each director of the firm and of the beneficial owners of 10 percent or more of the outstanding amount of its stock.

Even the presence of large bank holdings may be hidden in this way —not to speak of the proprietary controlling interests of the bank itself. Thus, in addition to the discrepancy between *Fortune*'s findings and Larner's, the Patman Committee's unprecedented studies (1968) suggest that three dozen corporations classified as "management-controlled" by Larner are really under the control of very large banks (pp. 13–15). Larner has rejected the Patman Committee's conclusions on the grounds that the banks do not hold at least 10 percent of the voting stock in most of the corporations named by the committee. There are six, however, in which more than 10 percent of the common stock is held by a single bank, and another in which 9.5 percent is held by a single bank. To Larner's 95 corporations controlled through ownership interests, then, we may add the 17 privately owned firms which the *Fortune* lists have excluded,[9] the 52 discovered by *Fortune* among the 500 to be under proprietary control through at least 10 percent minority holdings by an individual or family, and at least the six found by the Patman Committee to be under "bank minority control" by 10 percent or more stock ownership. This is a total of 170 firms, or 34 percent of the 500 largest nonfinancial firms which are controlled through ownership interests. Further, Larner (1970) correctly argues, as we noted earlier, that "control through a legal device" such as pyramiding, contrary to Berle and Means's view, is "more realistically seen . . . as a form of ownership control" (p. 132). He found 26 corporations in this category. Larner also classified two corporations as under "unknown" control; however, he believes "it is likely" that these are, in fact, privately owned. Adding these 28, we have a total of 198, or 39.6 percent of the top 500 firms controlled through a minimum of 10 percent ownership interest—a figure more than double Larner's original 95, or 19 percent.

It should be emphasized that we have so far used the criterion of 10 percent as the minimum proportion of the outstanding stock which an individual or cohesive group must have to exert minority control through ownership. This is the standard employed by Larner and other recent authorities (e.g., Monsen et al. 1968, 1969; Hindley 1970; Sheehan 1967; Vernon 1970), in place of the original 20 percent cutoff point used by Berle and Means, on the assumption that stock is now even more widely dispersed and that, therefore, a bloc of 10 percent should assure working control. However, on the basis of its investigations, the Patman Committee concluded that effective control could be assured with even *less* than a 5 percent holding, "especially in very large corporations whose stock is widely held" (1968), p. 91). Were this assumption correct, then another 14 corporations in which the Patman investigators found a single bank holding *more* than 5 percent but less than 10 percent of the voting stock would also clearly belong under proprietary rather than management control—bringing the total so far to 211, or 42.2 percent of the top 500 firms controlled by identifiable ownership inter-

---

9. I do not include all 26 privately owned firms named by *Fortune* (Sheehan 1966) because when the estimated sales of these firms are taken into account and they are ranked (and the others on the original 500 list reranked) by sales, only 17 belong in the top 500. If all 26 were included, and the number of "proprietary" firms (179) figured among the 526, the proportion would be the same: 34 percent. By sales, the 26 privately owned firms are ranked as follows: top 100, none; 101–50, 3; 151–200, 1; 201–50, 2; 251–300, 1; 301–50, 3; 351–400, 1; 401–50, 3; 451–500, 3; 501–26, 9.

ests.[10] Moreover, these findings do not consider "any of the various coalitions that may indeed assure working control for small groups in many companies" (Sheehan 1967). (For example, another six corporations which Larner classified under "management control" were found by the Patman investigators to have a group of two or three banks holding 10 percent or more of the common stock between them.) Indeed, the official sources of information ordinarily relied on in such investigations are highly unlikely to permit discovery of such coalitions. These coalitions moreover can scarcely be revealed by residual definitional modes of analysis, which merely classify by exclusion those corporations as management controlled in which no specified minimum proportion of shares has been found in the hands of a single individual or cohesive group. Genuine disclosure would require an investigation into the recent history of the corporation, and perhaps "inside information" which is not immediately accessible. At the least, information on critical phases of the founding, promotion, and expansion (or mergers) of the corporation—and the place in the present structure of control of individuals and families that played important roles during these phases —is needed to identify the implications of given shareholdings (Sweezy 1953, p. 160). Not since the NRC investigation of "interest groups in the American economy" has such a study been done in the United States.

However, most recently a very important study has been done which attempted—paradoxically—to systematically mine the publicly available "inside information" on the controlling interests in America's largest industrial corporations. Our own reference to *Fortune* and the *New York Times* (Sheehan 1966, 1967; Murphy 1967; Jensen 1971) has already indicated their possible value as sources of publicly available inside information. Thus, Philip Burch "searched carefully" through

---

10. Larner (1970) also apparently has some doubts concerning the adequacy of the residual definition of management control, using the less than 10 percent ownership criterion. He names five firms among the top 200 (and refers to "several others among the top 500") which, though he classified them as management controlled, "appear to be controlled, or at least strongly influenced, by a single family within their management. Yet these families owned only a very small fraction of the outstanding voting stock" (p. 19). With these included, there are 216 (not counting the unenumerated "several others"), or 43.2 percent, of the top 500 firms in the United States which are visibly controlled by identifiable individuals, families, or banks. We might note also that there are 335 industrial corporations among the top 500 nonfinancials. Of these, Larner found 89, or 27 percent, controlled through ownership; 19, or 6 percent, through ownership via a legal device; and another 2, or 1 percent, "unknown" which he believes likely to be privately owned. Fourteen of the "bank-controlled" corporations found by Patman among Larner's management-controlled corporations are industrials. Three of Larner's firms that he classified under management control but thinks are family controlled are also industrials. All 17 of the *Fortune* (Sheehan 1966) privately owned firms are industrials. This makes 144. We do not know (nor would *Fortune* provide the information when asked) the industrial classification of the 52 corporations *Fortune* (Sheehan 1967) found under proprietary control. Were they all industrials, 196, or 59 percent of the 335 top industrial corporations in the United States would be classified as controlled by identifiable individuals, families, or banks.

Fortune, Time, Business Week, Forbes and the business section of the *New York Times* over the period dating roughly from 1950 to 1971 in order to collect the information these business media contained on any of the 300 largest manufacturing and mining corporations (plus the next 200 largest less intensively) as well as the top 50 merchandising and transportation companies. He supplemented this information by *Moody's* manuals and Standard and Poor's *Corporation Records,* as well as SEC reports, though he found these of less use. "The results of this research and analysis," according to Burch (1972), "show a marked difference in stock ownership totals as contrasted with those arrived at through examination" of the SEC's *Official Summary of Securities Transactions and Holdings.* He found "disparities of very sizeable proportions" and is "of the firm opinion that the higher figures [using his business sources] are the more accurate ones" (pp. 25–27). He did a "company-by-company analysis of the control status of most [300] of America's large corporations . . . as of the mid 1960s" (p. 29); classified the corporations, ranked by *Fortune's* figures on sales, into three categories, "probably management control," "possibly family control," and "probably family control"; and he found that only among the 50 largest industrial corporations did his category of "probably management control" bulk largest, with 58 percent of them falling in that category. Of the total top 300, he found that 40 percent probably were under management control, 45 percent were probably under family control, and 15 percent *possibly* under family control (p. 70). Burch considers these "conservative figures," and it is his opinion that "they represent the most reliable findings that can be assembled on this difficult and important subject without resort to governmental subpoena and investigatory powers," and notes further that his study took no account of "vast blocks of corporate stock held by the big institutional investors, particularly the top 50 commercial banks and trust companies" (p. 17).

These findings obviously contradict the received view that the largest corporations are virtually all under management control—and which Larner purportedly showed in his own recent study. One question, then, aside from Burch's use of business sources not utilized systematically before, is by what criteria Burch classified the corporations under probable family control. Two conditions had to be met: (1) "that approximately 4 to 5 percent or more of the voting stock was held by a family, group of families, or some affluent individual" according to one or more of his sources; and (2) that he found representation "on the part of a family on the board of directors of a company, generally over an extended period of time" (Burch 1972, pp. 29–30). Whether this is a more or less valid index of proprietary control than using 10 percent as the required minimum (and using predominately official sources whose reliability has been shown to be questionable) cannot be determined in any simple manner—precisely because we have no independent criteria by which to measure "control" other than by the whole variety of hints, clues, and solid information we can get on the actual proprietary interests in a given corporation.

THE CONCEPT OF CONTROL

In short, how "control" is conceptualized is a critical question—apart from the problem of obtaining reliable and valid information. Following Berle and Means, "control" has generally been defined to refer to the "actual power to select the board of directors (or its majority)," although control may also "be exercised *not* through the *selection* of directors, but through *dictation* to the management, as where a bank determines the policy of a corporation seriously indebted to it" (Berle and Means 1967, p. 66; italics added). Thus control refers to the "*power* of determining the broad policies guiding a corporation and not to . . . the actual influence on the day to day affairs of an enterprise" (Goldsmith and Parmelee 1940, pp. 99–100; italics added). Control is not business management, or what Gordon (1966) has termed "business leadership" (p. 150). This would seem to be clear conceptually. However, in practice Berle and Means and their followers have simply assumed away the analytical issues by their operational definitions. They have merely assumed, rather than demonstrated, that once a cohesive ownership interest having at least a minimum specified proportion of the stock (whether 20 percent as in the original Berle and Means work or the current 10 percent criterion) disappears, the corporation slips imperceptibly and inevitably under "management control." At this point, presumably, the top officers, given the wide dispersion of stock among small shareowners and the officers' control of the proxy machinery, become capable of nominating and electing a compliant and subservient board of directors, of perpetuating themselves in office, and of abrogating, thereby, the control of proprietary interests (Gordon 1966, pp. 121–22; Larner 1970, p. 3; *Business Week,* May 22, 1971, p. 54). "In the mature corporation," as Galbraith (1968) sums it up, "the stockholders are without power; the Board of Directors is normally the passive instrument of the management" (pp. 59, 90–95).

However, as I have emphasized repeatedly, it is necessary to study the concrete situation within the corporation and the constellation of intercorporate relationships in which it is involved before one can begin to understand where control is actually located. The Berle and Means method of investigation, the definitions and procedures utilized, do not in fact even begin to accord with the actual content of their own concept. For this reason it seems advisable to conceptualize control in such a way as to link it inextricably with a method that is not reducible to a single criterion, such as a minimum percentage of stock held by a single minority bloc, but which requires instead a variety of interrelated yet independent indicators. The modalities of corporate control utilized by specific individuals and/or families and/or groups of associates differ considerably, vary in complexity, and are not easily categorized. Our concept of control must therefore compel attention to essential relationships. No less than the generic sociological concept of power, the concept of control, as Berle and Means (1967) themselves put it, is elusive, "for power can rarely be sharply segregated or clearly defined" (p. 66). The relationship between the actual locus of control, formal authority (bureaucratic executive posts), and legal rights (shareownership) is problematic. If control refers to the capacity to determine the broad policies of a corporation, then it refers to a social relationship, not an attribute. Control (or power) is essentially relative and relational: how much power, with respect to whom? (cf. Wrong 1968, p. 679; Etzioni 1968, pp. 314–15). Therefore, control is conceptualized here as follows: when the concrete structure of ownership and of intercorporate relationships makes it probable that an identifiable group of proprietary interests will be able to realize their corporate objectives over time, despite resistance, then we may say that they have "control" of the corporation (cf. Weber 1968, p. 926). To estimate the probability that a given individual or group controls a corporation, then, we must know who the rivals or potential rivals for control are and what assets they can bring to the struggle.

This has two obvious implications concerning the study of corporate control: it means that a specific minority percentage of ownership in itself can tell us little about the potential for control that it represents. We can discover this only by a case study of the pattern of ownership within the given corporation. However, it also means that confining our attention to the single corporation may, in fact, limit our ability to see the pattern of power relationships of which this corporation is merely one element; and it may restrict our understanding of the potential for control represented by a specific bloc of shares in a particular corporation. An individual or group's capacity for control increases correspondingly, depending upon how many other large corporations (including banks and other financial institutions) in which it has a dominant, if not controlling, position. The very same quantitative proportion of stock may have a qualitatively different significance, depending on the system of intercorporate relationships in which the corporation is implicated.

Of course, our reference here is to "structural" analysis rather than "behavioral" analysis of actual "struggles for control." Even such struggles, however, can rarely provide real insight concerning the question of control without the type of analysis emphasized here. Otherwise one cannot know who the contending powers actually are—what may look like a "proxy fight" between "management" and certain shareowners may in fact be a struggle between contending proprietary interests. The latter type of research, therefore, also requires the former, if it is to provide valid and reliable findings.

There remains the question as to what "broad corporate policies or objectives" are—over which control is to be exercised. I have found no usable definition in my studies of the writings on this question. Nor am I convinced it is amenable to definition apart from a specific theoretical framework in which it is conceptualized. We must have a theory of the objective necessities of corporate conduct and the imperatives of the political economy—and to attempt to outline such a theory here would take us rather far afield from the focus of this article. However, such questions as the following would be essential: what relationships must the corporations in an oligopolistic economy establish with each other? with the state? with foreign governments? with the workers? with sources of raw materials and markets? What common problems, which their very interaction creates, must they resolve? Then we may ask whether the individuals who actually decide among proposed long-range strategies and determine the "broad policies and objectives" of the corporations are merely members of "management."

We know, for instance, that the largest corporations in the United States are now typically "multinational" or "transnational" in the sense that the "sheer size of their foreign commitment," as *Fortune* puts it (Rose 1968, p. 101), and the "extent of their involvements is such that, to some degree, these companies now regard the world rather than the nation state as their natural and logical operating area." Is it the "managements" of these corporations that determine their broad policies? Or do the individuals, families, and other principal proprietary interests with the greatest material stake in these corporations impose their conceptions of the issues and demand that their objectives are pursued in order to maintain the "world . . . as their natural and logical operating area"? Here clearly we verge once again on the class questions raised at the outset of this article. To take a more limited issue, however: many of the multinational corporations face increasing risk of nationalization of their foreign properties. "Management" may plan for such contingencies, exercise their "discretion," and decide on the tactics to be adopted. When their planning goes awry or proves ineffective, however, must the management answer to their corporation's principal shareowners and other proprietary interests (such as banks) or not? Having left management in charge of the everyday operations of the corporations abroad with little or no interference, do the principal proprietary interests have the power to interfere when deemed necessary? Without an analysis of concrete situations and the specific control structure of the corporations involved, we cannot answer such questions—though occasionally particular events momentarily illuminate the actual relationships involved (though they may still remain largely in the shadows). Thus, for example, the Chilean properties of Kennecott Copper Corporation and Anaconda Company were recently (1971) nationalized in Chile. These two corporations, which owned the major copper mines of Chile, had adopted different long-range strategies to deal with the rising probability of nationalization. We cannot explore the details here, but suffice it to say that Kennecott's strategy was reportedly aimed at insuring, as Robert Haldeman, executive vice-president of Kennecott's Chilean operations, explained, "that nobody expropriates Kennecott without upsetting customers, creditors, and governments on three continents" (Moran 1973, pp. 279–80). Kennecott was able to "expand very profitably in the late 1960s with no new risk to itself and to leave, after the nationalization in 1971, with compensation greater than the net worth of its holdings had been in 1964. In contrast, Anaconda, which had not spread its risk or protected itself through a strategy of building transnational alliances, lost its old holdings, lost the new capital it committed during the Frei regime [preceding Allende's socialist administration], and was nationalized in 1971 without any hope of compensation" (Moran 1973, pp. 280–81).[11]

Now, according to Berle and Means (1967, p. 104) and Larner (1970, pp. 74–79), both Kennecott and Anaconda have long been under "management control." In Kennecott's case, there is relatively persuasive evidence that it is in fact probably controlled by the Guggenheim family and associated interests rather than by "management."[12] Whether this

---

11. The destruction of the constitutional government and parliamentary democracy of Chile, and the death of her Marxist president, Dr. Salvador Allende, at the hands of the armed forces on September 11, 1973, has once again given Anaconda (and other foreign corporations) "hope of compensation." The military regime's foreign minister, Adm. Ismael Huerta, announced within a week of the coup that the "'door was open' for resumption of negotiations on compensation for United States copper holdings nationalized by President Allende" (*New York Times*, September 30, 1973, p. 14).

12. Kennecott illustrates well our insistence on the importance of knowledge of a corporation's critical historic phases in disclosing the actual locus of control. The Guggenheim interests bought control of the El Teniente copper mine from the Braden Copper Company in 1908; in 1915 they sold it to the Kennecott Copper Corporation, in which Guggenheim Brothers was the controlling stockholder. In 1923, Utah Copper, in which the Guggenheims had a minority interest, also purchased a large bloc of Kennecott's shares (Hoyt 1967, p. 263). Yet for Berle and Means (1967) only six years later (their data were for 1929), Kennecott was "presumably under management control" (p. 104). When World War II began, as a historian close to the Guggenheim family has written, "the Guggenheims created a new Kennecott Copper Corporation, which would have three million shares. This corporation bought up the Guggenheim copper holdings," including 25 percent of Utah Copper Company's stock, and controlling interests in Copper River Railroad and other "Alaska syndicate holdings" (Hoyt 1967, p. 263). The Guggenheim Brothers also had (until purchased recently by the Allende government) the controlling interest in Chile's Anglo-Lautaro Nitrate Company, organized in 1931 out of previous nitrate holdings controlled by the Guggenheims (Lomask 1964, p. 281) and reorganized in 1951 by Harry Guggenheim (a senior partner of Guggenheim Brothers), to bring in two other smaller Guggenheim-controlled firms. Guggenheim presided as board chairman and chief executive officer of Anglo-Lautaro until his retirement in 1962. Previously, he had been "absent from the family business for a quarter of a century," until in 1949 his uncle enjoined him to reorganize Guggenheim Brothers (Lomask 1964, p. 65). In 1959 the Guggenheim Exploration Company, one of whose partners was a director of Kennecott Copper Corporation in which "the Guggenheim foundations" now also held large holdings, was also revived (Lomask 1964, p. 281). The son of one of the original Guggenheim brothers (Edmond A., son of Murry) "maintained an active interest in Kennecott Corpora-

is so or not, Kennecott's "successful tactics" in Chile did not test the reality of its alleged control by management. However, Anaconda's "management" was submitted to a rather clear test of the extent to which it had control. Within two months after the Chilean government "intervened" in Anaconda's properties and a month after it took over Anaconda Sales Corporation's control of copper sales, it was announced in the *New York Times* (May 14, 1971, p. 55) that Mr. John B. Place, a director of Anaconda and a vice-chairman of the Chase Manhattan Bank (one of its four top officers, along with David Rockefeller, chairman, and the president and another vice-chairman) was to become the new chief executive officer of the Anaconda Company. (Other Anaconda directors who were bankers included James D. Farley, an executive vice-president of First National City Bank, and Robert V. Roosa, a partner in Brown Brothers, Harriman, and Company.) As the *New York Times* reporter (Walker 1971) explained, Mr. Place had no mining expertise ("it is assumed he would not know a head frame from a drag line"), and though he had been an Anaconda director since 1969, he "lives in the East and has never attended the annual [stockholders] meeting held regularly in Butte, Montana," where Anaconda's most important American copper mines are located. In the wake of this Chase Manhattan officer's installation as Anaconda's chief executive officer, "at least 50 percent of the corporate staff," including John G. Hall, Anaconda's former president, "were fired. Chairman [C. Jay] Parkinson took early retirement" (*Business Week*, February 19, 1972, p. 55). The decimation of Anaconda's allegedly controlling management illustrates the general proposition that those who really have control can decide when, where, and with respect to what issues and corporate policies they will intervene to exercise their power.

PROFIT MAXIMIZATION?

Fortunately, some issues to which the question of control is relevant are somewhat more amenable to systematic, even quantitative, analysis than the ones just posed. Chief among these, which has occupied considerable theoretical, but little empirical, attention, is the proposition concerning "managerial discretion" (see and cf. Baumol 1959; Kaysen 1957, 1965; Marris 1963, 1964; Gordon 1966; Galbraith 1968; Simon

tion" as a director (Lomask 1964, p. 295), while Peter Lawson-Johnston, a grandson of Solomon Guggenheim, was (as of 1966) a partner in Guggenheim Brothers, a director of the advisory board of Anglo-Lautaro, a director of Kennecott, a director of Minerec Corporation, the vice-president of Elgerbar Corporation, and the trustee of three Guggenheim foundations (Hoyt 1967, p. 348). In the period from roughly 1955 to 1965, Burch (1972, p. 48) found Kennecott had "significant family representation as outside members of the board of directors," and concluded it was under "possibly" Guggenheim family control. This is certainly a cautious understatement, given the historic evidence presented here, drawn from works by two writers close to the Guggenheim family.

1957; Williamson 1963, 1970). It posits different motives and conduct for managers than owners, and thereby differences in the profit orientations of owner-controlled versus management-controlled corporations. "The development of the large corporations," as Gordon puts it (1966), "has obviously affected the goals of business decision-making. . . . It clearly leads to greater emphasis on the nonprofit goals of interest groups other than the stockholders," such as the management. The executives "do not receive the profits which may result from taking a chance, while their position in the firm may be jeopardized in the event of serious loss" (pp. xii, 324). Dahrendorf has stated the proposition succinctly. In his view (1959), the separation of ownership and control "produces two sets of roles the incumbents of which *increasingly move apart* in their outlooks on and attitudes toward society in general and toward the enterprise in particular. . . . Never has the imputation of a profit motive been further from the real motives of men than it is for modern bureaucratic managers. Economically, managers are interested in such things as rentability, efficiency, and productivity" (p. 46; italics added). This is an oft-asserted but rarely investigated proposition, on which Larner has recently provided systematic negative evidence. Drawing on his study of the separation of ownership and control, he found the following: using multiple-regression analysis and taking into account assets, industrial concentration, Federal Reserve Board indices of economywide growth and fluctuation of profit rates, and equity-asset ratios, Larner found that the rate of profit earned by "management" and "owner"-controlled firms was about the same; both were equally profit oriented. Second, the evidence on fluctuations in profit rates suggested no support for the view that allegedly nonowning managements avoid risk taking more than owners do. Third, Larner found that the corporation's dollar profit and rate of return on equity were the major determinants of the level of "executive compensation." Compensation of executives, he concluded, has been "effectively harnessed" to the stockholders' interests in profits. In Larner's words, "Although control is separated from ownership in most of America's largest corporations, the effects on the profit orientations of firms, and on stockholders' welfare have been minor. The magnitude of the effects," he concluded (1970), "appears to be too small to justify the considerable attention they have received in the literature of the past thirty-eight years" (p. 66).[13]

---

13. Similar findings are reported in Kamerschen (1968, 1969), Hindley (1970), and Lewellen and Huntsman (1970). Contrary findings, which show small but statistically significant differences in profit rates between allegedly owner-controlled and allegedly management-controlled corporations, appear in Monsen, Chiu, and Cooley (1968). The study by Lewellen and Huntsman (1970) differed from the others cited here, since no attempt was made to contrast performance by owner- versus management-controlled corporations. Their focus was on the specific question of whether a corporation's profitability or its sales revenue more strongly determined the rewards of its senior officers. By means of a multivariate analysis, they found that "both reported profits and equity market

Larner's findings contradict managerial theory, but are consistent both with neoclassical and neo-Marxian reasoning concerning corporate conduct: even where management is in fact in control, it is compelled to engage in a "systematic temporal search for highest practicable profits" (Earley 1957, p. 333). The conduct of the large corporation, in this view, whether under management control or ownership control, is largely determined by the market structure—the nature of competition, products produced, and the constraints of the capital markets (Peterson 1965, pp. 9–14; O'Connor 1971, p. 145). Growth, sales, technical efficiency, [and] a strong competitive position are at once inseparable managerial goals and the determinants of high corporate profits—which are in turn the prerequisites of high managerial income and status (Earley 1956, 1957; Alchian 1968, p. 186; Sheehan 1967, p. 242; Baran and Sweezy 1966, p. 33–34). Management need not spend "much of its time contemplating profits as such" (Peterson 1965, p. 9), so long as its decisions on pricing and sales and on the planning and organization of production must be measured against and not imperil corporate profitability. "This," argues Peterson, "is the essence of profit-seeking and of capitalist behavior in employing resources." Significant deviation from profit-maximizing behavior also would lead to the lowering of the mar-

---

values are substantially more important in the determination of executive compensation than are sales—indeed, sales seem to be quite irrelevant—[and] the clear inference is that there is a greater incentive for management to shape its decision rules in a manner consonant with shareholder interests than to seek the alternative goal of revenue maximization" (pp. 718–19). The use of multiple-regression analysis (Larner) or analysis of variance (Monsen) does not resolve the problem of causation (time-order). It merely shows, at one point in time, how corporations classified under different types of control differ on selected variables. It might plausibly be argued that a control group, whether an individual, family, or coalition of business associates, might gradually dispose of its holdings in a corporation precisely because its profit performance was not satisfactory over a period of time—for reasons not connected to how it was managed. This might be particularly the case for small control groups, to whom not the corporation's profits as such but the dividend yield and price appreciation of their stockholdings ("combined return") is primary. Thus, a finding that owner-controlled corporations were more profitable than management-controlled corporations (assuming the latter exist) might simply mean that control groups do their best to retain control of the more profitable corporations and get out of those that are less profitable. A genuine causal study requires information on changes over time in types of control and in corporate performance. Unfortunately, the nature of the data available probably precludes such a study. Are the same corporations that were once owner controlled more or less profitable once they come under management control? Take an extreme example. In 1923, Guggenheim Brothers sold control of Chile Copper Company, whose major asset was the Chuquicamata mine in Chile, to the Anaconda Copper Company, headed by John D. Ryan. The family was split over this issue: some of them thought that this would become an extraordinary profit-yielding asset—as it did; others were for accepting the immediate profits to be made by Ryan's offering price of $70 million for the controlling interest. The result was that, although they sold the controlling interest, the family retained a large block of stock as an investment (Hoyt 1967, pp. 258, 263). Did the loss of "family control" and its acquisition by Anaconda result in lessening effort at profit maximization in the Chile Copper Company? Posed in this way, the question appears (at least to me) to be rhetorical, though of course it is empirical.

ket price of the corporation's stock and make it an attractive and vulnerable target for takeover—and the displacement of the incumbent management (Manne 1965; *Business Week,* May 22, 1971, p. 55). Furthermore, some economists have suggested that professional management, particularly the use of "scientific budgetary planning" and the emphasis on the "time-value of money" (Earley 1956; Earley and Carleton 1962; Tanzer 1969, pp. 32–34), strengthens, rather than weakens, the drive toward profit maximization. Whether or not managers are actuated by the "profit motive," as a subjective value commitment, "profit maximization" is an objective requirement, since profits constitute both the only unambiguous criterion of successful managerial performance and an irreducible necessity for corporate survival (Peterson 1965; Tanzer 1969, pp. 30–32). In the words of Robin Williams, Jr. (1959), "the separation of ownership and control shows that the 'profit motive' is not a *motive* at all . . .; it is not a psychological state but a social condition" (p. 184).

This reasoning is persuasive and consistent with the findings that purportedly management-controlled and owner-controlled corporations are similarly profit oriented, and that profits and stock market values determine executive compensation. However, once again the difficulty is that since independent investigations concerning the control of the large corporations, including the two most recent and exhaustive studies by Larner and Burch, have come to very different conclusions, we cannot know if the "independent variable" has even been adequately measured. In reality, the allegedly management-controlled corporations may—appearances aside—continue to be subject to control by minority ownership interests and/or "outside" centers of control.

ENTANGLING KINSHIP RELATIONS AND SPHERES OF INFLUENCE

The problem is further complicated if, in fact, a number of seemingly independent corporations are under common control. Few today consider the concept of the "interest group" or "financial group" or "family sphere of influence" relevant to the workings of the large corporations. Indeed, Paul M. Sweezy (Baran and Sweezy 1966, pp. 17–20) has discarded the concept also, as noted earlier, although he was the principal author of the investigation for the NRC (1939) which provided one of the *two* most authoritative studies (the other by the TNEC) of the question to date (Goldsmith and Parmelee 1940, chap. 7). However, we know that the very object of such groups, as they were relatively well documented in the past, "is to combine the constituent companies into a system in such a way as to maximize the profits of the entire system irrespective of the profits of each separate unit," as Gardiner Means himself long ago pointed out (Bonbright and Means 1932, pp. 45–46).

Much as in the multinational corporation's relations with its affiliates and subsidiaries, the constituent corporations in a group may adjust intercorporate dealings in such a way as to raise or diminish the profit rates of the different ostensibly independent corporations (cf. Rose 1968, p. 101; Tanzer 1969, pp. 14 ff.). Under such circumstances, studies attempting to compare the conduct of corporations, several of which may in fact be involved in different groups to which their policies are subordinated, cannot provide valid or reliable results. We cannot be certain what is being measured.

In the United States today, the Mellons and DuPonts are among the most publicized instances of enduring "family spheres of influence." The TNEC found the Mellon "family . . . to have considerable shareholdings in 17 of the 200 corporations, 7 of which they controlled directly or indirectly" (Goldsmith and Parmelee 1940, p. 123). Today, according to *Fortune* (Murphy 1967; see also Jensen 1971) the Mellons, utilizing "various connections, and through a complicated structure of family and charitable trusts and foundations" and other "eleemosynary arrangements," have known controlling interests in at least four of the 500 largest nonfinancial corporations (Gulf Oil, Alcoa, Koppers Company, and Carborundum Company), as well as the First Boston Corporation, the General Reinsurance Corporation, and the Mellon National Bank and Trust Company (the fifteenth largest United States bank by deposits [Patman Report 1968, p. 79]). In turn (according to the Patman Report [1968], p. 14), Mellon National Bank holds 6.9 percent of the common stock in Jones and Laughlin Steel, another of the top 500.[14] It seems as reasonable to hypothesize that the Mellons are only instances of a less visible but prevalent situation among principal proprietary families as to assume they are "deviant cases" or historical vestiges. Moreover, given such family "spheres of influence" which radiate out among several large corporations, it should be understood that the same small proportion of the stock in the hands of such a family in a specific corporation carries different implications and potential for control than when held by a single individual with no other major resources and institutions to buttress his position. It is known that a great number of

---

14. Jones and Laughlin Steel was classified under "management control" by Larner. Aside from the 6.9 percent Mellon National Bank holding, the Bank also has two directors on the Company's Board. Koppers Company, in which *Fortune* (Murphy 1967) claims the Mellons held at least 20 percent was also classified as under "management control" by Larner, indicating the difficulty of locating "control" without access to "street knowledge" or insiders. This emphasizes again the secrecy in which holdings are shrouded and the fact that insufficient account of this is taken when considering "findings" about control centers. Larner himself notes, though without considering its possible general significance, that the Alcoa mandatory 10-K report filed with the SEC in 1963 states that no shareholder has more than 10 percent of the outstanding common shares, although from the proxy report and other sources he concluded that Alcoa was under Mellon control. *Fortune* (Murphy 1967) and the *New York Times* (Jensen 1971) estimate Mellon interests in Alcoa at 30 percent.

related individuals may participate in the ownership of a family bloc, utilizing a complex holding pattern to keep control concentrated, despite the diffusion of ownership. If control is exercised through entangling interests in several interrelated corporations, rather than limited to one, then such kinship information is vital to an understanding of the control structure. Indeed, the kinship relations between the top officers, directors, and principal shareholders of the large corporations (and banks) are the least studied but may be the most crucial aspect of the control structure.[15]

BANK CONTROL?

The banks are major institutional bases of economic power and corporate control which the managerialists, from Berle and Means to John Kenneth Galbraith, either have ignored or considered unimportant. Offering no substantial evidence to support his assertion, Gordon (1966) recently restated (in a new preface to his original study of the situation as of the 1930s) the accepted view that "large-scale industry is much less dependent on the banking community than it was a half-century ago, and such power as bankers have is less likely to be translated into corporate control than was true then" (p. ix). Noting the extensive interlocking between the largest banks and corporations, he simply claims that this is a "far cry from what was once meant by 'financial control'" (p. x). What implications such interlocking might have, Gordon fails to suggest. Galbraith's (1968) "commonplace observation" is that "the social magnetism of the banker" is "dwindling," and that the largest corporations are emancipated from reliance on bankers and outside sources of financing because they now have a source of their own capital, derived from their earnings, and "wholly under [their] own control" (pp. 68, 92).

Contrary to Galbraith's commonplace observations, however, uncommon but systematic research on the question does not seem to indicate decreased corporate dependence on external funds. For all U.S.

---

15. Larner's own statements in his notes on sources occasionally suggest how important, if not vital, is such kinship information if we are successfully to locate the actual centers of corporate control. Thus, for instance, Larner (1970) refers to *Moody's Industrials* as the source of his information that in the Dow Chemical Company, which he classified under "minority control," there were "78 dependents (plus spouses) of H. W. Dow [who] owned 12.6 percent of [the] outstanding common stock" (p. 75). Similar references were made to the Newberry Company, Cabot Corporation, and R. R. Donnelly & Sons Company, in which the descendants and kindred through marriage of the original founder are taken into account in establishing the share of these families in ownership. Clearly, systematic independent research of this type into the kinship interconnections of the principal shareowners, officers, and directors of the 500 largest corporations has not yet been done by anyone purporting to locate their centers of control. The outstanding recent unsystematic attempt to do this is, once again, the work of Ferdinand Lundberg (1968, chaps. 4–6).

firms whose assets exceed $5 million, John Lintner (1967) reports that "the dependence on outside liabilities for financing is about the same regardless of the size of the firm" and that the "relative shifts in the reliance on internal or external funds . . . have been remarkably stable over a full half-century" (pp. 179, 184). The Federal Reserve Bank of San Francisco reports a sharp increase in the past decade in reliance on external funds for financing, and if the bank's data are reanalyzed to exclude depreciation allowances—on the premise that only profits can be used to finance net investments to increase the firm's capital stock —the reported trend is even more clearly toward dependence on external financing. Most important, the largest corporations are found to be least self-financing (cited in Fitch and Oppenheimer 1970, no. 1, pp. 68 ff.).

If, contrary to managerialist assumptions, the large corporations must continue to rely on the capital market no less than in the past, this is of critical importance: since the distribution of banking assets and deposits is highly skewed, this means that "reliance on external financing" is, in fact, dependence on a small number of very large financial corporations. As of 1964, the 100 largest commercial banks in the United States held 46 percent of all the deposits of the 13,775 commercial banks in the country. The 14 largest alone, representing one-tenth of 1 percent of all commercial banks, held 24 percent of all commercial bank deposits (Patman Report 1966, p. 804). Thus the relationships between the large banks and corporations are essential to our understanding of the locus of corporate control. Where it might otherwise appear as if, lacking a visible controlling ownership interest, a corporation is under "management control," it may on the contrary be under the control of one or more banks and other financial institutions. Even in corporations in which a substantial minority of the stock (or even majority) is held by an identifiable ownership interest, this may not assure control: if the corporation has a long-term debt to a given bank or insurance company, has that institution's representatives on its board, and must receive prior approval of significant financial and investment decisions, then control of that corporation may be exerted from the "outside"; and this may be accentuated if several related financial institutions have a similar interest in that corporation. (The dismissal under the "prodding" of its bankers of Anaconda's chief executive officer and other top officers— discussed earlier—when their performance in Chile turned out to be inferior to Kennecott's and had led, in any case, to the company's deteriorating situation, seems to be a case in point [see *Business Week*, February 19, 1972, pp. 54–55]).

Whatever the dwindling "social magnetism" of the banker divined by Galbraith, this may be a questionable indicator of his economic power. Indeed, the Patman Committee, which gathered unprecedented information on the stockownership of large commercial banks, believes the power of the banks is growing. The committee found a "pattern of control whereby large blocks of stock in the largest *non*financial corporations in the country are becoming controlled by some of the largest financial corporations in the country." "This," the Patman Committee concludes, "is shifting economic power back to a small group, repeating in somewhat different manner the pattern of the trusts of the late nineteenth and early twentieth centuries." This "emerging situation" appears to the committee to be one involving increasing "bank minority control." The committee found that the largest banks surveyed in 10 major cities, not including the West Coast, hold 5 percent or more of the common stock in 147 (29 percent of the 500 largest industrial corporations. At least 5 percent of the common stock of 17 of the 50 largest merchandising companies and the same number of transportation companies is held by one or more of the 49 banks. These 49 banks are also represented on the boards of directors of 286 of the 500 largest industrial corporations. The same pattern appears among the 50 largest merchandising, utilities, transportation, and insurance companies (Patman Report 1968, p. 13). Whether or not and to what extent such fusion of financial and industrial capital indicates "financial" or "bank control" is an open question. However, it cannot be ignored if we want to understand its implications. Thus Peter C. Dooley (1969) found that precisely those corporations—the largest ones—which the managerialists claim to be most independent of the banks, are in fact, most closely interlocked with large banks and other financial corporations. Among the 200 largest nonfinancial corporations, the greater the assets of the nonfinancial corporation, the greater the incidence of interlocks between them and the 50 largest financial corporations (32 banks and 18 insurance companies). (p. 318).

This may mean that the conceptualization of the largest corporations, banks, and insurance companies as independent institutions may obscure the actual coalescence of financial and industrial capital which has occurred. On the one hand, as noted above, large banks and insurance companies frequently are themselves principal shareholders in the large corporations. On the other, the very same individuals and families may be principal shareowners in large banks and large corporations, even when these do not have institutional holdings in one another. Aside from the Mellons, with controlling interests in at least four of the 500 largest nonfinancial corporations and in an investment bank, insurance company, and the fifteenth largest commercial bank, whom we noted above, other well-known industrialist families in the United States may be cited who also have dominant and/or controlling interests in the largest banks. For example, there are both branches of the Rockefeller families, as well as other principal families in the Standard Oil corporations. The Rockefellers and associates reportedly (*Time,* September 7, 1962; Abels 1965, p. 358) held over 5 percent of the stock in the Chase Manhattan Bank (ranking second by deposits of all banks in 1963),[16] whose chairman of the board is David Rockefeller; the Stillman-Rockefeller families and associates are said to be dominant in the First National City Bank (ranking third in 1963) (*Fortune,* September 1965, p. 138). The Fisher and Mott families, among the principal shareowning families in General Motors, reportedly held over 5 percent of the stock of the National Bank of Detroit (U.S. Congress, 1963, pp. 227, 416), the country's sixteenth largest bank in 1963. The Henry Ford family owns 4 percent of the thirtieth ranking Manufacturer's National which, in turn, owns 7 percent of Ford Motor Company common stock (Patman Report 1968, p. 664). The M. A. Hanna family that controls at least two [of] the 500 largest corporations, National Steel and Consolidation Coal (Larner 1970, p. 120; Burch 1972, p. 58), has a dominant minority interest of at least 3 percent in the thirty-fourth-ranking National City Bank of Cleveland (U.S. Congress 1963, p. 165), which in turn holds 11 percent of the stock of Hanna Mining Company. These are, of course, merely instances, as I said, of prominent families whose interests overlap banking and industry. They illustrate the general theoretical issue, however, of the extent to which it is valid to speak at all of "bank control" of "industry"—as does the Patman Report, for instance, or other recent writers (Fitch and Oppenheimer 1970). Rather, these families' interests transcend the banks and corporations in which they have principal or controlling interests; and the banks may merely be units in, and instrumentalities of, the whole system of propertied interests controlled by these major capitalist families.

There appears, in fact, to be a special segment of the corporate world which represents the fusion of financial and industrial capital, to which Rudolf Hilferding (1974, chaps. 7, 14, and 23) long ago called attention, and whom he termed "finance capitalists" (cf. also Schumpeter 1955b, pp. 80–81; Lenin 1967, chap. 3; Sweezy 1942, pp. 261, 266). Hilferding was referring to "a circle of persons who, thanks to their own possession of capital or as representatives of concentrated power over other people's capital (bank directors), sit upon the governing boards of a large number of corporations. Thus there arises a kind of personal union, on the one hand, between the different corporations themselves [and,] on the other, between the latter and the banks, a circumstance which must be of the greatest importance for the policy of these institutions since a community of interests has arisen among them" (Hilferding [1947], as slightly reworded from the translation by Sweezy [1956], p. 261).

Do such "finance capitalists" or representatives of banks who sit on the boards of the large American corporations today have a special role

---

16. The 1963 rankings are given since this was the year of the House Select Committee's study. The source of the rankings is the *Fortune Directory for 1963.* The latest rankings by *Fortune* (July 1973) for 1972 are Mellon, 15; Chase, 3; First National City, 2; National Bank of Detroit, 18; National City Bank of Cleveland, 49.

in coordinating the interests of these corporations? Do they differ, for example, from other outside directors that interlock the largest corporations between themselves, as well as with other firms? These are critical questions which no single indicator can suffice to answer. We would need information concerning their own propertied interests, their relative wealth, [and] their kinship relations before being able to ascertain whether the "finance capitalist" represents a special social type in contrast to other officers and directors of the largest corporations and banks. One relevant issue, however, on which we do have some information is the extent to which they are likely to sit on a number of large nonfinancial corporation boards compared with "outside directors" (i.e., those who do not actually hold posts as officers in the corporate management) who are not bankers. I have analyzed raw data presented elsewhere (Smith and Desfosses 1972) on interlocking directorates among the 500 largest industrial corporations, ranked by sales, in 1968. What we find is that commercial and investment bankers are disproportionately overrepresented among the occupants of multiple corporate directorships (Table 21–2). Bankers constituted 21 percent of all outside directors in the 500 largest industrials, but well over twice that proportion among the outside directors with seats on three or more corporate boards. Indeed, the proportion of bankers who are outside directors rises directly with the number of corporate posts held. And among the select few ($N = 16$) outside directors having five or more posts, 56 percent were bankers; of the five outside directors with six or seven posts, four were bankers. Viewing the same relationship differently (Table 21–3),

Table 21-2. Principal Employer of Outside Directors of the 500 Largest Industrial Corporations in the United States in 1968 (percent)

Type of Principal Employer	Number of Seats Occupied						
	1	2	3	4	5	6+	Total
Other top 500 firm	13.9	25.9	15.7	12.9	18.2	0	15.4
Law firm	14.1	10.3	3.4	3.2	9.1	0	13.0
Bank	18.5	25.8	41.6	45.1	45.5	80.0	20.9
Commercial	10.8	14.5	19.1	29.0	36.4	40.0	12.0
Investment	7.7	11.3	22.5	16.1	9.1	40.0	8.9
Consulting firm	6.3	6.0	1.1	6.5	0	0	6.0
Other[a]	47.3	32.0	38.2	32.3	27.2	20.0	44.7
Total percent	100	100	100	100	100	100	100
Total N	1,932	282	89	31	11	5	2,350

Sources: Calculated from raw data given in Smith and Desfosses (1972, table 4, p. 65), on the composition of the outside directorships of the 500 largest industrials listed in *Fortune*, May 15, 1969, ranked by 1968 sales. Principal employer was obtained from information in the proxy statements of 460 corporations and from Standard and Poor's *Register of Corporations, Directors, and Executives*, 1970, for 35 corporations. Smith and Desfosses did not obtain information on five corporations.

[a]Types of employers which did not employ morethan 5 percent of the total number of outside directors in the 500 largest industrials, including utilities, merchandising, insurance, real estate, railroad firms, as well as educational institutions, foundations, government agencies, plus "unlisted companies."

Table 21-3. Number of the 500 Largest U.S. Industrial Corporations on Whose Boards Outside Directors Are Represented, by Type of Principal Employer, 1968 (percent)

Type of Principal Employer	Number of Seats Occupied				
	1	2	3	4+	(N)
Other top 500 firm	74	20	4	2	(361)
Law Firm	89	9	1	1	(306)
Bank					
Commercial	75	15	6	5	(283)
Investment	71	15	10	4	(208)
Consulting firm	86	12	1	1	(141)
Other[a]	87	9	3	1	(1,051)
All outside directors	82	12	4	2	(2,350)

Sources: See Table 21-1.
[a]See Table 21-2.

commercial and investment bankers stand out in marked contrast to other outside directors in the top 500 corporations: a far higher proportion of them have multiple corporation posts than do outside directors from other top 500 corporations, law firms, consulting firms, or other types of companies and institutions. Outside directors from other top 500 corporations are second only to the bankers in the proportion with multiple directorships. But well over twice the proportion of bankers occupy multiple posts: 11 percent of the commercial bankers and 15 percent of the investment bankers have seats on three or more top 500 corporate boards, compared with 6 percent of the directors from other top 500 firms.

WHO CONTROLS THE BANKS?

Who the controlling interests are in the largest banks is not publicly known. The Select House Committee report on chain banking (1963) and the Patman Reports (1964, 1966, 1967) for the first time provided an authoritative glance—however limited—inside. The 1963 and 1964 reports listed the 20 largest shareholdings of record (and the percentage of stock held) in each of the 200 largest commercial bank members of the Federal Reserve System in recent years. The 1966 Patman Report focused on commercial banks' holdings of their own shares and also listed the total market values (though without calculating the percentages) of the outstanding stock held by all financial institutions in the 300 largest commercial banks in 1966; and the 1967 Patman Report also focused on holdings in the banks by other financial institutions, particularly the major commercial banks in 10 metropolitan areas. The lists of the reported "beneficial owners" of the banks' shares obtained by the Patman Committee have not been released to date. With only the shareholdings of record available so far, the same difficulties arise here as have already been discussed earlier in detail. Any attempt to locate the actual ownership interests by identifying recognizable surnames alone, without knowledge of kinship relations, nominees, etc., cannot provide reliable and valid information. A recent study of this type, based on the 1963 Select Committee report, and utilizing the 10 percent minimum to define an ownership-controlled bank, came to the predictable conclusion that "management control had become the dominant form of control among the large member banks by 1962," accounting for 75 percent of the banks (Vernon 1970, p. 654). In contrast, Burch (1972) utilized other business sources of information cited earlier, as well as the 1963 Select Committee report, investigated representation on boards of directors, and consulted several family histories. However, like Vernon, he did not attempt any systematic investigation of kinship ties, so once again his are absolutely minimum estimates of control of these banks by ownership interests. He studied only the 50 largest, and concluded that 30 percent were probably under family control, another 22 percent possibly under family control, and 48 percent probably under management control (pp. 89–96). Vernon (1970) broke down his analysis into categories by total bank assets, rather than ranks, so no direct comparison is possible from their published reports. However, of the 27 largest banks having $1 billion in assets or more, he classified only two under "owner control," with the possible addition of another three in which he identified an interest greater than 5 percent but less than 10 percent (p. 655). Of the 27 largest banks listed by Burch, however, he classified eight as probably family controlled and four more as possibly family controlled. Once again the disparities in results by two different methods are striking. Other close students of the banks (aside from the Patman investigators [1968, p. 91] already cited) object to the ownership level of 10 percent as "arbitrary." Thus, Eisenbeis and McCall (1972), financial economists at the Federal Deposit Insurance Corporation, state that " 'minority control' can be achieved . . . through ownership of a much smaller proportion of stock than the arbitrary 10 percent levels" (p. 876).

In any event, the theoretical significance of such an alleged split between ownership and control in large banks was not suggested by Vernon, nor to my knowledge has any managerial theorist yet to suggest that the banks might somehow or other become non-profit-maximizing institutions, were they no longer under the control of specific ownership interests. Furthermore, neither Vernon nor Burch took account in their studies of the extent to which the banks themselves are interlocked and, most important, hold significant amounts of stock in each other. The Patman Committee (1966) did a survey, whose results have only been partially reported, which found that 57 percent of the 210 largest commercial banks hold more than 5 percent of their own shares and 29 percent hold more than 10 percent of their own shares. The banks (and other types of corporations) buy their own stock—sometimes termed "defensive buying" on Wall Street—to keep their shares out of the "unfriendly hands" of potential rivals for control.[17] If other financial institutions, including commercial banks, mutual savings banks, and insurance companies in which the same owning families appear among the principal shareholders, or which have long-standing business associations and common interests (including interlocks between banks and insurance companies), also hold the bank's stock, this further decreases the amount of stock which the principal individual and familial shareholders must own to maintain control. Nearly a third (30 percent) of the 275 large banks reported on by the Patman Committee had more than 10 percent of their shares which could be voted exclusively by other financial institutions. Nearly half (47 percent) had more than 5 percent of their shares similarly held (Patman Report 1966, p. 832). In addition, the extent and pattern of interlocking bank stockownership by the same principal shareowners is not known. Very preliminary data received by the Patman Committee found several "situations where the beneficial owners of large blocs of commercial bank stock are in fact holdings by a few families who have management connections with competitor banks in the same geographic area." Though banks may not legally interlock, officers and directors (and their families) of one bank may have principal shareholdings in other banks, and the preliminary data of the Patman Committee also revealed such situations (Patman Report 1966, pp. 878–79).

CONCLUSION

Our review of discrepant findings on the alleged separation of ownership and control in the large corporation in the United States,[18] and of the problems entailed in obtaining reliable and valid evidence on the actual ownership interests involved in a given corporation, should make it clear that the absence of control by proprietary interests in the largest corporations is by no means an "unquestionable," "incontrovertible," "singular," or "critical" social "fact." Nor can one any longer have confidence in such assurances as the following by Robert A. Dahl (1970): "Every *literate* person now *rightly takes for granted* what Berle and Means *established* four decades ago in their famous study, *The Modern Corporation and Private Property*" (p. 125; italics added). On the contrary, I believe that the "separation of ownership and control" may well be

---

17. Corporations may purchase their own shares for other reasons: (1) to maintain the price of their stock, (2) to prepare for possible mergers and acquisitions, (3) to allow them to convert bonds to shares, etc. Whatever the reasons, such holdings are of use in control, when necessary.

18. We have, of course, not reviewed empirical studies of the question in other countries. The principal study in England is by Florence (1961). The only other such systematic study of which I am aware is by Wheelwright (1957) on Australia, as well as my own forthcoming collaborative volume with Ewen and Ratcliff on Chile.

one of those rather critical, widely accepted, pseudofacts with which all sciences occasionally have found themselves burdened and bedeviled.[19]

News of the demise of capitalist classes, particularly in the United States, is, I suspect, somewhat premature. In place of such generalizations, extrapolated from an insufficiently examined American experience or deduced from abstract ahistorical theoretical premises, detailed empirical studies are necessary.

The methods and procedures and the basic concepts and units of analysis in such research will have to be quite different than those which have been most commonly employed in the past. Most important, such research must focus at the outset on the complex relationships in which the single corporation is itself involved: the particular pattern of holdings and their evolution within the corporation; and the relationships between it and other corporations; the forms of personal union or interlocking between corporate directorates and between the officers and directors and principal shareholding families; the connections with banks, both as "financial institutions" and the agents of specified propertied interests, including those who control the banks themselves; the network of intercorporate and principal common shareholdings. In a word, it will be necessary to explore in detail the institutional and class structure in which the individual large corporations are situated.

For these purposes, sociologists must reclaim the concept of class from the disuse and misuse into which it has fallen. Classes, as Dahrendorf (1959) rightly states, "are clearly not layers in a hierarchical system of strata differentiated by gradual distinctions. Rather, 'the analysis of social class is concerned with an assessment of the chances that common economic conditions and common experiences of a group will lead to organized action.' ... *Class* is always a category for purposes of the

---

19. An example of a critical unwitting pseudofact appears in two articles by Daniel Bell (1958, 1961). In both articles, Bell refers to the "X" family of "Middletown" as an instance of the end of family control. "[B]y and large," Bell wrote (1958, p. 248; and similarly 1961, p. 45), "the system of family control is finished. So much so that a classic study of American life like Robert Lynd's *Middletown in Transition,* with its picture of the 'X' family dominating the town, has in less than twenty years become history rather than contemporary life. (Interestingly enough, in 1957, the Ball family, Lynd's 'X' family, took in professional management of its enterprises since the family lineage was becoming exhausted.)" Perhaps Bell really knows who now dominates Muncie, Indiana, and what role the Ball Family plays there, but as an instance of "the breakup of family capitalism" and the end of family control, this is a singularly poor choice. Given the context in which Bell refers to the "X" family, his statement is quite misleading, since Ball Brothers, Inc., which is, according to *Fortune,* probably among the 500 largest corporations, ranked by sales, in the country today, continues to be privately owned. "Edmund F. Ball, a founder's son, is chairman of the company, but he has employed plenty of nonfamily talent. ... 'Ours is still,' says Edmund Ball, 'essentially a closely held, privately owned business' " (Sheehan 1966, p. 343).

analysis of the dynamics of social conflict and its structural roots, and as such it has to be separated strictly from *stratum* as a category for describing hierarchical systems at a given point in time" (p. 76).[20] If, as I think Daniel Bell (1958) argues correctly, a class system is maintained through the fusion of the family as an institution and extant property relations, and "capitalism . . . is a social system wherein power has been transmitted through the family," then we must make that an important focus of our empirical investigations (pp. 246–47). We should pursue Bell's (1961) own analytical starting point and original (though subsequently ignored) sociological emphasis on the relationship between "the peculiar cohesiveness of dominant economic classes" and "the linkage of the family and property system" (pp. 39–40). For this reason, it will also be necessary to focus, to use Parsons' term (1953) on the "members of the most *effective kinship unit*" (p. 120). This in turn means investigating the intricate network not only of general social interaction and shared concrete interests, but also the actual kinship relations between officers, directors, and principal shareholders within the same and different corporations.

This point is worth underlining, for it has been essential to our argument. If we are to locate the actual centers of corporate control, we must discover "the most effective kinship unit." Without research into the web of kinship relations binding apparently unrelated individuals into a cohesive owning unit for purposes of control, analysis of the locus of control of the large corporation is hobbled at the outset. Furthermore, by proceeding from such an analysis it will become possible to answer, on the most unambiguous empirical grounds, whether or not a capitalist "class" exists in the United States or similar countries and to what extent and in what ways that class has really been "decomposed" as the managerial theorists have assumed. Joseph Schumpeter (1955a) rightly argued that "the family, not the physical person, is the true unit of class theory" (p. 113). Classes are constituted of freely intermarrying families variously located in the social process of production and system of property relations. People similarly located economically are more likely to associate with each other freely than with others and, therefore, to freely intermarry. Particularly among the wealthy, a variety of specific institutions, from debutante balls to select social clubs, resorts, and assorted watering places, as well as the "proper" schools [and] colleges (fraternities, sororities, and "living groups"), assure their commingling and psychological compatibility—and, therefore, differential propensity to intermarry. Protection of the family's property (and "good name"), which injects a further note of caution in the selection of proper marriage partners, merely increases this "natural" social tendency (cf. Domhoff 1967, 1970, 1972; Mills 1957; Baltzell 1966a, 1966b). Our empirical

---

20. The phrase in single quotes is from Lipset and Bendix (1951), p. 248.

investigations of the separation of ownership and control must lead us, therefore, to investigate the extent to which the families of the officers, directors, and principal shareowners of the large corporations are bound by interwoven kinship ties—the extent to which, in other words, those who own and control the decisive units of production freely intermarry to form a social class.[21] Particularly relevant here is Baltzell's conclusion (1966a): "One of the functions of upper class solidarity is the retention, *within a primary group of families,* of the final decisionmaking positions within the social structure. As of the first half of the twentieth century in America, the final decisions affecting the goals of the social structure have been made primarily by members of the financial and business community" (pp. 183, 275; italics added).

Studies of the internal structure of capitalist classes will have to answer questions that include the following: what is the relationship between the "new group of managers who are utterly different from their capitalist predecessors" and the old owning families—from whom they are said (Dahrendorf 1959, p. 46) to be increasingly moving apart? How are the different strata and segments of this class, and the incumbents of the new roles brought about by the "decomposition of capital" and the growth of managerial functions, related? What role do the overlapping and interrelated interests of principal shareowning families in the large corporations play in class integration and corporate control? What is the relationship between formal authority in the bureaucratic administrative apparatus, ownership interests, and kinship status? What role do the banks, as institutions, play in the control structure of the class? By whom are the banks owned and controlled? Do those who sit at the center of the web of interlocking directorates between corporations, or in the decisive posts which unite the banks and nonfinancial corporations, have a special position in the class? How, in sum, is the class internally differentiated and integrated?

To none of these questions do we have anything like adequate answers. There have been significant contributions to our understanding of the formation of earlier historically dominant classes. Studies of existing ones, however, are rare and are usually limited to quantitative measurement of their social composition and to counting

---

21. Diverse authorities on kinship have noted that the "upper" classes everywhere, the United States included, tend to be characterized by an extended and tightly organized network of kin relations (see Goode 1964; Cavan 1963; Goode, Hobbins, and McClure 1971). Yet such findings have been ignored by sociologists in their discussions of the alleged "breakup of family capitalism" and the separation of ownership and control. Bert Adams (1970) is one of the few sociologists specializing in kinship relations to call specific attention to the interrelationship between kinship and "the entire debate regarding who rules or controls the U.S. economic system," stating that "the evidence points unquestionably to strong kin links among the extremely wealthy in the society." He suggests that "much exciting research lies ahead for those who would pursue the links between kinship and economics, not only in the middle and working classes, but among the wealthy or upper classes as well" (pp. 591–92).

the social mobility of individuals. These studies have not explored the relationships within the class, between individuals, families, "elites," strata, and segments of that class. They have—with few exceptions—ignored the structure of dominant classes.[22]

Such studies are necessary, among other reasons, if we are not to "read politics in an extraordinarily abstract fashion," bereft of the knowledge of the interaction and relationships between "concrete interest groups, or classes." I think it is correct, as Bell (1958) argues, that, "if the important considerations of power are *what people do with that power,* then we have to have more *particularized ways of identifying the groupings* than 'institutionalized orders,' 'domains,' 'circles,' etc." (p. 240; former italics in original; latter added). And this requires analysis of the internal relationships within the "dominant" or "upper" class —of the modes of articulation and association, as well as differentiation between given interest groups, class segments, etc.—so that we may be alert to possible internal structural sources of class cohesion and conflict. "Power," as William Kornhauser has put it (1966), "tends to be patterned according to the structure of interests in a society. Power is shared among those whose interests converge, and divided along lines where interests diverge," and this applies within a dominant class as it does in the society at large, though to what extent we can scarcely say, lacking such information as we are (p. 213).

The separation of ownership and control has meant at the least, its proponents argue, that whatever the capacity for organized action of the "full-blown capitalists" who constituted "a homogeneous capitalist class" in the past, this situation has been superseded by the "decomposition of capital" into a rather loose aggregate of fragmented groups having fundamentally different, often opposing, values and interests. "This is a peculiar state of affairs," in Dahrendorf's view (1959) "in which it is indeed virtually impossible to locate the ruling class" (p. 305). Once America had a "ruling class of businessmen [who] could relatively easily (though perhaps mistakenly) decide where their interests lay and what editors, lawyers, and legislators might be paid to advance them," as David Riesman has put the syllogism, but "the captain of industry *no longer runs business,* no longer runs politics," and that class has been replaced by "an amorphous power structure." Power in America has become "situational and mercurial; *it* [sic] resists attempts to locate *it*" (Riesman et al. 1953, pp. 247, 242, 257; italics

---

22. Aside from the works cited already by Domhoff, Mills, and Baltzell, Hunter's work (1959)—although not using the concept of class—contributes important information on interaction between corporate executives on a national level. Studies by Perlo (1957), Rochester (1936), and Lundberg (1946), as well as Lundberg's latest relevant work (1968), which is a mine of excellent ideas worth researching, are important nonacademic contributions. Barber and Barber (1965) contains excellent short historical studies. Other notable historical studies of dominant classes are by Bailyn (1955), Barber (1955), Ford (1953), Forster (1960, 1963), Edwards Vives (1927), Heise Gonzales (1950), and Rabb (1967).

added). Certainly these are no more than statements of the merely plausible; they are alleged social facts.

A contrary, and at least equally plausible, argument may be made that precisely because the individual capitalists of an earlier competitive era were compelled to struggle among themselves for economic survival, this also inhibited their acting in common, in comparison with the present relatively unified power and capacity for action possessed by those who own the principal portions and control the large corporations. Thus, for instance, Joseph Schumpeter (1955b) attempted to explain in political-economic terms what he considered the artificial conjuncture of capitalism and imperialism, as the result of the emergence of "monopoly capitalism" and the merger of formerly antagonistic "capitalists and entrepreneurs." In place of a "mass of capitalists competing with one another," there appeared what he termed "organized capital": the structural integration of large industrial enterprises and the "close alliance" of bankers and industrialists, "often going as far as personal identity. . . . Here capitalism has found a central organ that supplants its automatism by conscious decisions" (pp. 80–81). Therefore, it may be hypothesized that the social and economic interweaving of once opposed financial and industrial interests, increased economic concentration, the fusion of formerly separate large capitals, and the establishment of an effective organizational apparatus of interlocking directorates heightens the cohesiveness of the capitalist class and its capacity for common action and unified policies (see and cf. Hilferding 1910, chap. 23). Whether, as Riesman might claim, such a theory applied to contemporary America is a spectral survival of an earlier time is an empirical question.

We cannot know what "the capabilities and opportunities for cooperation among those who have similar interests, and for confrontation among those with opposing interests" (Kornhauser 1966, p. 213) are at the national level within the dominant class unless we investigate the internal differentiation and integration of that class through the best available techniques of empirical inquiry. The fact is that there is far more systematic information available on the poor—on farmers, workers, and black Americans—than on the men and women of the rich and the well-born, on those who make up the "upper strata"—if not the "capitalist class"—of our society. Yet by now it ought to be apparent, if only from our most recent past, that we must discover as much as we can about those who occupy the upper reaches of American society if we are to understand—and act effectively in—the present as history.[23]

---

23. Several years ago I wrote that "just as a society's class structure is a major basis of its political diversity and cleavage, so too is *intra*class social differentiation politically significant, and by exploring the structure of the working class it will be possible to locate fundamental sources of its political behavior. This does not mean that *inter*class differences or conflicting class interests are in any way secondary to the internal structure of

Studies of contemporary dominant classes elsewhere, including not only "advanced" but less developed and misdeveloped countries, are also essential. Such studies, aside from their intrinsic importance, may help reveal theoretical gaps and errors, as well as inadequate methodologies, in the present body of research and writing and allow us to clarify, elaborate, and specify given generalizations. These studies may provide the basis for a comparative theory of capitalist classes that is more comprehensive and valid than the extant one embodied in the "astonishing consensus" among social scientists. In place of abstract models based on ostensible "universal" elements in social structures, we need analyses of the structures of specific capitalist classes, analyses related to the actual historic processes within which they have been formed.

APPENDIX

Dahrendorf has taken Marx's writings in volume 3 of *Capital* to support his own theses concerning the dissolution of capitalism as the result of the separation of ownership and control. Not only does Dahrendorf (1959) explicitly reject what I have termed the "plain Marxist" proposition that the functionaries of capital and the owners of capital (when they are not identical individuals) belong to the same social class, but he also asserts that this "view is *clearly contrary* to Marx's own analysis" (p. 43; italics added). In volume 3 of *Capital,* Marx wrote briefly on the "credit system" (stock market) and "joint-stock companies," whose economic importance in England was increasingly evident. He noted that (1) they involved "an enormous expansion of the scale of production and of enterprises that was impossible for individual capitals" and that (2) capital is "here directly endowed with the form of social capital [capital of directly associated individuals] as distinct from private capital." However, it is two additional propositions, which anticipated the debate about the separation of ownership and control, that Dahrendorf and others consider supportive of their own managerial theory. Marx also wrote that (3) the corporations, being "social undertakings as distinct from private undertakings," mean "the abolition of capital as private property within the framework of capitalist production itself." (4) This means also the "transformation of the actually functioning capitalist into a mere manager, administrator of other people's capital, and of the owner of capital into a mere owner, a mere money-capitalist" (3:436).

---

the working class as the source of its politics. Quite the contrary. Any conflict between classes tends to erase or minimize the significance of *intra*class differences and to maximize *inter*class differences" (Zeitlin 1967, pp. 8–9). I take it as a working hypothesis that this statement applies equally well to a society's *dominant* class. A fine recent work which is replete with historical sociological interpretations that rest on, or require, analysis of the internal differentiation and integration of specific dominant classes is that by Moore (1966, e.g., pp. 36–39 on England; pp. 162–65, 192, on Imperial China; pp. 237 ff. on Japan).

Now, as to the first two propositions there can be no debate. Few would disagree that Marx correctly anticipated the profound significance of the corporation for large-scale production and rapid economic development. And the second point is an unexceptionable description of the obvious fact that pooling individual capital allows "undertakings" which smaller individual capitalists could not undertake separately. As to the third proposition, it is what I mean by "confusing Hegelian comments." For myself, its meaning is clear; for others it has been confusing (e.g., Bernstein, Schmidt, Bell, Dahrendorf, etc.). Marx had a penchant for Hegel's language and often used it precisely because he wished to honor that "mighty thinker" when others were currently treating him as a "dead dog." Therefore, he "coquetted with the modes of expression peculiar to him" (*Capital,* 1:19–20). One of Marx's oft-used Hegelian concepts was *"aufgehoben,"* or *"aufhebung."* In the volumes of *Capital* translated into English, this has usually been rendered "abolition." Yet this is clearly not its Hegelian meaning, nor the meaning Marx intended. As Ivan Soll (1969) explains, for Hegel, "the understanding's finite categories must be both preserved and negated—or to use a term favored by Hegel just because it possesses this double meaning, *aufgehoben*" (p. 134). Or in Hegel's own words "*Aufheben* exhibits its true double meaning . . . it negates and preserves at the same time" (cited from his *Logic* by Soll 1969, p. 134). Reinhard Bendix has written me in a private communication: "The implication [of *aufheben*] is to *recreate* in the process of *abolishing*—which is one of those conundrums Hegelians thrive on and the rest of us mortals despair over." The corporation as a new form of "social capital" negates "private capital" while preserving it. That this is Marx's likely meaning must be concluded. For in even greater exaggeration he goes on to say, "This is the abolition of the capitalist *mode of production* within the capitalist mode of production itself" (3:438). This can only be gibberish in English (or at best "confusing") unless it is understood in its Hegelian sense of negating while preserving, recreating while abolishing. In fact, Marx makes this clear in another passage: "However, this expropriation appears within the capitalist system in a contradictory form, as *appropriation of social property by a few.* . . . There is antagonism against the old form in the stock companies, in which the social means of production appear as private property; but the conversion to the form of stock still remains ensnared in the trammels of capitalism; hence, *instead of overcoming* the antithesis between the character of wealth as social and as private wealth, the stock companies merely *develop it in a new form*" (3: 440; italics added).

Further, it is in this context that Marx refers to the development which Hilferding was later to elaborate, as were many others, including Lundberg, Bonbright and Means, and then (though secondarily) Berle and Means. The latter authors laid out several types of control other than private ownership and control. In these types, "the separation of ownership and control" meant that the large property owners—those who owned the majority or predominant minority of shares in a corporation, directly or indirectly ('pyramiding')—appropriated control from the small shareowners. This was Marx's point when he stated that the form of the stock company and of credit offers the capitalist "absolute control within certain limits over the capital and property of others, and thereby over the labor of others" (3:439).

As to the fourth proposition, it too is quite consistent with the "plain Marxist" class analysis, for Marx, in elaborating this point, states: "profit is henceforth received . . . as compensation for *owning capital* that now is entirely divorced from the *function* in the actual process of reproduction, just as this *function* in the person of the manager is divorced from ownership of capital" (3:436–37; italics added). This, of course, is also the view I cited above from Weber. Further, from the standpoint of the analysis of social domination, class conflict, and surplus appropriation (exploitation), Marx's view, as already quoted here and as in the following passage, is directly opposed to the managerialist doctrine of "satisficing," "corporate conscience," "postcapitalist society," or "new industrial state." The role of the emerging corporation and stock market system, Marx wrote, was "to develop the incentive of capitalist production, enrichment through exploitation of the labor of others, to the purest and most colossal form of gambling and swindling, and to reduce more and more the number of the few who exploit the social wealth" (3:441).

REFERENCES

Abels, Jules. 1965. *The Rockefeller Billions.* New York: Macmillan.

Adams, Bert. 1970. "Isolation, Function, and Beyond: American Kinship in the 1960s." *Journal of Marriage and the Family* 32 (November):575–97.

Alchian, Armen. 1968. "Corporate Management and Property Rights." In *Economic Policy and the Regulation of Securities.* Washington, D.C.: American Enterprise Institute.

Bailyn, Bernard. 1955. *The New England Merchants in the Seventeenth Century.* Cambridge, Mass.: Harvard University Press.

Bain, Joe S. 1966. *International Differences in Industrial Structure: Eight Nations in the 1950s.* New Haven, Conn.: Yale University Press.

Baltzell, E. Digby. 1966a. " 'Who's Who in America' and 'The Social Register': Elite and Upper Class Indexes in Metropolitan America." In *Class, Status, and Power,* edited by Reinhard Bendix and S. M. Lipset. 2nd ed. New York: Collier-Macmillan.

——. 1966b. *Philadelphia Gentlemen: The Making of a National Upper Class.* New York: Macmillan.

Baran, Paul A., and Paul M. Sweezy. 1966. *Monopoly Capital.* New York: Monthly Review Press.

Barber, Eleanor G. 1955. *The Bourgeoisie in Eighteenth-Century France.* Princeton, N.J.: Princeton University Press.

Barber, Eleanor G., and Bernard Barber, eds. 1965. *European Social Class: Stability and Change.* New York: Macmillan.

Baumol, William J. 1959. *Business, Behavior, Value, and Growth.* New York: Macmillan.

Bell, Daniel, 1958. "The Power Elite—Reconsidered." *American Journal of Sociology* 64 (November):238–50.

———. 1961. "The Breakup of Family Capitalism." In *The End of Ideology.* New York: Collier.

Bendix, Reinhard. 1952. "Bureaucracy and the Problem of Power." In *Reader in Bureaucracy,* edited by R. K. Merton, Ailsa P. Gray, Barbara Hockey, and Hanan C. Selvin. Glencoe, Ill.: Free Press.

Berle, Adolph, Jr. 1954. *The 20th Century Capitalist Revolution.* New York: Harcourt, Brace.

Berle, Adolph, Jr., and Gardiner C. Means. 1967. *The Modern Corporation and Private Property.* New York: Harcourt, Brace & World (originally published in 1932 by Macmillan).

Bernstein, Eduard. 1961. *Evolutionary Socialism.* New York: Schocken (originally published in Germany in 1899).

Bonbright, James C., and Gardiner C. Means. 1932. *The Holding Company.* New York: McGraw-Hill.

Burch, Philip H., Jr. 1972. *The Managerial Revolution Reassessed.* Lexington, Mass.: Heath.

Business Week (no author given). 1971. "The Board: It's Obsolete Unless Overhauled." May 22, pp. 50–58.

———. 1972. "An Ex-Banker Treats Copper's Sickest Giant." February 19, pp. 52–55.

Cavan, Ruth. 1963. *The American Family.* New York: Crowell.

Dahl, Robert A. 1970. *After the Revolution?* New Haven, Conn.: Yale University Press.

Dahrendorf, Ralf. 1959. *Class and Class Conflict in Industrial Society.* Stanford, Calif.: Stanford University Press.

Domhoff, G. William. 1967. *Who Rules America?* Englewood Cliffs, N.J.: Prentice-Hall.

———. 1970. *The Higher Circles: The Governing Class in America.* New York: Random House.

———. 1972. *Fat Cats and Democrats.* Englewood Cliffs, N.J.: Prentice-Hall.

Dooley, Peter C. 1969. "The Interlocking Directorate." *American Economic Review* 59 (June):314–23.

Drucker, Peter F. 1971. "The New Markets and the New Capitalism." In *Capitalism Today,* edited by Daniel Bell and Irving Kristol. New York: Basic.

Earley, James S. 1956. "Marginal Policies of Excellently Managed Companies." *American Economic Review* 46 (March):44–70.

―――. 1957. "Comment." *American Economic Review. Papers and Proceedings* 47 (May):333–35.

Earley, James S., and W. T. Carleton. 1962. "Budgeting and the Theory of the Firm." *Journal of Industrial Economics* 10 (July):165–73.

Edwards Vives, Alberto. 1927. *La fronda aristocratica.* Santiago: Editorial del Pacifico.

Eisenbeis, Robert A., and Alan S. McCall. 1972. "Some Effects of Affiliations among Savings and Commercial Banks." *Journal of Finance* 27 (September):865–77.

Etzioni, Amitai. 1968. *The Active Society.* New York: Free Press.

Fitch, Robert, and Mary Oppenheimer. 1970. "Who Rules the Corporations?" *Socialist Revolution* 1 (1):73–107; also 1 (5):61–114; 1 (6): 33–94.

Florence, P. Sargant. 1961. *Ownership, Control, and Success of Large Companies: An Analysis of English Industrial Structure and Policy, 1936–1951.* London: Sweet & Maxwell.

Ford, Franklin L. 1953. *Robe and Sword: The Regrouping of the French Aristocracy after Louis XIV.* Cambridge, Mass.: Harvard University Press.

Forster, Robert. 1960. *The Nobility of Toulouse in the Eighteenth Century.* Baltimore: John Hopkins Press.

―――. 1963. "The Provincial Noble: A Reappraisal." *American Historical Review* 68 (April):681–91.

Galbraith, John K. 1967. *The New Industrial State.* New York: New American Library (also, "Introduction," 2nd ed. 1971). New York: Houghton Mifflin.

Goldsmith, Raymond W., and Rexford C. Parmelee. 1940. *The Distribution of Ownership in the 200 Largest Nonfinancial Corporations.* In *Investigations of Concentration of Economic Power.* Monographs of the Temporary National Economic Committee, no. 29. Washington, D.C.: Government Printing Office.

Goode, William J. 1963. *The Family.* Englewood Cliffs, N.J.: Prentice-Hall.

Goode, William J., Elizabeth Hobbins, and Helen M. McClure, eds. 1971. *Social Systems and Family Patterns: A Propositional Inventory.* Indianapolis: Bobbs-Merrill.

Gordon, Robert A. 1966. *Business Leadership in the Large Corporation.* Berkeley: University of California Press (originally published in 1945 under the auspices of the Brookings Institution).

Heise Gonzales, Julio. 1950. "La constitucion de 1925 y las neuvas tendencias politico-sociales." *Anales de la Universidad de Chile* 108 (80; 4th trimester):95–234.

Hilferding, Rudolph. 1947. *Das Finanzkapital.* Berlin: Verlag J. H. W. Dietz.

Hindley, Brian V. 1970. "Separation of Ownership and Control in the Modern Corporation." *Journal of Law and Economics* 13 (April):185–221.

Hoyt, Edwin P. 1967. *The Guggenheims and the American Dream.* New York: Funk & Wagnalls.

Hunter, Floyd. 1959. *Top Leadership, U.S.A.* Chapel Hill: University of North Carolina Press.

Jensen, Michael C. 1971. "A New Generation Comes of Age." *New York Times.* May 2, sec. 3, pp. 1, 5.

Kahl, Joseph. 1957. *The American Class Structure.* New York: Rinehart.

Kamerschen, David R. 1968. "The Influence of Ownership and Control on Profit Rates." *American Economic Review* 58 (June):432–47.

————. 1969. "The Effect of Separation of Ownership and Control on the Performance of the Large Firm in the U.S. Economy." *Rivista internazaionale di schienze economiche e commerciali* 16 (5):489–93.

Kaysen, Carl. 1957. "The Social Significance of the Modern Corporation." *American Economic Review* 47 (May):311–19.

————. 1965. "Another View of Corporate Capitalism." *Quarterly Journal of Economics* 79 (February):41–51.

Kolko, Gabriel. 1962. *Wealth and Power in America.* New York: Praeger.

Kornhauser, William. 1966. " 'Power Elite' or 'Veto Groups'?" In *Class, Status, and Power,* edited by Reinhard Bendix and S. M. Lipset. 2nd ed. New York: Collier-Macmillan.

Larner, Robert J. 1970. *Management Control and the Large Corporation.* Cambridge, Mass.: University Press, Dunellen.

Lenin, Nikolai. 1967. "Imperialism." In *Lenin: Selected Works.* New York: International Publishers (originally published in Petrograd in 1917).

Lewellen, Wilbur G., and Blaine Huntsman. 1970. "Managerial Pay and Corporate Performance." *American Economic Review* 60 (September):710–20.

Lintner, John. 1967. "The Financing of Corporations." In *The Corporation and Modern Society,* edited by E. S. Mason. New York: Atheneum.

Lipset, S. M., and Reinhard Bendix. 1951. "Social Status and Social Structure: A Re-Examination of Data and Interpretations." Part 1. *British Journal of Sociology* 2 (September):150–68.

Lomask, Milton. 1964. *Seed Money: The Guggenheim Story.* New York: Farrar, Straus.

Lundberg, Ferdinand. 1946. *America's Sixty Families.* New York: Citadel (originally published by Vanguard in 1937).

————. 1968. *The Rich and the Super-Rich.* New York: Bantam.

Luxemburg, Rosa. 1970. *Reform or Revolution.* New York: Pathfinder (originally published in Berlin in 1899).

Manne, Henry. 1965. "Mergers and the Market for Corporate Control." *Journal of Political Economy* 72 (April):110–20.

Marris, Robin. 1963. "A Model of 'Managerial' Enterprise." *Quarterly Journal of Economics* 77 (May):185–209.

————. 1964. *The Economic Theory of "Managerial" Capitalism.* London: Macmillan.

Marx, Karl. 1967. *Capital.* Vols. 1–3. New York: International (originally published in German in 1867, 1885, 1894).

Mason, E. S. 1967. "Introduction." In *The Corporation in Modern Society,* edited by E. S. Mason. New York: Atheneum.

Merton, Robert K. 1959. "Notes on Problem-Finding in Sociology." In *Sociology Today,* edited by R. K. Merton, Leonard Broom, and Leonard S. Cottrell, Jr. New York: Basic.

Metcalf, Lee. 1971. *Congressional Record* 117, pt. 17:22141.

Metcalf, Lee, and Vic Reinemer. 1971. "Unmasking Corporate Ownership." *Nation* July 19, pp. 38–40.

Miliband, Ralph. 1969. *The State in Capitalist Society.* New York: Basic.

Mills, C. Wright. 1957. *The Power Elite.* New York: Oxford University Press.

————. 1962. *The Marxists.* New York: Dell.

Monsen, R. Joseph, Jr., J. S. Chiu, and D. E. Cooley. 1968. "The Effect of Separation of Ownership and Control on the Performance of the Large Firm." *Quarterly Journal of Economics* 82 (August):435–51.

————. 1969. "Ownership and Management." *Business Horizons* 12 (August):45–52.

Moore, Barrington. 1966. *Social Origins of Dictatorship and Democracy.* Boston: Beacon.

Moran, Theodore H. 1973. "Transnational Strategies of Protection and Defense by Multinational Corporations." *International Organization* 27 (Spring):273–87.

Murphy, Charles J. V. 1967. "The Mellons of Pittsburgh." Part 1. *Fortune* 75 (October):120 ff.

National Resources Committee (NRC). 1939. *The Structure of the American Economy.* Washington, D.C.: Government Printing Office. Reprinted in Paul M. Sweezy. 1953. *The Present as History.* New York: Monthly Review Press.

Nichols, W. A. T. 1969. *Ownership, Control, and Ideology.* London: Allen & Unwin.

O'Connor, James. 1971. "Who Rules the Corporation?" *Socialist Revolution* 2 (January/February):117–50.

Parsons, Talcott. 1953. "A Revised Analytical Approach to the Theory of Social Stratification." In *Class, Status, and Power,* edited by Reinhard Bendix and S. M. Lipset. Glencoe, Ill.: Free Press.

Parsons, Talcott, and Neil Smelser. 1957. *Economy and Society.* London: Routledge & Kegan-Paul.

[Patman] Staff Report. 1964. *Twenty Largest Stockholders of Record in Member Banks of the Federal Reserve System.* 5 vols. U.S. Congress,

House, Committee on Banking and Currency, Domestic Finance Committee. 88th Cong., 2d sess. Washington, D.C.: Government Printing Office (cited as Patman Report).

————. 1966. "Bank Stock Ownership and Control" (reprinted in Patman Report 1968, vol. 1).

————. 1967. "Control of Commercial Banks and Interlocks among Financial Institutions" (reprinted in Patman Report 1968, vol. 1).

————. 1968. *Commercial Banks and Their Trust Activities: Emerging Influence on the American Economy.* U.S. Congress, House, Committee on Banking and Currency, Domestic Finance Committee. 90th Cong., 2d sess. Washington, D.C.: Government Printing Office (cited as Patman Report).

Perlo, Victor. 1957. *The Empire of High Finance.* New York: International.

Peterson, Shorey. 1965. "Corporate Control and Capitalism." *Quarterly Journal of Economics* 79 (February):1–23.

Playford, John. 1972. "Who Rules Australia?" In *Australian Capitalism,* edited by Playford and Douglas Kirsner. Harmondsworth: Penguin.

Rabb, Theodore K. 1967. *Enterprise and Empire: Merchant and Gentry Investment in the Expansion of England, 1575–1630.* Cambridge, Mass.: Harvard University Press.

Riesman, David, et al. 1953. *The Lonely Crowd.* Garden City, N.J.: Anchor.

Rochester, Anna. 1936. *Rulers of America.* New York: International.

Rose, Sanford. 1968. "The Rewarding Strategies of Multinationalism." *Fortune,* September 15, pp. 101–5, 180, 182.

Schumpeter, Joseph. 1955a. "Social Classes in an Ethnically Homogeneous Environment." In *Imperialism and Social Classes.* New York: Meridian (originally published in German in 1923).

————. 1955b. "The Sociology of Imperialism[s]." *Imperialism and Social Classes* (originally published in German in 1919).

Sheehan, Robert. 1966. "There's Plenty of Privacy Left in Private Enterprise." *Fortune,* July 15, pp. 224 ff.

————. 1967. "Proprietors in the World of Big Business." *Fortune,* June 15, pp. 178–83, 242.

Simon, Herbert A. 1957. *Administrative Behavior.* 2nd ed. New York. Macmillan.

Smith, Ephraim P., and Louis R. Desfosses. 1972. "Interlocking Directorates: A Study on Influence." *Mississippi Valley Journal of Business and Economics* 7 (Spring):57–69.

Soll, Ivan. 1969. *Introduction to Hegel's Metaphysics.* Chicago: University of Chicago Press.

Sorokin, Pitirim. 1953. "What Is a Social Class?" In *Class, Status, and Power,* edited by Reinhard Bendix and S. M. Lipset. Glencoe, Ill.: Free Press.

Sweezy, Paul M. 1953. "Interest Groups in the American Economy." In *The Present as History.* New York: Monthly Review Press.

————. 1956. *Theory of Capitalist Development.* New York: Monthly Review Press (originally published in 1952).

Tanzer, Michael. 1969. *The Political Economy of International Oil and the Underdeveloped Countries.* Boston: Beacon.

U.S., Congress, House, Select Committee on Small Business. 1963. *Chain Banking: Stockholder and Loan Links of 200 Largest Member Banks.* Washington, D.C.: Government Printing Office.

Vernon, Jack R. 1970. "Ownership and Control among Large Member Banks." *Journal of Finance* 25 (3):651–57.

Villarejo, Don. 1961/62. *Stock Ownership and the Control of Corporations.* Radical Education Project. Ann Arbor, Mich. Reprint of articles in *New University Thought* (Autumn 1961 and Winter 1962).

Walker, Robert. 1971. "A Banker for Anaconda." *New York Times,* May 23, sec. 3, pp. 3, 11.

Weber, Max. 1965. *Theory of Social and Economic Organization.* Edited by Talcott Parsons. New York: Free Press (originally published in German in 1925).

————. 1968. *Economy and Society.* Edited by G. Roth and C. Wittich. New York: Bedminster (originally published in German in 1921).

Wheelwright, E. L. 1957. *Ownership and Control of Australian Companies.* Sydney: Law Book.

Williams, Robin, Jr. 1959. *American Society.* New York: Knopf.

Williamson, Oliver E. 1963. "Managerial Discretion and Business Behavior." *American Economic Review* 53 (December):1032–57.

————. 1970. *Corporate Control and Business Behavior.* Englewood Cliffs, N.J.: Prentice-Hall.

Wrong, Dennis. 1968. "Some Problems in Defining Social Power." *American Journal of Sociology* 73 (May):673–81.

Zeitlin, Maurice. 1967. *Revolutionary Politics and the Cuban Working Class.* Princeton, N.J., Princeton University Press.

Capitalism, for Worse

22

By Paul M. Sweezy

With few exceptions, the economists of the capitalist countries, liberal and conservative alike, are agreed that in the nearly four decades since the publication of Keynes's *General Theory of Employment, Interest, and Money,* governments have been in possession of, and have successfully utilized, means to control the level of economic activity and prevent the occurrence of serious depressions. To quote Harvard's Nobel Prize—winning economist Kenneth J. Arrow:

> The new economic ideas of Keynes and his disciples have been translated into policy with almost unprecedented speed. The idea that the state, through its decisions to spend, tax, and regulate the supply of money, could reduce unemployment to levels far lower than those in the depths of previous depressions was accepted among both economists and political leaders, and has shown itself to work in practice with great success. In every advanced country, the post-World War II record is like that of a new economy. (*New York Times,* March 26, 1973)

Let us look for a moment at the U.S. record (I will return to the others later on). It is true that since World War II there have been no depressions comparable to that of the 1930s. But is this because economists and political leaders have put their heads together and decided upon appropriate spending, tax, and monetary policies to head one off every time it threatened? Or is it because there has been a tremendous increase in the general level of government spending, with armaments and war playing by far the largest part? (I presume that neither the economists nor the political leaders would wish to claim that the military spending is merely the form taken by Keynesian ideas when put into practice.)

To these questions our economist friends would probably reply that while for overriding political or foreign-policy reasons the requisite

282

amount of government spending has in fact been for milita
if this had not been the case it would have been possible to
deal more for welfare objectives, with much the same eco
In their eyes, the theory of the controllability of the level ot ੮
activity is therefore vindicated regardless of what the money is spen
on.

If this were really so, however, would we not expect that the controllers, helped by the large military budget, would have had an easy
time maintaining a reasonably satisfactory level of economic activity
throughout the postwar period? Surely with 20 percent or more of the
American people living below the officially defined poverty line and
with such projects as decent low-cost housing, pollution control, and
mass transportation crying out for vastly increased public outlays, there
has never been any lack of worthy purposes for the controllers to turn
their attention to. And yet it is a notorious fact that even in boom
periods, as at the time of writing in June, 1973, officially counted unemployment amounts to 5 percent or more of the labor force. Taking facts
like this into account, one could be pardoned for suspecting that the
whole "controllability" idea is a myth and that the military budget is
after all the only rational explanation of the relatively (i.e., relatively to
the 1930s) favorable economic record of the postwar period.

In order to test this hypothesis, my colleague Harry Magdoff and I
conducted an "experiment."[1] Using common sense and generally conservative estimating methods, we calculated for the year 1970 the number of workers who were either unemployed or directly and indirectly
dependent on military spending. We then added these figures and compared the result with the number of unemployed in 1938. (It should be
noted that both 1970 and 1938 were years of recession following a long
period of cyclical upswing and should therefore be fairly comparable.)

The first problem was to get an estimate of real, as distinct from
officially counted, unemployment, since everyone familiar with the
subject knows that there is a large discrepancy.[2] Working from official
data on labor force participation rates, which were steadily declining for
male workers during most of the 1950s and 1960s, and making an
adjustment for involuntary part-time workers, we concluded that a
conservative estimate of real unemployment was 8.1 million (9.4 percent of what would have been the labor force if jobs had been available).
To this we added those in the armed forces (2.9 million), civilian employees of the Defense Department (1.2 million), those employed in
producing goods for the Defense Department (3 million), and those

1. Reported in detail in "Economic Stagnation and the Stagnation of Economics,"
Monthly Review (April, 1971).
2. See, for example, the article on unemployment entitled "6 Pct. Is Only the Tip of the
Iceberg" by A. H. Raskin in the New York Times "Review of the Week" section, June 25,
1972.

employed because of what economists call the multiplier effect, i.e., workers employed in satisfying the demand generated by the incomes of those directly employed by the military budget (7.1 million). These items total 22.3 million. This is just over 25 percent of the 1970 labor force adjusted to include those not officially counted as unemployed.

This compares with an official unemployment figure of 19.0 percent in 1938. However, if we make adjustments for hidden unemployment at that time and add to the expanded total the relatively small number of defense-related employed, we would probably come up with a figure somewhere around 30 percent to compare with the 25 percent in 1970. All of which leads to the conclusion that, apart from military spending, things were a bit better in 1970 than in 1938. But not much, and certainly nowhere near enough to sustain the thesis that the economists and politicians are in effective control of the economy.

If my Keynesian friends wish to dispute these facts or estimates, I would be happy to hear from them. I confess, however, that I do not expect to. They like to talk about the record, but they are shy about subjecting it to a concrete historical analysis. In this connection it is worth noting, if only in passing, that they have not yet come up with a coherent theory of the Great Depression and why it was so much worse than any previous capitalist depression. Need I add that without such a theory it is quite impossible to provide any rational analysis of what might have happened in the postwar period in the absence of vastly expanded military spending?

At this point the Keynesians, with remarkable unanimity, shift their ground. What about the other advanced capitalist countries, they ask, and especially Germany and Japan, the two with the best growth and employment records and the lowest levels of military spending?

It is impossible to answer this question adequately in a brief essay, especially since, to the best of my knowledge, no one, and least of all the Keynesians, has made a serious effort to do so. I can therefore only indicate the general lines along which I believe an attempt at an answer should proceed.

Most fundamental here is the fact, too often forgotten by social scientists each working in his or her narrow speciality, that capitalism is a global system and not a collection of separate national economies. What happens in any part of the system affects to some extent what happens in all the others; and if the part in question happens to be by far the largest in the system, as is the case with the United States in world capitalism the effect on some or all of the other parts is likely to be large and even decisive. The question, then, is to what extent the performance of the world capitalist economy, and especially the economies of Germany and Japan, has been determined by the relative prosperity of the United States during this period.

It is, I believe, beyond dispute that both the German and the Japanese economic "miracles" were launched in the boom which accompanied the Korean War, i.e., as a direct result of U.S. military spending and involvement. In the case of Germany, Heinz Abosch has written: "For the West German economy, the Korean War proved to be a remarkable stimulant: while the big industrial powers had to step up the production of armaments, Germany, still subject to the restrictions of the Potsdam Agreement, was able to increase her entire industrial output, thanks to the orders that poured in from all sides. As Professor [Henry] Wallich remarks: 'it was sparks from the Korean War that set Germany exports alight.' "[3] What was true for Germany was even more so for Japan, which was the rear staging area for U.S. forces fighting in Korea and a direct recipient of large military orders. "In terms of the growth situation," writes Professor Tsuru, "the Korean conflict and the subsequent maintenance of 'special procurement' demand was a distinct boon."[4]

Of course it would not be possible to establish so close a continuing dependence of the German and Japanese economies on U.S. military spending. The booms touched off by Korea had much else to feed on: repair of war damage, renovation of capital equipment, and (perhaps most important) a veritable binge of "automobilization" similar to that which had sustained the U.S. economy in the 1920s. But continuing strong demand for German and Japanese exports remained a sine qua non of the prosperity of these countries, and it is difficult to believe that this export demand would have held up if the U.S. economy had once again sunk into a condition of low-level stagnation such as prevailed in the 1930s. It is well to remember that in that earlier period it was only military spending, first in Japan and Germany and only later in the United States, which pulled the capitalist world out of the Great Depression. In the post war period I would argue that it has been military spending (plus other similarly motivated outlays such as economic subsidies to puppet and client states), so far largely but by no means exclusively centered in the United States, which has prevented the capitalist world from sinking into a new Great Depression. As an historical interpretation of these strife-ridden decades, I submit that this makes vastly more sense than the notion that the postwar performance of world capitalism has been the brainchild of economists aided and abetted by wise political leaders. Economists may like to think that they

---

3. Heinz Abosch, *The Menace of the Miracle* (Monthly Review Press, 1963), p. 79.

4. Shigeto Tsuru, *Essays in Economic Development,* Economic Research Series No. 9 (Tokyo, 1968), p. 168. "Special Procurement" was the name given to U.S. purchases for military and related purposes. According to Professor Tsuru's figures (pp. 156–57) this item averaged 34.2 percent of Japan's total receipts from foreign sales of goods and services in the years 1951 to 1953.

are powerful, and political leaders that they are wise. But the sad truth is that there is precious little evidence to support these amiable conceits. True, they play a role, but not the one they think they play or would like to play; rather their role is that of instruments and agents of elemental forces generated by a blind and self-contradictory economic system which no one can control.

The real question to which economists ought to address themselves, but consistently refuse to do so, is why capitalism in the twentieth century has such a powerful tendency to stagnation that it requires increasingly massive forms of public and private waste to keep itself going at all. (As every reasonably sensitive observer of contemporary capitalism knows, military spending is only the leading species of a large genus.) Basically, the reason was stated by Marx with both eloquence and clarity more than a hundred years ago when he wrote: "*The real barrier of capitalist production is capital itself.* It is the fact that capital and its self-expansion appear as the starting and closing point, as the motive and aim of production, that production is merely production for *capital*, and not vice versa, the means of production mere means for an ever-expanding system of the life process for the benefit of the *society* of producers"[5] To put the point in another way, as long as the driving forces of production are profit and the expansion of profit-making enterprises, and as long as the incomes of working people are held down precisely to make possible an increase in profits and a more rapid expansion of enterprises, so long will the growth of society's power to produce tend to outstrip its power to consume. And if this contradiction is deeper and more pervasive today than it was in Marx's time, the reason is that in the intervening period the process of concentration and centralization of capital—which he recognized as inevitable features of capitalist development—has gone so far that dominant monopolies today have the power not only to exploit their own workers but all other strata of society as well, thus expanding the gap between wealth at one pole and poverty at the other, at the very time when there is, or soon could be, ample productive power to provide everyone without exception with the means to a decent human livelihood.

Under these circumstances economists have taken upon themselves the task of hiding the facts, of making the uncontrollable appear under control, of rationalizing a system which condemns hundreds of millions of people to lives of despair and starvation, and which through its unrestrained profligacy and violence threatens the very continuation of life on earth. It is not a task I envy them.

---

5. *Capital*, vol. 3, Kerr edition, p. 293. Italics in the original.

The Current Crisis: A Radical Analysis

23

David M. Gordon

Orthodox economists are fiddling with their models while the economy burns. We as radicals have been struggling to understand the roots and implications of the current crisis. As we learn more, our basic differences with orthodox economists have been clarified.

The *sources* of those differences can be easily understood. Orthodox economists seek to legitimate the capitalist system and to make it work better. We seek to understand its reproduction and contradictions in order to transform it. They study for capitalism. Most of us struggle for socialism. They sing of class harmony. We focus on class conflict.

Until very recently, the *reflection* of those differences in the current economic crisis has been muted. They have been confused and so have we. As we have begun to understand more about the current crisis, however, our basic differences with orthodox economists have been more and more sharply etched in our differing analyses of the current economic mess.

There seem to be four major levels of differences in analysis of the current crisis: the analysis of "accidents," the analysis of cycles, the analysis of history and structures, and the analysis of secular tendencies.

THE ANALYSIS OF "ACCIDENTS"

For orthodox economists and their voices in the government and media, "accidents" have played an important role in triggering the current crisis. Gazing at those accidents through the lenses of supply and demand analysis, they regard them as unfortunate disturbances of normal equilibria. Through market mechanisms, they assure us, the econ-

Reprinted from *Radical Perspectives on the Economic Crisis of Monopoly Capitalism* (New York: Union for Radical Political Economics, 1975), pp. 138–142, by permission of publisher.

omy will adjust and equilibrium will be restored. From this perspective, they have been able to blame parts of the crisis on bad weather conditions in 1972, the Soviet wheat deal, the Middle Eastern War, and the "greedy" Arabs. Focusing on those "accidents," they encourage us to scapegoat, to look elsewhere for the causes of the crisis.

Those events clearly happened. And they clearly had some effects on the developing economic crisis. They may even have been among the more important "triggers" which intensified the emerging crisis. Our own analysis of food and fuel inflation clearly indicate some of those effects.[1]

But our analyses of those events differ from orthodox views in two important ways.

First, we have a different view of the *ways* in which those short-term events influence the economy. Orthodox economists believe in equilibrium and regard the accidents as mild disturbances. We look for structural imbalances and can see, through that perspective, some of the ways in which the capitalist economic system, with its own characteristic instabilities, creates a special *vulnerability* to short-term disturbances.

The economy is vulnerable to disturbances, in our view, for two main reasons—the first abstract, the second concrete.

At the abstract level, capitalist economies tend intrinsically to display some of the manifestations of "anarchy" in production. Disruptions in the flow of production and realization in one sector may quickly spread to other sectors. A price rise in intermediate goods, for example, may lower profits in a final-good sector, forcing a lag in investment and consequently in employment. Disequilibria may be as likely as equilibria. The separation of production from consumption creates the formal possibilities of continual disruptions in the flow of capital through its cycle of expanded reproduction. Indeed, as Marx notes, proportional and steady accumulation seems more unlikely than the waves of cyclical fluctuation.[2] Equilibria themselves appear, from this perspective, as the true "accidents."

At the concrete level, our economy was vulnerable to recent short-term disturbances in several important ways. Those events did not occur in a vacuum. For example, the main reason why bad harvests around the world had such explosive effects on prices was that world grain reserves had been declining since the mid-1960s.[3] Grain reserves them-

---

1. These analyses are developed in the "food packet" and "energy packet" produced by URPE's Political Education projects. For more information about either packet, contact URPE/PEA, P. O. Box 331, Cathedral Station, N.Y., N.Y. 10025.

2. See in particular Marx's discussion of accumulation and crises in *Theories of Surplus Value*, Vol. II.

3. Data on declining grain reserves are provided in the article by Dale Hathaway in *Brookings Papers on Economic Activity*, 1974, No. 1.

selves had been declining, in large part, because American and Canadian grain companies had been consolidating their control over world grain markets by cornering and therefore partially limiting supplies. Foreign aid and PL-480 programs were used by the government to undercut the incentive of Third World countries to devote resources toward agricultural self-sufficiency. Acreage retirement and price subsidy programs in this country served simultaneously to subsidize large owners and to withhold potentially productive land from planting.[4]

Second, our own analyses of the recent short-term events reveal them to be *reflections,* in some instances, of more important trends in the world capitalist economy itself; in some cases, the so-called accidents were not really "accidents" at all. For instance, the Soviet wheat deal was not an isolated event, but part of a comprehensive strategy, energetically pursued by the government, to promote agricultural exports in order to balance the mounting trade deficit. Those trade deficits, in turn, reflected the erosion of American economic hegemony in the world market.[5] To pick a second example, the consequences of the OPEC oil price hikes flowed through the power and strategy of the major oil companies. For several years before those dramatic price increases, the "majors" had been jockeying both domestically and internationally to free themselves of reliance on the Arab supplies. They had been seeking to develop alternative energy sources, to break the back of environmentalist opposition to expansionist plans like the Alaskan pipeline, to consolidate their control over "downstream" refining and distribution. Providing an excuse for "crisis," for artificially withholding available supplies, the Middle Eastern price hikes simply provided an occasion, in an important sense, for the majors to pursue their longer-term strategies.[6]

THE ANALYSIS OF CYCLES

At a second level, radicals differ with orthodox economists in our interpretation and analysis of business cycles.

Orthodox economists, during the halcyon days of the neo-Keynesian revolution, promised us continually full employment. With careful government management of the economy, we could achieve stable growth with "full employment" and stable prices forever. During the

4. These points are developed in the "food packet," op. cit., and also briefly in Geoffrey Barraclough, "The Great World Crisis: I," *New York Review of Books,* January 23, 1975.

5. These points are also developed in some detail in the "food packet," and in an article by J. Crotty and R. Boddy forthcoming in *Socialist Revolution.*

6. These points are developed in the URPE "energy packet" and in Richard Kronish, "The Coming of the Energy Crisis," *Socialist Revolution* (September-October, 1973).

sixties, we heard more and more about the "obsolescence" of the business cycle.

We differ with that perspective in two important ways.

First, our view of contradictions in the economic system leads us to view skeptically the possibilities of "fine tuning." Orthodox macroeconomists take a typically "partial" approach to the problems of government policy, arguing that, *ceteris paribus,* perfect stabilization policies can be developed.[7] Experience has shown that the political economy confounds such *ceteris paribus* prescriptions. For instance, many orthodox economists argued, prophetically, that the Administration should institute some tax increases in 1966 to 1967 to begin to cool off the economy. But the government was not engaged exclusively in stabilization policies. It was also waging this little war. It couldn't control the costs of the war because there were these gritty fighters for national liberation who stubbornly refused to give up. It couldn't admit the true costs of the war because it was necessary to disguise the full magnitude and impact of that imperialist struggle. Engaged *both* in stabilization and in empire protection, the government was caught by the contradictions of political economic management of a world economic *system.*

Second, and more fundamentally, our analyses of the cycle suggest not only their continuing likelihood but their political necessity in a capitalist economy. If full employment continues too long, profits get eroded. While the government can try, through policies like accelerated depreciation allowances, to compensate for losses in retained earnings, hoping to forestall declines in investment, it cannot prevent the decline in profits forever. Ultimately serving the interests of capital in a capitalist economy, it must move sooner or later to curb workers' bargaining power through higher unemployment. Without a temporary bust of sufficient duration to dampen the demand for labor, given relative inelasticity of the supply of labor, wages will eventually increase to such a point that profits will erode, that capitalists' income will decline as a percentage of total national income. A full analysis of the *political economic business cycle* cannot ignore these tendencies.[8]

In short, orthodox economists have been able to pretend that the business cycle has become "obsolete" precisely because they ignore the contradictions and class struggles of a capitalist economic system. We have been able to recognize some of the important sources of the current crisis precisely through our attempts to understand those dimensions of contradiction and class conflict over the cycle itself.

---

7. This was their position during the mid-1960s and, despite a substantial loss of confidence, this remains their essential position today.

8. See R. Boddy and J. Crotty, "Class Conflict, Keynesian Policies, and the Business Cycle, *Monthly Review* (October, 1974).

THE ANALYSIS OF HISTORY AND STRUCTURE

At a third level, radical economists differ with orthodox economists in our analysis of the necessity and impact of longer-term structural shifts in the world economy.

Orthodox economists study the present as if it lasted forever. They take institutions for granted. They sleep upon ahistorical clouds. They focus almost exclusively on the behavior of individual economic units through the market within the context of a given institutional framework. Because their models do not usually permit the analysis of institutional changes themselves, they are usually forced, by their methodology, to pretend that structural changes have not occurred.[9]

Radicals begin with analyses of history, with analyses of the forms within which the content of economic life is reproduced and transformed. Over the broad sweep of history, we study changes from one mode of production to another. Within a period dominated by a single mode of production, we study structural changes as that form experiences stages of development. In our studies of capitalism, for instance, we have paid special attention to the kinds of structural changes which have resulted from the succession of stages of capital accumulation—as capitalism itself has passed through the period of commercial accumulation into its current stage of advanced corporate or monopoly accumulation.[10] Within any stage of development, we also recognize that capitalism is a world economic system, fundamentally interdependent, featuring shifting balances of political and economic power, passing through periods of single-nation hegemony to periods of intense international rivalry.[11] Through those lenses, we have been able to learn quickly that the current economic crisis reflects, at this third level of analysis, some fundamental structural shifts in the world political economy.

The glorious days of post-World War II affluence in the United States were fundamentally premised upon American political and economic hegemony in the world. Our corporations gained increasing international advantage. Our government could protect corporate penetration of foreign markets. Our international advantage provided

9. See, for example, the discussion of orthodox methodology in David M. Gordon, *Theories of Poverty and Underemployment* (Lexington, Mass.: D.C. Heath, 1972), Chap. 3.

10. This analysis of stages in the development of U.S. Capitalism is illustrated, for instance, in the analyses of the labor process and labor markets developed in David M. Gordon, Richard C. Edwards and Michael Reich, "Labor Market Segmentation in American Capitalism," unpublished paper, Harvard University, 1973.

11. These stages of international competition and dominance reflect the tendencies of capitalist economies to move, as if cyclically, from stages of relatively more dominant competition to more dominant monopoly. See some of the comments in Marx's discussion of the falling rate of profit and its counteracting tendencies in *Capital,* Vol. III.

a domestic cushion within which unionized workers could be rewarded with marginal increases in real wages. Political stability reigned and, as strikes became less and less frequent, so did economic tranquility.

During the 1960s, three important developments began fundamentally to limit American corporate power, bringing quickly to an end the short period of untrammeled American international economic dominance.

First, as multinational corporations grew in power, they began to move capital and investment so quickly around the world that the government itself began to lose some degrees of freedom in its ability to "fine-tune" the economy. Rapid capital movements brought about a convergence of the business cycles in the advanced industrial countries, amplifying the instability of international economic adjustments.[12] With the growth of the multinational corporations internationally, a shift clearly occurred. Up to the 1960s, the United States led the world economy. More and more, the United States both leads and responds. The tail and the dog are both doing a lot of wagging. Others are obviously sensitive to us, but we are also increasingly sensitive to others.

Second, oppressed people around the world began increasingly to limit the ability of the American behemoth to control its expansion and accumulation. National liberation movements in the Third World slowly began to limit the frontiers of expansion. At home the protests of blacks and other minorities forced the government to spend extra moneys to buy off the poor—which itself intensified the "fiscal crisis of the state" and further tightened the demand for labor as low-wage workers themselves began to find welfare a more remunerative possibility.[13]

Third, and fundamentally, the recovery of Europe and Japan began to erode American corporations' international competitive advantage. The days of "unconstrained" monopoly power began to be numbered. Corporations could no longer afford to pass on higher wages at home, forcing an intensification of work.[14] Corporations lost domestic markets and foreign markets to their foreign competitors. The American balance of payments deteriorated rapidly. The dollar itself collapsed as the single standard of the international monetary system. All those international developments intensified the effects of the postponed recession of the mid-1960s. When Nixon finally tried to cool off labor in 1969, international developments compromised the government's freedom of maneuver. Corporate profits, partly as a result of international competition, were already so low that corporations could not easily withstand

---

12. See Joyce Kolko, *America and the Crisis of World Capitalism* (Boston: Beacon Books, 1974).

13. See James O'Connor, *The Fiscal Crisis of the State* (N.Y.: St. Martin's, 1973).

14. See the analysis in my article, in this volume, on "Capital vs. Labor: The Current Crisis in the Sphere of Production."

a sustained recession—during whose first stages profits might drop even lower. On the other hand, balance of payments problems made a quick pull out of the recession into another expansionary period especially undesirable, since continuing inflation would further cripple our international position. Temporary controls were the only escape, and the simultaneous agricultural export drive and dollar devaluations generated additional inflationary pressures which, as controls were lifted, burst upon the domestic markets.

Taken altogether, these shifts in the structure of the world economy, reinforcing each other, help explain why this period of economic readjustment is so much more severe and complicated than others. They also help explain why the struggle over solutions to the crisis will itself be so intense.

THE ANALYSIS OF SECULAR TENDENCIES

Finally, at a fourth level, radicals ask whether there may be secular tendencies in capitalist development which, tend, over the long run, to generate fundamental crises. Orthodox economists try to avoid such questions.

Since the days of Keynes and Alvin Hansen, American orthodoxy has forgotten its earlier questions about permanent stagnation tendencies. American military spending and Keynesian economic management permitted that "short-term memory loss."

Radicals have not forgotten about such questions. Within the Marxian tradition, there has long been a focus on problems of underconsumption and falling rates of profit. These analyses have argued that such tendencies exist and that capitalist economies require counteracting tendencies in order to forestall periodic collapse. Although the traditional literature has not resolved some of the important problems raised by those fundamental questions, it has nonetheless helped us ask those kinds of questions about the background of the current crisis. As we have been studying the roots of the current crisis, it seems more and more obvious that we must press ahead in our search for concrete answers.

Take the hypothesis of the tendency for the average rate of profit to fall. It suggests that, in a period of apparent prosperity, profits will tend to fall as a result of the tendency of capitalists to substitute capital for labor, increasing the "organic composition of capital." Unless capitalists are also able to increase their exploitation of labor, profits will tend to fall because the basis for the creation of profits—the extraction of surplus value from labor in production—will shrink in relation to the sum of capital—both constant and variable capital—upon which rates of profit are calculated.

An interesting hypotheses indeed. In the United States, profits have been falling secularly since World War II, measured either in terms of their share of national income or in terms of rate of return.[15] At least three counteracting tendencies have clearly helped forestall the potentially disastrous impact on investment of those continuing declines in profit. Accelerated depreciation allowances have lowered the cost of capital through tax adjustments. A declining effective corporate tax rate has also lowered the cost of capital to compensate for the fall in profits. And corporations have rapidly and continually expanded their debt, compensating for falling retained earnings by increasing aggregate corporate indebtedness.[16]

In looking at those counteracting tendencies, we can surely recognize the dangers they pose for the longer-term stability of the capitalist economy. The post–World War II economy, particularly during the sustained boom of the 1960s, has been built upon a "house of credit cards." A shaky pyramid of paper money cannot rise forever into the sky. Sooner or later, it becomes clear, a powerful gust of wind may come along and blow the entire structure down. If that happened, we might tend to blame the moneylenders and coupon clippers who were calling in their debts, forcing foreclosure and bankruptcy. But they would only be acting as agents in a system. The system itself, if the hypothesis is correct, would have generated the problem for which moneylenders were one of the few available solutions. If the falling rate of profit has required credit expansion through the post–World War II period, then we must surely focus on the sources of the falling rate of profit in understanding the causes of a credit collapse if and when it occurs.

Thinking at this level, looking at secular tendencies, it becomes even clearer than it was at the first three levels that capitalist economies tend to create the conditions for continual crises. If and when we escape from this crisis, and the rules of the capitalist system still obtain, we shall to be able to anticipate another crisis before long. Before it comes, why not escape from the threat of crises for good? Who needs them?

THE CENTRAL ISSUE

While this summary of different levels of differences may help clarify the substance of our disagreements with orthodox economists about the causes and implications of the current crisis, it may also be a little misleading.

This summary has tried to trace the reflection of basic differences in perspective onto the plane of methodological and substantive discus-

15. See William Nordhaus, "The Falling Share of Profits," *Brookings Papers on Economic Activity*, 1974, No. 1.
16. See Review of the Month, *Monthly Review* (February, 1975).

sion of the crisis. That form of discussion may lead some to suspect that differences between most orthodox and radical economists are merely questions of methodology, focus, and inference. Underlying those differences resides a much more fundamental conflict, however, and we must return over and over again to that basic disagreement.

Orthodox economists either accept or more positively support the capitalist system. The capitalist system requires the protection of private property and the maintenance of opportunities for capital accumulation by the owners of the means of production. As the crisis develops, we are faced more and more starkly with a simple choice. Policies which are premised on the protection of private profit force the working people of this country to pay the costs of economic crisis. Policies which are premised on the protection of the living standards and working conditions of working people will necessarily force a sharper and sharper attack on the privileges and wealth of large corporations. So far, the first premise has continued to dominate. Its persistent claim is serving to intensify the objective basis of class struggle in this country—a direct conflict between the interests of capital and the interests of all the rest of us.

The time for a clear choice draws nearer. Which do we choose—our own lives and livelihood or the life of the capitalist system? The differences in our concrete analyses of the causes and implications of the current economic crisis only serves, in the final instance, to demonstrate the clear and insistent urgency of that basic choice.

Does the U.S. Economy Require Imperialism?

24

S. M. Miller, Roy Bennett and Cyril Alapatt

The United States, it is charged, is imperialist, neoimperialist, neo-colonialist.

The well-being of the economy, it is contended, requires the economic exploitation of and the draining of superprofits from weaker countries. Vietnam was no "accident." It was a logical continuation of inevitable economic drives that will be followed by "many more Vietnams."

If these contentions are valid, if the internal inconsistencies or the inherent contradictions of the American economy inexorably drive it to solve its problems through the exploitation of weaker countries, it follows that it would be extraordinarily difficult, if not impossible, to change U.S. foreign policy without first changing its economic and social system.

But if factors other than a basic economic thrust for foreign trade, sources of raw materials, and superprofits are involved, if political or military considerations are also levers—possibly prime levers—then a change in overseas policies might be possible without the prior shattering or destruction of the system itself.

The charge that economic imperialism is a necessity seems to have surface validity. How else can one explain the ubiquitous economic and military presence of the United States?

Starting with the premise that simple economic imperialism does not adequately explain U.S. foreign policy and the military interventions consequent to that policy, we have undertaken to question whether this theory's fundamental assumption is, in fact, valid.

Since the conclusion that imperialism is economically imperative for the United States is reached from a variety of viewpoints, it is therefore important that we specify what phenomena we are investigating.

1. The Domestic Significance. We are here concerned *only* with the domestic significance of U.S. overseas activity. We do not attempt to analyze its impact on the countries affected, however distorted their economies may be by the pattern of U.S. economic policies. We seek only to discover how important overseas activities are to this country without considering the extent to which the American economy dominates that of other nations. An asymmetry might prevail: while U.S. overseas economic activities may not be of overriding importance to this country, they may still be deeply significant and distorting to the nations at the other end.

2. The Third World Boundary. Our concern is with the importance of U.S. economic activity with low-income, or Third World, countries. We are not appraising the importance of its role in Western Europe, Japan, and other high-income or high-industrial countries.

Why this distinction? Because direct military intervention by the United States for economic reasons in the high-income countries has become highly unlikely. (Indeed, with the economic "miracles" of the Common Market countries and Japan, the 1970s will face the United States with serious competition abroad in the field of foreign-investment flows originating from Germany and Japan, among others.) The danger of military intervention or U.S.-directed coups is to the low income countries. While we recognize that for other purposes it would be important to consider all U.S. overseas economic activity, with our objective of assessing the likelihood of direct military activity the primary question is: Do U.S. economic interests in low income countries compel military-interventionist action?

3. Separating Military and Economic Activities. We do not presume that every economic activity necessarily requires, or can draw upon, military support, or that military action necessarily leads to expanding the economic importance of a territory for the United States. We wish here to examine economic reasons for intervention separately from military reasons. Obviously the two often coincide and it is worth examining when and why they do, but we do not attempt that important job in this paper.

Doubtless, some will assert that if these three perspectives shape our analysis, there is little sense in reading further. But bear with us. It is important to review data from many perspectives if we wish to have action programs that can change policy rather than merely sloganize it.

Magdoff's Approach. The most detailed analysis of the imperatives of economic imperialism for the United States is that presented by Harry Magdoff in his study *The Age of Imperialism.* Magdoff aggregates his data on overseas economic activity to show the importance of all foreign economic activity to the U.S. economy; thus, he lumps together trade and investment with high-income nations and with Third World countries. We do the opposite; that is, we disaggregate the data on overseas economic activities in order to see how important economic activity with low-income countries is to the United States.

High-income and Low-income Countries

In examining data on overseas economic activities, we have divided nations into high-income and low-income categories. We have included in high-income countries Canada, Western Europe, South Africa, Australia and New Zealand, and Japan. Low-income nations include all of Latin America (although countries like Venezuela, Mexico, and Argentina are on the borderline of the United Nations definition of developed countries) and all of Asia and Africa, except Japan and South Africa. Eastern Europe and the Soviet Union, which are not significantly involved economically with the United States, are considered outside these two categories.

Exports

The most common argument used to prove that export trade is not of central consequence to the American economy is its small relative size. While not a conclusive argument, it is not unimportant.

In 1968 U.S. exports were $34.7 billion, while GNP was $860.6 billion. Exports, then, constituted about 4 percent of total product. So it has been for generations: foreign demand takes a small relative percentage of the total output of U.S. goods and services.

But, more important, two-thirds of these exports were to high-income rather than low-income nations:[1] that is, most of our trade is with rich competitors, not weak dependencies. Moreover, exports to low-income areas dropped, between 1955 and 1968, from 37.1 percent of all exports to 31.4 percent, and preliminary figures for 1969 and 1970 indicate that this tendency continues.

Some point out that overall percentages may disguise the importance of foreign exports for particular U.S. industries. No doubt they do. But it is our view that the rise or decline of a particular industry, firm, or groups of firms does not necessarily have special significance unless it can be shown that this industry or group controls, or strongly influences, U.S. foreign policy.

In 1958 only two industries exported more than 20 percent of their output: chemicals and fertilizers (20.5 percent), and construction, mining, and oil-field machinery (26.9 percent). These are not, in dollar volume, large industries; nor are they politically potent groups.

In most industries, exports furnished less than 10 percent of demand. When one takes into account that these figures are for all countries, *the actual market sales to low-income countries do not exceed 3 to 3.5 percent of the output of American industry.*

1. Calculated from *Statistical Abstract of the United States,* 1969, p. 808.

A more detailed breakdown demonstrates, surprisingly, that agricultural products constitute a very significant component of total exports. In 1970, farm exports are expected to total $6.5 billion, almost 20 percent of all overseas shipments.[2] This is a continuation of a peculiar structural change in the U.S. export pattern, away from sophisticated goods and toward agricultural and primary products, an export pattern characteristic of the less, rather than the more, developed nations.

Of the six major commodity groups, the one showing the highest percentage of exports to low-income countries is the agricultural group: 46.7 percent in 1968. High-income nations receive at least half the exports of all other types; and in the case of sophisticated products—motor vehicles, auto parts, civilian aircraft, and pulp-paper manufacturers—the high-income nations recieve 73.4 percent of these exports.[3]

It should also be noted that the existence of high or low levels of trade does not, in itself, demonstrate anything about imperialism. All nations of all social systems trade. The United States, although in absolute numbers a large trader, is in relation to its economy one of the smaller trading nations. It is outranked by Japan, England, Germany, Italy, France, and a number of other countries. The important issue is the use to which a nation puts its trade. Therefore, it is not enough to show that a nation trades; one must show that trade exploits weaker nations. Thus, while it can be shown that the terms of trade favor *all* developed nations, the question to be answered is whether these benefits are so vital to the continued existence of the high-income imperialist nations that they cannot, for economic reasons, change this relationship.

Investments

Many find the strongest argument for the existence of economic imperialism to be the size of overseas direct investments. *In 1968 the total amount of overseas investment was $64.8 billion, a small percentage of the trillion dollars of all investments.*[4]

In 1964 low-income nations were the home of only 31.4 percent of all U.S. overseas investment—while the high-income nations absorbed almost 70 percent.[5] Furthermore, this percentage has declined since 1960, when low-income countries had 36.44 percent of overseas investment. This much-noticed changing trend indicates that the richer nations are finding it more profitable to do business with one another than with poorer nations.

---

2. Address of Assistant Secretary of Agriculture C.D. Palmby to the Sugar Club of New York, *The New York Times,* June 5, 1970.

3. Calculated from data in *Statistical Abstract of the United States,* 1969, p. 805.

4. *Survey of Current Business,* October 1969, p. 28.

5. $13.6 billion out of $44.3 billion total. This is $13 billion less than 2 percent of all U.S. invested capital at home and abroad. U.S. Department of Commerce. *Statistical Abstract,* 1967.

In a comparison of the values of direct investments abroad in 1968 by selected countries and industries, one striking fact stands out.[6] In that year more than $2 out of every $5 (42.2 percent) of U.S. investments in low-income nations were in petroleum. *If this figure were excluded, investment in all the poorer nations would be only 16.7 percent of U.S. total investments abroad. Yet, with this very high concentration of oil investments in low-income countries, absolute dollar investments are still greater in high-income than in low-income nations.*

Although the Latin American republics do contain considerable nonpetroleum investments (particularly Brazil, Mexico, and Argentina), these investments appear less massive when broken down by countries than when viewed in the aggregate for the region as a whole.

But are they at a level that requires the United States, for sheer economic reasons, to intervene to protect its investors from the threat of loss? Recent experiences with investments in Peru and Bolivia, and in Zambia and Libya in Africa, suggest that the State Department and the White House are less than eager at this point to intervene militarily to prevent nationalization of U.S. privately owned properties. No Latin American country—with the exception of Venezuela (oil)—had in 1968 a very high percentage of U.S. investments in any particular field. Even the Venezuelan investment is less than 10 percent of all U.S. overseas holdings in petroleum—a figure that surprised us.

For the Third World the general conclusion is that, with the exception of some Latin American countries, nonpetroleum investments are not high enough in any one country to warrant great economic concern by the United States. (The development of joint ventures, in which the poor country retains title to the enterprise, shares in its output, and at an agreed time assumes complete control, is a new factor and promises to affect the future investment picture importantly.)

The Effect on Individual Corporations

At this point it might be useful to point out again that we do not contend investments are not high for an individual U.S. company. When Chile nationalized Anaconda's copper mines in 1968 (and promised $500 million indemnification, which few expect will ultimately be paid), it cost Anaconda a large proportion of its earnings; its stock dropped over 60 percent in value. But that did not make it a national problem. It will help solve a national problem for Chile—which is good —but it is not of big enough proportion to affect negatively an economy the size of the United States. When Cuba, in 1960 to 1961, unceremoniously liberated a billion dollars in U.S. fixed assets, not a ripple appeared in the U.S. economy.

---

6. *Survey of Current Business*, op. cit.

A counterargument could be a version of the domino theory: investment in one nation may be low, but if it is lost in one, then other nations within the region may do likewise; therefore, an instructive lesson in deterrence is necessary. This is as much a political issue as a narrow economic one. We shall consider political issues in our concluding section, but we should point out here that the United States is already the victim of the domino effect. In financial circles there is considerable talk about the nationalization of the International Petroleum Corporation in Peru, Anaconda Copper in Chile, Occidental Petroleum in Libya, Roan Selection in Zambia; but there is no panic, except among speculators in those particular securities.

Income from Investments

Magdoff points out that two other types of analysis strengthen the case for the importance of overseas activity to the domestic economy. One is the level of income from overseas investment; the other is the importance of imports.

The total of overseas investment income in 1968 was *just under $5 billion,*[7] compared with *approximately $90 billion* from domestic operations of companies. But this figure is for all countries. Income from low-income nations totaled $2.9 billion, *about 3 or 4 percent of the total income of companies in the United States.* In relation to 1968s GNP of $850 billion, "imperialist earnings" in the same year from the underdeveloped countries amounted to *a little more than .033 percent.*[8] In addition, this represents a steady decline in the importance of investment income from low-income countries. In 1950 they furnished 65.1 percent of the income from all overseas investment;[9] in 1964, 60.4 percent;[10] in 1968, 59.5 percent.[11] But the most striking fact is that *71 percent of the investment income from low-income nations derives from petroleum!*[12] *If we exclude petroleum, only a little over 14 percent of overseas investments income, or less than $500 million total, comes from low-income areas.*

These recomputations weaken the impact of Magdoff's startling statement: "By 1964, foreign sources of earnings accounted for about 22

---

7. Ibid.

8. We know that official figures might be underestimates. But there is no way of adjusting for this. The point, however, is that even if one were to increase the return by doubling the figures, the relative importance of income or earnings remain small. The corporation profit figure (profit from all sources) does not include approximately $20 billion in interest income, $20 billion in rental income, and approximately $60 billion income of nonincorporated business.

9. U.S. Department of Commerce, *Balance of Payments Statistical Supplement, 1950–1960,* rev. ed., 1963, pp. 186–87.

10. Ibid.

11. *Survey of Current Business,* op. cit.

12. Ibid.

percent of domestic nonfinancial corporate profits." We have not succeeded in breaking down this figure on earnings, but our previous
analysis strongly suggests that rich countries make the substantial contribution to this outcome and that petroleum is the overwhelming
source of profit from low-income countries.

Imports

A very strong argument can be made for the importance of overseas
raw materials in American industrial production. Indeed, in "Scarce
Resources: The Dynamics of American Imperialism," a Radical Education Project pamphlet, Heather Dean dismisses the arguments we have
been analyzing and stresses the raw materials question exclusively:

> While not denying the existence of other economic motivations which are
> stressed by the Marxist left, I would argue that they are secondary to the
> total dependency of American production on foreign resources, that this
> dependency is sufficient in itself to explain U.S. policy, and that it leads to
> a fundamental conflict between the survival of the American economy in its
> present form and the drive for development in the Third World.

Magdoff, too, emphasizes the role of raw materials in U.S. overseas
activities, but he does not consider it the dominant factor.

In both accounts, one is struck by the extent to which U.S. industries
require basic materials, especially metals, from abroad and by the fact
that projections of potential need increase U.S. dependence upon materials produced or extracted in other nations. Of course this argument
cuts both ways. The low-income countries are vulnerable because they
are low-income. But the high-income countries are also vulnerable because they are big consumers of raw materials. This suggests that low-
income countries have some leverage against the imperialists. In recent
years this has become evident in the Zambian copper nationalization,
in much higher percentages for the low-income countries in petroleum
deals, and in the nationalization of U.S. oil and copper properties in
Bolivia, Chile, and Peru.

We have not gone into this question in depth, but we believe we first
have to learn which U.S. industries depend upon raw materials from
which other nations. Of course, "depend" is an unspecific term; an item
which is but 1 percent of the elements of a production process may be
more significant than one which provides 20 percent of the process if
it is difficult or very expensive to substitute another element for it.

This issue is basic to the question of "dependency," for it may be
possible to shift the process of production to accommodate changes in
the availability or costs of particular materials. Thus, the issue is not
only the current significance of materials, but the difficulty or ease of
substituting other materials for them. (Some obvious examples of sub-
stitutions are: synthetic rubber for natural, ceramics for high-tempera-
ture steel, aluminum for tin, and plastics for almost anything, including
copper, especially in corrosive petroleum chemistry.) Nor should it be

assumed that a particular product is used because it is the only one available. Cost factors are important in making choices. The unavailability of a particular commodity may not be a great problem; another may do as well, although at a higher price. And since raw materials are usually a small part of total costs, the resulting price rise may not be great. Even if it were, it need not be the main issue. U.S. publicly owned domestic shale oil reserves in the Rocky Mountain states are huge, amounting to 1.8 trillion barrels, 40 times other domestic reserves; and in the unlikely hypothesis that Latin American oil were not available, investment would be made in research and development to bring down the price.

Finally, on the question of oil dependency, Middle East petroleum, which is by far the largest income earner, is the one product on which the United States is *not* dependent. Middle East oil goes to Europe. The American source is domestic and Latin American. In the future it probably will be Alaskan and Rocky Mountain shale.

The question of substitution is also affected by possible shifts in the end products of American industry which, in turn, determine what materials are needed. The main change, of course, could be a reduction in military production. Magdoff cites a 1958 U.S. Department of Defense list of strategic materials indicating the high importance of imports for military production. If public pressure is effective in reducing military expenditures and in changing military technology, many of these materials would become less significant. The need for nickel, tungsten, titanium, tantalum, and other exotic metals for super-high-temperature military products would diminish markedly. Thus the demand for these and other materials is not unchanging.

It is, of course, wrong to approach the question of substitution as if one were suggesting the United States could or would adopt a policy of self-sufficiency. The substitution question is more serious for the low-income countries than it is crucial for the raw materials needs of the imperialist countries, as the matter is often placed. The issue is to find a way for the developing nations to exploit their own resources, deriving much greater revenue thereby, while recognizing that the market for this large raw materials output, for some time to come, will be in the developed—i.e., imperialist—nations. One does not expect Anaconda or the petroleum companies to cooperate in any such endeavor. But that does not mean it cannot be done without them. However, this is a political, not an economic, question and requires a separate study.

IMPLICATIONS

Let us recapitulate. Out of a total of direct investments abroad of $64.7 billion in 1968, 70 percent was invested in high-income countries —the Common Market, England, Canada, Australia, and to a small extent Japan. Only 30 percent, $18.6 billion, was invested in *all* the low-income countries. Out of the $18.6 billion invested, repatriated income was $2.9 billion.

What we question is that an economy approaching a trillion-dollar gross national product can, from any point of view, regard this $2.9 billion annually as critical to its existence. (Of the $2.9 billion in returned profit and interest, $2.1 billion is from petroleum investments, mainly in the Middle East.)

If one were to believe that this less than $3 billion income is vital to the existence of imperialism, one would have to accept that it is a mighty extraordinary tail to be able to wag a trillion-dollar dog.

We have been making a case against the imperialism argument, but a special kind of case. Our interest is focused on one question: How important is U.S. economic activity in low-income nations for the general level of economic production and growth in this country? We emphasize "general" for obviously particular firms or industries depend heavily on their activities in low-income countries, but the economy as a whole may not benefit to a marked extent from these activities. *Our conclusion*—subject to closer study of the import question—*is that the economy as a whole does* not *have a heavy dependence upon activites in low-income nations.*

This conclusion is similar to that of John Strachey in *The End of Empire,* and of Michael Barratt-Brown in *After Imperialism,* on British imperialism in the nineteenth century. Barratt-Brown argues that imperialism *retarded* the economic growth of Britain over the long run, and that trade and investment in Europe and America and the developed parts of the Commonwealth (Australia, Canada, New Zealand, South Africa) were more significant than were trade and investment with the colonialized part of the Empire. Strachey stresses that the costs of maintaining the Empire far overshadowed the economic gains from it. These arguments seem to have considerable validity in application to the United States. Foreign aid has been a cost to secure foreign trade. And the huge military costs so far outweigh the economic benefits of exploitation of weaker nations that one is compelled to consider whether political miscalculations rather than economic greed are not at the root of policy.

Much earlier this same perspective was debated at the Stuttgart Congress (1907) of the Second International. Both at the Congress and later, [Karl Kautsky attacked] Rosa Luxemburg's contention that imperialism was a "historical necessity" of capitalism. Kautsky argued, in the words of one of Luxemburg's recent interpreters, "that imperialism was not a necessary outgrowth of capitalism, but an abscess which the capitalists class as a whole would more and more wish to get rid of."[13]

---

13. Tony Cliff, *Rosa Luxemburg,* (London, 1969), p. 34.

Kautsky's theory was that imperialism was a method of expansion supported by certain powerful capitalist groups (the banks and the armament kings), contrary to the needs of the capitalist class as a whole; that expenditure on armaments reduced available capital for investment in the domestic economy. He argued further that the majority of the capitalist class would progressively increase its opposition to armed imperialist expansion. (We suggest the current attitude of Wall Street and big business to the Vietnam war is worthy of note, especially when Charles B. McCoy, president of DuPont, attacks the war for taking "a terrible toll in human life" and raises questions about the preservations of democratic values.[14] Or when Thomas B. Watson, Jr., of IBM tells a Congressional committee that the war presents "a major obstacle" to economic health and threatens "irreparable damage to society."[15] Or when Henry Ford II uses the forum of a stockholders' meeting to attack the Administration war policy as harmful to American business.

The Kautsky position, as thus described, comes close to ours, in contrast to the neoimperialist position, which continues to stress Lenin's 1917 analysis of imperialism. It is our belief that it is *economically* possible to curtail military production and U.S. interventionism. To do so presents a political problem, but it is not economically foreclosed.

Put another way, it has been the inability of critics up to this point to develop sufficient political support—rather than the heavy weight of economic necessity—which has kept U.S. policy moving in one direction rather than another.

Barratt-Brown has stated the problem forcefully:

> While there may be good original economic grounds for policies pursued, the whole structure of institutions, ideas, and purposes built up from these grounds takes on a life of its own and becomes its own justification. Those who claim to be Marxists need to be at least as Marxist as Marx in this matter and should not cite Marx's authority for the crudest type of economic determinism.[16]

For example, despite the importance of the oil companies and their overseas investments, they have not had unequivocal influence on U.S. policy in the Middle East since the formation of Israel. A strong case can be made that sheer economic interests and the political might of the oil companies should have led to Washington's support of the Arab nations rather than limited but unmistakable American support of Israel. Domestic political—not economic—considerations and the cold war led to the pro-Israel outlook of U.S. foreign policy.

We do not argue that economic interests are unimportant, or that they do not at times influence or determine U.S. policies. Obviously

---

14. *The New York Times,* June 4, 1970.

15. Ibid.

16. Michael Barratt-Brown, *After Imperialism,* (London, 1963), p. 204.

they do. Our argument is different: we are unconvinced that the U.S. economy so depends on overseas activities that it must protect them, even by military actions.

How then explain U.S. interventionism—in Cuba, in Vietnam? We think that today's interventionism springs much more from political-military than from economic roots. The cold war climate led to the imposition of "vital" military-political centers around the world, as in Southeast Asia, and to the defense or strengthening of those centers. A mindless anticommunism has considered any step toward radical change or revolution a pro-Russian, pro-Chinese, anti-American threat —a challenge to the American system—that must be confronted.

With the waning of the cold war, the prospective lowering of the "American profile" abroad, this counterrevolutionary reflex may also wane. Vietnam need not be followed by "other Vietnams." *If it is, the failure is political, not the result of inexorable economic necessity.*

The one clearcut case where "economic necessity" appears vital is the oil industry. This is one mighty industry dependent on overseas profits, especially from low-income nations. Greater sensitivity to the behavior of this industry, particularly abroad, is urgent. As the recent Peruvian, Bolivian, and Libyan examples show, there is already unwillingness, even in a Nixon Administration, to intervene militarily on behalf of oil companies. Close watch on the oil industry is essential, so that its imperatives do not become "economic necessity" and then political-military necessity for the nation. The oil industry should be totally nationalized, or turned into a public utility and regulated in the public interest. If progressive groups properly raised this issue, they would expose the very small political constituency of the oil barons.

The oil industry is politically vulnerable; they know it, and Congress knows it.

By the same logic, the armaments industry should also be nationalized. The public pays for it. Why shouldn't they own it?

Underlying our perspective is the contention that the U.S. economy could adapt to lower military budgets and a nonexpansionist policy abroad. Whether it does so or not largely depends, first, on the political strength to adopt policies that would expand the economy in other ways. If military outlays were cut, we do not doubt that policies could (not necessarily would) be followed which would produce growth rates of a relatively high level. We are less optimistic about policies to reduce inequality or improve the quality of life at home. For we do not see the problem of the U.S. economy as one of imminent crisis or collapse, but more in terms of whether or not it meets qualitative goals we think should be its target.

In general, we believe the economy has more flexibility than many left critics suggest. This does not mean that we are unmindful of the profound structural bias that operates against social change. However, this is not the place, nor is it our intention, to deal with the political strategy and tactics of turning the social system around.

We are aware that to assert that a billion dollars here or a billion dollars there is not significant sounds like playing with stage money. Any such sum is significant to those involved. Therefore, we are not arguing that economic activity between the United States and low-income nations is insignificant. Rather, our point is that this activity alone is not so dominating within our economy that political groups could not develop and offset the demands made by narrow, economically motivated interest groups. We do not think that the economy would collapse if particular economic interest groups were unable to control overseas U.S. political-military activities in certain areas.

A further note about high-income and low-income nations is in order. Our stress upon the relatively low significance of economic relations between low-income nations and the United States is not intended to downgrade foreign activities in the U.S. economy. The spectacular growth in U.S. foreign relationships is, however, with high-income nations. The most significant international economic institution—the multinational corporation—chiefly involves these countries. This development is likely to affect the American economy in many important ways. And one of its unfortunate effects may be, not further economic involvement with poor countries—which has helped as well as harmed them—but greater neglect of them. Rather than growing in importance for the rich nations, the poor countries are likely not only to fall further behind the rich but to become of even less concern to them. The rich will need one another more than they need the poor. Interventionism may be supplanted by unbenign neglect.

Fundamental Changes

Finally, we believe a nineteenth-century approach to imperialism, or even the twentieth-century variant of neoimperialism, misses the truly fundamental changes that are going on in the contemporary capitalist states. Galbraith tried to deal with the new phenomena in domestic terms in his *The New Industrial State,* but the task remains for analysts to deal with the virgin territory of foreign economic relations and their meaning.

Surely there is something new in the fact that 25 years have passed since World War II and no major economic crisis has occurred in the United States. Something is new when some Western capitalist nations are growing faster than the socialist growth states of China and the Soviet Union; something is new when contradictions and struggles among the rich nations for markets and sources of raw materials have diminished rather than sharpened.

All this is not to suggest that the developed capitalist Western nations have resolved their contradictions. It is to contend that papering over Lenin's *Imperialism* with neoimperialism does not begin to get at the new trends and developments taking place in the substructure of the world's economy.

A discontinuity, an abrupt change, has occurred in the functioning of the big industrial states since World War II. A simple linear projection of the past is not enough to explain the new phenomena. The degree of revolutionization of technology—its social, political, and economic implications—requires a comparable revolution in thinking.

Along with Barratt-Brown we do not hold that imperialism has never been a paying proposition. As in Great Britain, there were periods when it paid, and very well indeed. But periods change. What we are suggesting is that classical nineteenth-century economic imperialism has become a costly luxury that is far more politically than economically oriented, and that this is especially true for the United States.

The qualitative character of the change is dramatically illustrated in the following: In the nineteenth century a brigade of British soldiers easily and inexpensively held an entire Indian province; and a handful of gunboats dominated the whole of Mainland China. Today over a half-million U.S. troops and $100 billion cannot hold a half-sliver of a tiny nation in Southeast Asia, an area where the United States has no foreign investment at all.

A deeper study may suggest that U.S. imperialism since the 1890s was a product of a misperceived economic analysis, a belief that the domestic market problem could be solved only by expansion abroad.

The tempestuous growth of Japan and Germany in the postwar period without foreign investments or colonies suggests that solutions —other than the colonial, semicolonial, and neocolonial answer—are available for markets and raw materials. No one suggests that either West Germany or Japan has become less capitalist. But they may have become less imperialist, when imperialism is defined in the old terms.

It is worth examining whether some "unsolvable" internal market problems have not become susceptible to mitigation by different varieties of capitalist planning, as practiced in Western Europe or Japan. Japan's growth in living standards and GNP is rivaled only by the growth of her government-business-financial cohesion, to a degree unknown in the West. Indeed, there is some question whether there is as much directed, central planning in Peking or Belgrade as there is in Tokyo.

This question raises issues far beyond the scope of this small paper. But we hope the narrow slice we have chosen to point up will encourage others to delve more deeply than we have into what is manifestly a new and developing phenomenon.

The Logic of Imperialism

25

Harry Magdoff

How a question is formulated usually defines the limits of its answer. Hence, a most important aspect of scientific inquiry is discovering the right questions to ask. In this context, the very formulation of the question about imperialism by S. M. Miller, Roy Bennett and Cyril Alapatt takes us off the path of understanding modern imperialism.

Their article is directed to the question "Does the U.S. Economy Require Imperialism?" Imperialism, however, is so intertwined with the history and resulting structure of modern capitalist society—with its economics, politics, and ruling ideas—that this kind of question is in the same category as, for example, "Is it necessary for the United States to keep Texas and New Mexico?" We could, after all, return these territories to the Mexican people and still maintain a high-production and high-standard-of-living economy. We could import the oil, mineral ores, and cattle from these territories and sell U.S. goods in exchange. Any temporary decline in our Gross National Product would surely be a small price to pay for social justice. And given our growth rate and supposed ability to regulate our economy, continued economic growth should soon make up any losses resulting from the return of stolen lands.

Or one might ask, "Is Manhattan necessary for the United States?" It would surely be equitable to return land obtained from the Indians in a sharp deal. Such a transfer might at first have some small downward economic effect, but eventually should make for more prosperity. Manufacturing on the island is an insignificant percentage of total U.S. output. The profitable port activity could be shifted to New Jersey or other excellent Atlantic ports. Economic institutions—stock and commodity exchanges, investment and commercial banks, headquarters of large corporations—could be transferred lock, stock, and barrel to the interior. Such a move to wipe out a terrible blot on the conscience of white America could be socially useful. Moreover, a new financial headquarters of the United States (and the capitalist world) could be designed to avoid slum, smog, pollution, and traffic crises; the demand for buildings, housing, and transportation and communication equipment in the new "Manhattan" might spur the economy to new heights.

Such questions might be useful in the classroom to help stimulate students' imagination and to illustrate the contradictions of a capitalist economy. But they will not contribute to an understanding of the role of territorial expansion in the evolution and functioning of the economy, or the unique role of a financial center in the operations of a capitalist economy.

Our Critics[1] no doubt justify their question on the grounds that some popularizers on the Left formulate the issue purely in terms of "economic necessity"—as if every political and military action were in response to an immediate economic cause or to a telephone call from a corporation executive. Such a mechanical cause-effect approach is an obvious oversimplification, an inadequate guide to history, and more rhetoric than analysis. But when one merely meets an exaggerated rhetoric headon and makes the rhetoric the focus for debate, one departs from the tasks of scientific inquiry: one may thus be at a ball park, but not where the game is being played. The major task, in my opinion, for the study of imperialism is to discover and understand what Bernard Baruch described as "the essential oneness of [U.S.] economic, political, and strategic interests."[2] In such a study, we have to seek the main roots —the mainsprings—of this "oneness" as well as to understand the interactions and interdependence of the economic, political, and military drives.

It takes no deep perception to recognize the limits of the "necessity" formula. Thus, a substantial part of the world, notably the Soviet Union and China, has chosen the path of economic independence and therefore broken the trade and investment ties with the imperialist network. The advanced capitalist countries adjusted to these changes and have in recent decades achieved considerable prosperity and industrial advance. However, important as it is to recognize that such adjustments can take place, it is equally important to understand the route that these adjustments take: via wars, depression, and huge armaments programs. The economic adaptations emerged in the midst of recurrent struggles for control over spheres of influence—over other advanced countries as well as over Third World areas, it should be noted. And, most important, these adjustments have in no way lessened the intensity of the counterrevolutionary thrust of imperialist states, by wars and other

---

1. To avoid the awkwardness of listing the three authors at each reference, and to somewhat depersonalize the controversy, we will refer to them as the "Critics." We trust they will not take offense. "Critic," to our way of thinking, is an honorable designation.
2. Foreword by Bernard Baruch to Samuel Lubell, *The Revolution in World Trade and American Economic Policy,* (New York, 1955), p. xi.

means, directed to (*a*) prevent a further narrowing down of the territory in which they can freely trade and invest, and (*b*) reconquer the space lost to the imperialist world. Nor has this counterrevolutionary activity, which began during the first days of the Bolshevik revolution, diminished since the United States took the reins as leader and organizer of the capitalist world.

The relevant question is not whether imperialism is necessary for the United States, but to discover the "rationality" of the historic process itself: why the United States and other leading capitalist nations have persistently and recurrently acted in the imperialist fashion for at least three-quarters of a century.

The contrast between speculative hypotheses about the "necessity" of imperialism and the actual course of history is excellently demonstrated by the Critics themselves when they illustrate their interpretation of imperialism by referring to, and endorsing, the theoretical position of Karl Kautsky in his debate with Rosa Luxemburg. Kautsky argued, they point out, that imperialist expansion was sustained by only a small and powerful group of capitalists and that such expansion conflicted with the interests of the capitalist class as a whole. Because of this, Kautsky believed that the majority of the capitalist class would increase its opposition to, and eventually prevent, armed imperialist expansion.

It is strange indeed, in this day and age, to come across a revival of Kautsky's theory—a theory that has been devastatingly refuted by events. Our Critics refer to Kautsky's exposition at the 1907 Stuttgart Conference. But only seven years later the First World War broke out, to be followed at the earliest practical opportunity by the Second World War. It doesn't take much insight to recognize the role that Germany's expansionist aims played in both wars: Kautsky's optimism turned out to be mere illusion.

The Critics remind us of the current dissatisfaction of some U.S. businessmen with the Vietnam war. That there are shrewd businessmen who recognize that at times one must cut one's losses should hardly come as a surprise. The surprise is that it has taken them so long to awaken to the reality of a lost war and its social and economic consequences. However, the acid test of Kautsky's and the Critics' position would be: how many of these businessmen would agree to (1) an immediate pullout of U.S. forces from Vietnam, leaving the fate of Vietnam to the Vietnamese people, and (2) a complete withdrawal of all U.S. military forces and equipment from all of Asia?

The major weakness of Kautsky's theory was precisely the concentration on "necessity." By using this sterile framework, he distinguished between capitalists who "need" and those who "don't need" expansion. He thus ignored what was most important in explaining the course of militarism and imperialism: the industrial and financial structure of the economy, the strategic elements of change, and the special nature of the political system associated with successful monopoly capitalism. (It should go without saying that a full explanation of, say, German imperialism would have to take into account the special socioeconomic features and history of Germany.)

On their part, the Critics in effect adopt for their own economic analysis the same limited and crude economic interpretation of imperialism that they are criticizing. Accordingly, they look at only some of the relevant economic elements; those that they examine are treated as isolates, not as part of a social and economic organism; and then they whittle down even these isolates. This shrinking process takes on the following forms: (1) they eliminate from the realm of imperialism U.S. economic activity *in other advanced capitalist nations;* (2) they restrict the field of economic penetration in underdeveloped countries to *exports and direct private investment;* (3) *concerning foreign mineral resources,* they deal only with the so-called *national interest,* ignoring the drive for control over such resources by monopolistic interest groups.

IMPERIALISM AND THE RELATIONS BETWEEN DEVELOPED COUNTRIES

A large part of the Critics' article is devoted to statistical computations based on the assumption (and argument) that U.S. trade with, and investment in, other advanced capitalist nations has nothing to do with imperialism. Imperialism, they claim, involves only the relations between advanced and underdeveloped countries. This assumption misses an essential distinguishing feature of modern imperialism. The occupation and/or manipulation of a weaker by a stronger nation, and the building of empires by powerful military states, occur many times in human history, in ancient, medieval, and modern times. Moreover, the birth and adolescence of capitalism are marked by military penetration of noncapitalist areas to bring the latter into the trade and investment sphere of the dominant capitalists.

Because empire-building has been prevalent over long stretches of history, the use of the term "imperialism" to cover all such activities leads to definitions that stress the superficial and avoid the essential. The value of distinguishing different periods of history to which convenient labels are attached is to provide a useful analytical framework for discovering and understanding the main operating levers of the particular stage under study. For that reason, it seems to us, the term "imperialism" is best used to designate the international practices and relations of the capitalist world during the distinct stage of mature capitalism that emerged in the last quarter of the nineteenth century.

But even if one disagrees with this terminological approach, it still has to be recognized that the international economics and politics of the past seventy to ninety years have certain unique features. Hence, some historians follow the practice of calling the new stage "modern" or "new" imperialism, to distinguish it from that of mere empire-building. This should become clearer if we spell out some of the major phenomena of the new or modern imperialism:

1. As noted earlier, capitalism from its earliest days sank its roots in the noncapitalist world. It prospered by adapting (through force and economic pressure) the rest of the world to fit the needs of the more advanced capitalist nations. However, it is in the stage of modern imperialism that its "historic task" is fulfilled: the entire globe is fitted into the world capitalist system (until, in more recent years, parts of this system break away). Prices of commodities produced around the world become dominated by one world price established in the major financial centers. In this period of modern imperialism, there is a sharp stepup in the migration of commodities, men, and capital—in response primarily to the pressures of the most advanced centers of capitalism, including the pressures of competition among the advanced capitalist countries themselves.

2. The resulting world capitalist system of modern imperialism comprehends an intricate and interdependent set of relations between countries at various stages of industrial development. The outstanding aspect of this world system is the entrenchment of the so-called Third World countries as industrial and financial dependencies of key metropolitan centers—a dependency that is continuously reproduced by the normal behavior of the capitalist markets. In addition, among the more advanced capitalist nations, there are a variety of dependent relations of weaker nations on stronger ones.

3. The technical underpinning of the modern international world economy is the growth of what Veblen called the "technology of physics and chemistry": steel, electricity, oil refining, synthetic organic chemicals, internal combustion engines, etc. The technology of modern imperialism became the material base of decisive concentration of economic power in large industrial corporations and large financial institutions. The maturation of this economic concentration of power (called, for convenience, "monopoly capital") affected the economic and political structure of advanced capitalist nations. On the economic side, in contrast with the earlier stage of competitive capitalism, economic change and economic policy are primarily determined by the imperatives of monopolistic-type industries (oligopolies, to be technical). The latter, to protect their assets and maintain their leading positions, are impelled to seek control over supplies of raw materials and over markets —wherever these raw materials and markets may exist. Furthermore, the evolution of an economic structure based on monopolistic firms limits the alternatives of the political regimes of these countries. Gov-

ernments, whether liberal or conservative, can operate with a successful economy only if they assist, and help make more efficient, the major determinants of the economy: the monopolistic firms and the international financial arrangements with which these firms operate.

4. Finally, a distinctive feature of the new imperialism is the rise of intensive competitive struggle among advanced capitalist nations. It is this competitive struggle which helps determine the new world economic arrangements and is a major source of continual turbulence in the world capitalist system. Before the era of modern imperialism, Great Britain was the undisputed dominant nation in foreign trade, investment, and finance. The rise of industrialized nations, based on an advanced technology that enabled economic and military competition, led to the hectic struggle for conquest of those parts of the globe not yet incorporated into the international capitalist arrangements. It also led to struggles for redivision of colonies and spheres of influence. But, it should be noted most especially, the competitive struggle is not restricted to dominance over the underdeveloped world. It also entails struggle for dominance and/or special influence over other advanced capitalist nations, as was seen in two world wars. Present also as a major element in the power struggle between nations and between monopolistic firms of these nations is the use of investment in one another's territories and/or cartel arrangements for the division of markets.

Thus, if one sees modern imperialism in historical perspective, it should be clear that there are two attributes of the power struggles of this period: (1) the struggle for economic power vis-à-vis other industrial nations, and (2) the struggle for economic power over the underdeveloped nations. Furthermore, to understand the imperialist drives since the Second World War and the strategic alternatives confronting the decisionmakers of U.S. foreign policy, one must take into account the past and potential rivalries of the industrialized nations. Not the least aspect of the latter is the maneuvering of U.S. political policy and of U.S. firms to take over trade and investment channels of its former allies (as well as enemies) in the underdeveloped world.

Narrowing imperialism to trade with, and investment in, the Third World thus eliminates a vital sector of international economic and political activity: the imperialist rivalries associated with the investment operations of advanced capitalist nations across one another's borders. In addition, the Critics do not face up to the reality of world economic interdependence and the significance of U.S. international financial and military preeminence. The latter might be better appreciated if we consider the balance of payments situation.

The United States has had a deficit in its balance of payments for all but one or two of the past twenty years, and that deficit shows no signs of disappearing. This is unique in capitalist history. Any other country

—and the United States itself prior to its post–Second World War dominance—would have had to submit to the discipline of the international marketplace long, long before the twenty years were up. What does this discipline of the marketplace consist of? Adoption by the U.S. government of such measures as would produce deflation: a sharp rise in unemployment and downward economic adjustment. Instead, the United States has been able to maintain its kind of prosperity through the 1950s and 1960s without undertaking effective measures to eliminate the international payments deficit. Quite the opposite: its prosperity was sustained by the kind of activities made possible by the persistent deficit.

Why the deficit? As a rule, U.S. exports of goods and services (on current account) exceed imports. The deficit arises because the U.S. government and investors spend in international markets over and above their "means." The government spends huge sums for its military establishment around the globe, for its wars, and for military and economic assistance to other countries. Corporations spend on investment in foreign business undertakings—in advanced as well as underdeveloped countries. All of these activities, independent of the motives that induce them, contribute to the prosperity of the economy as it is constituted.

The nub of this whole development is that it is made possible by the fact that the other capitalist nations have, willingly and unwillingly, accepted the U.S. dollar as if it were as good as gold.

One need not follow too carefully the financial news to be aware that the other industrialized nations are not too pleased with the necessity of accepting the U.S. dollar as a substitute for gold; indeed, considerable friction has resulted, and still exists. Yet they do accept it, for several reasons. First, they fear that if they rock the boat too much, all the central bankers will sink in a sea of financial difficulties. Second, they are impressed with U.S. economic strength, though this confidence is being increasingly shaken. Finally, and not the least of the considerations, is U.S. military might and its global presence. In fact, the United States has undertaken the major responsibility for maintaining the world imperialist system. It first supplied the armaments, armies, and Marshall Plan aid to prevent social revolution in Western Europe. It has furnished naval and air bases around the world, sufficient not only to encircle the Soviet Union and China but to act as a threat of military intervention and for actual intervention in the Third World.

Thus the United States provides the main military might for the "security" of the Western world, including Japan. The quid pro quo has been the reluctant acceptance of the U.S. dollar as a reserve currency, despite the inability of the United States to provide adequate gold coverage for its dollar debts. And one of the results of this quid pro quo is that U.S. business can keep on investing in Western Europe, buying up European firms, paid for, in effect, by credit extended by other advanced capitalist nations to the United States.

Suppose, however, one does not accept this analysis of the interrelationship between U.S. investment in advanced capitalist nations (1) with the actual and incipient tensions between imperialist nations, and (2) with the maintenance of control and "stability" in the Third World. Would the Critics then be correct in isolating U.S. investments in advanced countries as a thing apart from economic and political concern with the Third World? In our judgment, they would still be mistaken in such a narrowing down of imperialism. The reason is simple: when firms invest in advanced countries they become directly involved in the ties between those countries and their part of the Third World. The more extensive U.S. investments in Europe and Japan become, the more extensive are their interests bound up with the spheres of influence and neocolonial arrangements of *the entire Third World*.

The simplest and most direct illustration is the oil industry. Some 24 percent of U.S. direct private investment in Europe is in oil: for oil refining, production of byproducts, and the marketing of these products to Europeans and their foreign customers. But where do they get the oil to refine? From the Middle East, of course. Note especially that the rapid rise in U.S. oil investments in Europe was accompanied by a decisive change in U.S. ownership of nearby oil deposits: before the Second World War, U.S. firms controlled some 10 percent of Middle East oil reserves; by 1967, this percentage rose to 59. The success and prosperity of U.S. investment in the European oil industry depend on access to the oil they extract from Third World countries. Conversely, they increase their profits on Middle Eastern oil by investing in oil refining and distribution in nearby Europe.

[Less dramatic], yet equally relevant, is the growing interest in the Third World entailed by other investments in the advanced nations. Thus, half of all U.S. direct investments in Europe and Japan are in manufacturing other than petroleum refining. Where do these firms get the raw materials to process? A significant portion must come from the Third World.

On top of this is the growing involvement of U.S. firms in the markets of the other advanced nations in the Third World. Through treaties and currency arrangements, manufacturers in the advanced countries have special preferences in some of these markets. Some of these preferred market outlets exist because of custom and distribution channels established in colonial days. U.S. firms thus extend their markets, getting a foothold in the preserves of other advanced countries, by investing in and thus becoming business "citizens" of the mother countries.

We have by no means exhausted the number of ways U.S. investment in advanced nations extends U.S. involvement in the economic affairs of the Third World. Let us look at just one other way. Quite recently, three U.S. banks made investments in England (a developed country, to be sure): Mellon National Bank and Trust Co. acquired a 25 percent stake in the Bank of London and South America Ltd. (BOLSA); New York's First National City Bank obtained a 40 percent share of National & Grindlay's Bank Ltd.; and Chase Manhattan Bank acquired a 15 percent interest in Standard Bank Ltd. Note, however, that while all three of these U.S. bank affiliates are based in London, "their main operations are in broad chunks of the underdeveloped world. National & Grindlay's operates in India, Pakistan, and the Middle East, Standard is in Africa, and BOLSA concentrates on Latin America." (The data and the quotation are from the *American Banker,* January 28, 1970.)

INVESTMENT IN UNDERDEVELOPED COUNTRIES

Having disposed of U.S. investment in advanced countries as unrelated to imperialism, the Critics fire their ammunition at the relative smallness of U.S. business interests in underdeveloped countries. In the statistical process of estimating the degree of U.S. economic interests, they reduce the dimensions of this involvement by restricting the discussion to exports and direct private investment. Perhaps they do so because of the availability of export and investment data and the lack of other adequate data. Whatever the reason, this concentration on direct private investment and exports results in overlooking other major involvement. For example:

1. Licenses of patents, processes, and trademarks granted to foreign manufacturers by U.S. manufacturing firms. This represents a growing business interest in the Third World as well as in advanced countries —in part a byproduct of the worldwide distribution of U.S. movies, TV, and advertising. One finds, for example, such ordinary products as inks and paints manufactured in the Philippines under licenses from U.S. manufacturers.

2. An important source of income to U.S. business is profit derived from shipping food and raw materials from the Third World to the United States, and the reciprocal trade. A considerable number of these ships are U.S. ships flying the flags of Liberia and Panama. Investments in such shipping companies are included in the Department of Commerce statistics under the category "International Shipping" and are excluded from statistics on direct private investments in underdeveloped countries. (Incidentally, control over shipping, and the insurance of this shipping, of Third World trade is an important element of the dependency relation of the periphery countries on the metropolitan centers.)

3. Excluded from direct private investment statistics are such significant and expanding areas of economic involvement as: (*a*) direct loans by U.S. banks to foreign governments and businesses; (*b*) many types of foreign bonds floated in the United States; and (*c*) loans made in foreign countries by Edge Act corporations (subsidiaries of U.S. banks). It should also be noted that a favorite form of financing by Edge Act corporations is the convertible bond, a financial instrument whereby the U.S. banking corporation can convert the bond to shares of ownership in the foreign company.

4. The data on direct private investment do not include or measure the degree of diffusion of U.S. business interests in the economic life of underdeveloped countries. This is especially evident in the case of the operations of foreign branches of U.S. banks and foreign banks owned by U.S. banks. (This is over and above items referred to in the preceding paragraph.) For example, direct private investment in banks abroad shows up in the catchall category of "other investments," which takes in a wide variety of activities, including such investments as those in sugar and banana plantations. Direct investment in Latin America (except Venezuela) for all "other invesments" amounted to $867 million in 1968. Thus, investments in banks, as calculated for Department of Commerce statistics, would be considerably below $867 million. However, one New York bank alone—the Chemical Bank—has $7.66 billion of deposits in its South American operations, excluding Venezuela (*American Banker*, January 28, 1970). The Chemical Bank, of course, is not the only U.S. bank operating in South America. Among just New York City banks, the following have extensive business operations in South America, as well as in other underdeveloped areas: First National City Bank, Chase Manhattan Bank, and Morgan Guaranty Trust Co. The size of the deposits controlled represents a diffusion of U.S. interests throughout the interstices of the Third World economies far beyond direct investments—in the day-to-day activities of the native firms as well as of other U.S. investors.

The importance of U.S. business interests in Latin America, for example, is indirectly reflected in the reason given for the partnership arrangement that Mellon National Bank made with BOLSA to enter the Latin American markets:

> By 1961 it was becoming obvious to the bank's management . . . that because of its lack of international banking facilities Mellon's share of the domestic market was being threatened. Huge banks from New York, California, and Chicago were taking advantage of their international expertise to obtain larger shares of the domestic business of Mellon's traditional customers (*American Banker*, January 28, 1970).

In this we can see several important aspects of U.S. involvement in the underdeveloped world: (1) it is becoming increasingly important—

important enough for banks to be able to win customers from each other based on the services they can give businesses dealing abroad; (2) the interconnection of domestic and international business activities—an interconnection that exists in nonfinancial business too; and (3) how competition within an industry spurs further penetration of the underdeveloped economies—also a factor in promoting pressure for investments other than banking in the Third World.

The Question of Size

The Critics based their interpretation of the current state of U.S. imperialism on the relative smallness of private investment in the underdeveloped world. We have tried to show that the economic involvement is considerably larger than one would infer merely from the statistics on direct foreign private investment. However, one needs to dig deeper. While the relative size of a particular economic sector is important, it is by no means the only consideration. It is necessary to understand the influence of the sector on the dynamics of an economy in motion. For example, the stock market in and of itself is a relatively small part of the U.S. economy. Yet what goes on in the stock market far exceeds its insignificant "statistical" contribution to the Gross National Product. The availability of this gambling casino is of the very essence of an advanced capitalist system. In addition: speculative fervor on the upside of the market can act as a goad and prop of inflation and prosperity; panic of speculators can spark and intensify a major economic decline.

The vagaries of the balance of payments are a significant illustration of the potential "bigness" of a statistically small category. The chronic deficit in our balance of payments since 1950 has ranged roughly between $1 billion and $4 billion a year. Now this is obviously an insignificant portion of the GNP. Statistically it is hardly worth mentioning: just the statistical error involved in measuring the GNP is surely larger than the balance of payments deficit. Yet this "statistically insignificant" deficit, due to its unique function and its cumulative effect, contains all the potentials of a major international crisis. Lack of cooperation by the governments and central banks of the other advanced industrial nations—that is, their decision to go off the "dollar standard" and back to the "gold standard"—would undoubtedly lead to a breakdown of the existing international payments system and consequently of international trade, with obviously serious consequences to the world capitalist economy. (Central bankers understand this; it is, in fact, an important reason for their reluctant endurance of U.S. financial hegemony. But such cooperation is a slim reed to depend on in a world of aggressive, competitive national and business interests.)

Once we recognize the role of the balance of payments deficit in maintaining U.S. prosperity and international financial stability, we can better appreciate the special advantages accruing from business involvement in the Third World. As noted earlier, the United States is able to sustain its wars, military posture, foreign investment, and military and economic assistance for two reasons: (a) the large surplus in the balance of its transactions in goods and services (technically, the "current account"), and (b) its relative freedom to accumulate deficits. We have already dwelt briefly on the politics of the latter. Let us now look into the former. Taking the last five years (1964–1968) for which complete annual data are available at the time of writing, we find that the surplus of goods and services in trade with the underdeveloped countries (including the profits on foreign investments) represented 66 percent of the total U.S. surplus on this account. For the last three of these years (years of full-scale war in Vietnam), the U.S. export balance on goods and services with the Third World was 85 percent of the total U.S. surplus.[3]

Examination of the ramifications of the balance of payments issue (for example, the interrelations between current and capital transactions and the ensuing contradictions) will take us too far afield. Suffice it to note here that business dealings with the Third World from the perspective of the balance of payments are an especially strategic element of the current capitalist economy of the United States. The balance of payments data, however, are a summation of many thousands of transactions. If we look into these "small" transactions, we will also find areas of significance that far outweigh statistical "smallness."

The business of individual firms in the Third World arises usually in response to these motives: (1) to obtain and maintain enlarged markets; (2) to get higher profit rates by taking advantage of lower production costs; and (3) to achieve control over sources of raw materials and food. Given the international maldistribution of income, it is only natural—indeed, inevitable—that trade (and investment for better access to a country's markets) will be much larger in the case of the rich than in that of the poor nations, despite the great disproportion of population in these two sectors. But this does not mean that interest in the markets of the poor nations has slackened or will in the future diminish—any more than one would expect a waning of business interest in the "peripheral" areas within the United States (e.g., Mississippi) in contrast with the metropolitan centers of this country (e.g., New York). Nor would the business community take with better grace the shutting off of the lesser foreign markets than they would countenance the secession of the poorer regions of the United States.

The economics of the business firm is dominated by the growth imperative: growth of profits, growth of sales, and growth of capital

---

3. Calculated from balance of payments statistics reported in *Survey of Current Business,* June 1967 and June 1969. The Third World was defined as Western Hemisphere countries, other than Canada; and Asian and African countries, other than Japan and South Africa.

investment. In the early stages of the evolution of a firm or a product, it is usually found that speediest results are obtained by concentrating on the upper-income segments of the native country and on those foreign countries that have a large upper-income population. However, no successful firm can afford to rest there. Under the pressure of competition, it must seek out additional and, if possible, more profitable markets. While these additional markets may be relatively small, their marginal effect can be unusually important because of their role in sustaining growth. This role of the marginal increase in the export market applies also to the marginal investment in a foreign country.

To liberal-minded observers, like our Critics, some of the percentages of business contributed by exports and investments may look small and unimportant. But these small percentages necessarily loom large in the eyes of the owners and managers of a business. The realities of the business world are such that these owners and managers must struggle doggedly not only to hang on to their share of the market but to constantly maneuver to increase their share. Their logic is necessarily different. And it is the logic of the owners and managers of business that insists on keeping as much of the world as possible free for capital investment and trade—to provide at least the possibility of still another marginal boost in sales, profits, and investment. By the same token, the closing down of any area to "free enterprise" is a threat to growth potential.

When the "free enterprise" world remains "free for private enterprise," opportunities do in fact arise for a new spurt in one business field or another—for a new source of growth. Thus the sober-minded *Business Week* (December 6, 1969), in its forecast for the 1970s, recognizes the differences in trade with the developed and the underdeveloped nations, but it also understands the new opportunities:

> As in the past, exports to industrial nations will rise faster than those to developing countries. In the 1960s, sales to industrial nations climbed from $13 billion to $24 billion, sales to developing countries rose from $7 billion to $11 billion. *An exception will be a boom in U.S. export and import trade with East and South Asia,* excluding Japan. (Italics added.)

The authors of this projection do not spell out their assumptions concerning the continuation or end of the Vietnamese war; nor do they specify any assumption about the nature of the U.S. military presence in Asia in the 1970s, as, for example, the replacement by the United States of British bases in Southeast Asia.

RAW MATERIALS AND THE THIRD WORLD

The Critics give two reasons for brushing aside the crucial question of the raw materials factor and the ties with the Third World: (*a*) they themselves have not studied the question of dependency on foreign raw materials in depth, and (*b*) the possibility of substituting one material for another. Their straightforward acknowledgment is commendable. And by all means they should look into the facts. We would suggest, though, that they not restrict their study to the "dependency" angle. The imperialism issue is not so much dependency as the compelling behavior of monopolistic-type business organizations.

That the drive for control of foreign resources extends beyond dependency can be seen in the way U.S. corporations sought, fought for, and obtained exploration and development rights for oil, copper, and other minerals *when the United States was blessed with a surplus of these minerals.* A major reason for the oil industry to invest abroad was specifically to protect its foreign markets. (In the 1870s, two-thirds of U.S. oil production was exported.) Here is how Raymond Vernon summarizes the early history of the global expansion of the U.S. oil industry:

> The more remote sources of crude oil, such as those of the Middle East and the Far East, were needed by the U.S. companies because of their proximity to established export markets in Asia and the Mediterranean basin. While these markets had been developed by U.S. companies in the latter part of the nineteenth century on the basis of U.S. exports, they were never wholly free from challenge by others. . . . For two decades before 1900, the American companies tried to counter this threat by capturing downstream facilities in some of the main markets in which they were challenged. By 1900, however, they seem to have decided that control of marketing facilities was not the appropriate strategy and that control of the crude oil was the key. It was then that the U.S. firms began aggressively to try for acquisition of foreign crude oil sources. More generally, however, the major oil companies had to take some interest in any potential source of oil wherever there was a risk that the source, when developed, might undersell existing supplies. . . . In economic terms, the cost of development could better be attributed to the hedging of risk—the risk of losing control of the price structure in established markets. . . . The early history of the major oil companies suggested another principle of a prudential sort. A well-diversified supply of resources, they rapidly discovered, was especially useful in dealing with blockages of supply, whether threatened or actual ("Foreign Enterprises and Developing Nations in the Raw Materials Industries," a paper presented to the American Economic Association, Dec. 30, 1969).

Foreign investment for the development and extraction of resources took place for many reasons. Just profit alone has been a sufficient motive for starting many plantations and mines in the underdeveloped world. But the investment in raw materials by monopolistic-type firms has added a new dimension—a dimension that goes a long way toward explaining what the era of modern imperialism is all about.

The concentration of economic power in a limited number of giant firms became possible in many industries precisely because of the control by these firms over raw materials sources. The ability to maintain this concentrated power—to ward off native and foreign competitors, to weaken newcomers, and to conduct its affairs in accordance with monopolistic price and production policies—depended on the alertness and aggressiveness of the giant firms to obtain and maintain control over major segments of the supplies of raw materials—*on a world scale.* This has been the underlying rationale of foreign investment in the extractive industries during the era of modern imperialism: not only in oil but in a spectrum of products, especially minerals.

The issue, therefore, is not dependency of the United States on foreign mineral supplies, but the dependency of monopoly industry qua "monopolies" on the control of these supplies. The data on the extent to which minerals used in the United States are obtained abroad are merely one measure of the farflung interests of U.S. monopolies. Necessarily, large firms that process "scarce" raw materials must be vitally concerned about the *world* production, distribution, and prices of these supplies, not merely the demand for these products in the United States.

On this subject, too, the issue of "smallness" raised by the Critics has little relevance. They point out that only the investment in foreign oil is large; the investment in other minerals is relatively small. The fact that the proportion of foreign investment in other minerals is small compared with oil has no bearing whatsoever on the depth of the concern and involvement of the firms using these other minerals. The proportion of foreign investment in iron ore, bauxite, and copper ore (among others) to investment in oil has little meaning, if any, to the steel, aluminum, and copper producers who seek to secure their leading positions and their special profit advantages by controlling a major segment of the foreign (as well as domestic) supplies of their products.

The second point on raw materials raised by the Critics concerns the possible substitution of one product for another, one that would result in a reduction of "dependency" on foreign supplies. Obviously, they do not mean the substitution of some ore other than iron to make steel or a bauxite substitute to make aluminum. Our alchemists have not learned this trick yet. What the Critics dwell on is the substitution of, say, aluminum and/or plastics for some uses of steel and of aluminum for copper. To a considerable extent substitution has been going on for years, if not centuries and millennia. Where technical substitution is feasible, competition between raw materials for the same or similar uses has been heated. This competition, however, has been accompanied not by a lessening of "dependence" on foreign sources but by an increase of such "dependence." The reason is quite simple. One cannot substitute at will—even if the price is right or even if the cost of the raw material is unimportant. For example, copper used in electric wire and cable can only be replaced by a material that conducts electricity. Steel, paper, and wood are therefore not usable as substitutes for wire requiring electrical conductivity. However, whereas aluminum is a possible substitute, the result of such substitution is an increase in "dependency" on foreign sources of supply: the proportion of foreign to domestic bauxite is considerably higher than the foreign to domestic ratio of copper ore.

Another reason for not relying on substitutability for removing, or diminishing, reliance on foreign sources can be seen in the case of steel. Steel has been on the losing end of many competitive battles, including the competition of plastics made from purely domestic sources. Nevertheless, the weakening competitive position of steel has been accompanied by an *increase* in the use of foreign ore. The reason is the depletion of the great Mesabi iron ore deposit. Furthermore, even though technical breakthroughs have made the conversion of domestic taconite ore economically feasible, the interest of U.S. steel firms in iron ore reserves in Canada, South America, Africa, and Asia has increased.

The upshot is that the problem of substitution of minerals, on the whole, is quite different from that of butter vs. margarine or synthetics vs. silk/cotton. At rock bottom, the replacement of one mineral by another is a technical problem. Economics is often involved, but the economic maneuverability is severely restricted by the technical determinants. One cannot, at the present stage of technology, send an electric current through matter that lacks the properties to transmit it. Nor can one make airplanes that carry passengers and freight without aluminum. Moreover, we don't know how to make an effective jet engine without getting columbium, tungsten, nickel, chromium, and cobalt from the four corners of the earth. Nor do politics and economics stand still, waiting on the sidelines for future imaginative technological breakthroughs.

The Critics, though, make a still more daring hypothesis on the substitution question: "The question of substitutability is affected by possible shifts in the end products of American industry which, in turn, determine what materials are needed. The main possibility is, of course, a reduction in military production." But why stop at military production? We could, for example, have our commercial jet airplanes made in France, England, Germany, and Japan. These countries would be happy to get the business and we would reduce our dependency on foreign raw materials. Better still, we could shift the end products of our society by restricting the use of automobiles in our crowded cities and reduce truck traffic by using subway rails. We could thereby lower the demand for cars, cut down on our dependence on foreign sources of minerals, and improve the air we breathe.

It is interesting to indulge in speculations on what a rational society would do to simplify the problem of foreign raw material dependency. Such speculation might even have educational value in exposing the limits and contradictions of a capitalist society whose modus vivendi is the profit motive. But if we want to understand what capitalist imperialism is all about, we had better pay attention to the mechanics and dynamics of *capitalism as a world system.*

FUNDAMENTAL CHANGES?

The Critics summarize their argument in a section entitled "Fundamental Changes"—changes which, in their opinion, point to the plausibility of a U.S. capitalist economy without imperialism. We do not have the space to tackle all the points made. But we shall try to comment in abbreviated form on a few.

First, they call on the authority of John Kenneth Galbraith's *New Industrial State* to support their contention that fundamental changes have occurred in capitalism which depart from the "necessity" of imperialism. But what are the changes that Galbraith deals with? The "new" capitalism, he claims, is and must be dominated by a limited number of giant corporations; the success of the "new industrial state" depends on the success of these giants. These industrial giants, in turn, have three imperatives: they must keep on growing; they must control their raw material supplies at consistent prices; and they must control their markets,[4] precisely. Galbraith, whether he knows it or not, is explaining the mainspring of the imperialism of monopoly capitalism.

Second, the Critics see a fundamental change in the absence of a major economic crisis since the end of the Second World War. If, however, one of the most important reasons for this "fundamental change" is the huge military machine built up and maintained by the United States,[5] then such a change is hardly an opener of a new dawn of a peaceful modern capitalism. Quite the contrary. It is a harbinger of wars and revolutions. The internal and external conflicts generated by such a "success" do indeed foretoken the end of imperialism and the decline of the U.S. empire—but not by a peaceful reform of monopoly capitalism.

Third, the Critics contrast the more rapid growth of a "nonimperialist" Germany and Japan with the slower growth of imperialist United States and Great Britain. (Incidentally, they refer to "the tempestuous growth of Japan and Germany in the postwar period, without foreign investments. . . ." They may wish to argue that foreign investments were not important for the growth rate, but there have been considerable foreign investments by Germany and Japan.) What is missing in this sort of correlation is an appreciation of the way capitalism works as a world system. Under *Pax Americana*, it is the United States that

---

4. See the author's review of Galbraith's book, "Rationalizing the Irrational," *The Nation*, (September 18, 1967).

5. See Paul A. Baran and Paul M. Sweezy, *Monopoly Capital* (New York, 1966). Also the author's "Militarism and Imperialism" in *Monthly Review* (February, 1970).

supplies the main military power and the police action to keep as much of the world as possible safe for "free" enterprise. In this arrangement, Germany and Japan, as major and strategic components of world capitalism, are special beneficiaries of the economic and military strategy of the United States. Japan in particular has benefited not only from the advantages of a prosperous U.S. market but also from U.S. purchases for the Korean and Vietnamese wars. There are of course special factors that have contributed to the German and Japanese growth rates, but the very possibility of growth is intimately related to *Pax Americana* and to a relatively successful U.S. economy based on militarism.

In sum, the Critics' analytical method is to separate out the various parts of the U.S. and world economy and to sever economics from politics. They arrive at the conclusion that, by tinkering with some of the parts through political pressure, capitalism can be reformed so that it can live and grow without imperialism. Our point of view is that the separate parts must be understood in the context of their interrelations with the social organism of world monopoly capitalism. Further, it is important to recognize the essential unity of the economics, politics, militarism, and culture of this social organism. We reach the conclusion that imperialism is the way of life of capitalism. Therefore, the elimination of imperialism requires the overthrow of capitalism.

Part5

The Structure of Power

There are an abundance of descriptive studies of various local "power structures" —from New Haven to Atlanta—in the United States, but the attempt to comprehend political power in our country at the national level has been as rare as "community" studies have been bountiful. This reflects both the complexity of the analytic task, and the prevailing unstated premises and underlying conceptions, as well as explicit theory, in academic social science concerning the nature of the state in America. If power is seen as amorphous or situational or located amongst a congeries of competing "elites," as has long been the prevailing view in American academia, then the analytic objective is to study "power" wherever "it" can be located; power at the national level, then, is largely constituted of the aggregated or interacting "power structures" studied.

The power structure of the United States, as Arnold M. Rose explains (Selection Number 26), is "highly complex and diversified (rather than unitary and monolithic)" and political power is pluralistic; it is constantly changing its locus, distribution, and manifestations. Rose's view of the political process in the United States is summed up in what he terms his "multi-influence hypothesis." Every level of American life has its own power structure, and these are certainly not unified into a single national power structure "even within the categories of the economic and the political, although occasionally semipermanent liasons develop among them." Within the various local power structures, a small number of persons exercise power at the community level and the various spheres of business, unions, voluntary associations, etc., also have their own elites, but the rank-and-file exercise "some restraining and modifying power" over each of them.

The point is, Rose argues, that in government there is "an ever-changing elite which exercises most of the power at any given moment." The two main national elites which influence each other are the political and economic elites—government officials and businessmen—but even these elites are not internally cohesive. The economic elite influences government successfully where there are no counterpressures, for instance, in the regulatory commissions. But in "general legislation," says Rose, "they have had an almost unbroken series of defeats" since the 1930s. Their ideology—which Rose says consists of business leadership in society and minimum government activity on behalf of others—has made no progress in government. Particularly because of the ascendance of the federal executive over the legislature and over state and local governments, he says, the power of business has been reduced.

The 1960s especially saw the breakdown of the conservative Republican and southern Democrat coalition, the rise of "new popular pressure groups," and the passage of a good deal of liberal legislation despite opposition from "economic elite pressure groups." Only in foreign policy, Rose believes, does a small group continue to control national decisions: it consists not only of the president and his official advisers, but also of "secret decision makers" in the CIA or the Council on Foreign Relations. In general, the two major political parties reflect less and less business influence. Indeed, "power is so complicated at the top businessmen hardly understand it," Rose contends, "much less control it." Since 1933, "the power position of businessmen" has declined while the spheres of the "elites of the federal administration" have risen. Certainly, he argues, "the political elites" are ascendant, yet they considerably check and balance each other. Similarly, if the two major political parties are "among the most powerful groups in the United States," they scarcely exist at the national level and differ considerably in relative cohesiveness at the state and local levels. This makes them accessible to influence by ordinary citizens; indeed, says Rose, their active "voluntary labor" for a candidate gives them access to political power greater than that of inactive wealthy citizens. In any event, Rose concludes, most congressmen and legislators vote their own convictions most of the time and "are only partially open to pressure of any kind." The main thing, then, in exerting influence is for citizens to elect legislators whose convictions accord with theirs.

The substance of Rose's view is that an active and diverse citizenry exercising influence in the political process in multiple ways assures that the United States, if not "completely democratic," comes as close as "any known other society—past or present." For Thomas R. Dye and L. Harmon Zeigler, in sharp contrast (Selection Number 27), "the irony of democracy" is that mass democracy requires "mass powerlessness." It is inherently not possible, say Dye and Zeigler, for individuals in a large, complex society to shape the political decisions which affect them. In a large society, the influence of individuals is "so tiny" as to render their political participation "fruitless." Elitism and mass powerlessness are necessary in the United States, as in all complex societies where the mass has to delegate governing responsibilities. This recognition is necessary, so they say, in order "to build an orderly, humane, and just society."

Everywhere, according to Dye and Zeigler, the delegation of responsibilities to governing authorities combined with the inherent inequalities in intelligence, ability, and drive among men creates a distinctive governing minority. "Organization inevitably means oligarchy." Moreover, democracy cannot rely on the people to govern, since they are antidemocratic, alienated, hateful, and violent. Therefore, "the future of American democracy," Dye and Zeigler maintain, "depends on the wisdom, responsibility, and resourcefulness of the nation's elite." Of course, "democracy is not always safe in the hands of elites" either, especially since their characteristic response to mass protest is "the abandonment of democratic values." For this reason, Dye and Zeigler assert, protest is dangerous—it provokes a "grim and repressive response" from both the masses and the elite, which is its only tangible accomplishment. Even "tinkering" with or trying to reform political institutions is "futile," because these reflect the dominant values of society. We are entering a "new age of scarcity" and the United States is increasingly beset by global problems like the "population explosion" or "inflation" over which it has no real control; it may therefore become necessary, Dye and Zeigler conclude, for us to entrust ourselves to rule by the experts, the "technological elites" who are capable of wielding the technological power necessary in the "struggle against scarcity." Thus, "an end to democracy," Dye and Zeigler believe," accompanied by a drastic restriction of individual liberty, may be the only course available."

According to Dye and Zeigler, then, the rule of elites is as inevitable as it has been eternal because it reflects the inherent incapacity of the people to govern themselves. This doctrine is in sharp contrast with the late C. Wright Mills's radical democratic critique of "mass society" in America. Writing in the 1950s, he saw the ascendance of the "power elite" as part of a lengthy historic process accelerated during and after the Second World War (Selection Number 28).

The decline of the old middle class of independent proprietors; the ascendance of the dependent new middle class (atomized and unorganized even on an economic level); the end of labor insurgence; and the decline of politics in mid-twentieth century America were among the factors involved in creating the situation in which the power elite established itself. The ideal of democracy, in Mills's view, became a legitimation of its opposite. Unified at the top, drifting and stalemated in the middle, and politically fragmented at the bottom, American society became a mass society.

It was particularly as America was transformed into a militarized capitalist country with a permanent war economy that the "power elite" was consolidated. In this militarized capitalism, Mills argues, the means of power—economic production, violence, and political administration—became enlarged, centralized, and increasingly coordinated and inseparable. Genuine "publics" and clashing political parties, civil servants of independence and integrity, and organized opposition movements bearing their own vision of things as they ought to be—these disappeared in the Cold War United States of the 1950s. Misplaced images of the past and celebrations of "balance" in the present served to justify the prevailing system.

The three hierarchical institutional orders—economic, political, and military— became joined in numerous ways into a triangle of power: the corporation executives, the political directorate, and the high military. As their domains increasingly coincided, as their decisions took on historical significance, and as the traffic between the three became frequent, they emerged, says Mills, as the power elite.

The country's economy is internally dominated by a few hundred corporations that are administratively and politically interrelated, and its principal economic decisions are made by corporation men who moved into the area of political direction during World War II. The apparently permanent military threat, according to Mills, fostered the ascendance of the higher military to a firm position of power among the power elite. This threat also made it possible for military definitions of reality to become the standard of judgment for virtually all political and economic actions.

The unity of the elite rests, says Mills, on their psychological similarity and social intermingling; their common backgrounds, interests, and perceptions; upon the intertwining of the institutional orders over which they preside; and upon "explicit coordination." The elite have taken advantage of the fact that their several interests can be realized through informal and formal arrangements. The so-called "veto groups" and "countervailing powers" have been relegated to the realm of the middle levels of power. The expanding hierarchies of the power elite replaced the old balance that included these groups.

Mills argues that responsible parties representing and clarifying policies do not exist; major decisions of war and peace are made in secret, with citizens knowing little about them and affecting them even less. The independent organizations which exist are either ineffective or irrelevant; the mass organizations, to the extent that they have become effective (and, therefore, larger), have become inaccessible to individual influence. These mass organizations, in Mills's view, are controlled from the top and integrated in many ways into the prevailing order dominated by the power elite.

Andrew Hacker also argues that power exercised administratively under contemporary capitalism has to be the focus of our understanding and the target of our critique of the edifice of power in America (Selection Number 29). Of course, tenure in the high administrative offices to which power attaches is insecure, says Hacker, so "there is no substitute for wealth." To be sure, "America has classes," and a rich propertied class of roughly 20,000 households owns a fifth or so of all personally held corporate stock in the country. "But," asks Hacker, "are they a ruling class, and a national one at that?" The answer, he says, is that the term "ruling class" is "historically inapposite." It is misleading to speak of a ruling class in America because "individual and family property play a much smaller part in our leading institutions" than in traditional ruling classes. Rather, the elites derive their power from their occupancy of high office in these leading institutions, particularly, Hacker avers, in the large corporations which are "the real centers of sovereignty" in the United States.

These large corporate bodies make the "major decisions in investment, innovation, and employment" that shape the regions, professions, public authority, and class configurations of our country. Since there are no alternative ways to organize the economy, the large corporations "get their way in Congress, the parties, and the bureaucracy." But, says Hacker, the rich propertied families whose fortunes are mainly held in corporate securities do not control the large corporations. To think that they do, he says, "implies an inability to understand and deal with power in its institutional form." What's more, the top corporate managers do not have a "cohesive culture" and do not overlap with the very wealthy, nor do they have "the kind of self-confidence that characterizes a bourgeoisie." Thus what rules America, Hacker concludes, is not a ruling class, but institutional power.

If Hacker does not wish to ignore the "deeper divisions of social life" in America and if he emphasizes that the large corporations control those parts of our country "that bear on their operations," he differs fundamentally with class theory because he denies that America has either a capitalist or dominant class. By speaking of a ruling class, Hacker says, we "look for power in the wrong places" —the rich do not control the large corporations. From the standpoint of class theory, however, Hacker is wrong on this critical question: under whose control and on behalf of which class in America is "power in its institutional form" deployed? Since he agrees with class theorists that public authority tends to be shaped and used to fit corporate ends, it follows that if Hacker also conceded that the large corporations are typically controlled not by "anonymous administrators" but by principal capitalist families and other cohesive ownership interests (as I argue in Selection Number 21), then he would also be compelled to conclude that we have not merely a "propertied" but a *dominant* class in this country. Perhaps unwittingly, then, Hacker's own focus on "power in its institutional form" serves to neutralize the question of class domination in America.

For G. William Domhoff, however, this is the main question to answer in order to understand the uses of power in the United States today (Selection Number 30). In his view, it is the "social upper class" made up of top wealth-holders that dominates our country. True, says Domhoff, some members of the upper class spend most of their time playing or engaged in the international social whirl, and some rulers are not members of the upper class. The latter, though, are carefully groomed and carefully selected employees of the upper class. Within that class there is a "leadership group" or "power elite" consisting, on the one hand, of active, working members of the upper class and, on the other, of their high-level employees in institutions they control. Domhoff argues that the members of the power elite hold the important government positions, especially in the executive branch, and that nonpartisan, seemingly objective discussion groups like the Council on Foreign Relations are really upper class policy planning organizations which develop the plans implemented by our government.

There are, he says, four interrelated political processes (special interest, policy planning, candidate selection, ideology) through which the ruling class rules. (1) Various private interests, particularly through trade associations, have taken over the piece of the government of greatest concern to them. (2) In upper class policy planning organizations like the Business Council, members of the national power elite come together to thrash out the issues, establish consensus, and set the framework for general government policies. They also try to create a climate of opinion favorable to such policies. (3) Selection of the candidates is the critical act, especially since American parties are merely used to fill political offices and have no genuine programs and few differences; these candidates have to be acceptable to the fat cats who make the huge campaign contributions. These candidates typically come from middle-class families anyway, and have no basic differences with the rich who own the country. (4) The dominant class maintains "ideological hegemony" (i.e., the ruled accept that rulers' view of the world) in great part by creating, spreading, and enforcing the hegemonic attitudes and values through a complex "dissemination network" which celebrates the present social arrangements under which we live. What's more, Domhoff argues, "pressure, intimidation, and violence" are used if gentle persuasion, material reward, or outright bribery are not enough to repress serious opposition to class rule.

For James O'Connor, whose categories are drawn from Marxian theory, the dominant class is an internally differentiated *capitalist* class with two main segments, "monopoly capital" and "competitive capital," with a host of rival interests organized along trade and industry lines. The basic social relations critical to the formation and implementation of state policy in the United States are those between labor and capital, particularly monopoly capital and organized labor; but such relations as those between monopoly and competitive capital and competitive capital and labor are also significant. In the capitalist class, interest consciousness alone—specific manufacturers' or retailers' associations pushing their own interests—results in contradictory policies. The attempt by regulatory agencies to maintain profitable conditions in particular industries, for example, tends to freeze resource allocation, reinforce monopoly power, and retard capital accumulation and expansion throughout the economy. Coordination and planning on behalf of monopoly capital as a whole is impossible in the highly specialized and interdependent productive system of contemporary capitalism. "Thus," argues O'Connor, "a class-conscious political directorate is needed to coordinate the activities of nominally independent government agencies" which otherwise would simply pursue the policies of the particularistic groups that dominate them. This role falls to the federal executive, since the legislature tends to represent regional and local capital as well as branches of organized labor. National capital relies mainly on the federal executive to "interpret class (as opposed to particular economic) corporate interests" and to implement appropriate policies. Both immediate interests and long-run relations between monopoly capital and competitive sector labor and capital have to be considered in policy formation and implementation. Thus, "monopoly capitalist class interests" emerge "unintentionally" within the state administration as the result of these contending political forces. In this sense, says O'Connor, "the capitalist state is not an 'instrument' but a 'structure.'"[1]

If monopoly capital and organized labor are the main contending forces and the state strives to regularize relations between them by transforming collective bargaining into an instrument of corporate planning, it must also control the "surplus population" (the poor and unemployed) and the workers in the competitive sector. For this, a host of special arrangements to protect particular commodity and labor markets are necessary, as are specific state expenditures for social consumption. These are often contradictory and are administered at different levels of the entire governmental system, federal, state, and local. In essence, then, the state has to fulfill two "contradictory functions," says O'Connor, accumulation of capital (profitable private economic expansion) and legitimation (loyalty of the population); and "it is the task of administrative rationality in every state agency to try to reconcile them." Particularly because special interest politics prevail at the state and local levels of government, class-conscious elements of monopoly capital have striven to make the federal budget "an instrument of national economic planning" and to subordinate particular to general class interests through executive power. Hence there has been a continual struggle by national capital since the turn of this century to gain centralized control over the budget and to appropriate city, county, state, and congressional prerogatives increasingly to the federal executive. In the process, O'Connor concludes, formal democracy has also declined at all levels of government in the United States.

---

1. This distinction between the state as "instrument" or "structure" is much debated recently among Marxian theorists. For a convenient critical summary of the debate, see David A. Gold, Clarence Y. H. Lo, and Erik Olin Wright, "Recent Developments in Marxist Theories of the Capitalist State," Part One, *Monthly Review* 27:5 (October, 1975):29–43; Part Two, *Monthly Review* 27:6 (November, 1975): 36–51. Also see Gösta Esping-Andersen, Roger Friedland, and Erick Olin Wright, "Modes of Class Struggle and the Capitalist State," and G. William Domhoff, "I am not an 'Instrumentalist,'" *Kapitalistate* No. 5 4–5 (Summer 1976): 186–220; 221–224.

Political Process in American Society

26

Arnold M. Rose

Political power in the United States, like any other social phenomenon, is changing its locus of concentration, its distribution, and its manifestations constantly.[1] Some of the observations and generalizations made in this book will be out of date by the time the reader is able to analyze and criticize them. Recent changes, for example, have occurred in the rural-urban distribution of power in state legislatures, in the strength of the Republican—southern Democratic "coalition" in Congress, and in the extent to which businessmen are to be found in key positions in the national administration. Nevertheless, most aspects of power have remained sufficiently stable for a student of the power structure to draw generalizations and to note slow-moving trends. In contrast to the major theses of C. Wright Mills and Floyd Hunter—that there is a secret, hierarchical, and unified power structure in the United States headed by an economic elite, that the political elite occupies only a secondary position in the power structure, and that the masses are apathetic and act in terms of false consciousness of their interests—we would assert the following propositions. Most of them are based on studies reported or summarized in this book; others are based merely on general or participant observation.

1. There is a power structure in every organized activity of American life and at every level—national, regional, state, and local. Power is the major means used by a large, heterogeneous society to effect or to resist change, and—except in simple face-to-face relations—power is structured, which is to say that there are different roles and role relationships, and a pattern into which these roles and relationships fit.

From Arnold M. Rose, *The Power Structure: Political Process in American Society,* Ch. 14, pp. 483–93. Copyright © 1967 by Oxford University Press, Inc. Reprinted with permission.

1. Even from the time the present study was begun, (in 1960), until it was sent to the publishers (in 1966), there were so many significant changes that additions, corrections, and qualifications had to be made regularly in the manuscript.

2. There are varying degrees of relationship and agreement among these varied power structures. They are certainly not unified into a simple power structure, even *within* the categories of the economic and the political, although occasionally semipermanent liaisons develop among them. Nor are they usually countervailing, because each operates primarily within its own sphere of influence, although countervailing (or check-and-balance) relationships occasionally do occur. The political party power structures—there are at least four major ones on the national level alone—probably have the largest number of relationships with other power structures, both because one of their specific roles is to mediate conflicts and because they have a large degree of control over the bureaucratic machinery of government, which in turn monopolizes most of the instruments of organized physical force.

3. Within each power structure, a small number of persons hold the largest amount of power. In community studies, this has been estimated to constitute less than 1 percent of the population, but such estimates refer to those who lead in communitywide political decisions, and not to power *within* the spheres of business, unions, voluntary associations, schools, churches, etc. While in any sphere of activity there are "leaders" who constitute a tiny proportion of all those affected by the activity, this does not mean that the others have no power whatsoever. Opposition groups occasionally form, and sometimes succeed in overturning the existing elite. In all cases where there are elections, the rank-and-file voters exercise some restraining and modifying power over the elite. Their power is a function of the extent to which they have interacted to create a public opinion, the extent to which the election machinery is honest, and the extent to which voters are equal. Under these criteria, most governmental elections accord a good deal of power to the electorate, most business corporation elections accord practically no power to the electorate, and labor union and voluntary association elections vary between these two poles. But even in government and in actively democratic trade unions, there is an everchanging elite which exercises most of the power at any given moment.

4. Each elite manifests its power mainly within its own domain. That is, the strongest powers of businessmen are exercised within their own businesses, and the strongest powers of politicians and public administrators are exercised within government. But particularly the political and economic elites, among all the elites, influence each other's spheres. Especially since the 1930s the government has set various restrictions and controls on business, and has heavily taxed business and the public to carry out purposes deemed to be for the general good— welfare programs, education programs, highways, war and military defense activities, etc. Business leaders use lobbyists, "business representatives" in legislatures, contributions to campaign funds, publicity designed to influence public opinion, the "political strike," and other

lesser techniques to influence government. Businessmen influence government more effectively than most nonbusinessmen, not only because they can afford lobbyists, advertisements and other costly techniques, but also because they are more educated, more knowledgeable, more articulate, and more activist than average citizens. The latter qualities give them an advantage quite compatible with a democratic society.

5. The economic elite has its greatest success in influencing government where there are no counterpressures from other sectors of the economic elite, from other noneconomic elites, and from public opinion. The result has been that the economic elite has been relatively successful in influencing government purchasing agents and the independent regulatory commissions. This is not quite an accurate way of stating the facts, however, since individual businesses often compete strongly with each other in influencing these factors of government, and there is a considerable turnover in the individual businesses benefited by these sectors of government. In pressuring or appealing to the top levels of the federal administration, to the Congress, or even to many state legislatures (especially outside the South), businessmen have been much less successful since the 1930s. In fact, as far as general legislation is concerned they have had an almost unbroken series of defeats, although they have succeeded in *delaying* the passage of certain bills for years. Thus while businessmen have gained certain economic benefits from government, their typical ideology—in favor of businessman leadership in the society and of a minimum of government activity for the benefit of other segments of the population—has made no progress.[2]

6. While the federal government has been gaining ascendancy over the state and local governments, and while the office of the president has been gaining power at the expense of Congress, it is far from true that the state governments and the Congress are powerless. Rather, it could be said that the "balance of power" doctrine envisaged in the Constitution has come into operation only since 1933, because the federal government (except for military activities) and the presidency (except in wartime) were relatively weak institutions before then. These two trends in political power have reduced the influence of the economic elite, for the federal government is less susceptible to influence from businessmen than are most of the state governments, and the presidency is less susceptible to such influence than are many of the congressmen.

7. In the early 1960s a coalition of several decades' duration between two major political power structures—the conservative leadership of

---

2. It has been argued that this businessman's ideology represents a "false consciousness" —that is, it claims to represent an economic interest, but is in fact contrary to the economic interest of businessmen. The factual argument is that businessmen gain most economic benefits when the government actively promotes the welfare and education of even its poorest citizens, when it maintains a regularly unbalanced budget, and when it reduces tariffs—all policies which most businessmen oppose.

the Republican party and the Democrats in power in most of the southern states—largely broke down. The southern Democrats, changing in membership and reduced in number by Republican inroads on their constituencies, drew closer to the northern Democrats, except publicly over the issue of civil rights. The South was rapidly becoming like the North—in its industrialization, urbanization, patterns of race relations permitted by Negro voting, and development of a two-party system.[3] The Republican party was sharply divided between its conservatives and liberals, on the one hand, and a smaller group of right-wing extremists with a vigorous ideology who seized control of the party's grassroots structures in the majority of states. The extremists—while occasionally ideologically supportive of business—were not as willing to make political compromises in behalf of business or as willing to trust leading businessmen as had been the previous conservative leaders of the Republican party. All these developments, coupled with the political skill of President Lyndon B. Johnson, permitted the permitted the passage of a great deal of "liberal" legislation in the 1964 to 1965 sessions of Congress, including "Medicare" for the elderly . . ., federal aid to education, the antipoverty program, tax reduction without a balanced budget, a comprehensive civil rights act, a voting rights act, elimination of national quotas for immigrants, creation of a new Department of Housing and Urban Development, aid to urban mass-transit programs and to highway and city beautification efforts, and a National Foundation on the Arts and Humanities. Further, the president had an unofficial price control policy which worked for a few years to keep major industries from raising prices.

8. In the passage of the above-mentioned legislation, interested economic elite pressure groups were mostly defeated. On the other hand, the major legislation sought by organized labor—repeal of Section 14(b) of the Taft-Hartley Act—was also defeated in the Senate. The one economic elite group that continued to reap major economic benefits from government activity was the armaments and space-exploration supply industries, although the Secretary of Defense made certain decisions on procurement (such as in favor of competitive bidding rather than cost-plus contracts) even in this area which were not favored by the leading manufacturers.

9. Through the Voting Rights Act of the Congress and the *Baker* v. *Carr* and *Reynolds* v. *Sims* decisions of the United States Supreme Court —including the giving of permission to the Attorney General to seek a Court review of the poll tax (which was consequently outlawed by the Supreme Court)—a major democratization of voting for state legislatures was occurring in many states. Both state and local government

---

3. The decline in the number of "safe" Democratic House seats has been documented by Raymond E. Wolfinger and Joan Heifetz, "Safe Seats, Seniority, and Power in Congress," *American Political Science Review* 59 (June, 1965):337–49.

activities were increasingly influenced by standards set by federal aid programs that covered ever wider spheres.

10. The pattern of legislation at both federal and state levels revealed the emergence of new popular pressure groups with considerable power, partly because of demographic shifts and partly because of growing political consciousness among these groups. These groups are the elderly, a portion of whom are now organized into many associations, the most politically active of which is the National Association of Senior Citizens; the Negroes, possibly a majority of whom are organized into various civil rights associations and activist churches; and the "resentful disaffecteds," practically all organized into a variety of leftist and rightist extremist organizations, of which the John Birch Society is the largest and the wealthiest. The political organization of voluntary associations representing these three categories of the "masses" provides increasing evidence of a thesis expounded in an earlier section [of the original work,] "Reactions against the Mass Society" (pp. 196–212).

11. The major area of small-group control of national policy remaining in the country was that of foreign policy. The most powerful arm of this small group—namely the president and his official advisers—are quite exposed to the public. But there are secret decisionmakers operating in this area also—secret in that their influence and processes of decisionmaking are not accessible to the public. These decisionmakers are the CIA, the foreign policy "experts" in the universities and in such organizations as the Foreign Policy Association and the Council on Foreign Relations, and the military supplies industrialists who exert their influence mainly through the military leaders. The last-named are the ones whom Mills placed at the pinnacle of the power elite in the United States; we identify them rather as one influence among several affecting the nation almost exclusively in the area of foreign policy. We are entirely skeptical about Mills's contention that the other "members" of the economic elite—say, for example, those organized in the Chamber of Commerce—have more influence on foreign policy than the workers organized into trade unions, especially when they engage in shipping boycotts.

12. Despite the fact that the Republican party's ideological move to the right after 1962 left the Democrats securely in command of the center, the program of the Democratic party remained as liberal as it had ever been. This can be seen not only by comparing national party platforms over the years, but by reviewing the legislation supported (and usually passed) by the majority of Democrats in Congress and by the Democratic presidents Kennedy and Johnson. This can be explained either as a long-run trend—in terms of the increasing strength of voters who favor liberal measures and generally support the Democratic party as the instrument to achieve them—or as part of a structural cycle.

Lipset specifies a version of the latter theory:[4] Republican presidents seek center support and so force Republican congressmen from safe conservative seats to behave in a more liberal fashion. When a Republican holds the presidency, the southern contingent of conservative Democrats have more power in their party. Thus, in a Republican presidency, the two congressional parties are not so far apart. But when a Democrat hold the presidency, he pulls his congressmen to the left, to respond to the needs of the greater number of voters there, while the Republican congressmen are free to follow their ideological inclination toward the right, and the two parties are quite far apart. It is difficult to judge from the facts which theory is correct, but this author tends to regard the former theory as more persuasive, especially in view of the decline of differences between South and North. In any case, there has been a significant difference between the platforms and policies of the two national parties at least since 1932,[5] and the difference in the mid-1960s was as great as could be found between democratic political parties anywhere in the Western world. The increasing number of differences between the two major political parties, and the growing ideological framework for those differences, will probably have profound implications for the political future of the United States—but it is still too early to foresee the future development. Nevertheless, from the standpoint of [our] thesis . . . we can say that there is little evidence that business is playing any significant role in the development of these trends. Business is a declining influence on the political power structures, except in the narrow area of its relationship to government procurement officials and the independent regulatory commissions—largely because business exerts its strongest efforts on these and because there are few countervailing influences on them . . .

13. The public's and the formal leadership's image of the power structure—if we can generalize from a study of the one state of Minnesota—does not include many people as seeing the economic elite as all-powerful, although the extent to which they do see business as influential may be somewhat exaggerated in terms of the facts. Judging from their public pronouncements, it is the political extremist—of both the right and the left—whose image of the American power structure includes a conspiratorial and all-powerful role for the economic elite. The extremist groups have different names for this "all-powerful

---

4. Seymour Martin Lipset, *Political Man* (New York: Doubleday, 1960), pp. 306–7.

5. The basic ideological difference between the leadership of the two parties, on the average, has been demonstrated by Herbert McClosky, Paul J. Hoffman, and Rosemary O'Hara, "Issue Conflict and Consensus Among Party Leaders and Followers," *American Political Science Review* 54 (June, 1960): 406–27. The public, also, sees ideological differences between the two parties. See, for example, the report of the Minnesota Poll in the *Minneapolis Sunday Tribune* (November 3, 1963), p. UM2.

group" but they refer to the same business elite: The "lunatic fringe" rightists call them "the hidden group behind the communists," the more rational extreme rightists call them "the Establishment"; the more rational extreme leftists also call them "the Establishment" or "Wall Street", but are more likely to use the Mills-Hunter terms "the power elite" or "the power structure," while the less rational extreme leftists either use the same terms or refer bluntly to "the big business conspiracy." While it is of considerable interest that the political extremists of both right and left—apparently along with many nonextremist intellectuals influenced by Mills and Hunter—have the same image of the top business elite as being all-powerful, it is of greater importance to note that the majority of the people and of the positional leaders of American organized society do not have this image. We have adduced much evidence in this book that the top business elite are far from having an all-powerful position; that power is so complicated in the United States that the top businessmen scarcely understand it, much less control it; and that since 1933 the power position of businessmen has been declining rather than growing.

14. Because the spheres of their organizations have grown in recent decades, the elites of the federal administration (including the military), of the federal courts, of certain voluntary associations, and of certain education and scientific institutions, have grown more powerful. While on rare occasions they supersede in power the top political elites—as when the United States Supreme Court order[s] the state governments to end racial segregation and to reapportion their legislatures in accord with population, or when the same Court declares unconstitutional a federal statute, or when the civil rights associations pressure Congress into voting for a statute as sweeping as the Civil Rights Act of 1964, or when the labor and old-age groups pressure Congress into voting for a statute as sweeping as the Medicare Act of 1965 (although both these statutes had the full support of that significant political elite—the president)—the political elites are usually ascendant over them. The political elites control the agencies of force and the instruments of legislation, have considerable access to the mass media, and have the support of public opinion. The political elites—the two major parties, the president, the factions in the houses of Congress, the executives and legislatures of the states and large cities—are not unified of course, and they check and balance each other to a considerable extent.

15. While the two major political parties are listed by us as among the most powerful groups in the United States, their structures are quite generally misunderstood by the public and by nonspecialized intellectuals and other leadership groups. They are structured mainly as voluntary associations, with grass-roots elections that range from being wholly democratic to being "controlled" from a self-perpetuating group at the top. In some states (e.g. Texas) they are highly fractionated and

schismatic. They are structured on the layer principle: ward or county, municipality, district, and state. They scarcely exist as voluntary associations at the national level—except for the quadrennial national nominating conventions—but they exist in the caucuses of Congress, where they are the most important single influence on congressmen's voting behavior despite the bifurcation within both political parties.

16. While money in the hands of rich people opens special opportunities to democratic political processes—such as through the use of lobbyists, advertisements, and campaign contributions—these processes are by no means closed to poor people. A volunteer campaign worker for a congressman will have more influence on him than most lobbyists, and as much influence on him as a campaign contribution equivalent to the voluntary labor, roughly speaking. The fact that the political party in most states is an open, if not entirely democratic, voluntary association, and the fact that it is the single most important influence on most elected officials, also gives the nonwealthy citizen access to political power often greater than that of the wealthy, but not politically active, citizen. In this context it should be understood that most elected officials, especially at higher levels, are only partially open to pressures of any kind. Practically all congressmen, and probably most state legislators, vote for bills in accord with their own personal convictions—when they have convictions with regard to specific bills—most of the time. Where they do not have convictions regarding a specific bill, the most important influence on them are the caucus leaders or committee chairmen of their own political party who are representing the party leadership's position. The "personal convictions" factor suggests that the *initial* selection of candidates and the means which they use to get elected to Congress are the two most important links in the chain leading to the passage of bills where influence can be most effectively applied. It is for this reason that we say that voluntary campaign labor, participation in the grass-roots party (as voluntary association), and monetary campaign contributions are the most powerful instruments to influence a legislator (or probably any other elected official).

In sharper summary, [our conclusions]—in contrast with those of Mills and Hunter—are that [the] power structure of the United States is highly complex and diversified (rather than unitary and monolithic), that the political system is more or less democratic (with the glaring exception of the Negro's position until the 1960s), that in political processes the political elite is ascendant over and not subordinate to the economic elite, and that the political elite influences or controls the economic elite at least as much as the economic elite controls the political elite. To arrive at such conclusions we must in part have a contrast conception: What should the American political power structure be compared to? We believe that Mills has implicitly compared the existing

American power structure to some populist or guild socialist ideal which has never existed and which we believe could never exist considering [such] basic sociological facts . . . as the existence of culture, the value of money to most people, etc. Our implicit comparison in this book has been to any known other society, past or present (with the possible exception of the contemporary Scandinavian countries). We do not say that the multiinfluence hypothesis is entirely the fact, or that the United States is completely democratic; we simply say that such statements are more correct for the United States today than for any other society.

While the whole first chapter of this book might be repeated in the summary, we wish merely to repeat in conclusion the statement of the multiinfluence hypothesis which has guided the studies reported in this book: Segments of the economic elite have violated democratic political and legal processes, with differing degrees of effort and success in the various periods of American history, but in no recent period could they correctly be said to have controlled the elected and appointed political authorities in large measure. The relationship between the economic elite and the political authorities has been a constantly varying one of strong influence, cooperation, division of labor, and conflict, with each group influencing the other in changing proportion to some extent, and each operating independently of the other to a large extent. Today there is significant political control and limitation of certain activities of the economic elite, and there are also some significant processes by which the economic elite use their wealth to help elect some political candidates and to influence other political authorities in ways which are not available to the average citizen. Further, neither the economic elite nor the political authorities are monolithic units which act with internal consensus and coordinated action with regard to each other (or probably in any other way): in fact, there are several economic elites, which only very rarely act as units within themselves and among themselves, and there are at least two (we prefer to think of them as four) political parties which have significantly differing programs with regard to their actions toward any economic elite and each of these parties has only a partial degree of internal cohesion.

The power structure of the United States is indeed so complex that this book only touches on certain aspects of it, rather than providing full empirical evidence for these aspects. We believe, however, that enough empirical documentation has been provided to give basic support to the multiinfluence hypothesis as a general statement about what is true of the power structure of the United States.

The Irony of Democracy

27

Thomas R. Dye and L. Harmon Zeigler

The elitism [of] . . . American society is not a unique corruption of democratic ideas attributable to capitalism, war, "Watergate," the "military-industrial complex," or any other events or people in this nation. Elitism is a necessary characteristic of *all* societies. There is no "solution" to elitism, for it is not *the* problem in a democracy. There have been many mass movements, both "left" and "right" in their political ideology, which have *promised* to bring power to the people. Indeed, the world has witnessed many "successful" mass movements which have overthrown social and political systems, often at great cost to human life, promising to empower the masses. But invariably they have created new elite systems which are at least as "evil," and certainly no more democratic, than the older systems which they replaced. Revolutions come and go—but the masses remain powerless. The question, then, is not how to combat elitism or empower the masses or achieve revolution, but rather how to *build* an oderly, humane, and just society.

Let us summarize some of the reasons why mass democracy is not really feasible. First of all, in a large society the influence of a single individual on societal decisions, even assuming political equality, is so tiny as to render participation in mass democracy fruitless. As the society grows larger, the individual shrinks—in influence, power, liberty, and the capacity for shaping the decisions which affect his life. As Rousseau observed: "Thus, the subject remaining always one, the relation of the sovereign increases in proportion to the number of citizens. From which it follows that the more the state grows, the more liberty diminishes." The chance that a particular individual in a society of 200 million people can affect the outcome of an election, a referendum, or other societal decision is infinitesimal. An individual who has only one two-hundred-millionth of a say in the outcome of issues cannot be personally effective. This would be true even under conditions of perfect equality.

Inequalities among men are inevitable, and these inequalities produce differences in political power. Men are not born with the same abilities, nor can they acquire them by education. Modern democrats who recognize that inequality in *wealth* is a serious obstacle to political equality propose to eliminate such inequality by taking from the rich and giving to the poor, to achieve a "leveling" which they believe is essential to democracy. But despite their mass appeal, these schemes consistently run astray—in part because of the ingenuity of the men who have acquired wealth in defeating them. But *even if* inequalities of *wealth* were eliminated, differences among men in intelligence, organizational skills, leadership abilities, knowledge and information, drive and ambition, and interest and activity would remain. Such inequalities are sufficient to assure oligarchy, even if wealth were uniform. Moreover, de Tocqueville's warning about equality deserves consideration:

> I believe that it is easier to establish an absolute and despotic government among a people in which the conditions of society are equal than among any other; and I think that if such a government were once established among such a people, it not only would oppress men, but would eventually strip each of them of several of the highest qualities of humanity.[1]

Moreover, it is impossible for a mass to govern. The mass must delegate governing responsibilities to representatives, and by so doing they create a governing minority who will be distinguished from the masses in behavior, role, and status. This is true no matter what system of accountability is established. Delegation of authority creates a governing elite. Yet delegation is essential, if for no other reason than that people are unwilling to spend all of their time in decisionmaking activity—attending meetings, acquiring information, debating, and so on. Organization inevitably means oligarchy. Mosca demonstrated that even European socialist parties espousing democracy were in fact oligarchies:

> When his work is finished, the proletarian can think only of rest, and of getting to bed in good time. His place is taken at meetings by the bourgeois, by those who come to sell newspapers and picture postcards, by clerks, by young intellectuals who have not yet got a position in their own circle, people who are glad to hear themselves spoken of as authentic proletarians and to be glorified as the class of the future.[2]

---

1. Alexis de Tocqueville, *Democracy in America,* vol. 2 (New York: Vintage Books, 1955), p. 336.
2. Gaetano Mosca, *The Ruling Class* (New York: McGraw-Hill, 1939), p. 332.

The authoritarianism of "revolutionary" parties today confirms Mosca's earlier observations. Participatory democracy is a romantic fiction.

THE FUTILITY OF PROTEST

Many students who read this book lose their innocence. "How can I, an 18-year-old freshman from Central Oregon, ever attempt to wage battle against the all-powerful elite?" "*The Irony of Democracy* certainly does not make me eager to take advantage of the opportunity to register to vote. I almost feel it is futile." Obviously, there is frustration, a sense of helplessness, and anger over our claim . . . that "the future of American democracy depends upon the wisdom, responsibility, and resourcefulness of the nation's elite."

"Revolutionary" movements are led by elites, and even the much-heralded "counterculture' is dominated by a few intellectuals. The only way to avoid elite rule is to decentralize decisionmaking to the point of absurdity. (Even the New England town meeting drew sparse attendance.) A particularly relevant example of the inevitability of elite rule is community control over schools and other governmental functions, now so much in demand. The phrase itself is illusory, because there is really no *community* as such, but rather an articulate group of community leaders who wish to contest for power with an established elite (in most cases the central administration of schools). Paul Goodman's definition of decentralization, while not incorrect in its assumptions, misses the point: "Decentralizing is increasing the number of decisionmaking units and the number of the initiators of public policy; increasing the awareness of individuals of the whole function in which they are involved; and establishing as much face to face association with decisionmakers as possible. *People are directly engaged in the function.*"[3] Goodman's point is correct, up to a point, for (obviously) increasing the number of decisionmaking centers increases opportunities to influence decisions. But do not assume that the word "people" means "masses," for it does not. Further, do not assume that the content of decisions would be altered appreciably by a shift in the locus. A social system which has institutionalized . . . consensus values . . . is not likely to be appreciably changed by tinkering with political institutions.

At this point in the development of our society, institutional reforms (e.g., making political parties "more democratic," abolishing the seniority system in Congress, etc.) are futile. Political institutions are not agencies of change but rather reflections of the dominant values of

---

3. Paul Goodman, "Notes on Decentralization," in Irving Howe (ed.), *The Radical Papers* (Garden City, N.Y.: Doubleday, 1966), p. 190 (emphasis added).

society. Changing the shape of an institution without changing its underlying value structure accomplishes nothing.

One short-term method of change is protest. But protest are prima facie evidence of little political power. (The protests of the 1960s and early 1970s, beginning with the civil rights demonstrations and culminating in student uprisings, have in every case been undertaken because of the realization that "normal" channels of political influence were not possible.) Consequently, one cannot expect that long-term social change can develop out of protest activity.

Protest, even peaceful protest, is not viewed with favor by either elites or masses. In spite of overwhelming evidence on this point, student protesters persist in the belief that their actions will "awaken the public." Indeed, these actions will awaken the public, and its elite representatives will respond, but the response will be grim and repressive. That the backlash to protest, especially student protest, is inevitable must be understood if our argument against the possibility of radical change through protest is to be understood. As Wilson and Lipsky have argued, the protestors' basic problem is that they have no resources to exchange for political benefits, and their protests reduce even further the opportunities for coalition with groups who have actual or potential resources.[4] It is consequently of little political significance that blacks and students form an alliance, for both groups suffer from the same problem: no exchangeable resources. Take, for example, protests about the Vietnam war. According to the Survey Research Center, adult "doves" were quite antagonistic toward Vietnam War protesters: A clear majority were negative, and almost one-fourth declared themselves extremely hostile. Thus the natural target for a coalition—that part of the adult population opposed to the war—was alienated.[5]

Whether or not student protesters consciously sought coalition with those who shared their values, their tactics achieved the opposite effect. That any alternative tactic of protest could succeed in building coalitions is doubtful. But clearly the fierce hostility of the mass suggests that it is in no mood to tolerate dissent, even when peaceful. It may be helpful to potential protesters to know that, in spite of media coverage sympathetic to the youthful protesters, adults (even doves) approve of what has been labeled a police riot at the 1968 Democratic Convention in Chicago. The adult population also thought that the four slain Kent State students *got what they deserved.* That part of the electorate which was *not* alienated by students (and which agreed with their goals) came to less than 3 percent.[6]

---

4. James Q. Wilson, "The Strategy of Protest: Problems of Negro Civic Action," *Journal of Conflict Resolution* 3 (September, 1961): 291–303; Michael Lipsky, "Protest as a Political Resource," *American Political Science Review* 68 (December, 1968):1144–58.

5. Philip E. Converse et. al., "Continuity and Change in American Politics: Parties and Issues in the 1968 Election," *American Political Science Review* 69 (December, 1969):1087.

6. Ibid, p. 1088.

Student protest leaders practice selective perception with consummate skill. If there were to be "power to the people," then the student protesters would find themselves in a far worse situation than those who were so brutally attacked at the Chicago convention. A genuine "people's revolution" in America would begin with a reign of terror in which first radical students and then blacks would be threatened with brutal extermination. Of course, this is precisely the point of *The Irony of Democracy,* and why radical political movements accomplish only repressive political responses. As Slater puts it: "If the matter is left to a collision of generational change it seems to me inevitable that a radical right revolution will occur as a last-ditch effort to stave off change."[7]

A further point to be made about the "youth revolt" is that it is not anything of the sort. The vanguard of the new generation is exactly that —an elite, or "an elite-to-be." The evidence is clear that, at least politically, there is no youth culture. For instance, outside the South, Wallace captured a disproportionately high vote among those under 30. While expressing in extreme form the values of traditional America, Wallace attracted large numbers of younger voters. So let the college radical avoid deceiving himself:

> Although privileged young college students, angry at Vietnam, saw themselves as sallying forth to do battle against a corrupted and cynical older generation, a more headon confrontation at the polls, if a less apparent one, was with their own agemates who had gone from high school to the factory instead of college, and who were appalled by the collapse of patriotism and respect for the law that they saw around them.[8]

Charles Reich asserts that there is an emerging culture that is noncompetitive, more "humane, and less materialistic and confining (he calls it Consciousness III), which will spread through the entire population by the force of its own appeal and without the need for broad-gauged, concerted proselytizing.[9] He finds the new-left activism of the 1960s a failure but offers another alternative: "when self is recovered the power of the corporate state will be ended as miraculously as a kiss breaks a witch's evil enchantment."[10] But students should not take such statements seriously. If those who reject the old culture simply conduct their personal lives in a manner somewhat different from the traditional style (even to the point of living in communes), then, unless one seriously expects most adults to reverse their values, social change will be left to participants in the "old culture." Further, Consciousness III is hardly as idyllic as it is portrayed to be by Reich. Although it includes some genuinely humane values, it also includes hard narcotics, terror-

7. Philip E. Slater, *The Pursuit of Loneliness* (Boston: Beacon Press, 1970), p. 126.

8. Converse, et. al., op. cit, p. 1104.

9. Charles A. Reich, *The Greening of America* (New York: Random House, 1970).

10. Ibid., p. 295. For an alternate, more realistic appraisal, see Joe Olexa, *Search for Utopia* (doctoral dissertation, University of Oregon, 1971).

ism, violence (presumably Charles Manson and Patricia Hearst are liberated persons), but more often only superficial changes in life-style. For example, Reich attaches considerable importance to clothes and rock music. We cannot find much evidence that such symbols of change are very meaningful. That someone wears his hair long, likes rock music, and smokes grass are not usually good indicators of his political values. So the spread of Consciousness III beyond the campuses of our colleges and universities is superficial, and it contains no viable political expression.

THE DILEMMA OF AMERICAN POLITICS

The dilemma of American politics today is not really much different from that faced by the Founding Fathers in 1787—how to protect individuals in a democratic system where majorities rule from the excesses and injustices of both *majorities* and *minorities.* James Madison warned that protection against *majority* oppression "is the real object to which our inquiries are directed." But the question is not only how to restrain the masses, but also how to control elites. The threat to democratic values arises not only from unrestrained majorities, but also ruling minorities.

The masses are antidemocratic and therefore cannot be relied upon to govern democratically. Despite a superficial commitment to the symbols of democracy, the people are not attached to the ideals of individual liberty, toleration of diversity, freedoms of expression and dissent, or equality of opportunity. On the contrary, these are more likely to be the values of elites. Masses are authoritarian, intolerant, anti-intellectual, nativistic, alienated, hateful, and violent. Mass politics is extremist, unstable, and unpredictable. The masses are not committed to democratic "rules of the game"; when they are politically activated, they frequently go outside these rules to engage in violence. Moreover, mass politics frequently reflects the alienation and hostility of the masses by concentrating upon scapegoats. The scapegoats can be any minority who are somehow differentiated from the majority of the masses—Jews, blacks, Catholics, immigrants, students, intellectuals, etc.

The masses are fatally vulnerable to tyranny. Extremist movements —reflecting authoritarianism, alienation, hostility, and prejudice—are more likely to be based in masses than elites. Hannah Arendt writes: "A whole literature on mass behavior and mass psychology demonstrated and popularized the wisdom, so familiar to the ancients, of the affinity between democracy and dictatorship, between mob rule and tyranny."[11] The masses, feeling in themselves the power of the majority,

---

11. Hannah Arendt, *The Origins of Totalitarianism* (New York: Harcourt Brace Jovanovich, 1951), pp. 309–10.

cannot be trusted to restrain themselves in dealing with dissenting minorities. Tolerance of diversity is a quality acquired only through years of socialization. The authoritarianism of the masses is unavoidable, given their authoritarian childhood experiences and family relationships, their limited education and restricted cultural opportunities, their monotonous job experiences, and their orientation toward immediate gratification. Efforts to reeducate or resocialize the masses are futile. Two hundred years ago Jefferson proposed universal free public education as a prescription for mass ignorance, incompetence, and alienation. Today the masses in America average twelve years of free public education, but, if anything, they appear less capable of governing in a wise and humane fashion than the masses of Jefferson's time.

Yet we have also learned that democracy is not always safe in the hands of elites—even democratically elected elites. Throughout this nation's history elites themselves have posed threats to democracy—from the Alien and Sedition Acts, to Woodrow Wilson's "Red Scare," to Roosevelt's incarceration of thousands of Japanese-Americans, to Truman's "loyalty" programs, to the present Watergate "horrors." Restrictions on mass political activity—the forcible breakup of revolutionary parties, restrictions on the public appearances of demagogues, the suppression of literature expressing hatred or advocating revolution or violence, the equipping and training of additional security forces, the jailing of violence-prone radicals and their coconspirators, and so on—are continuing threats to a democratic society.

Elite repression—the abandonment of democratic values by the nation's established leadership—is a characteristic response to mass protest activity. While it may be comforting to argue that Watergate was unique and unprecedented, or that it was a product of a conservative ideology, neither statement is true. *All* elites are capable of repressive measures when they feel threatened by mass unrest.

Of course, repression in a free society is a contradiction. We cannot logically curtail liberty—even the liberty of a demagogue—in order to preserve a free society. James Madison considered and rejected repression as a means of controlling mass movements, and pointed out the inconsistency of repression in a free society:

> Liberty is to faction [mass movements] what air is to fire, an element without which it instantly expires. But it could not be less folly to abolish liberty, which is essential to political life, because it nourishes faction, than it would be to wish the annihilation of air, which is essential to animal life, because it imparts to fire its destructive agency.[12]

In short, repression is not really a serious instrument for an elite committed to the values of individual dignity, personal freedom, and tolerance of diversity.

---

12. James Madison, Alexander Hamilton, and John Jay, *The Federalist,* No. 10.

If this dilemma—the protection of individual liberties against the assaults of majority and elite excess—is troublesome today, there is every indication that it may become even more serious in the future.

In the winter of 1973 to 1974, as Americans shivered in the dawn waiting for a few gallons of gasoline, suddenly the warnings of ecologists became alarmingly real. Similarly, as inflation cut deeply into the earning power of the average wage-earner, the predictions of economists became tangible and terrifying. Americans perceived not only an abstract decline in the quality of life, but a tangible deterioration. Nineteen seventy-three may prove to be a year which—in retrospect—divided one age (the age of affluence) from another (the age of scarcity).

The political processes of the first age may prove to be luxuries which cannot be afforded in the second. In an age of affluence, democracies—albeit the symbolic variety described in these pages—could be tolerated because there had been considerable slack in the system. The economic problems of industrial societies—how to achieve an appropriate distribution of existing and future wealth—was one that could be debated and subjected to interelite negotiation. The problem was one of *distribution*. The stakes of the dispute was serious, but not too serious. Thus, "wars on poverty" come and go, the distribution of wealth remains stable, but protest is confined and isolated, as was the case with the riots of the 1960s.

In an age of scarcity, hardship is much more widespread, as the problem shifts from distribution of abundant resources to *conservation* of scarce resources. Chillingly symptomatic of the protest of the new age was the truckers' strike of 1974, in response to scarce and expensive fuel. Truckers—previous beneficiaries of the age of affluence or "middle-Americans"—became so outraged that they engaged briefly in the techniques of protest previously confined to the ghetto. Two truckers were killed, and dozens were injured by gunshot, rocks, and bottles. National Guardsmen were called out in eight states.

There are several significant aspects to the truckers' strike. First, as previously mentioned, it was led by frustrated *middle*-Americans. Second, the source of the truckers' frustration was *not* the policy of the United States or any political subdivision. Rather, the scarcity of fuel —and the attendant rise in price—were caused by a complicated *international* reallocation of resources. In the 1960s, the national government at least had the authority to provide symbolic satisfaction to rioters. In the 1970s, the nation-state may no longer be the effective decision-maker.

In an age of scarcity, problems which materially affect an individual's quality of life may be so linked with international systems that national decisions are futile. Examples come readily to mind. Consider, for instance, the "population explosion." World population is approximately 3.6 billion. However, one-third of the population lives in areas —such as the United States—where population stability is being achieved. For such areas, population will become stable at about 50 percent larger than it is now. For the remainder of the world, the balance of population and available resources is approaching a grim solution; mass starvation. Assuming, therefore, that the "developed" nations effectively stabilize population, will they not in any case be victims of the scarcity which ensues as the world's resources are exhausted?

Similarly, pollution is a global problem, as is inflation. In these cases there is little that a nation-state, acting individually, can do. Additionally, there is the problem of the technology, or competence, required to understand, much less influence, the problems which accompany the age of scarcity. We know that masses have little knowledge of contemporary politics; what can we expect them to understand about international reallocation of scarce resources? Indeed, we now know that even recent American presidents, especially Nixon, found themselves incapable of understanding the complexities of the international monetary system.

Size and complexity, then, reduce the notion of participation by masses-and in some cases, elected elites—to an unrealistic dream. Moreover, the continued inability of national governments to provide relief can lead to widespread civil unrest, of which the truckers' strike is indicative. Necessarily, governments' attention would shift from resource allocation to controlling civil unrest. In times of anxiety, the pressures toward authoritarianism are intense, as we learned from Watergate.

However, even assuming no widespread social unrest, there are other reasons why "democracy" may be unsuitable to an age of scarcity. An end to democracy, accompanied by a drastic restriction of individual liberty, may be the only course available. As Heilbroner predicts: ". . . the passage through the gantlet ahead may be possible only under governments capable of rallying obedience far more effectively than would be possible in a democratic setting. If the issue for mankind is survival, such governments may be unavoidable, even necessary."[13]

If the present political game is survival, rather than the division of abundant resources, the power of *technological elites* over elected elites may relegate government "by the people" (even when "the people" are the elite) to antiquity. The greater the technological power we bring to bear in the struggle against scarcity, the more the political power of existing elites must be sacrificed to the technological elite. In a world where only the most careful planning can prevent rapid deterioration of the quality of life, social control, drastic restrictions in individual freedom, and rule by "experts" are inevitable. Bargaining among competing elites, much less mass participation, could not be tolerated.

---

13. Robert L. Heilbroner, *An Inquiry into the Human Prospect* (New York: W. W. Norton & Co. Inc., 1974), p. 110.

The Structure of Power in American Society

28

C. Wright Mills

I

Power has to do with whatever decisions men make about the arrangements under which they live, and about the events which make up the history of their times. Events that are beyond human decision do happen; social arrangements do change without benefit of explicit decision. But in so far as such decisions are made, the problem of who is involved in making them is the basic problem of power. In so far as they could be made but are not, the problem becomes who fails to make them?

We cannot today merely assume that in the last resort men must always be governed by their own consent. For among the means of power which now prevail is the power to manage and to manipulate the consent of men. That we do not know the limits of such power, and that we hope it does have limits, does not remove the fact that much power today is successfully employed without the sanction of the reason or the conscience of the obedient.

Surely nowadays we need not argue that, in the last resort, coercion is the "final" form of power. But then, we are by no means constantly at the last resort. Authority (power that is justified by the beliefs of the voluntarily obedient) and manipulation (power that is wielded unbeknown to the powerless)—must also be considered, along with coercion. In fact, the three types must be sorted out whenever we think about power.

In the modern world, we must bear in mind, power is often not so authoritative as it seemed to be in the medieval epoch: ideas which

From *Power, Politics and People: The Collected Essays of C. Wright Mills,* edited by Irving Louis Horowitz. Copyright © 1963 by The Estate of C. Wright Mills. Reprinted by permission of Oxford University Press, Inc.

justify rulers no longer seem so necessary to their exercise of power. At least for many of the great decisions of our time—especially those of an international sort—mass "persuasion" has not been "necessary"; the fact is simply accomplished. Furthermore, such ideas as are available to the powerful are often neither taken up nor used by them. Such ideologies usually arise as a response to an effective debunking of power; in the United States such opposition has not been effective enough recently to create the felt need for new ideologies of rule.

There has in fact come about a situation in which many who have lost faith in prevailing loyalties have not acquired new ones, and so pay no attention to politics of any kind. They are not radical, not liberal, not conservative, not reactionary. They are inactionary. They are out of it. If we accept the Greek's definition of the idiot as an altogether private man, then we must conclude that many American citizens are now idiots. And I should not be surprised, although I do not know, if there were not some such idiots even in Germany. This—and I use the word with care—this spiritual condition seems to me the key to many modern troubles of political intellectuals, as well as the key to much political bewilderment in modern society. Intellectual "conviction" and moral "belief" are not necessary, in either the rulers or the ruled, for a ruling power to persist and even to flourish. So far as the role of ideologies is concerned, their frequent absences and the prevalence of mass indifference are surely two of the major political facts about the western societies today.

How large a role any explicit decisions do play in the making of history is itself a historical problem. For how large that role may be depends very much upon the means of power that are available at any given time in any given society. In some societies, the innumerable actions of innumerable men modify their milieux, and so gradually modify the structure itself. These modifications—the course of history —go on behind the backs of men. History is drift, although in total "men make it." Thus innumerable entrepreneurs and innumerable consumers by ten-thousand decisions per minute may shape and reshape the free-market economy. Perhaps this was the chief kind of limitation Marx had in mind when he wrote, in *The 18th Brumaire*, that: "Men make their own history, but they do not make it just as they please; they do not make it under circumstances chosen by themselves. . . ."

But in other societies—certainly in the United States and in the Soviet Union today—a few men may be so placed within the structure that by their decisions they modify the milieux of many other men, and in fact nowadays the structural conditions under which most men live. Such elites of power also make history under circumstances not chosen altogether by themselves, yet compared with other men, and compared with other periods of world history, these circumstances do indeed seem less limiting.

I should contend that "men are free to make history," but that some men are indeed much freer than others. For such freedom requires access to the means of decision and of power by which history can now be made. It has not always been so made; but in the later phases of the modern epoch it is. It is with reference to this epoch that I am contending that if men do not make history, they tend increasingly to become the utensils of historymakers as well as the mere objects of history.

The history of modern society may readily be understood as the story of the enlargement and the centralization of the means of power —in economic, in political, and in military institutions. The rise of industrial society has involved these developments in the means of economic production. The rise of the nation-state has involved similar developments in the means of violence and in those of political administration.

In the western societies, such transformations have generally occurred gradually, and many cultural traditions have restrained and shaped them. In most of the Soviet societies, they are happening very rapidly indeed and without the great discourse of western civilization, without the Renaissance and without the Reformation, which so greatly strengthened and gave political focus to the idea of freedom. In those societies, the enlargement and the coordination of all the means of power has occurred more brutally, and from the beginning under tightly centralized authority. But in both types, the means of power have now become international in scope and similar in form. To be sure, each of them has its own ups and downs; neither is as yet absolute; how they are run differs quite sharply.

Yet so great is the reach of the means of violence, and so great the economy required to produce and support them, that we have in the immediate past witnessed the consolidation of these two world centers, either of which dwarfs the power of ancient Rome. As we pay attention to the awesome means of power now available to quite small groups of men we come to realize that Caesar could do less with Rome than Napoleon with France; Napoleon less with France then Lenin with Russia. But what was Caesar's power at its height compared with the power of the changing inner circles of Soviet Russia and the temporary administrations of the United States? We come to realize—indeed they continually remind us—how a few men have access to the means by which in a few days continents can be turned into thermonuclear wastelands. That the facilities of power are so enormously enlarged and so decisively centralized surely means that the powers of quite small groups of men, which we may call elites, are now of literally inhuman consequence.

My concern here is not with the international scene but with the United States in the middle of the twentieth century. I must emphasize "in the middle of the twentieth century" because in our attempt to understand any society we come upon images which have been drawn from its past and which often confuse our attempt to confront its present reality. That is one minor reason why history is the shank of any social science: we must study it if only to rid ourselves of it. In the United States, there are indeed many such images and usually they have to do with the first half of the nineteenth century. At that time the economic facilities of the United States were very widely dispersed and subject to little or to no central authority. The state watched in the night but was without decisive voice in the day. One man meant one rifle and the militia were without centralized orders.

Any American as old-fashioned as I can only agree with R. H. Tawney that "whatever the future may contain, the past has shown no more excellent social order than that in which the mass of the people were the masters of the holdings which they ploughed and the tools with which they worked, and could boast . . . 'It is a quietness to a man's mind to live upon his own and to know his heir certain.' "

But then we must immediately add: all that is of the past and of little relevance to our understanding of the United States today. Within this society three broad levels of power may now be distinguished. I shall begin at the top and move downward.

II

The power to make decisions of national and international consequence is now so clearly seated in political, military, and economic institutions that other areas of society seem off to the side and, on occasion, readily subordinated to these. The scattered institutions of religion, education, and family are increasingly shaped by the big three, in which historymaking decisions now regularly occur. Behind this fact there is all the push and drive of a fabulous technology; for these three institutional orders have incorporated this technology and now guide it, even as it shapes and paces their development.

As each has assumed its modern shape, its effects upon the other two have become greater, and the traffic between the three has increased. There is no longer, on the one hand, an economy, and, on the other, a political order, containing a military establishment unimportant to politics and to moneymaking. There is a political economy numerously linked with military order and decision. This triangle of power is now a structural fact, and it is the key to any understanding of the higher circles in America today. For as each of these domains has coincided with the others, as decisions in each have become broader, the leading men of each—the high military, the corporation executives, the political directorate—have tended to come together to form the power elite of America.

The political order, once composed of several dozen states with a weak federal center, has become an executive apparatus which has taken up into itself many powers previously scattered, legislative as well as administrative, and which now reaches into all parts of the social structure. The long-time tendency of business and government to become more closely connected has, since World War II, reached a new point of explicitness. Neither can now be seen clearly as a distinct world. The growth of executive government does not mean merely the "enlargement of government" as some kind of autonomous bureaucracy; under American conditions, it has meant the ascendancy of the corporation man into political eminence. Already during the New Deal, such men had joined the political directorate; as of World War II they came to dominate it. Long involved with government, now they have moved into quite full direction of the economy of the war effort and of the postwar era.

The economy, once a great scatter of small productive units in somewhat automatic balance, has become internally dominated by a few hundred corporations, administratively and politically interrelated, which together hold the keys to economic decision. This economy is at once a permanent-war economy and a private-corporation economy. The most important relations of the corporation to the state now rest on the coincidence between military and corporate interests, as defined by the military and the corporate rich, and accepted by politicians and public. Within the elite as a whole, this coincidence of military domain and corporate realm strengthens both of them and further subordinates the merely political man. Not the party politician, but the corporation executive, is now more likely to sit with the military to answer the question: what is to be done?

The military order, once a slim establishment in a context of civilian distrust, has become the largest and most expensive feature of government; behind smiling public relations, it has all the grim and clumsy efficiency of a great and sprawling bureaucracy. The high military have gained decisive political and economic relevance. The seemingly permanent military threat places a premium upon them and virtually all political and economic actions are now judged in terms of military definitions of reality; the higher military have ascended to a firm position within the power elite of our time.

In part at least this is a result of an historical fact, pivotal for the years since 1939: the attention of the elite has shifted from domestic problems—centered in the thirties around slump—to international problems—centered in the forties and fifties around war. By long historical usage, the government of the United States has been shaped by domestic clash and balance; it does not have suitable agencies and traditions for the democratic handling of international affairs. In considerable part, it is in this vacuum that the power elite has grown.

1. To understand the unity of this power elite, we must pay attention to the psychology of its several members in their respective milieux. In so far as the power elite is composed of men of similar origin and education, of similar career and style of life, their unity may be said to rest upon the fact that they are of similar social type, and to lead to the fact of their easy intermingling. This kind of unity reaches its frothier apex in the sharing of that prestige which is to be had in the world of the celebrity. It achieves a more solid culmination in the fact of the interchangeability of positions between the three dominant institutional orders. It is revealed by considerable traffic of personnel within and between these three, as well as by the rise of specialized go-betweens as in the new style high-level lobbying.

2. Behind such psychological and social unity are the structure and the mechanics of those institutional hierarchies over which the political directorate, the corporate rich, and the high military now preside. How each of these hierarchies is shaped and what relations it has with the others determine in large part the relations of their rulers. Were these hierarchies scattered and disjointed, then their respective elites might tend to be scattered and disjointed; but if they have many interconnections and points of coinciding interest, then their elites tend to form a coherent kind of grouping. The unity of the elite is not a simple reflection of the unity of institutions, but men and institutions are always related; that is why we must understand the elite today in connection with such institutional trends as the development of a permanent-war establishment alongside a privately incorporated economy inside a virtual political vacuum. For the men at the top have been selected and formed by such institutional trends.

3. Their unity, however, does not rest solely upon psychological similarity and social intermingling, nor entirely upon the structural blending of commanding positions and common interests. At times it is the unity of a more explicit coordination.

To say that these higher circles are increasingly coordinated, that this is *one* basis of their unity, and that at times—as during open war —such coordination is quite wilful, is not to say that the coordination is total or continuous, or even that it is very surefooted. Much less is it to say that the power elite has emerged as the realization of a plot. Its rise cannot be adequately explained in any psychological terms.

Yet we must remember that institutional trends may be defined as opportunities by those who occupy the command posts. Once such opportunities are recognized, men may avail themselves of them. Certain types of men from each of these three areas, more farsighted than others, have actively promoted the liaison even before it took its truly modern shape. Now more have come to see that their several interests can more easily be realized if they work together, in informal as well as in formal ways, and accordingly they have done so.

The idea of the power elite is of course an interpretation. It rests upon and it enables us to make sense of major institutional trends, the social similarities and psychological affinities of the men at the top. But the idea is also based upon what has been happening on the middle and lower levels of power, to which I now turn.

III

There are of course other interpretations of the American system of power. The most usual is that it is a moving balance of many competing interests. The image of balance, at least in America, is derived from the idea of the economic market: in the nineteenth century, the balance was thought to occur between a great scatter of individuals and enterprises; in the twentieth century, it is thought to occur between great interest blocs. In both views, the politician is the key man of power because he is the broker of many conflicting powers.

I believe that the balance and the compromise in American society —the "countervailing powers" and the "veto groups" of parties and associations, of strata and unions—must now be seen as having mainly to do with the middle levels of power. It is these middle levels that the political journalist and the scholar of politics are most likely to understand and to write about —if only because, being mainly middle class themselves, they are closer to them. Moreover these levels provide the noisy content of most "political" news and gossip; the images of these levels are more or less in accord with the folklore of how democracy works; and, if the master-image of balance is accepted, many intellectuals, especially in their current patrioteering, are readily able to satisfy such political optimism as they wish to feel. Accordingly, liberal interpretations of what is happening in the United States are now virtually the only interpretations that are widely distributed.

But to believe that the power system reflects a balancing society is, I think, to confuse the present era with earlier times, and to confuse its top and bottom with its middle levels.

By the top levels, as distinguished from the middle, I intend to refer, first of all, to the scope of the decisions that are made. At the top today, these decisions have to do with all the issues of war and peace. They have also to do with slump and poverty which are now so very much problems of international scope. I intend also to refer to whether or not the groups that struggle politically have a chance to gain the positions from which such top decisions are made, and indeed whether their members do usually hope for such top national command. Most of the competing interests which make up the clang and clash of American politics are strictly concerned with their slice of the existing pie. Labor unions, for example, certainly have no policies of an international sort other than those which given unions adopt for the strict economic protection of their members; neither do farm organizations. The actions of such middle-level powers may indeed have consequence for top-level policy; certainly at times they hamper these policies. But they are not truly concerned with them, which means of course that their influence tends to be quite irresponsible.

The facts of the middle levels may in part be understood in terms of the rise of the power elite. The expanded and centralized and interlocked hierarchies over which the power elite preside have encroached upon the old balance and relegated it to the middle level. But there are also independent developments of the middle levels. These, it seems to me, are better understood as an affair of entrenched and provincial demands than as a center of national decision. As such, the middle level often seems much more of a stalemate than a moving balance.

1. The middle level of politics is not a forum in which there are debated the big decisions of national and international life. Such debate is not carried on by nationally responsible parties representing and clarifying alternative policies. There are no such parties in the United States. More and more, fundamental issues never come to any point or decision before the Congress, much less before the electorate in party campaigns. In the case of Formosa, in the spring of 1955 the Congress abdicated all debate concerning events and decisions which surely bordered on war. The same is largely true of the 1957 crisis in the Middle East. Such decisions now regularly bypass the Congress, and are never clearly focused issues for public decision.

The American political campaign distracts attention from national and international issues, but that is not to say that there are no issues in these campaigns. In each district and state, issues are set up and watched by organized interests of sovereign local importance. The professional politician is of course a party politician, and the two parties are semifeudal organizations: they trade patronage and other favors for votes and for protection. The differences between them, so far as national issues are concerned, are very narrow and very mixed up. Often each seems to be fifty parties, one to each state; and accordingly, the politician as campaigner and as Congressman is not concerned with national party lines, if any are discernible. Often he is not subject to any effective national party discipline. He speaks for the interests of his own constituency, and he is concerned with national issues only in so far as they affect the interests effectively organized there, and hence his chances of reelection. That is why, when he does speak of national matters, the result is so often such an empty rhetoric. Seated in his sovereign locality, the politician is not at the national summit. He is on and of the middle levels of power.

2. Politics is not an arena in which free and independent organizations truly connect the lower and middle levels of society with the top levels of decision. Such organizations are not an effective and major part

of American life today. As more people are drawn into the political arena, their associations become mass in scale, and the power of the individual becomes dependent upon them; to the extent that they are effective, they have become larger, and to that extent they have become less accessible to the influence of the individual. This is a central fact about associations in any mass society; it is of most consequence for political parties and for trade unions.

In the thirties, it often seemed that labor would become an insurgent power independent of corporation and state. Organized labor was then emerging for the first time on an American scale, and the only political sense of direction it needed was the slogan, "organize the unorganized." Now without the mandate of the slump, labor remains without political direction. Instead of economic and political struggles it has become deeply entangled in administrative routines with both corporation and state. One of its major functions, as a vested interest of the new society, is the regulation of such irregular tendencies as may occur among the rank and file.

There is nothing, it seems to me, in the makeup of the current labor leadership to allow us to expect that it can or that it will lead rather than merely react. In so far as it fights at all, it fights over a share of the goods of a single way of life and not over that way of life itself. The typical labor leader in the U.S.A. today is better understood as an adaptive creature of the main business drift than as an independent actor in a truly national context.

3. The idea that this society is a balance of powers requires us to assume that the units in balance are of more or less equal power and that they are truly independent of one another. These assumptions have rested, it seems clear, upon the historical importance of a large and independent middle class. In the latter nineteenth century and during the Progressive Era, such a class of farmers and small businessmen fought politically—and lost—their last struggle for a paramount role in national decision. Even then, their aspirations seemed bound to their own imagined past.

This old, independent middle class has of course declined. On the most generous count, it is now 40 percent of the total middle class (at most 20 percent of the total labor force). Moreover, it has become politically as well as economically dependent upon the state, most notably in the case of the subsidized farmer.

The *new* middle class of white-collar employees is certainly not the political pivot of any balancing society. It is in no way politically unified. Its unions, such as they are, often serve merely to incorporate it as hanger-on of the labor interest. For a considerable period, the old middle class *was* an independent base of power; the new middle class cannot be. Political freedom and economic security *were* anchored in small and independent properties; they are not anchored in the worlds of the white-collar job. Scattered property holders were economically united by more or less free markets; the jobs of the new middle class are integrated by corporate authority. Economically, the white-collar classes are in the same condition as wage workers; politically, they are in a worse condition, for they are not organized. They are no vanguard of historic change; they are at best a rear guard of the welfare state.

The agrarian revolt of the nineties, the small-business revolt that has been more or less continuous since the eighties, the labor revolt of the thirties—each of these has failed as an independent movement which could countervail against the powers that be; they have failed as politically autonomous third parties. But they have succeeded, in varying degree, as interests vested in the expanded corporation and state; they have succeeded as parochial interests seated in particular districts, in local divisions of the two parties, and in the Congress. What they would become, in short, are well-established features of the *middle* levels of balancing power, on which we may now observe all those strata and interests which in the course of American history have been defeated in their bids for top power or which have never made such bids.

Fifty years ago many observers thought of the American state as a mask behind which an invisible government operated. But nowadays, much of what was called the old lobby, visible or invisible, is part of the quite visible government. The "governmentalization of the lobby" has proceeded in both the legislative and the executive domain, as well as between them. The executive bureaucracy becomes not only the center of decision but also the arena within which major conflicts of power are resolved or denied resolution. "Administration" replaces electoral politics; the maneuvering of cliques (which include leading Senators as well as civil servants) replaces the open clash of parties.

The shift of corporation men into the political directorate has accelerated the decline of the politicians in the Congress to the middle levels of power; the formation of the power elite rests in part upon this relegation. It rests also upon the semiorganized stalemate of the interests of sovereign localities into which the legislative function has so largely fallen; upon the virtually complete absence of a civil service that is a politically neutral but politically relevant depository of brainpower and executive skill; and it rests upon the increased official secrecy behind which great decisions are made without benefit of public or even of Congressional debate.

IV

There is one last belief upon which liberal observers everywhere base their interpretations and rest their hopes. That is the idea of the public and the associated idea of public opinion. Conservative thinkers, since the French Revolution, have of course Viewed With Alarm the rise of the public, which they have usually called the masses, or something to that effect. "The populace is sovereign," wrote Gustave LeBon, "and the tide of barbarism mounts." But surely those who have supposed the masses to be well on their way to triumph are mistaken. In our time, the influence of publics or of masses within political life is in fact decreasing, and such influence as on occasion they do have tends, to an unknown but increasing degree, to be guided by the means of mass communication.

In a society of publics, discussion is the ascendant means of communication, and the mass media, if they exist, simply enlarge and animate this discussion, linking one face-to-face public with the discussions of another. In a mass society, the dominant type of communication is the formal media, and publics become mere markets for these media: the "public" of a radio program consists of all those exposed to it. When we try to look upon the United States today as a society of publics, we realize that it has moved a considerable distance along the road to the mass society.

In official circles, the very term, "the public," has come to have a phantom meaning, which dramatically reveals its eclipse. The deciding elite can identify some of those who clamor publicly as "Labor," others as "Business," still others as "Farmer." But these are not the public. "The public" consists of the unidentified and the nonpartisan in a world of defined and partisan interests. In this faint echo of the classic notion, the public is composed of these remnants of the old and new middle classes whose interests are not explicitly defined, organized, or clamorous. In a curious adaptation, "the public" often becomes, in administrative fact, "the disengaged expert," who, although never so well informed, has never taken a clearcut and public stand on controversial issues. He is the "public" member of the board, the commission, the committee. What "the public" stands for, accordingly, is often a vagueness of policy (called "openmindedness"), a lack of involvement in public affairs (known as "reasonableness"), and a professional disinterest (known as "tolerance").

All this is indeed far removed from the eighteenth century idea of the public of public opinion. The idea parallels the economic idea of the magical market. Here is the market composed for freely competing entrepreneurs; there is the public composed of circles of people in discussion. As price is the result of anonymous, equally weighted, bargaining individuals, so public opinion is the result of each man's having thought things out for himself and then contributing his voice to the great chorus. To be sure, some may have more influence on the state of opinion than others, but no one group monopolizes the discussion, or by itself determines the opinions that prevail.

In this classic image, the people are presented with problems. They discuss them. They formulate viewpoints. These viewpoints are organized, and they compete. One viewpoint "wins out." Then the people act on this view, or their representatives are instructed to act it out, and this they promptly do.

Such are the images of democracy which are still used as working justifications of power in America. We must now recognize this description as more a fairy tale than a useful approximation. The issues that now shape man's fate are neither raised nor decided by any public at large. The idea of a society that is at bottom composed of publics is not a matter of fact; it is the proclamation of an ideal, and as well the assertion of a legitimation masquerading as fact.

I cannot here describe the several great forces within American society as well as elsewhere which have been at work in the debilitation of the public. I want only to remind you that publics, like free associations, can be deliberately and suddenly smashed, or they can more slowly wither away. But whether smashed in a week or withered in a generation, the demise of the public must be seen in connection with the rise of centralized organizations, with all their new means of power, including those of the mass media of distraction. These, we now know, often seem to expropriate the rationality and the will of the terrorized or— as the case may be—the voluntarily indifferent society of masses. In the more democratic process of indifference, the remnants of such publics as remain may only occasionally be intimidated by fanatics in search of "disloyalty." But regardless of that, they lose their will for decision because they do not possess the instruments for decision; they lose their sense of political belonging because they do not belong; they lose their political will because they see no way to realize it.

The political structure of a modern democratic state requires that such a public as is projected by democratic theorists not only exist but that it be the very forum within which a politics of real issues is enacted.

It requires a civil service that is firmly linked with the world of knowledge and sensibility, and which is composed of skilled men who, in their careers and in their aspirations, are truly independent of any private, which is to say corporation, interests.

It requires nationally responsible parties which debate openly and clearly the issues which the nation, and indeed the world, now so rigidly confronts.

It requires an intelligentsia, inside as well as outside the universities, who carry on the big discourse of the Western world, and whose work is relevant to and influential among parties and movements and publics.

And it certainly requires, as a fact of power, that there be free associations standing between families and smaller communities and publics, on the one hand, and the state, the military, the corporation, on the other. For unless these do exist, there are no vehicles for reasoned opinion, no instruments for the rational exertion of public will.

Such democratic formations are not now ascendant in the power structure of the United States, and accordingly the men of decision are not men selected and formed by careers within such associations and by their performance before such publics. The top of modern American society is increasingly unified, and often seems wilfully coordinated: at the top there has emerged an elite whose power probably exceeds that of any small group of men in world history. The middle levels are often a drifting set of stalemated forces: the middle does not link the bottom with the top. The bottom of this society is politically fragmented, and even as a passive fact, increasingly powerless: at the bottom there is emerging a mass society.

These developments, I believe, can be correctly understood neither in terms of the liberal nor the Marxian interpretation of politics and history. Both these ways of thought arose as guidelines to reflection about a type of society which does not now exist in the United States. We confront there a new kind of social structure which embodies elements and tendencies of all modern society, but in which they have assumed a more naked and flamboyant prominence.

That does not mean that we must give up the ideals of these classic political expectations. I believe that both have been concerned with the problem of rationality and of freedom: liberalism, with freedom and rationality as supreme facts about the individual; Marxism, as supreme facts about man's role in the political making of history. What I have said here, I suppose, may be taken as an attempt to make evident why the ideas of freedom and of rationality now so often seem so ambiguous in the new society of the United States of America.

What Rules America?

29

Andrew Hacker

Why can't we deal with class? Terms like "upper middle" and "lower middle" refer to style and sophistication, not the deeper divisions of social life. On the whole we prefer to circumvent the question of class. We think of cities as being composed of "ghettos" and "white ethnics" and "the aged." Discussing families on welfare or crime in the streets, we speak of blacks and Puerto Ricans. Sociologists neutralize the subject by referring to "stratification." Or they tell us it is "ambiguous" and "complex." The Census once reported that 70 percent of all Americans show some "inconsistency" between their earnings, education, and occupations. We all know Yale graduates who are driving taxis.

Yet we know America has classes, and that they are more than temporary way stations. No matter how we divide up Americans according to culture, careers, even income, power is at the heart of the question. Some people have more freedom, more independence, than others. Some are buffeted about from birth to death, never in a position to bend events or answer back to authority. Class may confer power over others; but in personal life it affects how you can make the world work on your behalf. Traditionally class has depended on property. In the classical couplings—patrician and plebeian, lord and serf, guild master and journeyman—one class had holdings of substance. When Marx spoke of the bourgeoisie, he meant people owning a mill with at least 100 workers and living in a town house with servants.

Nowadays one can go a long way in America without property. Indeed, a person can achieve influence and independence without ever accumulating an estate of six figures. Hence all the emphasis, in writing about influence, on officials and administrators whose power derives from office rather than ownership. Hence too the stress on seniority,

Reprinted with permission from *The New York Review of Books* 22, No. 7 (May 1, 1975): 9–13. Copyright © 1975 Nyrev, Inc. Footnotes have been renumbered.

tenure, and professional certification: securities upheld by law even if
not entirely transmissible to one's heirs. However, the current state of
the economy has shown how flimsy some of these underpinnings can
be. Seniority isn't worth much if one's company goes out of business.
Having an architect's license this year is hardly a guarantee of comfort.
After floating through the sixties on whimsical balance sheets, we are
again learning that there is no substitute for wealth. Moreover the desire
to accumulate holdings is still strong: witness Spiro Agnew, William
Ronan, and Otto Kerner. Doctors, lawyers, and businessmen, as they
reach their forties, see the prospect of a cool million they can call their
own, notwithstanding neglected wives, disaffected children, and involvements in dubious projects.

Which Americans should we call rich? The richest 5 percent of our
population holds 40 percent of the nation's wealth. However, 5 percent
of the population is three million families, or anyone earning at least
$30,000 a year. G. William Domhoff—of whom more later—concen-
trates on the top 1 percent, which still means 600,000 households and
a bottom line of about $60,000. The trouble with both estimates is that
they include too many people who, while well off, are still what we
think of as upper-middle-class.

A surprising amount of information on income is available, so long
as we realize that agencies collect figures in different ways and for
different purposes. Moreover, by the time the tables get published the
statistics can be out of date. The 1970 census, for example, has some
interesting figures; but they are based on incomes for 1969, which is a
long way back. At that time, 390,708 of the country's seventy million
households had incomes in excess of $50,000, the top category in the
census summaries.[1] (A "household" for the census consists either of a
family or a single person living alone or with an unrelated roommate.
Two unmarried people who share the same bed are counted as two
households.) Almost half of these $50,000 households had at least two
and often three wage-earning members. So along with affluent executives, the bracket includes families in which on Friday night everyone
empties his pockets onto the kitchen table. The census also found that
in 1969 the country contained 13,457 households with incomes of over
$50,000, even though none of the members worked. This is apparently
what we have in the way of retired, widowed, and otherwise idle rich.

Still, as was intimated earlier, within a top bracket beginning as low
as $50,000 will be many salaried and professional people who are well
off but still not what we mean by rich. For more detailed information
on the higher reaches, our best information comes from the Internal
Revenue Service, which does a lot of unpublicized things with our tax

1. *Census of Population, 1970: Detailed Characteristics.* Final Report PC(1)-D1 (U.S. Government Printing Office, 1973), Table 252.

returns. (Even when the rich pay little or no taxes, they still submit returns.) As a result, IRS statistics are not precisely comparable with those of the census. Thus while the census uncovered 390,708 households with over $50,000 in 1969, the Internal Revenue Service received 410,521 such returns that year. One reason for the discrepancy is that in some cases wives and husbands file separately; another is that IRS does a better job than the census at finding certain kinds of people. (The evidence indicates that citizens are about equally truthful in answering the two arms of government.) IRS uses its "adjusted gross income" figure rather than the full total. However, for most households the difference between the two is not great. The latest IRS breakdowns cover 1972 incomes, as listed on 78 million returns.[2] These include 43 million joint husband-wife declarations, with most of the remaining 35 million coming from single persons, of whom 3.6 million were heads of families. (See Table 29–1.)

While $50,000 clearly puts one at the top of the pyramid—only three-quarters of 1 percent of the country's households reach that level —most people in that bracket still get most of their income from salaries and other payments for services. It is only when one passes the $200,000 mark that property becomes the major source of income. Most of the households in the $50,000 to $200,000 range represent the executive and professional explosion we have experienced since World War II. These people tend to be experts and administrators rather than owners; and because they earn their money, a disproportionate part of it goes straight to the government in taxes. Moreover when they do invest, they are not terribly good at it. Their ratio of capital losses to capital gains is over twice that for households above $200,000.

All things considered, the country's propertied class can be defined as the individuals or families or households who file the top 22,887 returns. Representing three one-hundredths of 1 percent of all filings, their average income ($407,000) amounted to forty-two times the national average ($9,600) for 1972, and their unearned income ($290,000) came to 337 times that for the average household ($860). But all this simply lets us know what people took in during a given year. Indeed, in the case of the rich, it tells only what they *decided* to take in. It does not apply to the extent and distribution of personal holdings.

On wealth itself we have no reliable information. Neither the census nor Internal Revenue has ever asked people to declare their holdings. What you own is nobody's business while you still have breath in your body, the only exception being if you happen to run for or hold office in a jurisdiction where disclosures are mandatory. Among our rights to privacy, this one seems paramount. And were we to require account-

---

2. *Statistics of Income, 1972: Individual Income Tax Returns,* Internal Revenue Service (U.S. Government Printing Office, 1974), Table 4.

ings, there would still be problems. The cash value of real estate, mineral rights, or art objects often depends on which appraiser you retain. Moreover a labyrinth of brokers, dealers, street names, holding companies, and family foundations can keep the curious from knowing a particular person's holdings. It takes the researchers at *Fortune* and *Business Week* the better part of a year to run down estimates on well-known families, and even there the chief source is gossip.

Hence we should be grateful to Professor James D. Smith of Pennsylvania State University for his efforts in this matter.[3] He analyzes estate records—the sums people declare when they die—to obtain an idea of how much is still held by the living. The method has plenty of pitfalls, of which Smith is painstakingly aware. Still it is the best technique we have. Unfortunately it takes time to collect and compute the figures. (His new book works with 1969 data.) Even so, Smith and his colleagues have given us some information where previously we had none whatever. . . . Vito Natrella calculates that in 1969 some 120,000 people had a net worth of at least $1 million. However, this valuation includes everything from yachts and villas to gas leases and sculptures, in addition to equities in self-owned business and practices. To get more accurate figures it is probably best to shelve the hardware and count only negotiable securities. By and large this means corporate stocks. (Despite tax breaks, the rich put only about $15 into bonds for every $100 they hold in stocks.) According to Smith, approximately 55,000 living Americans had stocks worth $1 million in 1969, and of these 5,000 held more than $5 million.[4] Together these 55,000 people owned about 18 percent of the country's personally held corporate stock. If we want evidence of concentrated wealth, this is probably the best statistic to use. Happily, it approximates the Internal Revenue total on $200,000 filings. Rather than Ferdinand Lundberg's legendary sixty families, America's rich consist of 50,000 to 60,000 people, representing perhaps 20,000 households.

Who are these people? Many of course are retired, and one can see them entering and leaving their East Seventies town houses and Palm Springs condominiums. The largest single group, however, are local proprietors. They own the largest department store in Duluth, the second biggest bank in Memphis, and lettuce fields in the Salinas Valley. In the larger cities their holdings extend into newspapers, real estate, and brokerage houses. This is our best counterpart of a classical bourgeoisie, and its members have a major say in controlling civic affairs. Generally their influence stops at the state line, however. Owning half of downtown Wichita doesn't usually gain you a dinner invitation from the White House.

---

3. Smith, ed., *The Personal Distribution of Income and Wealth,* National Bureau of Economic Research. (Columbia University Press, 1975).

4. James Smith, Stephen Franklin, and Douglas Wion, *The Concentration of Financial Assets in the United States* (Urban Institute, 1973), Table 6.

But are they a ruling class, and a national one at that? Perhaps the most prolific exponent of this view has been G. William Domhoff . . . He began his inquiries in 1967 with *Who Rules America?* Three years later he published his answer: *The Higher Circles.*[5] His most recent book, *The Bohemian Grove,* carries the subtitle "A Study in Ruling Class Cohesiveness" and examines clubs, associations, and similar gathering places. When Domhoff says, "There is a ruling social class in the United States," he means to be taken literally. He is not simply saying that people in top positions bump into one another at the Council on Foreign Relations or clubs like the Links and Pacific Union. Rather, he contends, they form a distinctive stratum whose members frequent the same resorts and send their children to connected prep schools. These linkages lead to friendships and marriages, ensuring hegemony for the future. Interlocking directorates are not enough for Domhoff: he cites bloodlines and debutante parties to thicken the fusion.

Table 29–1. High Income Tax Returns: Who Made How Much

Income Ranges	Returns	Percent of Income Unearned	High Income Returns as Percent of:		
			All Returns	All Income	All Unearned Income
$1 million & over	1,011	91	.0013	.3	3
$500,000 to $1 million	2,646	78	.0034	.2	2
$200,000 to $500,000	19,230	62	.025	.7	5
$100,000 to $200,000	91,423	39	.12	1.6	7
$50,000 to $100,000	482,964	24	.6	4.3	12
Incomes over $50,000	597,274	36	.75	7.1	29
Incomes over $200,000	22,887	72	.03	1.2	10

Source: *Statistics of Income, 1972 Individual Income Tax Returns,* Internal Revenue Service, Washington, DC, 1974.

Domhoff has a following, especially among younger teachers of political science who agree with his analysis and want something more recent than C. Wright Mills. Unlike Mills, however, Domhoff can be rather casual about his facts, leading to the suspicion that he may be in over his head. Take the basic question of who belongs to his ruling class. At one point he claims that its members own "25 to 30 percent of all privately held wealth in America." However, James Smith's calculations indicate that to account for 29 percent of the country's holdings one must extend the list of owners to include almost four million persons. At another time, Domhoff's upper class embraces "one percent of the population," which gives us two million people, including everyone who earns $35,000 a year. At the back of *The Bohemian Grove* he lists 2,000 names (an "Appendix of Heavies") ranging from Kingman Brewster and David Rockefeller to Jacques Barzun and Edgar Bergen.

---

5. *Who Rules America?* (Prentice-Hall, 1967), *The Higher Circles* (Random House, 1970).

It is not easy to conceive of Domhoff's "rulers" as a class. Still, his questions are important; power in America can be understood through the people who participate in its exercise. But indiscriminately throwing statistics into a stewpot only confuses the issues.

Domhoff makes corporate executives the central members of his ruling class. I have been following his and other arguments to this effect for some time, and I still cannot see the point of giving them that label. Mills called them an "elite," a term referring to people whose power accompanies their occupancy of certain offices—bishops, generals, judges, salaried managers of public and private enterprises. Most have little in the way of property and their influence lasts only so long as they sit at a particular desk. Members of this elite are easily replaceable; in many cases it is impossible to distinguish an officeholder from his predecessor or successor. Ruling classes, in contrast, have traditionally consisted of persons who can be named and remembered. Since both individual and family property play a much smaller part in our own leading institutions, it is misleading to keep on speaking of a ruling class. For one thing, it prompts us to look for power in the wrong places. For another, it is historically inapposite. We will not understand the institutions of our times if we cling to an old conception of class rule. We do indeed have classes; but their arrangement reflects the corporate structure.

Most executives come from modest middle-class backgrounds, having majored in accounting at, say, Ohio State or in engineering at Purdue. They spend most of their adult lives climbing the company ladder, with periodic promotions but no spectacular leaps. Only those who rise to a top vice presidency begin to accumulate assets of any substance. Robert Murphy, the recently chosen chairman of General Motors, owned less than $300,000 in stock at the time of his elevation, which came after thirty-seven years with the firm. Clifton Gavin, Exxon's president after twenty-eight years' service, had $380,000 at the time of the last proxy statement.[6] Neither makes the millionaire list even though they each hold one of the most powerful jobs in America.

Administrative officers like these do not overlap to any great extent with the world of inherited wealth. Their children grow up in the suburbs of mid-America and are more apt to attend Bloomfield Hills high school than Foxcroft or St. Paul's. Only about a third of their sons end up at institutions like Yale or Williams; most send their children to freshwater colleges like Lehigh and Ohio Wesleyan and Iowa State. A far cry, certainly from the debutante circuit. Those who carry on the dynasty do so in the special cases of a founding family: Sarnoff at RCA, Bronfman at Seagram, Ford of Ford, and the Watsons in IBM. But even

---

6. Proxy statements list only executives' shares in their own companies. But given in-house loyalty, these probably represent the bulk of their stock holdings.

in companies like these an outsider now has an open chance for the most powerful job. Irving Shapiro, no less, currently occupies the corner office at Du Pont. On the whole the men who get to the highest corporate positions have nothing distinctive about them. Simply listing their names diverts attention from the real structure of power.

The description of America as fifty states may best be left to high-school civics courses. Our real centers of sovereignty are corporate bodies with inelegant names like Esmark, Tenneco, and Transamerica. We still leave to these institutions the major decisions on investment, innovation, and employment. In that sense, Union Carbide and Amerada Hess are more "necessary" to our prosperity than West Virginia or Arizona. When a recession comes, we ask what we can do to help companies create more jobs.) The shape of regions, professions, public authority, indeed such class configurations as we have—all these reflect directions charted in corporate board rooms.

It would be incorrect to say that these institutions run the entire country; they control only those parts of it that bear on their operations. That they get their way in Congress, the parties, and the bureaucracy derives mainly from the fact that we have no alternative ways to organize the economy. Of course the big corporations also move things along with a little underwriting. Where once Commodore Vanderbilt helped out Mark Hanna, business school graduates at American Airlines, Minnesota Mining, and Goodyear Rubber did some laundering for Charles Colson and Maurice Stans.

This is not to deny that rich families invest most of their fortunes in corporate securities. The question is whether by so doing they gain control of the economy. Domhoff, along with several other analysts, wants us to believe that they do. Last December, for example, he told the House hearings on the then vice-president designate that "15 employees of the Rockefellers have been identified on the boards of nearly 100 corporations . . . with combined assets of some $70 billion."[7] Gerard Zilg has a similar finding in his new book, *DuPont: Behind the Nylon Curtain,* where he lists "over 100 multimillion dollar companies in which the Du Ponts have a controlling interest." The list includes Boeing Aircraft, the Chemical Bank, Coca-Cola International, Continental Can, and Uniroyal.[8]

Sad to say, there is less here then meets the eye. That Rockefeller people are on the boards of companies worth $70 billion may sound impressive on first hearing. But a single person could reach that figure with *four* directorships—say, of General Motors, Exxon, General Electric, and IBM. Indeed, he could come close to it simply by sitting on the board of AT&T, which alone has assets of $67 billion. If Rockefeller

7. *The New York Times,* December 5, 1974.
8. Gerard Zilg, *Du Pont: Behind the Nylon Curtain* (Prentice-Hall, 1974), pp. 549ff.

agents need a total of 100 directorships to reach $70 billion, they aren't even near the major leagues. Zilg's book contains a lot of home truths about the Du Ponts, who emerge as a mean-fisted and nastyminded lot, a heavy influence on the state of Delaware. However, his claim that they have "a controlling interest" in 100 companies turns out to refer to the number of firms having a clanmember on their board. One board seat doesn't give you "control" unless you have quite a few shares in your pocket; and there is no evidence that the Du Pont directors on Zilg's list are in a position to have their way at Chemical Bank or Coca-Cola.

There are of course people who have built up their own enterprises into billion-dollar corporations: Norton Simon, Edwin Land, Howard Hughes. However, I can think of only one case where a single family largely owns and controls a series of great companies. These are the Mellons, who keep away from publicity by sticking close to Pittsburgh. Gulf Oil and Alcoa are essentially Mellon properties, as are the somewhat smaller Koppers and Carborundum companies, the First Boston Corporation, and the Mellon National Bank. For example, the Mellons own 20 percent of Gulf, well over the amount needed for control, and have four of the ten seats on its board. (Alcoa won't reveal the share the Mellons control, but the family has three of the twelve board seats.)

But who are the "Mellons"? Since the death of Richard King Mellon five years ago, the family has had neither strong leaders nor any discernible common purpose. Functionaries handle the directorships as well as the trusts and foundations which form a perpetual pool of Mellon capital. In a real sense all the Mello   nieces and nephews and second cousins have themselves become a kind of corporate body, not very different from pension funds and other investing institutions that want a steady return on their money. There is no evidence of a peculiar "Mellon" stamp on the policies of First Boston or Gulf or Alcoa. In the way their money is deployed, Mellon family members seem indistinguishable from a consortium of banks or insurance companies.

Why, then, the desire to see control as a matter of kinship? Maurice Zeitlin . . . makes a more convincing case for a ruling class than Domhoff does by extending his ambit beyond family to "groups of associates . . . and other cohesive ownership interests."[9] This makes sense to the extent that he includes banks and brokerage houses and corporate check-signers without all the gossip about who belongs to which clubs and whose sons "date" whose daughters. Yet even Zeitlin ends up by trying to find a ruling class of "freely intermarrying families." "If we are to locate the actual centers of corporate control," he writes, "we must discover the most effective kinship unit."

But who says we must? There seems little point in using a term like "kinship" to link anonymous administrators like Garvin of Exxon and

---

9. "Corporate Ownership and Control: The Large Corporation and the Capitalist Class," *American Journal of Sociology* (March, 1974):1098. [Reprinted in this volume.]

Murphy of General Motors. C. Wright Mills's conception of an elite was convincing because the kind of people who now ascend to presiding positions are in fact different from their propertied predecessors. Nelson Rockefeller, who buys people when he needs them, is more a throwback to J. P. Morgan or William Randolph Hearst than he is akin to the modern corporate types who tend toward civil service routines. Even though their paths undoubtedly cross in the course of business, our top managers are not linked together in ways that make them a cohesive culture. Nor have they the kind of self-confidence that characterizes a bourgeoisie. Balzac would find nothing to write about here.

It is entirely possible to engage in rule without being part of a ruling class. If we assume that corporate capitalism deserves all the criticism it can get, must there be particular malefactors to receive that indictment? All this listing of names, bloodlines, and marriages implies an inability on our part to understand and deal with power in its institutional form. Apparently we cannot visualize power as exercised administratively. Instead of the edifice of Chase Manhattan, our eyes seek out Rockefellers in the flesh. Indeed we often ignore an even more powerful bank, First National City, because the name of its chairman escapes us.

Of course corporate power appears in several constellations. Some companies present themselves as being solidly established and yet "modern" in outlook, especially those that join the Committee for Economic Development and other pronouncementmaking bodies. But just as the railroads got an early start through federal land grants, so entire new industries have been created by war, space, and covert contracts. This has been especially true of the more freebooting firms in the South and far West. Once public money gets transfused into Global Marine and McDonnell Douglas, taxpayers find themselves the powerless junior partners of operating executives. When Elizabeth Tudor commissioned Drake and Frobisher to do her dirty work, she at least kept the upper hand.

By concentrating on families, clubs, [and] personalities, the criticism of contemporary capitalism is in deeper confusion than its target. Blaming "the rich" or a "ruling class" no longer makes much sense. People have sometimes shown themselves ready to direct their resentments at institutions: suspicious attitudes toward oil companies and utilities show that. Even so, it has yet to be demonstrated how deeply one can hate American Cyanamid or Rockwell International. The class struggle is easier with an enemy of flesh and blood, as we know from countries like China and Cuba, where local landlords were an everyday sight. Our own capitalism's demise seems slated for yet another postponement until its attackers find ways of rousing mass anger against an edifice whose power depends neither on the personal qualities of those who hold it nor on their membership in a ruling class.

State and Ruling Class in Corporate America

30

William Domhoff

On top of the gradually merging social layers of blue and white collar workers in the United States, there is a very small social upper class which comprises at most 1 percent of the population and has a very different life-style from the rest of us. Members of this privileged class, according to sociological studies, live in secluded neighborhoods and well-guarded apartment complexes, send their children to private schools, announce their teenage daughters to the world by means of debutante teas and debutante balls, collect expensive art and antiques, play backgammon and dominoes at their exclusive clubs, and travel all around the world on their numerous vacations and junkets.

There is also in America an extremely distorted distribution of wealth and income. Throughout the twentieth century, the top 1 percent or so of wealth-holders have owned 25 to 30 percent of all wealth and 55 to 65 percent of the wealth that really counts, corporate stock in major businesses and banks. But even that is not the whole story, for a mere 0.1 percent have at least 19 percent of all the wealth in the country—190 times as much as they would have if everyone had an equal share. As for income, well, the maldistribution is not quite as bad. But one recent study argues that if income from capital gains is included, the top 1.5 percent of wealthholders receive 24 percent of yearly national income. And, as all studies on matters of weatlh and income are quick to point out, these estimates are conservative.

It is not hard for most of us to imagine that the social upper class uncovered in sociological research is made up of the top wealth holders revealed in wealth and income studies. However, it is not necessary to rely on our imaginations, for it is possible to do empirical studies linking the one group to the other. The first systematic studies along this line

Reprinted from G. William Domhoff, "State and Ruling Class in Corporate America," *The Insurgent Sociologist* 4:3 (Spring, 1974): 3–16, by permission of the publisher.

were reported by sociologist E. Digby Baltzell, but there have been others since.

In most countries, and in most times past in our own country, it would be taken for granted that an upper class with a highly disproportionate amount of wealth and income is a ruling class with domination over the government. How else, it would have been argued, could a tiny group possess so much if it didn't have its hooks into government? But not so in the United States of today. This nation is different, we are assured. It has no social classes, at least not in the traditional European sense, and anyhow there is social mobility—new millionaires are created daily. Besides, many different groups, including organized labor, organized farmers, consumers, and experts have a hand in political decisions—at least since the New Deal. There is no such thing as a ruling class in America.[1]

In this paper I am going to suggest that in fact a ruling class does dominate this country, a suggestion which not only flies in the face of prevailing academic wisdom, but raises problems for political activists as well. To support this suggestion, I will describe four processes through which the wealthy few who are the ruling class dominate government. Let me begin by defining two terms, "ruling class" and "power elite." By a ruling class, I mean a clearly demarcated social upper class which:

a. has a disproportionate amount of wealth and income;
b. generally fares better than other social groups on a variety of well-being statistics ranging from infant mortality rates to educational attainments to feelings of happiness to health and longevity;
c. controls the major economic institutions of the country; and
d. dominates the governmental processes of the country.

By a power elite I mean the "operating arm" or "leadership group" or "establishment" of the ruling class. This power elite is made up of active, working members of the upper class and high-level employees in institutions controlled by members of the upper class.

Both of these concepts, I contend, are important in a careful conceptualization of how America is ruled. The distinction between ruling class and power elite allows us to deal with the everyday observation, which is also the first objection raised by critics of ruling-class theory, that some members of the ruling class are not involved in ruling, and that some rulers are not members of the upper class. Which is no problem at all, in reality. There always have been many members of ruling classes who spent most of their time playing polo, riding to

1. For typical expressions of this view, consult sociologist Arnold Rose, *The Power Structure* (Oxford University Press, 1967), political scientist Robert Dahl, *Pluralist Democracy in the United States* (Rand McNally, 1967), or political scientist Grant McConnell, *Private Power and American Democracy* (Alfred A. Knopf, 1966).

hounds, or leading a worldwide social life. And there always have been carefully groomed and carefully selected employees, such as Dean Rusk of the Rockefeller Foundation, Robert McNamara of Ford Motor Company, Henry Kissinger of the Council on Foreign Relations, and Herb Stein of the Committee for Economic Development, who have been placed in positions of importance in government.

Now, many other criticisms have been raised about ruling-class theory, and many different kinds of evidence have been put forth to deal with these criticisms. One typical criticism is that the ruling class is never specified in a way that it can be studied empirically. But this argument can be met by reputational, positional, and statistical studies which show that certain social registers, blue books, prep schools, and exclusive clubs are good indicators of upper-class standing.

Another usual comment is that there is no reason to believe the alleged ruling class is "cohesive" or "class conscious," a criticism which can be countered by pointing to systematic evidence on interregional private school attendance, overlapping club memberships, interlocking corporate directorships, and nationwide attendance at annual upper-class retreats like the Bohemian Grove and the Ranchero Visitadores.

Then there is the assertion that members of the upper class have lost control of corporations and banks to middle-class managers and technocrats, which flies in the face of facts on corporate ownership, on the social backgrounds of corporate directors, and on the motives and goals of corporate managers.

Perhaps the most important criticism, however, is that championed by political scientists, who say proponents of ruling class theory do not spell out the mechanisms by which the ruling class supposedly dominates government. Not content to infer power from such indicators as wealth and well-being statistics, they want the case for governmental domination by a ruling class demonstrated in its own right, without appeal to statistics on wealth, income, health, and happiness.

My first attempt to satisfy the political science fraternity on this score was to show that members of the power elite hold important governmental positions, especially in the executive branch of the federal government, which I assume everyone now agrees is the most important part of American government.[2] But critics were not satisfied by a sociology-of-leadership approach, which infers "power" to be present when a disproportionate number of people from a given class [or] ethnic, racial, or religious group appear in positions of responsibility in a given institution. Although no one questions the findings of this method when it is used to show antiethnic or antiracial discrimination on the part of banks, corporations, and universities, weaknesses are discovered

2. G. William Domhoff, *Who Rules America?* (Prentice-Hall, 1967).

in it when it is used to study the powerful instead of the powerless. Now the critics want to see the position holders in action, to see the various means by which they supposedly rule in the interests of themselves and their class.

Such critics often argue, as sociologist Arnold Rose did in his earlier-cited book on *The Power Structure,* that members of the power elite may not act in the interests of the ruling class while in governmental positions. Instead they may act in the "national interest," a claim that probably strikes many people as a little empty when they contemplate oil industry tax favors, subsidies to corporations and rich farmers, defense contract overruns, loans to failing corporations, and the general social science finding that most human beings rarely if ever transcend their class, religious, and/or ethnic background in viewing the world.

In my second effort to satisfy the concerns of those who wonder about the precise relationship between the state and the ruling class in corporate America, I turned to the problem of policy formation, developing information which suggests that nonpartisan, seemingly objective discussion groups like the Council on Foreign Relations and the Committee for Economic Development are in fact exclusive policy-planning organizations wherein members of the power elite join together with their hired experts to develop plans which are then brought to the government through blue ribbon commissions, position papers, friendly politicians, and not least, governmental appointees who are members or employees of these groups.[3] But this was not quite good enough either, mostly because it did not deal with the role of political parties and elections.

Despite the generally negative response I have received from political scientists, I would like to take another stab at satisfying their major criticism of ruling-class theory. Perhaps it is masochism that motivates this near-hopeless task, but I have a new way of thinking about the problem of ruling class and government that may put things in a new light. Simply put, I think there are four general processes through which economically and politically active members of the ruling class, operating as the leaders of the power elite, involve themselves in government at all levels. I call these four processes:

1. the special-interest process, which has to do with the various means utilized by wealthy individuals, specific corporations, and specific sectors of the economy to satisfy their narrow, short-run needs;
2. the policy-planning process, which has to do with the development and implementation of general policies that are important to the interests of the ruling class as a whole;

---

3. G. William Domhoff, *The Higher Circles* (Random House, 1970).

3. the candidate-selection process, which has to do with the ways in which members of the ruling class insure that they have "access" to the politicians who are elected to office; and
4. the ideology process, which has to do with the formation, dissemination, and enforcement of attitudes and assumptions which permit the continued existence of policies and politicians favorable to the wealth, income, status, and privileges of members of the ruling class.

Let me now turn to each of these processes to show their role in ruling class domination of the government. Although my focus will be on the federal government in Washington, I believe the general schema can be applied, with slight modifications, to state and local governments.

The special-interest process, as noted, comprises the several means by which specific individuals, corporations, or business sectors get the tax breaks, favors, subsidies, and procedural rulings which are beneficial to their short-run interests. This is the world of lobbyists, Washington superlawyers, trade associations, and advisory committees to governmental departments and agencies. This is the process most often described by journalists and social scientists in their exposés and case studies concerning Congressional committees, regulatory agencies, and governmental departments. This process also has been the target of the excellent investigations by Ralph Nader and his colleagues.

I do not think I need spend any time giving examples of how this process works. Indeed, each reader will have his or her favorite studies for demonstration purposes. For myself, I am partial to what Richard Harris, in *The Real Voice,* and Morton Mintz, in *By Prescription Only,* have revealed about the machinations of the drug industry, and to the superb study of *The Politics of Oil* by Robert Engler. My favorites among the Nader studies, by a small margin, are Robert Fellmeth's *The Interstate Commerce Omission* and James Turner's *The Chemical Feast.* For a panoramic view, I prefer relatively recent books like Joseph Goulden's *The Super-Lawyers,* Drew Pearson and Jack Anderson's *The Case Against Congress,* Morton Mintz and Jerry Cohen's *America, Inc.,* and Robert Sherrill's *Why They Call It Politics.* But I stress that there are many other fine studies of this process, and that more are appearing all the time.

The information in these studies might seem on its face to be impressive evidence for ruling-class theory. After all, it shows that members of the ruling class are able to realize their will on innumerable issues of concern to them. They can gain tax breaks, receive subsidies, subvert safety laws, and dominate regulatory agencies, among other things. However, in the eyes of most political scientists this is not adequate evidence, for it does not show that the various "interests" are "coordinated" in their efforts. Moreover, it does not show directly that they dominate policy on "big issues," or that they control either of the political parties. This typical view is even expressed by Grant McConnell, the political scientist most sensitive to the many ways in which various private interests have taken over the piece of government of greatest concern to them. After concluding that "a substantial part of government in the United States has come under the influence or control of narrowly based and largely autonomous elites," he then asserts there is no need to talk of a power elite because

> These elites do not act cohesively with each other on many issues. They do not rule in the sense of commanding the entire nation. Quite the contrary, they tend to pursue a policy of noninvolvement in the large issues of statesmanship, save where such issues touch their own particular concerns.[4]

Moreover, the big interests do not dominate the government as a whole. The political parties and the presidency seem to be beyond their reach:

> Fortunately, not all of American politics is based upon this array of small constituencies. The party system, the presidency and the national government as a whole represent opposing tendencies. To a very great degree, policies serving the values of liberty and equality are the achievements of these institutions. Public values generally must depend upon the creation of a national constituency.[5]

In order to deal with the kind of argument presented by McConnell, it is necessary to consider next the policy-formation process, the process by which policy on "large issues" is formulated, for it is in the policy process that the various special interests join together to forge general policies which will benefit them as a whole. The central units in the policy network are such organizations as the Council on Foreign Relations, the Committee for Economic Development, the Business Council, the American Assembly, and the National Municipal League, which are best categorized as policy-planning and consensus-seeking organizations of the power elite. I will not repeat here the information on the financing and leadership of these organizations which shows beyond a doubt that they are underwritten and directed by the same upper-class men who control the major corporations, banks, foundations, and law firms.[6] More important for our purpose is what goes on in the off-the-record meetings of these organizations.

The policy-planning organizations bring together, in groups large and small, members of the power elite from all over the country to discuss general problems—e.g., overseas aid, the use of nuclear weapons, tax problems, or the population question. They provide a setting in which differences on various issues can be thrashed out and the

---

4. McConnell, op. cit., p. 339.
5. Ibid., p. 8.
6. Domhoff, *The Higher Circles,* op. cit.

opinions of various experts can be heard. In addition to the group settings, these organizations also encourage general dialogue within the power elite by means of luncheon and dinner speeches, special written reports, and position statements in journals and books.

It was in groups such as these that the framework for a capital-labor detente was worked out at the turn of the century, that the bill for a Federal Trade Commission was drafted, that the plans for social security were created, that the ideas behind the Marshall Plan were developed, that national goals for the 1960s were projected, and the "population problem" was invented.[7] I do not have the space in this paper to spin out any of the case examples that are available in the works I just cited. Let me be content to summarize the policy-planning network by means of the diagram on the next page, and to list some of the most important functions of this process:

1. They provide a setting wherein members of the power elite can familiarize themselves with general issues.
2. They provide a setting where conflicts within the power elite can be discussed and compromised.
3. They provide a setting wherein members of the power elite can hear the ideas and findings of their hired experts.
4. They provide a "training ground" for new leadership within the ruling class. It is in these organizations that big businessmen can determine which of their peers are best suited for service in the government.
5. They provide a framework for commissioned studies by experts on important issues.
6. Through such avenues as books, journals, policy statements, press releases and speakers, they can greatly influence the "climate of opinion" both in Washington and the country at large.

There are several points for political scientists and other critics of ruling-class theory to consider in contemplating the policy-planning network. First, it provides evidence that businessmen, bankers, and lawyers concern themselves with more than their specific business interests. Second, it shows that leaders from various sectors of the economy do get together to discuss the problems of the system as a whole. Third, it suggests that members of the power elite who are appointed

---

7. On the capital-labor detente and the Federal Trade Commission, see James Weinstein, *The Corporate Ideal in the Liberal State* (Beacon Press, 1968). On social security, see Domhoff, *The Higher Circles,* op. cit. On the ideas behind the Marshall Plan, see David Eakins, "Business Planners and America's Postwar Expansion," in *Corporations and The Cold War,* David Horowitz, ed. (Monthly Review Press, 1969). On national goals, see G. William Domhoff, "How The Power Elite Set National Goals," in *The Triple Revolution Emerging,* Robert Perrucci and Marc Pilisuk, eds. (Little, Brown and Co., 1971). On the "population problem" see Steve Weissman, "Why the Population Bomb Is a Rockefeller Baby," *Ramparts,* (May, 1970), and William Barclay, Joseph Enright, and Reid T. Reynolds, "Population Control in the Third World," *NACCLA Newsletter* (December, 1970).

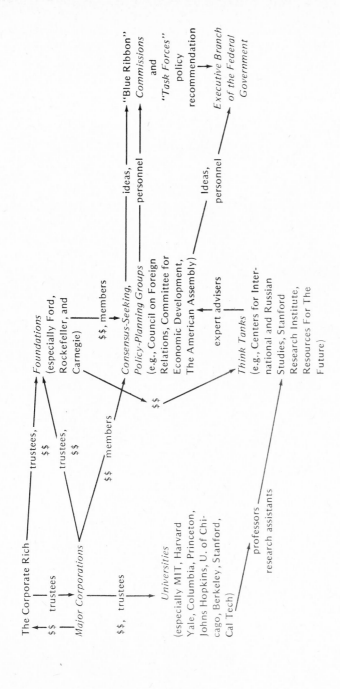

Figure 30–1. The Power Elite Policy-Making Process

to government are equipped with a general issue-orientation gained from power-elite organizations that are explicitly policy oriented. Fourth, it reveals that the upper-middle-class experts thought by some to be our real rulers are in fact busily dispensing their advice to those who hire them.

In short, if political scientists were to take the idea of a policy-planning process seriously, they would not be able to agree with Grant McConnell when he downgrades the importance of the Business Council by saying "the really effective participants in business politics are those [organizations] which direct their energies almost wholly to hard, specific matters of immediate economic concern to business firms."[8] Instead, they would say that trade associations are among the most important influences in the special-interest process and that the Business Council is one of the Archimedean points of the policy process.

If I am right that members of the ruling class gain their narrow interests through the well-known devices of the special-interest process and their general interests through the little-studied policy-planning process, then the question immediately arises: how is all this possible when we have a government elected by the people? Shouldn't we expect elected officials to have policy views of their own that generally reflect the wishes of the voters who sent them to office? There is certainly one group of political scientists who believe this to be the case—they have developed a detailed argument to suggest that the deep-seated political ambitions of individuals and parties lead them to take the policy stands which will get them a majority of the vote, thereby insuring that the policy views of politicians will reflect more or less the views of the people.

To answer questions about our elected officials, we must examine the political parties and the candidates they nominate. When it comes to the parties, political scientists have suggested that a fully developed political party fulfills four functions: (1) integrating conflicting regional, ethnic, and class identifications; (2) selecting candidates to fill offices; (3) political education; and (4) policymaking. In the United States, however, the parties have little or nothing to do with political education or policy making: "Particularly in our own century," writes political scientist Walter Dean Burnham, "American political parties have been largely restricted in functional scope to the realm of the constituent [integrative function] and to the tasks of filling political offices."[9] Another observer, the executive director of the National Committee for an Effective Congress, puts the matter even more strongly:

8. McConnell, op. cit., pp. 292–93.
9. Walter Dean Burnham, "Party Systems and the Political Process," p. 279, in *The American Party Systems*, William Chambers and Walter Dean Burnham, eds. (Oxford University Press, 1967).

For all intents and purposes, the Democratic and Republican parties don't exist. There are only individuals [candidates] and professionals [consultants, pollsters, media advisers].[10]

It is because American politics is restricted largely to office-filling functions that I prefer to talk about the candidate-selection process rather than the political process. The term political process gives the impression that more is going on in our electoral system than is really the case. And it is precisely because the candidate-selection process is so individualistic and issueless that it can be in good part dominated by means of campaign contributions from members of the ruling class. In the guise of fat cats, the same men who direct corporations and take part in the policy groups play a central role in the careers of most politicians who advance beyond the local or state legislature level in states of any size and consequence. To quote again from Walter Dean Burnham: "Recruitment of elective elites remains closely associated, especially for the more important offices and in the larger states, with the candidates' wealth or access to large campaign contributions."[11] Moreover, the role of the wealthy middlemen seems to be especially crucial in the nomination phase of the process. At least this was the conclusion of one of the most thorough studies ever done of campaign finance, by political scientist Alexander Heard:

> The necessity for obtaining essential election funds has its most profound importance in the choosing of candidates. The monies can usually be assured, and often can be withheld, by the relatively small corps of political specialists whose job it is to raise money.... As a consequence, money probably has its greatest impact on the choice of public officials in the shadow land of our politics where it is decided who will be a candidate for a party's nomination and who will not. There are many things that make an effective candidate, but here is a *choke point* [my italics] in our politics where vital fiscal encouragement can be extended or withheld.[12]

The fat cats, of course, are by and large hard to distinguish in their socioeconomic outlook whatever their political party. Indeed, most corporations, banks, and law firms try to have personnel who are important donors to both parties. Then too, many of the fattest cats of the opposing parties join together as leaders of such policy-planning groups as the Council on Foreign Relations and Committee for Economic Development. For example, in 1968 there were 144 members of tbe Council on Foreign Relations who gave $500 or more to the Republicans, 56 who

---

10. John S. Saloma III and Frederick H. Sontag, *Parties* (Alfred A. Knopf, 1972), p. 295.
11. Burnham, op. cit., p. 277.
12. Alexander Heard, *The Costs of Democracy* (Doubleday, 1962), p. 34.

contributed $500 or more to the Democrats. One hundred twenty-six members of the National Council of the Foreign Policy Association donated sums of $500 or more to Republicans, 71 gave to Democrats. At the Committee for Economic Development, there were 95 Republican donors and 16 Democratic donors. Although well-connected in both parties, we can see a power elite preference for the Republican Party, at least in 1968. There is one other difference among fat cats worth noting—southern and Jewish members of the upper class are more likely to be Democrats than are their WASP-y counterparts.[13]

What kind of politicians emerge from this individualistically oriented electoral politics that has to curry favor with large contributors? The answer is available from several studies. Politicians are first of all people from the higher levels of the social ladder: "The wealthiest one-fifth of the American families contribute about nine of every ten of the elite of the political economy."[14] They are secondly, at least among those who wish to go beyond local and state politics, quite ambitious men who are constantly striving for bigger and better things. They are thirdly people who are by and large without strong ideological inclinations; the exceptions to this statement are well-known precisely because they are so unusual. Finally, with the exception of the local level, where businessmen are most likely to sit on city councils, they are in good part lawyers, an occupational grouping that by training and career needs produces ideal go-betweens and compromisers. The result of the candidate selection process, in short, is (1) men who know how to go along to get along; and (2) men who have few strong policy positions of their own, and are thus open to the suggestions put forth to them by the fat cats and experts who have been legitimated as serious leaders within the framework of the policy-planning network.

When we consider the interaction between the policy process and the political process, it is not surprising that there is a considerable continuity of policy between Republican and Democratic administrations. As columnist Joseph Kraft wrote about the Council on Foreign Relations, "the Council plays a special part in helping to bridge the gap between the two parties, affording unofficially a measure of continuity when the guard changes in Washington."[15] Nor is it surprising that Hubert Humphrey would reveal in early 1973 that he had asked Henry Kissinger before the election in 1968 to serve as *his* foreign policy adviser should he win the Presidency. But David Halberstam's *The Best and The Brightest* best reveals the degree to which politicians defer to representatives of the policy process. After winning an election based upon "new frontiers" and nonexistent missile gaps, President-elect John

13. G. William Domhoff, *Fat Cats and Democrats* (Prentice-Hall, 1972), for the information in this paragraph.

14. Kenneth Prewitt and Alan Stone, *The Ruling Elites* (Harper & Row, 1973), p. 137.

15. Joseph Kraft, "School for Statesmen," *Harper's Magazine,* July, 1958, p. 68.

F. Kennedy called in Republican Robert Lovett, a Wall Street financier who hadn't even voted for him, and asked him for his advice as to whom should be appointed to important government positions. Kennedy did this because he only knew mere politicians, not the kind of "serious men" who were expert enough to run a government:

> He had spent the last five years, he said ruefully, running for office, and he did not know any real public officials, people to run a government, serious men. The only ones he knew, he admitted, were politicians, and if this seemed a denigration of his own kind, it was not altogether displeasing to the older man. Politicians did need men to serve, to run the government.[16]

Among Lovett's suggestions were Dean Rusk of the Rockefeller Foundation, Robert McNamara of Ford Motor Company, and Douglas Dillon of Dillon, Read, who, as we all know, ended up as Kennedy's choices to head the state, defense, and treasury departments.

So politics in America has little to do with issues and public policy. It is an exercise in imagebuilding, namecalling, and rumormongering, a kind of carnival or psychological safety valve. Thus, a Richard M. Nixon can unctuously claim he is dealing with the issues in the 1972 campaign, when in fact even the *Wall Street Journal* has to admit that all he does is wave the flag and accuse people who disagree with him of being traitors.[17] And at about the same time he is pretending to discuss the issues, he can quietly tell his campaign strategists not to worry about what the platform says because "Who the hell ever read a platform?"[18] Then, after the election, the president's press secretary can calmly admit that the issue of spending cuts in domestic programs was purposely hidden during the campaign. It would have been "naive" to raise this issue, explained Herb Klein when he was asked why the president did not mention his plans to cut back domestic programs during the campaign. "You don't raise unnecessary issues in the middle of a presidential campaign," Klein explained.[19]

I conclude that the notion of public policy being influenced to any great extent by the will of the people due to the competition between the two political parties is misguided. "Politics" is for selecting ambitious, relatively issueless middle- and upper-middle-class lawyers who know how to advance themselves by finding the rhetoric and the rationalizations to implement both the narrow and general policies of the bipartisan power elite.

At this point I can hear the reader protesting that there is more to American politics than this. And so there is. I admit there are serious-

16. David Halberstam, *The Best and The Brightest* (Random House, 1972), p. 4.

17. James P. Gannon, "Is GOP Campaign Rhetoric Too Hot?" *Wall Street Journal,* Sept. 8, 1972, p. 8.

18. "Republicans: Cloth-Coat Convention," *Newsweek,* August 7, 1972, p. 23.

19. "Post-Election Candor," *Newsweek,* March, 26, 1973, p. 15.

minded liberals who fight the good fight on many issues, ecologically oriented politicians who remain true to their cause, and honest people of every political stripe who are not beholden to any wealthy people. But there are not enough of them, for there is also a seniority system dominated by ruling class–oriented politicians who have a way of keeping the insurgents off the important committees and out of the centers of power. There is in addition a southern Democratic delegation which retains its stranglehold on Congress despite all the claims of the mid-sixties that its star was about to fade. Then there are the machine Democrats who aid the Southerners in crucial ways even while they maintain a liberal voting record. And finally, there are the myriad lobbyists and lawyers who are constantly pressuring those who would resist the blandishments of the power elite. As former Congressman Abner Mikva once said, the system has a way of grinding you down:

> The biggest single disappointment to a new man is the intransigence of the system. You talk to people and they say, 'You're absolutely right, something ought to be done about this.' And yet, somehow, we go right on ducking the hard issues. We slide off the necessary confrontations. This place has a way of grinding you down.[20]

In short, even though there is more to American politics than fat cats and their political friends, the "more" cannot win other than headlines, delays, and an occasional battle. The candidate-selection process produces too many politicians who are friendly to the wealthy few.

Contemplation of the ways in which the special-interest, policy-planning, and candidate-selection processes operate brings us to the sixty-four dollar question: why do we, the general public, acquiesce in this state of affairs? Why is it, as Marx warned, that the ruling ideas of any age are the ideas of the ruling class? Why does the ruling class have what the Italian Marxist Antonio Gramsci called "ideological hegemony," by which he meant that "the system's real strength does not lie in the violence of the ruling class or the coercive power of its state apparatus, but in the acceptance by the ruled of a 'conception of the world' which belongs to the rulers?"[21] Unfortunately, no one has given an adequate answer to these interrelated questions. Such an answer would involve insights from a variety of disciplines including history, anthropology, and psychology as well as political science and sociology, and would quickly lead to ageold problems concerning the origins of the state and the general nature of the relationship between leaders and led.

However, at the sociological level which concerns me in this paper, we certainly can see that members of the ruling class work very hard at helping us to accept their view of the world. Indeed, we can be sure from past experience that they will stop at nothing—despite their pro-

---

20. Robert Sherrill, "92nd Congress: Eulogy and Evasion," *The Nation*, February 15, 1971.
21. Giuseppe Fiori, *Antonio Gramsci: Life of a Revolutionary* (NLB, London, 1970), p. 238.

testations of "democracy" and "liberalism"—to get their views across.[22] Through the ideology process, they create, disseminate, and enforce a set of attitudes and "values" that tells us this is, for all its defects, the best of all possible worlds. At the fount of this process are the same foundations and policy-planning groups which operate in the policy process. For in addition to providing policy suggestions to government, these policy-planning organizations also provide the new rationales which make the policies acceptable to the general public. Thus, in the case of the ideology process we must link these organizations not to the government, as in the policy process, but to a dissemination network which includes middle-class discussion groups, public relations firms, corporate-financed advertising councils, special university and foundation programs, books, speeches, and various efforts through the mass media.

The dissemination apparatus is most readily apparent in the all-important area of foreign policy. Perhaps most critical here is the Foreign Policy Association and its affiliate, the World Affairs Council.

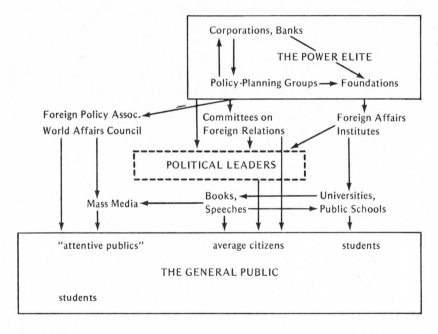

Figure 30–2. The Flow of Foreign Policy Ideology to the General Public: Political Leaders Play an Intermediary Role

22. G. William Domhoff, "The Power Elite, the CIA, and the Struggle for Minds," *The Higher Circles* (Random House, 1970), for an account of how moderates and liberals within the power elite subverted various American institutions in their efforts to "save" an "open" society.

Tightly interlocked with the Council on Foreign Relations, the Foreign Policy Association provides literature and discussion groups for the "attentive public" of upper-middle-class professionals, academics, and students. For local elites, the Council on Foreign Relations sponsors Committees on Foreign Relations in over 30 cities around the country. These committees meet about once a month during the nonsummer months to hear speakers provided by the Council on Foreign Relations or the government. The aim of this program is to provide local elites with information and legitimacy so they may function as "opinion leaders" on foreign policy issues. In addition to the Foreign Policy Association and the Committees on Foreign Relations, there are numerous foreign affairs institutes at major universities which provide students and the general public with the perspectives of the power elite on foreign policy. Then too, political leaders often play an intermediary role in carrying foreign policy positions to the general public.

The enforcement of the ideological consensus is carried out in a multitude of ways that include pressure, intimidation, and violence as well as the more gentle methods of persuasion and monetary inducement. Those who are outspoken in their challenge to one or another of the main tenets of the American ideology may be passed over for promotions, left out of junkets, or fired from their jobs. They may be excluded from groups or criticized in the mass media. If they get too far outside the consensus, they are enmeshed in the governmental law enforcement apparatus which is shaped in the policy-formation process with a special assist from the ruling-class-dominated American Bar Association and its affiliated institutes and committees.[23] But I do not think we need spend much time considering the bitter details of ideology enforcement, for they are all too fresh in our minds after years of struggle over civil liberties and the war in Southeast Asia.

---

23. The bottom level of the enforcement apparatus, the police, didn't do their job quite right in the late sixties. While injecting the required amount of fear into many citizens, they also created many new dissenters among students, Blacks, and Chicanos by their heavyhanded tactics. So the Ford Foundation spun off a $30 million Police Foundation to fund the university programs, special institutes, consultants, and books which are being used to teach the police to be more sophisticated in their containment of dissent in the future.

Political Power and Budgetary Control in the United States

31

By James O'Connor

INTRODUCTION

Capital organizes production for the market and employs labor power only if there is a reasonable expectation of profit. The state administration organizes production as the result of a series of political decisions.

These political decisions are made within a definite framework of social relationships and as a consequence of social, economic, and political conflict. Two systems of social relationships must be considered: first, those between and within economic classes, and second, those between economic classes and state power (including the legislative and executive branches of government). We must analyze the general relationship between labor and capital and also that between capital and the state. There is no necessary and direct connection between the economic might and needs of monopoly capital and state budgetary priorities. Monopoly capital must work within the political framework of the federal system. In other words, it is compelled to work within the framework of different political systems at different levels of government.[1]

The relationship between monopoly capital and organized labor is the dominant production relation or social relation of production in U.S. society. Less significant relationships include those between monopoly capital and competitive capital, competitive capital and competitive labor, and so on.

We will describe the main relationships between private power and state power. We also will describe the centralizing tendencies that are at work in both the executive and legislative branches of the federal government. We will examine the relationship between the executive

Reprinted from James O'Connor, *The Fiscal Crisis of the State* (New York: St. Martin's Press, 1973), pp. 64–95, by permission of the publisher, St. Martin's Press, and the author. Footnotes have been renumbered.

1. The varying strategies and tactics that monopoly capital employs when dealing with different levels and branches of government gave rise to the theory of pluralism, which dominated American political thought during the 1950s and early 1960s.

branch (which increasingly is under the dominance of class-conscious monopoly capital) and the legislative branch (which still is powerfully influenced by interest-conscious competitive capital and to a lesser degree by monopoly capital). Finally, we will review the politics of budgeting at the state and local levels.

A POLITICAL FRAMEWORK FOR BUDGETARY ANALYSIS: THE FEDERAL GOVERNMENT

What are the channels through which economic class relationships find their political expression in the federal government? Whose interests does the national government serve? The large number of power centers within the national state, each with a measure of autonomy, mitigates against any simplistic analysis of federal power in budgetary matters. One political scientist notes:

> In federal government alone, it may be necessary to consider the reactions of at least ten institutions to any major changes in taxing and spending: the Ways and Means Committee in the House of Representatives, the Finance Committee in the Senate, Appropriations Committees in both Houses of Congress, the Council of Economic Advisors, the Bureau of the Budget, the Treasury Department, the Internal Revenue Service, the General Accounting Office, and the Federal Reserve Board.[2]

... The first and most powerful influence in the national government is the capitalist class—owners and controllers of the monopoly corporations and state contractors. The members of this class have organized themselves along interest-group and class lines (competitive capital organizes itself mainly along interest-group lines).

Interest-group organization and participation in the national state have been studied by McConnell, Hamilton, Kolko, Engler, and many other social scientists and historians. In Hamilton's words:

> there are currently associations of manufacturers, of distributors, and of retailers; there are organizations which take all commerce as their province; and there are federations of local clubs of businessmen with tentacles which reach into the smaller urban centers and market towns. All such organizations are active instruments in the creation of attitudes, in the dissemination of sound opinion, and in the promotion of practices which may become widespread.[3]

An example is the national committee of the U.S. Chamber of Commerce, which is charged with reviewing the federal budget (state and

---

2. Ira Sharkansky, *The Politics of Taxing and Spending* (Indianapolis-New York: 1969), pp. 34–35.

3. Walton Hamilton, *The Politics of Industry* (New York: 1957), p. 9. Other representative works dealing with interest group politics are: Grant McConnell, *Private Power and American Democracy* (New York: 1966); Gabriel Kolko, *Railroads and Regulation, 1877–1916* (Princeton, N.J.: 1965); Robert Engler, *The Politics of Oil* (New York: 1961).

local budgets too) and federal operations and recommending budgetary or operational changes.

These self-regulatory private associations normally are organized along industry, not regional, lines because of the national character of most commodity markets. More often than not, they use the state to mediate between their members (e.g., conduct elections to determine the form and extent of farm commodity price support programs) as well as to provide needed credits, subsidies, technical aid, and general support. Key industry groups include the highway lobby (automobiles, oil, rubber, glass, branches of construction, etc.), the military lobby, oil, cotton, textiles, railroads, airlines, radio and television, public utilities, and banking and brokerage. Wheat, cotton, sugar (among other growers), and cattle ranchers also are organized into associations.

Interest groups have appropriated many small pieces of state power through a "multiplicity of intimate contacts with the government."[4] They dominate most of the so-called regulatory agencies at the federal, state, and local levels, many bureaus within the Departments of Agriculture and Interior (Agriculture was the first Department established to serve a special clientele), the Bureau of Highways, and a number of congressional committees. Their specific interests are reflected in the partial or full range of policies of hundreds of national and state government agencies—for example, the Interstate Commerce Commission and other regulatory bodies, the Department of Defense, the Corps of Engineers, the U.S. Tariff Commission, and the Federal Reserve System. In a summary of the politics of interest groups McConnell writes that

> What emerges as the most important political reality is an array of relatively separated political systems, each with a number of elements. These typically include: (1) a federal administrative agency within the executive branch; (2) a heavily committed group of congressmen and Senators, usually members of a particular committee or subcommittee; (3) a private (or quasi-private) association representing the agency clientele; (4) a quite homogeneous constituency usually composed of local elites. Where dramatic conflicts over policy have occurred, they have appeared as rivalries among the public administrative agencies, but the conflicts are more conspicuous and less important than the agreements among these systems. The most frequent solution to conflict is jurisdictional demarcation and establishment of spheres of influence. Logrolling, rather than compromise, is the normal pattern of relationship.[5]

In other words, the interpenetration of private economy and the state and the growth of the federal bureaucracy have transformed polit-

---

4. *Private Power and American Democracy,* op. cit., p. 279. "Other interest groups" include professional associations such as the professional educators who dominated the Office of Education in pre-Sputnik days.
5. Ibid., p. 244.

ical economic issues and conflicts into problems of administration. Historically, pressure-group activity and conflict have characterized not only the legislative branch but also the executive branch of government.

By itself, however, interest-group politics is inconsistent with the survival and expansion of capitalism. For one thing, "the interests which keep the interest groups going are too disparate, and the least common denominator of action is too passive to bring into being a completely cohesive union."[6] For another, interest consciousness obviously leads to contradictory policies, making it difficult or impossible to plan the economy as a whole. Thus, a class-conscious political directorate is needed to coordinate the activities of nominally independent government agencies. Paradoxically, enduring interest groups require a sense of "responsibility"—that is, class consciousness. For example, the attempt by regulatory agencies to maintain profitable conditions in a particular industry tends to freeze the pattern of resource allocation and establish monopoly conditions, which, in turn, retard capital accumulation and expansion throughout the economy. Another example is planning for overseas expansion which clearly requires a class-conscious political directorate.

The class organization of monopoly sector capital—both its private activity and participation in the state—have been studied by Williams, Weinstein, Kolko, Domhoff, Eakins, and others.[7] These writers have shown that the instability and inefficiency attendant upon capitalist production in the past increased investment risk and uncertainty, contributed to crises and depressions and deficiencies of aggregate demand, and created other economic problems. By the turn of the century, and especially during the New Deal, it was apparent to vanguard corporate leaders that some form of rationalization of the economy was necessary.[8] And as the twentieth century wore on, the owners of corporate capital generated the financial ability, learned the organizational skills, and developed the ideas necessary for their self-regulation as a class.

Thus, it was a class-conscious political directorate that controlled the War Industry Board during World War I, parts of the National Recovery Administration and the Agricultural Adjustment Administration, and

---

6. *The Politics of Industry,* op. cit., p. 9.

7. William Appleman Williams, *The Contours of American History* (New York: 1961); James Weinstein, *The Corporate Ideal in the Liberal State, 1900–1918* (Boston: 1968); Gabriel Kolko, *The Triumph of Conservatism, 1900–1916* (Glencoe, Ill.: 1963); William Domhoff, *Who Rules America?* (Englewood Cliffs, N.J.: 1967); David Eakins, "The Development of Corporate Liberal Policy Research, 1885–1965," (Ph.D. dissertation, University of Wisconsin, 1966). . . .

8. "The New Deal tried to frame institutions to protect capitalism from major business cycles and began in an unclear sort of way to underwrite continuous economic growth and sustained profits" [Paul K. Conkin, *The New Deal* (New York: 1967), p. 75]. As Ellis W. Hawley has shown, however, "partial, piecemeal, pressure-group planning" rather than corporate class planning mainly characterized the New Deal [*The New Deal and the Problem of Monopoly* (Princeton, N.J.: 1966), p. 480].

the Office of War Mobilization, the last of the World War II planning agencies. Class-conscious politicians and administrators today influence or control the Department of Defense, agencies within HUD, HEW, and the Departments of Commerce, Transportation, and Treasury, and State, the Council of Economic Advisors (CEA), and the Bureau of the Budget. Because conflicts within the corporate ruling class must be reconciled and compromised and because of the complex and wide-ranging nature of the interests of this class, policy is dictated not by a single directorate but by a multitude of private, quasi-public, and public agencies. Policy is formulated within the highly influential Business Council, in key universities and policy-planning agencies such as the Foreign Policy Association and the Committee for Economic Development (CED), and by the corporate-dominated political parties. This policy is a key input in the formulation of legislation initiated by the executive branch. But the president and his key aides must remain independent; they must interpret class (as opposed to particular economic) corporate interests and translate these interests into action, not only in terms of immediate economic and political needs, but also in terms of the relations between monopoly capital and competitive sector labor and capital. Monopoly capitalist class interests (as a social force rather than as an abstraction) are not the aggregate of the particular interest of this class but rather emerge within the state administration "unintentionally." In this important sense, the capitalist state is not an "instrument" but a "structure."

The second way production relations are expressed politically is in the regulation of interclass social relations to ensure that the technical level of the work force will be reproduced and expanded (social capital) and the social order as a whole maintained (social expenses). Around the turn of the century, populist, labor, and socialist forces posed a potentially serious threat to American capitalism. In a series of political steps designed to prevent popular movements from (in Marx's words) "removing the extremes of society" (capital and wage labor), corporate leaders and the political directorate sought "to weaken their antagonisms and transform them into a harmonious whole." The state must try to integrate all elements of the population into a coherent system, win mass loyalty, and legitimate itself and society. Far and away the most important element is monopoly sector organized labor, which gradually was taught to adopt responsible attitudes and behavior toward monopoly capital and capitalist society. This required regular cooperation between the leaders of organized labor, the corporations, and the state to head off mass social movements, transform collective bargaining into an instrument of corporate planning, strive for a high level of employment and wages commensurate with productivity advances, and maintain labor's reproductive powers, with regard not only to the level of private consumption but also to social consumption (social insurance, health, housing, etc.).

The need to develop and maintain a "responsible" social order also has led to the creation of agencies and programs designed to control the surplus population politically and to fend off the tendency toward a legitimization crisis. The government attempts to administer and bureaucratize (encapsulate) not only monopoly sector labor-management conflict but also social-political conflict emerging from competitive sector workers and the surplus population. The specific agencies for regulating the relations between capital and organized labor and unorganized workers are many and varied—for example, agencies within HUD and HEW, the Department of Labor, the National Labor Relations Board (NLRB), the National Mediation Board and Federal Mediation and Conciliation Service, the Social Security Administration, various congressional committees, state employment agencies (or human resource development agencies), and so on. Some of these agencies were established primarily to maintain social control of the surplus population (e.g., HEW's Bureau of Family Services); others serve mainly to attempt to maintain harmony between labor and capital within the monopoly sector (e.g., the Bureau of Old Age and Survivors Insurance). In both cases the state must remain independent or "distant" from the particular interests of capital (which are very different from the politically organized interests of capital as the ruling class). The basic problem is to win mass loyalty to insure legitimacy; too intimate a relation between capital and state normally is unacceptable or inadmissable to the ordinary person.

The state also regulates the relations between big and small capital (e.g., the Small Business Administration, various farm agencies, etc.), between capital based in different regions (e.g., TVA), and between capital in expanding and contracting sectors of the economy (e.g., the Maritime Administration within the Department of Commerce). Relations between small-scale capital and the working class also must be regulated (e.g., Department of Agriculture programs designed to protect consumers). Because it requires their political support for national and international programs, monopoly capital cannot afford to antagonize local and regional capital needlessly. Subsidies must be granted to declining industries (e.g., fishing) and to capital in underdeveloped regions (e.g., Appalachia). The Department of Agriculture, Department of Commerce agencies, many congressional committees, and federal grant-in-aid programs are deeply involved in managing relations within the business classes, and permanently engaged in financing small-scale capital's political support for large-scale capital's programs.[9]

---

9. There is a final aspect of state power—the state's dependence on banks and other financial institutions to float the state dept. In times of national emergency this dependence has dissolved—for example, during World War II, when the treasury compelled the Federal Reserve to support federal bond prices, and during the Vietnam War, when the treasury borrowed from federal trust funds (i.e., from itself). At the state and local government levels the dependence of the state on finance capital for capital funds is great . . .

Finally, the state administration itself has its own logic or rationality. As we know, the state has two major functions—"accumulation" and "loyalty." These two functions are contradictory and it is the task of administrative rationality in every state agency to try to reconcile them. . . .

These functions of the national state, which are not unique to modern capitalism, but which have taken new forms during the twentieth century, are extremely expensive. Further, these functions require effective central executive control over the federal budget and administrative machinery. The exception is interest-group economic needs, to which the legislative branch and many executive agencies are highly responsive. Modern capitalism, a system of highly specialized and interdependent production, also requires central coordination and control. Finally in the context of the conflict between capitalism and world revolution and socialism, the leading capitalist powers (chiefly the United States) require a highly centralized system of military production and distribution—a military-industrial complex—that functions more or less independently of the legislative branch.

The growth of the executive branch, the development of class politics within both the executive and legislature, and the decline of "particularism" in Congress, is a familiar story. Less familiar, but important for understanding the fiscal crisis are the corresponding changes in budgetary control and policy. . . .

STATE CAPITALIST BUDGETARY PRINCIPLES AND CONTROL

A brief review of the changing relationships between and within the legislative and executive branches of the federal government is needed to appreciate the significance of the revolutionary developments in the budgetary principles of modern capitalism. In Britain the rising middle classes transformed the budget into an instrument of financial control over the crown during their struggle for political representation. In the United States a revolution eliminated the crown, removing any analogous development. From the very beginning there existed a relatively close harmony between Congress and the executive because both closely represented the interests of local and regional capital. The budget was from the beginning the expression of the particular interests of the farmer, planter, and merchant classes (and later the industrialists), and was always a source of private profit. By the early twentieth century, the ascendancy of national capital and the regional interest groups began to drive a wedge between the power of local or particular interests and the legislative and executive branches. The latter finally became the representative of national capital. The former still largely represents regional and local capital (and branches of organized labor). Congress became increasingly unable or unwilling to exercise its prerogatives and voluntarily or involuntarily helped transfer them to the executive and to class-conscious congressional leaders. Since the turn of the century congressional control over appropriations has become increasingly weak. Congress has disabled itself in several ways—for example, by establishing revolving funds, creating government corporations, refusing to prohibit transfers between appropriations, authorizing the use of departmental receipts without limitation of amount, and voting lump-sum appropriations.[10] Attempts to reestablish control by voting specific appropriations, "far from securing to Congress that completeness of financial control which is ... its constitutional birthright, has served only to make the law less certain and to satisfy Congress with the name rather than the substance of power."[11] Congressional control after funds have been appropriated has been equally weak, especially in comparison with Britain, where the House of Commons is able to ensure that its policies are carried out "accurately, faithfully, and efficiently."[12]

Meanwhile, class-conscious elements within the executive (and to a lesser degree the legislative) branch have been eager to transform the budget into an instrument of national economic planning. The executive branch has consolidated its own financial powers by mingling appropriations, bringing forward the unexpended balance of former appropriations and backward the anticipated balance of future appropriations, and impounding appropriations it does not want to spend.[13]

However, the executive branch has long recognized that securing financial control requires changes in the formal character of the budget. Between 1912 and 1956, four presidential commissions made essentially the same recommendations for budgetary reform. A key figure was Frederick Cleveland, chairman of President Taft's Commission on Economy and Efficiency, whose work subsequently became extremely influential in higher corporate circles. Summarizing the ideas of these commissions, Sharkansky writes,

> The Cleveland-Buck school of reformers would have the agencies present their budget requests to the president, together with detailed information about past accomplishments of each program and the accomplishments to be expected from a given level of expenditures. The president and his Bureau of the Budget would edit these requests for the purpose of developing a budget coinciding with their policy intentions. Then a single Executive Budget would go to a single Appropriations Committee in the House and Senate, together with supporting data about agency accomplishments and expectations.[14]

---

10. Lucius Wilmerding, Jr., *The Spending Power, a History of the Efforts of Congress to Control Expenditures* (New Haven, Conn.: 1943), p. 193.

11. Ibid., p. 195.

12. Basil Chubb, *The Control of Public Expenditures* (London: 1952), p. 1.

13. *The Spending Power,* op. cit., p. 194.

14. *The Politics of Taxing and Spending,* op. cit.

Finally, the unified Appropriations Committee and Congress as a whole would review and act on these requests. Cabinet members would be given the privileges of the floor in Congress to explain and defend their past actions and present proposals.

The thrust of these proposals is to force congressmen to act "responsibly" in budgetary matters—that is, to act in the interests of the society as a whole (meaning monopoly capital). Behind-the-scene deals would be eliminated, congressmen would be forced out into the open, and the special interests they represent would be exposed to public view. Needless to say, these proposals have not been implemented because they would eliminate the raison d'être for Congress—the game of give and take it plays.

However, at least three major budgetary changes have been made—each a step in the direction of centralized executive budgetary control. The first was the creation of the Bureau of the Budget by the Budget and Accounting Act of 1920 and the introduction of the administrative budget, which coordinates expenditures proposed by the executive. Coordinated executive expenditures were recommended by Alexander Hamilton, the first Secretary of the Treasury, but individual executive departments and agencies dealt directly with congressional committees until 1920. In effect, there was no federal budget, but rather a series of "congressional budgets" which were developed by particular economic and political interest groups and combined into a budget bill which was then signed by the president.

What enabled the executive branch to make this change? Dave Eakins has established that the origins of the federal administrative budget can be found in the municipal reform movement which began in the 1890s and reached its zenith in the 1920s. By 1890, as a result of immigration and industrialization, a large and growing proletariat was crowded into the urban centers. The urban working class was organized by political machines, which were by no means models of democracy, but which did "deliver the goods" to their constituents. Corporate liberal reformers (lawyers, businessmen, professionals, et al.) agitated against the corrupt machines and the ward system and working-class representation on school boards; in general they sought to give more authority to the city executive—the mayor or city council (or city managers). Established in 1905, the New York Bureau of Municipal Research pushed for city commission government, a strong mayor's office, and a centralized city budget. During the first three decades of the twentieth century, the Bureau exported some of its experience to other cities and the municipal reform movement was widely successful. Subsequently, the reformers turned their attention to the federal government. A new organization, the corporate-dominated and class-conscious Institute for Government Research (later to become the Brookings Institution, which was set up and staffed by many who had been active in municipal reform) led the way in convincing business-men, Congress, and the public that a national budget was indispensable for "efficient" national administration. One move was to reorganize and streamline the executive branch with the aim of trying to establish effective administrative control from the top. Another was to create an administrative budget, the basic instrument for coordinating congressional committees, which remained responsive to the needs of special interests within the owning classes.

The administrative budget has been described as the chief mode of "management and control by the executive and Congress over activities financed with federal funds . . . [This] (once approved) becomes a tool of executive control over the spending of the various departments, agencies and government corporations."[15] Although executive agencies continued to prepare their own estimates, the locus of responsibility was shifted by the 1920 act from Congress to the president, who was made formally responsible for initiating an annual budget through his new staff agency, the Bureau of the Budget (now the Office of Management and Budget—OBM). In sum, it was not until well into the twentieth century that monopoly capital was strong and well-organized enough for the state to try to impose the monopoly sector's class interests on society. And the working class could not resist successfully either the municipal reform movement in most cities or the centralization of national political power and budgetary control accomplished by the Budget and Accounting Act.

The second major step toward class-conscious and executive domination of the national budget has been the gradual shift from line-item budgets to program budgets. Line-item budgets classify expenditures in terms of the items to be purchased, whereas *program budgets* classify outlays in terms of the outputs that will be produced by a given program (or services provided). Program budgeting is a device for steering the economy as a whole and centralizing the allocation of budgetary resources—and for ameliorating the fiscal crisis. Beginning in 1961, program budgeting was introduced in the Department of Defense in the more elaborate program-performance-budgeting system (PPBS). By combining program budgeting with detailed measurement of costs and performance efficiency ("performance budgeting" was first introduced in 1951), PPBS permits expenditure decisions to be based on comparisons of the costs and effectiveness of alternative ways of achieving the objectives of "public policy." It assumes that public policy is already determined and thus that there are no political conflicts, or that political conflicts that do arise concern the allocation of scarce resources, which always can be rationalized.

---

15. David J. and Attiat F. Ott, *Federal Budget Policy* (Washington, D.C.: 1965), p. 6. European fiscal planning has undergone similar changes.

In 1968, twenty-three major departments and agencies prepared program budgets, and many other departments were encouraged to do so.[16] The Bureau of the Budget, which was supposed to monitor PPBS programs, was in fact, the main user of PPBS. A few class-conscious senators (e.g., William Proxmire) have endorsed it, but most congressmen and agency heads have been either hostile or indifferent to the system: The special interests of powerful agency constituencies would not be served, and might be undermined, by such policy analysis.[17]

Because of resistance to PPBS, contained specialization and incremental decisionmaking remain the two main budgeting devices. *Contained specialization* refers to the takeover of budgetary decisions by specialists who are guided by professional and technical criteria. *Incremental decisionmaking* means that budget experts accept programs and policies presently in force, and strive mightily to avoid political disputes or otherwise upset the status quo. With the widespread use of these devices political expertise and professional competence replace "partisan infighting"—in other words, budgetary decisions tend to be taken out of the realm of politics and become bureaucratized.[18]

Specialization and incremental decisionmaking appeal to many economists in policymaking positions. For example, Arthur Smithies writes that "budgeting is essentially an economic problem in solving as it does the allocation of scarce resources among almost insatiable and competing demands."[19] This school of thought denies that budgetary issues are political in character and sees little or no difference between the allocation of resources by the household or business firm, on the one hand, and the state, on the other. Critical analysis of the state and the budget is replaced by an implicit acceptance of the given balance of private interests and relationships. "Certainly," writes another economist, "the most fruitful systems analyses have not indulged in argument about objectives for argument's sake, but have been forced to review existing objectives and priorities as inconsistencies among them have appeared or because they proved to be inappropriate under changing conditions."[20]

Superficially, the whole purpose of PPBS (which sees process politics and incremental decisionmaking as interferences in the planning process) is to reveal and rationalize conflicting or inconsistent objectives,

16. David Novick, ed., *Program Budgeting-Program Analysis and the Federal Budget* (Cambridge, Mass.: 1965), passim.

17. Keith E. Marvin and Andrew M. Rouse, "The Status of PPBS in the Federal Agencies: A Comparative Perspective," in Robert Haveman and Julius Margolis, eds., *Public Expenditures and Policy Analysis* (Chicago: 1970), pp. 451–52.

18. *The Politics of Taxing and Spending*, op. cit., p. 34. "The norms of technical competence and professionalism seem more prevalent than partisan infighting in the [Ways and Means] Committee deliberations" (ibid., p. 39).

19. Arthur Smithies, *The Budgetary Process in the United States* (New York: 1955), pp. xiv–xv.

20. *Public Expenditures and Policy Analysis*, op. cit., p. 426.

but underlying this is the state-corporate planners' desire to serve state-corporate planning as a whole by forcing compromises when conflict arises within or between economic classes over particular issues. The real significance of program budgeting, however, is that it is a step toward strengthening the executive office in relation not only to the federal agencies but also to special interests in the Congress. The program budget, Jesse Burkhead correctly states, "becomes a technique, not for management at the operating level, but for the centralization of administrative authority."[21]

As suggested above, the application of program budgeting has been limited. The basic reason is that PPBS by itself cannot challenge or change underlying power relations. Congress has insisted on maintaining the radical disjuncture between the legislation and the funding of new programs. Enabling or authorizing legislation is not handled by the appropriations committees in the two houses, but rather by substantive committees such as Public Works. The power of particular interests in the substantive committees and executive agencies is described by Wiedenbaum as

> institutional obstacles to improving the allocation of public resources.... The end result . . . is that the process of public resource allocation is hardly deliberate and systematic choice among alternatives that economists try to envision. Rather, it is a fragmented and compartmentalized affair. Many of the key decisions are not made during the budget process or within the budgetary framework at all.[22]

In a nutshell, as Wildavsky writes, at the highest level of government it is "difficult to get and find a national consensus" on priorities and goals, "The 'grand objectives'—how much health, how much education, how much welfare, and which groups in the population shall benefit—are questions of value judgment and politics. Yet [PPBS] analysis cannot make much contribution to their resolution."[23] In terms of budgetary priorities for social consumption and welfare (i.e., in areas where priorities are determined by the relations of production) there can be no consensus on national goals. In these spheres PPBS is particularly irrelevant. But it has also been difficult (although less so) to establish

---

21. Jesse Burkhead, "Review of David Novick, ed., *Program Budgeting-Program Analysis and the Federal Budget," American Economic Review* 56:4 (September, 1966): 943.

22. Murray Wiedenbaum, "Institutional Obstacles to Reallocating Government Expenditures," in *Public Expenditures and Policy Analysis,* op. cit., p. 233.

One reflection of these "institutional obstacles" is that little more than one-half of federal expenditures are relatively controllable; the remainder are made out of trust funds or are permanent or indefinite expenditures or fixed charges. Wiedenbaum estimates that only 12 percent of the Labor Department and HEW's budget is controllable; 30 percent of the Agriculture's; 56 percent of HUD's budget. Interestingly enough, the Defense Department's budget contains the largest amount of controllable expenditures—97 percent (ibid., p. 239, table I).

23. Aaron Wildavsky, "Rescuing Policy Analysis from PPBS," in *Public Expenditures and Policy Analysis,* op. cit., p. 320.

national goals for social investment and military spending. (Under the Nixon administration systems analysis has suffered a decline even in the Defense Department.) The scope for the determination of budgetary priorities by special interests remains fairly wide, albeit not as wide as in the past. Thus, PPBS has had "limited application [because of] the inability of the (Budget) Bureau to significantly overhaul its own or the bureaucracy's budget traditions."[24]

In sum, even after widespread experimentation with program budgeting, budgetary priorities still are based on a mixture of class and special-interest needs. Overall budgetary planning based totally on monopoly capital's class needs is not an accomplished fact, but a future goal which will not be realized until administrative power is effectively centralized within the executive branch.

There is one important exception to this conclusion—*aggregative fiscal policy,* or the determination of the total volume of spending and taxation. The federal budget is closely connected with general economic movements (revenue, e.g., is determined by ups and downs in the tax base). In turn, general economic conditions are determined in part by the federal budget (by changes in the tax rate and level of spending). As federal spending and taxation have grown in absolute and relative terms, the executive (the only branch structurally capable of fiscal planning) has had to take into account the two-way movements between total taxation and spending and total employment, income, and production. This has required even greater executive control over state finances —and a third step toward centralization of budgetary authority.

The budget contained the first analysis of expenditures and receipts on a national-income accounting basis. As early as 1947, the CED recommended the adoption of a cash-consolidated budget as a guide to fiscal planning and policy. But the national-income budget introduced in 1963 is a superior measure of the impact of federal spending on general economic activity because it excludes purely financial credit transactions and accounts for receipts and expenditures at the time of their economic impact rather than when cash receipts and payments occur. It explicitly recognizes the integral relation between the budget and the private sectors and is an essential tool of overall fiscal planning. In 1967, a presidential commission recommended a unified budget concept to eliminate the confusion that had arisen from the simultaneous use of the administrative budget, the consolidated-cash budget (which included trust funds), and the national-income accounts budget. And in 1972, fiscal planning reached a new apex with the adoption of the full-employment budget—a guide to federal spending based not on revenues collected but on revenues that would be yielded by a full-employment economy.

---

24. Allen Shick, "The Budget Bureau That Was: Thoughts on the Rise, Decline, and Future of a Presidential Agency," *Law and Contemporary Problems* 35 (Summer, 1970): p. 520.

CONGRESS AND THE EXECUTIVE:
CONTEMPORARY RELATIONSHIP

Special-interest elements within Congress, by and large, have not resisted the increasing centralization of power within the executive branch, mainly because there has been no immediate sense of loss of power. Until the fiscal crisis compelled Nixon to attempt to limit federal spending to $250 billion in 1972, the executive has been pushing for across-the-board budgetary expansion, which delights the typical representative and senator (the economyminded House Appropriations Committee excepted). More, the executive has not sought to abolish any formal legislative procedures or functions, and attempts by class-conscious congressmen to reform the congressional committee structure and thus centralize authority within the legislative branch have been a near-total failure.[25]

Most congressmen still prefer the administrative budget concept to the unified format, and few members have accepted such Keynesian concepts as full-employment surplus and fiscal drag. Congress is still inclined to emphasize the fiscal or dollar-level aspect of the budget, at the expense of its program orientation.[26] And Congress has developed its own specialized committees and its own bureaucracy (e.g., the General Accounting Office), and its appropriations procedures have remained unchanged for decades. The budget is still not considered a single piece of legislation; it is still referred to the appropriations committees where it is separated into parts which are sent to different subcommittees. "Taxes and expenditures are (still) decided separately by the separate committees in each house; although the bills on taxes and appropriations are passed by vote of the whole House and whole Senate, there is little evidence that the two groups of bills are related closely to each other when they are considered."[27] Similarly, the benefits and costs of programs authorized in specific appropriations bills are never evaluated in relation to one another. Nor are bills discussed or studied in detail by the full committees, and full House debate is rare. Each House Appropriations subcommittee is still concerned with a different division of the government, and "it is quite natural that a group of men familiar with a particular division of the executive branch will be inclined to take a parochial interest in its welfare."[28] The ex-

---

25. The Legislative Reorganization Act of 1946 attempted to create a joint committee of members of the House and Senate tax and appropriation committees. Joint committees on the budget also have been suggested at various times during the past twenty years. These and other efforts to improve the allocation of public resources have been challenged and defeated by members in both houses.

26. Aaron Wildavsky, *The Politics of the Budgetary Process* (Boston: 1964), p. 60; Richard F. Fenno, Jr., *The Power of the Purse: Appropriations Politics in Congress* (Boston: 1966), p. 316.

27. *Federal Budget Policy*, op. cit., p. 36.

28. James R. Schlesinger, *The Political Economy of National Security* (New York: 1960), p. 111.

treme example is the military budget, which has been determined by the Pentagon and the armed services committees with hardly any critical examination by Congress.

That Congress still effectively represents sundry parochial interests, and thus still views the budget as a set of individual and unrelated parts, has been particularly galling to monopoly capital. Various "reforms" that would substitute class-conscious for special-interest budgeting have been suggested by the Committee for Economic Development.[29] Corporate planner and former Budget Director Charles Schultze has denounced the "absurdity of what we are doing now," referring to the plethora of short-run budgets and appropriations bills.

Nevertheless, the executive has succeeded in exercising more and more informal controls over congressional budgetary initiatives and authority (in addition to the formal changes in budgeting already discussed). In the past any bill initiated by a congressman without "legislative clearance" from the Budget Bureau faced enormous obstacles. The Bureau had considerable control over the direction and timing of federal obligations because it reviewed each executive agency's budget requests from Congress and controlled the allocation of treasury funds to the agencies. This further enhanced the Bureau's and the executive's powers. And there has been more overall executive fiscal planning, with new agencies created to discipline Congress. In 1938, Roosevelt set up a temporary Monetary and Fiscal Advisory Board, made up of the Director of the Budget Bureau, the Chairman of the Federal Reserve System, the Secretary of the Treasury, and the Chairman of the Advisory Committee of the National Resources Commission. Later, the Office of Emergency Planning was established to deal with problems cutting across departmental lines. During the Kennedy years, the Budget Bureau, the Treasury, and the CEA were organized into an informal but powerful group responsible for overall fiscal planning (and implicitly, control over Congress). The most recent "reform" at the top was the creation of the Domestic Council to direct program planning for the president and the transformation of the Budget Bureau into the Office of Management and Budget (OMB) by the Nixon administration. Because of the persistence and strength of special-interest executive agencies and congressmen, "the budget process tends to operate as a constraint on presidential power."[30] The OMB was set up to insulate the president from the budgeting process. Nixon desired more "coordination and evaluation" of federal programs, and OMB is "a sort of elite mini-Government [which] other agencies feel is running roughshod over them." More, Congress "finds [OMB] blind to grass-root realities

---

29. See, for example, CED, *Control of Federal Government Expenditures* (New York: 1955), p. 24.

30. "The Budget Bureau That Was" op. cit., p. 521. "The capability of the Bureau to function effectively in a presidential role was impaired by the close identification of many examiners with the agencies they were assigned to review" (ibid., p. 533).

or complains that it is partly immune to Capitol Hill influence . . ."[31] Thus, budget policy is increasingly formulated by the executive without any attempt to revolutionize or modernize the congressional appropriations process. The effect of this shift in financial control to the executive has been succinctly described by Schlesinger:

> The Congress, secure in its belief that the basic legislation has established policy, may view its annual consideration of the budget formulated by the experts simply from the standpoint of assuring the most economical attainment of legislative goals. Thus policy formulation, which is so intimately connected with the appropriations levels, may slip into organizational limbo and finally be unconsciously seized by the Bureau of the Budget [today, Domestic Council and OMB]—the one organization that, in theory, should be concerned with economy and efficiency, and should be divorced entirely from policy formulation.[32]

The general result is that budget issues cease to be political issues, and the budget becomes a better planning instrument for the executive. If and when the President's Advisory Council on Executive Reorganization (Ash Council) plans to reorganize the federal executive along functional rather than program lines, administrative power will be centralized even further.

One effect is increasing executive resistance to programs tailored by Congress to local and regional interests—the interests of small-scale capital. In the long run these interests must give way to those of "society as a whole"—a euphemism for the needs of monopoly capital. Thus, for example, there is a long-run tendency for agricultural price supports and water subsidies to decline, and for federal land giveaways to be curbed. And attempts have been made to check guarantees and subsidies to railroads, airlines, waterways, and the merchant marine and to develop a comprehensive federal transportation policy. Another effect is that overall budgetary priorities change very slowly regardless of the wishes of the "current" administration. Thus, until the peak of the fiscal crisis in 1972–1973 over the past two decades, no major program introduced by previous administrations has been eliminated. For example, eight years of Republican administration in the 1950s failed to reverse the upward trend in federal spending; in fact outlays on health, education, and welfare were expanded. Now only the executive can interpret and effectively act on the needs of private capital and private interests. With regard to the operation of democratic institutions, one economist has concluded, "The relationship between the legislative and executive branches largely determines the success or failure of democratic govern-

---

31. *Wall Street Journal,* January 29, 1971.
32. *The Political Economy of National Security,* op. cit., p. 107.

ment."[33] Is it necessary to add that formal democratic government has declined in proportion to the decline of the budget as an "important instrument of legislative control"?

POLITICAL POWER AND BUDGETARY CONTROL: STATE AND LOCAL GOVERNMENT

Although the federal government frequently acts in the interests of particular industries and capitalist groups, the executive branch (and increasingly Congress as well) devotes itself to controlling the social and production relations between capital and labor. In the past, the main domestic problem was the relationship between monopoly capital and organized labor. Today, the executive is more and more preoccupied with the conditions of unorganized labor in the competitive sector, particularly black and other minority workers condemned by racism to the competitive sector and to poorly paid jobs in the monopoly sector. In addition to the relations between labor and capital in the monopoly and competitive sectors, the federal government must regulate those between labor in the competitive sector and the rest of society.

Budgetary control and determination at the state and local levels also is many-sided. The political economies of the fifty states and the economic and social structures of the thousands of local governments, special districts, supramunicipal authorities, and the rest of the 116,000 governmental units vary widely. There is, for example, a near bewildering array of types and amounts of taxes collected at the state and local levels, and there are vast differences in the percentage of funds that originate in federal, state, and local revenue sources. Then there are the variations in taxes per capita, which can be attributed not to variations in wealth and income but to social and political factors such as the strength of organized labor or the prevalence of institutionalized racism. Another factor is the "wide range of responses in the budgets of individual states" to depression, war, and postwar reconversion—and the "similar responses made by states with widely different economic and political characteristics."[34]

Nevertheless, most states share certain political-economic features; some are unique to government at the state level, others are shared by state and local government. These similarities permit us to generalize and describe the essential features of budgetmaking in the great majority of states.

First, although economic and political power are formally separated in capitalist economies, there is an intricate web of informal relations

---

33. Harold D. Smith, "The Budget as an Instrument of Legislative Control and Executive Management," *Public Administration Review* 4:3 (Summer, 1944):181.
34. *The Politics of Taxing and Spending,* op. cit., pp. 128, 138, and 173.

between state and economy, government official and businessman. Such connections exist at the federal level, but the ties between special interests and state and local bureaucracies are far more numerous and intimate. Most state legislatures are instruments of business and commerce, including specific industries and corporations. For "constituents" many state legislators have a cross section of private business—banking, oil and gas, ranching and agriculture, utilities, gambling, wholesale and retail trade, and so on. Businessmen, labor officials, professional groups, [and] lobbyists visit the state capitol not to represent an abstract "social order as a whole," but rather to advance the interests of industry, trade, or corporation. Special-interest politics and budgetary control are central to state and local as well as federal government. But at the state and local levels the special interests prevail.

Who are these "special interests"? Typically there is a one-to-one relationship between local capital in competitive industries and local power elites. At the state level the special interests represent capital not only in the competitive sector but also in the monopolistic and state sectors. Businessmen with statewide or region wide economic interests constitute the dominant stratum of the capitalist class within state political boundaries and regional economic boundaries. The political-economic perspective of regional capitalists normally reaches beyond the local level and often to the national level, which reinforces special-interest structures within the federal government.

Perhaps the most famous example of the scope and power of regional capital is the symbiotic relationship between the Nevada gambling industry and the state legislature. Other well-known examples are the industries—for example, oil, agriculture and lumbering, mining, [and] shipping—that are dependent on geography and climate. California state universities and colleges work closely with the cattle industry on such programs as crossbreeding, land conservation, animal nutrition, disease prevention, and parasite control, and the Colorado School of Mines serves the mining industry. The Texas Railroad Commission is the instrument of the oil industry, and in Oregon the lumber interests and the legislature work hand in hand. In Illinois

> among the taxpayers' group is a powerful bloc composed of business organizations such as the State Chamber of Commerce, the Illinois Manufacturers' Association, the Chicago Association of Commerce and Industry, and the Illinois Association of Retail Merchants. . . . In general, all (of these groups) stand for maintaining the status quo and the retention of a "favorable business climate" in tax matters.[35]

---

35. Glenn W. Fisher, *Taxes and Politics: A Study of Illinois Public Finance* (Urbana, Ill.: 1969), pp. 178–179. Fisher's is one of the few studies that does more than suggest the symbiotic relationship between particular economic interests and state government power.

The political economy of state government is complex. Under the federal system, "the powers not delegated to the United States by the Constitution, nor prohibited by it to the states, are reserved to the states respectively, or to the people." Local government, thus, is subordinate to—dominated by and dependent on—state government. Accordingly the businessman in the competitive sector (local capital), whose economic interests are confined to a particular city or metropolitan area, normally adopts a statewide political perspective because political power is located in the State House.

Thus, for example, in order to win favorable legislation, local capital in retail trade is compelled to organize trade associations on a statewide basis even in the absence of statewide markets or investments.

The second characteristic of state budgetmaking is its limited perspective. Both federal and state governments attempt to regulate the relationships between labor, capital, and government officials, but state governments are not responsible for macroeconomic planning. Further, capitalists and organized labor perceive such issues as collective bargaining, minimum wages, or hours laws in regional terms. For these reasons, the production relations are administered to serve particular industries or sectors of the economy, not the social order. Construction, the most important state and local industry, is organized by regional and local capitalists and is allied with real estate, agriculture, banking, and other industries. Contractors, building suppliers, and construction unions form powerful lobbies in every state capitol and city hall. Each year state legislatures and city councils pass prolabor legislation and budget items. A notable example is the preservation and strengthening of archaic codes that protect markets for building materials and labor power. Such measures underscore the different political economic functions of federal and state (and local) "labor " legislation. The purpose of the former is to maintain social and economic peace throughout the social order. The latter "favors" workers employed by particular industries which themselves are afforded privileged treatment by law and budget. Finally, it should be added that monopoly sector capital and labor, which often are in agreement on national issues, are divided in state and local politics: Taxes required to finance pro labor programs—property taxes, business income taxes, and so on—cannot be shifted as easily as the federal corporate income tax is shifted.

How is state budget making shaped by local and regional capital and organized labor? First, workers in the competitive sector who are not represented by strong unions (or special-interest groups) have negligible direct or indirect influence. Consequently, little is appropriated for welfare, health, and other services needed by these workers. In this way the federal system deepens divisions between monopoly sector workers and organized, skilled workers in industries such as construction, on the one hand, and unorganized competitive sector workers, on the other. The latter often not only are "passively" excluded from the budgetmaking process, but also are actively opposed when they attempt to organize and gain political influence. Powerful regional and local businessmen rely on low-paid wage labor, high rents for slum properties, high interest rates on personal loans, high prices in ghetto retail establishments, and so on. Powerful unions are determined to protect hard-won privileges and exclusive spheres of influence. Thus, for example, organized labor normally seeks to keep welfare costs down in order to minimize property and sales taxes, and other local levies paid by workers. Or black organizations that seek public funds for ghetto reconstruction (and oppose urban renewal designed to serve downtown business interests) run athwart the politically powerful alliance between white contractors and white-dominated labor unions.

Second, a high priority is given to "economic development programs"—that is, direct and indirect subsidies granted to particular industries and economic sectors. Summarizing the findings of a comprehensive study of the New York metropolitan area, Robert C. Wood writes that

> the attitudes of the participants [in government], the nature of the political process, and the rules of the political game strengthen the economic trends in being. They leave most of the important decisions for regional development to the private marketplace. They work in ways which by and large encourage firms and households to continue "doing what comes naturally."[36]

Wood continued:

> the system of quasi-governmental agencies, the authorities and public corporations with programs which leap over municipal boundaries buttresses the marketplace ... as a matter of conscious design. ... Success seems to smile on the transport agencies that favor the auto, the housing project that reclaims a potentially profitable downtown site, the water resources program which responds to a present need rather than anticipating—and helping to shape—the future pattern of development.[37]

The fiscal function of state governments and agencies thus is chiefly to provide social capital and social investment ... State and local budgets emphasize education and highway transportation—and the education budget itself is focused on supplying a work force for private capital.

Special interests are even more powerful at the local level. City and local junior colleges train skilled and technical manpower for local industry; downtown business interests (utilities, large retail establish-

---

36. Robert C. Wood, "The Political Economy of the Future," in Benjamin Chintz, ed., *City and Suburb* (Englewood Cliffs, N.J.: 1964), p. 151.
37. Ibid., p. 152.

ments, banks, etc.) normally determine urban renewal priorities and expenditures; local transit systems and zoning and license laws are designed to serve local business and property owners. Beyond this, local government is also responsive to the needs of regional and national monopoly capital with local plants, offices, and other facilities. Thus, Detroit city government cannot afford to ignore the automobile companies; downtown renewal in St. Louis was shaped by the Busch interests; the Mellons wield great power in Pittsburgh; Wilmington (indeed all of Delaware) in many respects is the private preserve of the du Ponts; the Rockefellers are not without influence in shaping Manhattan's political economy; and so on.

[Referring to] the intimate relationship between big business and local government in American cities . . . Oliver Williams has termed this the "investor city"—one of four basic types of local government in America. Dominated by local or national capitalists who view it is an instrument of capital accumulation (or as a corporation that should be run in accordance with business principles), the investor city "stands ready to enact zoning variations, reduce tax assessments, provide subsidies, develop industrial parks, install utilities, and do whatever else may be required to keep labor costs low and promote production."[38] In this kind of city the distinction between private and public power is unclear and public investment is a special form of private investment. Several studies of local power in America suggest that the investor city is very common.

Power in the investor city has been consolidated by the development of city manager and commission government, nonpartisanship, and special district government. Corporate liberal businessmen and business-oriented civic reformers introduced commission government and nonpartisanship in the late nineteenth century because of the increasing importance of the city's economic and social functions. Shortages of good streets, electric lighting, public transportation, water and sewage disposal systems, and other facilities were developing. Business wanted forms of local government in which economic and social issues could be resolved in an atmosphere of nonpartisanship—that is, they wanted institutions in which these issues could be settled administratively or bureaucratically. The proliferation of nonschool special districts from the 1940s through the 1960s (special districts make up about two-thirds of U.S. governmental units) has placed more local decision making on an administrative rather than political basis. This development troubles even orthodox political scientists. "One serious argument against [special districts]," John Bollens writes, "is the inability of the public to exert adequate control over them."[39]

---

38. Oliver Williams, "A Typology of Comparative Local Government," *Midwest Journal of Political Science* (May, 1961): 160.

39. John C. Bollens, *Special District Governments in the United States* (Berkeley, Calif.: 1957), p. 252.

Although thousands of municipalities are directly or indirectly controlled by local, regional, or national capitalists, alone or in alliance, the largest cities are controlled by "arbiter governments" (to use Williams' categories). In New York, Chicago, Philadephia, and other major cities, local government perceives its basic task as managing social and economic conflict between and within economic classes. The fundamental characteristic of arbiter cities is the domination of a political machine or charismatic leader. The size of the working class, the influence of local labor organizations, and the heterogeneous character of the business and commercial interests combine to make it difficult or impossible for business to establish clearcut control. As a consequence, capital has been compelled to establish supramunicipal authorities (e.g., Bay Area Rapid Transit District and Port of New York Authority), economic development corporations, and other agencies that make budgetary decisions outside of the normal political process and hence are relatively insulated from and indifferent to working-class majorities.

Keeping in mind the political framework in state governments and investor or arbiter city governments, budgeting procedures and controls are readily comprehensible. The dominant private interests (particularly the leading industries) predetermine the volume of state spending and the major budgetary priorities. There is little planning at the state and local levels, and the role of financial expertise and integrated decision-making (so important at the federal level) is minimal.[40] Although there has been a greater emphasis on "executive leadership" throughout the twentieth century, state agencies still tend to be more or less independent of the governor (and thus more amenable to the influence of special interests). This clearly limits the possibility of an integrated approach to budgeting. In many states earmarking of funds protects the special interests from both the governor and the legislature. In Alabama, to cite the most extreme example, almost 90 percent of all state revenue is earmarked for specific purposes. Over 50 percent of state taxes is earmarked in twenty states; and in another twenty states between 30 and 50 percent is earmarked. One student of state budgeting concludes that "chief executives and legislators have surrendered much of their potential for innovation for a more limited role as reviewers of administrators' requests. State legislators seem to have accepted a more limited supervisory role than the governors."[41] Similar conclusions were drawn by another student of state budgeting after an investigation of the restricted role of the state legislature in the budgetary process in Illinois.

---

40. *The Politics of Taxing and Spending,* op. cit., p. 84. In the eighteenth and early nineteenth centuries, when the property tax was the only (or nearly the only) revenue source, there was a close relationship between taxes and expenditures and correspondingly close legislative control of the budget.

41. Ibid., p. 111.

Despite its formal authority over appropriations, the 1963 General Assembly was virtually powerless in the determination of State expenditures. . . . The legislature had no criteria of its own to apply to [appropriations] bills other than the fact that they were appropriations and therefore worthy of passage. In the absence of such criteria legislative behavior could only produce a stamp of acceptance for decisions made elsewhere. As an institution the legislature was incapable of doing more.[42]

Routine appropriations and incremental budgetary changes are more typical of local than of state government. Normally, current appropriations are kept in line with past spending, and every effort is made to balance the budget, in part because local budget makers are more dependent upon economic conditions within their narrow jurisdiction than their counterparts at the state level.[43] But it is also partly due to the near-total domination of local government by special interests. At the state level the oil industry, the freeway lobby, the railroads, the utilities, the liquor interest, the food chains, and other segments of the economy are forced to haggle for what they want. But at the municipal level mayors, city councils, and city managers tend to be directly responsible to the dominant local industries (which frequently are allied with organized labor). Thus, local budgetary initiatives and planning normally are introduced through the back door in the form of new special districts and/or new federal government aid tied to innovative programs.[44]

Williams identified two other types of local government. "Caretaker government" is found in small towns and rural communities where business interests are marginal and require little or no state-financed infrastructure and where population density is small, education is relatively neglected, and farm or rural families provide many or most of their own services—wells, cesspools, and so on. In other words, caretaker government creates conditions under which residents can take care of themselves; it provides little social investment or social consumption. Caretaker government, which was characteristic of nineteenth-century America, is dying out. The fourth type is rapidly growing in number and size. This is the middle-class and working-class residential suburb which defines its main task as providing life's amenities and specializes in social consumption.

THE "CHALLENGE TO FEDERALISM"

Because of growing regional and national economic integration, the development of regional economic units with distinct social and eco-

---

42. Thomas J. Anton, *The Politics of State Expenditures in Illinois* (Urbana, Ill.: 1966), pp. 246–47. Anton continues that "decisions with regard to large [expenditures] increases, and all other major decisions made in 1963, were determined by the Governor, or persons acting in his name" (ibid.)
43. *The Politics of Taxing and Spending*, op. cit., p. 126.
44. Ibid., p. 96.

nomic problems (e.g., transport, education, land-use, health, etc.), and increasing economic concentration and centralization, monopoly capital requires more top-down administration and budgetary planning, especially around regional needs. But because of the persistence of small-business control of state and local governments, the proliferation of special districts and authorities, and the general fragmentation of local political and budgetary power (together with the regressive character of local tax systems), the struggle for centralized political administration and fiscal planning has been a protracted one. At the local level the long-term trend is unmistakable—mayors' terms have been lengthened and their powers of appointment and removal have been broadened. In the larger cities the mayor has been given authority to formulate and execute the municipal budget (New York City has attempted to use PPBS). Similarly, the trend is clear at the state level: Most states have created a more powerful governor and have adopted centralized budgeting systems. And interstate compacts, which are unresponsive to the general public but which are highly responsive to specialized interests, are proliferating.[45]

Far more ominous from the standpoint of small business and other local and parochial interests (not to speak of community-control insurgency movements) is the usurpation of local political and budgetary power by the national state—a trend that is well advanced in developed capitalist societies. In France parliamentary control of the national budget continues to decline.[46] In Japan during the 1950s and 1960s "the amalgamation of cities began to be promoted by the government in connection with regional development plans . . . [T]he development of capitalism demands . . . a widening of administrative areas."[47]Local government and political federalism in West Germany are under attack by big business and the national state (the official 1966 Report on Financial Reform states that "certain problems of decisive importance cannot be satisfactorily resolved within the limits of the traditional structure of Federalism").[48]

There has been a gradual erosion of the traditional federal system in the United States. Monopoly capitalist groups and the federal executive have been working together to increase federal power in local affairs and, step-by-step, to dismantle local government. The expansion of federal political and fiscal power has ranged from national clean air and

45. Marian E. Ridgeway, *Interstate Compacts: A Question of Federalism* (Carbondale, Ill.: 1971), p. 296.

46. Andrew Shonfield, *Modern Capitalism* (Oxford: 1965), pp. 130 and 145.

47. "Local Governments and their Financial Administration in Post-War Japan," op. cit., p. 117.

48. Elmar Altvater, "West Germany: The Soul Message," *International Socialist Review* 3:16–17 (November, 1966): 394–95.

water standards and the thousands of federal guidelines that are part of grants-in-aid packages[49] to programs for national coordination of police activity.

Various business-oriented groups and commissions are attempting to "reform" local government and fiscal system. The influential Advisory Commission on Intergovernmental Relations has endorsed broadening local jurisdictions, transferring functions between governments, and sharing fiscal and other responsibilities.[50] And the CED has long sought to create the basis for federal and monopoly capital budgetary planning on the local and regional levels. In a report released in the 1950s, the CED strongly emphasized the importance of local capital budgeting, putting away sums from annual budgets for capital improvements, and increasing debt and developing centralized marketing arrangements to help small municipalities and other local governments raise more money more cheaply.[51] Since the 1950s the deterioration of local government, mounting regional needs, the worsening fiscal crisis, and the growing power of the people's insurgency movements at the local level have compelled big business to make bolder and more far-reaching recommendations for "reform." In 1966, the CED urged that overlapping layers of local government be curtailed and that only members of policymaking bodies be selected (which would sharply reduce the number of elected local officials). It also recommended that one chief executive (either elected or appointed) be placed in charge of all administrative agencies and that all department chiefs be appointed, and that 54,000 of the country's 80,000 local government units be abolished.[52]

The recommendations outlined above are formulas for federal and big business control of the country's principal regions. Monopoly capital–directed regional planning and government (which ultimately will require that the power to tax be granted regional agencies) and federal spending and tax programs have developed hand in hand. . . .

---

49. See, for example, HEW, *A Guide for Local Government Agencies: Establishing Cost Allocation Plans and Indirect Cost Proposals for Grants and Contracts Within the Federal Government* (Washington, D.C., 1970). The issue of revenue sharing and federal power is discussed in more detail in chap. 8.

50. Advisory Commission on Intergovernmental Relations, *Metropolitan America: Challenge to Federalism* (Washington, D.C., 1966).

51. Committee for Economic Development, *Defense Against Recession,* March 1954, pp. 45–46.

52. CED, *Modernizing Local Government,* July 1966, pp. 8–16.

Part 6

Social Conflict and the Struggle for Power

Every theory of political power has an underlying conception not only of the rulers but of the ruled—of who "the people" are and what they might be, of the potential that lies within them to transform themselves and the conditions under which they live. In short, a theory of political power is also a theory of social conflict and what the struggle for power is all about. These are the central issues in this final part of our book. In particular, the issues concern, first, the source and meaning of the black uprisings in our cities in the late 1960s and, second, whether these presaged the emergence of an even more profound social movement in America made up of ordinary working men and women, black and white alike, bent on consciously making their own history.

Thus Col. Robert B. Rigg, Ret., U.S. Army, argues (Selection Number 32) that "racial issues, poverty, political unrest among minorities, the population explosion, and the rapid growth of strip cities that absorb the decaying old core cities—all these represent a combination of future factors and trends that could plague metropolitan areas." The future is grim, he believes, because a new frame of mind is emerging among American minorities, "an outlook that visualizes rebellion against society and authority as a successful venture for the future." America's cities, argues Rigg, could soon become the center of a special brand of internal warfare bearing the unique label, "Made in USA." Given leadership, organization, and political direction, unrest that once led only to sporadic "riots" could be transformed into an urban insurrectionary movement.

You need not point to the "red flag of communism," Rigg says, to appreciate the fact that violence, dissidence, and disaffection can threaten the United States from within. National Guard units could end up being on active duty in many of our cities as activists of the left who protested against the war in Vietnam and "communist elements" turn to foment and organize "urban unrest and trouble" by whites and blacks alike to protest against poverty and their environment. Militancy, he believes, has replaced defeatism and complacency in the slums.

From a military standpoint, Rigg claims, successful warfare against urban-based guerrillas in American cities could be as difficult and prolonged as the fighting was in Vietnam if the insurrection is well organized. Thus, there are several problems to confront: "political and intelligence penetration" as well as disruption of the insurrectionary forces; provision of accurate information on the facilities used by the urban guerrillas; development of a whole new manual of military operations for such urban warfare; coordination of the police, FBI, Army, National Guard, and local political authority; and the establishment of vital communications networks. "Limited wars" are likely right here in our own country; therefore, Rigg urges, U.S. Army units must be trained to know every American city intimately. American troops must be fully prepared to go to war against their fellow Americans.

Evidently "political and intelligence penetration" of left organizations and efforts "to disrupt organization itself," were already well underway when Rigg was writing. In 1971, as Senator Frank Church observes, "the Senate Subcommittee on Constitutional Rights exposed the massive surveillance of Americans by the U.S. Army intelligence system," and in Senate Intelligence Committee hearings from late 1974 through 1975 it was disclosed that nationwide "surveillance of law-abiding citizens and groups" was carried out by the FBI and CIA.[1] The Army and FBI maintained files on "dissident groups" and "prominent persons" who might "sympathize" with them—civil rights activists, black militants, folksingers, ministers, priests, professors, students, union leaders, senators, and congressmen. Between the mid-1960s and 1971, over 100,000 politically active Americans were under Army surveillance, and well over half a million by the FBI. "Yet not a single individual or group" was prosecuted under the alleged statutory basis for these investigations. The FBI employed 1,500 informants and engaged in "warrantless invasions" of personal affairs through "squealers," "finks," and "stool pidgeons" in 85 percent of its domestic intelligence cases. FBI informants and "turncoats" infiltrated and reported on antiwar, civil rights, and women's liberation organizations across America. There was not only widespread investigation, but also warrantless wiretapping and bugging; both the FBI and CIA broke into hundreds of homes and offices during the 1960s alone. "In some cases, these breakins were to install microphones; in other cases, they were to steal such items as membership lists from organizations considered 'subversive' by the bureau." The FBI also "squelched" or "forestalled" publication of articles about its own activities, as well as favorable ones about political dissenters (e.g. Dr. Martin Luther King).

There was also widespread "harrassment" of people simply on the basis of their political beliefs and life-styles. The FBI had "programs to disrupt, discredit, and destroy groups and individuals," according to the Senate Intelligence report, and "to prevent dissenters from meeting or engaging in protest activity." The FBI purposely interviewed New Left activists "to enhance the paranoia endemic in these circles" and "get the point across there is an FBI agent behind every mailbox," as an FBI internal memorandum put it; and it mailed anonymous derogatory letters and made threatening phone calls as if from others in the movement. (Stokely Carmichael left for Africa the day after his mother got an anonymous FBI phone call telling her falsely that the Black Panther Party intended to kill him.) The IRS began special audits on the basis of political rather than tax criteria and opened files on over 11,000 people between 1969 and 1973.[2] The FBI used special "COINTELPRO" (Counterintelligence Program) techniques against political dissenters and movement leaders, including "efforts to neutralize people by breaking up their marriages or ruining their jobs," risking "the death of suspect individuals by intentionally exacerbating tensions between groups," and "anonymously and

---

1. My summary of the findings on the "domestic intelligence" activities of the FBI and other government agencies (and all quotations) is drawn, unless otherwise noted, from the Select Intelligence Committee hearings and reports, U.S. Congress, Senate, 94th Cong., 1st Sess. *Hearings Before the Select Committee to Study Governmental Operations With Respect to Intelligence Activities,* Vol. 6 (Washington, D.C.: U.S. Government Printing Office, 1976), particularly the testimony by F. A. O. Schwarz, Jr., Chief Counsel, and Curtis R. Smothers, Minority Counsel, of the Senate Committee Staff, pp. 4–60; and the *Final Report* of the Committee, 94th Cong., 2nd Sess. *Intelligence Activities and the Rights of Americans,* Book II (Washington, D.C.: U.S. Government Printing Office, 1976), particularly the "Introduction and Summary," pp. 1–20.

2. IRS Commissioner Donald C. Alexander, confronted with the Senate Intelligence Committee's Report on the IRS carrying out illegal missions from the FBI, CIA, and White House, told a House committee hearing "he would like to make 'the biggest bonfire' in Washington to destroy 11,500 IRS intelligence files rather than show the files to the Americans involved," according to a UPI story, *Wisconsin State Journal,* May 12, 1976, p. 2.

falsely labeling" activists as government informants. The FBI also created "wholly fictional organizations" and "pseudopublications" of the left to attack other left organizations, including one with the quaint name "Committee for the Expansion of Socialist Thought in America." And it held in ready and put together list after list of political critics and activists to be rounded up in case of "national emergency." At one point, the list had over 26,000 individuals on it.

In 1972, at the height of the "ghetto informant program" requested by the White House, there were reportedly 7,402 undercover spies employed by the FBI alone as "listening posts" in black urban areas. It even had agents or spies in such organizations as the Southern Christian Leadership Conference, which was led by pacifist ministers characterized as "violence prone." SCLC was labeled a "Black Hate Group" and targeted for attacks "designed to destroy and disrupt" it; and the long-established moderate National Association for the Advancement of Colored People was also infiltrated. In fiscal 1976, the FBI reportedly programmed about $7.5 million for secret political intelligence informants. This was over twice as much as it budgeted for its entire organized crime informant program.

The FBI was particularly successful, according to a special staff report of the Senate Intelligence Committee, in covert action against the Black Panthers, provoking bloody and sometimes fatal clashes between the Panthers and rival organizations in a secret drive to destroy the black power movement in the late 1960s.[3] The FBI, said the special report, deliberately inflamed existing rivalries that led to threats, beatings, bombings, shootings, and at least four murders in California. The report also said that the FBI set up the Black Panthers for the raid by the Chicago police in which leaders Fred Hampton and Mark Clark were shot to death in 1969, supplying them with information on where the Panther apartment was, who used it, what the floor plan was, and what weapons were supposed to be inside. Memoranda quoted in the special report reveal that FBI agents credited their own "counter intelligence action" with contributing to "a substantial amount of unrest" in black ghettos. One FBI memorandum referred to its agents' own contribution to the "overall situation" in San Diego, California, in which "shootings, beatings, and a high degree of unrest continues to prevail in the ghetto area." The special Senate Intelligence Committee report concluded that "the chief investigative branch of the federal government [the FBI], which was charged by law with investigating crimes and preventing criminal conduct, itself engaged in lawless tactics and responded to deep-seated social problems by fomenting violence and unrest."

An imagery of violence runs through Col. Rigg's article and the FBI memoranda and reports on black protest. In contrast, the government's National Advisory Commission reported that most of the "civil disorders" in black urban areas did not involve major violence and damage, nor were the disorders directed against white persons. Instead, their targets were "symbols of white American society— authority and property"—in black neighborhoods. Indeed, according to the commission, "despite extremist rhetoric, there was no attempt to subvert the social order of the United States." The disorders broke out after cumulative underlying grievances became linked in the minds of many, so that the specific incident that sparked the disorder was "often routine or even trivial." The source of these grievances according to the commission, is the severely disadvantaged situation of

---

3. *Final Report* of the Select Intelligence Committee, Book III.

the black population and discrimination against them. Thus, "the typical rioter was not a hoodlum, habitual criminal, or riffraff; nor was he a recent migrant, a member of an uneducated underclass, or a person lacking broad social political concerns," as many commentators have maintained. Rather, claims the commission, he was usually better-educated than his neighbors, underemployed or menially employed, proud of his race, "informed about politics, [and] highly distrustful of the political system and of political leaders." The "counterrioters" who walked the streets telling people to "cool it" were even better educated and had a higher income than both the rioters and noninvolved. Finally, the commission concludes, the status quo of daily life was quickly restored after the disorders, but "little basic change" took place in the conditions underlying the disorders.

Contrary to the commission's view, Robert Blauner argues (Selection Number 34) that the ghetto struggles were not aimed mainly against discrimination and for integration into American life, but were preliminary forms of mass rebellion against colonial status—against the alien presence of white businesses and officials and against the police who protect the ghetto's "outside exploiters." The real historic import, Blauner suggests, of the 1964 to 1968 revolts may have been the impetus given to organizing in the black urban areas—to taking control of the businesses, social agencies, schools, and police operating there. The prisons, particularly, have been the focus of new black nationalist and revolutionary organization.

Since there "really is no black economy," however, and since most Afro-Americans work outside the ghetto, black leaders are trying increasingly to strike a balance between increased community autonomy and integration by such means as ethnically oriented school curricula and local control of police. Because the police "enforce the culturally repressive aspects of Afro-American and other minority subcultures," Blauner contends, and prevent blacks from attacking "the larger power structure" by confining them to skirmishes in the ghetto, the elimination of "police colonialism" is essential. Three measures of increasing degrees of radicalism, Blauner says, have been proposed to handle the police: (1) increase the percentage of black officers to match the black population's percentage of metropolitan residents; (2) require the police to live in the communities they patrol; and (3) withdraw the metropolitan police, substituting an independent indigenous police force responsible to a ghetto governing body.

Of course, so-called "black power programs" for ghetto control of property, business, schools, social agencies, and police could become a form of indirect or neocolonial rule by corporate capital. There are three major white stakes in racism and the retention of the black urban areas, according to Blauner: (1) a small minority of whites have "private and corporate interests in land and residential property of the black community"; (2) a larger minority gain from the absence of competition for their jobs, while the public employees who "administer the lives of the ghetto poor" depend on maintaining the status quo; and (3) "the political power and bureaucratic security" of the middle classes require the ghetto. The real issue, then, Blauner concludes, is how to increase ghetto autonomy and also open the doors for black Americans to "full participation in the institutions of the mainstream."

Class and Class Conflict in the United States

Some writers argue that the black struggles, although clearly rebellions against institutional racism and the exploited "colonial" situation of ghetto populations, reflect an even more basic split in American life between labor and capital. The ghetto revolts, they say, were centered among young black workers, distinguished from other workers only by their color and especially exploited class situation. These young blacks are an integral part of the American working class of men and women who are compelled to sell their labor power in order to live.[4] This raises the critical question: are the concepts of class and class struggle applicable to social reality in the United States, and will the workers one day put socialism on the historic agenda in America? These are the issues debated in the following selections.

The notion that there are "two armies massed on an industrial battlefield— 'labor' on the one side, 'capital' on the other"—is rejected by Harold. L. Wilensky (Selection Number 35). Instead, he says, there is "immense variation in interest and attitude within the ranks of each, and a consequent decline in the solidarity of each." Much of the behavior and many attitudes said to be rooted in class are instead a matter of race, religion, ethnic origin, education, age, and stage in the family life cycle. Members of any one of these groups, Wilensky claims, display more homogeneity of behavior and belief than all manual workers or even union members. Insofar as class categories remain useful for understanding social reality in the United States, it is the line which divides the regularly employed, well-paid workers from the lower class that is becoming more important than the split between upper working class and lower middle class. In general, Wilensky argues, class consciousness in rich countries like the United States is a transitional phenomenon characterizing workers not yet accustomed to the modern metropolis and work place. A clearly defined working class no longer exists in the United States, if it ever did.

Wilensky views class in functionalist terms as a system of distribution of so-called "rewards" in society—who gets whatever is valued, and why. The idea of class consciousness in Marxian theory—which refers to an awareness in the members of a class of their common interests and of the opposing interests of another class (or classes) and the readiness to act collectively to realize their class interests —is not applicable to American labor, he says except sporadically and in brief periods of its early history, especially during rapid industrialization. Such consciousness is fading into memory.

Depending on how you ask the question, Wilensky says, Americans will tell you there are no classes, many classes, that they belong to the middle class, that they belong to the working class. There is considerable cross-class identification and little class allegiance, except in the upper strata, where identification and allegiance are considerable. Political identification, however, tends along class lines: workers (especially union workers) are likely to vote Democratic. Labor unions do much to mobilize the committed vote, activate class disposition, and reinforce party appeals. This happens, suggests Wilensky, through interrelated steps in which the development of prolabor orientations leads to the acceptance of union discipline, development and transfer of political skills, and increased political interest.

Not only are American workers rarely class conscious, Wilensky argues, but they are becoming less so, especially compared to European labor. Union leaders

---

4. See, for instance, Earl Olfari, "Marxism-Leninism: The Key to Black Liberation," *Black Scholar* 4:1 (September, 1972):35–46, and also his *The Myth of Black Capitalism* (New York: Monthly Review Press, 1970); Donald J. Harris, "The Black Ghetto as Colony: A Theoretical Critique and Alternative Formulation," *Review of Black Political Economy* 2:4 (1972):3–33. Cf. also William K. Tabb, *The Political Economy of the Black Ghetto* (New York: W. W. Norton, 1970).

and rank and file have become integrated into the system as the result essentially of the impact of continued economic growth on the structure of opportunity.

John Kenneth Galbraith carries the argument further with the thesis that "labor-management relations have undergone a fundamental change in the heartland of the modern industrial system—the area of the large industrial corporations" (Selection Number 36). The effect is to limit and even dissolve class conflict, he says, while exporting social tensions elsewhere. Where large corporations bargain with large unions, tension tends to disappear because of four main relevant changes in the large corporation and the economy itself, according to Galbraith: (1) Power has passed from the capitalist to the corporate bureaucrat, or, more properly, the "technostructure" (which we encountered already in Part Four). The inherent conflict between labor and capital over "revenue" diminishes because the techno-structure can allocate revenue between stockholders and labor. Indeed, Galbraith contends, "the goals of the corporate bureaucracy are less opposed to those of labor than to those of corporate capitalism," since the new corporate goal, growth, simultaneously rewards the worker and the bureaucrat with new opporunties and higher pay while it "modifies the concern for profit maximization." (2) Technology itself reduces conflict by replacing blue-collar with white-collar workers who identify with the firm and making the remaining blue-collar workers mere "sedentary operatives sitting at a console." Thus, their number, their identification with other workers, and their militancy are reduced. (3) Affluence also makes identification with the union tenuous; for, with increased mobility and enlarged alternatives, says Galbraith, "the affluent worker" is not driven to cling to his union. (4) Finally, and most important, when demand is strong and reliable and employment high, differences between the large corporation (which exercises extensive control over prices) and the union can usually be resolved by passing along the increased labor costs to the public in higher prices. Thus, the "inescapable conclusion," according to Galbraith, is that "industrial conflict has been extensively dissolved or absorbed by the system."

This results, though, in increased tensions among public employees and in the middle income brackets to whom the costs of dissolved conflict in the heartland have been exported. Public employees are involved in a zero-sum game with the taxpayers, and their gains cannot be shoved off for others to pay. The result is rising labor militancy in the public sector, with government the target instead of capital. The middle income malaise is also a consequence of the fact that their incomes respond only slowly to the increased costs passed into them directly by the corporations and indirectly through taxes, says Galbraith. If this is to be resolved, then "some mechanism of public price determination of wages and prices" has to replace the unhampered determination by corporations and unions. Fiscal and monetary policy cannot reconcile high employment with price stability. A wage-price or price-wage spiral is inevitable without public intervention, Galbraith believes.

There is another conflict that is replacing the class struggle, says Galbraith: its foundations are in the corporations' need for a highly educated but bureaucratic personality, an objective incompatible with the university ideal of independent thought. Galbraith concludes that the abandonment of "unremitting pursuit" of increased production and a higher standard of living may be necessary if "personality is to be expressed."

Those like Galbraith and Wilensky who argue that class struggle is a "dwindling phenomenon" in the United States also typically assume that underlying the dwindle is the plain "fact" that blue-collar workers have been increasingly replaced by white-collar workers in the class structure. This is Galbraith's "second factor" reducing class conflict. As he puts it, "the number of white-collar workers in the United States almost 15 years ago overtook the number in the blue-collar working force and is, of course, now far greater." Similarly, Wilensky implies the same when he states: "a clearly defined working class no longer exists, if it ever did." Examining such "centrist" claims about "the transformation of the class structure" by analyzing census and survey data systematically, Richard F. Hamilton and James Wright (Selection Number 37) reject the claim that the "working class" has been disappearing and is now a minority while the "middle class" has shown a continuous increase in size. The confusion comes, they say, from not distinguishing between occupational composition and class lines and from lumping together the figures on men and women in the labor force, rather than examining the occupational changes of the sexes separately. In fact, the proportion of manual workers among nonfarm men has declined quite modestly over the 70 year span since the beginning of this century, from 69.9 percent in 1900 to 57.5 percent in 1970. In the past decade, this has been stable; in 1960, the comparable figure was 58.7 percent. Thus, a substantial majority of men in the labor force today outside of farming are manual workers. Instead of the "oft-touted 'middle class majority,' " Hamilton and Wright point out, what has happened is that women have vastly increased their share of the labor force, and most of them have become so-called white-collar, or clerical and sales, workers. Four-fifths of the nonfarm women employed outside the home were manual workers in 1900, compared to less than two-fifths in 1970. Not only are women usually not the main earners in the family, Hamilton and Wright argue, but the white-collar wives of workers probably work in the urban center or in offices near the factories, as well as in small stores in working class neighborhoods; and their family, friendship, and neighborhood contexts are working class anyway. So, Hamilton and Wright suggest, their life-styles and political outlooks are not likely to have changed much.

Aside from the claim that the working class has become a minority, it is also often argued (as does Wilensky, for example) that the split between an "upper working class" and "lower class" is becoming the major one in the class structure. Hamilton and Wright find, however, that there is no systematic tendency for the "upper" working class to be more "conservative" than the "lower" one. In fact, the sharpest line of class differentiation in political outlooks, they say, is between the white Protestant upper-and upper-middle-class segment on one side and those "below" them on the other, or even between them and their Catholic, Jewish, or black peers. The core group of conservative Republicans are white Protestant upper- and upper-middle-class Americans. Even though they are a small minority, Hamilton and Wright contend, they win many state and national elections because almost all vote. As a group, they are much more politically active than other Americans, and they back their candidates financially. If they are conservative compared to other Americans, it is probably the result of a combination of self-interest and encapsulation in socially homogeneous conservative communities. It should also be clear, say Hamilton and Wright, that the evidence does not support the oft-heard claim (see, for instance, the selection in this book by Dye and Zeigler) that, politically, this upper-middle class is particularly "responsible" compared to the "intolerant" or "authoritarian" working class. On civil rights, for example,

Hamilton and Wright do not find that the upper-middle-class Americans surveyed in national opinion polls are "distinguished by any special sense of responsibility." In fact, as they report, Chandler Davidson found in his analysis of a wide range of elections in Houston, Texas, our sixth largest city, that *poor whites* were the *most* likely to vote for black candidates *and* for white candidates and measures which would improve the situation of the black population. Some national surveys also show that support of government guarantees for job equality was stronger among poor whites, even in the South.

Perhaps it is not so much an absence of class consciousness, let along alleged intolerance, that characterizes American workers as it is "downright cynicism," argues Donald Clark Hodges (Selection Number 38). The workers have become politically indifferent because they believe they are politically impotent. Cynicism, argues Hodges, is a constant feature of the labor movement, an informal philosophy of labor which results from the workers' awareness that they are exploited and used for the benefit of the bosses. It is a reflection of their disillusionment with the labor movement and with collective struggle, their resignation to getting what they can for themselves and their families, and their contempt for all movements, parties, and principles. Cynicism is the conception of the political world as essentially hostile to the interests of manual workers. Young workers are especially likely to be cynics, claims Hodges, having been least affected by labor's earlier struggles and most affected by the ethos of individual gain.

Cynicism is essentially the worker's response to his alienation from his work and from a society that exploits him. In the United States, Henry Miller has embodied this cynicism in his novels, summed up in the phrase "I don't want it when I'm dead. I want it now." According to Hodges, this form of cynicism fortifies demands for higher wages and better working conditions by undermining the authority of the boss and the "system"; yet it is not akin to the Marxian concept of class consciousness because the latter glosses over the fundamental opposition between manual and intellectual workers. Manual workers are a group, cynics say, whose interests defy constant and faithful representation. The philosophy of working class cynicism is hostile to both capitalism and socialism because it embodies the workers' experience of betrayal by their leaders and exploitation by the system, and their resentment of their social status. Cynicism, Hodges argues, is a variant of the philosophy of anarcho-syndicalism, but without the ideals or ultimate illusions.

Underlying the sense of impotence and cynicism among American workers, though, may be one "ultimate illusion"—that significant changes in their lives on or off the job can take place while they confine themselves to unionism based on "collective bargaining." This is one major reason for the workers' "betrayal" by their leaders, according to Stanley Weir (Selection Number 39), himself a long-time active trade unionist. Even when "young, idealistic people, fresh from the ranks" replace the old union officials, they are confined by national arbitration and grievance procedures and a contract which together deny them and the rank and file the right to strike at the local level. Under the present union-management setup in the United States, the workers in a particular workplace cannot themselves decide to strike that workplace. This has been the real issue in the continuing revolts in labor's ranks since the 1960s. Representing a profound "break in the experience of submission," says Weir, the workers' revolts have aimed at winning union democracy and expanding their common control over their working lives.

The top labor officials who left the shops long ago are not sensitive to the workers' need for control over their conditions of work, which explains why almost all the unions that came together in the CIO have experienced revolts against their old officialdom in recent years. There have been revolts in the automobile industry, among longshoremen on both coasts, among steelworkers, electricians, oil, gas, and atomic workers, coal miners, seamen and maritime workers, airline mechanics, painters, paper and pulp workers, teamsters, and transport workers. Usually, and at best, the split among officials is between the "hard" and "soft" line: between those who ignore or repress the rank-and-file revolt and those who maintain that concessions from the top are the only means by which the revolt can be checked. Weir argues that a genuine response from union officials to these pressures from below—the adoption of a new program dedicated to fundamental changes in work methods and conditions and to opposition to technological disemployment (which would mean a long and difficult struggle against the largest corporations)—has been almost nonexistent. These revolts have usually been channeled into electoral struggles, several of which have resulted in the replacement of old top bureaucrats by secondary bureaucrats more responsive to such pressures. There have also been splits between large locals and the international union, some of which have resulted in disaffiliations and the establishment of new unions. Independent labor leaders have been threatened, assaulted, and even killed. Disaffiliation, says Weir, may result in the workers' finding themselves involved in a struggle merely to maintain their new unions, rather than expanding them and winning new gains.

Throughout the country, Weir contends, there are workers whose conditions and wages are artifically depressed because of captive affiliations with conservatively led unions to which there are no progressive alternatives. The fight for better conditions, Weir says, cannot be waged at periodic intervals, as can the fight for wage increases; it must be fought every day inside the plants. During such fights, the base and authority of the union moves from the union hall back inside the plant. Workers who are willing to fight their employer to obtain a better life on the job have to be prepared to fight their union leaders as well. To be successful, Weir argues, they will have to break out of their local isolation and unite the ranks horizontally, workplace by workplace, and this will require them to articulate an alternative vision of society and of workers' control of production that directly challenges capitalist social relations.

One principal source of the soaring number of wildcat strikes during the late 1960s, according to David M. Gordon (Selection Number 40), was the large corporations' strategy for coping with rising international competition during a period of continuous growth and "prosperity." That strategy, and the economic crisis of the mid-1970s, reflects the inherent conflict between labor and capital in "the sphere of production" itself.

Sooner or later, "prosperity" cuts into corporate profits because of workers' increased militancy and decreased productivity when their bargaining power is enhanced with fuller employment. Ordinarily, the large corporations have been able to respond by "hiking the price of their products," says Gordon, but rising international competition during the 1960s made this too risky. The result was that between 1965 and 1969, the ratio of profits to wages and of the share of profits in national income plunged. With demand high but profits squeezed, the corporations found it difficult to compensate for reduced profits by labor saving investment because existing plant and equipment had to be used to the optimum while retained earnings also declined. To maintain the level of investment, borrowing became necessary. Thus, corporate indebtedness (external financing) rose dramatically in the late 1960s, which meant vastly increased interest payments and another continuing drain on profits. Given this, and faced with international competition, the corporations tried to speed up production so as to get more output from each worker per day. This precipitated the first rise in the rate of industrial accidents in fifty years and a leap of 28 percent between 1963 and 1970 alone. In response, workers' wildcats and other forms of resistance rose even more dramatically.

With the boom continuing but profits eroding as workers resisted speedup, it became necessary, argues Gordon, to attack the workers directly through government policy. The wage-price freeze was imposed to discipline the workers so profits could recover. The purpose of the controls, as the government's administrator put it bluntly, was "to zap labor." Strike activity fell as wages fell, and by 1973, work stoppages were at the level of the early 1960s. The point is that if structural instabilities promoted the mid-1970s crisis, it was explicit government policy to induce the recession so as to discipline labor at a time when "major" contracts were expiring throughout industry. This merely postponed the crisis and when political pressures forced abandonment of controls in mid-1964, the economic crisis "exploded" around the world.

Recession has many causes, says Gordon, but calculated political decisions made at the top are critical in its timing, with the objective of making the workers sacrifice their wages, jobs, and living conditions to restore profits. Since this may be politically dangerous, the corporations and government now recognize the necessity for more long-range "planning." This involves government management of investment and credit policies in the interests of the corporations and the establishment of a legal framework for containing worker militance, including the imposition of "no strike agreements" and compulsory arbitration, as well as punishing wildcat strikers. This makes it clear, Gordon concludes, why the workers have to fight on two levels: the uses of state policy and control of production itself.

However, "state policy" in our country is mediated through a complex structure which combines legislative, executive, judicial, and police/military components not only at the federal, but also at the state and local levels of government; and each of these levels also constitute the political terrain of class conflict. In particular, Alexander Hicks, Roger Friedland, and Edwin Johnson argue (Selection Number 41) that public policy in state governments is significantly affected by the *organized* presence of labor and capital—of major unions and large corporations —in a particular state. The fact is, they note, state governments play a crucial role in the redistribution of income; on the average, state governments spend about a third of total expenditures and raise a quarter of the total tax revenues at all levels of government in our country. The question is, what impact does the presence of organized labor and capital have on the redistributive policies of state governments? In particular, Hicks, Friedland, and Johnson ask, what impact do they have on redistribution of income to and from poor households? Utilizing the sophisticated techniques of multiple regression analysis and taking into account a variety of variables which other studies or theories suggest are relevant in public redistributive policy, they find that the unions and corporations have significant *opposite effects* on state governmental redistribution. The presence of major unions in a state has a significant positive impact in favor of state government policies which redistribute income to the poor whereas the corporations have a negative impact. These findings suggest, according to Hicks, Friedland, and Johnson, how critical class power and class conflict are in the formation of public policy; yet few social scientists have bothered to study them in America in the past quarter-century.

This, of course, reflects the prevalent situation in our national political life for class conflict is usually subterranean and rarely surfaces in our country or becomes the focus of widespread debate. Yet, as we have seen, there are constant struggles in workplaces across America, that but these are rarely glimpsed or insightfully reported in academic studies and media fare. What's more, the men and women who work in the shops, factories, mines, and mills of our country appear, if at all, as vague and evanescent, yet strangely stereotypical, figures.[5] It is fitting, then, at the end of this volume of studies which debate the nature of American reality, that we have deft and sure portraits of some of these workingmen and their common struggles in Steve Packard's "Steelmill Blues" (Selection Number 42)—a report of what he learned while trying to organize rank-and-file workers at the Gary Works by "talking common sense to everyone."

---

5. Fortunately there are some fine recent exceptions, among them the books by Richard Sennett and Jonathan Cobb, *The Hidden Injuries of Class* (New York: Alfred Knopf, 1972); Studs Terkel, *Working* (New York: Pantheon Books, 1974); and Andrew Levison, *The Working Class Majority* (New York: Coward, McCann, and Geoghegan, 1974).

Made in U.S.A.

32

Col. Robert B. Rigg

During the next few years organized urban insurrection could explode to the extent that portions of large American cities could become scenes of destruction approaching those of Stalingrad in World War II. This could result from two main causes:

1. Man has constructed out of steel and concrete a much better "jungle" than nature has created in Vietnam.
2. There is the danger and the promise that urban guerrillas of the future can be organized to such a degree that their defeat would require the direct application of military power by the National Guard and the active Army.

This degree of destruction can easily come about because of these two circumstances. After all, we have seen many square blocks totally ruined in Watts, Detroit, and elsewhere, where there was no organized resistance. Were organized insurrection to break out and military power needed to suppress it, destruction in city square miles could mount tremendously over what we have seen.

However, while application of pure military firepower would be a poor solution, political efforts might prove not much better. There are measures that offer a better solution if we are to keep our cities from becoming battlegrounds: penetration by police intelligence, application of military intelligence, and reliance on traditional FBI methods. Such efforts must begin now so as to prevent organized urban guerrilla violence from gaining momentum.

To prevent and to curb urban violence of any order we must establish an effective system of intelligence in the ghettos of urban America.

From *Army* magazine, January 1968. Copyright © 1968 by the Association of the U.S. Army and reproduced by permission.

If penetration were professionally effective, such a system could warn of any plans for organized violence by subversive elements. Further, should organized violence break out, such an espionage system would be able to keep riot control and counterviolence forces informed during a disturbance.

The real prevention of urban violence and insurrection begins with social, economic, and political efforts. But alongside these measures and efforts there must be the "peripheral insurance policy" of an inside intelligence system that can warn of serious outbreaks and help curb them.

Furthermore, there will also be needed among the well established political-tactical-military informants those who can help guide troops and police through the maze of buildings, stairwells, streets, alleyways, tunnels, and sewers that may be the key to tactical success. In the countryside we would call this elementary or "grass-roots" intelligence; in the city there will be a similar need.

Just as China was plagued with rural guerrilla warfare from the 1920s to the late 1940s, so too, if present trends persist, could the United States experience similar strife and violence. The singular difference is that the fighting would be urban in nature. Furthermore, it is likely to be of such a special brand that can bear only the unique label, "Made in the USA." Thus the United States may inadvertently provide the world with a new brand of internal warfare that could haunt and harass large metropolitan areas for decades to come.

This possibility is alarming in light of the population explosion and the urban growth which by the 1980s may result in strip cities extending from Miami to Boston, from Chicago to Detroit, from San Francisco to San Diego—not to mention similar areas abroad. Of further import for the near future is the fact that the older "core cities"—such as Chicago, New York, Detroit, Newark, Oakland, Los Angeles, and others—could become concrete jungles where poverty could spread with their growth. Additionally, such cement-and-brick "jungles" can offer better security to snipers and city guerrillas than the Viet Cong enjoy in their jungles, elephant grass, and marshes. This suggests protracted warfare of a very new kind if city guerrilla forces become well organized by dissident and determined leaders.

City warfare is not new. What would make this type of conflict new, different, and more terrifying would be two elements. One would be the very geographical extent of the concrete jungles that are now simply called ghettos: such slum areas can expand rapidly as suburbia grows and absorbs the more affluent. The other would be lawless forces intoxicated by the ease and security with which they might successfully defy police, National Guardsmen, and Army regulars. The concrete blocks of our great ghettos have vertical acreage and horizontal mileage that offer such tactical protection and vantage points as to make future snipers much "braver" and city guerrillas much bolder than unorganized rioting mobs have been so far.

These are only a few of the trends in the United States which flash warning that our nation could be in for such violent street disorders that to suppress them would ultimately require the civil use of military power on a scale never heretofore visualized.

Racial issues, poverty, political unrest among minorities, the population explosion, and the rapid growth of strip cities that absorb the decaying old core cities—all these represent a combination of future factors and trends that could plague metropolitan areas and breed more violent and better organized disorder. That urban violence has spread significantly makes the outlook grim, because street violence has found acceptance among minorities.

Today's riots bring more than temporary disorder. They instill a new frame of mind among minorities—an outlook that visualizes rebellion against society and authority as a successful venture for the future. So far the unruly elements, with no real organization, have demonstrated that they can do unusual damage wantonly and indiscriminately. But the sick seed can grow into a menacing weed if in the future the potentials of organization are exploited.

So far the causes of urban violence have been emotional and social. Organization, however, can translate these grievances into political ones of serious potential, and result in violence or even prolonged warfare. Thus we may find that the danger to a free America is greater from within than from without.

If present trends persist, it is possible that in the next decade at least one major metropolitan area in the United States could be faced with guerrilla warfare of such intensity as to require sizable U.S. Army elements in action and National Guard units on active duty for years. No doubt such an urban conflict could be contained, subdued, and defeated, but the effort could possibly require years of concerted military action before even effective social improvements could have impact. This is what the war in South Vietnam has demonstrated. Further, if organized guerrilla resistance spreads to several cities and requires the use of many military units, a national paralysis of very serious proportions might ensue.

The strange thing about the ominous prospect is that such warfare in alleys, streets, cellars, sewers, and rooftops could erupt and be carried out initially by organized guerrillas with no prodding by communists or other political movements. It could erupt simply from poverty or racial or local issues, and expand into more blood-spilling violence during which a more overriding political issue—communist or other—could be conveniently inserted by subversive leaders.

Today you need not point to the red flag of communism to appreciate that violence, dissidence, and disaffection of other sorts can threaten the United States from within. A future political brand of internal guerrilla threat may now be so faceless as to not appear on the attorney general's black list for some time to come. Yet the potential threat could be so ominous as to rank alongside communism. Nevertheless, the threat of future communist exploitation of American urban unrest remains potent.

Communist China and Cuba represent potential grave internal threats to the United States. They can covertly subsidize insurgent elements within our urban areas, although so far, according to the FBI, they have not done so. However, in some intelligence circles of our government it is known that the more dangerous conspirators in ghettos are being prompted by members of the pro-Chinese wing of the American Communist party.

The riots in Newark and Detroit have opened new opportunities for these communist nations which have a well-known record of exporting revolution. Suddenly they learn that there are ill-disciplined elements in the continental United States which can engage in violence without even a political cause. Snipers who will fire from rooftops and highrise windows out of nothing more than the urge to violence and vengeance against society are certainly ripe for political coercion by Red China's and communist Cuba's secret agents who seek men of this type the world over.

Some advocates of Black Power regard outbreaks of violence as a necessary part of what Adam Clayton Powell called "the black revolution that is going to purge American democracy." Powell pronounced this on 26 July 1967, just as the Detroit riot began to subside. On the same day, Black Power leader Stokely Carmichael issued a similar manifesto from Cuba, at the very time when the Organization of American States was announcing that Castro was continuing his support of communist terrorists and guerrillas in Venezuela. In its report, the OAS special committee made the main point that Cuba's activities include training, arming, and transporting guerrillas for operations in other countries.

Extremely bitter since the Bay of Pigs invasion, Castro has become a would-be exporter of revolution. With Carmichael at his elbow, Castro gave his "blessing" to riots in U.S. cities and called for guerrilla warfare there.

On 3 August, while still in Cuba, Carmichael repeated his prediction of "urban guerrilla warfare" against the U.S. government: "Our only answer is to destroy that government or to be destroyed while trying to destroy the government." At any rate, "we are going to start with guns to get our liberation."

A few days later in New York another advocate of violence, H. Rap Brown, called on Negroes to arm themselves against a white "conspiracy of genocide," while labeling riots in Newark, Detroit, and Plainfield as "dress rehearsals for revolution."

These are straws in the wind, but nevertheless many hundreds applaud locally, and millions listen nationally, while would-be Nazis and members of the American Communist party draw much smaller crowds, generate only token enthusiasm, and represent a weak threat, internally. But these groups can exploit advocates of Black Power and violence. Responsible Negro leaders work elsewhere with real power and purpose for more meaningful progress, but they may end up as "Uncle Toms" if the advocates of violence persist.

In the future, forceful leaders—or even careless ones—could easily evoke and provoke protracted violence so as to cause National Guard units to be on almost permanent active duty in many of our cities.

Every nation at times has its would-be Hitlers. So far the United States has been able to survive the extreme rantings of such radicals who have never been able to muster political forces of consequence, much less military forces. But the appeal, and sometime success, of guerrillaism is an intoxicant that could "inspire" urban minority leaders or future would-be Hitlers—men of ruthless purpose and gnawing ambition.

Time, and the crowding circumstances of the population explosion, can breed wholesale urban violence. Social and economic progress promise to be of help here, but we cannot be too certain that such efforts will always succeed. For example, not long ago modern housing in Anacostia, D.C., was vandalized by youthful gangs of the community. With no unified leadership, they smashed and destroyed property wholesale and so intimidated storeowners and passersby that one of Washington's major newpapers wrote a series of articles of this modern-day phenomenon which portends problems in future communities. Why? Because here was a state of mind that manifested itself very boldly. Its overtones for the future are obvious.

Urban riot has been established as an instrument of racial rebellion. But the riots have not been strictly one of Negroes clashing with whites; often the rioters were relieving their frustrations at their ghetto surroundings and relative poverty, and upon authorities. It is important to remember this, especially where it pertains to slums. Violence in the future may even be by whites protesting against poverty and their environment. White or black, here is where the political aspect looms large because communist elements can penetrate urban American and foment serious trouble.

The future brand of trouble may not necessarily be communist-inspired. Activists of the left who now expend their energies in protesting against the Vietnam war could become a growing source of urban unrest and trouble. The future problem of city violence bears no particular political label at the moment, but it does indicate that trouble can arise from the left or right, or from black or white. Poverty and social problems exist in rural areas, but they can reach explosive and serious proportions only in our cities.

The personal right to own firearms is being seriously debated in Washington today. The argument will linger, and probably with no conclusive results, for a long time. The stark fact remains that from Chicago to the Congo anyone who wants to shoot can buy small arms and even mortars. World War II, the many limited wars since, and all the military aid programs have flooded the world with arms and ammunition. If a subversive force or organization wants arms, they are available. If their leaders want them on a wholesale scale, arms for the urban guerrillas of the United States will not be hard to obtain.

Today, one trend is self-evident: metropolitan police cannot cope with even disorganized violence where it reaches high proportions. Tomorrow, police and National Guard units may not be able to cope with urban violence that is well organized.

Another trend is toward organization for violence. Over the past two decades organization has spread in the ghettos of America. It began with street gangs who boldly formed semiuniformed clubs and deliberately engaged in "rumbles" for "sport" or diversion. Now the overtones of racialism and the more public recognition of poverty-area-contrast with other communities have brought movements designed to "fight their way up and out." In short, the trend is toward organization designed for aggression in behalf of racial and poverty issues. Militancy prevails in slums where heretofore there was only the defeatism of complacency. For the future, militancy can be expected to prevail. Elements of American poverty have discovered the ally of aggression. Added, however, will be organization behind the militancy, and the second ingredient of arms in place of rocks and bottles. A disorganized mob throws rocks, bricks, and bottles. An organized mob of the future will be armed, and will not be content to gather its armament from street rubble.

"Fight for something" is an old American tradition. Any time hence, people in a large slum in a congested metropolitan area could fight in guerrilla fashion for their own local aims. They might not be fighting the federal government, but merely the city or the state. As in Vietnam today, the fighters by night could be workers by day. Rooftops, windows, rooms high up, streets low down, and back alleys nearby could become a virtual jungle for patrolling police or military forces at night when hidden snipers could abound, as they often do against U.S. and allied forces in Vietnam in daylight. Could local police or National Guard units carry out search-and-destroy campaigns in the cement-block jungles of highrise buildings?

Even in the face of large-caliber artillery, the battle of Stalingrad demonstrated that a city of steel, concrete, and brick offers unusual protection to its defenders and great obstacles to its assailants. Consider a creeping guerrilla war by night in a typical portion of the old core of an American city. Police patrols and National Guardsmen could be sniped at by night for months and suffer heavy casualties from determined but hidden foes. Such warfare would not need to be fought by lone guerrillas in the lower streets. Vietnam's jungles have no elevators and stairwells in their treetops, but city buildings do—and a multitude of vacant rooms to which to flee. No jungle's tree branches are as secure. The degree of security for city guerrillas is almost too imposing to suggest. Mao Tse-tung's concept of prolonged war could be applied— by city guerrilla forces so determined—to the same extent that he waged it about China's countryside.

Police, National Guard, and active Army units could hardly carry out successful clear-and-hold operations in the steel-and-concrete jungle of highrise buildings without resorting to a campaign that would almost reach the destruction experienced by Stalingrad. The problem is difficult enough in the sometimes peaceful countryside of Vietnam today, but what tank or bulldozer is going to flatten an old twenty-story apartment or office building that is sniper-ridden by night and vacant by day? Here, urban guerrillas could shoot down into the streets, drop fire bombs, and not even need mortars. Plainly, the finest "jungle" for insurrection was not created by nature; it has been built by man.

From a military standpoint, successful warfare against urban-based guerrillas in American cities could be as difficult and prolonged as the fighting in Vietnam if the insurrection is well organized.

Unless the decay of core cities can be cured by social, economic, and political means, Detroit's relatively small square mileage of violence of 1967 could look insignificant in military and damage terms, compared to what could be a virtual Stalingrad in an American city by 1970 or 1980.

While the patterns of future urban insurrection may vary, there will be certain problems to confront, if the violence is organized.

Problem No. 1 would be organization itself. To combat this would require political and intelligent penetration of high order and expertise. Here, penetration must be deep enough so as to warn of secret subversive plans, to pinpoint leaders, and to disrupt organization itself.

Problem No. 2 would concern the identification of hideouts, areas where weapons are stored, sources of arms, guerrilla means of transportation, access and escape routes, and probable resistance spots. In other words, we must have intimate and accurate information on the facilities used by urban guerrillas before and during trouble.

Problem No. 3 relates to tactical military action against organized resistance once conflict begins. Hopefully, this assumes that at least fair intelligence and espionage would continue to meet the problems mentioned. But no intelligence report has ever been prepared that included complete information on the enemy *after* the fighting started. Tactical action has always had to rely on what little was known and what could be learned through intelligence gathered by scouting and combat. Imagine a building or a block of buildings that houses innocent people but is used at night by snipers and insurrectionists with fire bombs. Tactical action here would take on the proportions of search-and-plant operations by day, and retaliation, maneuver, and fighting by night. Night fighting will call for a very delicate decision as to which darkened window to shoot at and which rooftop to blast by mortar fire or to assault by helicopter. A whole new manual of military operations, tactics, and techniques needs to be written in respect to urban warfare of this nature. There are none on the subject today.

Problem No. 4 includes police-Guard-Army and local authority (particularly political) coordination, communications, and control. Here also is a very big problem that can be greatly aggravated by chaos and street fighting. For every city, for every emergency, this one requires much planning in depth. Planning is vital, particularly in terms of political and military control and coordination of all efforts. Once chaos and conflict ensue, command and coordination become even more crucial and necessary. Communications in terms of standing operating procedure, integrated radio networks, liaison, procedures, and the like are big problems that must be solved before conflict, and modified to meet the demands of the situation.

Problem No. 5 can be termed "Mixture X." It includes everything from control and safety of a few dozen (or hundreds) of refugees fleeing from buildings to hostages being held by seasoned guerrillas or being used by them as escape shields. It includes the sick and wounded among the innocent. It includes the supply of food and medicine—and medical treatment—to trapped people. It includes evacuation by helicopters and by fire fighters of people trapped in burning buildings. It includes the protection of firemen from sniper fire, the need of which last summer's Detroit riot demonstrated in very grim and dramatic fashion. Plainly, firemen need the Red Cross badge of safety to protect them in their valor and work. They didn't have even this in Detroit. They may suffer heavy casualties during organized urban insurrection of the future unless they are somehow more respected by some agreement or other measure.

Success in coping with organized urban warfare will not rest on agreements, but rather depend on tactics and techniques yet to be formulated. The overall problem, and success in meeting it, depend heavily on a new measure of organization, coordination, and study among officials of the city, state, National Guard, police, active Army, and FBI. While these organizations understand the problem and are alert to it, much work lies ahead.

The implications are clear. American military and political plans must now, more than ever before, be based upon meeting a new kind of internal violence.

The most delicate type of so-called "limited war" lies ahead. Military force and military restraint of a new order call for new types of training and discipline. Traditionally, and normally, soldiers are taught to fire back, to gain the objective, and to seize the high ground. These tactical principles can no longer be applied unless we want to see street blocks become battlegrounds of utter destruction. Greater firepower and more troops have already raised the ante of escalation in Vietnam.

There is one lesson we must learn from even this type of limited war. When urban guerrilla warfare strikes, meeting it will require the highest degree of calmness ever demanded of the American soldier since the traditional "don't one of you fire until you see the white of their eyes." This means that the active Army, National Guard, and police must use the pressure of their presence, the force of probing, and the expertise of military intelligence, without resorting to serious outbreaks of firepower, much less wanton shooting. The implications here are serious in respect to military training and operations. Each unit and each soldier must be expected to endure the highest incidence of sniping, apply the utmost of maneuvering and—at times—resort to the least firing. This is a large order for any force, but only through such disciplines and techniques can urban guerrilla warfare be contained within bounds, limited in destructive powers, held within limits, and destroyed by the most singular means—and that is through seizure rather than through destruction by firepower. Military intelligence, police and detective efforts, and FBI penetration can make greater progress toward defeating future urban guerrillas than any military firepower.

Such planning must include training troops for urban insurrection. For the National Guard this means a complete change of direction in training as something of first priority. For the active Army, such training has serious overtones to the extent that it must train for the concrete jungle as well as for the other kind. Further, it means that Army units must be oriented and trained to know the cement-and-asphalt jungle of *every* American city. It means that maneuvers and exercises, heretofore carried out about the countryside, in the future can be conducted in large cities. Possibly the sight of such maneuvers in several cities could prove a deterrent to urban insurrection. Today's trend implies that very soon American troops will be maneuvering in metropolitan areas to an extent more than ever before imagined. Here they will be required to learn about and memorize details of many metropolitan communities, their buildings, streets, alleyways, rooftops, and sewers, just as once they learned the use of terrain features of open country. This is the only way to solve the intelligence, social, economic, and political problems associated with serious Third Front warfare which could bear the unfortunate label of "Made in the USA."

Patterns of Disorder

33

National Advisory Commission on Civil Disorders

Disorders are often discussed as if there were a single type. The "typical" riot of recent years is sometimes seen as a massive uprising against white people, involving widespread burning, looting, and sniping, either by all ghetto Negroes or by an uneducated, southern-born Negro underclass of habitual criminals or "riffraff." An agitator at a protest demonstration, the coverage of events by the news media, or an isolated "triggering" or "precipitating" incident is often identified as the primary spark of violence. A uniform set of stages is sometimes posited, with a succession of confrontations and withdrawals by two cohesive groups, the police on one side and a riotous mob on the other. Often it is assumed that there was no effort within the Negro community to reduce the violence. Sometimes the only remedy prescribed is application of the largest possible police or control force as early as possible.

What we have found does not validate these conceptions. We have been unable to identify constant patterns in all aspects of civil disorders. We have found that they are unusual, irregular, complex, and, in the present state of knowledge, unpredictable social processes. Like many human events, they do not unfold in orderly sequences.

Moreover, we have examined the 1967 disorders within a few months after their occurrence and under pressing time limitations. While we have collected information of considerable immediacy, analysis will undoubtedly improve with the passage and perspective of time and with the further accumulation and refinement of data. To facilitate further analysis we have appended much of our data to this report.

We have categorized the information now available about the 1967 disorders as follows:

Reprinted from National Advisory Commission, *Report of the National Advisory Commission on Civil Disorders* (Washington, D.C.: U.S. Government Printing Office, 1968), pp. 63–65.

- The pattern of violence over the nation: severity, location, timing, and numbers of people involved;

- The riot process in a sample of 24 disorders we have surveyed:* prior events, the development of violence, the various control efforts on the part of officials and the community, and the relationship between violence and control efforts;

- The riot participants: a comparison of rioters with those who sought to limit the disorder and with those who remained uninvolved;

- The setting in which the disorders occurred: social and economic conditions, local governmental structure, the scale of federal programs, and the grievance reservoir in the Negro community;

- The aftermath of disorder: the ways in which communities responded after order was restored in the streets.

Based upon information derived from our surveys, we offer the following generalizations:

1. No civil disorder was "typical" in all respects. Viewed in a national framework, the disorders of 1967 varied greatly in terms of violence and damage: while a relatively small number were major under our criteria and a somewhat larger number were serious, most of the disorders would have received little or no national attention as "riots" had the nation not been sensitized by the more serious outbreaks.

2. While the civil disorders of 1967 were racial in character, they were not *inter*racial. The 1967 disorders, as well as earlier disorders of the recent period, involved action within Negro neighborhoods against symbols of white American society—authority and property—rather than against white persons.

3. Despite extremist rhetoric, there was no attempt to subvert the social order of the United States. Instead, most of those who attacked white authority and property seemed to be demanding fuller participation in the social order and the material benefits enjoyed by the vast majority of American citizens.

4. Disorder did not typically erupt without preexisting causes as a result of a single "triggering" or "precipitating" incident. Instead, it developed out of an increasingly disturbed social atmosphere, in which typically a series of tension-heightening incidents over a period of weeks or months became linked in the minds of many in the Negro community with a shared reservoir of underlying grievances.

---

* The Statement on Methodology in the Appendix of the Report describes the survey procedures.—Ed.

5. There was, typically, a complex relationship between the series of incidents and the underlying grievances. For example, grievances about allegedly abusive police practices, unemployment and underemployment, housing, and other conditions in the ghetto, were often aggravated in the minds of many Negroes by incidents involving the police or the inaction of municipal authorities on Negro complaints about police action, unemployment, inadequate housing, or other conditions. When grievance-related incidents recurred and rising tensions were not satisfactorily resolved, a cumulative process took place in which prior incidents were readily recalled and grievances reinforced. At some point in the mounting tension, a further incident—in itself often routine or even trivial—became the breaking point, and the tension spilled over into violence.

6. Many grievances in the Negro community result from the discrimination, prejudice, and powerlessness which Negroes often experience. They also result from the severely disadvantaged social and economic conditions of many Negroes as compared with those of whites in the same city and, more particularly, in the predominantly white suburbs.

7. Characteristically, the typical rioter was not a hoodlum, habitual criminal, or riffraff; nor was he a recent migrant, a member of an uneducated underclass, or a person lacking broad social and political concerns. Instead, he was a teenager or young adult, a lifelong resident of the city in which he rioted, a high school dropout—but somewhat better educated that his Negro neighbor—and almost invariably underemployed or employed in a menial job. He was proud of his race, extremely hostile to both whites and middle-class Negroes and, though informed about politics, highly distrustful of the political system and of political leaders.

8. Numerous Negro counterrioters walked the streets urging rioters to "cool it." The typical counterrioter resembled in many respects the majority of Negroes, who neither rioted nor took action against the rioters; that is, the noninvolved. But certain differences are crucial: the counterrioter was better educated and had higher income than either the rioter or the noninvolved.

9. Negotiations between Negroes and white officials occurred during virtually all the disorders surveyed. The negotiations often involved young, militant Negroes as well as older, established leaders. Despite a setting of chaos and disorder, negotiations in many cases involved discussion of underlying grievances as well as the handling of the disorder by control authorities.

10. The chain we have identified—discrimination, prejudice, disadvantaged conditions, intense and pervasive grievances, a series of tension-heightening incidents, all culminating in the eruption of disorder at the hands of youthful, politically-aware activists—must be understood as describing the central trend in the disorders, not as an explana-

tion of all aspects of the riots or of all rioters. Some rioters, for example, may have shared neither the conditions nor the grievances of their Negro neighbors; some may have coolly and deliberately exploited the chaos created by others; some may have been drawn into the melee merely because they identified with, or wished to emulate, others. Nor do we intend to suggest that the majority of the rioters, who shared the adverse conditions and grievances, necessarily articulated in their own minds the connection between that background and their actions.

11. The background of disorder in the riot cities was typically characterized by severely disadvantaged conditions for Negroes, especially as compared with those for whites; a local government often unresponsive to these conditions; federal programs which had not yet reached a significantly large proportion of those in need; and the resulting reservoir of pervasive and deep grievance and frustration in the ghetto.

12. In the immediate aftermath of disorder, the status quo of daily life before the disorder generally was quickly restored. Yet, despite some notable public and private efforts, little basic change took place in the conditions underlying the disorder. In some cases, the result was increased distrust between blacks and whites, diminished interracial communication, and growth of Negro and white extremist groups. . .

Internal Colonialism and Ghetto Revolt

34

Robert Blauner

It is my basic thesis that the most important expressions of protest in the black community during the recent years reflect the colonized status of Afro-America. Riots, programs of separation, politics of community control, black revolutionary movements, and cultural nationalism each represents a different strategy of attack on domestic colonialism in America. Let us now examine some of these movements from this perspective.

RIOT OR REVOLT?

The so-called riots are being increasingly recognized as a preliminary if primitive form of mass rebellion against colonial status. There is still a tendency to absorb their meaning within the conventional scope of assimilation-integration politics; some commentators stress the material motives involved in looting as a sign that the rioters want to join America's middle-class affluence just like everyone else. That motives are mixed and often unconscious; that black people want good furniture and television sets like whites is beside the point. The guiding impulse in most major outbreaks has not been integration with American society, but an attempt to stake out a sphere of control by moving against that society and destroying the symbols of its oppression.

In my critique of the McCone Report, . . . I observe that the rioters "were asserting a claim to territoriality, making an unorganized and rather inchoate attempt to gain control over their community turf."[1] In succeeding disorders also the thrust of the action has been toward

Excerpted from Robert Blauner, "Internal Colonialism and Ghetto Revolt," in *Racial Oppression in America*, pp. 89–91, 95–104. Reprinted with permission of Harper & Row, Publishers. Copyright © 1972 by Robert Blauner. Footnotes have been renumbered.

1. *Racial Oppression in America*, chap. 6.

ridding the community of the alien presence of white officials, rather than killing white people as in a conventional race riot. The main attacks have been directed at the property of white businessmen and at the police who operate in the black community "like an army of occupation," protecting the interests of outside exploiters and maintaining the domination over the ghetto of the central metropolitan power structure. The Kerner Report misleads when it attempts to explain riots in terms of integration: "What the rioters appear to be seeking was fuller participation in the social order and the material benefits enjoyed by the majority of American citizens. Rather than rejecting the American system, they were anxious to obtain a place for themselves in it" (p. 71). More accurately, the revolts pointed to alienation from the system on the part of many poor, and some not-so-poor, blacks. Again as I argue with respect to Los Angeles: the sacredness of private property, that unconsciously accepted bulwark of our social arrangements, was rejected. People who looted—apparently without guilt—generally remarked that they were taking things that "really belonged" to them anyway. Obviously the society's bases of legitimacy and authority have been attacked. Law and order has long been viewed by Afro-Americans as the white man's law and order; but now this characteristic perspective of a colonized people is out in the open. The Kerner Report's own data question how well ghetto rebels have been buying the system: in Newark only 33 percent of self-reported rioters said they thought this country was worth fighting for in the event of a major war; in the Detroit sample the figure was 55 percent (Kerner Report, p. 178).

One of the most significant consequences of the process of colonization is a weakening of the individual and collective will to resist oppression. It has been easier to contain and control black ghettos because communal bonds and group solidarity have been weakened through division among leadership, failures of organization, and a general dispiritment that accompanies social oppression. The riots were a signal that the will to resist had broken the mold of accommodation. In some cities they represented nascent movements toward community identity. The outbursts stimulated new organizations and movements in several riot-torn ghettos. If it is true that the riot phenomenon of 1964 to 1968 has passed its peak, its historical import may be more for the "internal" organizing momentum that was generated than for any profound "external" response by the larger society in facing underlying causes.

Despite the appeal of Frantz Fanon to young black revolutionaries, America is not Algeria. It is difficult to foresee how rioting in our cities can function in a manner similar to the situation of overseas colonialism, where such outbursts were an integral phase in a movement for national liberation. By 1968 some militant groups (for example the Black Panther Party in Oakland) had concluded that ghetto riots were self-defeating for black people in the present balance of organization and gunpower

—endangering their lives and their interests—though they had served to stimulate both black consciousness and white awareness of the depths of racial crisis. Such militants have been influential in "cooling" their communities during periods of high riot potential. Theoretically-oriented black radicals see riots as spontaneous mass behavior which must be replaced by a revolutionary organization and consciousness. Despite the differences in objective conditions, violence seems to have served the same psychic function for young ghetto blacks in the 1960s as it did for the colonized of North Africa described by Fanon and Albert Memmi—the assertion of dignity and manhood.[2]

In the past few years riotlike political action appears to have shifted from the urban ghetto streets to more limited and focused institutional settings. One has been the high schools and colleges, where a white European cultural system carries out the psychic and intellectual colonization of people of color. The second has been the prisons, whose inmates are disproportionately black, brown, and lower class. In confining within its walls a significant segment of those who have reacted against racial and colonialism overtly and aggressively, although not always with political consciousness, the prison is a concentrated essence of the colonial relationship. It is therefore not surprising that it has become a new breeding ground for nationalist and revolutionary organization. . . .

THE MOVEMENT FOR GHETTO CONTROL

The call for black power unites a number of varied movements and tendencies. Although agreement on a unified program has not yet emerged, the most important emphasis seems to be on the movement for control of the ghetto. Black leaders and organizations are increasingly concerned with owning and controlling those institutions that exist within or impinge upon their community. The colonial model provides a key to the understanding of this movement; indeed, advocates of ghetto control have increasingly invoked the language of colonialism in pressing for local home rule. The framework of anticolonialism explains why the struggle to put poor people in control of poverty programs has in many cities been more important than the content of these programs, and why it has been crucial to exclude whites from leadership positions in black organizations.

The key institutions that anticolonialists want to take over or control are business, social services, schools, and the police. Though many spokesmen have advocated the exclusion of white landlords and small businessmen from the ghetto, the idea has evidently not caught fire

2. Frantz Fanon, *Wretched of the Earth* (New York: Grove, 1963); Albert Memmi, *The Colonizer and the Colonized* (Boston: Beacon, 1967).

among the blacks, and little concrete movement toward economic expropriation has as yet developed. Welfare recipients have organized in many cities to protect their rights and gain a greater voice in the decisions that affect them. Larry Jackson observes that "there is no organizational structure in the black community which can equal (on a national level) the number of troops that the National Welfare Rights Movement can politically engage in literally hundreds of cities across the country."[3] However, because the problems of welfare do not cut across class lines, whole communities have not mounted direct action against this form of colonialism. Thus, schools and the police have been the crucial issues of ghetto control politics.

The Schools

In many cities during the late 1960s, educational priorities shifted from integration to community control, New York and Brooklyn being the most publicized examples. Afro-Americans demanded their own school boards, with the power to hire and fire principals and teachers and to construct a curriculum that would be relevant to the special needs and culture of ghetto youth. Black students across the country have been active in high schools and colleges, protesting in behalf of incorporating black power and black culture into the education system. Consider how similar the spirit behind these developments is to the attitude of the colonized North African toward European education:

> He will prefer a long period of educational mistakes to the continuance of the colonizer's school organization. He will choose institutional disorder in order to destroy the institutions built by the colonizer as soon as possible. There we see, indeed, a reactive drive of profound protest. He will no longer owe anything to the colonizer and will have definitely broken with him.[4]

Protest and institutional disorder over the issue of school control in New York City came to a head in 1968. The procrastination in the Albany State legislature, the several crippling strikes called by the teachers' union, and the almost frenzied response of Jewish organizations made it clear that decolonization of education faces the resistance of powerful vested interests. Funding for the experimental school districts was ended after one year, and the limited autonomy that had been granted these districts was incorporated into a more general plan of decentralization. The defeat of "community control" in New York may have contributed to its failure to spread rapidly to other major cities.[5]

---

3. Larry R. Jackson, "Welfare Mothers and Black Liberation," *Black Scholar* 1:5 (April, 1970):35.

4. Memmi, op. cit., pp. 137–8.

5. Major documents in the school controversy, various viewpoints and analyses are included in Maurice R. Berube and Marilyn Gittell, eds., *Confrontation at Ocean Hill-Brownsville* (New York: Praeger, 1969).

The movement reflected some of the problems and ambiguities that stem from colonization within the borders of the "mother country." The Afro-American community is not parallel in structure to the communities of colonized nations under traditional colonialism. The significant difference here is the lack of fully developed indigenous institutions other than the church. Outside of some areas of the South there is really no black economy, and most Afro-Americans are inevitably caught up in the larger society's structure of occupations, education, and mass communications. Thus the ethnic nationalist orientation, which reflects the reality of colonization, exists alongside an integrationist orientation, which reflects the reality that the institutions of the larger society are much more developed than those of the incipient nation. As would be expected, the movement for school control reflected both orientations. The militant leaders who spearhead such local movements may be primarily motivated by the desire to gain control over the community's institutions—they are anticolonialists first and foremost. Many parents who support them may share this goal, but the majority are probably more concerned about creating a new education that will enable their children to "make it" in the society and the economy as a whole; they know that the present school system fails ghetto children and does not prepare them for participation in American life.

In many communities black leaders are now struggling for measures that fall between the poles of integration and community autonomy: for example, control over special programs, ethnically oriented curricula, and "alternative schools" within a racially heterogeneous institution or district. And by 1971 the ways and means of achieving integration had reappeared as a major national controversy as the Nixon administration backtracked on the busing issue. As more cities and school systems move toward black majorities, however, demands for community control are likely to emerge again.

The Police

There has been a growing recognition that law enforcement is particularly crucial in maintaining the colonized status of black Americans. Of all establishment institutions, police departments probably include the highest proportion of individual racists. This is no accident, since central to the workings of racism are attacks on the humanity and dignity of the subject group. The police constrict Afro-Americans to black neighborhoods by harassing and questioning them when they are found outside the ghetto; without provocation they break up groups of youths congregated on corners or in cars; and they continue to use offensive and racist language no matter how many seminars on intergroup understanding have been built into the police academy. They also shoot to kill ghetto residents for alleged crimes such as car thefts and running from officers of the law. According to a recent survey:

In the predominantly Negro areas of several large cities, many of the police perceive the residents as basically hostile, especially the youth and adolescents. A lack of public support—from citizens, from courts, and from laws —is the policeman's major complaint. But some of the public criticism can be traced to the activities in which he engages day by day, and perhaps to the tone in which he enforces the "law" in the Negro neighborhoods. Most frequently he is "called upon" to intervene in domestic quarrels and break up loitering groups. He stops and frisks two or three times as many people as are carrying dangerous weapons or are actual criminals, and almost half of these don't wish to cooperate with the policeman's efforts.[6]

Thus the police enforce the culturally repressive aspects of middle-class American values against the distinctive ethnic orientations of Afro-American and other minority subcultures. It has been observed that few whites are arrested for gambling despite its popularity in a variety of forms; blacks, however, are arrested unduly for this offense and similar crimes like making noise in public. The Detroit officer David Senak as described by John Hersey[7] well exemplifies how individual policemen can become moral crusaders against "deviant behavior" and how the black community is particularly vulnerable to such cultural aggression.[8]

Police are key agents in the power equation as well as in the dramas of dehumanization and cultural repression. In the final analysis they do the dirty work for the larger system by restricting the striking-back of black rebels to skirmishes inside the ghetto, thus deflecting energies and attacks from the communities and institutions of the larger power structure. In a historical review, Gary Marx notes that since the French revolution, police and other authorities have killed large numbers of demonstrators and rioters; the rebellious "rabble" rarely destroys human life. The same pattern has been repeated in America's recent revolts.[9] Journalistic accounts suggest that police see themselves as

---

6. Peter Rossi, et al., "Between Black and White—The Faces of American Institutions in the Ghetto," in *Supplemental Studies for the National Advisory Commission on Civil Disorders* (July, 1968):114.

7. John Hersey, *The Algiers Motel Incident* (New York: Bantam, 1968).

8. In the trial of Huey Newton, the definition of the widely used expression "pig" became germane to the case. As a number of witnesses testified, in the language of the ghetto the term connotes a spectrum much wider than that of policeman. As one man put it succinctly, a pig is any outsider who comes into an oppressed community to direct the lives and activities of people whose feelings and culture he neither understands nor respects.

9. "In the Gordon Riots of 1780 demonstrators destroyed property and freed prisoners, but did not seem to kill anyone, while authorities killed several hundred rioters and hung an additional 25. In the Reoellion Riots of the French Revolution, though several hundred rioters were killed, they killed no one. Up to the end of the summer of 1967, this pattern had clearly been repeated, as police, not rioters were responsible for most of the more than 100 deaths that have occurred. Similarly, in a related context, the more than 100 civil rights murders of recent years have been matched by almost no murders of racist whites." G. Marx, "Civil Disorders and the Agents of Social Control," in Marx, ed., *Racial Conflict* (Boston: Little, Brown, 1971).

defending the interests of white people against a tide of black insurgence; the majority of whites appear to view "blue power" in this same light.[10] There is probably no other opinion on which the races are today so far apart as they are on the question of attitudes toward the police.

Set off in many cases by a confrontation between an officer and a black citizen, the ghetto uprisings have dramatized the role of law enforcement and the issue of police brutality. In their aftermath, movements have arisen to contain police activity. One of the first was the Community Alert Patrol in Los Angeles, a group organized to police the police in order to keep them honest and constrain their violations of personal dignity. This was the first tactic of the Black Panther Party, which originated in Oakland—perhaps the most significant group to challenge the police role in maintaining the ghetto's colonized status. The Panthers' later policy of openly carrying guns (a legally protected right) and their intention of defending themselves against police aggression brought on a series of confrontations with the Oakland police department. In 1968 when I first drafted this chapter I wrote: "All indications are that the authorities intend to destroy the Panthers by shooting, framing up, or legally harassing their leadership—diverting the group's energies away from its primary purpose of self-defense and organization of the black community to that of legal defense and gaining support in the white community." Within three years all these "indications" had materialized into hard fact. The Panthers [had] suffered critical losses to their leadership and organizational unity, and their cofounder Huey Newton . . . publicly criticized his party for isolating itself from the problems and concerns of the black community.

There are three major answers to "police colonialism," which correspond to reformist and more radical approaches to the situation. The most elementary, and most superficial, focuses on the fact that ghettos are overwhelmingly patrolled by white rather than by black officers. Therefore, the first proposal—supported today by many police departments—is to increase the numbers of blacks on local forces to something like their distribution in the city, making it possible to reduce the use of white cops in the ghetto. This reform should be supported for a variety of obvious reasons, but it does not get to the heart of the role of the police as agents of colonization.

The Kerner Report documents the fact that in some cases black policemen can be as brutal as their white counterparts. I have not found data on who polices the ghetto, but statistics showing the proportion of blacks on the overall force are available for many cities. In most places

10. Jerome H. Skolnick, ed., *The Politics of Protest* (New York: Ballantine, 1969), esp. chap. 7, "The Police in Protest."

the disparity is so striking that white police must predominate in patrolling black neighborhoods. Among the 30 cities listed by *Ebony* magazine, in the modal case the proportion of blacks in the population was three to four times as great as their proportion on the police force; for many cities this ratio was 5, 10, and even 20 times. In Oakland 34.5 percent of the population was black; only 4.7 percent of the policemen were black. For Boston the percentages were 16 and 2, for Cleveland 39 and 5, Dallas 25 and 2, Birmingham, 42 and 2! There were only five cities where the ratio was less than 2 to 1, that is, where the proportion of black cops was slightly more than one-half their percentage in the town as a whole: Gary, Washington, D.C., Atlanta, Philadelphia, and Chicago.[11] These figures suggest that both the extent and the pattern of colonization may vary from one city to another. It would be useful to study how black communities differ in degree of control over internal institutions as well as in economic and political power in the metropolitan area.

A second more radical demand is that the police must live in the communities where they work. The idea is that black officers who lived in the ghetto would have to be accountable to the community; if they came on like white cops then "the brothers would take care of business" and make their lives miserable. In many cities large numbers of policemen, like other public employees, reside in adjacent suburbs; they have resisted the demand of political leaders and pressure groups that they live where they work on the grounds that it singles out their occupation for discriminatory treatment.

The third, or maximalist, position is based on the premise that the police play no positive role in the ghettos. It calls for the withdrawal of metropolitan officers from black communities and the substitution of an autonomous indigenous force that would maintain order without oppressing the population. The precise relation between such an independent police, a ghetto governing body that would supervise and finance it, the city and county law enforcement agencies, and the law itself is as yet unclear. It is unlikely that any major city will soon face these problems as directly as New York did in the case of its schools. Of all the programs of decolonization, police autonomy will be most resisted. It gets to the heart of the way the state controls and contains the black

---

11. *San Francisco Sunday Examiner and Chronicle* (May 9, 1971), sec. A, p. 19, summarizing "The Dilemma of the Black Policeman," *Ebony* (May, 1971). Comparing the 1971 figures with the 1968 data reported in the Kerner Report (p. 321) shows very little change in the overall pattern. Some cities made absolute and relative gains in police integration; others, including two of the "leaders," Philadelphia and Chicago, lost ground.

That black officers nevertheless would make a difference is suggested by data from one of the supplemental studies to the Kerner Report. They found Negro policemen working in the ghettos considerably more sympathetic to the community and its social problems than their white counterparts. Peter Rossi, et al., "Between Black and White—The Faces of American Institutions in the Ghetto," op. cit., chap. 6.

community by delegating the legitimate use of violence to police authority.[12]

The various black power programs that are aimed at gaining control of individual ghettos—buying up property and businesses, running the schools through community boards, taking over antipoverty programs and other social agencies, diminishing the arbitrary power of the police —can serve to revitalize the institutions of the ghetto and build up an economic, professional, and political power base. These programs seem limited; we do not know at present whether they are enough in themselves to end colonized status. But they are certainly a necessary first step.

Yet they have dangers and pitfalls. Just as the limitation of a riot "strategy" became apparent, and just as the cultural movement bears a potential tendency toward antipolitical withdrawal that would have little impact on the condition of the poor and dispossessed, so ghetto control politics—indeed "black power" itself—faces the possibility that its programs and political thrust could be coopted by the larger system of power. A number of radical political analysts already see a new stage of neocolonialism in which Afro-American leaders, under the black power banner, exercise a form of "indirect rule" over their internal communities, whose people are then more efficiently exploited and controlled by an ever-flexible corporate capitalism.[13] While this eventuality is not to be discounted, I do not look for such a pat and facile solution to what Franz Schurmann has called a key contradiction of American capitalism—that between the emerging black cities and the white suburbs.[14]

---

12. As far as I know, the only locale where these problems have been at least considered is Berkeley, California. In April, 1971, a measure to divide the police department into autonomous units, each controlled by one of the city's three major social areas (the white middle-class "hills," the predominantly black South and West sides, and the youth-oriented campus section), was placed on the ballot. The plan received about 32 percent of the vote in the city as a whole. It did not receive the support of black Berkeley, where not a single precinct was carried. In my judgment this was because the project did not arise out of the experience and politics of the black community, but was chiefly engineered and organized by the white left and students. Others have stressed the middle-class character of Berkeley's minority population and the sophistication and liberal image of its police force.

13. See for example, Earl Ofari, *The Myth of Black Capitalism,* op. cit., Robert Allen, *Black Awakening in Capitalist America* (Garden City, N.Y.: Doubleday, 1969); Martin Oppenheimer, *The Urban Guerilla* (Chicago: Quadrangle, 1969); William K. Tabb, *The Political Economy of the Black Ghetto* (New York: Norton, 1970); and Jan Dizard and David Wellman, "I Love Ralph Bunche But I Can't Eat Him for Lunch: Corporate Liberalism, Racism, and Reform—Emerging Strategies for Ghetto Control," *Leviathan* 1 (Summer, 1969): 46–53.

14. Franz Schurmann, "System, Contradictions, and Revolution in America," in Roderick Aya and Norman Miller, eds., *The New American Revolution* (New York: The Free Press, 1971).

THE ROLE OF WHITES

What makes the Kerner Report a less-than-radical document is its superficial treatment of racism and its reluctance to confront the colonized relation between black people and the larger society. The report emphasizes the attitudes and feelings that make up white racism, rather than the system of privilege and control which is the heart of the matter. With all its discussion of the ghetto and its problems, it never faces the question of the stake that white Americans have in racism and ghettoization.

It is not a simple question, but this [article] should not end with the impression that police are the major villains. All white Americans gain privilege and advantage from the colonization of black communities.[15] The majority of whites also lose something from this oppression and division in society. Serious research should be directed to the ways in which white individuals and institutions are tied into the ghetto. Let me in closing suggest some possible parameters.

1. It is my guess that only a small minority of whites make a direct economic profit from ghetto colonization. This is hopeful, in that the ouster of white businessmen may become politically feasible. Much more significant, however, are the private and corporate interests in the land and residential property of the black community; their holdings and influence on urban decisionmaking must be exposed and combated.[16]

2. A much larger minority of whites have occupational and professional interests in the present arrangements. The Kerner Commission reports that 1.3 million nonwhite men would have to be upgraded occupationally in order to make the black job distribution roughly similar to that for whites. The commission advocates such upgrading without mentioning that 1.3 million specially privileged white workers would lose in the bargain.[17] In addition, there are those professionals who carry out what Lee Rainwater has called the "dirty work" of administering the lives of the ghetto poor: the social workers, the schoolteachers, the urban development people, and of course the police.[18] The social problems of the black community will ultimately be solved only by people and organizations from that community; the emphasis within these professions must shift toward training such a cadre of minority personnel. Social scientists who study and teach

---

15. See Blauner, *Racial Oppression,* chap. 1.

16. On the network of interests in the ghetto, see Harold Baron, "The Web of Urban Racism," in Knowles and Prewitt, eds., *Institutional Racism,* op. cit.

17. *Report of the National Advisory Commission on Civil Disorders,* op. cit., pp. 253–56.

18. Lee Rainwater, "The Revolt of the Dirty-Workers," *Trans-Action* 5:1 (November, 1967): 2, 64.

courses on problems of race and poverty likewise have an obligation to replace themselves by bringing into the graduate schools and college faculties men and women of color who will become the future experts in these areas. For cultural and intellectual imperialism is as real as welfare colonialism, although it is currently screened behind such unassailable shibboleths as universalism and the objectivity of scientific inquiry.

3. Without downgrading the vested interests of profit and profession, the real nitty-gritty elements of the white stake are political power and bureaucratic security. Although few whites have much understanding of the realities of race relations and ghetto life, I think most give tacit or at least subconscious support for the containment and control of the black population. And whereas most whites have extremely distorted images of black power, many—if not most—would be frightened by actual black political power. Racial groups and identities are real in American life; white Americans sense they are on top, and they fear possible reprisals or disruptions were power to be more equalized. There seems to be in the white psyche a paranoid fear of black dominance; the belief that black autonomy would mean unbridled license is so ingrained that such reasonable outcomes as black political majorities and independent black police forces will be bitterly resisted.

On this level the major bulwark of colonization is bureaucratic security, which allows the middle classes to go about life and business in peace and quiet. The black militant movement is a threat to the orderly procedures by which bureaucracies and suburbs manage their existence, and I think today there are more people who feel a stake in conventional procedures than there are who gain directly from racism. In their fight for institutional control, the colonized are not playing by the white rules of the game. These administrative rules have kept them down and out of the system; therefore blacks are not committed to running institutions in the image of the white middle class.

The liberal, humanist value that violence is the worst sin cannot be defended today if one is committed squarely against racism and for self-determination. Some violence is almost inevitable in the decolonization process; unfortunately racism in America has been so effective that the greatest power Afro-Americans wield today is the power to disrupt. [(This is because racism has fractionated the black population, making unity of political action difficult. A unified people and movement would have power to implement its goals and force changes on the society that would go far beyond disruption.)] If we are going to swing with these revolutionary times and at least respond positively to the anticolonial movement, we shall have to learn to live with conflict, confrontation, constant change, and what may be either real or apparent chaos and disorder.

A positive response from the white majority needs to be in two major directions at the same time. First, community liberation movements should be supported in every way by pulling out white instruments of direct control and exploitation and substituting technical assistance to the community when this is asked for. But it is not enough to relate affirmatively to the nationalist movement for ghetto control without at the same time radically opening doors for full participation in the institutions of the mainstream. Otherwise the liberal and radical position is little different from the traditional segregationist position. Freedom in the special conditions of American colonization means that the colonized must have the choice between participating in the larger society and in independent structures of their own.

Class,
Class Consciousness, and
American Workers

35

Harold L. Wilensky

For centuries, social critics and social scientists have given us the images
with which we construct our picture of the world. Among the concepts
that have done the most to mislead us in our search for an understanding of social reality are "class" and "class consciousness." European students of labor—*théoricien et militant* alike—take for granted
the utility of such ideas. In America, academic journals and the press are
filled with references to the "middle class" or "working class"; discussions of the affluent worker becoming "middle class" are commonplace.
And the constitutions of many American unions only yesterday contained the ringing slogans of class warfare.

This rhetoric—whether it is tolerated by nostalgic exsocialists who
head a few modern labor unions or whether it is taken more seriously,
as in popular discussions of the affluent worker—obscures more than it
reveals of the shape of American society. I should like to ask, "Where
do the ideas of class and class consciousness fit the situation of American labor well, and where do such ideas fit badly?" I shall argue that,
in the United States and in other rich countries, class consciousness
among manual workers is a transitional phenomenon—characterizing
workers not yet accustomed to the modern metropolis and the modern
work place; that a clearly defined working class no longer exists, if it
ever did; that much behavior and many attitudes said to be rooted in
class are instead a matter of race, religion, ethnic origin, education, age,
and stage in the family life cycle. Indeed, almost any of these traditional
groupings of the population display more homogeneity of behavior and
belief than "labor," if by the latter term we mean all manual workers
or even all union members.

Reprinted from Harold L. Wilensky, "Class, Class Consciousness, and American Work-
ers," Chapter 2 in William Haber, ed., *Labor in a Changing America* (New York: Basic
Books, 1968), pp. 12–28, by permission of the publisher. Copyright © 1968 by Basic
Books, Inc., Publishers, New York.

Finally, if we want to use economic classifications that yield uniformity in ideology or mentality, we must turn to such categories as "small entrepreneur" (a small part of the lower middle class) or to particular crafts (a small part of the upper working class) and to the established professions (a minority of the upper middle class). Insofar as class categories remain at all useful, the line that divides stably employed, well-educated, well-paid workers from the lower class is becoming more important than the split between upper working class and lower middle class. Whether we are witnessing the *embourgeoisement* of the workers or the sinking of the middle class into the proletariat, the top of one and the bottom of the other seem to form a new middle mass, a population that increasingly shares common values, beliefs, and tastes. And the process goes on in every rich country.

In general, I hope that all this will add up to a more realistic picture of the position, prospects, and mentality of that minority of the urban labor force that we customarily label "manual worker" or "working class" and its relation to other classes.

THE IDEA OF SOCIAL CLASS

All students of stratification are concerned with the distribution of rewards in society—who gets whatever is valued and why. They are also interested in the effect of the distribution of rewards on human behavior.[1] But there is no agreement about what rewards shared by what strata and what positions held by what groups are significant in explaining social structure and change; for instance, how we decide

---

1. The necessity of specialization—universal differences in role based on sex, age, work, and authority—leads everywhere to social stratification. People classify one another in categories and place these categories above or below one another on a scale of superiority and inferiority. The criteria of ranking vary; anything valued and unequally distributed may suffice: wealth, power, magic, women, and so on. Despite the recurrent dream of absolute equality—for example, the "classless society"—every society past or present has had some system of stratification. Distinctions are made. Some positions are honored, others not. Some are accorded more authority than others. Who is and who is not honored —the priest, the workman, the scholar, or the warrior—the distance between top and bottom positions; the difference between rich and poor, leader and rank-and-file; these and other features of stratification systems vary from place to place, time to time. But power and prestige differences do appear everywhere. Among the reasons are these: (1) Any society has to distribute people among its different positions and induce them to perform essential duties. (2) Every society has a hierarchy of values based on the fact of scarcity. (3) Differences in the distribution of these values (for example, income, power) move people to go after positions and to perform once they are in them. (4) As long as the family has anything to do with bringing up children and as long as some of the behavior and possessions unequally valued and unequally distributed are learned or acquired in the family, then some inequality will be perpetuated. (5) The various criteria of stratification are related—power differences among men are universal; those with power can use it to obtain for themselves and their kin those things which are valued (a man of power can use connections to get his son a good job; a man of wealth can buy his son a good education). Cf. K. Davis and Wilbur E. Moore, "Some Principles of Stratification," *American Sociological Review* 10 (1945): 242–49.

whether a man is a member of the working class or whether the working class is becoming middle class.

Karl Marx's definition of class, although imprecise, tends to emphasize, not sources of income (wages, profit, rent), not amount of income, not type of occupation, but what he called "the relations of production" —that is, *authority relations rooted in the distribution of property rights,* political power anchored in economic power.[2] Individuals form a class only insofar as they are locked in political combat with another class. Marxist discussion of "class consciousness" has since followed this line, emphasizing three critieria. In the Marxian view, a man is said to be class conscious when he is (1) rationally aware of his own class interests and identifies with them; (2) aware of other class interests and rejects them as illegitimate; and (3) aware of and ready to use collective political means to realize his class interests.[3]

In this Marxian sense, is American labor class conscious?

MARXIAN CLASS CONSCIOUSNESS IN AMERICAN LABOR HISTORY

Surely, for brief episodes during our most rapid industrialization, American labor displayed a militancy that fits the Marxian model and that has its contemporary counterpart in the labor movements of less developed countries. In the last quarter of the nineteenth century, American labor protest was intermittently tame and violent, economic and political; labor organizations were unsteady, easily diverted to elaborate political programs (from greenbackism to the single tax, from revolutionary anarchism to Marxian socialism, from Owen's "estate guardianship" to producers' and consumers' cooperation). Obstinate employers used private armies; the courts declared unions to be criminal conspiracies (until use of the injunction in the late nineteenth century gave them a better weapon); and the government broke strikes by use of local, state, and federal troops. In the 1880s, especially during and just after the depression of 1884–1885, labor protest began to sweep the land. Skilled and unskilled, women and men, native and foreign-born —never before (and not again until the 1930s) had American labor displayed such a drive to organize.

The peak of immigration was reached that decade, and streams of

---

2. For the best recent discussion of Marx's theory of class, see Ralf Dahrendorf, *Class and Class Conflict in Industrial Society* (Stanford: Stanford University Press, 1959), chap. 1. The task of evaluating Marx is beyond the scope of the present essay. Note, however, that by Marx's own definition of class, the abolition of private ownership of the means of production cannot lead to the "classless society" because authority is obviously neither tied to the legal title of property nor confined to the industrial sphere. For a balanced summary of sociological critiques of Marx, see ibid., chap. 4.

3. C. Wright Mills, *White Collar* (New York: Oxford University Press, 1951), chap. 15.

newcomers caught the enthusiasm. "Labor organizations assumed the nature of a real class movement. . . . General strikes, sympathetic strikes . . . nationwide political movements became the order of the day."[4] Employer associations quickly counteracted with lockouts, blacklists, armed guards, and detectives. When the wave of strikes failed, a consumer boycott movement of epidemic proportions got under way. This was a time of great upheaval, when the Knights of Labor, an inclusive labor organization espousing the ideal of producers' cooperation, spearheaded a mid-eighties mass movement culminating in an unsuccessful nationwide strike for the eight-hour day. It was the time, too, of the famous bomb explosion on Haymarket Square, which touched off a period of hysteria and police terror in Chicago and resulted in the unjust conviction and execution of innocent men.[5] The strength of employer opposition and the unwieldiness of the Knights' own organization threw the labor movement into decline.

As the movement broke up, the American Federation of Labor (AFL) was established to organize workers on straight trade-union lines, for better wages, hours, and working conditions through collective bargaining—foreshadowing the form in which labor protest was to be cast during the next century. The last gasp of nineteenth-century working-class militancy came in the form of the Homestead strike of 1892 (which involved a violent battle between an army of 300 Pinkerton detectives hired by Andrew Carnegie and armed strikers, including women and boys, who were finally overcome by the militia) and the great Pullman strike of 1894, which was broken with the aid of federal troops, a federal injunction, and the imprisonment of its leaders.

This enormous thrust upward from the people of poverty and low status was again repeated in the early days of Franklin Roosevelt's New Deal and provoked much the same militant fear on the part of the wealthy and well-born. In the 1930s, with almost revolutionary fervor, autoworkers in Flint, Michigan, seized control of corporate property in the famous sit-down strikes.

Marxian class consciousness? Yes, sporadic, loosely organized, and, as America has grown richer, fading into memory. Today, some of those sit-down strikers—or their sons—peacefully negotiate contracts with employers, serve on community welfare council boards, run for municipal office (and occasionally win), and live the modestly comfortable middle-class life of trade-union officials. The spontaneous protest movements of yesterday have become the "business unions" of today

---

4. Selig Perlman, *A History of Trade Unionism in the United States* (New York: Macmillan, 1928), p. 84.

5. Ibid., pp. 68–105; and Charles A. Beard and Mary R. Beard, *The Rise of American Civilization* (New York: Macmillan, 1933), chap. 2, pp. 73, 220ff.

—large stable organizations sanctioned by contracts and the law. American labor today has limited goals: better wages, shorter hours, and improved conditions of employment. Its means are mainly economic: the establishment of collective bargaining agreements enforced in part by arbitration of grievances. Occasional legal strikes over the terms of the agreement occur, but these have become the accepted alternative to massive state control of labor relations. A decreasing proportion of union members and of the total labor force is now drawn into strikes. The strike weapon, though not obsolete, has been blunted.

Similarly, in politics, the period of early industrialization saw many efforts to base political parties on distinctive working-class interests and membership. But, in recent decades, American labor has taken its place in the coalition of interest groups that dominates the Democratic party nationally and in the machinery of both major parties at local levels.

ATTITUDES TOWARD CLASS TODAY

The theme that class consciousness in American labor has dwindled is consistent with what we know of the attitudes of the American population toward social class and class conflict. Keeping in view the Marxian sense of class consciousness, what can we say about awareness of classes? Surveys using a variety of questions, leading and neutral, fixed and openended, indicate that most Americans think that classes exist, but there is little agreement about their nature and number, and there is great variation in how people on the same income and occupational level identify themselves.

In such research, the pitfalls are many and the results not very gratifying. There is the well-known problem that phrasing affects response: the researcher gets what he asks for. Thus, if you suggest that "some people say that there are social classes in the U.S.A. They call them lower, middle, and upper social classes," and then ask, "Which would you put yourself in?" the vast majority will choose the comfortable "middle." Add "working class" as one of your alternatives and a third to half of these "middle class" identifiers will switch to "working class." Leave the matter open—"What social classes do you think there are [in this city]" and "which one of them are you in?"—and as many as half the population will either deny the existence of classes or in some way indicate that the idea is meaningless.[6]

If you now confine yourself to those who think that classes exist and ask them for the number and characteristics of the classes, you will tap

6. Cf. Richard Centers, *The Psychology of Social Class* (Princeton: Princeton University Press, 1949), and Joseph A. Kahl, *The American Class Structure* (New York: Rinehart, 1957), chap. 6. Using four census tracts in Minneapolis representing four rental levels, Gross asked 935 subjects all three questions described above. Here is a comparison of percentages using one or another label by form of question, along with results from other studies using roughly comparable questions:

a great range of rather vague ideas. Few Americans see labor and capital as the classes; few see them at war. Various groups and strata emphasize various criteria of ranking—the value of material possessions (house, furniture, cars, clothing), type of job or job opportunities, amount of education, income or economic security (the lower strata emphasize this more), refinement of taste and manners (college people sometimes emphasize this), "morals" (the thrift-spendthrift theme is strong here among some members of the lower-middle class), or social origins. The number of classes named is similarly variable.

Finally, the context of questioning and the area of life covered by the questions affect criteria for the definition of the classes. If you go to a man in the evening and ask about the neighbors, he will think about status symbols and styles of life—consumption, house, car, leisure uses; if you talk to him on the job and ask about the people there, he will think of authority—the authority of bosses, of skill and expertise.[7] The average American is a Veblenian at home, a modified Marxist at work.

In assessing class consciousness in American labor, it is perhaps more important to examine the types of people who label themselves upper, middle, or working class. By any objective measure, there is considerable cross-class identification. About a fifth of all professional, business, and white-collar people identify as working class.[8] The clearest and most consistent awareness of class is at the top; a hard core of business,

	Form of Question and Sample						
Percentage saying:	UML Minnea-polis[a]	UMWL Minnea-polis[a]	UMWL U.S.A.[b]	UMWL U.S.A.[c]	Open Minnea-polis[a]	Open U.S.A.[d]	Open Tallahassee[e]
Upper	5	2	3	4	1	3	2
Middle	76	42	43	36	31	47	43
White-collar	—	—	—	—	—	—	3
Working	—	45	51	52	11	11	6
Lower	10	3	1	5	3	4	2
No classes	2	1	1	—	14	—	25
Don't know	4	2	1	3	20	28	—
Other classes	3	5	—	—	15	8	9
No response	—	—	—	—	5	—	10
Total	100	100	100	100	100	100	100
	(935)	(935)	(1,097)	(1,337)	(935)	(5,217)[f]	(320)

[a]Neal Gross, "Social Class Identification in the Urban Community," American Sociological Review, 18 (1953):398–404. Four census tracts chosen to represent four rental levels.

[b]Richard Centers, op cit., p. 77. Centers reports on two national samples. These samples were cross sections of white males. These are the results which Centers obtained in his sample of July, 1945.

[c]Ibid., p. 77. This is Centers' cross section of February, 1946.

[d]"The People of the U.S.—A Self-Portrait," Fortune, 21 (1940):14. A national cross-section quota sample.

[e]John L. Haer, "An Empirical Study of Social Class Awareness," Social Forces 36 (1957):117–21. Area probability sample.

[f]Total, not reported in the Fortune article, is cited in Haer, op. cit., p. 119.

7. Cf. Kahl, op. cit., p. 86.

8. Ibid., pp. 161–62. In my study of the Detroit area, about two in five of the white men in the upper working class (defined by income and occupation) aged 21 to 55 identify as middle class given the four choices; even one in four of the men on relief say that they are middle class.

professional, and technical people plus some of the clerical and sales people call themselves middle class no matter how you ask the question. Among workers, the more skilled are the most class conscious—consistent with the fact that labor organization emerged first among employees in a strategic market or technical position (printers, locomotive engineers, cutters in the garment industry).

What about the rejection of other class interests as illegitimate and the willingness to act out such sentiments politically? The few recent American studies that have looked for this evidence of class consciousness have turned up precious little of it. For instance, a sample of white men in Philadelphia, half Protestant, half Catholic, was asked in 1953: "To which one of these groups do you feel you owe your allegiance— business or labor?" They were also asked whether they agreed or disagreed with six policy statements, three taken from the CIO, three from the NAM. To be scored class conscious, a man had to choose sides, agree with all his side's policy statements, and disagree with the others. By this measure, only minorities of every group were class conscious: 40 percent of the big businessmen in the sample, 25 percent of the small businessmen, 28 percent of unionized workers, and only 13 percent of nonunionized workers. On the allegiance question, more union workers were neutral than were prolabor.[9]

A similar study of unionized textile workers in Paterson, New Jersey, a highly industrialized city with a long history of industrial conflict, showed similar results. "How do classes get along?" these workers were asked. "In general are they like enemies, or like equal partners, or like leaders and followers?" As Table 35–1 suggests, the most common responses to this and similar questions reflect more a pattern of paternalism than one of class warfare. One worker said, "If the bosses would treat the working people right, they would get along all the time. It's like a dog with a bone. If you give him food, he will be all right. Just treat us right and we'll follow right along." Another expressed his

Table 35–1. Attitudes about Class Relations among Ninety–five Textile Workers in Paterson, New Jersey (Including Multiple Answers)

Paternalism	27
Enemies	21
Partnership	19
Snobbish or jealous	12
Vague	8
Don't know	14

9. Oscar Glantz, "Class Consciousness and Political Solidarity," *American Sociological Review* 23 (1958): 375–83. The sample of 201 Protestants and 199 Catholics was a multistage sample of households, stratified and purposive at the first stage (precincts of varying occupational and religious composition) and random, with different probabilities, at the second stage.

general approval of the class system in this most un-Marxian way: "The people who have money own businesses, and the rest of the people work for them. If there were no rich people, who would the poor people work for?" Twenty-eight percent expressed such paternalistic views. One in five saw classes as partners; about one in five, as enemies. Over one in three held some other view, mostly vague. Most of these unionists felt that the class system was both inevitable and desirable. And although one in three thought that the system was becoming more rigid, half thought that it was becoming more open, especially for the next generation.[10]

The most intensive recent survey of the political expression of working-class consciousness was carried out among 375 blue-collar men in Detroit. If we are to uncover Marxian class consciousness anywhere, it would be in this study.[11] The sample was chosen from seven ethnically homogeneous neighborhoods: one of them northwest European, three mainly Negro, three Polish—generally overrepresenting the economically deprived and uprooted. They were interviewed when severe unemployment was a fresh memory—down from a recession peak of 20 percent of the labor force in 1957–1958 to 6 percent at the time of the interview in 1960. All but 10 percent used class imagery in response to at least one of eight unstructured questions designed to elicit spontaneous expressions of class symbolism (who was his favorite president and why, etc.). The closer one pushed these men to a Marxian model, however, the smaller the fraction that one could call class conscious. From mere class verbalization, characterizing 26 percent of the sample, the measure moved toward militancy as follows: (1) "When business booms in Detroit, who gets the profits?" Answers such as "rich people" or "big business" were considered indicators of moderate "skepticism" and covered 30 percent. (2) Favoring a statement about picketing a landlord was scored "militant radicalism"; 23 percent went this far. (3) Agreeing with the statement that the wealth of our country should be divided up equally so that people would have an equal chance to get ahead counted as militant egalitarianism. Only 10 percent would go all the way, the same tiny fraction that failed to verbalize in class terms at all.

Do class attitudes affect a man's politics? Do class-conscious union members, however few, act out their militancy?

---

10. Jerome Manis and Bernard Meltzer, "Attitudes of Textile Workers to Class Structure," *American Journal of Sociology* 60 (1954):30–35. The sample: 200 randomly selected members of the TWUA-CIO in Paterson, New Jersey. Ninety-five men were interviewed, including sixty-seven operatives, nineteen craftsmen, and nine laborers. Median age: fifty. Median residence in Paterson: forty years.

11. John C. Leggett, "Uprootedness and Working-Class Consciousness," *American Journal of Sociology,* 68 (1963):682–92. Cf. Alfred W. Jones, *Life, Liberty and Property* (New York: J. B. Lippincott, 1941), a sophisticated study of attitudes among Akron residents on such issues as the sit-down strikes of 1936.

THE LABOR VOTE

During the presidential campaign of 1948, when President Truman was running for office, I had an opportunity to study political action in a local union of the autoworkers in southeast Chicago. A local officer recounted an incident in a plant across the street that was discussed during the campaign by members of his local. He was telling me about the union shop, not politics, and he said he would give me an example of how important it was "from the standpoint of discipline" that workers be prounion:

> There was a guy over there who was bitterly against Roosevelt. . . . Then Roosevelt died and the boys in the shop felt pretty bad. They decided that they would have three minutes' silence on the day Roosevelt was buried. Well, this old guy had it all figured out ahead of time. When the bell rang all the fellows stood up at their machines in absolute quiet. . . . And then this old geezer bagan to . . . make as much noise as he could. . . . The funny thing is that [the workers] didn't do a thing. They just turned away from him and wouldn't even speak to him afterwards. . . . They came over to the union and the first thing was they insisted that he be thrown out of the union or at least suspended for a couple of months. We had a big meeting about that and I told the boys that that wasn't a real punishment, that the agony of having to work with the men would be a lot worse than having a leave of absence. I told them that they should fine him and make him keep on working. So that's what they did. They fined him $100 and the money went for a fund to build a statue of Franklin Roosevelt . . . [When he came to the local meeting to pay the fine, he] stood right up there in front of all his fellow workers and he said that he had been wrong and that he was sorry. . . . It took a lot of courage to admit that he was wrong. That made a terrific difference. You have no idea. He's made a good union man.

The Democratic New Deal tradition was still strong among the union activists in 1948 and—as in the case of the story—they slid easily from problems of discipline on strictly union matters to problems of discipline on strictly political matters. The president of Local 166, one member commented, "can't get it through his head that a guy can be Republican and still be for the union."[12]

For a quarter of a century, studies of voting and political orientation have shown that American labor unions have, with their emphasis on issues rather than man or party, solidified the political direction of those

---

12. Harold L. Wilensky, "The Labor Vote: A Local Union's Impact on the Political Conduct of Its Members," *Social Forces* 35 (1956):114. The following discussion of the labor vote is drawn from this article, which also assesses evidence on political behavior of union members and activists up to 1956.

exposed to their influence, helping to keep their active members in the old New Deal–Fair Deal coalition revived in President Johnson's "Great Society." The years 1944–1952 saw the emergence of a new postwar, post-Roosevelt political generation—a loosening of the ties that bind ethnic Catholics to the urban Democratic machines[13] and a breakup of the lower middle class—working class coalition that formed the basis of Democratic strength for two decades. There is some evidence that, nationally, the lower half of the working class, including the Negro minority, had politically significant elements that were becoming alienated from both the Democratic party and the political process.[14] For the minority involved directly with unions, however, the old ties to the liberal-labor wing of the Democratic party remained strong. From 1936 to 1952, comparisions between the candidate and/or party preferences and participation of union and nonunion voters on roughly the same socioeconomic level consistently show that the union voters are less apathetic and are more inclined to vote Democratic.[15] For example, Louis Harris, analyzing poll results for 1952, concludes that: (1) while the rest of the nation was going 3 to 2 for Eisenhower, union members were voting over 3 to 2 for Stevenson ("the labor vote held remarkably well"); (2) fewer than one in ten Catholic union members bolted the Democrats, compared to three in ten of the nonunion Catholics; (3) labor and economic issues were a bit more salient for union members and their families than for the rest of the population; (4) union members were solidly convinced that their economic welfare was tied to continued Democratic rule; but (5) the families of union members voted 9 to 8 for Eisenhower, slipping from their normal 2 to 1 Democratic inclination. (Two out of every ten members of union families bolted from the

---

13. Samuel Lubell, *The Future of American Politics* (New York: Harper, 1951) and Seymour M. Lipset, et al., "The Psychology of Voting," in *Handbook of Social Psychology*, ed. Gardner Lindzey (Cambridge, Mass.: Addison-Wesley, 1954), chap. 2.

14. An analysis by Morris Janowitz and Dwaine Marvick of the Survey Research Center data on the 1952 election campaign shows that nonvoting among lower lowers (defined by income and occupation) reached 45 percent, and those who voted gave Stevenson only a 5 percent plurality. Catholics as a whole gave Stevenson a similarly small plurality. Like the farmers, the lower middle class made major shifts to Eisenhower. *Competitive Pressure and Democratic Consent* (University of Michigan, Institute of Public Administration, 1956). President Johnson's even more overwhelming victory over Barry Goldwater in 1964 similarly cut across class lines; every bloc of voters moved to the Democrats because of fear of extremism in domestic affairs and recklessness in foreign affairs.

15. See Gallup poll results reported for 1936, 1940, and 1944, in V. O. Key, Jr., *Politics, Parties, and Pressure Groups* (3rd ed.; New York: Crowell Co., 1952), p. 79. On 1948, see David Truman in F. Mosteller, et al,, "The Pre-Election Polls of 1948," *Social Science Research Council Bulletin* 60 (1949):229–30; and Angus Campbell and Robert L. Kahn, *The People Elect a President* (Ann Arbor: Survey Research Center, 1952), pp. 27–28. On 1952, see Angus Campbell, G. Gurin, and Warren E. Miller, *The Voter Decides* (Evanston: Row, Peterson, 1954), pp. 72–73.

voting pattern of their household breadwinner.)[16] These studies suggest that although labor unions change few votes (the John L. Lewis endorsement of Willkie is often cited),[17] they do much to mobilize the committed vote, to activate class disposition, and to reinforce party appeals.[18]

That class consciousness can combine with union activity to yield uniform voting is shown in an analysis of the hard-core supporters of G. Mennen Williams, the liberal Democratic governor of Michigan from 1948 to 1960, now Assistant Secretary of State in charge of African affairs. Recognizing Governor Williams' strong commitment to civil rights, almost all of the Negroes, union and nonunion, militant and tame, voted for him in 1958. But when we look at the Williams vote among whites, we find: (1) militant unionists, 81 percent; (2) moderate unionists, 72 percent; (3) nonmilitant unionists (the ones who merely mention class in discussing issues or avoid class symbolism entirely), 52 percent; (4) militant nonunionists (only 5 cases); (5) moderate nonunionists, 50 percent; (6) nonmilitant nonunionists, 38 percent.[19] Clearly, that minority of workers who are highly class conscious and are exposed to a lively union act out their ideology in the political arena.

We can see the process by which this takes place. Comparison of the political orientation of members and nonmembers or of union actives and inactives suggests that: (1) routine experience in union social and economic affairs leads to a generalized prolabor orientation; (2) this orientation leads to acceptance of union discipline in strikes and collective bargaining; (3) the younger, more ambitious, better educated and

---

16. "Labor Was Not an Issue in the Election," in *Labor and Nation Timely Papers,* 1:1 (1953):15–25, and Louis Harris, *Is There a Republican Majority?* (New York: Harper, 1954), pp. 148–49. R. W. Dodge, using interviews with an area probability sample of the adult population in Detroit in 1951–1952, found that about 80 percent of the people in union families who indicated a political preference favored the Democratic party, while the nonunion segment had only a slight Democratic majority. The contrast held for the labor-backed mayoralty candidate in 1951, whose main support, however weak, came from persons in union (especially CIO) families. "Some Aspects of the Political Behavior of Labor Union Members in the Detroit Metropolitan Area" (unpublished doctoral dissertation, University of Michigan, 1953). Only two of these studies—Harris, op. cit., and Bernard R. Berelson, Paul F. Lazarsfeld, and W. H. McPhee, *Voting* (Chicago: University of Chicago Press, 1954)—use controls for such politically relevant social categories as race, ethnicity, and religion.

17. E.g., see Irving Bernstein, "John L. Lewis and the Voting Behavior of the CIO," *Public Opinion Quarterly* 5 (1941):233–49.

18. Cf. Key, op. cit., pp. 79–80. Berelson, et al., op. cit., pp. 37–53, report that in Republican Elmira, in 1948, not only did union members vote more Democratic than nonmembers of the same occupation, class, education, age, or religion, but also that the more prounion workers were more Democratic, and, in an IAM-AFL local studied, the more interaction the members had with other union members the more Democratic the vote. Also those FDR voters who were identified working class remained most loyal to Democrats in 1948, ibid., pp. 253–73.

19. John C. Leggett, "Working-Class Consciousness, Race, and Political Choice," *American Journal of Sociology* 69 (1963):171–76. Three in four of the sample belonged to a union; eight in ten of these were members of a CIO union.

sometimes more skilled workers who become involved in local union activity and take charge of union affairs develop transferable political skills in the union office and come to see political action as a necessary extension of the collective-bargaining process; (4) locally, they cultivate political influence to protect their institutional privileges—gain police support in the maintenance of picket lines; (5) in national campaigns, they articulate the national union line at a local level in informal ways, and, less often through precinct organization, see discipline in the political sphere as a normal part of trade-union loyalty; (6) all this adds up to increased political interest and activity both in and out of the union, and, when the available "friends of labor" are mainly liberal Democrats, it gives the political focus of the activists a broader "labor-liberal" flavor.[20]

STRUCTURAL ROOTS OF IDEOLOGICAL DIVERSITY: THE LIMITS OF CLASS ANALYSIS

That we find some workers who are class conscious even in a Marxian sense, that we can point to a labor vote which prolabor politicians count on, should not obscure equally important and perhaps increasingly important facts about American society. The membership of American labor organizations is only about a third of all nonagricultural employees, compared with more than half in England and more than two-thirds in Sweden. American labor is conservative. Compared to European labor, it shows a low degree of class consciousness. Its leaders have become integrated into the power and status structure of a private-enterprise economy and a pressure-group polity. The mass of unorganized wage and salaried workers is similarly integrated into the mainstream of community life.

---

20. Harold L. Wilensky, "The Labor Vote," op. cit., p. 120. Cf. two sample surveys of the Detroit area—Dodge, op. cit., and Arthur Kornhauser, A. J. Mayer, and H. L. Sheppard, *When Labor Votes* (New York: University Books, 1956). The latter found, for a general UAW population, what appeared in the Chicago local that I examined. Cf. two case studies which showed a positive relation between activity and acceptance of labor political effort. Arnold Rose, *Union Solidarity* (Minneapolis: University of Minnesota Press, 1952), pp. 79, 165 and J. Seidman, J. London, and B. Karsh, "Political Consciousness in a Local Union," *Public Opinion Quarterly* 15 (1951/52): 692–702. Though popular speculation is abundant, systematic analysis of the character of labor as a political force is rare. In addition to Seidman, et al., Kornhauser, et al., and Wilensky, see F. Calkins, *The CIO and the Democratic Party* (Chicago: The University of Chicago Press, 1952); and H. E. Freeman and M. Showel, "Differential Political Influence of Voluntary Associations," *Public Opinion Quarterly* 15 (1951/52):703–14. The latter, on the basis of a preelection survey in 1950 in the state of Washington using an area probability sample, concludes that business, political, and veterans' associations exert *widest* positive influence; labor and church organizations, *narrowest*. Unions, like the Catholic Church, apparently achieved high saturation of a small target; positive influence was confined to their own membership; in fact, labor's hypothetical endorsement has a negative effect on candidate preference among nonmembers.

These characteristics of American labor can be explained in large part by the impact of continued economic growth on the structure of opportunity. If, on the whole, the rich were getting richer and the poor poorer; if occupations were becoming more manual and less skilled; if depressions were frequent and severe; if, in short, the opportunity to rise in the social and economic scale was declining while mass aspirations were rising, we might expect American labor to swing in a politically class-conscious direction. The evidence suggests just the opposite.

Occupational and income changes have brought a vast heterogeneity to the labor force. This heterogeneity is epitomized by the growing middle layers of American society—the new middle class of white-collar and professional people, the increasingly skilled upper crust of manual workers. Advanced specialization has made for finer distinctions of status and a multiplication of occupational worlds. Instead of two armies massed on an industrial battlefield—"labor" on one side, "capital" on the other—we have immense variation in interest and attitude within the ranks of each, and a consequent decline in the solidarity of each.[21] On the management side, the complexity of internal cleavages follows the increased complexity of organization—with increased bargaining over power and budget between staff advisors of specialized knowledge and power-conscious executives, between levels of authority, or on the same level of authority between rival advisors and rival supervisors. Although it is still useful to distinguish between the managers and the managed, the lines are becoming a bit blurred. On the labor side, even unionized workers divide on age, sex, seniority, and skill lines, not to mention the division by religion, nationality, and race. Union or nonunion American workers display much diversity in values, beliefs, and ways of life.

---

21. Wilbert E. Moore, "Occupational Structure and Industrial Conflict," in *Industrial Conflict,* edited by Arthur Kornhauser and others (New York: McGraw-Hill, 1954), pp. 221 ff.

What Happened to the Class Struggle?

36

By *John Kenneth Galbraith*

Anyone who foresees a decline in tension between capital and labor, employer and employee, is intellectually suspect, and so it has been for a long while. The class conflict is part of our cultural heritage. Moreover, in the last two centuries a great many employers have proclaimed fulsomely a new era of good feeling in their labor relations. Many thereafter have been burned in effigy by their employees, who have regretted only the need for a surrogate.

The claim of reactionary politicians that they have eliminated labor strife, and the claim of reactionary philosophers that the interests of the worker are being cared for by God, have added similarly to the bad reputation of the prophet of labor peace.

It is in this obdurate environment that I find myself today. I am about to argue that labor-management relations have undergone a fundamental change in the heartland of the modern industrial system—the area of the large industrial corporation. The effect is to limit and even dissolve conflict where we are most accustomed to expect it. The classical class struggle at the center of our industrial life is a dwindling phenomenon. But those who feel that without conflict life would be unduly dull should be of good cheer. As tension diminishes in this part of the society, it burgeons in others.

Tension diminishes in that part of the industrial economy where large corporations bargain with strong unions. This is the classical area of conflict—that part, indeed, where socialists of a half-century ago would have foreseen the ultimate facedown between capital and labor. The reason lies not with the mellowing of the trade unions, the tendency of the union with passing years to become senile as some would suggest. Unions, like all other institutions, have a life design; they are

Reprinted with permission from *Washington Monthly*. Copyright by the Washington Monthly Co., 1028 Connecticut Ave., N.W., Washington, D.C. 20036.

463

certainly not the same when old as when young. But the relevant changes occur in the corporation—and in the economy itself. Four changes have a claim on our attention.

There is, first, the transmigration of power within the corporation itself. To a point this is not subject to dispute. Power has been passing from the owner to the manager, from the capitalist to the corporate bureaucrat. Capitalist goals are sharply juxtaposed to those of labor. Both capitalist and worker want revenue; speaking broadly, both want the same revenue. This is a condition well calculated to induce conflict. One should not make complicated what has a simple clarity of line.

With the passage of power to the corporate bureaucracy, to what I have called the technostructure, the conflict is a good deal less stark. In degree the technostructure has the choice between allocating revenue to stockholders and to labor. There are risks of disturbance to the technostructure in underpaying the stockholder. Up to a certain size they risk a takeover. But there are also risks of disturbance in underrewarding the unions. Peace is worth paying for.

Additionally, the goals of the corporate bureaucracy are less opposed to those of labor than to those of corporate capitalism. Growth, bringing new opportunity, promotion, prestige, and higher pay is what best rewards the technostructure. Concern for growth thus modifies the concern for profit maximization. In reliability of employment, opportunity for overtime and even, in degree, opportunity for advancement, corporate growth also rewards the worker in a way that profits do not.

The second factor reducing conflict is technology. This has numerous mitigating effects. Blue-collar are replaced with white-collar workers. White-collar workers identify themselves with the firm and do not organize. (The number of white-collar workers in the United States almost 15 years ago overtook the number in the blue-collar working force and is, of course, now far greater.) And technology converts many of the blue-collar workers who remain to sedentary operatives sitting at a console. Identification tends to be with the machine and the process rather than with a fellow working stiff. All of these changes reduce the militancy of the worker and the union man and also the number who are available to be militant. We have here a probable reason why a fair number of highly technical firms—IBM, the advanced electronic enterprises serving the Pentagon, and NASA—are not even organized.

Third, we have the effect of general affluence. This may not make people less interested in income. But for the worker it does increase mobility and enlarge alternatives. For the worker who is dependent as a matter of life and death on his job, the union is the alternative to something only marginally superior to slavery. (The difference between starvation and a whip for compelling toil, as I have argued elsewhere, is mostly a matter of taste.) The compelled worker clings desperately to his union, suffers for it, rises angrily to its cause and command. It, literally, guarantees what liberty he has. The affluent worker is not similarly so driven.

Fourth and finally and most important, the Keynesian context has greatly reduced the role of the union. I need not emphasize the stress that this system places upon high employment and economic growth. Underwriting such employment and growth is a high and reliable level of aggregate demand. In the industrially developed part of the Keynesian economy, firms are large. This is a normal aspect of capital intensive production with high technology. Such firms exercise extensive control over prices; stable price and cost parameters are a requirement of highly technical, highly capitalist production. If demand is strong and reliable, differences between firm and union can usually be resolved by meeting the union demand and passing along the resulting price increase to the public. On occasion some company situation or policy will lead to resistance and a strike. The recent General Electric dispute is a case in point but, I think, an exceptional one. Or the wage and price increase may be opposed under public pressure because it is against public policy—because it is inflationary. And this can also lead to strikes. But a wage dispute that involves public policy invokes the government or the society, not the employer, as the antagonist. It is not a conflict in the context of the classical class struggle. Nor does it raise temperatures as does a struggle over profits. The latter is a zero-sum game; what one side wins the other loses. A conflict in the context of high demand and employment can leave both the employee and employer better off than before and often does.

There is a considerable vested interest in the classical labor/employer confrontation. It is something we understand; our perceptions of social matters are not so numerous that we can let go easily of those we have. The unions that deal with the large firms resist any notion that they are less vital, less embattled, that they live less dangerously than, say, half a century ago. Men concerned with labor relations do not wish to seem less heroic than their precursors. Yet the conclusion is inescapable. In the heartland of the industrial system—in the automobile, steel, nonferrous metal, rubber, chemical, oil, petrochemical, and large-scale consumer product industries—industrial conflict has been extensively dissolved or absorbed by the system. Much as it may be regretted, it will never be the same again.

But although conflict has been greatly reduced in this part of the economic society, it has reappeared or been intensified in other parts of the society. But this is not all. The very process by which tension has been absorbed in the heart of the industrial society has brought about an increase in tension elsewhere. It has exported its problem to other parts of the economy. This is a development, I venture to think, of first-rate importance. To it I now turn.

The heartland of the industrial system resolves its differences at high employment by raising prices—by passing the cost of settlement along to the public. This is to say, the cost is passed along to the public employee, the pensioner and, less dramatically, to the white-collar worker in the private sector of the economy. These all live under the price pressures emanating from the heart of the system. And there is here no similarly easy solution. There is no equally easy way by which the teacher, patrolman, fireman, civil servant can have an amicable negotiation with *his* employer and then pass the cost along to someone public. In relation to the taxpayer it *is* a zero-sum game. In recent years by far the most rapid increase in trade-union membership has been the public sector. And, farm workers apart, it has been the most important area of trade-union militancy. In very large measure, this has been the result of the method by which tension has been reduced in the industrial sector.

There continues to be a feeling that unions in the public sector of the economy are somehow less legitimate than in the private sector. And there is a stronger belief, reinforced generally by law, that if they exist they should not strike. These attitudes are obsolete—and also socially damaging—and also unjust. We reduce tension in the industrial sector by passing the cost to these people. And we say it is improper, even unpatriotic, for them to react. And this attitude is exceedingly damaging to the public interest. For if the public services cannot act on their own behalf their compensation will fall ever further behind. And good manpower, skills, and talent will not be attracted to these services. Schools, law enforcement, municipal services, other government services, will suffer in consequence. And this is not hypothetical. They have already suffered for precisely this reason. Few things, it seems to me, are now socially so necessary as strong trade-union organization in the public services. And organizations, except in the most extreme cases, should not be denied the use of any bargaining instrument in their own behalf. Far better occasional teachers' strikes than no teachers. Far better an occasional garbage collectors' strike than no garbage collectors. If we deny the right to strike to policemen and firemen it should only be because we have made manifestly certain that they do not need it. For here too the difference to the public between a strike and a situation in which policemen and firemen cannot be hired will eventually become rather theoretical. To thieves and arsonists it will be even more academic.

The industrial heartland does not export its tensions only to the public sector. All whose incomes respond slowly are in some degree recipients. This has something to do with the middle-class, middle-income malaise of our time. And in the case of both the public sector and the white-collar community it raises important questions about larger economic policy. For why should we cause trouble here by the way we settle disputes in the industrial sector?

This line of thought suggests that even at the cost of some trouble, even anguish, in the industrial heartland we should stop this export of tension (and inflation) to the rest of the economy. I believe we should. And I believe that sooner or later we will admit the need to do so. It means some system of wage and price restraint wherever strong unions bargain with strong employers in a strong market. Though many countries now accept it, the notion of an organized system of wage and price restraint is still greatly resisted by the present administration. In part this responds to the power, including the power of suggestion, of the large corporations and the unions. They do not need it. In part the resistance is theological. There is reluctance to admit the decline of the market. This concedes economic sin. There is aversion to recognizing the role of the modern corporation and the modern union in wage and price determination. This concedes further wickedness. There is the belief, as I have elsewhere said, that God is a conservative gentleman who will not let His side down. There is the undying faith of the modern high church economist in macroeconomic measures—in fiscal or monetary policy.

This belief that fiscal and monetary policy can reconcile high employment with price stability, a belief asserted against all the force of both experience and logic, will be counted without question the most unforgivable error of the present generation of American economists. Until we agree on substituting some mechanism of public price determination of wages and prices—which I do not think need be very complicated—for unhampered determination by corporations and unions, the strongest parts of the economy will continue to export their tensions to the weakest. Or they will be kept from doing so by yet greater social injustice. That, of course, is recession and unemployment with even more damaging implications for the weaker members of the community.

One further form of conflict is replacing the classical class struggle. It is of a very different sort.

The modern industrial heartland is highly technical, highly organized, and highly planned. It has, in consequence, a large and insistent demand for highly qualified people. This talent, not the supply of capital, not workers skilled or unskilled, diligent or otherwise, has become the touchstone of industrial success. It has brought into being everywhere in the industrial world a very large educational establishment. There is, I think, no real doubt as to the cause and effect. When capital was vital for industry we multiplied banks and savings institutions. The educational system supplied unlettered proletarians. Now that industry needs educated men, we marvel at our enlightenment.

But the ethic of the modern educational system has not yet been successfully accommodated to that of the industrial society. That ethic sets store by personality and independent thought. It celebrates the sovereignty of the individual in markets and equally in the political process. The industrial system is, in contrast, highly organized, highly bureaucratic. And so is the state that, in considerable measure, sustains it. The ethic of the industrial heartland requires the individual it has called into existence to subordinate his personality to the goals of organization and the truths of organization—to the goals and truths of General Motors, General Dynamics, and the generals who comprise the Joint Chiefs.

Here we have the foundations of the conflict that is replacing the class struggle. It comes to sharpest focus, not surprisingly, in the universities but has far wider implications. Not having to do with money, men who are identified with the classical class struggle think it frivolous, even adolescent. This is the particular and natural reaction of many unions. It is not frivolous.

The form and dimensions of this conflict—of personality with organization, of individuals with what they believe to be bureaucratic arrogance or matters ranging from environment to weaponry—is still far from clear. Its ultimate resolution is even less so. I am beginning to believe that it may eventually involve some retreat from some of the rewards of massive industrial organization—a decision, if personality is to be expressed, to subordinate or abandon some of our concern for more goods, more production, a higher standard of living. The price of an unremitting pursuit of these we may one day decide is too high to pay.

But this conflict I must, for the purposes of this article at least, put out on the plate and leave. Let me insist only as to its reality. It is not the passing neurosis of a few people in the universities. In one form or another it is the crisis of all the industrial countries. More immediately, I am persuaded, it is going to involve a very sharp reaction to bureaucratic power and bureaucratic arrogance, especially as these are expressed by the large industrial corporation and its public allies. The political effort to assert other values, to protect the individual against organization, to curb organization power, to frustrate bureaucratic convenience in the private sector as in the public, will be central to our public debate and our political effort for a long time. Those who fear that life in the advanced industrial society is becoming too peaceful should relax. There is, I think, no danger.

But let me content myself with a summary reminder of two more immediate points. The industrial system eases its tension by shifting it to the public employee and to the white-collar worker. Let us be certain that we do not keep the public employee, simply because he is so valuable, from defending himself and defending therewith recruitment for the services he renders. And beyond this let us cease to solve problems of labor relations in one part of the economy by exporting inflation and tension to the rest. Let us accept that no combination of conventional economic policy with prayer and incantation reconciles high employment with price stability in what I have called the industrial heartland. There will be a price-wage or a wage-price spiral. Having recognized this and the damage that results, let us be practical and act accordingly.

The Transformation of the Class Structure

37

Richard F. Hamilton and James Wright

Central to both Marxist and [centrist . . .] formulations [about American society] are a number of questions concerning current class arrangements and their origins: Has the class structure changed? If so, in what ways? Has the blue-collar or working-class rank become a minority? Is the middle class showing a continuous increase in relative size? In other words, is the key assumption of the centrist position, the assumption of a dominant emerging "center," a valid one . . .?

Most presentations of evidence bearing on this claim are based on data for the entire labor force. Laying aside the farm population (where the long-term decline is clear and unambiguous) and focusing only on those in nonfarm employment, one does find support for the [centrist] claim—if one takes the entire labor force and counts all jobs as being of equal importance. If, however, one recognizes that the occupations of heads of households (or of main earners) are of greater importance to the welfare and social condition of the family than those of second and third earners, then a different approach to the question is warranted. The second and third earners are wives or children whose contributions to family welfare are both smaller and more likely to be temporary. Given the current organization of families and work, the main earners are usually male and the second earners are overwhelmingly, but not entirely, female. For this reason it is appropriate to examine the occupational trends for males and females separately rather than to focus on the entire labor force.

Reprinted from Richard F. Hamilton and James Wright, *New Directions in Political Sociology* (Indianapolis: Bobbs-Merrill Studies in Sociology, 1975), pp. 15–23. [Footnotes and references have been omitted. Detailed evidence in support of the authors' conclusions appears in Robert F. Hamilton, *Class and Politics in the United States* (New York: John Wiley, 1972), esp. chaps. 4–6, 11, and 18. Also see his *Restraining Myths* (Beverly Hills: Sage Publications, 1975), chap. 4.—Ed.]

A markedly different result occurs when one makes this distinction between main and secondary earners. Examining the trend among the traditional blue-collar categories (the U.S. Census categories: craftsmen, operatives, laborers, and service), one finds a rather modest decline in the course of the century from 69.9 percent in 1900 to 57.5 percent in 1970. There is no "rapid social change" occurring in recent years: the 1960 figure, for example, was 58.7 percent. For a number of reasons which are too complicated to consider here, it seems unlikely that any great transformations will occur in the forthcoming decade. The conclusion, then, is that a majority of the nonfarm males are in blue-collar or working-class occupations. The much-discussed "class shift" has still not occurred.

Support for the claim is found on the female side of the labor force. In 1900 an overwhelming majority (78 percent) of women were in blue-collar employment. Two major developments occurred in the subsequent decades: there was a considerable increase in the number of employed women and there was a change in the location of their employment, that is, a shift to white-collar work. By 1950 the transformation of the majority had already occurred, only 45.6 percent then being in manual jobs. This trend has continued to the present. The 1970 census shows only 37.4 percent of employed women in manual jobs.

In many instances what this development means is that working-class wives (that is, those whose husbands are in blue-collar employment) come to be engaged in white-collar work. The husband goes to work in the factory and the wife goes to an office. It seems unlikely that these women would be employed in the front offices, in the financial or commercial centers of cities, or in the new office locations in suburbia. These white-collar workers from working-class families are probably to be found in warehousing and transportation, in locations surrounding the urban center, or in offices located adjacent to the factories. Rather than being in the elegant downtown shops, they would be located in the smaller stores on the main streets of working-class neighborhoods.

For a number of reasons, it seems unlikely that working-class women employed in these "middle-class" settings would be led to change their life styles or their political outlooks. They probably would not be subject to any significant middle-class influence while on the job. The number of middle-class persons (meaning here middle-class males or women of middle-class families) employed with these working-class women would be very small. There would be little incentive for the women to change politics, to become moderate or Republican, because there would be little positive stimulus to do so and because they would still be enmeshed in family, neighborhood, and friendship patterns that would reinforce the values and orientations held before taking the job. Where the job supplements income and allows an increase in consumer spending, it seems likely that the result would be an embellishment of a working-class life style rather than an imitation of the distant upper-middle classes. In short, and in clear contrast to the received expectation, the oft-touted middle-class "majority" is in fact constituted by white-collar women whose family, friendship, and neighborhood contexts are very likely to be working class. For this reason one may conclude that the middle-class majority is yet to arrive.

THE BLUE-COLLAR–WHITE-COLLAR DISTINCTION

What about the related assumption, the belief that the blue-collar–white-collar division is the most significant one in contemporary industrial societies? Are political orientations more sharply differentiated along this line than any other?

An examination of some relevant evidence (the Survey Research Center's national election studies) yields little support for this claim. The difference in party identification between the lower-middle-class white Protestants and the equivalent well-off workers was a matter of four percentage points. In the case of 1964 voting, the difference was one of twelve percentage points. The examination of class differences in the other groups (Catholics, Jews, blacks) shows a reversal with the lower middle class being somewhat more Democratic in both identification and voting. Instead of sizable differences appearing along this "line" in the class structure, the actual differences prove to be rather inconsequential.

A sharper division in attitudes and political preferences appears between the lower and the upper middle classes. This was most clearly the case among the white Protestants. Among the Catholic, Jewish, and black populations, similar outlooks and preferences were found in all class levels with only a limited tendency in a conservative direction among the upper middle segments. It is among the larger and less cohesive group, the majority white Protestants, that the upper-middle–lower-middle cleavage was most pronounced.

A similar exploration was conducted of the attitudes of "lower" and "upper" working classes. Contrary to the expectations of those who anticipate "conservative" sentiment among the well-off workers, no systematic tendency in this direction has been found. There are variations from study to study but the available evidence does not show either sizable or consistent differences in support of the thesis. The further implication here, as far as political attitudes and choices go, is that the so-called middle-mass hypothesis is also lacking support.

The actual pattern then is one of fairly substantial Democratic sentiment in three segments: the lower working class, the upper working class, and the lower middle class. The same groups also show relatively high levels of support for various liberal welfare-state–type measures.

There are consistent differences between the white Protestants on the one hand and the other major minority groups on the other hand. Despite a persistent focus on "class," the differences between socioreligious groups have been greater than those between classes.

The sharpest line of differentiation proves to be that "line" which circumscribes the upper-middle-class white Protestant segment. They are more conservative than the white Protestants "below" them in the class structure. And they are considerably more conservative than their Catholic, Jewish, or black peers in the upper middle class. In fact, this part of the white Protestant category contains the core group of conservative Republican supporters. In 1964, for example, they were very solid in their support for Goldwater. They were solid in their opposition to extension of medical care, to a guaranteed living standard, and to federal aid for education. And they were extremely alarmed about the threat of "government power."

It may seem paradoxical that a party with a "political base" this small is able to win statewide elections and also, with considerable frequency, national elections. Part of the explanation is to be found in the level of activity of this group. They make maximum use of their political resources. Republicans in this context, for example, come close to 100 percent participation in elections. They talk politics with greater frequency than any other group; they attend meetings, give money, and so forth. A similar but less pronounced tendency appears among the Republicans in other segments of the society. Some limited media effect favorable to the Republicans also appear to play a role. Then too, the choices made by Democratic administrations have also provided some help to the minority Republicans. The involvements in World War I, in the Korean War, and in Vietnam were no doubt significant factors in the subsequent Republican victories in 1920, 1952, and 1968.

Why is the basic division found between the upper and lower middle classes? Why is the division there and not elsewhere as some have claimed?

One immediate answer is that the two groups live in different communities, in settings which share different political traditions. Those in the upper-middle-class communities, especially the white Protestants, come from families that were Republican and conservative. In their rather isolated circumstances in the upper-middle-class suburbs, they are sheltered from events in the larger society and, at least until recently, received no compensating "education" as to those larger problems from the mass media. They have been trained in a special conservative tradition and, located in relatively isolated and segregated communities, they have not been subjected to lessons or influences that might lead them to adopt a different outlook. The separation of the white Protestants from the Catholics and Jews within the upper-middle-class suburban communities allowed the perpetuation of a liberal tradition within the latter two groups. The patterns of encapsulation, in short, allowed the continuation of all three subgroup traditions.

A parallel question may be raised as to the situation of insular lower-middle-class communities. A limited exploration of this question in two American cities casts some initial doubt on this formulation of the problem. A very large portion of the lower middle class lives in working-class neighborhoods. It also seems likely that they are kin to their working-class neighbors, have gone to school with them, and have friends and associates in the neighborhoods and in community organizations. Rather than attempting to "maintain distance" from their working-class neighbors (that is, from their friends and relatives), this alternative reading suggests that they would have a normal human interest in maintaining and improving their links with that community. Rather than making a fetish of their "middle-class" position, it seems more likely that their loyalties would be to those in the immediate milieu. Some studies have shown considerable numbers of the "lower-middle-class" population, roughly half in some cases, calling themselves "working class" when given a choice between that and a "middle-class" label.

One other feature of the lower-middle-class existence that deserves mention is the typical pattern of income over the career. The upper-middle-class family can ordinarily anticipate increased income over the entire active career. These earners begin in relatively low positions in the bureaucracies, but it is part of the plan for such careers that promotion to the middle and higher levels will occur with appropriate increases in pay. For the lower middle and working classes, on the other hand, the family income follows a different line of development. Their incomes begin at a low level and increase up to the middle of the career, when the main earner is in his forties. Thereafter some decline takes place as individual earnings diminish and as the second and third earners either leave the family or cease their employment. Most of the increased earnings in midcareer are due to the presence of second and third earners. In great measure, the explanation for working-class affluence is the presence of two or more employed family members. The presence of multiple earners, in turn, is a function of position in the family cycle. This pattern appears to have been a part of working-class and lower-middle-class life for more than a century; it is not some new development which has appeared with "advanced industrialism."

The much-discussed fact of "blurred class lines" or, more specifically, of white-collar workers earning less than blue-collar workers, needs reconsideration in the light of the above observations. If the affluent workers and the marginal middle classes live in the same community, come from the same family backgrounds, and have similar life experiences, it may mean that they do not "resent" their lower income. It might be a simple and easily understood fact of life, one which is viewed as a just and equitable arrangement; skilled workers, after all, have more training and they do more onerous work than the white-collar workers. The relationship would be very clear in the working-class communities. One could have "models" who had followed both alternatives among one's neighbors (or among one's brothers or uncles) so that the "fact" of lower income would come as no surprise either to the lower-middle-class white-collar worker or to the skilled worker. It most certainly would not be a source of alarm or "status panic." It would, on the other hand, be problematic for the social relationships of the white-collar worker or the neighborhood shopkeeper if he suddenly began putting on airs, keeping his distance, or supporting unusual polit-ical movements. Whether the white-collar worker in these "integrated" communities makes more or less than the skilled worker would be a fact of little importance because the backgrounds, the politics, and the out-looks of both groups are very similar. The image of the two groups being separated by a "line"—as with a territorial boundary—appears to be mistaken.

To summarize, the reasons for the centrality of the lower-middle–upper-middle cleavage are as follows: differences in territorial locations, differences in the typical family backgrounds and in the associated training, differences in the education provided by schools and peer groups, and differences in the typical pattern of earnings over the career. When people casually speak of "the middle class," they are actually referring to the upper-middle class, and that group constitutes only a small portion of the population—roughly one-sixth of the total. For reasons of their incomes alone, the working class and the lower-middle class are not able to achieve the upper-middle-class life-style. And, not having informal social contact with upper-middle-class people, they are in a poor position to envy or emulate their "betters."

MIDDLE-CLASS 'RESPONSIBILITY'

Related to the centrist claims of the fundamental importance of the blue-collar–white-collar distinction and the "class shift" argument is the view that the upper middle class is the politically "responsible" class and that the workers and lower middle class groups are characterized by various degrees of authoritarianism and protofascistic tendencies.

Recent Survey Research Center (SRC) studies have asked about government supported medical care, about a living standard guarantee, and about school aid. While a guaranteed living standard might in current circumstances be viewed as a very ambitious, almost "utopian" undertaking, that certainly cannot be said about government medical care programs or education aids. Comprehensive medical care programs exist in all industrially advanced countries with the single exception of the United States. If the upper middle class is, as has been alleged, a group characterized by a distinctive sense of responsibility, we ought to see that indicated in the responses to these questions. The upper-middle-class white Protestants, however, show the lowest percentage of support for that option of all the groups being reviewed here. The responsible position on federal school aid also gains little support from those ranks, although in this case both upper-middle- and lower-middle-class white Protestants have equal disdain for this option. The most responsible groups in respect to both of these options prove to be the poor.

One might argue that such matters are not central to the claims about upper-middle-class responsibility. The heart of the matter is in the civil rights area, and here, it is said, the evidence is clear. But a review of Survey Research Center materials and some Gallup studies showed essentially no difference in the outlooks of non-South blue-collar and white-collar workers. A second review covering a later SRC study and a large range of questions from National Opinion Research Center studies revealed a similar result. Outside of the South, no significant differences were found between blue-collar and white-collar workers in those issues which had been the subject of recent public discussion. These studies did show some differences when the question concerned closer, more intimate personal relationships, but even here they were far from the categoric differences suggested in some of the recent literature. Outside of the South there also appeared to be little systematic difference between the lower middle class and the upper middle class. Again the upper middles did not appear to be distinguished by any special sense of responsibility. Some of the questions from the Gallup studies, in fact, showed the lower middle class to be more tolerant than the more educated and "sophisticated" upper middle class.

The results for the South did provide support for the received hypothesis, although even here they were not consistent. In 1956, for example, just under two-thirds of blue-collar, lower-middle-, and upper-middle-class white Southerners supported government intervention to ensure fair treatment in jobs and housing.

The best conclusion one can draw from this evidence is that outside of the South there is no clear and systematic indication of a "working-class authoritarianism," of an intolerant lower middle class, or of an especially responsible upper-middle class. For three-quarters of the nation the best conclusion is that there is "no difference."

If one failed to make the distinction by region, the class differences in the South would come through and affect the overall or "national" findings. It is not entirely clear what causal factors yield this result in the South. The white working class is disproportionately located in middle-sized and smaller communities, whereas the upper middle class is highly urban. The whites who migrate into the South, for the most part, are found in the upper middle class and they may well import more positive attitudes although even this does not appear to suffice as an explanation. One possibility, still to be explored, is that the tendency in the South may be linked to the past efforts of Protestant clergy who for decades taught the inferiority of blacks.

Before leaving this subject, it is worth noting another recent study of the Southern white populations. This is a study of the voting of whites in elections in which there were black candidates or white liberal candidates, or in the referenda where there were options providing for improvement of the circumstances of the black population. A review of a wide range of such elections in Houston, Texas, the sixth largest city in the United States, showed "problack" voting to vary inversely with class level. That is, the poor whites were the most likely to vote for such candidates or measures and the rich whites were least likely to make such choices.[1] Some survey evidence shows a pattern consonant with this result; support for government guarantees of job equality was stronger among poor whites in 1956 and 1964, both in the South and elsewhere.

SUMMARY

The claims made about cleavages in the contemporary United States rather seriously distort one's understanding of the American reality. There is, first of all, the persistent focus on the blue-collar–white-collar line, the claim that it provides the most important division in the society. There is also the variant on this which claims that the line has shifted "downward" so that the well-off skilled workers are now part of the middle class. Both the original claim and the variant are not supported by recent evidence. The major cleavage in the society appears to be between the dominant upper and upper middle classes on the one hand and the combined working class and lower middle class on the other. This division is based on differences in the location of the respective communities, the informal social, cultural, and political lessons received in these communities, the character of the respective careers, and the patterns of income over those careers.

Rather than the much-predicted "blurring of class lines," one might well anticipate a sharpening of the division. If no serious attempt is made to bridge the geographical distances between these "two nations" (in other words, to integrate them), it seems likely that the differences in outlook will persist and, over time, will be accentuated.

The finding that the major division is between the upper and lower-middle classes is *consonant with* the original Marxist viewpoint. The

1. [Chandler Davidson, *Biracial Politics: Conflict and Coalition in the Metropolitan South* (Baton Rouge: Louisiana State University Press, 1972).]

major owners of the means of production would be found in the upper class and they would constitute only a tiny minority (if represented at all) in all of the studies reported here. The upper middle class, however, would contain many persons who are fractional shareholders. The evidence is consonant with the view that their conservatism represents a defense of their own personal interests. . . .

There are other readings of the motivations, however, which are equally plausible. The upper middle class, more than any other group in the society, is likely to have contacts, no matter how limited, with the upper class and elites. They are more likely than other groups to be readers of journals and periodicals put out by or sponsored by upper class groups. There might be a personal influence factor and a media effect might operate to yield this result. Self-interest, personal influence, and media effects, it should be noted, are not mutually exclusive hypotheses. They might all contribute to generating the observed conservatism.

Still another possibility is that a special subgroup tradition is passed on and maintained within the class. Such a tradition, because of the peculiar isolation of these groups, is relatively immune to changing events, changing social needs, or even to the group's own changing interests. The importance of such traditions is indicated by some of the findings reported here. The received claims, as noted, lay considerable stress on "class." The attitudinal and behavioral differences associated with class, however, have never been very great. Much of the research and analysis in the area has tried to discover why the differences are not greater. One remarkably consistent characteristic of political differentiation in the United States and elsewhere is that the cleavages along religious and ethnic lines tend to be more significant than those following class lines. Within a given class—working class, lower middle, or upper middle class—there are divisions between Protestants and Catholics, the former tending more toward the Republicans, conservative economic policies, and opposition to a federal government role in guaranteeing civil rights. The Jews are even more liberal in all of these areas than the Catholics. . . .

In the Marxist tradition, the role of class determinants is thought to be so sweeping that it overwhelms any ideal or traditional factor. One could pay attention to the presence of a subgroup tradition, but because of the dynamics of advanced capitalist societies, any such tradition or group base would be a transitory thing, solely of aesthetic or passing historical interest. The same conclusion derives from some non-Marxist perspectives, particularly those which assume the presence of some considerable "homogenization" processes integrating or assimilating all subgroups into the "larger" society. If one assumes a process of this sort, the study of any subgroup would again be a matter of passing historical interest. It might be useful for "capturing the moment." It would not be of use, however, in predicting the future development of the country.

. . . Given that these communities and their traditions have persisted well into the "postindustrial" age, the responsibility of the researcher, the theorist, and, the commentator is to recognize the fact, to build it into fundamental descriptions of the society, and to provide some explanation for the persistence of these "premodern" forms. However, if there is some dynamic which is destined to eliminate these extraclass concerns, those processes ought to be demonstrated. The unsupported prediction will not suffice.

Another way of expressing the concern here is to note that it is not an either/or matter. It is not as if one were obligated to focus only on class factors to the exclusion of traditional communal concerns. It is not as if the concern with class were "hard" and "realistic" and the concern with ethnic loyalties and religious belief (or the attitudes correlated with religion) were "soft" or "ephemeral," a lesser order of being. Both appear to be real things, hence both are deserving of attention. It complicates the analysis somewhat, but if the reality is complicated by the existence of both factors, nothing is served by omitting consideration of one of them.

Cynicism in the Labor Movement

38

Donald Clark Hodges

There is an increasing tendency among the working classes to become politically indifferent. In the face of the bureaucratization of public life, the average laborer has tended to give up struggling for collectively improved conditions of work in favor of improving his individual circumstances and those of his family. His interest in the public has waned in proportion to belief in his own political impotence. All classes show the effects of increased bureaucratization, but in different degrees. Despite labor's increased gains, anyone who has worked on the assembly line or as a shop steward knows that political apathy is more prevalent in the ranks of labor than anywhere else.[1] Moreover, this indifference of the worker to politics is an expression not merely of apathy but of downright cynicism.[2] White-collar workers tend to be merely indifferent to politics; denim workers are irreverent, bitter, and scornful. The white-collar worker does not have a long tradition behind him of criticism and social protest, so that his political indifference is comparatively mild. The bitter struggles of manual workers against capital, management, and the State have fostered disillusionment of an altogether different stamp.

Reprinted from *The American Journal of Economics and Sociology*, Vol. 21, No. 1 (January 1962), pp. 29–36, by permission of the publisher and the author. Footnotes have been renumbered.

1. The author is an ex–industrial worker and a former shop steward of Local 201, United Electrical, Radio and Machine Workers of America (C.I.O.), Bridgeport, Conn.

2. The most recent studies of the sociology of cynicism include: Ely Chinoy, *Automobile Workers and the American Dream* (Garden City: Doubleday, 1955), pp. 83–86, on the laborer's "alienation from his work" and resentment at taking orders; C. Wright Mills, *The New Men of Power* (New York: Harcourt, Brace, 1948), pp. 266–74 on the developed habits of submission, low level of aspiration, and apathy of unskilled laborers—the underdogs of American labor; Hadley Cantril, *The Politics of Despair* (New York: Basic Books, 1958), pp. 35–46, 68–76; Karl Bednarik, *The Young Worker of Today: A New Type*, ed. J. P. Mayer, tr. R. Tupholme (Glencoe: Free Press, 1955), pp. 28–73, 128–30.

The manual laborer is still the best authority on where the shoe of management pinches and the heel of capital treads. The most bitter cynics are manual laborers imbued with anachist and syndicalist ideas. Some are revolutionary romanticists; others, realists disillusioned with the lofty hopes and vain promises of militant trade unionism. The cynicism of labor intellectuals tends to be abstract and impersonal because it seldom arises directly from a life of manual labor. Although it helps to clarify the workers' sense of futility, it is not the source of cynicism in the labor movement. That source is the degradation of the laborer to an appendage of the machine and to an instrument of another's gain. To fully appreciate the philosophy of cynicism it helps to have been a laborer oneself, to have worked for lower wages in proportion to the unskilled character, monotony, and drudgery of labor, to have paid for wage boosts, health and social insurance plans by speedups and by rises in the cost of living, to have suffered from the comparison between manual and intellectual work, and to have lost faith in the leadership of labor bureaucrats and exworkers who have made a career out of trade unionism.

I

Unlike radical and conservative philosophies of labor, which follow the ebb and flow of economic prosperity and depression, cynicism is a constant feature of the labor movement. It is tied neither to the fortunes of revolutionary trade unionism nor to the ups and downs of business unionism, but is an informal philosophy of labor that is endemic to the working classes. As a philosophy of unorganized as well as organized labor, it is common to strikebreakers and scabs as well as to militant trade unionists. Unorganized workers, who constitute the poorest and most demoralized stratum of the proletariat, cannot afford to turn down jobs and to assist in the struggles of organized workers who offer them no assistance. (Their sympathies may be with the strikers, but their stomachs favor their employers.) Cynicism is common not only to free trade unionism, but also to the labor movements in fascist and communist countries. Since the experience of industrial workers is similar everywhere, resentment against the bosses becomes articulate as a philosophy of labor that is independent of all political parties.

"There are two wings to every bird of prey" (Eugene Debs). In American public life the right wing corresponds to the Republican party and the left wing to the Democratic party. Unlike Republicans and Democrats, cynics have no faith in political creeds, which to civic minded and public spirited citizens is even worse than atheism. On the one hand, left-wingers are impatient with reality in insisting that workers should preserve a spirit of militancy under all circumstances. On the other hand, right-wingers are uncritical of social conditions even when they have the power to change them. In contrast to both, and to liberals who hew to the middle of the road, cynics are distinguished by their contempt for all movements, parties, and principles, which is another way of saying that they are politically unprincipled.

Cynicism is a conception [that views] the political world and everything it represents as essentially hostile to the interests of manual labor. As an inseparable feature of the labor movement, it comes closest to expressing the informal philosophy of the workers. It shows up in the observations of American workers "in the sad comment, 'The only reason a man works is to make a living'; in the occasional overflow of resentment, 'Sometimes you feel like jamming things up in the machine and saying goodbye to it'; in the cynical observation, 'The things I like best about my job are quitting time, pay day, days off, and vacations. . . .' "[3]

The term "cynicism" is used by Bednarik to describe the psychological condition of the young worker in a Welfare State.[4] The young worker's withdrawal from public life, his escape into privacy and into pleasure hunting is attributed partly to the higher standard of living made possible by the Welfare State and partly to his disillusionment with it for not having provided an even higher standard. The young worker, writes Bednarik, constitutes a new type that is more cynical and more independent than the old: "he disregards all the artificial higher social systems and aims at a group system on anarchic lines . . . the new type feels himself to be largely independent of and superior to society, even though he may acknowledge and take into account the real power of that society and of the State."[5] The young worker is cynical of social norms and draws his personal ideal from the distractions of age, i.e., from the artificial wealth of films and advertising.[6] Unreserved egoism is believed necessary in order to combat the selfishness of the world. "The one idea of the modern worker is to 'grab all you can get hold of.' "[7] This personal ideal is the expression of what Bednarik calls "socialized father hate": "The young worker of today, in his detached attitude towards the State and its social institutions, is like a son who is always demanding and taking; and the only reason why he has not become totally estranged from his father is that he is obliged at least to listen to his orders and admonitions, if only the better to circumvent them. The same goes for his attitude towards industrial society in general, the factory where he is employed and the party and trade-union

---

3. Chinoy, op. cit., p. 85.
4. Bednarik, op. cit., pp. 109, 111–12.
5. Ibid., pp. 33–34.
6. Ibid., p. 34.
7. Ibid., p. 56.

organizations which form part of his working world. For him they all represent a sort of father-world ... the advantages of which he uses without feeling himself deeply committed."[8]

The philosophical equivalent of this type of cynicism among young workers is perhaps best exemplified by Max Stirner's *The Ego and His Own.* Unlike Proudhon, who equated property with theft (the belief of anarchists who are moral idealists), Stirner does him one better by calling alien property a "present": "Why so sentimentally call for compassion as a poor victim of robbery, when one is just a foolish, cowardly giver of presents? Why ... put the fault on others as if they were robbing us, while we ourselves bear the fault in leaving the others unrobbed. The poor are to blame for there being rich men."[9] This is not necessarily a call to robbery, but it is a plea that the workers should liberate themselves from any reverence for the rights of property and the State, and that they should take advantage of any and every opportunity to reimburse themselves for losses. This type of cynicism has become increasingly popular among young workers.

II

Much of modern cynicism is suggestive of ancient Cynicism, which has also been called by historians "a philosophy of the proletariat." The Cynics were irreverent toward culture, disloyal to the State, resentful toward authority, antiintellectual, and scornful of conventional morality. Like the Hebrew Prophets, they regarded the love of money as the root of all evil.[10] Like the Prophets, they championed the interests of the underdog. To its critics, Cynicism has been equated with a philosophy of degeneracy: "The Cynic differed from the modern hobo in having a vocation; but, like the hobo, was sometimes a robber, sometimes a thief, sometimes a beggar and had no inhibitions except against useful labor.... Greek Cynicism was chiefly a relaxation of the ordinary restraints of civilized man and freeing of the natural impulses; among these impulses are indolence, selfishness, envy, and ill-nature."[11] This is decidedly an unsympathetic account. It fails to consider that Cynicism was also a response to the alienation of the worker from his work and from a society that exploited the laborer for all he was worth. Manual labor, according to Lucian, is an evil not because it is intrinsically contemptible (the Platonic and Aristotelian view), but because it implies an injustice to the laborer. To the upper classes, he says: "All that costly

---

8. Ibid., p. 52.

9. Max Stirner (pseud. for Caspar Schmidt), *The Ego and His Own,* tr. by S. T. Byington (New York: Boni and Liveright, n.d.), pp. 33–32.

10. Farrand Sayre, *Diogenes of Sinope* (Baltimore: J. H. Furst, 1938), p. 25.

11. Ibid., p. 47.

array of means of enjoyment which you so gloat over is obtained ... through how many men's blood and death and ruin. To bring these things to you many seamen must perish; to find and fashion them many laborers must endure misery. ..."[12] Dudley, the historian of Cynicism, also notes the similarities between ancient and modern cynicism: "In modern times the movement most akin to Cynicism is Anarchism. ... It is especially interesting to find Kropotkin recognizing the 'best exposition from the Ancient World of the principles of Anarchism' is the *Republic* of Zeno, which was of course composed when Zeno was under the influence of Cynicism."[13]

Henry Miller is one of the few Americans to have given expression to the informal philosophy of cynicism of the workers. He stands almost alone among self-conscious and philosophically articulate cynics in this country. He has been acknowledged as the "minnesinger of the lumpen-proletariat" because his outraged sympathies are for the oppressed stratum of unorganized unskilled laborers and because his books and essays idealize the values of the unemployed vagrant, "hobo," or "bum." Yet his cynicism is an attack upon the social system for taking advantage of all "producers," skilled as well as unskilled, whom he identifies with the "little" or "common" man, i.e., "the man who does the dirty work."[14] Miller's cynicism is directed against the joy-killers of the western world and is summarized in the statement: "I don't want it when I'm dead. I want it now."[15] In part, his message is sex instead of sacrifice. Miller is already widely known for his apotheosis of sexual freedom. However, just as important to an understanding of his writings is his constant note of cynicism: "To be sure, it is the general expectation among those who believe in a new order that the common man will eventually inherit the fruit of all the inventions and discoveries now being made. But over whose dead body, I'd like to ask? ... The great bugaboo here in America is the 'dictatorship of the proletariat.' Looking at the rank and file ... does any one honestly believe that these men and women will dictate the future of America? Can slaves become rulers overnight? These poor devils are begging to be led, and they are being led, but it's up a blind alley."[16]

The cynicism of manual workers is constructive in serving the purpose of higher wages and better conditions of work. However, it is even more fundamentally destructive in undermining the authority of the boss and the "system." The cynic's dominant sentiment is that of resentment. ... Class hostility of this kind is founded upon the sense of

---

12. Quoted by Sayre, ibid., p. 8.
13. Donald R. Dudley, *A History of Cynicism* (London: Methuen, 1937), pp. 211–12.
14. Henry Miller, *To Remember to Remember* (New York: New Directions, 1947), p. xxxvi.
15. Ibid., p. xxxv.
16. Ibid., p. xviii.

inferiority in being a worker, in having to take orders, in being treated like a machine instead of a human being of the same value and importance as the employer. The worker's psychology is based upon a comparison: "I get the smallest part of the money which my employer makes. . . ."

By this comparison the worker is a "sucker," a "fall guy." " 'What they call honest toil is a mug's game. . . . You know that as well as I do.' "[17] By the same comparison the employer is on top of the antheap because he has a "racket." Although he operates within the law, his mentality is fundamentally criminal, i.e., aimed at taking advantage. If the boss accedes to the demands of the workers for higher wages, it is only because he has something sinister up his sleeve, such as higher prices or speedups. Writes Celine: " 'Commiseration of the fate and the condition of the down-at-heel? I tell you, worthy little people, life's riffraff, forever beaten, fleeced, and sweating, I warn you that when the great people of this world start loving you, it means that they are going to make sausage meat of you." '[18]

III

Cynicism is not a philosophy of the proletariat in Marx's meaning of the term. For the proletariat, in the Marxian sense, includes engineers and technicians besides manual laborers. The Marxian concept of the working class glosses over the fundamental opposition between manual and intellectual workers, so that it is consistent for a Marxist to argue that the leadership of the proletariat is the prerogative of its intellectuals. On the contrary, the cynic holds that manual laborers are a group whose interests defy constant and faithful representation. It is possible to represent faithfully and constantly the interests of professional workers because their interests, like those of their representatives, are the interests of white-collar workers generally. But it is impossible, the cynic argues, to do the same for the class of manual laborers because their representatives, whether political officials or trade union bureaucrats, are white-collar workers imbued with white-collar values.

Cynics are critical not only of capitalism but also of socialism. Cynicism is neither a movement nor a school, in the strict sense, but the inchoate philosophy of labor of the unknown and unsung manual laborer. "A plague on all your houses" is the attitude of cynics toward political movements which place the welfare of the business and professional classes above the interests of the plodders and grubbers. The tendency is for manual laborers to become increasingly cynical about

---

17. Celine (pseud.), *Journey to the End of the Night,* tr. by J. H. P. Marks (Boston: Little, Brown, 1934), p. 308.
18. Ibid., p. 64.

the pretensions of labor leaders to lead them toward a better future. Socialists of every hue and variety, whether democratic or authoritarian, utopian or scientific, are regarded with suspicion; so also are trade-union bureaucrats who believe in the principles of business unionism. Cynicism is the expression of the attitude of manual laborers disillusioned with the claims of anyone to better their conditions without profiting in the meantime at their expense. It is a symptom of resentment against the entire world of white collar workers, against higher education as well as higher salaries.

Industry cannot survive without a class of manual laborers. Yet this class is becoming progressively disaffected with the world of white collars and white hands, so that it serves it with increasing reluctance. With greater mechanization, the unskilled laborer shows less respect for drudge labor. With the increasing tendency to cynicism, businessmen and politicians are regarded as worse than ordinary criminals, and techniques of illegitimately earning a living are regarded with tolerance and even approbation. For the cynic, the world owes him a living, so that he feels justified in violating the law as long as there is no injury to his fellow workers. It is noteworthy that the modern tradition that helped to justify this attitude overtly championed industrial sabotage and assassination of key political figures, while idealizing such epic but criminal heroes as the Russian bandit, Pugachev, and the English legendary figure of Robin Hood.[19] That tradition is generally known as anarchosyndicalism or revolutionary trade unionism, and is the tradition that inspired the Industrial Workers of the World (I.W.W.) in this country.

Cynicism is a variant of anarchism—anarchism without ideals or ultimate illusions, apathetic, easygoing instead of strenuous, nonsectarian; hence, more broadly appealing and far more suitable to the conditions and mentality of contemporary workers than the older tradition of militant idealism and self-sacrifice. In this country cynicism is a realistic acquiescence in the fact that social idealism has already received its funeral rites. It is a sad commentary upon the promise of American politics that the dream of a classless society has reality only as a museum piece, and that few Americans in public life pay anything but lip-service to the ideal of social justice. Indeed, there has been only one eminent American in recent years who was capable of declaring publicly: "While there is a lower class I am in it; while there is a criminal element I am in it; while there is a soul in prison, I am not free."[20]

---

19. Robert Hunter, *Violence and the Labor Movement* (New York: Macmillan, 1914), p. 278; Eugene Pyziur, *The Doctrine of Anarchism of Michael A. Bakunin* (Milwaukee: Marquette University, 1955), pp. 101–9.

20. Miller, op. cit., pp. 170, 196, quoted from Eugene V. Debs. [Debs was the leader of the early twentieth century mass socialist movement in the U.S., and its candidate for President before World War I.—Ed.]

U.S.A.: The Labor Revolt

39

Stanley Weir

The rank-and-file union revolts that have been developing in the industrial workplaces since the early 1950s are now plainly visible. Like many of their compatriots, American workers are faced with paces, methods, and conditions of work that are increasingly intolerable. Their union leaders are not sensitive to these conditions. In thousands of industrial establishments across the nation, workers have developed informal underground unions. The basic units of organization are groups composed of several workers, each of whose members work in the same plant-area and are thus able to communicate with one another and form a social entity. Led by natural on-the-job leaders, they conduct daily guerrilla skirmishes with their employers and often against their official union representatives as well. These groups are the power base for the insurgencies from below that in the last three years have ended or threatened official careers of long standing.

During the same period, farm laborers, teachers, professionals, white collar, service, and civil service workers, who were not reached by labor's revolt of the 1930s, have demonstrated an adamant desire to organize themselves into unions. For the first time in over three decades the United States faces a period in which the struggles of the unionized section of the population will have a direct and visible effect on the future of the entire population. Because the press coverage of the revolts has been superficial and because they have been ignored by the liberal and a majority of radical publications, it is necessary that the major revolts be examined in some detail.

Reprinted, with author's revisions, from the *International Socialist Journal* Nos. 20, 21 (April and June 1967), pp. 279–86, 465–73, by permission of the author. Copyright 1967 by Stanley Weir. Footnotes have been renumbered. "Epilogue, 1976," was written especially for this edition of *American Society, Inc.*

WIDESPREAD REVOLT BEGINS IN AUTO INDUSTRY

The General Motors Corporation employs as many workers as all other auto manufacturers combined. In 1955, [the] United Automobile Workers' president, Walter Reuther, signed a contract with GM which did not check the speedup or speed the settlement of local shop grievances. Over 70 percent of GM workers went on strike immediately after Reuther announced the terms of his agreement. A larger percentage "wildcatted" after the signing of the 1958 contract because Reuther had again refused to do anything to combat the speedup. For the same reason, the auto workers walked off their jobs again in 1961. The strike closed every GM and a number of large Ford plants.

The UAW ranks' ability to conduct a nationwide wildcat strike is made possible by a democratic practice that has been maintained by GM workers since the thirties. Every GM local sends elected delegates to Detroit to sit in council during national contract negotiations. They instruct their negotiators and confer with them as the bargaining progresses. Ideally the council and negotiators arrive at an agreement on the package that the latter have been able to obtain from the employer and both the rank-and-file delegates and leaders recommend ratification by the ranks at the local union level. In 1961, when the council unanimously recommended rejection and strike, Reuther notified the press that the strike was official, that he was leading it and that it would continue until all grievances concerning working conditions had been settled in separate local supplemental agreements rather than in the national contract. He thus maintained control. The ranks were outmaneuvered and angered.

Just prior to the negotiation of the 1964 contract, a development took place in the UAW that is unique in American labor history. Several large Detroit locals initiated a bumper sticker campaign. In all cities across the country where UAW plants are located the bumpers of auto workers' cars pushed the slogan: "Humanize Working Conditions." Lacking the support of their official leaders, they were attempting to inform the public of the nature of the struggle they were about to conduct and that its primary goal would be to improve the condition of factory life rather than their wages.

Their attempt to bypass Reuther failed. Contrary to established practice, he opened negotiations with Chrysler, the smallest of the Big Three auto makers. He imposed the pattern of this contract on the Ford workers and announced that the Chrysler-Ford agreements would be the pattern for the GM contract. The dialogue of the GM workers with their president was brief. They struck every GM plant for five weeks and were joined by thousands of Ford workers. They returned to work under a national contract no better than those signed with Ford and Chrysler. Their strike won the settlement of a backlog of local grievances, created pride in the knowledge that it was primarily and publicly directed against Reuther's maneuver, and made possible the further development of rank-and-file leaders. They demonstrated that they would not give ground in their efforts to make their national contract a weapon against the speedup and to rid themselves of a grievance procedure that allows the settlement of individual grievances to take up to two years.

Aware that the ranks would be continuing their fight and seeking revenge at the UAW's September, 1966, convention in Long Beach, California, Reuther sought issues that could be used to divert their wrath. In early 1965 the ballot count in the election between incumbent International Union of Electrical Workers (IUE) President James B. Carey and his challenger Paul Jennings was in doubt. Reuther issued a statement to the press announcing his offer to merge the IUE with the UAW. The merger might have salvaged Carey's reputation and employment in the labor movement. It could also have been used as a major agenda item necessitating extended discussion at the UAW convention, but Carey rigidly turned down the offer, claiming that he had learned of Reuther's offer only hours before it was made public.

The Long Beach UAW convention in May of last year was the first labor convention experience for over 60 percent of the delegates. Many of the faces that had become familiar to Reuther during previous conventions were absent. None of the delegates got a chance to discuss what was the main issue of the ranks who elected them—the demands they want to make and win in the negotiations for the 1967 contract; that point on the agenda was postponed to a special conference in April, 1967. Reuther won more than a breathing spell at Long Beach. In the months preceding the convention the rebellion in the UAW's 250,000 man Skilled Trades Department had reached crisis proportions. Their wages had fallen behind those of craft union members doing comparable work in other industries. They threatened to disaffiliate and join the rival International Society of Skilled Trades (independent). The convention amended the UAW constitution to give the Skilled Trades Department, containing less than 20 percent of the UAW's members, veto power over all national contracts. It is likely that they will get a substantial wage increase in the 1967 contract. They do not work under the same conditions as the semiskilled who buck the assembly lines and who are the majority and now second-class citizenry of the UAW. Reuther has obtained an aristocratic power base and laid the foundation for another and more violent rupture in the UAW.

For more than a decade it has been absolutely clear that the UAW ranks demand top priority be given to the fight to improve working conditions. Their efforts to make Reuther lead this fight have been herculean. At this late date it is almost paradoxical that he remains rigid in his refusal to make that fight. And so he must try to go into the April conference equipped with a diversionary tactic of gigantic proportions —based on more than a transparent maneuver that will only further enrage his ranks. His recent resignation as first vice-president of the AFL-CIO and his open split with that body's president, George Meany, has among other things armed him with such a diversion. The question of total withdrawal from the AFL-CIO is the first point on the agenda of the April conference which is now scheduled to last only three days.

Leaflets circulated by UAW members in Detroit auto plants last January and prior to the split ridiculed Reuther's inability to stand up to Meany. They were picked up by the national press and significantly hurt Reuther's prestige. Evidence mounts to indicate that Reuther was finally driven to sever his distasteful relationship with Meany for two principal reasons: (1) the demands of the UAW's revolt and internal struggle, and (2) the widespread revolts throughout the labor movement, particularly in the unions that form Reuther's domain in the AFL-CIO (Industrial Union Department). The latter may include a third principal factor. The revolts are numerous enough to have given Reuther the vision that the revolts in the 1930s gave to John L. Lewis —the formation of a powerful new labor confederation through the organizational centralization of the unions that are in rebellion—a confederation that could now include white collar, professional, service, and farm workers.

The wildcat strike of UAW-GM Local 527 in Mansfield, Ohio, in February revealed the depth of the liberal stance Reuther has taken in his fight with Meany. The total walkout at Mansfield occurred because two workers were fired for refusing to make dies and tools ready for shipment to another plant in Pontiac, Michigan. GM has long followed a policy of transferring work out of plants where workers have established better working conditions, or are conducting a struggle to improve them, to other plants with less militant work forces. The Mansfield workers had long observed this practice in silence. To be forced to participate in the transferral and their own defeat was the final indignity.

Mansfield is a key GM parts feeder plant and their strike idled 133,men in over 20 shops. Instead of utilizing this power to win his men's demands, Reuther declared the strike illegal. Moreover, he threatened to put the local into trusteeship and suspend local democracy. In an all-day session on February 22, his leadership pressured Local 727 leaders into asking their men to return to work without winning a solution of their grievances. The local leaders were told that the strike was poorly timed because it came on the eve of the UAW's big push for annual salaries and profit-sharing in 1967 bargaining. These two demands are to be given preference over all others. It is probable that the Mansfield strike has prematurely revealed the argument that Reuther will use in the April Conference against rank-and-file demands that the big push be to eliminate the speedup and inoperable grievance machinery.

The above probability is reinforced by the February 8 UAW Administrative Letter issued to elaborate upon Reuther's position on his split with Meany. It contains a long and detailed "Outline of UAW Program for the American Labor Movement." Under its section on collective bargaining it stresses the "development of a sound economic wage policy." No mention or hint is made of the need to improve working conditions which to this moment is the cause of the major crisis for Reuther's leadership.

Under "Aims and Purposes of a Democratic Labor Movement" the February 8 letter stresses collective bargaining and "appropriate progressive legislation" as the methods to be used to advance the interests of union members and their families. But Reuther's current policies insure that direct action, including wildcat strike and minor acts of sabotage in the plants, will daily continue to interrupt production. His program's concessions to the revolt can only encourage the fight against conservative union leadership and does not include goals that will enable him to lead and contain it. His failure to champion an improvement of working conditions will create a consequent dimming of enthusiasm and support for Reuther's new program for American labor, both within the UAW ranks and the ranks of unions whose support he hopes to win. His actions will tend also to undercut the possibility of success for the many good policies the program contains.

LONGSHOREMEN AND STEELWORKERS

In 1964 the ranks of the International Longshoremen's Association (east and Gulf coasts) conducted a strike-revolt against both their employers and union officials that was identical to and almost simultaneous with that accomplished by the UAW rank and file. The stevedoring companies and ILA officials had negotiated what appeared to be an excellent contract. It contained, by past standards, a significant wage increase. It guaranteed every union member a minimum of 1,600 hours of work per year and minor economic fringe benefits. The dockers struck immediately upon the announcement of the terms. Their president, Thomas W. Gleason, hurriedly toured all locals at the request of George Meany on a mission called "Operation Fact." Gleason claimed his ranks wildcatted because they didn't understand the contract. They understood only too well. In return for the recommended settlement the number of men in each work gang was to be cut from 20 to 17. The employers originally demanded a gang size reduction to 14 men, a size more nearly in line with manning scales negotiated by International Longshoremen's and Warehousemen's Union President Harry Bridges for west coast longshoremen. The ILA ranks did not give in to this or the many other undercutting pressures. President Johnson declared a national emergency and invoked the 80-day "cooling-off" period under the provisions of the Taft-Hartley Act.

Wildcat strikes resumed on December 21, one day after the "cooling-off" period ended and continued through January. All ports were on strike at the same time for over 18 days, and longer in southern and Gulf ports where separate and inferior contracts were offered. Longshoremen in New York and northern east coast ports returned to work, having lost on the main issue of gang size, but their defeat in this battle was not accompanied by a deep demoralization. Their union has long been unofficially divided into separately led baronies. For the first time in the history of the ILA, the entire membership initiated and conducted an all-union strike.

The United Steelworkers Union revolt deserves special attention because it demonstrates how long it takes in some instances for a revolt to develop. In 1946 the steelworkers conducted a 26-day strike; in 1949, 45 days of strike; in 1952, 59 days; in 1956, 36 days. All of these strikes were conducted with only reluctant or forced support from the international leadership.

In 1957 an obscure rank-and-file leader named Ronald Rarick ran against USW President David MacDonald. Rarick, a conservative who has since become a reactionary, based his entire program on opposition to a dues increase and increase in the salaries of officials. As the campaign for the presidency developed, the rank-and-file could see that Rarick was not a militant unionist. Militants couldn't vote for Rarick with enthusiasm. His candidacy was used in the main to record opposition to MacDonald. He beat MacDonald in the Pennsylvania region by a slight margin, but lost nationally. The vote ran 223,000 for Rarick, 404,000 for MacDonald. I.W. Abel, running for Secretary-Treasurer, got 420,000 and his opposition got 181,000. In effect, Rarick disappeared after the election, but the vote he received alarmed the leaders of the large unions.

Four years later, MacDonald ran unopposed and received only 221,000 votes. It was obvious that MacDonald had been able to win a large vote against Rarick because he was able to utilize the treasury and resources of the International. To beat MacDonald a candidate had to be recruited from inside the International who also had access to its facilities.

As early as the Special Steelworkers Conference of 1952, the regional and local union leaders of the USW had warned MacDonald that he would have to do something about the deterioration of working conditions in the plants. They further warned that the resulting rank-and-file anger was threatening their position and they might have no other alternative than to transmit this pressure to him.

Twelve years later many of these same secondary and tertiary leaders realized that they could not survive under MacDonald's leadership. They picked I.W. Abel, a man who had not worked in a mill for 25 years, to challenge MacDonald. After a long dispute over the ballot count, Abel was declared the winner. Under his leadership a significant democratization of the negotiation process has begun. Delegates to the 1966 USW convention terminated the union's participation in the joint employer-union Human Relations Committee whose function was to study plant working conditions and to determine how they could be changed in order to cut the cost of production and speed the automation process. The union's 165 man Wage Policy Committee which had the power to ratify contracts was also completely stripped of its power. A new and somewhat liberalized method for allowing the ranks a voice in negotiations was instituted. The policy of last minute "shotgun" bargaining a few days prior to contract expiration was substituted for MacDonald's practice of beginning negotiations a year in advance of deadline.

ELECTRICAL WORKERS AND THEIR SECONDARY LEADERS UNITE

James B. Carey, President of the International Union of Electrical Workers, was removed from office in a struggle similar to that which deposed David MacDonald. By 1953 he had been out of contact with his membership for many years. He had failed to lead them in a fight for improved working conditions against the General Electric and Westinghouse corporations. He had been less successful than Reuther or even MacDonald in obtaining wage increases to ease his ranks' anger. However, he felt the pressure of coming rebellion and sought to oppose rather than appease it. He proposed a constitutional change for his union that would have had the employers collect union dues and send them directly to the union's Washington, D.C., headquarters, which would in turn dispense to the locals their stipulated share.

The secondary leaders recognized the danger to themselves and in 1964, with the backing of the ranks, organized an opposition to Carey. In Paul Jennings of the Sperry local in New York they found a candidate with a good union reputation. Jennings beat Carey, but a majority of the ballot counters were Carey supporters and they declared Carey the winner. Jennings forces challenged the count and Carey supporters readied a second set of ballots to show the challengers. They would have given Carey the victory. Because of the ease with which Carey made enemies, even among men like George Meany, the supporters of Jennings were able to obtain aid in a world unfamiliar to the union's ranks. The U.S. Department of Labor impounded the original ballots before a ballot switch could be made.

The struggle for rank-and-file autonomy in the IUE did not end with Jennings's 1964 part-coup victory. In a very short time Jennings did more to improve wages than his predecessor, but he too neglected the fight for working conditions. Under his leadership the IUE engineered a united effort of eleven unions in the 1966 negotiations and subsequent strike against GE. A showdown was long overdue. GE had a 1965 volume of $6.2 billions, up one billion over 1964. It spent $330 million for capital expansion and still netted $355 million after taxes. Profits after taxes for the 1960 to 1965 period were up 52 percent. They had grown accustomed to docile union negotiators. The IUE-led united front broke GE's Boulwarist approach to bargaining, i.e., GE's practice of making their first settlement offer their last settlement offer under Board President Boulwaris' chairmanship. It also broke President Johnson's 3.2 percent wage guideline and obtained a 5 percent wage increase. However, after the contract was signed, major locals of all unions in the front, including thousands of workers of the IUE, UAW, International Brotherhood of Electrical Workers, and the independent United Electrical Workers, stayed out on strike. Jennings and the leaders of the other unions had failed to negotiate an improvement of grievance machinery and working conditions. A Taft-Hartley injunction was necessary to end the strike of those involved in defense production.

Carey and MacDonald were not the only leaders of large industrial unions to be felled since 1964. In that year O.A. "Jack" Knight, President of the Oil, Gas, and Atomic Workers, retired three years early in the face of a developing rank-and-file revolt. During the Miami convention of the United Rubber Workers' Union in September, 1966, the widespread unrest and revolts in the local unions that had preceded the convention forced incumbent President George Burdon to withdraw his candidacy for renomination. In an emotional speech he conceded the "serious mistakes" made during his administration. The major criticisms leveled against him were: loss of touch with the ranks, lack of personal participation in negotiations, and an attempt to have the union pay his wife's personal traveling expenses. Veteran vice president Peter Bommarito was swept into office by acclamation. He immediately pledged to take a tougher position against the employers.

COAL MINERS AND THE LEWIS LEGACY

The 1963 to 1966 and still-continuing revolt in the United Mine Workers' Union did not unseat its president, W. A. "Tony" Boyle, the hand-picked successor of John L. Lewis. However, the insurgent nominees for all top offices at the 1963 UMW convention, standing firm in spite of the violence committed against them, provided the first formal opposition to top UMW incumbents since the 1920s. Steve "Cadillac"

Kochis (Boyle's challenger from Bobtown, Pennsylvania) and his supporters lost as they predicted. They knew they had decisive strength in
the Ohio-Pennsylvania-West Virginia region, but they also knew the
dangers of the very loose UMW balloting system. They knew that the
Boyle forces would build up a commanding block of votes in far away
districts that they found impossible to monitor.

Boyle inherited the revolt. Immediately after World War II, John L.
Lewis turned from his policy of leading militant strikes for demands
closest to the desires of his membership to an all-out program to speed
the mechanization of the richest mines. The shift was hailed in the press
for its technological progressiveness, but the human cost was staggering. Between 1947 and 1964 the UMW lost over 380,000 members.
Lewis retained as members only those who worked in mines that could
afford to automate; the rest were cut loose.

The abandoned did not all lose their jobs. More than 100,000 remained in the small mines or after a period of unemployment found
work in mines that had been shut down because their veins were near
exhaustion. The Lewis shift enabled them to reopen by hiring displaced
miners at low pay. In West Virginia, Pennsylvania, and Ohio there are
now a large number of mines that have a headroom that is often no more
than 36 inches. The miners who work them literally spend their lives
on their hands and knees. By 1965, the production of coal in the poorer,
nonautomated and nonunion mines accounted for 30 percent of total
U.S. coal production. Their owners are again making fortunes. They
employ embittered and impoverished former UMW members who have
top experience and skill, at $14 a day, little more than half the union
rate, and do not have to pay pension or fringe benefits. Thus, a small-
scale mechanization of the small mines has been made possible.

The increase in the strength of the competitive position of the
nonunion mines has in turn forced the large mine operators to impose
a speedup on their employees. Pressure is applied, resulting in a deterioration of protective working and safety conditions. Fatalities are as high
as they were during World War II when 700,000 men were working coal
underground.

During the summer of 1965 in the Ireland Mine near Moundsville,
West Virginia, five local union leaders refused to work under unsafe
conditions and were fired. An unauthorized strike ensued which in one
week spread over the West Virginia, Ohio, and Pennsylvania region.
Roving bands of pickets easily shut down mine after mine, including
United States steel's large captive Robena mine. The UMW International leadership, including the grievance processors they appoint at the
local levels, lost all control. The halfhearted legal efforts of the U.S.
Department of Labor, that had the year before attempted to increase the
democratic rights of the local and regional UMW organizations, had
failed. The local leaders, the only authority the rebel ranks would follow

in a disciplined and responsible manner, were labeled "instigators of anarchy."

The main reason for this large unauthorized strike was the jam of unsettled grievances in mine after mine; in addition, the rank-and-file miners were angered that their top officials had negotiated a wage increase in the previous contract at the expense of improving working conditions. The main demands of the rebels became the right to elect their own local business agents and a democratized union structure from bottom to top. They felt that only by obtaining these rights could they find ways of helping themselves and their friends, relatives, and former union brothers in the small mines. They returned to work only after being promised a greater voice in the negotiation of the next contract. In what was a major departure from past practice in the UMW, Boyle sent out a call for the Contract Policy Committee to meet *before* the opening of formal negotiations with the operators in 1966.

The contract obtained a 3 percent wage increase for the 100,000 soft-coal miners who are left in the UMW. Their economic fringe benefits were slightly improved, but they are still far behind the workers in auto and steel. They won the right of first preference to any job openings in other mines in their district if laid off. During the negotiations they had to conduct a series of wildcat strikes to obtain these gains and their only satisfaction lay in the knowledge that the contract was an improvement over the one negotiated two years earlier. The revolt and the conditions that generate it persist. "Nonunion" union men work for poverty level wages under nineteenth century conditions. In this period between contracts, sporadic acts of all forms of sabotage are on the increase.

BRIDGES, AUTOMATION AND B-MEN

In 1960 International Longshoremen's and Warehousemen's Union President Harry Bridges negotiated the first six year "Mechanization and Modernization" contract with the Pacific Maritime Association. Like the contract that John L. Lewis negotiated for the automation of Big Coal, Bridges's contract allowed the unrestricted introduction of containerization of cargo, the use of vans, and automated cargo handling machinery. At the same time, it eliminated thousands of jobs. Primarily because of increased maritime activity due to war shipments, widespread unemployment up to now has been avoided.

Just as in coal, however, the human costs have been staggering. In the first year of the contract, the accident rate in what has become the nation's most dangerous industry went up 20 percent.[1] In the same year the longshore accident rate on the east coast declined one-half percent.

1. *Longshore Bulletin,* ILWU Local 10, February 8, 1962.

To obtain this contract Bridges gave in to the employer's request that they be allowed to "buy" the elimination of the major working and safety conditions improvements won in the militant struggles of the 1930s. The long-established manning scales and the 2,100 pound sling load limit were eliminated. These provisions were not only eliminated for labor performed on containerized cargo, but on the still very sizeable amount of cargo manhandled piece by piece and sack by sack.

Even more than Lewis, Bridges won the respect of employers everywhere, admiration in many liberal circles, and from the press the title of "labor statesman." The contract established one gain for only one section of the longshoremen: during the six-year life of the contract those who entered the industry before 1948, had achieved union membership prior to 1960, had reached the age of 65, and who additionally had 25 years of service, could retire with a $7,900 bonus in addition to their unimproved pension. They could retire earlier if disabled and receive a smaller bonus on a prorated basis. Or, if they had 25 years in the industry at age 62 they could collect the $7,900 in monthly installments until they reached 65 when the regular pension payments began.

Although the fund that pays the bonuses is created by the tonnage worked by all longshoremen, the recipients are older union members who work little more than half that tonnage. The balance is moved by B-men and casuals working under the jurisdiction of the union and the younger men who became union members (A-men) after 1960, none of whom are allowed to share in the fund.

The B-men are a permanent and regular section of the work force who get the pick of the dirtiest and heaviest jobs that are left over after the A-, or union, men have taken their pick. After the B-men, casuals hired on a daily basis get their turn at the remainders. The casuals get none of the regular fringe benefits and are not compensated for that loss.

The B-man system was created simultaneously with negotiations for Bridges's automation contract. The production of B-men is appreciably higher than that of the union men because they lack union representation on the job. They pay dues but have no vote. In Bridges's San Francisco base and home Local (No. 10) they can attend union meetings providing they sit in a segregated section of the meeting hall's balcony. These eager-to-be-organized nonunion men do most of the work that is performed deep in the holds of the ships, the area of production that produced the militants who built the ILWU in the thirties.

Bridges fears these young men. In 1963, in collusion with the employers, he led the Kafkaesque purge that expelled 82 of them from the waterfront jobs they had held for 4 years. (Over 80 percent of the 82 are Negroes.) They were tried in secret. The charges against them were not revealed. Their number, but not their identities, was made known to ILWU members. Bridges's witch-hunt methods and double standards make the bureaucratic procedures used to expel his union from the CIO, and the insidious tactics used by the government to prosecute both him and James Hoffa, bland by comparison. Hoffa and Bridges at least had the right to counsel, to produce witnesses, to know the charges, and to formal trial prior to judgment or sentencing.

The atmosphere of intimidation resulting from the framing of the 82 has, until now, successfully silenced open opposition among B-men and younger men. However, to Bridges's surprise, a revolt against his automation contract and leadership has recently developed among the older men. Unlike B-men and casuals, most of them work on the ships' decks and the docks rather than down in the hold where the major burden of the current speedup is being carried. It appeared for a time that the prospect of their receiving a bonus upon retirement and lighter daily labors would conservatize them; but 42 percent of all ILWU longshoremen (union or A-men) on the coast voted against the second six-year "Mechanization and Modernization" agreement negotiated in July, 1966. The speedup had reached these men as well. The contract won a majority in the large San Francisco local where retired members (pensioners) are allowed to vote, but lost in the other three large Pacific coast ports of Los Angeles, Portland, and Seattle. Had the B-men been allowed to vote, there is little doubt that it would have been overwhelmingly defeated.

The dissension that has developed between Bridges and other top ILWU leaders since last July has become so deep that news of it has appeared in the San Francisco press. Rumors persist that the fall out is over the question of how to handle the growing revolt in the ranks. Whether Bridges continues to pursue the automation policies in which he has staked his entire reputation or abandons it to pursue a rewinning and improvement of the working conditions desired by his ranks, the effect will be to stimulate a continuance of the revolt. He is now plagued by lawsuits, including one filed by the expelled B-men and another filed in federal court several years ago by ILWU Local 13 in the name of all members in the large port of Los Angeles. James B. Carey and David McDonald learned, and now Bridges is learning, that the pursuit of policies that alienate the ranks can isolate a top leader from his coofficials and hasten his fall from power.

MORE TROUBLE IN MARITIME

The accelerated advancement of cargo-handling technology during the last decade has in the last two years created an opposition to the leadership of Joseph Curran, president of the National Maritime Union. There has been a sharp decrease in the time that ships remain in American ports and the seamen are allowed ever shorter time with their families. The seamen's anger has been increased by the small monetary compensation for the special sacrifices of family and social life demanded by their industry. Curran has not responded to these problems, but instead has attempted to improve his position with the large New York membership by announcing plans for the construction of rent-free housing built with the union's pension fund. The announcement—an example of a positive and conservatizing reform initiated from above to quiet dissatisfaction—did not quell the revolt.

An aspirant to office in the NMU must already have served a term as a paid official. James M. Morrissey was one of the few oppositionists who could meet this requirement. The press has done nothing to inform the public of the fight made by Morrissey and his supporters. To this date the only source of printed information about it comes from Issue No. 23 of editor H. W. Benson's respected journal, *Union Democracy in Action,* published in New York. In an election [of questionable] honesty . . . , the incumbent officialdom conceded that Morrissey got 34 percent of the total vote and 14 percent of the New York vote in his struggle to unseat Curran.

Morrissey got close to what is the full treatment risked by rank-and-file opposition leaders in unions, whose democratic practices are limited. Last September three unidentified assailants beat him with metal pipes outside his union hall. No arrests have been made. His skull was shattered in several places and the bone over one eye was crushed. He still lives as does the opposition he leads. Curran is still [involved] in his fight to retain the job that pays him $83,000 annually.

By the autumn of 1966 it was possible to observe that, with the exception of the United Packinghouse Workers (UPW), every major union that contributed to the creation of the CIO in the 1930s had experienced a major revolt. Conditions in the coal, auto, rubber, steel, electric, and maritime industries in the sixties are now renovating the unions whose formation they stimulated in the thirties. It should also be observed that most of the unions being renovated belong to and are a majority in the AFL-CIO Industrial Union Department, headed by Walter Reuther. The reasons for the UPW's exemption from the revolt process thus far are apparent: to the credit of its president, Ralph Helstein, the first day of its 1966 convention was thrown open to the delegates to voice their gripes about conditions in both their union and industry.

THE AIRLINE MECHANICS STRIKE

Most of the major industrial union revolts broke into the open prior to last summer. The press reported each as an individual phenomenon, if it reported them at all, and the full significance was missed. It took the five week July-August strike of the airline mechanics, who are affiliated with the International Association of Machinists (IAM), to make the general American public conscious of what *Life* magazine's

August 26, 1966, strike-end issue called the "New Union Militancy," and the November issue of *Fortune* documented as a period of "dramatic shift from the familiar faces to the facelessness of the rank and file." This strike of less than 30,000 men did what the much larger strike-revolts failed to do. By stopping 60 percent of the nation's air passenger travel they directly touched the lives of the nation's middle class.

Without advance signalling from liberal social analysts, who are usually among the first to call attention to signs of labor unrest, the daily press gave recognition to labor's new era—and no wonder. The mechanics made it impossible for reporters to ignore the observation. But the press stressed wages as the issue. Robert T. Quick, President and General Chairman of IAM District 141, gave an indication of the real issue in one of his strike press releases: "We're working under chain gang conditions for cotton picking wages."

The public had not witnessed a stance like that taken by the mechanics since the 1930s. They rejected the first contract proposed by their new president P. L. Siemiller. They rejected a second contract worked out under the direct intervention of the Johnson administration. Siemiller stated he was sure his ranks could live with this contract, but the strike continued without pause. They went further: not only did they make plain their opposition to Johnson's intrusion in their affairs, they rejected labor's allegiance to the Democratic party. The four largest mechanics locals on the Pacific coast—Los Angeles, San Francisco, Portland, and Seattle—sent telegrams to George Meany, Walter Reuther, James Hoffa, and Harry Bridges asking that "immediate action be taken to form a third political party that will serve the best interests of labor."

The mechanics returned to work, having broken more than the 3.7 percent wage guideline of the nation's chief executive. More than damaging his prestige, they increased their own. It is certain that back on the job they will be treated with more respect by their immediate supervisors and that it will be easier for them to unofficially institute improvements of their "chain gang" working conditions.

REVOLT AGAINST HOFFA RULE

The revolts have not all been national or unionwide in scope, but this does not diminish their potential or importance. In the latter months of 1965, James Hoffa's Teamster leadership became unable to restrain the rebellion of the Philadelphia Teamsters. Local 107, City Freight Drivers, have a long tradition of opposition to their international. The leader of their local in 1963 to 1964 was Ray Cohen, a Hoffa supporter. The ranks were dissatisfied with the representation he supplied. Two caucuses existed in the local: "The Real Rank-and-File Caucus" (pro-Hoffa) and "The Voice Caucus," so called because of its publication.

The opposition to Cohen became so great that Cohen became a liability to the international. Hoffa made his first appearance in Philadelphia, after becoming International Brotherhood of Teamsters president, to announce Cohen's demotion. The elimination of Cohen evidently created no basic changes in the local. In June, 1965, at Roadway Express Incorporated's freight loading dock, a young worker, 18 years old and a son of a night over-the-road teamster's shop steward, was helping to load a big box into a trailer. He refused to work under conditions he considered unsafe. The foreman said: "If you don't do it, I'll fire you." The young freight handler answered: "Screw you. Fire away." He was fired. Four other men were ordered to do the same job, they said the same and were also fired. The five men left the job together and went to the union hall. They told their story to the ranks standing around the hall and to the local leaders. A meeting was held. The Voice Caucus took the lead away from its opponent caucus and made a motion for a general strike of all Philadelphia Teamsters; it carried and the strike was on: from five men to a strike of every driver and handler in the city and outlying region in less than 24 hours. Now to insure that the strike was totally general, the Teamsters patroled the streets, stopped trucks and made out-of-town drivers get off their trucks. As a main location for the latter activity, they chose the area in front of Sears and Roebuck's department store. There is an immense lawn and the highway widens out allowing room to parallel park trucks and trailers in large numbers. After several days of this activity, the police attacked the local drivers. The out-of-town drivers joined the strikers against the police. A pitched battle ensued. Within five minutes, the boulevard in front of Sears and Roebuck was impassable due to overturned trailers. This guerrilla-type warfare continued in many areas of the city for several days. Finally by injunction and because *both* factions of the leadership backed down, the strikers were forced back to work. Although none of their strike gains have been contractualized, they are working under better conditions because they are able to express their strike-won strength on the job.

At present, both caucuses—Real Rank-and-File and the Voice—are in disrepute among the ranks because both backed down in the face of local authorities. Hoffa has threatened to take the local under trusteeship. The rank and file, to demonstrate that it is not defeated, had a meeting and passed a resolution which stated that such an attempt would be met by another strike.

THE PAINTERS AND DOW WILSON

The 1965 Building Trades strike in northern California's giant homebuilding industry was particularly important because it involved skilled workers with relatively high wage scales. Plumbers, laborers, sheet-metal workers, and painters struck against the wishes of their international union leaders. All but the painters settled within a few days. Ten thousand painters stayed out for 37 days.

San Francisco Painters' Local No. 4 is the largest local in the International Brotherhood of Painters. It was led by Dow Wilson and Morris Evenson. Its strike demands, including coffee time, were some of the most radical ever made by painters. Painting labor processes, due to the rapid advances in paint chemistry, are more rationalized than those of any other trade in the building industry. Time studies and resulting speedups are the rule. Paint foremen, rushing to make new tracts ready for the developers' sales forces, stand over painters with blank wage checkbooks protruding from their pockets. If a man falls behind he can be summarily fired and paid off in full. Tension of all kinds is high. Unsatisfied, the employers have for some time been pressuring the union to allow them to institute the use of new methods of paint application—the elimination of brushes for rollers, pressure rollers, and spray guns.

During the strike the leaders of the international union publicly sided with the employers' automation demands. Local No. 4 and its leadership stood firm. Leaders in several other northern California locals backed down and their ranks rebelled. Less than halfway through the strike Dow Wilson, in effect, became the leader for the entire strike and a majority of San Francisco Bay area locals. The painters won their strike, their coffee time, a big wage increase, and temporarily checked the advance of technological unemployment.

Wilson knew that the international leaders would be vindictive and that they would try to get at the ranks through him. The strike filled out his reputation as a model union leader, unique in these times. He was an independent political radical who was unhampered by dreams of wealth. He saw himself as a servant of the ranks, had exposed collusion and corruption in the painting of government housing that was cheating the taxpayers of millions of dollars, and had used his prestige to bring Negro workers into the industry. He was a threat to the international union and employers. Wilson realized he would have to carry his ranks' fight for union democracy to the international convention.

In the early morning hours of April 6, 1966, Dow Wilson was assassinated in front of the San Francisco Labor Temple—gangster style, by a shotgun blast in the face. A month later Lloyd Green, president of the nearby Hayward local and a colleague of Wilson's, was killed in an identical manner. The leaders and ranks of Local No. 4 accompanied by Wilson's widow and children demonstrated on the main streets of San Francisco and in front of the homes of city and federal authorities. Arrests were made shortly thereafter.

An official of a painting employers' association confessed a major role in authoring the assassinations and driving the murder car. His trial made it clear that his power in labor relations came from money he stole from the painters' pension fund and by threatening recalcitrants with a visit from his friend Abe "the Trigger" Chapman, whose name was formerly identified with Murder Incorporated. He also indicated a top regional union official who is a supporter of the international union's policies. The official's guilt has not been proven; legal proceedings continue.

In a matter of weeks after the burial of the assassinated leaders, the international officials of the painters union made their first unsuccessful attempt to take several Bay Area locals into trusteeship and suspend local autonomy. The courts have refused to grant an injunction against further attempts of the International to take control, but the rank-and-file painters and their remaining leaders, headed by the courageous Morris Evenson, continue to show a willingness to protect their independence in every way.

DISAFFILIATION AS A REVOLT TOOL

The revolt of California, Oregon, and Washington pulp and paper workers in 1964 received little publicity. However, it caught the attention of labor leaders nationally. In compliance with National Labor Relations Board requirements, workers in locals that were affiliated with two aging and eastern based AFL-CIO internationals (International Brotherhood of Pulp Sulphite and Paper Mill Workers and the United Papermakers and Paper workers) broke away to form the independent Association of Western Pulp and Paper Workers (AWPPW). The old unions lost face and $500,000 a year in dues monies.

The AWPPW members, whose work in 49 mills accounts for 90 percent of pulp and paper production on the Pacific coast, set up headquarters in Portland, Oregon. They announced the birth of their union through the publication of a monthly newspaper, *The Rebel.* They elected a president who is typical of the new union's staff; before taking office he was a mill electrician.

Since its initial organization, the AWPPW has had strong support from regional and local unions in areas where they set up locals, but life has been hard for this new union. Its newness and small membership has made it impossible to build the large treasury needed to operate a union today. It is not just the high cost of routine operation, collective bargaining against large corporations and legal costs that have created problems. The AWPPW is continually harassed by the two bureaucratized unions from which it split, both of which have the support of George Meany and the conservative AFL-CIO hierarchy. As their isolation increases and the official support they receive from other unions shrinks, owing to pressure from Meany, their energies are expended in a fight for existence rather than growth.

Throughout the United States there are large numbers of workers in local and regional units whose position is similar to that of the Pacific coast pulp and paper workers, prior to their establishment of independence in 1964. Their working conditions and wages are artificially depressed because of what amounts to captive affiliations with conservatively led international unions. Their tolerance of their captivity seems unlimited only because at present there is no progressive alternative available.

WHY WORKERS REVOLT

Almost without exception, the revolts were conducted primarily to improve the conditions of life on the job. This is absolutely contrary to what the public has been led to believe. Newspaper, television, and radio reporting rarely relate the existence, let alone the details, of labor's noneconomic demands. The following statement by the Director of Research in Technology and Industrial Relations at Yale University stands as a classic definition of strike causes in American industry:

> In 1936 and 1937, a wave of sit-down strikes swept through the rubber and automobile plants of the United States. The workers on strike wanted higher wages, union recognition, and an organized machinery for the handling of day-to-day grievances, but, above all, they were striking against what they called the "speedup" of work as governed by the assembly line. The causes of every major strike are complex and frequently so interwoven as to be inseparable. But somewhere among the causes (and frequently basic to the others, as in the sit-downs) are work methods and working conditions.
>
> Two years before the first sit-down strike the country experienced a nationwide walkout of textile workers. Here, discrimination against union members, wages, and many other issues were involved, but the dynamic origin of the disturbance (not only in 1934, but through the remaining thirties and after) was the introduction of new work methods and machinery, all of which were generally lumped by the workers and denounced as the "stretchout." If particular work methods or undesirable working conditions may sometimes cause a national walkout, they are also the common origin of innumerable lesser conflicts in the world of industry. The net result of a minor conflict over a work method may be a day's slowdown or a grievance fought through the local's plant grievance machinery or, perhaps, hostilities expressed in low-quality work or by a high rate of absenteeism. . . . When neglected or misunderstood, these merely local disturbances can, with surprising rapidity, grow into a national emergency.[2]

2. Charles R. Walker, "Work Methods, Working Conditions, and Morals," *Industrial Conflict,* eds. A. Kornhauser, R. Dubin and A. Ross (New York: McGraw-Hill, 1954).

Walker does not deny the importance of issues other than those involving working conditions, he simply says that they are secondary. Work methods and conditions are not the only issues in the current revolts. Wage increases have not kept up with price increases since the end of World War II. Americans have become accustomed to the pattern and have adjusted to it. Workers have maintained or increased their purchasing power by working long overtime hours, "moonlighting" (working two jobs) or putting their wives to work. This is not to say that the unusually big jump in the cost of living that occurred last year failed to increase anger, frustration, and discontent. It did, but the American working class has not yet found an effective way to oppose price increases. Workers in the larger and stronger unions in particular have come to believe that wage increases are a defensive or holding action. Even when they have won substantial raises, price increases have wiped them out in a matter of months. They no longer believe that a collective bargaining contract whose major achievement is a wage increase represents a victory of more than temporary progress.

The above belief notwithstanding, it is always difficult and often impossible for workers to make the improvement of working conditions the formal as well as primary goal of contract negotiation.[3] It is absolutely impossible for the employed near-poor and poor to do so. For example, the conditions of work of the farm laborers in California's central valley are brutal and improvements are sorely needed, yet the United Farm Workers Organizing Committee headed by Caesar Chavez continues to give the wage demands top priority. His ranks would have it no other way. In a sense, the farm worker puts aside his own most immediate need because he has responsibilities to his wife and children. Then too, it should not be forgotten that workers who have incomes twice as large as the farm workers find it difficult to keep their wives in good spirits or their creditors patient during a strike whose major goal is anything other than a sizable wage increase.

Employers take the attitude that their authority over work methods and conditions is unchallengeable and sacrosanct. Most of all they fear any kind of employee control over the production process. No matter that the union sometimes forces them to grant sizeable wage boosts, they cover their increased costs and more by getting more work out of their employees. American employers have made it clear that they will make a principled stand against any demand that would give a union any authority over the methods, conditions, and speed of production. Union officials fear fighting so determined an enemy, and they fear the new union leaders that would be developed in such a fight. The fight for better conditions cannot be made every one, two, or three years like

3. An informative discussion of this point is contained in Alvin W. Gouldner, *Wildcat Strike* (Yellow Springs, Ohio: Antioch Press, 1954).

the wage fights; it must be fought every day inside the plants. During such a fight the base and authority of the union would be moved from the union hall back inside the plant. Workers who are willing to fight their employer to obtain a better life on the job have to be prepared to fight their union leaders as well.

The struggle of American industrial workers to improve the conditions under which they perform their labors is not an effort simply to obtain a better physical work environment. The goals go far beyond clean air and surroundings. Work paces and safety take higher priority.

Of equal, if not greater, importance is the drive to obtain formal contractual control over the methods whereby they are forced to perform their productive duties and to control their relationship to the machines with which they live. Cheated of the opportunity to make decisions of any kind, they are unable to take responsibility for what they do. In many cases, they are not told the identity of the product part which they help produce, let alone its function. Yet they may be forced to remain at that labor for years, denied the right to transfer to other jobs that would allow a break in the monotony and increased knowledge of both the end product and total technology involved in its manufacture. Alienated, adjuncts to the machine, they resent the respect the machinery commands from their employers. In a word, industrial workers are fighting for dignity. Without it there is no daily gratification in their lives.

It was precisely this struggle that in the early 1930s caused mass-production workers to organize independent local unions on a plant for plant basis without outside help and which inspired John L. Lewis to create the CIO by centralizing the power of those locals in the mid 1930s. But the CIO was not to become a weapon that would win significant improvements of work conditions, methods, and controls. Those goals had to be subordinated to more immediate ones. The first priority of the CIO had to be the winning of collective bargaining recognition and the negotiation of corporation or industrywide contracts so that workers in one plant would not be forced to compete against those in others.

By 1941, the industrial unions had accomplished these immediate goals to a substantial degree. The time had arrived when the workers, through their new unions, could be free to return their attention to the problems of the work process. World War II cheated them from doing so.

The war provided employers with an opportunity to check the momentum of the CIO. With the exception of John L. Lewis, the official labor leadership, especially those who were pro-Communist, pledged that for the "duration," their unions would not strike. The employers responded by trying to win back organized labor's recent gains. Alone, workers were forced to defend just the fundamental victories of the 1930s. The attempts to do so were often branded as "aid to the enemy."

The war, however, by its very totality, had a far more crippling effect on labor's ranks than those directly imposed on them by their employers, the government, and their official leaders. Within a year after it had begun, the war atomized the rank-and-file's on-the-job union cadres. It took large numbers of experienced local union leaders and shop stewards from the workplaces. It decimated the personnel of labor's most fundamental organizational unit, the informal work groups created by the productive process. These groups, with their informal leaders, form a social unit able to discipline their members and restrict production. The CIO was born in these groups. They pyramided their power, plant-wide, and an independent local union was formed. The process was called "self-organization." A typical example of the effect of World War II on the groups was as follows: A group of ten welders and grinders who worked in close contact with one another were employed in a plant that unionized in the late 1930s. Half of them became employed there in the late 1920s or early 1930s. Others came later, but all participated in a portion of the long fight that brought the union into the plant, and more importantly, to obtain the right to *openly* bargain with their immediate supervisor—the foreman. By 1943, five of them had gone into the armed forces and two had gone to the shipyards on the west coast. They were replaced by two housewives, a draft-exempt youth, and four men beyond draft age from farms and marginal jobs. How could the three remaining members of the original group impart to the newcomers the history, tradition, and knowledge of their group's struggles or the union lessons learned in years of fighting? They could not. Before it sustained war losses the group was able to conduct actions that would tame a foreman. They could participate in that process which keeps union leaders militant. If they saw a local president softening in his attitude toward management he would be told: "Look, remember when you worked with us and how it was, and how you complained louder than anybody else? And now you're talking out of both sides of your mouth and letting us live under these conditions." Neither did they spare their own members who showed signs of weakening. A failure to attend union meetings brought jibes, serious but with smiles, that reminded the absentees of what they had all been through together and the need to continue. No such pressures could be applied to their group's wartime replacements. To the new members, the union officials were unapproachable "big shots."

When the war was over, the reconversion to peacetime consumer production once again broke up the personnel of the work groups. Large numbers who had entered the armed forces or war industries did not return to their old jobs. The old groups could not reestablish themselves. In plant, after workplace, the workers were divided into segments with three major identities: old timers, vets, and kids, so-called. For a time their attentions focused primarily on stockpiling home furnishings. Who could blame them? For the first time in American history a majority of workers were able to consume a large number of the products made. But the brightness of that goal diminished. The routine drudgery of workers' lives soon reestablished its monotonous predictability. Besides, television sets and dishwashers at home did not bring gratification to life on the job. And the workers were getting to know one another again. They were learning who, among those near them, liked to bowl, sew, garden, repair cars, and fish. The questions had been asked: "How many kids do you have?" and "Where do you want to go next vacation?" The social cohesion and the work eliminated the separate identities. Work groups again attained leaders. The selection, as always, was natural. No formal elections were held. The vote was by a nod, by the raising of a brow, or by a silent consensus that at first is not always conscious. Someone in a group emerges as courageous and articulate, stands up to a foreman, and the rest support him or her, with the result that it is once more a fighting unit involved in guerrilla warfare.

By the mid-1950s, American workers, particularly in the mass production, transportation, and maritime industries, were ready once more to resume the struggle that had caused the revolts of the 1930s. They found, however, that the leadership created during the rise of the CIO was not responsive to their desires. There was an unwillingness among the official leaders to give up the control they had so easily attained during the war. The workers had no choice but to conduct a fight on two levels. Inside the workplaces, they fought their employers, and at the same time conducted a campaign to win the in-plant local union officials—the only section of the labor leadership with whom they have daily and direct contact—to their cause. Officials who identified with them were supported. Every possible pressure was brought to bear on those who would not. By 1964, the tactic had achieved enough success to separately pit large numbers of individually unified local unions against their regional leaders who, in turn, were forced to apply pressure on those top leaderships that were not responsive. Thus the revolts broke into the open. They were created, grew, and became a fact visible to the public, first because of the need and secondly *because the rank and file of American unions had been able to build from their work groups the basic organizational vehicle for them.*

The revolts continue to grow in both depth and magnitude. Wildcat strikes show a steady increase. Each year the Federal Mediation and Conciliation Service enters nearly 8,000 disputes. Last year union rank-and-file members rejected 11.7 percent of the contracts negotiated with the Service's aid, an all-time high that is still rising. In the first month of fiscal 1967 the rejections rose to 19.3 percent. There is continued increase in the number of elections in which long-time incumbents are being challenged from below.

The present struggle to improve work conditions, methods, and controls is far more desperate than that of the 1930s, and represents a far deeper potential crisis for the nation. The productivity of the entire labor force is far higher. Employers have retained the right to establish the speed at which assembly lines will travel and the methods by which work shall be performed. No major union, including the UAW, has made a concerted effort to restrict that right. Workers in most modern automobile assembly plants often turn out between 60 and 70 cars an hour. Neither the human anatomy nor mentality was designed to endure such strain or monotomy.

A manifestation of this may be the reported increase in the use of drugs within the plants:

> Pep-pill use by factory workers draws increasing concern as a hidden hazard. Plant medical directors and safety specialists fear scattered signs of drug use by production workers are symptomatic of an underground factory safety problem. A major farm equipment maker, a big food processor, detect increased use of pep pills in their plants. One worker's tool box turns up a hundred bennies (benzedrine capsules). One executive suspects "there are several pushers in our plants." "The problem is most acute in California," he adds, "but we've found a little of this to be countrywide."

> Los Angeles narcotics authorities turn up a well-supplied pusher in an auto plant; they aid big aerospace companies seeking remedies to the problem. One California narcotics specialist figures pills are pushed in all plants with assembly line operations. Some executives blame today's fast production pace and excessive moonlighting for driving workers to stimulants. One detective says that employers don't want to attack the problem for fear of stirring unfavorable publicity.[4]

The increased use of speedup methods in industry now threatens the safety and health of workers in the most literal sense. According to the National Safety Council's 1966 report on U.S. industry, "14,500 workers died and another 2.2 million were temporarily or permanently disabled in 1966." The U.S. Public Health Service recognizes the crisis is greater than at any time in the nation's history and is spending a record $6.6 million on occupational health this year. Syndicated columnist Sylvia Porter recently discussed a "top-level" report to the U.S. Surgeon General that argued that $50 million a year is needed to reduce hazards by 20 percent; she further argued that doing so "would add $11 billion a year to our production."[5]

The problems of speedup and increased safety hazards have been largely ignored by the official union leaders. Workers have been forced to seek solutions outside official union grievance machinery. Production, particularly in heavy industry, is plagued by slowdowns and minor acts of sabotage. Bolts are dropped into the slots in which the chains travel that pull the assembly lines; machinery is not maintained or is

4. *Wall Street Journal,* November 22, 1966, p. 1
5. *San Francisco Chronicle,* April 13, 1967.

handled in a way that will hasten its breakdown. The quality of the product is harmed by shortcuts that allow a momentary breathing spell; creativity and efficiency are withheld. The object is revenge, release from boredom, and the rest that results while repairs are awaited.

For brief periods after each guerrilla victory (and under management's increased surveillance) the glee is limitless though no trace of it can be found on the facial expressions of the participants. Nevertheless it is a difficult war. Victories are short-lived. The tension saps energies and the speedup continues. In many plants employees hired as spies openly take notes. While there are few mortalities (firings), there are many casualties. Suspected trouble-makers are sometimes temporarily laid off for real or for alleged infractions of rules unrelated to the actual charge. Most often they are transferred to other departments of the shop. They sustain no loss in pay, but must accustom themselves to new foremen, new repetitive tasks, and undergo a period of initiation in their new work groups.

The widespread introduction of automated machinery since World War II has increased the existing alienation of American workers. When new machines and methods are substituted for the old, new job classifications and rates must be defined. The employers make every attempt to reclassify jobs so as to downgrade wages. Then too they sometimes meet outbreaks of worker militancy with threats of automating jobs out of existence. It is impossible to measure the anger that results.

Automation qualitatively increases nervous tension on the job. A worker at a machine on which he or she can produce one hundred pieces a day is placed at a machine that can be made to turn out five hundred. A mistake that previously made it necessary to scrap one piece becomes one that necessitates the scrapping of five. At the same time, the new machine cheats the worker of the opportunity to use the skills needed to operate the old one. The deskilled worker loses individual bargaining power, freedom in the job market, and a daily loss of work gratification —a damage to self-image.

Even though armament production has absorbed the jobs lost because of automation, workers bitterly hate the automation process. In it they see future joblessness. They reject all claims that it represents progress. They are aware of the human price. It uproots them and requires that they transplant themselves to another workplace and often to another geographic area. If their work area is automated and they are lucky enough to retain their employment, they may face an even more dismal prospect: an on-the-job loneliness for which there is no compensation. The friends that once surrounded them, providing an on-the-job family, disappear or no longer work within earshot. Increased absenteeism and loss of morale are inevitable. What once made the job just bearable has been eliminated. Also, the fighting weapon, the informal work group, has been destroyed; new ones must be built.

The final indignity of the process for the workers is that they and their leaders are seldom if ever consulted before automated change is introduced. They are presented with an accomplished fact—change designed by humans who have no conception of an industrial worker's life experience, on the job or off.

But the consequences of automation give workers weapons they did not previously have. Probably, like the British workers during the beginnings of Luddism in the late eighteenth century, American workers now note the demoralization of industry's middle class. Computerization, automation's companion, is stripping middle executives and immediate management of their power to make decisions. Meaningful decisions are increasingly made at the top.

Automation creates problems for management in still other ways. Automated machines represent a far larger capital investment than their predecessors. They are far more vulnerable to neglectful treatment. Their complexity provides increased opportunities for the minor acts of sabotage that are already widespread and difficult to detect. A slowdown or stoppage of an automated machine causes a production loss several times over the loss caused by a similar crisis involving the machines it replaced. One worker is able to restrict production to a degree that earlier would have involved a half dozen.

The rapid disappearance of family-owned companies and the growing number of corporate mergers contribute to the rank-and-file revolts in a manner similar to that of automation. In industries run from the top by professionals for multi-absentee owners, the symbol of authority is no longer human, with a consequent effect on the contents and enforcement of directives from the main office. Embattled from above and below, the vise on middle and lower management twists tighter. The problem is exaggerated in corporations of the conglomerate type owning factories of productive units in a number of nonrelated industries. Top managers directing units making steel, candy, silk stockings, and chemicals lose contact with the production processes. They are in the business of managing.

The unique character of the conglomerate gives their managers a new weapon in their dealings with organized labor. If a particular union strikes in one of their industries, the others—in different industries under contract to different unions—are free to operate and profit. It is much easier to put union against union.

According to Federal Trade Commission figures, over 70 percent of all important mergers and acquisitions (involving $10 million in assets) between 1960 and 1965 were conglomerate. Only 13 percent of the mergers were with firms producing similar or related products. The same trend continued into 1967. (The FTC estimates that at the current merger pace, 75 percent of all corporate assets in the nation will be in the hands of 200 corporations by 1975.) International unions (so called because they include Canadians) are thus forced to negotiate contracts for larger and larger numbers of their members. By their very nature, these negotiations become more and more attentive to wage and economic fringe benefit payment patterns, less and less concerned with the working conditions that vary so widely from workplace to workplace. The conditions of daily life in industry degenerates. It is absolutely necessary and proper that American workers permit the top leaders of their international unions more centralized power. There is no other way to challenge growing corporate power during the negotiation of master collective bargaining agreements. At the same time, the ranks want to determine the goals of those negotiations and to use their power in the workplace to increase their control over the nature of work. How to simultaneously centralize labor's total power on the one hand and decentralize it on the other is a decisive issue of the revolts. No sense can be made of them unless this is recognized.

There is another objective condition in industrial society that affects the revolts and must be mentioned briefly: the labor shortage. It became a major problem for industry in 1966, or after the revolts began, but this is not to downgrade its effect. It allowed a greater degree of independence for those already in the workforce when it began. Probably more important, however, it caused industry to hire hundreds of thousands of youths who would in the past have had to wait years longer to get what has long been considered "adult employment." The attitudes of the new young workers have been a revelation to the older workers. They, like their middle-class counterparts in the universities, are free of the wounds that the Depression inflicted on previous generations. For large numbers of them a good self-image is not dependent upon having a reverent attitude toward employment. They rebel against doing what has dulled and shortened the lives of their parents. The following experience in today's factories is not uncommon: A young worker is offered a higher paying job, discovers it requires a faster pace or involves an onerous condition and turns it down—preferring to live easier at less pay. The older workers observe such an action in shocked respect. They would not have dreamed of taking such a step. It reveals to them the sacrifices they have long endured. The experience can widen but more often helps to narrow gaps. Today's young are armed with mirrors.

The revolt of university students has had a radicalizing effect on the entire society. This includes industrial workers. Many of them are repulsed by the attire and conduct of some of the students, but dissent of any kind has a contagion. Besides, the repulsion is an initial and surface reaction. The workers' rebellion creates tolerances and even feelings of kinship for others doing the same.

Will the students develop new alliances now that they have lost a base in the civil rights movement? Already, radical students have begun to reevaluate their attitudes toward unions. They have been taught, often by formerly radical social scientists, that American workers are now fat on beer, barbecue, and television, and no longer capable of struggle for social progress. The rank-and-file revolts are destroying the cynical myth and providing opportunity for alliances. The initiative will not always be from the students. It must not be forgotten that during the Free Speech Movement's revolt on the Berkeley campus in December, 1964, it was the San Francisco local of the Service Employees International Union that provided the FSM with its first public support in the Bay Area and paved the way for public support from the powerful San Francisco Central Labor Council. During the FSM strike that in the same month closed that campus, rank-and-file Teamsters respected the students' picket lines until ordered to cross them by their leadership. The Cement Truck Drivers East Bay Teamsters local, however, officially honored the strike. Early in 1965, when Mario Savio and the other FSM leaders were under attack from the entire establishment in the state, Paul Schrade, the west coast director of the United Automobile Workers, visited the Berkeley campus and before press and public declared that he would greet the presence of students like Savio inside his union.

The most decisive crisis for American unions is the alienation that lies between them and members of the black community: particularly the black youth, but also the black union members. The main cause of the crisis is twofold: White rank-and-file workers are, in the main, but to varying degrees, racially prejudiced; the leadership of labor has generally failed to provide the leadership that could solve the crisis. In the broadest sense of the term the crisis is one of leadership. The top officials of labor have failed to provide adequate leadership for any of the major problems facing workers. Walter Reuther provides a good example. He has many times provided segments of the civil rights movement with valuable aid. Those admirable actions are cheated of their full educational value for the UAW ranks—both white and black. "He is helping them, but what about us?" A Reuther who conducted a more than rhetorical battle against the speedup in the auto plants could increase his union's support of the black revolution tenfold without incurring the wrath of the white workers in his ranks. At first they would forgive him his trespasses because he was also delivering for them. Only then could there be the receptivity that allows for education in the best sense. Also, the black UAW members, who suffer from the speedup as much as do the white workers, could begin to take Reuther seriously.

Almost invariably, when labor leaders make speeches asking that their white ranks champion the rights of blacks in industry, they are asking the whites to give up something without offering them anything in return. White workers involved in the formation of the CIO welcomed the presence of blacks because it won an industrial union for them. For that time, the appearance of substantial numbers of blacks in mass production industries with full union membership was progress.

As a result, the prejudice of the whites who experienced it was diminished. As always, morality followed necessity. Tragically, the initial progress was not built upon. The CIO bureaucratized and lost its momentum. The blacks lost a vehicle for major progress and organized labor lost a natural ally.

The momentum of the movement for black liberation and labor's lack of responsiveness dictate that black workers will organize, as such, within industry and unions. If this attempt at organization is grounded in demands for an improvement of work life as well as black freedom it will find sympathies among white workers. The organizations they form will help stimulate the formation of internal union opposition movements in general. The present weakness of the rank-and-file revolts is that they are localized and isolated from one another. If the revolts continue to grow in scope, it is likely that it will mean the beginning of the end of labor's leadership crisis. Only the failure of the revolts and the consequent demoralization can create the basis for the development of a major racist movement among white industrial workers.

The isolation of labor from its natural allies is closely related to its political failures. The politics which join the official labor leadership to the Democratic party contribute to its impotency in serving its membership. There is hardly a major labor negotiation that fails to demonstrate this fact. There is not one aspect of labor's leadership crisis that has not contributed to the cause of the rank-and-file revolts.

Thus far, these pages have discussed those causes of the revolts that are in some way internal to industry and the unions, due mainly to policies and conditions that affect workers as such. But there are developments in our society that have a radicalizing effect on a major portion of the population—workers included. Although it is difficult to measure the impact of these broader developments, it is doubtless that they are among the principal causes of the revolts. Or, to put it another way, the rank-and-file union revolts are the industrial workers' expression of a more widespread radicalization process taking place in America.

The active development of the process begins with a question that Americans increasingly ask themselves and each other: "Is this all there is to life?" The absence of life satisfaction in an era of instant communication and atomic miracles seems a tragic contradiction. The question was not formulated yesterday, nor inspired by just the experiences of the 1960s. It reaches much deeper into our past and the institutions, ideas, and values on which our society operates. The conscious pursuit of happiness via government programs is not new to Americans. We have tried a number of governmentally sponsored attempts at what was claimed would be a new society. All of these attempts were characterized by an ideological vagueness. Yet, for a time, they instilled hope.

The New Deal of Franklin Roosevelt instilled more optimism than all its successors. However, it was production for World War II, rather than the New Deal, that brought full employment. Regardless of the cause of full employment, there was not a New Deal supporter whose inspiration was not dulled by that program's destruction of food at a time when there were Americans who were starving.

Americans fought World War II with an enthusiasm instilled by the promise of a "better life" after victory. The Fair Deal of Harry Truman did no more than provide a faint echo of the New Deal and we marked time until the Korean War—fought with far less enthusiasm than World War II. The New Frontier of John Kennedy gave many Americans a moment of hope. The president was youthful. He surrounded himself with professional intellectuals. No basic change was accomplished. The Great Society has done no more. The impatience of Americans has grown. Lyndon Johnson is no longer a popular president. The impatience is based on more issues than the war in Vietman.

None of the promises from the top, of a newer and greater society, have been kept. A period of war, hot and cold, H-bombs, nerve gas and bacteriological weapons, is not one in which people can live on hope for the distant future. Americans have more and more sensed that their leaders are without program, answers, or clear idea of where we are headed. This and an increased awareness of corruption in higher places has stimulated initiatives from below.

Dissent initiative in the population mystifies many national political figures. They have always operated on the idea that if a majority of the population enjoyed a degree of prosperity, there could be political stability. But the general public has developed an awareness of what it previously paid little attention to. There are millions of Americans who live in material and therefore spiritual poverty. Whatever lessons have not been learned from the War on Poverty have been taught by the struggles of black, Mexican, Indian, and poor white Americans.

It is only since the end of World War II that a majority of Americans have experienced a relatively high standard of consumption. Yet, there exists an uneasiness and an insecurity. How is it possible to enjoy a large well-balanced meal that stimulates overeating when others are denied this right? Guilt can cheat a dinner table of its warmth. And then, how safe is a wealth not enjoyed by all? The problem is not limited to the United States. For the first time in history and in many parts of the world the idea that progress toward happiness can be individually instead of collectively achieved through material plenty is beginning to be challenged, given actual test. It is logical, however, that the major challenge should be made in the most advanced industrial nation.

The problems of an atomic and computer era automatically pose the question of collective solution, in all problem areas. Collective action and the need for decisions made collectively and more democratically immediately follows. The major factor that propels a society into a period of accelerated social change is the existence of an "ever increasing divorce between reality and the law, between institutions and men's way of living, between the letter and the spirit."[6] When the divorce becomes wide enough, all practices that oppress and all institutions that are not responsive get challenged. Blacks, for example, cannot live with racism in any of its forms; students cannot live in multiversities operating on century-old methods; and the new middle class cannot abide the unilateral decisions which factoryize professional work. Industrial workers are unable to utilize unions with aged organizational structures and a low degree of internal democracy. The broad social action program of the UAW, for example, has wide public appeal. It is vastly superior to those of most other unions. In contrast, the UAW, like most other unions, is structured so that its power lies outside the factories: in the international headquarters and local union halls rather than primarily on the shop floor. The auto corporations have a foreman-to-worker ratio of approximately one to fifteen. The ratio of bargaining UAW shop stewards to workers in most plants is one to 250. Regardless of the quality of the steward, it is physically impossible to provide adequate representation. Nevertheless, it is the stewards, more than any other section of union officials, who are in constant contact with the ranks and who perform the primary official function of the union. They are not cut into the official union power structure as an organizational unit; this automatically preserves the open gap between top leadership and ranks. The gap exists in all American unions. Long absent from the place of work, the top leaders live in an atmosphere that makes it easy for them to accept or tolerate management philosophies. For some time, management and top union leaders have operated on the premise that, in order to grant wage increases, the employers must be free to get more production from workers. It is difficult to find a worker who accepts the idea, but the union provides no builtin vehicle—such as a shop stewards' council system—that allows constant expression of this rejection in top leadership echelons.

What of the future of the rank-and-file union revolts and their ability to wrest change? Their weakness lies in their lack of more than local level organization or program. Their main strength is that they do not exist in societal isolation. They have broken into the open in a period when other segments of the population are also in revolt. This was far less true in the revolts of the 1930s: at that time there were no black or student rebellions. One other condition is brand new: unlike the 1930s, for the first time intellectuals have the means to build their own organizational base within labor. Teachers, professionals of all

---

6. Albert Mathiez, *The French Revolution* (New York: Alfred A. Knopf, 1928); (New York: Grosset and Dunlap, 1964), p. 3.

kinds, white-collar workers, and government employees at all levels are forming unions of their own. In return for the support they are getting from blue-collar unions they are bringing to labor's ranks a degree of cultural and technical expertise never before available.[7]

7. In a recent series of articles on the Black Revolutionary Union Movement in Detroit's auto plants, Robert Dudnick (a reporter for the independent radical weekly, *The Guardian*), argues that the principal purposes of the black workers' movement are quite similar to those advocated by Weir for labor as a whole. See Dudnick's pamphlet: "Black Workers in Revolt" (*The Guardian,* 197 E. 4th Street, New York).—Ed.

Epilogue : 1976

A dozen years have passed since the "new era" began. The workers' revolts have won small victories here and there, but nowhere have they succeeded in making the institutional changes needed to increase and sustain rank-and-file power in American unions. The character of collective bargaining remains the same, with total dependency on arbitration of grievances and denial of the right to strike at the local level. Union governments and internal structures remain adaptations to collective bargaining as it is now institutionalized. Thus, even where long incumbent union officials have been replaced with young idealistic people, fresh from the ranks, change has not been qualitative. The new officials have been thrown into the same institutional framework that imprisoned and bureaucratized the old ones. Tragically, quickly, and inevitably, they have become bureaucrats themselves.

The major accomplishments of the revolts and rebellions have been that for millions of workers they meant a break in the experience of submission, and they put an end to the myth that unions are monolithic organizations. By making the fight, the ranks made clear that there is a considerable gap separating the ranks and top officials of the unions. Beyond those accomplishments there is the very substantial but never mentioned victory that was won by the revolts: they were not crushed. They were checked, contained, and even "put down," but they were strong enough to assure that no major segment of the American working class has yet experienced decisive defeat and demoralization.

It is important to examine the strengths of the revolts, particularly those that were demonstrated during their first five years, from 1964 through 1969. The power of the revolts was in the unanimity with which the workers acted. This, in turn, gave the revolts the appearance of spontaneity. Seldom were they led by organized factions within the union. The revolts were so popular and their power base so broad that they were often led by the natural leadership that arises in the social relationships created by the production processes. This meant that during the course of the actual revolt, the workplace leadership had maximum protection, whether the fight took the form of a wildcat strike, unsanctioned extension of an official strike, a sit-down, a slowdown, a temporary speedup designed to sabotage complex production coordination systems, a mass campaign of minor acts of sabotage, or refusal to ratify a contract. Wherever the structure of the rebel organization was based on the informal work group network of the workplace, the communication system for most types of actions was preexisting and natural.

The main strength of the revolts and the major reason for their massive popularity in the ranks, across entire national industries, was the underlying idea that sustained them. Prior to World War II, and particularly during the Depression years, the view that the key to happiness was a "steady job" that could provide "three square meals a day, a roof over the head, and clothes on the back" was dominant among the workers. At the end of World War II and to the surprise of most, there was no return to depression. Instead, the vast majority of the population had steady jobs. For the first time in American history the working class in large part was able to buy many of the things it made. By 1956, and the emergence of "16 Ton" as the biggest pop-record hit of all time, there was broad recognition that society's prewar values had not stood up to test. The majority of American workers had refrigerators, clothes closets, and garages, all under substantial roofs by depression standards. But still they had not found the way to the "good life."

They were coming home from work each day with frustrations and stress exhaustion that took the pleasure out of consuming the products they purchased. Roger Miller's "King of the Road," a song about an industrial worker who dropped out and walked away from it all, was on 15 million juke boxes in the same year that the rank-and-file revolts broke into the open. There were few who did not envy the hero of the song and fewer still who could afford to emulate him. We were a nation of people who were now stuck with the steady jobs we once wanted so much. In the early 1960s, Americans switched the focus of their drive to obtain a good life from a home based consumerism to a fight to improve the quality of life where most spend the bulk of their waking hours, on the job. Nothing could have been more logical and the revolts were proof of that change of focus. The dismay among industrial relations experts is that until the recession of the 1970s, few of the revolts were conducted to obtain more money. The goal, in a word, was dignity. The rebels wanted and want the right to make some of the decisions about the speeds and methods of production that so affect every hour of their lives. A shift of focus has taken place: millions of Americans are no longer content to seek individualistic solutions to social problems. They now seek goals that can only be obtained through collective efforts. In extending the pursuit of happiness from home to workplace, the ranks have had to make the sorts of demands that necessitate expansion of workers' control over job conditions. These demands by their very nature go beyond the confines of existing capitalist property relations; and more to the point, they are demands that are alien and unnatural to the present contractual system of collective bargaining and its organizations on the union and on the employer side. This indicates the scope of change that is to come as rank-and-file forces increasingly see the inadequacy of the present objectives of militant struggles.

Shortly after the 1966 airline-mechanics strike demonstrated the full potential of the revolts, the employers, top union officials, and government forces moved into a coalition that has with few exceptions contained the revolts at the local union and workplace level. After militant actions have passed the peak of their ability to sustain avid interest, leaders or suspected leaders get disciplined or offered union or management jobs. Rebel departments get bought off temporarily by liberal incentive schemes or privileges. The officials call "showcase strikes," the employers sit back and wait, the government threatens injunction or intervention, and finally the ranks go back to work with considerable energies and bank savings spent. If the ranks hold out for a better contract than the leadership has negotiated, the leadership goes back to the bargaining table only to reemerge with the old contents in a new pail. An example is provided by the ILWU West Coast longshoremen. In 1975, they twice rejected a contract negotiated by their president Harry Bridges. They accepted it the third time. He simply refused to go after the demands they wanted to make. He wore the membership down. They continue to work under a contract that does not protect jobs from automation and allows employers to bypass union hiring hall procedures. He has been free to do so because, even if the ranks were able to mount a movement to recall him from office, a new leadership with an alternative vision has not emerged in opposition to the Bridges regime.

This is the typical failing of all the revolts so far. In no instance has any segment of the rank-and-file leadership yet articulated any major new ideas or program.

Therefore, the revolts have not been able to break out of local isolation and develop an organization that could link the efforts of the ranks horizontally, workplace for workplace. The working class visionaries of our time have yet to come forth. It has been two years since Joe Germano, kingmaker and duke of the United Steelworkers' giant Chicago-Gary area District 31, retired and saw his handpicked successor Sam Evett defeated by the young oppositionist Ed Sadlowski. It was clear to most that Sadlowski is a man of integrity who wants to make a more militant fight against the employers. But he assumed leadership in the most powerful steel region as an individual rather than the leader of a movement. His main campaign appeal was made around "getting the old guys out and the young blood in." The idea was popular but not sufficient to stir imaginations about a better future. The forces of the international union isolated Sadlowski in his own offices and even removed the grievance and arbitration files. His intentions had been to put the existing collective bargaining apparatus to better use. He became its captive, and with fewer resources to operate it than did his predecessor. Sadlowski has sometimes offered the idea that there is little that can be done to change the nature of the current institution of collective bargaining as long as the market economy remains intact. But there is still no movement for Sadlowski to "lead" or to draw strength, leadership, and protection from.

The massive coal miners wildcat in February, 1968, put long isolated locals of the UMW into contact with each other. In the following months the Black Lung Movement, extremely important in itself, became the organizational vehicle for the revolt against the remnants of the John L. Lewis regime led by Tony Boyle. A number of important reforms came with Arnold Miller's assumption of leadership —staff Cadillacs were sold off, inflated salaries were cut, District trusteeships ended, and in many instances District officials had to stand for election for the first time in half a century. But Miller's reforms were not enough to even begin to bring to the ranks what they had fought so hard for, and so in 1975 they (in effect) struck against Miller for the right to strike at the local level in order to obtain redress of grievances. What Miller had actually done was "Reutherize" the UMW. Its financial scandals were cleaned up, District officials were no longer appointed, and for the first time, like the auto workers, the miners had the right to vote to ratify their contracts. In return, however, Miller wanted what Reuther had and current UAW President Leonard Woodcock now has, central control over the right to strike. As always, every crisis in labor organizations is, at bottom, one of democracy. The ranks of the UMW are the first to have conducted a national strike explicitly for the right of the workers of a particular workplace to decide to strike that workplace. This is the fundamental issue across American industry today, in steel, auto, rubber, transportation, and the building trades, yet no section of the current rank-and-file leadership in any of those industries has been able to get the message clearly to the public. By itself, the issue has little in it to attract attention in the general population.

The United National Caucus (UNC) in the UAW has sustained itself as an opposition grouping for almost a decade. This is no small feat. But it has never really caught on. Afraid to dream a little, its program remains essentially within the confines of status quo collective bargaining. It has found no fundamental way of breaking out of existing boundaries. It seeks to mobilize on the basis of anger rather than hope. The same is true of the Teamsters for a Decent Contract (TDC). Though small, they constituted the only national opposition to Teamster President Fitzsimmons during the contract negotiations in March to April, 1976. We have to respect their courage, but not their main idea, which is "we can do it better than Fitz." Their literature failed to contain even the minimum required in order to conduct responsible opposition to a corrupt incumbent machine. No analysis was made of the unique nature of collective bargaining in the trucking industry, of the structure and nature of the industry itself and its power mechanism; no analysis was made of how the union actually works and is structured. During his career, Walter Reuther often moved further into verbal proposals for radical change than any of the concepts in the TDC program. Now that the contract is signed and Fitzsimmons is still in power a question is posed: how much luck will the top Teamster leadership have in winning over or intimidating some of the key members that TDC won to its ranks? How well are they armed with the ideas and resulting morale that makes principled resistance possible?

The League of Revolutionary Black Workers emerged from a series of wildcat strikes at Mahwah, New Jersey, Ford plant in the late 1960s. It linked with related developments mainly in the Detroit area that resulted in the formation of the Dodge, Ford, Eldon Avenue Chrysler, and other Revolutionary Union Movements (DRUM, FRUM, ELRUM, and several more). For a time it appeared that blacks might use their struggle to special advantage and build an organization in which oppositionists of any skin color could obtain cover and protection from victimization by union and employer officials. Understandably but tragically these organizations suffered initial defeats, then narrowed the constituency to which they were appealing and finally failed even to sustain their backing among young black assembly line workers with the lowest seniority.

On March 23 and 24, 1974, another opportunity was missed. On those two days, active labor-union women met in Chicago to form the Conference of Labor Union Women (CLUW). Here was a chance to channel some of the inspired energies of the new women's movement into sagging existing unions. Just for a start, America has thousands of workplaces containing hundreds of thousands of women who are not unionized. What could have happened if the existing union and federation leadership had given these women the freedom to go out and organize on the basis of their newfound sense of sisterhood? This is precisely what was denied to CLUW. The bureaucracy of labor allowed it no meaningful autonomy. The restrictions were not imposed on the conference merely through the efforts of women representing the male leadership of what are often referred to as the "conservative" unions. The fight to make CLUW an appendage was led by women from the "sophisticated left of center" unions like the UAW and AFSCME. They were able to win a majority of the conference. Those who opposed them had no alternative ideology or program. And so CLUW has withered.

Present in all the revolts and revolt organizations have been representatives, usually no more than a handful, of one or more of the sectarian leftwing groupings. Their statements and literature reflect considerable anger against the "system," but they have not led or aided any attempt to develop a vision of what might constitute the "good life" of the future in the context of a particular industry and workplace. Calls for a shop stewards movement, a labor party, or a workers' or workers'-and-farmers' government seem to fall on deaf ears at the same time that a deep radicalization is occurring in the American working class. Commonly young workers band together informally, having found that they are not able to relate to either the union officials or the leftists. The unions and the left, each in their own way, are into institutions and ideas built long ago which have become divorced from the way women and men live now. They are expert at national and international level problems and possible solutions. They are able to describe how workers' control might work at the national level. Never discussed is how "workers' control" might work in the workplace of their employ. That is a question on which every one of their fellow workers could speak with knowledge, expertise, and insight. If they did, who knows what new ideas might emerge? Also never debated in the labor movement is the widespread idea that "you can't fight progress." It has become commonplace for employers to introduce new machines and automated methods and then use the change in technology as cover for a speedup campaign that eliminates jobs. Workers disappear from the workplace with no more than token severance money. Those who remain often find their work considerably more routinized and barren. They complain but find no alternative vision to justify opposing the introduction of new machinery that eliminates jobs. They find no precedent even for the discussion of such a topic. Contained by old ideas, the revolts of the "new era" are still in their primitive and initial form, waiting for the awakening of native workplace activists who finally dare to voice their dreams.

Capital vs. Labor

40

David M. Gordon

Everyone is feeling the pinch of the current economic crisis. Consumers still face soaring prices. Workers face layoffs. Workers' real incomes have fallen back to 1964 levels. The poor suffer continuing cutbacks in essential social services. Even corporations—oh, pity their impoverished coffers—fear liquidity crises.

Most economic discussions have focused on the *appearances* of the crisis in the sphere of circulation. They have talked almost exclusively about the behavior of monetary variables like prices, wages, profits, and interest rates.

But there is another equally important dimension to the dynamics of the current crisis hiding beneath the surface of those economic aggregates [and] underlying policies and strategies [that frames] the growing struggle between corporations and working people in this country. The crisis *also* involves the conflict between capital and labor in the sphere of *production.* In order to understand the current situation, in order to discuss strategies for defending our own interests, we must focus clearly on these struggles in production as well.

IN THE BEGINNING

Conflict between capital and labor began to sharpen during the sustained boom of the mid 1960s.

From the corporations' perspective, prosperity continued longer than it should have. Continuous growth, however productive of jobs, is bad for profits. Continuous prosperity eventually threatens profits through the market mechanism. Individual capitalists—profit junkies

Reprinted from *Radical Perspectives on the Economic Crisis of Monopoly Capitalism* (New York: Union for Radical Political Economics, 1975), pp. 31–39, by permission of publisher.

on prosperity highs—invest feverishly during a boom. Sooner or later, they begin to exhaust the reserve supplies of workers. The labor market tightens. This overinvestment has two shattering consequences: wages begin to rise rapidly, *cutting into profits,* and workers take advantage of their scarcity by resisting the corporations' drive for profits more militantly and more effectively; worker productivity slows, *directly undercutting capitalist control of the production process.*

This was exactly what began to happen between 1965 and 1969. The economy had been growing steadily for almost five years. It was due for a cooling bath. The government could not afford to admit the costs of the war in Vietnam by raising taxes. The boom continued.

With labor markets tight, wages began to rise rapidly.[1] As the scarcity of labor sharpened, workers' resistance to corporate control of production grew. The growth of productivity slowed to one-quarter its rate of increase during the first half of the boom.[2] With their relative bargaining power increased, workers were slowing down the pace of their own work in resistance to corporate expansion.

In the age of monopoly capitalism, corporations normally try to protect profits through their practice of markup pricing. They try to pass on higher costs in higher prices, maintaining their margin of profits over average costs.[3] During the 1960s, however, international economic competition was intensifying. As a result of that growing competition, the risks to corporations of continually raising their prices had mounted. Especially in those industries like auto and steel where international competition was having its most direct effects, the limits on continuing price increases were clearly felt. Corporations found it more and more difficult to respond to rising labor costs and sagging worker productivity by hiking the price of their products.[4]

As a result, corporate profits suffered their classic decline during the last half of the boom.[5] Between 1965 and 1969, corporate profits as a

---

1. During the first half of the boom, from 1961 to 1965, wages increased an average of 3.9 percent a year. During the second half, from 1965 to 1969, they increased an average of 6.5 percent a year. See R. Boddy and J. Crotty, "Class Conflict, Keynesian Policies, and the Business Cycle," *Monthly Review,* (October, 1974): Table I.

2. During the first half of the boom, labor productivity rose at 6.5 percent a year. During the second half, it rose at 1.6 percent a year. Loc. cit.

3. William Nordhaus provides useful evidence that corporations had been following average cost markup pricing practices throughout the fifties and the early sixties. See W. Nordhaus, "The Falling Share of Profits," *Brookings Papers on Economic Activity,* Number 1, 1974.

4. Nordhaus (ibid.) also shows, from his own estimations, that the gap between aggregate prices and aggregate estimated "average total normal cost" fell to its lowest point in 1968 to 1969 since the mid-1950s. See Figure 5, p. 196.

5. This pattern repeated itself through all the postwar business cycles. See the data presented in Boddy and Crotty, op. cit.

share of national income began to fall and the ratio of profits to wages plunged.[6]

From the traditional Marxian perspective, capitalists will respond to rising wages by trying to substitute capital goods for labor, striving to increase relative surplus value by increasing the productiveness of workers.[7] During a continuing boom, however, corporations are reluctant to abandon current capacity, however inefficient, because the tight demand for their goods means that they can earn at least some profit on that production. As the profit squeeze continues, moreover, they find it increasingly difficult to salvage retained earnings for new investments in labor-saving machinery. When profits fall during periods of prosperity, in short, corporations find it difficult to compensate for the profit squeeze by labor-replacing investment.

During the late sixties' boom, typically, many corporations tried to overcome some of these problems by increasing their borrowing. They hoped to make up for the drop in internally generated retained earnings. Taking loans from someone else, they hoped to maintain their levels of investment in structures and equipment. The evidence of that borrowing is clear. Corporate indebtedness skyrocketed during the 1960s. Corporate debt/equity ratios soared. Corporate loans as a percentage of corporate product increased steadily.[8]

External financing of investment does not by itself provide a magic solution to the problems of the profit squeeze, however. Borrowing to finance investment brings heavy interest payments. By 1973, corporate interest payments had reached fully a quarter of total profits, eight times greater than their share immediately after World War II.[9] As the borrowing continued, interest payments began to represent nothing less than another source of the continuing drain on profits.

The character of capital accumulation, in these respects, had produced the seeds of sharper conflict between corporations and workers. Corporations had characteristically overinvested during the boom, sowing the seeds of a squeeze on their own profits. Workers had seized the time, taking advantage of their increasing strength (through scarcity) to resist the corporations' "werewolf hunger" for profits.

In the late sixties, it appears, that conflict became increasingly mani-

---

6. Absolute profits fell by 4.0 percent per year (in real terms) from 1965 to 1969. The ratio of profits to wages fell from .165 to .09 and the share of profits in gross corporate product fell from roughly 17 percent to 10 percent over the same period. See Boddy and Crotty, op. cit., and Nordhaus, op. cit.

7. This refers to the analysis in Volume I of *Capital*, Part V on the "Production of Absolute and Relative Surplus Value."

8. Complete data on the increase in corporate loans and on the increasingly shaky credit structure are presented in "Banks: Skating on Thin Ice," review of the month, *Monthly Review* (February, 1975).

9. See Nordhaus, ibid., p. 171.

fest in one particular and predictable form. In that kind of situation, Marxian theory would predict that corporations would seek to maintain and restore profits by *seeking to increase relative surplus value through the "intensification" of labor*—by trying to *speed up* the pace of production in order to get more output from workers in any given hour of the working day. Employer efforts to speed up production always encounter worker resistance. Brought about by an emergent intensification of capital-labor conflict in production, speedup was bound to intensify that conflict even more deeply.

And, by a variety of indications, that was precisely what began to happen in the late sixties. Especially in those industries suffering increasing international competition, evidence of speedup and worker resistance abounds.

One interesting indication of speedup involves industrial accidents. When corporations are trying to substitute capital for labor, industrial accidents appear to fall.[10] Indeed, the incidence of industrial accidents had been falling in this country since World War I, a period during which corporations had been turning more and more to automation.[11] But during the sixties, as speedup began to replace or complement labor-saving investment, the rate of industrial accidents began to rise for the first time in fifty years. The rate of industrial accidents in manufacturing was 27.7 per cent higher in 1970 than it was in 1963.[12]

Workers do not endure such speedups and accidents without pro-

---

10. Marx had argued, in Volume I of *Capital,* that employers' ability to increase relative surplus value through the intensification of labor was indeterminate, in part, because workers might get worn out or injured by speedup too quickly and would have to be replaced. Increasing their productiveness as a means of increasing relative surplus value did not suffer that indeterminacy, clearly, because workers were much less likely to get injured.

11. One consistent series on work injuries in manufacturing extends from 1926 to 1970. The incidence of injuries, measured as hours lost through disabling work accidents over millions of man-hours worked, fell from its peak in 1926, at the beginning of the series, almost continuously to the early 1960s, when it began to level off at exactly half the 1926 peak. See the U.S. Bureau of Census, *Historical Statistics of the United States, Colonial Times to 1957* (Washington, D.C.: U.S. Government Printing Office, 1960), p. 100, for data up to 1956; and the *President's Report on Occupational Safety and Health* (Washington, D.C.: U.S. Government Printing Office, 1972), Appendix B, Work Injury Rates by Industry, 1958–1970, pp. 71ff. for more recent data.

12. See the *President's Report on Occupational Safety and Health,* ibid., Appendix B. There is further evidence from that table that the increases in injury rates came especially in those industries which had previously experienced the most substantial labor displacement through automation. In what Robert Averitt calls "core industries," those concentrated industries in which market power and capital/labor ratios are highest, the average increase in the incidence of industrial accidents between 1963 and 1970 was nearly 50 percent, or almost twice the overall increase in manufacturing. See Robert Averitt, *The Dual Economy* (N.Y.: W. W. Norton, 1968) for the distinction between core and peripheral industries; and David M. Gordon, "Class and Segmentation in the United States: A Methodological and Empirical Review," New School for Social Research, 1975 in progress, for the basis for the empirical distinction between the two sectors.

test. They feel it in their muscles and they suffer it when they get hurt. At least partly in response to speedup, wildcat strikes began to increase during the late 1960s. Workers marched out of the plants protesting working conditions. Reflecting their anger, the index of aggregate strike activity began to climb along with the rate of accidents. Work time lost through strikes climbed in 1970 to 3½ times its 1963 levels.[13] The number of workers involved in work stoppages waged in protest over "speedup" itself increased by 350 percent from 1965 to 1969 and absolute work time lost through stoppages over "speedup" increased by 240 percent during the same years.[14]

Corporations began to panic. Their profits were being squeezed and workers were beginning to resist their efforts at intensification. "Many manufacturing executives . . . [had] openly complained in recent years," the *Wall Street Journal* observed, looking back from 1972, "that too much control had passed from management to labor." So we began to hear the hue and cry of the famous "productivity crisis." America was losing its position of international economic advantage, we were told, because our workers weren't working hard enough. All those lazy workers, taking off Mondays and Fridays! To save America, we all had to work a little harder. The National Commission on Productivity posted billboards along the highways, urging us to knuckle down.

The workers' struggles at the GM Vega plant in Lordstown, Ohio, were symptomatic of these developments. The auto industry had been suffering especially hard from international competition. They had been hiring into new segments of the labor force. Throughout the industry, tremors of concern about "absenteeism" were spreading. In response to that concern, the GMAD division of GM—the tough guys, the marine corps of the company—had assumed management of the Lordstown plant in 1971. As *Business Week* had reported, "The need for GMAD's belt-tightening role was underscored during the late 1960s when GM's profit margin dropped from 10 percent to 7 percent."[15] Among its "modernizing" innovations, GMAD increased the speed of the line from 60 cars per hour to over 100—as pure an example of speedup as one finds in modern industry. The workers protested and finally struck. The press talked innocently about changes in workers' attitudes, about some new, mystifying preoccupation with nonmonetary issues. The workers talked quite simply about the speed of the line. As the local

13. For these aggregate strike data, see the U.S. Bureau of Labor Statistics, *Handbook of Labor Statistics,* Bulletin 1923, 1974, Table on Work Stoppages in the United States, 1927–1972. The complete series is reproduced in Table 40–1.

14. Data on strikes by objectives and grievance are compiled in *Handbook of Labor Statistics,* ibid., pp. 373ff.

15. Quoted in Stanley Aronowitz, *False Promises* (N.Y.: McGraw-Hill, 1974), p. 22.

union president observed, "people refused to do extra work. The more the company pressured them, the less work they turned out. Cars went down the line without repairs."[16]

CONTROLS SHIFT THE TERMS OF STRUGGLE

As the boom continued, as profits eroded, as workers resisted speedup, it become more and more obvious to corporations and the government that workers' strength had to be directly attacked. When the Nixon administration assumed power in 1969, it moved quickly. Nixon knew the classic remedy. He slammed on the fiscal and monetary brakes immediately. The recession of 1969 to 1970 followed quickly.

But time was short. Because the boom had continued so long, it would take several years for the recession to exercise its fully "restorative" powers, curbing workers' strength, paring away inefficient enterprises. That was too long to wait it out. Nixon was afraid to campaign for president with millions out of work. Corporate profits had fallen to such low levels by 1969 that few businesses could easily countenance the prospect of a sustained recession.

So the administration restored the juice in late 1970. The meters indicated by early 1971 that the economy was still racing too fast. Prices were climbing. Workers were resuming their strikes. Huge labor contract settlements, as high as 15 percent, chilled corporate spines. More important, profits fell in 1971 to their lowest share of national income since World War II.[17]

The administration had few options. It had refused to wait out a sustained recession. Untempered boom could prove disastrous for profits; workers' strength and militance would continue. Continually rising prices would also poison the balance of payments, whose trade deficits were deteriorating every month. "Caught in this trap," as *Business Week* editorialized at the time, "there is only one thing the administration can do."[18] Nixon established his New Economic Policy as a compromise. Stimulative measures would continue, but a wage-price freeze would hopefully contain the fires which short-lived recession had failed to cool.

The president assured the public, of course, that controls were designed to protect us all from the ravages of inflation. In fact, their purpose was quite different. Workers had to be disciplined so that profits could recover. Explaining the exclusion of profits from the freeze, Nixon said that "all Americans will benefit from more profits." Arnold

---

16. Quoted in ibid., p. 42.
17. See the tabulations in Nordhaus, op cit.
18. *Business Week,* August 14, 1971, p. 110.

Weber, the freeze administrator, wrote later in sanitized language that "The Cost of Living Council was reluctant to control profits at a time when . . . they were already at a relatively low level."[19] He admitted more candidly in a recent interview with Clayton Fritchey that business "had been leaning" on the administration "to do something about wages." "The idea of the freeze and Phase II was to zap labor and we did."[20]

They did indeed. Wages were carefully controlled while price increases, more difficult to control, permitted profits' momentary recovery by late 1972. Equally important, wage controls also curbed workers' militance. Strike activity began to fall rapidly as workers recognized the impossibilities of improving their living standards by exercising their right to strike. By 1973, during the last year of the guidelines, the index of work time lost through work stoppages had fallen back to its levels of the early sixties before the conflict had sharpened.[21]

The timing of controls was important too. Large numbers of important contracts were expiring in late 1971 and early 1972. By racing to institute controls in August, 1971, the government helped corporations forestall a bitter round of bargaining negotiations at precisely that point when workers' anger was rising most dramatically. For many industries, the timing of the controls bought the corporations a three-year lease on life—most major contracts have three-year terms—a respite during which they were assured of at least wage moderation. At the time, many hoped, the controls would be temporary, necessary for the moment to get corporations over the hump of a difficult bargaining period. "Next year," as *Business Week* reasoned soothingly in August, 1971, "there are not as many large contracts coming up as this year."[22] It was precisely at this point that the public relations campaign announcing the "productivity crisis" reached its peak, seeking to convince workers to settle into a more intense pace, to tolerate their loss of bargaining power over wages.

While the controls worked for the moment, they did not restore economic stability. Indeed, they largely compounded prevailing distortions by freezing them. When Phase IV guidelines were lifted in March, 1974, the economic crisis exploded around the world. Many corporations raced to increase their prices as soon as they were permitted. Workers were beginning to experience the sharp decline in their real

19. Arnold Weber, *In Pursuit of Price Stability: The Wage-Price Freeze of 1971* (Washington, D.C.: The Brookings Institution, 1973), p. 38.

20. Quoted in Clayton Fritchey's column, *The New York Post,* September 19, 1974.

21. Data on work stoppages since 1972 come from Bureau of Labor Statistics, *Current Wage Developments,* 26-12 (December, 1974): 32. Putting the separate sources together, I have tabulated the incidence of strike activity over the whole period in Table 40–1.

22. *Business Week,* August 7, 1971.

earnings by May. In protest, workers marched out on strike again.[23] By 1974, it seems clear, we were still suffering the consequences of the postponement of recession in the mid-1960s. No substitute had yet been found for the normal functions of recessions. Corporations were still looking for ways of squeezing more profits out of workers. Workers were growing angrier every month, more and more strenuously resisting those corporate efforts. We were still living with an economy, in *Business Week*'s muted words, "that had yet to go through normal business cycle adjustment."[24]

Table 40-1. The Incidence of Strike Activity, 1960-1974

Year	Percent of Total Man-Days Idle
1960	0.14
1961	.11
1962	.13
1963	.11
1964	.15
1965	.15
1966	.15
1967	.25
1968	.28
1969	.24
1970	.37
1971	.26
1972	.15
1973	.15
1974	.22[a]

Source: Cited in footnotes 13 and 21.
[a]The figure for 1974 is an approximate weighted average of the monthly data, with actual figures through September and estimated figures through December.

What to do?

Business leaders and the business press appreciated the magnitude of the moment. *Business Week* editorialized in October, 1974:[25]

It is inevitable that the U.S. economy will grow more slowly . . . Some people will obviously have to do with less . . . The basic health of the U.S. is based on the basic health of its corporations and banks . . . Yet it will be a hard pill for many Americans to swallow—the idea of doing with less so that big business can have more. It will be particularly hard to swallow because it is quite obvious that . . . they are in large measure the cause of . . . what ails the Debt Economy.

23. The monthly strike data soared during June and July. See the source in footnote 21 above.
24. *Business Week*, February 3, 1975, p. 66.
25. *Business Week*, October 12, 1974.

THE INVISIBLE HAND'S LAST STAND

The Ford administration appeared indecisive. But the Ford administration made its clear choice. Dominated by the advice of free marketeers like Alan Greenspan and William Simon, the administration vowed to stage the Invisible Hand's Last Stand. They understood that the basis for corporate profits could only be restored if labor's strength was broken and inefficient corporations were eliminated. If the modern economy had dulled the market's razor, then sharpen it!

The administration made its choice in 1973. Production bottlenecks were about to force the discontinuation of wage-price guidelines. The economy had not yet cooled.

Worse yet, corporations were about to face an extraordinarily intense period of collective bargaining. During 1974 and the first half of 1975, contracts covering two-thirds of all workers protected by "major contracts" were expiring.[26] Many of these contracts, lasting three years, had been negotiated just after controls had been imposed in August, 1971. Workers in those unions were bristling for a fight, anxious to try to compensate for the real wage losses they suffered during contracts negotiated under the club of controls.

More specifically, corporations looked ahead in early 1974 to the expiration, among others, of the Communication Workers' contract in July, the Steelworkers' contract in August, scores of aerospace contracts in October, the Mineworkers' contract in November, the railroad contracts in December, hundreds of construction, utilities and food workers' contracts throughout the early part of 1975.

In many of those negotiations, workers were not only going to be struggling to make up for past real wage losses but were also going to be demanding cost-of-living escalator clauses which would automatically adjust their contractual wages to rises in the cost-of-living index. (As of October, 1974, only 45 percent of workers covered by major contracts were protected by cost-of-living escalator clauses, and none of these clauses provided for a penny-for-penny full adjustment.[27]) The administration and the mine companies expected that at least the miners would strike and that an expensive settlement in the mines would set the trend for more expensive settlements later on.

If wage controls could not be continued politically, then it must have seemed fairly clear, in the early months of 1974, that another return to a period of recession was necessary, *if for no other reason* than to curb

---

26. For information on contract expiration, see U.S. Bureau of Labor Statistics, "Wage Calendar 1974." Bulletin #1310, 1974, p. 2. There were 10.3 million workers in the United States covered by major contracts including 1,000 workers or more in early 1975.

27. Cost-of-living clause information comes from "Wage Calendar, 1974," ibid., p. 4. Only about 6,000,000 workers not covered by major contracts have escalator clauses so that, of all 85 million workers in the United States, only about 4.6 million—or barely more than five percent—received such protection in early 1975.

labor's bargaining power during the negotiations in the months ahead. As a British banker admitted during the same period, in arguing for a recession with somewhat more candor than we Americans are accustomed to, "We've got to get some discipline back into this country's work force, and the only way to do it is to make the blokes damn grateful to have any sort of job at all."[28]

The administration moved quickly. Government spending was cut sharply in the middle of 1973, with the "full-employment budget" falling quickly from deficit to surplus. The monetary screws were tightened soon after. In a fact sheet accompanying Ford's economic address last fall, the White House regretted that "twice within the past decade, in 1967 and in 1971 to 1972, we let an opportunity to regain price stability slip through our grasp."[29] The administration vowed not to repeat the mistake. As Pierre Rinfret, a leading economic consultant to the business world, put it, the administration's policy was one of "benign neglect—there is no program and it has been done on purpose. Greenspan wants to let the economy take a deep bath to correct inflation."[30]

From the corporate perspective, of course, the strategy is working while it lasts. Real wages have fallen sharply. Workers seem subdued, with the incidence of strike activity down. As one American labor leader explained, "Layoffs take the steam out of members. . . . They take away the urge to strike."[31]

Perhaps even more crucially, the combination of the administration's sweet-talking public relations campaign and the impact of the recession has had an impact on some of the crucial bargaining sessions of the period. The United Mine Workers Union did strike, as expected, in November. Demanding substantial wage recovery, they were able to win large wage increases. But in the last stages of their negotiations, despite those successes, the union leadership began to soften some of its demands. Many rank-and-file mineworkers had been demanding a concrete contractual protection of their right to engage in wildcat strikes. The leadership met several times with the Ford administration and, according to informal reports, began to wear down under the insistent argument that a prolonged strike would irreparably deepen the recession. We were all in this together, the UMW leaders heard for the 600th time, and the litany softened their determination. Much to the dismay of large blocks of the rank-and-file membership, who actually

28. Quoted in the *Wall Street Journal*, November 18, 1974, p. 1.
29. Quoted in R. Boddy and J. Crotty, op. cit.
30. Quoted in *Newsweek*, February 28, 1975.
31. Quoted in the *Wall Street Journal*, December 18, 1974.

opposed ratification of the contract, the leadership gave in on the wild-cat strike protection issue.

It would be a mistake to exaggerate the importance of government policy in dealing with the economic crisis. Structural instabilities promoted the present crisis and world economic instability may cause a much deeper collapse than the administration "intended." It is nonetheless important to be clear about the factors which affect the *timing* of changes in government policies.

The present plunge began as a politically induced recession in late 1973. A crucial period of collective bargaining was approaching. Recession represented a necessary stage in the evolving corporate and government attempt to restore labor discipline. By now, if political pressures force the administration to abandon its recessionary strategy and re-stimulate the economy, circumstances make them much more amenable than they were. After June, 1975, the bargaining calendar will be virtually empty for more than a year. Major contracts covering only 500,000 workers, or five percent of workers covered by major contracts, will expire in the second half of 1975. In the first half of 1976, only the Teamsters among major unions will be negotiating. After June, 1975, that is, the need for a cool economy to cool workers will have diminished. Combining the velvet glove of moral suasion and the iron fist of recession, corporations and the government will have played out their moves during this first stage of the crisis.

During that stage, working people in this country are being asked to provide the basis for restoring profits by sacrificing their jobs, their social services, their livelihoods, and their standards of living. Recession has had many causes, but recession has also been permitted and exacerbated by conscious, calculated *political* decisions made at the top. Those of us attacked by those decisions must take direct *political* action to overcome that strategy. They know that the political risks of a long recession are high. We must prove them right.

When we do, and the government is forced to pull out of the recession, the economy will still be skidding in an inflationary direction. What next?

STATE PLANNING LOOMS

It seems clear, from reading the business press, that corporations will begin to press very quickly for a new kind of economic management in this country. Recession to cool out the economy will be too costly. Normal expansion, in this time of crisis, will involve too much inflation and dislocation. Expansion with price controls will be necessary. But most people admit that the first stage of wage-price controls, from 1971 to early 1974, fell apart at least partly because bottlenecks and shortages developed. This time around, corporations recognize that more extensive management of the economy will be required. Wage and price controls will be insufficient. It will also be necessary to exercise government management over investment policies and credit policies—in short, over the allocation of resources.[32]

It will be important to remember, as we approach that stage of management, that corporations will be seeking planning for their own benefit. And such corporate planning will, as always, have two aspects.

One aspect will focus on the distribution of income between profits and wages. If prices and wages will be controlled, corporations will obviously seek to manipulate the planning process in order to protect profits at the expense of wages. Looking ahead, foreseeing this direction, some unions are racing to negotiate their contracts before controls begin. Negotiating during recession is bad enough, but negotiating during controls may be worse. The west coast dock workers, for instance, are requesting early expiration of their contract in order to get a new contract before controls resume. As Harry Bridges, the longshoremens' union leader, explained recently, "We've got to worry about controls because controls won't be equitable."[33]

Another aspect of the struggle in a period of planning will necessarily involve the sphere of production. If prices, wages, and profits are controlled during a period of planning, corporations will be seeking—among other tactics—to deepen their control over the production process in order to get as much surplus value out of workers in production as they can. Their degrees of freedom for protecting and improving their profits in the sphere of exchange will be more limited. Correspondingly, they will seek to reorganize and intensify production in order to make up for whatever they may lose under price controls.

Some of these kinds of developments seem to have occurred during the first, more limited, stage of wage-price controls from 1971 to 1974. Facing limited price controls, corporations appear to have tried to change work rules in order to get more work out of their employees. During 1972, the first full year of wage-price controls, workers' wildcat strikes over "work-rules" grievances soared, climbing to ten times their levels in 1965 and 1966 and almost four times their levels during 1968 in the peak of speedup.[34] If and when these contests in production begin, workers will depend fundamentally on their right to strike over grievances, on their right to protest attacks in production by withholding their labor. Corporations recognize that crucial fact, of course. Slowly but surely, the first signs of an attack on workers' right to strike

---

32. See the piece by Bill Tabb on economic planning in *Radical Perspectives on the Economic Crisis of Monopoly Capitalism* (New York: URPE, 1975).

33. Quoted in the *Wall Street Journal*, December 18, 1974, p. 27.

34. Based on the data cited in footnote 14 above.

have begun to appear. Two recent legal decisions provide the barest hint of that attack.

The first involves the right of workers to strike over outstanding issues in contract negotiations. During negotiations in the steel industry last year, the corporations convinced the steelworkers union leadership to accept a "no-strike agreement," under the terms of which the union agreed not to strike over outstanding bargaining disagreements but to submit them to compulsory arbitration. Rank-and-file steel workers challenged that agreement in court. The no-strike agreement was upheld by the U.S. District Court in which the case was heard. In supporting the corporations and the union, the District Court judge argued that "in any system of self-government, in theory and in practice, even the most precious of rights may be waived . . . In denying plaintiffs the relief they seek, this Court does no more than permit the [no-strike] negotiating procedures to proceed as, at least potentially, an evolutionary step forward in labor relations."[35]

The second precedent involves the right to wildcat strike over specific grievances during the terms of contract. A Supreme Court decision of 1962 had ruled that federal district courts could *not* issue injunctions against wildcat strikes even though such strikes represented a breach of a no-strike provision in a contract which guaranteed binding arbitration of the dispute. In a potentially historic decision in 1970, the new Nixon Supreme Court overturned that earlier decision. It argued that district courts could and should issue injunctions halting wildcat strikes in such situations. The intent of the decision was clear. Arbitration must prevail and strikes must not. The majority decision argued that "the very purpose of arbitration procedures is to provide a mechanism for the expeditious settlement of industrial disputes without resort to strikes, lockouts, or other self-help measures."[36] Since almost all contracts currently provide for arbitration, the decision potentially provides the basis for court injunctions against all wildcat strikes over any issues *unless* the contract explicitly guarantees, in writing, the workers' right to engage in wildcat strikes. It was such protection which many rank-and-file mineworkers sought in their 1974 negotiations—explicitly mindful of the 1970 Court decision—and which they were unable to obtain.

In this context, armed with these kinds of court precedents, employers will undoubtedly press ahead with their public relations campaigns during the stage of planning if and when it arrives. Talk of the "produc-

---

35. Hubert I. Teitelbaum, "Opinion of Court," Aikens et al. vs. I. W. Abel et al., No. 74-17 Civil Action, in the United States Court for the Western District of Pennsylvania, pp. 22–33.

36. See Boys Markets, Inc. v. Retail Clerks Local 770, 398 U.S. 235, 90 S. Ct. 1583, 26 L. Ed. 2d (1970), opinion reprinted in *Labor Relations Law,* ed. R. A. Smith et al., *1973 Cumulative Supplement* (N.Y.: Bobbs-Merrill, 1973), p. 147.

tivity crisis" will undoubtedly resume. Workers will once again be asked to pay the costs of economic crises with their muscles and their sweat in production.

In short, if and when planning comes workers must recognize that, as before, the economic crisis will continue to unfold at two levels. In the sphere of circulation, political struggle will take place over the division between profits and wages through the mechanisms of wage and price controls. In the sphere of production, necessarily, political struggle will take place over how hard workers must labor in the service of employers' surplus value. Through every stage, at every moment, workers must maintain their strength and their militance in both these spheres, at both those levels, to protect their rights.

Big Business vs. Organized Labor: Class Conflict and Governmental Redistribution in the United States

41

Alexander Hicks, Roger Friedland, and Edwin Johnson

This paper summarizes some of our research on the determinants of public policy in the 48 mainland states of the United States. Our preliminary findings suggest that large corporations and labor unions have significant and opposite effects upon redistributive policy in the United States.[1]

Governmental redistribution is defined here as the extent to which the total spending and taxing activities of a governmental unit redistribute income (whether as cash, goods, or services) to a particular income group or class. During the last thirty years, governmental redistribution in the United States has resulted in net transfers of income *to* the poor, involving sizeable portions of national income.[2] Redistributive policies have been important features of governmental policy in all of the more advanced industrialized nations since, at least, the early post-World War II period.[3] Some typical policies that have contributed to levels of

---

This article was written especially for this edition of *American Society, Inc.*

1. See Alexander Hicks, Roger Friedland, and Edwin Johnson's "The Political Economy of Redistribution," unpublished paper, Department of Sociology, University of Wisconsin, Madison, 1976; and also Roger Friedland's *Class Power and the Central City*, unpublished Ph.D. dissertation, University of Wisconsin, Madison, 1976.

2. See Morgan Reynolds and Eugene Smolensky's "The Post-Fisc Distribution 1961 and 1970 Compared," *The National Tax Journal* 27 (December 1974):515–30; and see the same authors' *Public Expenditures, Taxes and the Distribution of Income: The U.S.: 1950, 1961, and 1970* (New York: Academic Press, forthcoming). Our definition and measure (cf. Booms and Halldorson below) of redistribution is limited to so-called "first order" tallies of net values more or less directly taxed from or allocated to households, and does not take account of the impact of government fiscal activities upon distributions of wages and earnings. A complex debate is now emerging which focuses upon the latter kind of impact of governmental spending and taxing upon income distributions. See Jeffrey G. Williamson's "Who Pays for the Services of America's Working Poor?" Discussion Paper 334–76, *Institute for Research on Poverty*, University of Wisconsin, Madison, 1976.

3. See, for examples, Andrew Schonfeld's *Modern Capitalism* (New York: Oxford University Press, 1966), pp. 3–18, and Andrew Martin's *The Politics of Economic Policy in the United States* (Beverly Hills, Calif.: Sage, 1972).

governmental redistribution have been social insurance pensions, unemployment compensation, and progressive income taxes. State governments have been highly important for governmental redistribution in the United States. State governments on the average have spent about a third of U.S. governmental expenditures and raised about a quarter of total U.S. tax revenues during the past quarter-century.[4]

We expected national business corporations and organized labor to have opposite effects upon governmental redistribution in the American states. The impact of organized labor would be positive, while the corporations would have a negative impact. Our reasoning is based on theory and research about their *interests* in governmental redistribution and their political *resources* for realizing these interests by influencing redistributive policies. The direction and significance of a set of organizations upon public policies largely derive from their policy interests and political resources.

We expected large corporation interests to be antiredistributive for several reasons: Information on business-elite attitudes and accounts of the political activities of big business show that large corporations oppose redistributive policies. Further, the political resources of large corporations are numerous and substantial. Well-financed public relations and lobbying specialists, effective monopolies of governmentally required information and expertise, control over the dispensation of many forms of monetary and status rewards, and discretionary power over tax bases and credit decisions upon which governments depend for their fiscal solvency are but a few of the resources they have to realize their political interests.[5]

The opposite applies to the overall interests of labor unions in governmental redistribution. They are proredistributive, according to survey research of labor leader attitudes and case studies of organized labor's political activities. Organized labor's political resources are also considerable. It has the capacity and reputation for being able to mobilize the vote of union members and its own well-financed public relations and lobbying specialists. In some contexts, it may make effective use of its power to strike.[6]

---

4. See Ira Sharkansky's *The Maligned States* (New York: McGraw-Hill, 1972).

5. See Allen H. Barton's "Consensus and Conflict Among American Leaders," *Public Opinion Quarterly* 38 (Winter 1975):507–30 on business elite attitudes; see Duane Lockard's *New England State Politics* (Princeton, N.J.: Princeton University Press) for one of many accounts of business' political activities at the state level of government; and see Robert R. Alford and Roger Friedland's "Political Participation," *Annual Review of Sociology*, Vol. I (1975), published in Palo Alto, California by Annual Review incorporated, edited by Alex Inkles, James Coleman and Neil Smelser, for an incisive discussion of political power.

6. See Allen H. Barton, op. cit., on the redistributive attitudes of labor elites; and see J. David Greenstone's *Labor in American Politics* (New York: Knopf, 1971) on political attitudes.

Governmental redistribution was measured using an index which measures the ratio of net expenditure benefits to net revenue burdens for households with incomes under $4000.[7] The presence of national business corporations and of organized labor in states was measured using summary indices, each based on several indicators. Each index emphasized organizational attributes related to centers of policy making (e.g. the number of the largest 500 manufacturing corporations with national headquarters in a given state) and political resources (e.g. the number of AFL-CIO members in a given state).

The results of a statistical (i.e. regression) analysis of determinants of governmental redistribution in the American states are presented in Table 41–1.

Along with measures of governmental redistribution and of the presence of large corporations and organized labor we have included a summary measure of state income, education, and occupational composition (labeled "socioeconomic development"), the proportion of households below the 1961 poverty line, "governor tenure potential" (an indicator of gubernatorial centralization of state political systems) and "policy innovativeness" (or how quickly states adapt new policies).[8] The signs (plus or minus) of the B-coefficients of Table 41–1 may be interpreted as statements of the directions in which given variables influence governmental redistribution (e.g., plus signs denote positive influences). The absolute sizes of these coefficients may be interpreted as approximate indications of the strength of such influences.

As can be seen by perusing Table 41–1, the influences of national business corporations and of organized labor upon governmental redistribution are in the directions that we had hypothesized. The presence of organized labor has a significant positive impact on governmental

---

7. For an explication of the Booms and Halldorson index, see their "The Politics of Redistribution: A Reformulation," *American Political Science Review* (September 1973): 920–33; for explications of the other variables and measures used in this Paper see Hicks, et al., op. cit.

8. These "additional" variables are included in this model primarily in order to minimize a kind of distortion that would have resulted for our B-coefficients for national business corporations and organized labor had they not been included. The kind of distortion at issue is called specification bias. It results when independent variables that are related to a given dependent variable in a regression equation *and* are also correlated with the equation's dependent variable are excluded from the equation. Our "additional" variables would have fit these conditions for specification bias. The "additional" variables presented in Table 41–1 are a subset of a selection of all of the variables from the wide ranging analysis of governmental redistribution in Booms and Halldorson, op. cit., that either had statistically significant ($p > .05$) or large ($B > .20$) impacts upon redistribution. Those "additional" variables that were not statistically significant in one prior run including all of the "additional" variables selected were excluded from the second run, the results of which are presented in Table 41–1.

It should be noted that we have elsewhere run more elaborate models of governmental redistribution, including a number of new variables and measures and multiplicative as well as additive specifications. The results of such runs expand on and refine but do not contradict the results of the simple model presented here. Hicks, et al., op. cit.

Table 41-1. Results from the Multiple Regression of Governmental Redistribution Upon "National Business Corporations," "Organized Labor," and Some Additional Variables ($N = 48$)

Independent Variables	B or Standardized Regression Coefficients	Statistical Significance Level
National Business Corporations	−.342	.041
Organized Labor	.418	.036
Poverty	.648	.008
Development	.456	.004
Governor Tenure Potential	.260	.012
Policy Innovativeness	.486	.045

Note: R^2 = Coefficient of determination correcting for degrees of freedom. R^2 = .656

redistribution, while the impact of the corporations is negative. As the standardized coefficients show, these influences are moderate to large.[9] The above state findings, of course, do not address the question of *how* business corporations exercise their influence upon redistributive policies.[10]

Large corporations and labor unions have received very little attention in the study of public policy, especially in studies disciplined by quantitative data and statistical techniques. Hopefully this paper not only provides important findings on the political process but also will stimulate rigorous scholarly attention to the roles of corporations and labor unions in generating public policy.

The question remains, what do our findings mean from the standpoint of a class analysis of politics? In brief, we regard large corporations as capitalist class organizations to the extent that they are directed at their highest policymaking levels *by* members of the capitalist class and, primarily, *toward* capitalist class goals. We consider as constituting the capitalist class those families and individuals who receive the bulk of their income in the form of profits, dividends, capital gains, rents and interest. The generation of such asset income is the overriding goal of this class. In contrast, labor unions are working class organizations insofar as they are directed by working-class persons and toward working-class goals. The families and individuals who have no income from

9. A comparable analysis of America's 130 largest central cities found that large corporations and organized labor had opposing impacts upon local War on Poverty funding levels. See Roger Friedland, op. cit.

10. Because of space constraints we will leave the evaluation and interpretation of the impacts of "Poverty," "Development," "Governor Tenure Potential," and "Policy Innovativeness" to the thought and judgement of our readers, who may find it useful to consult Fry and Winters, "The Politics of Redistribution," *American Political Science Review* 49 (June 1970):508–22 and Hicks et al., op. cit., 1976.

property and no authority in workplaces constitute the working class. One major objective, then, of the working class is to maintain and increase its share of the national income as opposed to the interests of the capitalist class in reducing real labor costs.

Thus, the impacts of corporations and unions upon governmental policy are *class* impacts and manifestations of *class power.* Our findings show opposing class impacts upon redistributive policy and, consequentially, indicate *the presence of class conflict in the contemporary United States.*

Of course, the findings presented here concern the influences of different social forces on existing variations in redistributive policies in American states around 1960. Our findings do not speak to the extent to which different social forces actually determine the limits within which "realistic" policy options are constrained. Nor do our findings necessarily challenge the received opinion that class politics in the United States are relatively moderate, even when measured by so limited a yardstick as the class politics of western Europe. What is clear, however, is that the impact of class power and class conflict on public policy in the United States has received little systematic attention in American society during the past quarter-century.[11]

11. For clear but detailed explications of the concept of class, see Erik O. Wright and Lucca Perrone, "Marxist Class Categories and Income Inequality" and Erik O. Wright "Class Boundaries in Advanced Capitalist Societies," unpublished papers, Department of Sociology, University of Wisconsin, Madison, 1976. For a more detailed discussion of the relation of class to policy, see Hicks et al., op. cit.

Steelmill Blues

Steve Packard

Matt calls. Bad connection. But his voice gets through, wild almost with a sort of ecstasy, and I'm going to have to decide fast. He says they're sure to hire him and me and another guy if we go tomorrow.

"Gary, Indiana?" I say. "Isn't that a whole long . . ."

"Sure it is!" he jumps back at me through the buzzing, clicking lines. "It'll take more than an hour, maybe an hour and a half, each way. But it's the perfect organizer's job. And really, my idealistic friend, how far is it? Some middle-class executive would go that far for a little money. Yes?"

I've been resisting this. But my life sure does need a new direction. I think my basic reaction is: thrilled.

Matt and John pick me up early next morning in an old Chevy. Matt's eyes truly shine—like this job will be one of life's great blessings, the pure smile of a kid's birthday party or a fisherman setting first boot into a trout stream on his one-week vacation.

At the first break in the joking and small talk, I ask Matt where he's taking us. Yesterday he wouldn't say because the phones are tapped and secret listeners all too easily could warn big business that we're coming. (Members of his collective have been fired recently, following visits to their plants by FBI agents.) But even now Matt relishes his secret. Finally he pauses, looks across to me, tilts back his head, and says, "Gary Works." In fact he says it with such a note of triumph I don't dare admit it means nothing to me. I just keep talking and look for clues.

Matt gives an analysis of the situation we're getting into. "Now the strike's coming up, you know. They'll hire anything white that's strong enough to walk in the door. Most predictions say it should be a long one, which means a heightened political situation between now and August when the contract runs out, and a potentially explosive situation after that. There's no better time for you to learn!" He pauses for questions. Then continues, "You guys'll be surprised in the mill. You'll see that Negroes do the hardest and dirtiest jobs, sure. But they have tremendous power, because they're organized, and the mill stops without them. Without steel the whole country stops. And the Negroes know it."

"So should I expect blacks to play a leading role in the, you know, rank-and-file caucuses that fight the unions?" I can't wait to really get into all this stuff.

But Matt's smile fades. "Look Steve," he says slowly, "I think that there's a lot in the collective's politics you could learn from. Rank-and-file caucuses are no way to organize anything. No power there. They always *say* that they're fighting the union. But I. W. Abel's bunch was a rank-and-file caucus before he got to be president of the steelworkers. He did what he had to, to make a name for himself. Now he's in, and it hasn't meant a damn. Even if Able had the Ivory Snow purest heart in all of capitalism, it wouldn't mean a damn, because the whole union System is what's wrong. If you want to organize real worker's power, you organize it right on the shop floor. Wildcats, job actions, whatever. No contracts. No white-shirted men in offices. It's the workers who are going to have to overthrow the place and run it."

I'm sure I do have a lot to learn. But I manage to fake my way through personnel quite well. Take off my clothes and put them back on with forty other assorted applicants, and listen to a lecture about hard work and how all the country's problems are because workers are lazy. That seems to be the big test. But I don't throw up, and neither does anyone else, and they hire us all.

Gary Works. United States Steel. Biggest plant in America. When you get a new job, so many things are happening at the same time you get a little stoned. Maybe you manage to steer your way through, but only vaguely in touch with half of what flows by.

I work in Merchant Mills. The main warehouse building is just a couple of blocks wide. But it's so long, if you stand in the middle you can't see halfway through the gloom to either end. Huge doors are everywhere, always open, snow piles in around the edges.

On the long east side of the place are the twelve "mills" sticking out from the main building like the teeth of an Afro comb. Each long skinny rolling mill is the length of a football field; red-hot ribbons of steel come snaking streaking down it. By the time the ribbons get to us they're usually gray, but still hot enough to cook your lunch on. Our job is to cut them to the right lengths. To test and inspect them for special uses. To straighten or flatten them in enormous noisy machines. To finally tie piles with steel wire, or bind them with metal bands.

Every morning I get to Gary about fifteen minutes before work. The whole city-sized mill complex is surrounded by a high metal fence and a dark moat of chemical-smelling water, once a river, now the lower end of the alimentary canal that feeds U.S. Steel's waste products into Lake Michigan. The inner defense perimeter consists of a guard house and a gate where armed men look at our I.D. cards, make sure we match our pictures, then give us our daily IBM cards. I write my name and company number on the top of it.

Next, to the gray washhouse and filthy clothes. After one day these clothes are the kind of dirty that lets them stand in the locker by themselves. I get into my regulation metatarsal shoes with the metal plates over the top so it's harder to break your foot. I put on a couple of sweatshirts and an army coat. On the way to Merchant Mills, I gather the long hair off my shoulders, twist it around a few times, and trap it under my hardhat where it stays all day. My hair is so long now not a bit falls back out. Finally the safety glasses—little wire screens fold back against your temples—special adjustable rims curl securely around your ears and hurt in every possible position.

The foreman's name is Chuck. He looks us over, who's here today and who's not. Then he mentally figures everyone's seniority against the jobs that need doing. He makes notes on his clipboard, and reads off orders. "Packard, Quintana, Lewis, Pritchet: coil trimmer!" We give him our IBM cards and he makes a note on each, since different jobs get different pay. Most of the jobs I get rate $2.81 per hour for day shift and $2.89 at night.

As each of us hands him our IBM card, the foreman reads aloud the top "safety check" card on his deck, and then puts it on the bottom. Little cards, like the Community Chest pile in a Monopoly game. "Watch for slippery grease spots on floor." "Wear your hardhat at all times."

For the first two weeks, I ride to work with Matt and John. Matt was once a major SDS leader. Back then I used to think his side was too cynical, and slow. And they, of course, said the rest of us were too impetuous and naive, and maybe they were right. We sure tried to do too much. Moved too fast. And got smashed.

So now he's trying to recruit me into his Sojourner Truth Collective. He's spent hours at my place, laughing, playing chess, and arguing that his Dictatorship of the Proletariat really *would* fulfill my ideals. Driving back and forth to the mills we continue our talks, but somehow they never turn out right. For example, John describes the guys in his own part of the mills with disgust, he says they hate him, they all seem to be racists and right-wingers. I suspect he just talks leftist jargon at them, and that's what they hate. But when I try to rap about how I'm talking radical common sense to everyone and how fast I make friends and everyone seems ready to agree when you come on plain and friendly, Matt turns up the radio.

Then he jumps on me. "You think you're getting somewhere, Steve, but you're wasting your time on these hippies." I've told him about my coworker on the coiltrimmer who reads Herman Hesse. And the millwright who wants to send his kid to a Free School. And José who reads Che Guevara and who resisted the draft. "These guys won't stick around," he says. "It's the Negroes and older workers—the guys who are going to be here for their life—that have a real sense of class responsibility for this place."

I try to throw in a good word for Youth Culture. Matt comes back with: "If I ran Chicago, the first thing I'd do is wipe out Lincoln Park and turn it back into a neighborhood." (Lincoln Park is the half-hippie area where I live.) The car rolls along in empty silence; not even radio noise can fill it up.

Hostile chills descend on me and Matt pretty often, it seems. We try to wait them out. Our car heads north on 94. It's March, and today a little flock of goldeneyes are swimming through beer cans and tires on what remains of Wolf Lake.

Finally I try to pick it up again: "How are *you* talking to people, Matt."

He's ready too. "Speedup seems to be the issue in my part of the mill," he says with full determined sparkle back.

"Really? I've been more bored than tired," I say.

Matt is driving. But he lets the car go blind long enough to give me a powerful and hard look. "You're going to have to work up more proletarian spirit than that, my friend. Speedup is as big a part of the class struggle as anything you can name. Always has been, always will be."

I try an appeal to the facts—although with no real confidence. "Didn't you tell me yesterday that the guys you work with spend hours fishing for perch in the creek beside their furnace? And that they have a whole library of dirty books they sit around and read? You said that they even cook up a lazy barbecue at lunch every day. Isn't that right?"

He sighs, then gives it a last try. "Steve, do the men where you are complain about working too hard?"

"Of course they do. But I get to feel it's more like a ritual. I mean, they don't really objectively work so damn much."

"Right! They complain about it! They complain because they're oppressed! See if you can't listen a tiny bit to what some regular workers are trying to tell you, Steve. If they complain about it, you can organize them around it!"

Matt's wondering why he's cursed with a collective of such drips. I don't say anything.

So he does. "You understand that?!" Threateningly.

"No, I don't think I do." Obstinately. Defensively.

In the third week, we go on different shifts, and I have to find another ride. Asking around and putting notes on cars in the parking lot, I find enough people so that I've got a ride for any shift, and I never ride with Matt again.

Forty years ago, workers fought to unionize these mills. Gary has a proud and powerful history where the army was called out many times to suppress militant workers and to prevent the establishment of a union. But people fought on and sacrificed for many years, and the union was finally established.

Or at least that's what I read in radical history books.

No one from the union has ever talked to me. I've never been issued a "union card." (What would I do with it if I had one, I wonder.) I've never seen a sign, a poster, a leaflet, or an announcement passed out or posted up by the union. People don't discuss the union. I wonder, does it have meetings? Do they vote? Is there a union hall? And the heroism and bloodshed, the years of hard organizing work, what were they for?

Actually I was afraid the union would be racist and conservative, and we would have to struggle against them. I didn't expect that there would just be no union. I ask people if they know who our grievance man is, and almost nobody does. The union takes a few bucks out of my paycheck; I can see it listed over by the taxes and the F.I.C.A. and all the other paycheck leaks. That's my only evidence it still exists.

Is this mill just unorganized chaos, basically a scene of individual workers against the company? Now I've been here awhile, and I'm slowly learning. Gary Works is a very complex organism, thousands of people and machines making up a living, changing thing. It's not organized too clearly by the company, not organized by the union at all. But very organized, just the same. I got my first sense of it from this story, told by my friend Spider, a black craneman who I often ride to work with.

Most of the cranemen are black. Although it's a pretty good job, there's no way you can "move up" from a crane job to a softer one, which is what most white guys aim for. The blacks know they don't have a chance at the no-work-at-all jobs, so the older, smarter men go after the crane jobs.

One day, a white craneman was assigned to a good crane that should have gone to a certain black. The foreman made some little excuse to explain it, but basically he was doing a favor for a white friend and at the same time showing everyone who's boss. This foreman was new or he would never have been so foolish.

Black cranemen decided to sabotage production until this bullshit was straightened out. They had mild support from most white cranemen, who also thought the foreman was wrong.

Nothing can operate long without the cranes bringing and taking steel, and the blacks quickly stopped the whole mill. They kept the cranes in lowest gear and worked in super-slow-motion. Foremen soon began coming out of their offices, looking around, rubbing their eyes in disbelief. It was like the whole building popped LSD—or the air turned to some thick jelly—everything moving at one-tenth normal speed.

Steel was piling up, and men stopping work. Foremen were yelling, and cranemen explaining all the complex problems their machines had somehow suddenly developed. Calls were coming in from the main office in Pittsburgh, where the computer showed that our statistics had all stopped. So of course the company quickly called the union.

Union sharpies swooped down magically from nowhere. "Men. Men. Come on now. What is the problem? Let's go through the channels on this thing. Right? Submit a grievance. What you're doing is an illegal strike!" But everyone knew that grievances take months, and that the day this foreman had to be wised up was today.

After a couple of hours the company backed down. Higher-level bosses appeared and announced that the foreman had "made a mistake." They switched around the white and black cranemen, the slowness thawed right out, and the mill began to hum again at its normal rate. According to the rules. The workers' rules.

Big wildcats like that are less common than small, partial ones. The most used weapon is sabotage. From the wholesale wrecking of machines to trickier, more selective actions—endless sabotages go on every day. I'm on many jobs where the foreman tries to hustle us too much or insists that we do a job in some dangerous or unpleasant way, and somebody breaks a machine. Nothing can ever be proved—only the workers know just what combination of speed, pressure, change of pace, and angle of feed is sufficient to make some dirty old monster start to shake and throw sparks and smoke to a crunching halt. How fast the millwright fixes it depends on what vibrations he feels from the waiting men. And of course the foreman swears, and fumes, and groans, but he can't really do anything. If he is not overly dumb, he learns the limits beyond which he cannot go.

The men don't usually talk about this stuff; communication is carried out through undercurrents and understandings. But everyone in the mill agrees that the workers are right, which is why there's nothing the boss can do. We know the ins and outs of the machines enough to use them, undetected, against the boss whenever necessary.

The only way a foreman can survive—the only way he gets a fair amount of work done in his zone—is to understand this communication-by-sabotage. It is the workers' police and court of law, by which we struggle to enforce our code of what's right and fair. It is part of a system laboriously built up over the decades.

Our collective's strategy is that we should each become part of the direct action leadership in the mill. Then we can find ways to sharpen and intensify this struggle.

I feel I'm doing well, so far. I've already played good roles in a number of little actions, and have growing mutual respect and good feelings with guys in all parts of our mill. This process is a tricky one though, because the place is strongly divided up into minority groups. At lineup every morning all the workers are either black, or Latin, or hillbilly, or old ethnic European, or young white hippy-type. I'm hippy-type.

Nearly every foreman is "middle-American" white. Other older whites have skilled jobs and don't line up with our "labor gang." The workers most mistrusted by the other minorities are hillbillies and hippies—because we occasionally get transformed into bosses.

Yesterday Hendrickson, one of the foreman's sidekicks and henchmen, drew me aside and gave me a little pep talk about a new job he wants me to learn: the job of "inspector."

Hendrickson explains that "it's a real smart job to learn, Steve, and I think you can do it. The work's not hard. You don't have much time (seniority), that's true. But people here like you; I don't think anyone will complain. And it's a good way to get started out of this labor gang." What he means is that young whites should want to get ahead, and this inspector's job is a first step toward having my head fitted for a foreman's blue hat.

Today Chuck, the foreman, sends my friend Chico and me to the inspection tables together. Hendrickson takes me aside again and says, "Look Steve, here's your clipboard, and I'm going to show you how to do this job. Give it your best, son, O.K.? We really could use another inspector. Most of these guys, you know . . ." He looks around to see that no nonwhite is listening and then says, "Most of these guys— fucking Puerto Rican and the colored—don't even know how to read and write."

The picture becomes even clearer. Hendrickson shows me a couple of simpleminded things to do with a micrometer, a pencil, and that clipboard. Then he says, "Sanchez here is your helper." That's my friend Chico, who is scowling. "Your job, Packard, is to tell him when to move steel for you. Have him spread out each bundle of rods on this bed. Then you check them, and have Sanchez pull them down into that trough and wire them up again. You inspect. That's all. You don't do this other work. Understand?"

Once or twice the thought flashes through my mind, why not become an inspector? Get a little more pay, maybe even more freedom to organize. (In his last job, Matt organized from the privileged position of a tool and die maker, and did well.)

But this ambitious thought don't trouble me for long. I decide to do the job badly so I won't be asked again, and Chico is a big help in this. He won't work.

I say, "What a drag. I can't dig this 'inspecting' bullshit. But I got to finish out the day at it. Let's work slow." Chico doesn't go for this line. No matter what I do or say, I am neck deep in hostility. Chico doesn't lift a finger. He says, "I don't think you make a good inspector, hippy." The other two Spanish guys always call me hippy, but Chico never has before.

He moves slow, uncooperative, messes things up on purpose. Most of the time he's in the wash house or canteen or sitting around half-asleep. He teases me, wants me to break down and order him to work. Chico was my friend, but now he's baiting me—waiting, almost wanting me to use that angry pissed-off commanding voice. If I say, "For Christ sakes, Chico, we got to do some work today! Let's go!" he'll start working real fast, and be my enemy forever.

Twice they catch me doing the job Chico is supposed to do. "Oh! Packard. I guess you didn't understand. You don't move the steel, you have your helper do that. You inspect, all right? Have Sanchez do the rest." Sure.

I don't push Chico. We get almost nothing done, and Chuck is freaked. The next day he puts me back on inspecting with a new helper, a black man about forty years old. For some reason this guy thinks he's supposed to work hard. Has he just arrived from the South? I can't talk to him very well.

We do five or six times as much steel as I did with Chico, but I save my skin by rejecting two-thirds of it. The reject pile grows bigger than I've ever seen it. Chuck comes, furious. With him is the chief inspector, who's friendly and fatherly. The chief looks over my steel and admits it's not quite up to the specifications in the book, but says that we might stretch the limits just a bit (wink) and go ahead with accepting most of this stuff.

I say thanks. And continue to reject two out of three loads. I think of the various bombshells or defoliation sprayers this steel might be destined to make. I think about how much I hate being Mr. Inspector. The cranes hoist load after shiny load back to the scrap cars.

Days come and days go. I never get an upwardly mobile job again.

One of my favorite guys to work with is Billy. Billy will be a skilled worker one day, but he's in no hurry. He's generous, hates privilege, learned a lot of politics in Vietnam, always sides with the minorities against the foreman.

To watch him work is to watch a performance. He's a master. Billy runs his gray, hulking band-leveler like he's playing an organ. He knows every possible subtle adjustment, combination of lubricants, point of strain, and everything else necessary to play this massive thing like no one else alive.

He knows what effect X or Y or Z lubrication in the bearings in front will have on the permissible tension of angle lever way down the other end. (And so of course he uses these to magnificently cripple the mother whenever Chuck steps out of line. Which isn't often.)

Another area of brilliance is the contraptions Billy devises out of coke cans, scrap wood, cardboard, etc. Once he rigged up a plastic milk carton and a long bent nail to do 95 percent of the job I was assigned that day (this automation was removed when Chuck lurked about, of course). If you asked Billy, he'd tell you he constructs these inventions to make his work easier, but it's clear to me he does them for the sheer joy and challenge.

Billy doesn't produce a lot of steel. He quickly admits he could get out two or three or more times as much with little sweat. But every experienced man who works this machine turns out the same small amount. It's part of our speedup war with the company, and it would betray the other workers if you did more.

So my friend uses his energy to teach new people tricks, or to build a fire in the salamander for the crew on the next shift; to perform, and to clean his machine with thorough tenderness, scrub and oil it like a prized sports car, or a precious baby, for a good hour at the end of every day.

I would like to understand Billy. He talks reluctantly about his bored television-watching marriage. Less reluctantly about the nutty things he spends his money on. And then there are the virtual hymns of devotion to Lake Michigan trout and to his boat. She's the only thing in his life he really speaks of fondly, that boat, and he worked a hell of a lot of overtime to buy her. (Though now Billy works overtime to get a bigger one.) I have a feeling from Billy, and from many people here, that the things they buy with their money are often more excuses to spend than real needs or wants. I think Billy doesn't know what to do with himself. I think he spends money so he'll have to work. I begin to toy with a new slogan: "Work is the opiate of the people."

It's lucky I feel some sense of mission in this mill. Without it I'd go nuts. A lot of young guys are doped on regular chemical opiates. I might have been too.

But it's the middle-agers and the older guys that I really feel worst about. Scattered here and there in the gloom are tall, thin heavy steel hole-filled garbage cans packed with burning coal to provide a little heat. For some reason they're called salamanders. Circles of older guys sit on kegs and benches around the salamanders for three or four hours a day. Just sit their with their lights out. It's like they're watching TV, but no TV.

The foreman can't make you work. They've given up trying, but they won't let you do anything else. You can't play music, you can't fool around, if they catch you reading you get yelled at. Sometimes I use my time to write all these ideas down, and I always put "Dear Carol" at the top of the page so people won't ask questions. But I can't let a foreman catch me writing. The only thing they let you do here is sit like a vegetable.

Once a foreman came by a salamander where seven or eight of us were sitting around, one of us snoozing. The foreman kicked the guy's foot, shook him and said, "What's this?! A sleepin?! Look a little bit alive here!!" So the guy opened his eyes and sat up straight. He looked a little bit alive. The foreman was satisfied—and walked slowly on. We chuckled.

One day toward the tail end of winter, I finish my job in an hour, and go walking through the mill yards, through U.S. Steel's Forbidden City, slowly toward the shore of Lake Michigan. I walk through enormous railroad yards, wide weedy prairies struck with room-sized blocks of black rusting solid steel. It seems like the surface of a strange planet. Or the burial ground of an ancient civilization. On my walk I stop to watch the work in the wheel mill (where steel train wheels are made); I prowl around the plate mill where ping-pong-table sized and shaped ponds of molten steel burn out silently in heat and color. I watch technology and poetry and spectacle of these places; I think of how my spirit would glow with pride at this incredible mass of human accomplishment if it was all being done for the good.

At the cold water's edge, wind and spray have piled crude icebergs bigger than the steel block behind me. Crashing waves, white and grey and winter blue-black, bright sun, purple sky with intense red-orange clouds from the mill's smokestacks. The water is filthy and the icebergs speckled with oil and cans and boxes and crap, but if you squint your eyes, they are towering white and beautiful. I get back to Merchant Mills two-and-a-half hours after I left. No one has missed me. I'm bored.

The next day I begin my time-and-motion study, a little bit of "social science" like I learned in college. I walk up and down the aisles noting on a piece of paper who's doing what, being careful that no one sees me and decides I'm a company spy.

In one half-hour I collect the following data:

Men apparently working	80
Men walking around (some may have been doing a job, but most were just killing time like me)	29
Men sitting around salamanders	64
Men standing around doing nothing	53
Men dancing	1

Over half are wasting their time away. I guess I knew it would be this bad. They think they're getting away with something. I have no crocodile tears about how the war effort won't have enough steel, but these numbers are about the emptiness of people's lives.

I make my survey again, picking times when it is most likely people will be working, if they ever work. The last day of this I have plenty of time, because my job for eight hours is to sweep a little dirt, steel filings, and cigarette packages out of an area the size of a living room. Here's the total:

People working	366
People doing nothing	600

Someone's been writing chalk slogans on the wall of the washhouse. "Keep the faith, baby" ... "Work ½ out of eight hours and you will KEEP THE FAITH" ... "Be a soul man, not a Co. man ... Work ½ out of eight hours." They are all signed by "Cadillac Louis." A general feeling among all but the hillbilly workers is that it's right to sluff off. And there's something revolutionary about the workers controlling the pace of their work this way.

But there is something deadening and enslaving here too. I look around at the circles of soot-black hulking shapes sitting joyless, motionless, around the salamanders. They are like the molted skins of insects left by the shore of a pond. As if their souls have left them.

It's a strange atmosphere the coming strike makes. No one talks about it, no concern or excitement. We have been producing huge stockpiles of steel so that our strike won't hurt the company, even if we stay out for months. Everyone knows, and no one cares.

Still, a strike mentality has set in. Energy gets lower and lower as we prepare to turn ourselves off. My own life here is puttering to a stop.

In the last weeks the company has already started laying off men. There is so much steel now that no one knows what to do with it, and half the men hired after me are already gone. We throw goodbye parties every afternoon and take turns bringing the treats. One day I chip in a watermelon, next day Charles brings little cakes and ice cream, next day it's Otis with spareribs and cokes. About a half-hour before quitting time ten of us start our party. Chuck would stop us if he could, but everyone is in a weird frame of mind these days, and he doesn't dare get tough. Some of the oldest men come over and ask questions about what we're doing. We explain, and they put mixed expressions on their faces, thinking about the days when a layoff or strike was a serious thing, and how times have changed.

I only learn about the strike vote meeting from a radical friend who works in the coke ovens. No one else in Merchant Mills seems to know a thing so I call up the union, and the voice says impatiently, "Yes, the strike vote is Tuesday. Everybody's been informed." I tell her that not a damn person in Merchant Mills knows about it, and she promises that the union will look into this. That night I see there's one dim leaflet tacked up in the glass case by the foreman's office. I try to talk the meeting up, but nobody cares. One older black guy sums up the feeling pretty well: "What difference? Meeting, no meeting. Strike, no strike. They going to do it just like they want anyhow." By "they" he means the union and the company.

Tuesday. The union hall of local 1014 of the United Steelworkers of America is packed by the time I arrive, and I have to sit in the front. (I'm told later that my picture is on the cover of the union newspaper. But I've never seen our union newspaper.) About 400 people are at the meeting out of 15,000 members.

Harry Piasecki, the union president, starts by announcing in a tough and determined voice that the company is going to be real scared to hear of the big militant turnout tonight. From what I hear, this meeting is about eight times bigger than most local meetings, which means that Piasecki is probably quite as scared as the company right now.

He and other union officials give long empty reports about the strike talks, and it's obvious they want to drag this thing out until we become confused and bored and hopefully we'll go home. After a half-hour some of the guys on the floor start to yell out. Piasecki takes a big sheaf of papers out of his briefcase and shouts, "Brothers! I hope we are going to register a big strike-vote here tonight, to give our union leadership the backing they deserve." He raises the messy sheaf in the air. "You men know the company is stalling and won't cooperate. And I'd bet you are wanting to know just how these negotiations stand."

"Yeah." "Yeah," "Tell us," the shouts ring out.

He begins. "I have a copy of our bargaining position right here. It has fourteen categories of demands on it, and the company has only agreed to *talk* about six of them. Even to talk. That's the kind of bad faith we are up against."

"What is it?" "What are they offering?" the cries go up.

"Right. Right," says the president. "And I'm going to tell you exactly what these categories are." He shuffles through papers some more, while we wait. Finally he says, loud and decisive, "Number three!" Then silence, and, after more shuffling and a brief consultation with another official sitting at the microphone-covered table, "Number five! Number six!" Then more silence and more shuffling and heads out in the audience are looking back and forth, and asses are shifting around in their chairs. Eventually he gets out the rest of the six numbers. Nothing more, just the numbers. This is union democracy in action. Most of the audience is looking passive, but a few start to yell again. "Hey, what's with these numbers?!" "What are they offering?!" "What's the old age benefit?" "Come on! What's going on?"

The gavel goes rap rap rap rap and Piasecki says, "O.K. brothers, let's keep it orderly, every man will have his chance to speak." But the uproar continues and finally he shouts, "Do you men want to know what's in those categories?" Clearly they do. So he consults, and shuffles more papers, and then begins to read out the answers. "Wages and Hours! Retirement Plans!" He goes on like this, with the category titles. That's all. Just the titles. Confusion and passivity increase. Some men yell. Some leave. Most just sit.

Now the microphone on the floor is opened up, but those who ask good questions don't get answers, and many of the speakers are minor union officials. They remind us that the union charter doesn't allow us to vote on the terms of the contract; it only allows us to authorize Piasecki to authorize Abel to call a strike. They talk drivel, but use tough, labor-movement language: "Brothers and sisters," "Standing bravely on the picket line," "We're not going to knuckle under to that goddam company until Mother fucking Hell Freezes Over, excuse me if there are ladies present."

It's getting late, and more people leave. Those who thought this meeting was actually going to mean something are frustrated and disappointed. At just the right point, Piasecki calls the vote. "All right men, how many are in favor of authorizing a strike against this company, if the negotiators feel it is necessary? Let's hear it!" There is a thunderous "Aye." How could you vote anything else? Does anybody here want to vote in favor of the company? That's what he seems to ask as he shouts, "Those opposed?" We all look around, but no hands are raised. How could they be? This is union democracy.

Still, I can't feel too superior to the union when I look back over my own six months here. The direct actions I took part in were for more bonus money or less work, and these are things the workers have already—with their job security and other past gains protected by the union.

This current setup can pretty much handle the traditional issues. There's a need for radicals here, but it's around whole new types of things.

Just before the strike, Billy and I have a little talk about "life." To make some point, I ask about his boat.

He says, "When the strike comes, I may finally have time to paint her up and get her into the water." It's almost August and he hasn't used it yet. Billy gives me a sheepish look.

I think the deepest needs of my friends here, the needs that require radical changes, are those same unclear things that brought me into the Movement long ago. I felt then that history was ready for the development of a whole new kind of person. Somehow things like community, art, sex roles, justice, participatory democracy, creativity—somehow things like this were almost remolded into a new vision.

We were almost *too* successful at first. But with "the revolution" came some real heavy pressures. A lot of us got clobbered in one way or another. Then we began to think we had to "get practical," to appeal to the "material self-interest of the working class," and abandon our most radical ideas. But it's exactly that newer, free-er, wider, higher vision that the average people really need. That's the only thing Billy and my other friends could really throw their lives into.

On July 31, the day before the strike is to begin, newspaper headlines trumpet: The union and the company have! reached! an! agreement! At the same time the company announces a layoff of practically everybody in the plant—for three, four, possibly five months. I realize that I have just witnessed the Great Steel Strike. Or the Great Steel Layoff. It's a farce, or a ritual. Matt says we should organize unemployed-councils to demand jobs or money, but what he describes sounds grim and lifeless. He's on the wrong battlefield.

I walk around the mill saying goodbye to friends everywhere— Hester, Sammy, David, Chico, Tom-bone, Cook, and many more. There is such a mixture of hope, high spirits, and sadness. U.S. Steel. I steal my hardhat for a keepsake when I leave.

Name Index

Subject Index

Abels family, 260

Absentee corporations, 125, 172

Absenteeism, 529

Absolute poverty, 121
  See also Poverty

"Accidents," economic, 285–97

Accidents, industrial, 528, 528n

Accumulation vs. legitimation, as
    state function, 393

Acquisitions and mergers, 17–24
  distribution of, 23
  and financial status of
      acquired firms, 23–24
  involving 1,000 largest
      manufacturing firms,
      20–21
  involving 200 largest
      manufacturing firms,
      21–22

AFDC, 192

Agrarian revolt, 359

Airline industry, 499–500

Alaskan pipeline, 287

Alienation, political, 162–62

Alienation, work, 421, 509–10,
    551–54

"Alternative schools," 442

American Assembly, 377

American Bar Association, 386

American Federation of Labor,
    453

American Stock Exchange, 41

Anaconda Copper Company,
    251–53, 254n, 259, 298

Anarcho-syndicalism, 421, 486n

Anarchy of production, 199

Anglo-Lautaro Nitrate Company,
    252n

Appalachia, effects of mining in,
    172–86

Arbiter governments, 408

Arbitration, 537

Army, U. S., training of and
    urban warfare, 433

Assembly line workers, benefits
    from war of, 231

Assets
  concentration of, 3–4, 10–12
  as a measure of concentration,
      8
  See also Trust assets

Association of Western Pulp and
    Paper Workers (AWPPW),
    503

Auger mining, 125
  advantages for miners, 179
  effects on environment of, 179
  growth of, 180–81
  process described, 179
  vs. strip mining, 178–79

Authoritarianism of the masses,
    346–47